Economic Development: The Critical Role of
Competition Law and Policy
Volume II

Wherever possible, the articles in these volumes have been reproduced as originally published using facsimile reproduction, inclusive of footnotes and pagination to facilitate ease of reference.

For a list of all Edward Elgar published titles visit our website at
www.e-elgar.com

Economic Development: The Critical Role of Competition Law and Policy Volume II

Competition Law and its Architecture

Edited by

Eleanor M. Fox

Walter J. Derenberg Professor of Trade Regulation
New York University School of Law, USA

and

Abel M. Mateus

Professor of Economics
New Lisbon University, Portugal

An Elgar Research Collection
Cheltenham, UK • Northampton, MA, USA

Published by
Edward Elgar Publishing Limited
The Lypiatts
15 Lansdown Road
Cheltenham
Glos GL50 2JA
UK

Edward Elgar Publishing, Inc.
William Pratt House
9 Dewey Court
Northampton
Massachusetts 01060
USA

A catalogue record for this book is available from the British Library

Library of Congress Control Number: 2010939207

ISBN 978 1 84980 046 4 (2 volume set)

Printed and bound by MPG Books Group, UK

Contents

Acknowledgements

The editors and publishers wish to thank the authors and the following publishers who have kindly given permission for the use of copyright material.

Chicago-Kent Law Review for articles: William E. Kovacic (2001), 'Institutional Foundations for Economic Legal Reform in Transition Economies: The Case of Competition Policy and Antitrust Enforcement', *Chicago-Kent Law Review*, **77**, 265–315; Ignacio De León (2008), 'Latin American Competition Policy: From Nirvana Antitrust to Reality-Based Institutional Competition Building', *Chicago-Kent Law Review*, **83** (1), 39–65.

Hart Publishing Ltd for excerpts: Elina Cruz and Sebastian Zarate (2009), 'Building Trust in Anti Trust: The Chilean Case', in Eleanor M. Fox and D. Daniel Sokol (eds), *Competition Law and Policy in Latin America*, Chapter IX, 157–88; John M. Connor (2009), 'Latin America and the Control of International Cartels', in Eleanor Fox and D. Daniel Sokol (eds), *Competition Law and Policy in Latin America*, Chapter XIV, 291–323.

International Bank for Reconstruction and Development/The World Bank for excerpt: Rafael del Villar (2008), 'Competition and Equity in Telecommunications', in Santiago Levy and Michael Walton (eds), *No Growth Without Equity? Inequality, Interests, and Competition in Mexico,* Chapter 9, 321–64.

International Lawyer for article: Eleanor M. Fox (2009), 'Linked-In: Antitrust and the Virtues of a Virtual Network', *International Lawyer*, **43** (1), Spring, 151–74.

Juris Publishing Inc for excerpt: David Lewis (2008), 'Chilling Competition', in Barry E. Hawk (ed.), *2008 Fordham Competition Law Institute*, Chapter 17, 419–36.

Kluwer Law International for articles: Frédéric Jenny (2006), 'Cartels and Collusion in Developing Countries: Lessons from Empirical Evidence', *World Competition*, **29** (1), 109–37; Giacomo Di Federico (2009), 'The New Anti-monopoly Law in China from a European Perspective', *World Competition*, **32** (2), 249–70; Abel M. Mateus (2010), 'Competition and Development: Towards an Institutional Foundation for Competition Enforcement', *World Competition*, **33** (2), 275–300.

Oxford University Press for articles: Joel P. Trachtman (2003), 'Legal Aspects of a Poverty Agenda at the WTO: Trade Law and "Global Apartheid"', *Journal of International Economic Law*, **6** (1), March, 3–21; Aditya Bhattacharjea (2008), 'India's New Competition Law: A Comparative Assessment', *Journal of Competition Law and Economics*, **4** (3), 609–38.

Southwestern Journal of Law and Trade in the Americas for article: Eleanor M. Fox (2007), 'Economic Development, Poverty and Antitrust: The Other Path', *Southwestern Journal of Law and Trade in the Americas*, **13**, 211–36.

Taylor and Francis Books, UK for excerpt: Robert Anderson and Frédéric Jenny (2005), 'Competition Policy, Economic Development and the Possible Role of a Multilateral Framework on Competition Policy: Insights from the WTO Working Group on Trade and Competition Policy', in Erlinda M. Medella (ed.), *Competition Policy in the East Asia Pacific Region*, Chapter 4, 61–85.

United Nations Conference on Trade and Development for excerpts: Simon J. Evenett (2005), 'What Can We Really Learn from the Competition Provisions of RTAs?', in Philippe Brusick, Ana María Alvarez and Lucian Cernat (eds), *Competition Provisions in Regional Trade Agreements: How to Assure Development Gains,* Chapter 2, 39–65, Doc. number UNCTAF/DITC/CLP/2005/1; Thulasoni Kaira (2008), 'The Role of Competition Law and Policy in Alleviating Poverty – The Case of Zambia', in Hassan Qaqaya and George Lipimile (eds), *The Effects of Anti-Competitive Business Practices on Developing Countries and their Development Prospects,* 133–77, Doc. number UNCTAD/DITC/CLP/2008/2; Michael Adam and Simon Alder (2008), 'Abuse of Dominance and its Effects on Economic Development', in Hassan Qaqaya and George Lipimile (eds), *The Effects of Anti-Competitive Business Practices on Developing Countries and their Development Prospects,* 571–631, Doc. number UNCTAD/DITC/CLP/2008/2.

Wisconsin Law Review for article: Philippe Brusick and Simon J. Evenett (2008), 'Should Developing Countries Worry About Abuse of Dominant Power?', *Wisconsin Law Review*, **2**, 269–94.

Every effort has been made to trace all the copyright holders but if any have been inadvertently overlooked the publishers will be pleased to make the necessary arrangement at the first opportunity.

In addition the publishers wish to thank the Library of Indiana University at Bloomington, USA, for their assistance in obtaining these articles.

A Guide to the Readings and a Perspective on the Literature

Eleanor M. Fox and Abel M. Mateus

Introduction

Volume I presented the political economy framework for our study of the role of competition in economic development. Volume II presents the law and legal strategies for harnessing competition to advance development goals. As we see in the readings, the goals chosen by the various nations may include notions of fairness and justice as well as efficiency. The bundle of goals are commonly seen as synergistic in helping to lift up the developing countries and their peoples and to enhance the legitimacy of markets.

As reflected in Volume I, developing countries are not homogeneous. 'Bottom billion' countries[1] have different needs and prospects from the BRIC tigers – Brazil, Russia, India, and China. Nations have different demographics of poverty. They have different levels of infrastructure, trade, human resources, corruption, cronyism, good governance, peace, democracy, trustworthy institutions and rule of law – all of which influence prospects for effective competition law and policy as well as development.

Some articles included in this volume address a threshold question: Are developing countries (or some of them) not yet ready for competition law? As Paul Collier observes, an island of good market policy can have little effect in the sea of a failed state. Good competition law and policy needs the support of good institutions.

The collection in this book largely – but not entirely – by-passes the threshold question. Most of the chapters simply take on board the fact that competition laws exist in so many developing countries; assume or argue their virtues, and sometimes reference their costs. They ask both descriptive and normative questions: What are the recurrent types of anticompetitive practices that harm their nation? What are the governmental and business structures that give rise to the need for and usefulness of competition law and advocacy? Has globalization increased or diminished the need? How does the competition law of particular nations address their competition problems? Does it do so wisely and adequately, and with what shortcomings and challenges? Are there gaps in coverage or effectiveness of the law, and do developing countries have the capacity to fill them? Are there needs for supranational law or collaboration, and how can those needs be met? Are there characteristics of developing countries, or lesser or least developed countries, that may suggest that we in the developed world refocus the lens through which we see good antitrust law and good antitrust institutions?

Several authors begin their chapters with the plight of developing countries, the poorest and weakest of which are targets of anticompetitive practices launched from the shores of the developed world and as well are victims of cronyistic conduct by their own governments.

Authors in this volume generally ask: How can developing countries use competition law and advocacy to make their people better off?

The volume is organized along the following lines.

Part I is devoted to competition law and advocacy. Competition authorities have a dual role: (1) to enforce and illuminate the law, and (2) to be the voice for competition within the government even outside the bounds of competition law proper; thus, the advocacy role. Advocacy might variously involve convincing the government to lower trade and regulatory barriers, convincing the legislature to grant necessary powers to the competition authority, and publicizing the benefits of competition and the costs of its suppression. Chapters in Part I provide insight into the scope of the problem of suppressed competition in developing countries, insight into the nature of the practices that systemically victimize the peoples in these countries, and analysis of legal rules derived from or tailored to endemic problems and circumstances, such as scarce resources, both human and financial.

Part II deals with institutions. Strong, transparent, accountable, non-corrupt institutions are seen as critical to effective competition law and policy. Achieving this aspiration is one of the huge challenges of developing countries.

Part III addresses international architecture. Globalization has highlighted the plight and prospects of developing countries in the world. Transnational and international institutions promise synergies, and they provide fora for cooperation and opportunities for information and know-how. Blueprints have been proposed for global systems that could make the world, and developing countries, better off. The chapters in this section deal with existing and possible transnational systems, and as well they confront the practical realities that may limit their adoption.

Finally, Part IV turns inwards; it is more microscope than telescope. It presents experiences of selected countries at different stages of development; namely China, India, Chile, Mexico and Zambia. The country experiences add a critical dimension, for law and policy ultimately grow from ground up.

Part I   Competition Law and Advocacy

A.   *Foundational perspectives – Are developing countries different?*

In this section we present two papers, one by Eleanor Fox, professor of law and co-editor of these volumes, and one by Ignacio De León, professor of economics and first president of the Venezuelan Competition Authority. In one sense, these papers present vivid contrasts with one another, both descriptively and normatively. At the same time, they share enormous common ground.

The Fox chapter stresses the stacked deck facing developing countries. It discusses the need for a competition policy compatible with a policy for efficient, inclusive development, much in the spirit of the later Spence Growth Report (Volume I, supra). Fox argues for a contextual competition law/policy that will free markets both from repressive government and restrictive private barriers to opportunity and mobility.

Fox observes that the current US paradigm for determining whether conduct is anticompetitive has narrowed in the direction of laissez faire in the last few decades, and argues that it may be too limited for developing countries, with their much weaker markets and much larger problem of abuses by state monopolies and government-privileged dominant firms. She queries whether developed-country antitrust rules and standards may not be the best for developing countries. Sensitivity to context may require some simpler rules, informed not only by regard for efficient outcomes but also by the need to nurture incentives likely to enhance entrepreneurship, innovation and creativity of people without market power. Context may also suggest a greater need for intervention to open blocked markets. Noting that state restraints are often more debilitating than private restraints in suppressing entrepreneurial incentives, having reference to the work of Hernando de Soto, and drawing from the work of Bill Kovacic, she encourages competition agencies to take an aggressive role in advocacy to remove regulatory and other state barriers to competition, engagement, entry, participation and thus innovation.

The de León chapter argues that static price theory is a poor metric for determining what is anticompetitive; a notion that Fox shares. De León writes: '[T]he ultimate purpose of economic liberalization in transitioning and developing countries is promoting entrepreneurial creativity, innovation, and economic growth, all of which were stifled during previous decades of burdensome regulations, trade protectionism, and government dirigisme' (p. 42). '[T]he ultimate goal of competition must be connected to the development of competitiveness, innovation, and economic development' (p. 64). De León argues for strong advocacy, and he urges intervention against state restraints. Yet, quite differently from Fox, he argues for constraint in applying antitrust law to competitor collaboration (and implicitly to dominant firm conduct), which, he suggests, is likely to be the means to advance the search for knowledge; it is likely to be the spur to an evolutionary, knowledge-and-information-based market process. Drawing inspiration from Hayek and Schumpeter and invoking the context of Latin America, de León is concerned that antitrust law is dangerously likely to be applied to block creativity and innovation and to restore government dirigisme by the back door.

The reader may wish to read, also, Wolfgang Kerber, 'Competition, Innovation and Maintaining Diversity through Competition Law'.[2] Kerber, like de León, elaborates a theory of evolutionary economics, but, unlike de León, is sympathetic to antitrust interventions to protect the process of evolutionary learning.

In the vein of de León, the reader may also wish to read Lucas Sebastián Grosman, 'Piedras en el camino: una breve reflexión sobre el lugar de los consumidores y los competidores en la defensa de la competencia',[3] arguing that Fox's proposal for an antitrust system copious enough to protect economic opportunity and mobility is bound to have a chilling effect on robust competition, especially in a context of little legal certainty and weak institutions.

B. Monopolies and Abuse of Dominant Position

Dominant firm abuses is one of the most fraught subjects of competition law. Jurisdictions experience the dominant firm problem differently, often depending on their state of development, their history of state ownership and control, the robustness or sluggishness of their markets, the trustworthiness of their institutions, and the embeddedness of disparity of wealth and opportunity. Accordingly, jurisdictions make different trade-offs between efficiency (e.g., allocative or productive) on the one hand, and equity on the other; they use different default presumptions as to what structure of the market or allocation of freedoms is most likely to produce efficiency, and they apply different perspectives on the probable costs and benefits of government antitrust intervention. Consequently, perspectives range from the US nearly hands-off approach to unilateral conduct by dominant firms, in expectation that firms will do good and the market will punish them if they err or exploit, to distrust of dominant firms, in expectation that they will use their power to exclude emerging rivals and exploit the public.

In this section we include three articles. The first is by Michael Adam of UNCTAD and Simon Alder, then a student at the University of Zurich. Adam and Alder identify the sometimes conflicting factors and objectives that developing countries face. These include trade-offs within efficiency (is efficiency more likely to be produced by more rivalry or by greater expectation of profit?), and the quest for a less extreme maldistribution of wealth and opportunity. The authors then give historical, economic, legal and political background. They offer a wide range of examples of both facts and legal principles, in jurisdictions as diverse as Zambia, Kenya, Korea and Jamaica. They deal separately with state-created monopolies and national champions. In each case, Adam and Alder muster data from the various jurisdictions, giving the countries' own assessment of, for example, why they maintain state monopolies, why they have unilateral conduct laws and what methodologies they use to identify dominance.

The second piece, by Philippe Brusick and Simon Evenett, must be seen against a background of claims, often by US Americans, that the only egregious private restraint is a hard core cartel and that single firm conduct, even by dominant firms, is likely to be efficient and procompetitive.[4] Brusick, former head of Competition and Consumer Policies at UNCTAD, and Evenett, professor of international trade and economic development at St Gallen, Switzerland, ask: Should developing countries worry about abuse of dominant power? Their answer (like the quite different article of Adam and Alder) is Yes. The authors state both the theoretical and the evidentiary case. They compile extensive evidence of abuses of dominance, especially in Latin America, sub-Saharan Africa and southeast Asia.

Brusick and Evenett explain the characteristics that make developing countries prone to abuse. They catalog, in particular, abuses by state-owned monopolies and recently privatized firms. Well aware, however, of political realities, they reference the problem of vested interests in concluding: 'injecting the discipline of competition and limiting the exercise of market power into economies where vested interests have strong links to policy makers is unlikely to be easy … ' (p. 294).

Third, we include David Lewis' essay, 'Chilling Competition'. David Lewis was the first chairman of the Competition Tribunal of South Africa and is the immediate past chair of the Tribunal; thus, he led the body in its formative years. The Lewis paper takes its place in a larger debate, telescoped above. In the larger debate, the multinational business community questions whether dominant firm abuses are a problem. They assert that *antitrust challenges* to large firm conduct are a much bigger problem than private abuses of power. They contend that antitrust lawsuits are commonly triggered by inefficient rivals seeking protection, and they argue that antitrust lawsuits and prospects of them, not dominant firm strategies, chill competition.

One forum for this debate is the International Competition Network (ICN). The ICN has an ongoing project on unilateral conduct. The first step in condemning conduct as an abuse of dominance is proof that a firm is dominant. Thus, the first item on the ICN agenda of its unilateral conduct project was how to assess dominance. For example, is proof that the putative dominant firm has a large market share sufficient for the plaintiff's prima facie case? In the ICN working group, voices in the negative prevailed. High market shares do not necessarily signal dominance. Many factors are relevant.[5]

David Lewis offers a different perspective. In the article included in this collection, he argues that the likelihood and consequences of anticompetitive antitrust intervention are 'vastly exaggerated', and that the likelihood and consequences of the authorities' failing to challenge anticompetitive unilateral conduct are 'significantly understated'. Lewis shows why this is especially the case in countries with certain historical and structural features such as pervasive historical state ownership, privilege and suppression of merit-based competition. Failures to challenge anticompetitive abuses perpetuate the suppression of competition. John Fingleton and Ali Nikpay similarly argue that, where markets are sluggish, costs of non-intervention are more likely to outweigh costs of intervention.[6]

C.   Cartels

Hard core cartels (also called cartels herein) are agreements among competitors to fix prices, divide markets, rig bids or otherwise stop competing. To keep the cartel from self destructing in the face of outsiders' competition, cartel members often erect roadblocks or facilitate boycotts.

In the developed world, cartels are commonly regarded as the most heinous anticompetitive conduct, robbing buyers and ultimately consumers of many millions of dollars each year. How directly and substantially do cartels impact developing countries? Is the international cartel problem also of central concern to developing countries?

Pioneering empirical work has been done in this area by Valerie Suslow, Margaret Levenstein, Simon Evenett and John M. Connor. A seminal paper by Suslow and Levenstein points out that, before the last decade, the research on cartels and developing countries addressed how much developing countries' commodities cartels harmed the developed world. Suslow and Levenstein turn the telescope around. The authors report that, in 1997, developing countries imported $51.1 billion in goods from industries internationally cartelized during the 1990s, an amount greater than all foreign aid to developing countries that year.[7] Their work is readily accessible and we do not include it in this volume, but we suggest it to the reader.

We do include a chapter by Frédéric Jenny, and another by John Connor.

Frédéric Jenny is professor of economics, judge of the Court de Cassation of France and chairman of the Competition Committee of the OECD. In his chapter, Jenny observes: 'Much to the chagrin' of competition officials, 'there are no convincing macroeconomic studies demonstrating the existence of a positive and strong correlation between the intensity of competition law enforcement and the rate of economic growth (in developed or developing countries)' (pp. 110–11). Nonetheless, says Jenny, there is an available line of inquiry that can shed light on the correlation. He refers to the line of reasoning initiated by Levenstein, Suslow and Evenett. Jenny presents a compelling mass of anecdotal and empirical evidence of anticompetitive practices in the developing world. Reporting data from countries as disparate as Peru, Brazil, Egypt, Zambia and Cambodia, Jenny finds that 'the results are stunning with respect to the scope and importance' of the anticompetitive practices revealed (p. 113).

John Connor, a professor of industrial economics, is a prolific researcher, empiricist and writer on the proliferation of international cartels, their price effects, and the relationship between sanctions and deterrence. Connor identifies the inadequacy of sanctioning systems in the common quest for deterrence. Thus, he says, in the chapter we include in this volume: 'The phenomenon of historically high and highly-touted monetary sanctions imposed on international cartels in the past decade is obscuring major deficiencies in world anti-cartel efforts' (p. 322). In a number of articles, Connor relates his research to competition law systems of various parts of the world. The chapter included in this volume references not only the three jurisdictions credited with the most effective anti-cartel enforcement – the United States, the European Union and Canada – but applies his work to Latin America.

The evidence amassed by all of the authors above shows that cartels – international, cross-border and domestic – seriously and persistently harm the peoples of developing countries. Moreover, developing countries are often targets of international and off-shore cartels precisely because the country is ill equipped to enforce the law against them in meaningful ways. In large part as a result of the work of Jenny, Evenett, Connor, Levenstein and Suslow, international and local communities now understand the immensity of antitrust harms occurring every day in developing countries, and the conversation has turned from: Where is the problem? to How can we solve it? Numerous countries, including developing countries, have adopted leniency programs, designed to encourage cartel members to come forward and expose their cartels in return for amnesty. Policy makers in many nations are considering criminalizing the cartel violation and the possibility of jail, while others ponder the appropriateness of criminal penalties to their culture, as well as the effectiveness of due process safeguards in their country, and some express concern that raising the offense to a criminal level might unduly increase the authorities' burden of proof.

Part II   Institutions

We turn in section D to institutions. It is now well accepted that, in adopting and applying a system of law, institutions centrally matter. Douglass C. North crystallized this principle in his seminal work, Institutions, Institutional Change and Economic Performance (1990). North asks why some societies perform far better than others. He contrasts institutional structures that induce investment in education and reward industriousness with very different institutional structures in many developing countries:

> Now if I describe an institutional framework with a reverse set of incentives [i.e., not investment in education, industriousness and adaptability] ... , I will approximate the conditions in many Third World countries today as well as those that have characterized much of the world's economic history. The opportunities for political and economic entrepreneurs are still a mixed bag, but they overwhelmingly favor activities that promote redistributive rather than productive activity, that create monopolies rather than competitive conditions, and that restrict opportunities rather than expand them. They seldom induce investment in education that increases productivity. The organizations that develop in this institutional framework will become more efficient – but more efficient at making the society even more unproductive and the basic institutional structure even less conducive to productive activity. (p. 9)

North cautions:

> Institutions are not necessarily or even usually created to be socially efficient; rather they, or at least the formal rules, are created to serve the interests of those with the bargaining power to devise new rules. In a zero-transaction-cost world, bargaining strength does not affect the efficiency of outcomes, but in a world of positive transaction costs it does and given the *lumpy* indivisibilities that characterize institutions, it shapes the direction of long-run economic change. (p. 16)

Does neoclassical economics help to identify and solve the problem? It has made a significant contribution to models explaining increase in output at the margin given the existing stock of capital; but, says North, 'surely this neoclassical formulation has begged all the interesting questions' (p. 133). The neoclassical formulation depends on the existence of an assumed incentive structure. 'To attempt to account for [differential performances of economies] ... without making the incentive structure derived from institutions an essential ingredient appears to me to be a sterile exercise' (p. 134).

North's insistence on the centrality of institutions is echoed in several essays, articles and reports in Volume I, particularly by Spence, Khemani and Rodrik. Those chapters (1, 2, 3, 4 and 8 of Volume I) bear rereading.

In this section, in the spirit of North, we present two chapters. The first is by William Kovacic, commissioner of the US Federal Trade Commission. The Kovacic article is a classic in examining institutional foundations for legal/economic reform in transition and developing economies. As Kovacic observes, transitional economies confront difficult choices, such as how to allocate scarce human resources and scarce political capital. Jurisdictions must set and follow basic priorities, which include establishing property and contract rights and building the institutions that support them. They need, especially, a well-functioning judiciary, honest and transparent government administration, university training of specialists and regulatory frameworks.

Kovacic explores the claim of a link between democracy, economic growth and freer markets. He then turns more centrally to competition law and policy and asks what should be the place of antitrust enforcement on the nation's agenda. (It does not necessarily merit a place at the top). He surveys the literature and arguments for and against early incorporation of antitrust law, including arguments for only limited antitrust powers at the start, depending on the context. Echoing Khemani (Volume I, supra) and de León, Kovacic explains how the competition agency can be an 'institutional counterweight' to resist 'efforts to sabotage market-oriented reforms' (p. 291).

Kovacic then reviews common initial conditions in transitional and developing countries and explores their implications for law design, implementation and technical assistance. In concluding remarks he observes that 'issues of institutional capability deserve far greater attention in designing laws and timing their application' (p. 315).

Abel Mateus, co-editor of these volumes, professor of economics and immediate past president of the Portuguese Competition Authority, contributes a different but complementary perspective on institutions. His chapter is informed by three strands of contributions: (1) models of the political economy of development that incorporate the effects of interest groups and vested interests; (2) decision theory suggesting the appropriateness of different legal regimes depending on the extent to which the objectives of the regime will be subverted by (for example) corruption and cronyism, calibrated with the level of damages necessary to make the enforcement system pay off in the face of the subversion; and (3) the level of the jurisdiction's institutional development charted according to a composite index of governance and government capture. Using these calibrations, Mateus proposes three developmental levels of competition law regimes. At level 1, a nation should not have competition law at all; at level 2, the nation is ready for a simple set of clear rules; and at level 3, the nation is ready for more nuanced rules and principles of law and a system of remedies to match.[8]

Part III   International Architecture

Three phenomena are at play. First, national enforcement systems are limited, not only by the gaps that constrain effective governance of a nation's own internal market, but also by forces exerted by international trade and competition. Cross-border effects, and the appreciation of problems as world problems, have naturally led to designs for global collaborations and world systems.[9]

In the 1990s, the international competition dialog turned to a possible global system in the context of the World Trade Organization (WTO). Many detractors emerged, in the name of sovereignty and fear of bureaucracy. They argued for soft convergence as a substitute.

Second, small and developing countries faced different problems. They were so small and so short of resources that they struggled to construct even credible national enforcement. They could hardly hope for effective enforcement to counter foreign acts that hurt their citizens. Was regional cooperation and perhaps regional integration an answer?

Third, consciousness rose about the pervasiveness of dire poverty and its impact in forestalling the poorest countries' quest for growth. It became common cause that the gains of the successive trade rounds disproportionately benefited the developed nations. Moreover, it was noted that the immense and growing disparity between rich and poor, combined with the stagnation of the poorest nations, fed into the terrorist agenda. Dialog turned to the place of poverty on the world trade agenda, giving rise to initiatives including the Millennium Development Goals.[10] Should the WTO confront the global maldistribution of the benefits of trade?

Robert Anderson and Frédéric Jenny, in their chapter on 'Competition Policy, Economic Development and the Possible Role of a Multilateral Framework on Competition Policy', draw from their experience on the WTO Working Group on the Interaction between Trade and Competition Policy. (Jenny was chairman of the Working Group; Anderson was a counselor in the WTO Secretariat.) The Working Group was in operation from 1997 to 2004, when it was discontinued after competition was jettisoned from the Doha Development Round trade agenda.

The Working Group produced a wealth of information, including submissions by many developing countries on numerous trade and competition issues. The submissions and discussions led to the insights presented in the Anderson/Jenny chapter. The central theme of the chapter is 'the fundamental complementarity of competition policy, trade liberalization and domestic economic reform, and their importance for development' (p. 61).

The Anderson/Jenny chapter analyzes the relevance of competition policy for developing countries, and considers applications of law as well as advocacy. It articulates arguments in favor of competition policy in the WTO. As well, it notes the reservations expressed by developing countries, in particular that a world agreement would limit their policy space and development strategies. The authors proceed to analyze why the fears identified with a multilateral system are not likely to materialize. Finally, the authors consider the Doha proposals for a multilateral competition framework (now in abeyance).

For a dissenting point of view, see Ajit Singh, 'Multilateral Competition Policy and Economic Development: A Developing Country Perspective on the European Community Proposals'.[11] Singh argues that a liberal, open-market competition regime is against the interests of developing countries at this stage of their development. He observes that the advanced countries used market-protecting instruments at earlier stages, and argues that developing countries are entitled to those opportunities now. Singh commends to developing countries industrial policy along lines implemented by Japan and Korea in their earlier stages of development, along with competitor cooperation and government–business cooperation. He proposes a multilateral agreement limited to the anticompetitive conduct and mergers of the world's largest multinational corporations.

Even before 2004 when the Working Group was disbanded, the star of world antitrust had dimmed. Opposition was led both by the United States, which feared loss of sovereignty, and developing countries, which feared imposition of Western rules. A proposal was made for a counter-enterprise – a grass-roots, virtual cooperation of the competition authorities of the world, with no power to make or impose rules, much less to enforce them, and with the aspiration to converge law and process through voluntary interaction. This virtual, networking organization was formed. It is the International Competition Network, or ICN. The formation, evolution and work of the ICN are explored in the chapter by Eleanor Fox, 'Linked-In'. The chapter not only discusses the birth of the ICN, but describes how recommended principles and practices emerge in the context of the ICN. The author hypothesizes that, despite the absolute openness and inclusiveness of the ICN, in view of the scarce resources and thus the infeasibility of deep participation by developing countries, the principles and practices that emerge may tend to be those most fitting to the mature, developed economies.

Meanwhile, even during the debate on a competition agreement in the WTO, developing countries entered into, and they continue to enter into, free trade and regional trade agreements (RTAs) with a competition dimension. RTAs with competition provisions are multiplying. In a 2005 study, the OECD concluded that 47 such agreements had been recently concluded, 36 percent of which were between developing countries.

Competition provisions in RTAs are generally adopted as flanking protections to prevent market-opening undertakings from being undermined by anticompetitive agreements. Even so, can RTAs be a useful vehicle for developing countries' overcoming size and resource problems in competition law enforcement? RTAs may provide a trade-and-competition framework that can support competition law systems on their own bottom.[12] Many nations have ambitious plans for regional competition systems through RTAs. However, coordination problems are difficult and few such systems are yet operational in a meaningful sense.[13]

We include in this section an essay by Simon Evenett, who asks: What can we learn from competition provisions in developing countries' RTAs about their interest in a multilateral competition agreement? Evenett explores the competition clauses in RTAs of developing countries and their content. Do they include abuse of dominance? Special and differential treatment? dispute resolution? Or only non-discrimination, due process, transparency and voluntary cooperation? Do developing countries obtain or resist competition clauses in their RTAs, and would resistance tend to explain their opposition to the multilateral agreement that might have evolved from the Doha agenda? Evenett examines these questions, analyzes the data, and urges caution in drawing lessons from developing countries' RTAs about their level of enthusiasm for a multilateral system.

The final entry on international architecture is Joel Trachtman's article on a poverty agenda within a world institution such as the WTO. Trachtman identifies poverty as 'the overwhelming moral, economic, legal and political issue facing us' (p. 3). Trachtman quotes Thabo Mbeki, then president of South Africa, who described the distribution of wealth in the world as 'global apartheid'. Global apartheid, says Trachtman, locks people into a position of poverty, inequality and disenfranchisement. Even while it is liberalizing and thus should be opportunity-increasing, the world trade system perpetuates global apartheid. Trachtman explores both ethical and selfish foundations for embedding redistributive policies in the WTO, and proposes how this effort might proceed.

Trachtman's article is not about competition policy. But the analysis and message are highly relevant to competition policy, at least equally with, for example, environmental policy; and perhaps more so, since competition rules themselves can advance opportunity, mobility and access to markets. Freedom from tariffs and duties fits tightly into both a pro-competition and a pro-poor agenda. The Trachtman article raises consciousness about the urgency to 'dismantle the barriers that form "global apartheid"'.

Part IV   Selected Country Experiences

In the last section, we present studies anchored in competition problems of selected countries; namely, China, India, Chile, Mexico and Zambia.

As globalization deepens, many eyes are on the BRIC countries – Brazil, Russia, India and China. Their competition regimes, or revised regimes, are young, and all four nations are on the cusp of dynamic economic change. They are rising players in the world economy. They are seen as leaders among developing or transitional countries, engaging in the world economic system and using the world system to enhance their growth and development. In view of the fact that the BRIC countries – in particular China – are changing the world economic landscape, the question is asked: Do they or will they offer a new model of competition law/policy for developing countries or even the world? What is such a model likely to be?

We present here chapters on two of the BRIC countries – China and India. Brazil's competition regime has been treated in a number of other articles and documents.[14] A peer review of competition law and policy in Brazil by the Organization of Economic Cooperation and Development is also available.[15] For Russia, too, an OECD peer review is available.[16]

We include in this section a paper by Giacomo Di Federico on the new antimonopoly law of China. The chapter is written from a European perspective, and helpfully so, because important aspects of the text and concept of the Chinese law are drawn from the European Treaty. This is so not only regarding much of the substantive law but also regarding the relationship between free competition and free trade within China.

Di Federico's paper presents, first, the background of China's political economy, and it reflects on the sometimes uneasy fit between China's form of government and pure competition principles. He identifies the Chinese Anti-Monopoly Law (AML) as 'an admirable synthesis (in substantial and procedural terms) of the struggle between marketplace needs and the socialist regime' (p. 251). Yet, he worries about the conflicting pulls and opportunities for non-transparent use of discretion by the Chinese authorities. Di Federico derives his observations from a close analysis of the law and its institutions. He makes numerous observations and suggestions about the challenges that lie ahead.

Since the article was published in 2009, a major case cited by Di Federico has been decided. China prohibited the proposed merger of Coca Cola and Huiyuan, China's big juice company (note 46 of the article). The competition authority, MOFCOM, cited harm to competition as the basis for the prohibition, although by modern international standards applied to this conglomerate merger, the competitive (consumer) harm was not apparent. In a second case, AQSIQ, cited in the article at note 56, suit was brought for abuse of administrative power by a state administrative agency. The agency required consumer product manufacturers to subscribe to the product authentication service of its own subsidiary, rather than that of competitors. The Chinese court dismissed the suit on grounds that the statute of limitations had run. The court held that the statute of limitations runs from the date the abuse begins. Thus in all cases of long-standing administrative abuse, the statute of limitations has run long before any victim has the opportunity to press a challenge. The resolution of both cases seems to confirm the concerns of Di Federico.

But there is also reason for optimism. China's antitrust enforcement authorities are in touch with, and are continually seeking knowledge from, antitrust authorities and experts in many jurisdictions around the world. In formulating its rules and regulations for mergers, for example, China is adopting international perspectives and standards. The merger authority MOFCOM has shown a high degree of activity and interest in multijurisdictional mergers with a Chinese dimension. China is now one of the several major jurisdictions to which merging parties pay heed.

Much has been written on the Chinese antimonopoly law, both in the run-up to its adoption and in the aftermath. A useful reference is volume 75 of the *Antitrust Law Journal*, issue 1, 2008, containing articles by Rodney J. Ganske, H. Stephen Harris, Jr, Huang Yong, Bruce M. Owen, R. Hewitt Pate, Sun Su, Wang Xiaoye, Wen Xueguo, Wu Zhenguo, Zheng Wentong and Eleanor Fox. The article by Huang Yong, 'Pursuing the Second Best', welcomes the competition law despite its flaws. Commenting on China's new mission to enforce competition policy in the face of traditions that may not align with a first best solution, Huang invokes the words of the late premier Deng Xiaoping: 'crossing the river by feeling for the stones'.

India is the other BRIC country represented in this volume. We include the article by Aditya Bhattacharjea. Bhattacharjea (like Huang for China) wrote his article before the new competition law became effective. As he states in his note preceding the article, enforcement under the new law has barely begun and the issues he identifies in his article have yet to be resolved.

India's Competition Act replaces its 1969 Monopolies and Restrictive Trade Practices Act (MRTPA). Bhattacharjea takes a critical look at the new act. He reviews the history under the MRTPA (which was largely an unfair competition act); he notes decisions under that act that attempted to enforce fair business conduct at the expense of competition, and he worries that the deficiencies of the past might haunt the future. But India and its new competition commission are positioning themselves firmly in the international community of antitrust. Vinod Dhall and others take an optimistic view that India will apply modern, pro-competition standards.[17]

The chapter on Chile reflects yet a different culture. In their chapter, 'Building Trust in Antitrust: The Chilean Case', Elina Cruz and Sebastian Zarate delve into the cultural background of Chile. They describe the impact of liberalization (starting in 1973) on the national psyche, and the motivation of Chileans to protect freedom of competition even against the efforts of the competition enforcers themselves. Thus, the general mistrust in the antitrust system. See also a theoretical basis for mistrust expressed in the De León article, supra.

Cruz and Zarate argue that distrust, combined with an institutional design that has allowed Chilean Supreme Court jurists to second-guess the specialist tribunal, has led to weak and inadequate enforcement against competitor collusion. They offer proposals for building trust in Chilean antitrust.

Thus far we have not yet examined sector regulations, and we do so now. Sector regulation has a critical link with competition policy. Indeed, in many developing countries, sectoral regulation may be a first home for competition law and policy; that is, antitrust provisions and considerations may first appear in regulatory statutes. However, sectoral regulation may be used perversely to reward and privilege the insiders.

Our example in this area is drawn from Mexico and the regulation of telecommunications. We include the essay of Rafael del Villar, 'Competition and Equity in Telecommunications', which is a chapter in the compelling book edited by Santiago Levy and Michael Walton, *No Growth Without Equity?*[18] Levy and Walton set the stage for their book with an important essay on the link between inequality and low growth, illustrated by the history, politics and performance of Mexico. They make the important observation that 'market failures hurt those with lower incomes more, and institutions and policies dominated by the rich will not correct market failures because they have no incentives to do so' (pp. 16–17). They explain by example 'how unequal power and influence shape economic institutions in ways that lead to outcomes that are both inequitable and a source of slow growth' (p. 17). Levy and Walton postulate that Mexico faces a 'growth-equity puzzle' – a high-inequality and low-growth equilibrium. Their book is devoted to analyses and ideas to help solve the puzzle.

The del Villar essay, which provides rich empirical detail, nicely illustrates possibilities to produce positive change in policy design and implementation, in the spirit of Levy and Walton. It describes the Mexican telecommunications industry, the fact of Mexico's privatization before regulation, and the ways in which the design of the regulation opened the system to regulatory capture. According to del Villar, the procedure for and the sequencing of the privatization sabotaged the capacity of Mexico's competition and consumer protection laws to protect the public from the exploitative abuses that followed. The sabotage is most unfortunate because the competitive functioning of telecommunications is crucial to both equity and efficiency. Del Villar suggests possibilities for counteracting the Mexican telecommunications monopoly.

The reader may be interested also in a companion chapter on telecommunications reform by Roger Noll,[19] and in the account by Eleanor Fox of the case against Mexico for violating WTO antitrust prohibitions by facilitating a Telmex-led cartel that raised the cost of terminating cross-border calls into Mexico.[20]

The final chapter is devoted to sub-Saharan Africa – one of the poorest parts of the world. Thulasoni Kaira, director of the Zambian Competition Commission, contemplates the role of competition law and policy in alleviating poverty in Zambia.

Kaira undertakes the ambitious task of examining whether and how competition policy can alleviate poverty. The project of poverty alleviation would have to be accomplished, he says, in one of three ways: by creating wealth, as through efficiencies; by creating jobs, as through new entry; and by reducing prices, as through competition. 'Where competition enforcement efforts do not lead to these results, then the existence of this law should be questioned' (p. 136).

Kaira turns specifically to Zambia. He asks: Where are the extreme poor, and why is there still extreme poverty despite strong progress towards macroeconomic stability?

Some 80 percent of the extreme poor in Zambia work in agriculture and related industries. What can help them the most? Kaira finds an answer to this important question, drawing not only from his educated instinct but from surveys: the remote poor need infrastructure. They are disadvantaged and exploited by the high cost or impossibility of getting to market. Bid-rigging and collusive tendering on road construction projects are endemic. Competition law enforcement and advocacy can help. Road construction is just one of the many examples that Kaira identifies – others being drawn from the cotton, horticulture and floriculture, poultry, beef and tobacco industries. In each of his examples, Kaira pinpoints means by which competition policy can provide an effective remedy against exclusions and exploitations, including opportunistic uses of monopsony power by large multinationals against the poorest segments of the population; for example small farmers. He commends tools for opening channels for better information and transparency, and access to modern technology.

Whether competition policy can really contribute to poverty alleviation in Zambia remains debatable, Zaira says; yet his entire article exudes not only the hope but the conviction that it can.

Conclusion

The articles included in this volume present some contrasting perspectives. In particular, in developing countries, how much antitrust law intervention against private power is wise? How applicable are international standards and priorities, and at what stage of development?

But the larger message is not the differences but the common ground. Competition law/policy has the potential to play a critical role in enhancing economic development. Developing countries' economies and peoples are gravely harmed by practices, both from off-shore and on-shore, both by their own governments and private actors, that are anticompetitive by any definition of that word. Vested interests do what they can to preserve their privileges. Weak institutions conspire against positive change. What can break the barriers to healthy competition? Inspiration, perseverance and perhaps some luck in the political economy environment. Critical ingredients include information, knowledge, know-how and a decent prospect of institutional reform. As the articles in these volumes show, paths to reforms are being identified and opened, and competition authorities in developing countries around the world are rising to the challenge.

Notes

1. See Paul Collier, Volume I, Chapter 9.
2. Drexl et al. (2010).
3. Grosman (2007).
4. See also Grosman (2007).
5. See Recommended Practices for Dominance/Substantial Market Power Analysis, available at http://www.internationalcompetitionnetwork.org/uploads/library/doc317.pdf. See also Bernard (2009) and Bourgeois (2009).
6. Fingleton and Nikpay (2009).
7. See Levenstein and Suslow (2004). See also Evenett et al. (2002).
8. See also, for institutions of antitrust and a suggested simple design of substantive law for transitional countries, Fingleton et al. (1996).
9. Beginning in the 1970s, the United Nations Conference on Trade and Development (UNCTAD)

became a forum for the negotiation of The Set of Multilaterally Agreed Equitable Principles and Rules for the Control of Restrictive Business Practices, now called The United Nations Set of Principles and Rules on Competition. The Set was adopted as a voluntary code in 1980. TD/RBP/CONF/10/Rev.2, available at http://www.unctad.org/Templates/Page.asp?intItemID=4106&lang=1. See also the UNCTAD Model Law on Competition, with draft commentaries, available at http://www.unctad.org/Templates/WebFlyer.asp?inItemID=4108&lang=1. The reader may wish to become familiar also with the work of UNCTAD's committee on Competition Law and Policy in providing 'a development-focused intergovernmental forum for addressing practical competition law and policy issues'; http://www.unctad.org/Templates/StartPage.asp?inItemID=2239&lang=1.

See generally, for an analysis of the principal international institutions of antitrust, including UNCTAD, the WTO, OECD and ICN, Sokol (2007) Berkeley Business Law Journal, **4**, 37–122.

10.   See http://www.un.org/millenium/.
11.   Available at http://unctad.org/en/docs/ditcclp200310_en.pdf.
12.   See generally Brusick et al. (2005).
13.   See the efforts of CARICOM (the Caribbean Community), Stewart (2005) p. 333. See also Lee (2009).
14.   See, for example, de Paula (2007), Chapter 7.
15.   See http://www.oecd.org/dataoecd/62/35/35415135.pdf.
16.   See http://www.oecd.org/dataoecd/10/60/32005515.pdf.
17.   See Dhall (2007), Overview and Chapter 23.
18.   Levy and Walton (2009).
19.   Noll (2009).
20.   See Fox (2009).

References Other than the Articles Printed Herein

Bernard, Kent S., (2009), 'Monopolization/Abuse of Dominance and the Research-based Pharmaceutical Industry – The Chilling Effect of Uncertain Rules of Enforcement', in Barry Hawk (ed.) *International Antitrust Law & Policy: Fordham Competition Law 2008*, Huntington, NY: Juris, pp. 343–8.

Bourgeois, Hendrik (2009), 'The Chilling Effects of Article 82 Enforcement', in Barry Hawk (ed.) *International Antitrust Law & Policy: Fordham Competition Law 2008*, Huntington, NY: Juris, pp. 349–84.

Brusick, Philippe, Ana María Alvarez and Lucian Cernat (eds) (2005), *Competition Provisions in Regional Trade Agreements: How to Assure Development Gains*, United Nations Conference on Trade and Development (UNCTAD), New York and Geneva: United Nations.

de Paula, Germano Mendes (2007) 'Competition Policy and the Legal System in Brazil', in Paul Cook, Raul Fabella and Cassey Lee (eds) *Competitive Advantage and Competition Policy in Developing Countries*, Cheltenham, UK and Northampton, MA, USA: Edward Elgar, pp. 109–35.

Dhall, Vinod (ed.) (2007), *Competition Law Today: Concepts, Issues, and the Law in Practice,* Delhi, Oxford: Oxford University Press.

Drexl, J., W. Kerber and R. Podszun (eds) (2010) *Economic Approaches to Competition Law: Foundations and Limitations*, Cheltenham, UK and Northampton, MA, USA: Edward Elgar.

Evenett, Simon, Margaret Levenstein and Valerie Y. Suslow (2002), 'International Cartel Enforcement: Lessons from the 1990s', World Bank Policy Research Working Paper No. 2680, http://ssrn.com/abstract=265741.

Fingleton, J., E. Fox, D. Neven and P. Seabright (1996), *Competition Policy and the Transformation of Central Europe*, London: Centre for Economic Policy Research.

Fingleton, John and Ali Nikpay (2009), 'Stimulating or Chilling Competition', in Barry Hawk (ed.) *International Antitrust Law & Policy: Fordham Competition Law 2008*, Huntington, NY: Juris, pp. 385–419.

Fox, E. (2006), 'The WTO's First Antitrust Case – Mexican Telecom: A Sleeping Victory for Trade and Competition', *Journal of International Economic Law*, **9**(2), 271–92.

Gal, Michal S. (2009), 'Antitrust in a Globalized Economy: The Unique Enforcement Challenges Faced by Small and Developing Jurisdictions', *Fordham International Law Journal*, **33**(1), 1–56.

Grosman, Lucas Sebastián (2007), 'Piedras en el camino: una breve reflexión sobre el lugar de los consumidores y los competidores en la defense de la competencia', *Revista Jurídica de la Universidad de Palermo*, **8**, September, 185–9.

Lee, Barbara (2009), *Caricom Competition Commission: Enhancing Competition Enforcement in the Caribbean Community*, IDRC Pre-ICN Forum on Competition and Development: Competition Principles Under Threat, Ottawa: International Development Research Centre. Also available at http://www.crdi.ca/uploads/user-S/12458757281Pre-ICN_presentation_-_Barbara Lee.doc.

Levenstein, Margaret and Valerie Y. Suslow (2004), 'Contemporary International Cartels and Developing Countries: Economic Effects and Implications for Competition Policy', *Antitrust Law Journal*, **71**, 801–52.

Levy, Santiago and Michael Walton (2009), *No Growth Without Equity? Equality, Interests, and Competition in Mexico*, Washington, D.C.: Palgrave Macmillan/World Bank.

Mehta, Pradeep and Simon Evenett (2009), *Politics Trumps Economics? Political Economy and the Implementation of Competition Law and Economic Regulation in Developing Countries*, New Delhi: Academic Foundation.

Noll, Roger (2009), 'Priorities for Telecommunications Reform in Mexico', in Santiago Levy and Michael Walton, *No Growth Without Equity? Equality, Interests, and Competition in Mexico*, Washington, D.C.: Palgrave Macmillan/World Bank, pp. 365–388.

Roberts, Simon (2010) 'Competition policy, competitive rivalry and a developmental state in South Africa', in Omano Edigheji (ed.) *Constructing a Democratic Developmental State in South Africa*, South Africa: HSRC Press, pp. 222–37, also available at http://www.hsrcpress.ac.za.

Rodriquez, A.E. and Ashok Menon (2010), *The Limits of Competition Policy: The Shortcomings of Antitrust in Developing and Reforming Economies*, Netherlands: Kluwer Law International.

Sokol, D. Daniel (2007), 'Monopolists Without Borders: The Institutional Challenge of International Antitrust in a Global Gilded Age', *Berkeley Business Law Journal*, **4**, 37–122. Also available at http://ssrn.com/abstract=961380.

Stewart, Taimoon, (2005) 'Special Cooperation Provisions on Competition Law and Policy: The Case of Small Economies', in Philippe Brusick, Ana María Alvarez and Lucian Cernat *Competition Provisions in Regional Trade Agreements: How to Assure Development Gains*, United Nations Conference on Trade and Development (UNCTAD), New York and Geneva: United Nations, pp. 329–60.

UNCTAD (2000), *'The United Nations Set of Principles and Rules on Competition': The Set of Multilaterally Agreed Equitable Principles and Rules for the Control of Restrictive Business Practices*, United Nations Conference on Trade and Development, Geneva: United Nations.

Part I
Competition Law and Advocacy

A
Foundational Perspectives –
Are Developing Countries Different?

[1]

ECONOMIC DEVELOPMENT, POVERTY AND ANTITRUST: THE OTHER PATH

*Eleanor M. Fox**

"Technocrats may be inclined to ignore distributional issues, but no one else will."

Harvard Institute for International Development, 1991[1]

ABSTRACT

Antitrust law is a multi-faceted discipline. It guards against certain creations and misuses of economic power. It facilitates the functioning of markets. Sometimes it pries open closed markets, wresting them from public and crony control. In some jurisdictions it empowers David to compete against Goliath. In others, it shields David from being trampled by Goliath. In matters of antitrust, protection of the weak from the powerful is a refrain most loudly heard in connection with the asserted needs of developing countries.

Meanwhile, in developed countries, it is often insisted that antitrust is only "for efficiency," defined as aggregate consumer or total wealth and applied with the assumption that markets increase aggregate wealth. Developing countries retort that antitrust for developing countries must also address concerns of distribution and power. Developed countries rejoin that global efficiency demands that laws converge, and laws should converge toward that of the developed world, lest they protect inefficiencies, drive prices up, and increase risks of arbitrary enforcement power, defeating the promise of markets.

  * Eleanor Fox is the Walter J. Derenberg Professor of Trade Regulation at New York University School of Law.

  The author thanks Dennis Davis, John Fingleton, Frederic Jenny, Wolfgang Kerber and D. Daniel Sokol for their very helpful comments. She thanks the members of the symposium in honor of Lawrence Sullivan sponsored by Southwestern Law School. She thanks Gauri Chhabra and Meredith Laitner for their research assistance. Also, she is grateful to the Filomen D'Agostino and Max E. Greenberg Foundation for its generous research support.

  1. REFORMING ECONOMIC SYSTEMS IN DEVELOPING COUNTRIES 3 (Dwight H. Perkins & Michael Roemer eds., 1991).

This article wrestles with this tension. It argues that antitrust should not be used to protect David from Goliath, but it may be used to empower David against Goliath. The article suggests factors, principles, queries and strategies that may help developing countries in their quest for an antitrust law that is fair and efficient for them.

I. INTRODUCTION

This article is about competition, antitrust law, poverty and economic development.

It asks: What is the foundational perspective that should inform competition law in developing countries?

Important scholarship argues that context matters in designing and applying competition law and its supporting institutions for developing countries.[2] This literature commonly begins with the model of antitrust law of industrialized countries. It then asks what changes are warranted by context such as weak institutions, lack of funding, high barriers, and weak capital markets. This article takes a next step. It advocates the need for placing a developing country's antitrust in the broader context of development economics, and it asserts the relevance of the developing country's plight in the storms and bargains of world trade and competition.

Spokespeople for developing countries often express the need for an antitrust paradigm different from that of the developed world.[3] Spokespeople for the developed world tend to argue for universal

---

2. Ground-breaking work has been done by William Kovacic. *E.g.*, William Kovacic, *Capitalism, Socialism, and Competition Policy in Vietnam*, 13 ANTITRUST 57 (1999); William Kovacic, *Getting Started: Creating New Competition Policy Institutions in Transition Economies*, 23 BROOK. J. INT'L L. 403 (1997); William Kovacic, *The Competition Policy Entrepreneur and Law Reform in Formerly Communist and Socialist Countries*, 11 AM. U. J. INT'L L. & POL'Y 437 (1996); William Kovacic, *Designing and Implementing Competition and Consumer Protection Reforms in Transitional Economies: Perspectives from Mongolia, Nepal, Ukraine and Zimbabwe*, 44 DEPAUL L. REV. 1197 (1995); William Kovacic, *Competition Policy, Economic Development, and the Transition to Free Markets in the Third World: The Case of Zimbabwe*, 61 ANTITRUST L.J. 253 (1992); William E. Kovacic & Robert S. Thorpe, *Antitrust and the Evolution of a Market Economy in Mongolia*, in DE-MONOPOLIZATION AND COMPETITION POLICY IN POST-COMMUNIST ECONOMIES 89 (Ben Slay ed., 1994).

3. *See* AJIT SINGH, U.N. CONF. ON TRADE & DEV., COMPETITION AND COMPETITION POLICY IN EMERGING MARKETS: INTERNATIONAL AND DEVELOPMENTAL DIMENSIONS (2002).

norms,[4] which may apply differently when facts are different. Moreover, they commonly describe antitrust as "for efficiency."[5]

This article takes a different starting point. It asks: If you were a policymaker in a country whose principal economic problem was deep systemic poverty, aggravated by corruption, cronyism, selective statism, weak institutions, and often unstable democracy,[6] what is the foundational perspective on which you would formulate your country's antitrust law? In particular, would you choose a foundational principle that trusts liberalization and free enterprise ("first model"), or would you choose a foundational principle that centrally takes account of the opacity, blockage and political capture of your markets, and includes some measure of helping to empower people economically to help themselves ("second model")? There are, of course, other formulations. There are also formulations within the formulations.[7]

---

4. *See, e.g.,* Makan Delrahim, *The Long and Winding Road: Convergence in the Application of Antitrust to Intellectual Property*, Remarks at George Mason Law Review Symposium (Oct. 6, 2004), *in* 13 Geo. Mason L. Rev. 259 (2005) ("consensus-based antitrust enforcement is vital to global business and consumer welfare").

5. By one common formulation, antitrust is only for efficiency. One common formulation of the efficiency standard is that antitrust law should proscribe only that which disserves consumers and is inefficient, as judged by output limitation. Business conduct other than hardcore cartels is presumed efficient; it is argued that, apart from cartels, the law should proscribe only conduct that has an output-limiting outcome and is not a legitimate business response to consumers.

There are alternative ways to regard efficiency and how to achieve it. One major alternative would focus on preserving the structure and forces of competition, positing that the process of competition is most likely to create incentives to compete and invent. Diversity and openness are thought to promote knowledge and experimentation and to function as a feedback mechanism that facilitates adaptation and dynamic change. *See* Wolfgang Kerber, Competition, Experimentation, and Legal Rules and Institutional Framework (Dec. 2, 2006) (unpublished manuscript, on file with author); *see also* Eleanor Fox, *What is Harm to Competition? Exclusionary Practices and Anticompetitive Effect*, 70 Antitrust L.J. 371 (2002).

6. Mark Dutz and R. Shyam Khemani wrote on the "tyranny of predatory vested interests":

> These factors [high market concentration, high barriers to entry, high ownership concentration and weak corporate governance] tend to reinforce one another and give rise to inflexible, inefficient industrial and financial market structures. They also have adverse implications not only for fostering effective competition and competitiveness, but also for governance at both the state and corporate levels – and for the persistence of an anti-competitive nexus mutually supporting vested interests between incumbent firms and government, with some of the earned rents used to entrench market power by buying government favoritism. Since firms tend to be large in size and few in number, they have organizational and financial advantages in influencing legislation and regulation.

Mark Dutz & R. Shyam Khemani, Competition Law & Policy: Challenges in South Asia 11 (2007).

7. For example, one mainstream perspective assumes that markets work well and that government interventions work badly (neo-liberal assumptions). At the other end of the contin-

214 *SOUTHWESTERN JOURNAL OF LAW & TRADE IN THE AMERICAS* [Vol. 13

The answer is not uncomplicated. Even if the second model might seem more legitimate to a developing economy in the abstract, the first model is a path well-traveled, and reinventing a path is difficult and costly. Moreover, the first model offers some clear and relatively simple rules without risking the costs of too much intervention and costs of excessive discretion by officials.

The article concludes by suggesting that reliance on markets is critical for economic welfare; that the neo-liberal principles that animate much of antitrust law in this age of "modernization"[8] are not necessary for efficiency and could run contrary to it; and that developing countries might wish to explore a path more sympathetic to their context.

This article is written at a time when "convergence" is repeatedly referenced as an imperative objective of antitrust in a globalized world. Convergence implies universal standards, or at least universal norms implemented in common ways. The phrase "universal standards" normally refers to the standards of the United States and Europe.[9] This article suggests that developing countries should nonetheless consider the benefits of their own perspective. It further suggests that substantial convergence can be achieved and will naturally occur even in the face of varying perspectives.

II. THE CHOICE

Approximately one hundred nations in the world have adopted antitrust laws. Perhaps a quarter of these nations are developed countries. Yet other developing countries have not adopted antitrust laws; some are considering doing so.

---

uum, analysts may acknowledge that market structures may be "skewed in favour of entrenched elites with inequitable distributions of wealth with social stratification drawn along racial or ethnic lines," a situation that competition law might exacerbate. TAIMOON STEWART, JULIAN CLARKE & SUSAN JOEKES, COMPETITION LAW IN ACTION: EXPERIENCES FROM DEVELOPING COUNTRIES iv (2007), *available at* http://www.idrc.ca/en/ev-111677-201-1-DO_TOPIC.html.

8. Both the United States and the European Union have launched commissions or projects to consider how competition law should be modernized. Moreover, in the United States, successive Supreme Court opinions have narrowed the purview of U.S. antitrust law. *See, e.g.*, Leegin Creative Leather Prods., Inc. v. PSKS, Inc., No. 06-480, 2007 WL 1835892 (U.S. June 28, 2007); Weyerhaeuser Co. v. Ross-Simmons Hardwood Lumber Co., Inc., 127 S. Ct. 1069 (2007); Volvo Trucks N. Am., Inc. v. Reeder-Simco GMC, Inc., 546 U.S. 164 (2006); Ill. Tool Works Inc. v. Independent Ink, Inc., 547 U.S. 28 (2006).

9. This is the case even while the standards of the United States and Europe are changing, as institutions in both jurisdictions embark on "modernization" projects, and as the United States Supreme Court successively narrows the scope of the law. Yet with the economic rise of China and India, one might expect the American and Euro-centric center of gravity to shift and to do so in ways not predictable today.

By one perspective, all of these nations should adopt antitrust laws;[10] and all of these nations should adopt the developed world's framework: free markets and antitrust in their service. Much like the developed countries, developing economies are riddled with cartels and other restraints that obstruct their markets and hurt their people. Globalization has lowered barriers and paved the way to the efficiency benefits from markets and, it is argued, liberalization and antitrust should work hand-in-hand to anchor these benefits.[11]

This paper argues that antitrust for developing countries must be seen in a larger context. The canvas includes the dire economic conditions of developing countries and the treatment they receive from the world community. Developing countries often see free-market rhetoric and aggregate wealth or welfare goals as inappropriate to their context because of the tendency of free-market policies to disproportionately advantage the already advantaged in every game played.[12]

This does not imply that antitrust for developing countries would or should look dramatically different from a developed country's antitrust. There are reasons why it might look much the same, as I develop below; but there are also reasons why the perspective might differ from the neo-liberal one that currently informs many antitrust laws of developed countries – a perspective that has "relatively little resonance for the great majority of the population that is poor."[13]

III.   THE STACK OF THE DECK: A FEW SYMBOLS

In the mid-1990s, the symbol of globalization was both cast and burnished by a concept and epithet called the "Washington Consen-

---

10. *Compare* A.E. Rodriguez and Mark D. Williams, *The Effectiveness of Proposed Antitrust Programs for Developing Countries*, 19 N.C. J. INT'L L. & COM. REG. 209 (1994) (arguing that antitrust law is largely inappropriate for developing countries and that the liberal effects of the law will be overwhelmed by interest-group politics procuring protection), *with* Craig W. Conrath and Barry T. Freeman, *A Response to "The Effectiveness of Proposed Antitrust Programs for Developing Countries,"* 19 N.C. J. INT'L L. & COM. REG. 233 (1994) (arguing that antitrust law and advocacy will benefit consumers).

11. Efficiency is usually seen as the measure of antitrust benefits. At this point I do not raise differences between consumer welfare and total welfare in measuring efficiency. I stress aggregate concepts – whether defined in terms of all consumers or all consumers and producers: Do the winners win more than the losers lose? And if so, should we disregard distributional consequences?

12. *See* Nancy Birdsall, *Inequality Matters: Why Globalization Doesn't Lift All Boats*, BOSTON REV., Mar.-Apr. 2007, at 7; Francis Fukuyama, *Keeping Up with the Chavezes*, WALL ST. J., Feb. 1, 2007, at A17; Peter Sutherland, *The Doha Development Agenda: Political Challenges to the World Trading System—A Cosmopolitan Perspective*, 8 J. INT'L ECON. L. 363 (2005).

13. Fukuyama, *supra* note 12.

216 SOUTHWESTERN JOURNAL OF LAW & TRADE IN THE AMERICAS [Vol. 13

sus."[14] The Washington Consensus prescribed deregulation, privatization, liberalization, clear property rights, and fiscal discipline. Following this prescription, it predicted enhanced growth for the economies of developing countries.[15]

Citizens and advocates of the developing world quickly observed the other side of the coin. Globalization also tended to increase the disparity of wealth and opportunity to the harm of some of the poorest people.[16] In certain least developed countries it made many producers worse off as their exported commodities faced more com-

---

14. John Williamson wrote THE PROGRESS OF POLICY REFORM IN LATIN AMERICA, the book that gave rise to the epithet, Washington Consensus. The book emphasizes the importance of reliance on market forces and sound fiscal and monetary policies for Latin American countries. The epithet became a generalized neo-conservative prescription. JOHN WILLIAMSON, THE PROGRESS OF POLICY REFORM IN LATIN AMERICA (1990).

15. *See* JOSEPH E. STIGLITZ & ANDREW CHARLTON, FAIR TRADE FOR ALL: HOW TRADE CAN PROMOTE DEVELOPMENT 2 (2005); *see also* Dani Rodrik, *Feasible Globalizations, in* GLOBALIZATION: WHAT'S NEW? 196 (Michael W. Weinstein ed., 2005); Jeffrey D. Sachs, *Globalization and Patterns of Economic Growth, in* GLOBALIZATION: WHAT'S NEW? 214 (Michael W. Weinstein ed., 2005). All three sources contest or qualify the premises and efficaciousness of the Washington Consensus

16. *See* Anna Bernasek, *Income Inequality and its Cost*, N.Y. TIMES, June 25, 2006; *cf.* David Dollar, *Globalization, Poverty and Equality, in* GLOBALIZATION: WHAT'S NEW?, *supra* note 15, at 96 (suggesting that opening up trade "has been a good strategy" for countries such as China, Mexico, and Uganda); *id.* at 97; *but see* Birdsall, *supra* note 12 (distinguishing good inequality, which incentivizes people who are able to respond to incentives and "is consistent with efficient allocation of resources," from "destructive inequality [which] reflects privileges for the already rich and blocks potential for productive contributions of the less rich."). Birdsall notes that while globalization has produced rapid economic growth in India and China, moving millions of people out of poverty, it has also left millions of the poorest, even in India and China, equally or worse off and has caused inequality to rise.

India is in persistent poverty: "[T]he increasingly common, business-centric view of India suppresses more facts than it reveals. Recent accounts of the alleged rise of India barely mention the fact that the country's $728 per capita gross domestic product is just slightly higher than that of sub-Saharan Africa . . . . Malnutrition affects more than half of all children in India and there is little sign that they are being helped by the country's market reforms, which have focused on creating private wealth . . . . Feeding on the resentment of those left behind by the urban-oriented economic growth, communist insurgencies . . . have erupted in some of the most populous and poorest parts of north and central India [in districts that the government no longer effectively controls]." Pankaj Mishra, *The Myth of the New India*, N.Y. TIMES, July 6, 2006, at A1.

See also Pascal Lamy, Dir. Gen., WTO, Making Trade Work for Development: Time for a "Geneva Consensus," Emil Noel Lecture, New York University School of Law (Oct. 30, 2006) (transcript available at http://www.nyulawglobal.com/events/documents/emilenoellecturefall06.pdf). Pascal Lamy recounts the bias in the prior trade rounds against developing countries. He notes the persistence of "economic colonization" and the developing countries' "bitter" "potion" of intractable adjustment problems. Developing countries' problems of adjustment to the onrush of free trade are particularly serious "because [trade openings] often hit larger parts of the population and because the countries have little capacity to handle the much needed accompanying policies to assist the victims of globalization." *Id.* at 6, 7, 10. Moreover, developing countries usually lack safety nets, and lack of safety nets means that job loss causes

petition in world markets, their value-added exports faced high tar-iffs,[17] and the prices demanded for value-added imports were often supra-competitively high.

Moreover, while talking the talk of liberalization, developed countries often liberalized where convenient and resisted liberaliza-tion where inconvenient. This has been particularly true in the case of agriculture, where developing countries often have significant com-parative advantage. Industrialized countries flooded African markets with deeply subsidized cotton, displacing and threatening the liveli-hoods of African farmers who produced cotton at two-thirds of the importers' cost.[18] Thus, even though developed countries gave mil-lions of dollars for development[19] and insisted that the poor should work to help themselves, they continued to block opportunities for efficient but poor foreign producers who attempted to help them-selves by competing on the merits.[20] Journalist Martin Wolf calls this phenomenon the "Hypocrisy of the Rich."[21]

Persistent world-game strategies tend to keep the advantaged on top and the disadvantaged on bottom.[22] For this, there are several symbols. One is "Seattle."[23] Seattle evokes the memory of the riots that opposed the prospect of freer trade under the aegis of the World Trade Organization ("WTO") without giving the usual losers a signifi-cant voice; the losers are those who consistently get an unfair and meager share of the gains from trade unleashed by globalization and liberalization.

In the wake of Seattle and subsequent flash points, the greatest economic problem in the world – deep systemic poverty and its link to inequality – could no longer be pushed to the margins. Nearly twenty

---

severe hardship. Further, the promised benefits of market openings are harder to capture: the time and costs to market (e.g., trucking goods to a port) can overwhelm gains.

17. RALPH KAPLINSKY, GLOBALIZATION, POVERTY AND INEQUALITY: BETWEEN A ROCK AND A HARD PLACE 57 (2005).

18. *See* MARTIN WOLF, WHY GLOBALIZATION WORKS 212-218 (2005).

19. *See* WILLIAM EASTERLY, THE WHITE MAN'S BURDEN: WHY THE WEST'S EFFORTS TO AID THE REST HAVE DONE SO MUCH ILL AND SO LITTLE GOOD (2006).

20. Competition on the merits is competition that is based on cost and quality.

21. *See* WOLF, *supra* note 18; *see also* Dani Rodrik, *Goodbye Washington Consensus, Hello Washington Confusion? A Review of the World Bank's Economic Growth in the 1990s: Learning from a Decade of Reform*, 44 J. ECON. LITERATURE 973 (2006) [hereinafter *Goodbye Washington Consensus*].

22. *See* Birdsall, *supra* note 12.

23. *See, e.g.*, JOSEPH STIGLITZ, THE ROARING NINETIES: WHY WE'RE PAYING THE PRICE FOR THE GREEDIEST DECADE IN HISTORY 238 (2003) (identifying the Seattle meeting as the occasion for "the backlash against globalization" and as a "civil demonstration of a magnitude that had not been seen in more than a quarter century").

percent of the world's population lives on less than one dollar a day, and in sub-Saharan Africa this figure rises to more than forty percent.[24] Persistent poverty reduces the physical and mental capabilities of large populations.[25] It saps the work force and productivity in the poorest nations, undermining their promise of efficiency (no less, humanity). It increases spending on health care, which decreases savings and investment.[26] Moreover, income inequality breeds corruption.[27] It activates a spiral that leads to more economic and political inequality.[28]

In the year 2000, the heightened global concern with poverty produced the United Nations' Millennium Development Goals (MDGs). The MDGs aspired to halve the percentage of the world's severely poor by 2015. We are halfway there by years but not by performance, although rates of extreme poverty are falling, especially in Asia.[29]

Most of the specified strategies for reaching the anti-poverty goal are in the nature of benefits and public goods – health, school meals, education, infrastructure, debt forgiveness.[30] This paper, however, will focus on MDGs and markets.[31] "MDGs" is a gripping symbol.

It is fair to ask: Have we met a clash of symbols?

This paper argues:

---

24. A dollar a day is a translation of income levels based on a measure called "purchasing power parity." *See* KAPLINSKY, *supra* note 17, at 27-30.

25. *See* Editorial, *A Better Way to Fight Poverty*, N.Y. TIMES, May 5, 2005, at A34.

26. Bernasek, *supra* note 16.

27. *See* Charles W. Calomiris, *Capital Flows, Financial Crises, and Public Policy, in* GLOBALIZATION: WHAT'S NEW? 36 (Michael W. Weinstein ed., 2005); William Easterly, *The Rich Have Markets, the Poor Have Bureaucrats, in* GLOBALIZATION: WHAT'S NEW? 170 (Michael W. Weinstein ed., 2005).

28. As one economics professor from Harvard observed, with greater wealth comes greater political influence: "If the rich can influence political outcomes through lobbying activities or membership in special interest groups, then more inequality could lead to less redistribution rather than more." Bernasek, *supra* note 16 (quoting Edmond Glaeser).

29. U.N., Millennium Development Goals Report 2006 (2006).

30. *See* The Secretary-General, *Report of the Secretary-General: Road Map Towards the Implementation of the United Nations Millennium Declaration*, U.N. GAOR, 56th Sess., U.N. Doc. A/56/326 (Sept. 6, 2001).

See SIMON J. EVENETT, COMPETITION AND THE MILLENNIUM DEVELOPMENT GOALS: NEW "EVIDENCE" FROM OFFICIAL SOURCES (2006) (stating that the policy makers do not see a strong link between competition and the Millenium Development Goals [hereinafter "MDGs"] and other indicators of development although these links exist), *available at* http://www.evenett.com/working/CompandMDGs200206.pdf.

31. I do not argue that antitrust should become poverty law. Rather, I argue that antitrust for developing countries that ignores poverty and maldistribution risks 1) being a hostile law that does not command legitimacy and does not take root, or 2) inducing, to fill the gap, an unfair competition law that has no market consciousness as a rudder.

1. Market tools are a very important part of the panoply of tools needed to address world poverty and should be used liberally. These market tools include market-freeing measures that reduce prices. They also include antitrust priority-setting that targets conspiracies that raise the price of staples, such as milk, bread, transportation and utilities, helping the poor[32] as well as those who are better off. Moreover, as observed by Professor Simon Evenett, "the conceptual arguments and available empirical evidence by and large support[ ] the view that promoting inter-firm rivalry enhances the dynamic economic performance of developing economies."[33]

2. At the same time, outside of the area of cartels, there are limits to the modern Western antitrust framework, especially when applied to developing countries and populations mired in poverty. For macroeconomics, the limits of the neo-liberal approach have been well-documented.[34]

The deck is stacked in favor of those on high rungs of the ladder in skill, education, capital, and mobility; it is stacked in favor of those who live in an economy with a supportive infrastructure, composed of non-corrupt and well-funded institutions.[35] Moreover, certain modern versions of industrialized countries' antitrust, and even qualified versions that recognize the weaknesses of institutional structures and markets, focus only on the allocation of resources and the size of the pie. The guiding concern is that inefficient anticompetitive practices may cause the pie to shrink, even while it is posited that non-cartel acts almost never cause the pie to shrink.[36] Proponents of this per-

---

32. *See* WORLD BANK, WORLD DEVELOPMENT REPORT 2000/2001: ATTACKING POVERTY 61 (2000), *available at* www.worldbank.org/prem/poverty/wdrpoverty/report/ch4.pdf.

Lower agricultural prices can of course hurt poor farmers. This is a cost of competition and markets. It is a relatively short-term cost that even poor societies should probably choose to bear for a better future; but they may find it difficult to do so; and the political power of farmers might prevail over consumer choice.

33. SIMON J. EVENETT, U.K.'S DEP'T FOR INT'L DEV., LINKS BETWEEN DEVELOPMENT AND COMPETITION LAW IN DEVELOPING COUNTRIES (2003), *available at* http://www.evenett.com/reports/dfidpaper.pdf; *see also* Ana Maria Alvarez, Simon J. Evenett & Laurence Wilse-Samson, *Anti-Competitive Practices and the Attainment of the Millennium Development Goals: Implications for Competition Law Enforcement and Inter-Agency Cooperation, in* IMPLEMENTING COMPETITION-RELATED PROVISIONS IN REGIONAL TRADE AGREEMENTS: IS IT POSSIBLE TO OBTAIN DEVELOPMENT GAINS? 60 (2007).

34. *See, e.g.*, STIGLITZ, *supra* note 23, at 228-240; Rodrik, *Goodbye Washington Consensus, supra* note 21.

35. *See* Lamy, *supra* note 16; Birdsall, *supra* note 12.

36. *See* Verizon Commc'ns Inc. v. Law Offices of Curtis V. Trinko, LLP ("Trinko"), 540 U.S. 398 (2004); Bus. Elecs. Corp. v. Sharp Elecs. Corp., 485 U.S. 717, 727 (1988). In *Trinko* the Court said: "The mere possession of monopoly power, and the concomitant charging of monopoly prices, is not only not unlawful; it is an important element of the free market system. The

spective on aggregate efficiency or wealth do not grapple with deontological questions of power and how opportunity is distributed. They normally presume that an antitrust approach on the distribution of opportunity and wealth will shrink the size of the pie and make even the poorest worse off. Developing countries, however, may disagree.[37]

By contrast, the Millennium Development Goals are centrally *about* distribution.[38] Achieving the goals is perceived to be central to the well-being of the developing world and indirectly, all the world. This article argues that if policy is to be friendly to economic development, it must look dire poverty in the eye.[39] This means not only harnessing market forces to keep prices competitive; it also means building a ladder of mobility from the lowest rung up to enable mobility, incentivize entrepreneurship,[40] and stimulate invention.[41] It implies a consciousness about not expanding the moat between rich and poor, the enabled and the powerless. The mobility imperative[42] applies to economic policy. In particular, it applies to competition law and policy. If competition law in developing countries threatens to widen or preserve the inequality moat rather than build the mobility ladder, there is a serious question whether free-market competition law beyond anti-cartel law[43] should be advocated for the developing world.

---

opportunity to charge monopoly prices – at least for a short period – is what attracts 'business acumen' in the first place; it induces risk taking that produces innovation and economic growth." *Id.* at 407.

37. *See* Ajit Singh, *Multilateral Competition Policy and Economic Development: A Developing Country Perspective on the European Community Proposals* (paper presented at the fifth session of the Intergovernmental Group of Experts on Competition Law and Policy, Geneva, July 2-4, 2004), *available at* http://www.networkideas.org/feathm/aug2003/MCP.pdf; STEWART ET AL., *supra* note 7.

38. This is so even though allocative measures are likely to have a positive effect on the plight of the severely poor by reducing the price of necessities provided by market actors.

39. This was the tenet of the faltered Doha Development Trade Round. *See* Lamy, *supra* note 16.

40. *See* Mark Dutz, Janusz Ordover & Robert Willig, *Entrepreneurship, Access Policy and Economic Development: Lessons from Industrial Organization*, 44 Eur. Econ. Rev. 739 (2000).

41. The ladder metaphor is also used in JEFFREY D. SACHS, THE END OF POVERTY: ECONOMIC POSSIBILITIES FOR OUR TIME 73 (2005).

42. *See* DUTZ & KHEMANI, *supra* note 6, at 6 ("By helping to lower public . . . and private barriers to entry and [removing] restraints to trade, competition law and policy can help create opportunities for broadly based participation in the economy.").

43. Anti-cartel law responds to both the neo-liberal and liberal sentiments: neo-liberal because it removes barriers to efficiency; liberal because it responds to sentiments of fairness and fair rules of governance, i.e., that markets should be governed by impersonal forces and not by a few powerful people.

IV. THE COMPETITION CHALLENGE

A. Introduction

We put poverty at the center of our concerns. Related is the "left behind" or marginalization problem. We assume that developing countries, on the whole, wish to become part of the increasingly integrated world economy with the hope of increasing their economic opportunities, generating higher rates of profit and growth, and inducing a higher rate of investment in their countries.

Do all nations want to follow this path of globalization and integration? Becoming a part of the world market system may entail a dramatic shift, with the fear of homogenization and loss of community.[44] This essay is focused on nations that choose the more integrated route, as do most nations today.

It is hard for the advantaged to put poverty and inequality at the center of our concerns. It is hard because we are drawn ineluctably to the models of law that we know and not because we resist the challenge; we are drawn to imagine that our sun is the center of the universe. From this perspective, we would propose the model we know, modified slightly to take account of flawed capital markets, to make competition law friendlier to developing countries. This approach is often taken, and this is a problem that must be examined.

Assuming that developing countries choose to increase economic interconnection, we should ask: First, to what extent will competition and the market help developing countries develop efficiently for the good of their people? Second, to what extent will antitrust law help? Third, if antitrust law, what form of antitrust law?

B. To What Extent Will Competition and the Market Help?

Freeing up the market has been shown to hold great economic benefits for developing and transitional countries. The converse approach to freeing the market, command-and-control, so ill served Russia and Eastern Europe that it fell of its own weight.[45]

---

44. *See* CHINUA ACHEBE, THINGS FALL APART (1962).

45. A third option – among others along the continuum – is a combination of competition and industrial policy. Some commentators argue that industrial policy in Japan and Korea put those nations on a sound footing before they fully exposed their businesses to the winds of competition. Others observe, however, that vibrant competition within the borders of both nations co-existed with government-managed external competition; and these commentators credit the countries' successes to the market and not to its suppression. *See* Working Group on the Interaction between Trade and Competition Policy, *Study of Issues Relating to a Possible Multilateral Framework on Competition Policy,* ¶¶ 168-257, WT/WGTCP/W/228 (May 19, 2003), *available at* http://www.jmcti.org/2000round/com/doha/wg/wt_wgtcp_w_228.pdf; *see also* Singh, *supra*

Hernando de Soto, in *The Other Path*, eloquently demonstrates the benefits of tearing down barriers to free market participation. He catalogued and studied the barriers, such as dense licensing requirements, that kept the poorest Peruvians outside of Peru's market system, relegating them to their own informal economy. Alienated by the exclusion and their dismal lives, many joined the terrorist Shining Path. To counter the Shining Path and its destructive forces, de Soto proposed another path ("el otro sendero"): tearing down the barriers to participation in the recognized economy; giving people hope and chance; enabling the poor to participate in markets on their merits. *The Other Path*[46] is a blueprint for building the ladder of mobility. It envisions a society that values mobility; that opens the door to inclusion, from the poorest up; and it proposes to do so for pragmatic reasons of building a better society.

The counter viewpoint – hospitality to government control and indifference to the plight of the excluded – blocks the market through excessive regulation, privilege, and cronyism. The powerful insiders protect their friends at the expense of the public and often at the particular expense of the poor. This was the story of Telmex in Mexico. Owned by a crony of presidents, Telmex was guaranteed a monopoly price for incoming cross-border telecom connections; but the monopoly price was guaranteed at the expense of poor Mexicans who migrated to the United States for work and whose telephone life-line was to Mexico.[47] As for small new telecom companies in Mexico, the

---

note 37 (developing countries often query whether they should follow the model of Japan and Korea).

Free markets are regarded with some skepticism by the new left in several South American countries, wherein the populace complains that it has not seen the benefits of liberalization. The economic, social and political reforms in Latin America beginning in the 1980s had not delivered their promises of economic growth and there was resentment among the people because the reforms had not reduced poverty and inequality. This produced a populist shift towards socialism, returning more power to the state and rolling back whatever achievements were made. *See* Jorge Castañeda, *Latin America's Left Turn*, FOREIGN AFFAIRS, May-June 2006, at 28.

46. HERNANDO DE SOTO, THE OTHER PATH: THE INVISIBLE REVOLUTION IN THE THIRD WORLD (1989).

47. Not only do the poor suffer from prices that are too high, but they suffer from suppressed growth. "[T]he rest of the country suffered from [Telmex's] favored position. In a modern age when businesses need low-priced, high-quality telecommunications to compete in a global economy, Mexican growth has borne the cost of Mr. Slim's privilege. Any genuine effort to help the poor necessarily requires more healthy competition, starting in the telecom market." *See* Mary Anastasia O'Grady, *A Telecom Monopoly Cripples Mexico*, WALL ST. J., Feb. 10, 2006, at A19.

entrenched system deprived them of the right to price-compete against Telmex for incoming calls.[48]

Thus, not only does globalization tend to stack the deck against developing countries and those who are least able (least educated, skilled and monied, and lacking infrastructure) to ride the wave of globalization's opportunities;[49] but globalization also allows cronyistic governments to block upward mobility and entrench the condition of the poor.

Antitrust can help. But what form of antitrust?

C. *Antitrust*

(1) What Form of Antitrust?

Antitrust law is a subset of competition policy. Liberalization helps to open markets so they can work. In the vision of de Soto, liberalization tears down barriers, especially those barriers facing the people who are the least well off. It invites these often alienated individuals into the economic system, giving them hope, dignity and self worth.

Antitrust law cures artificial obstructions market players create on the market. But nations disagree on the types of acts that constitute an artificial obstruction. Are they only acts that shrink the size of the pie, decrease aggregate wealth, and are allocatively inefficient?[50] Or are they also acts that block the channels of mobility and which keep worthy actors down and moats wide?[51] If the latter, obstructions can be seen in more human terms and perhaps antitrust policy and its language can be better aligned with efficient development.[52]

There is good reason why mobility factors should play a role in the antitrust laws of developing countries. The marketplace should give firms, including smaller and younger firms, a fair chance to compete on the merits of their product, free from artificial and unneces-

---

48. *See* Eleanor Fox, *The WTO's First Antitrust Case – Mexican Telecoms: A Sleeping Victory for Trade and Competition,* 9 J. OF INT'L ECON. LAW 271 (2006).

49. *See* Lamy, *supra* note 16.

50. It is important for an antitrust agency to identify and target anticompetitive acts that shrink the pie. I do not imply the contrary.

51. *See* Eleanor Fox, *What is Harm to Competition? Exclusionary Practices and Anticompetitive Effect,* 70 ANTITRUST L.J. 371 (2002).

52. Protecting mobility and opportunity on the merits need not and should not imply protecting inefficient competitors from competition or handicapping efficient firms. *See* Eleanor Fox, *We Protect Competition, You Protect Competitors,* 26 WORLD COMPETITION 149 (2003); *see also* DUTZ & KHEMANI, *supra* note 6.

See Michael Boudin, *Antitrust Doctrine and the Sway of Metaphor,* 75 GEO. L.J. 395 (1986), for a discussion as to the power of metaphor.

224 *SOUTHWESTERN JOURNAL OF LAW & TRADE IN THE AMERICAS* [Vol. 13

sary foreclosing restraints by powerful firms. Empowerment to engage in markets free of unnecessary business restraints is the counterpart to de Soto's vision of empowerment to engage in markets free from unnecessary government restraints. Undue market restraints, whether public or private, retard efficient development. They may also harm allocative efficiency and surely do not advance it. To the extent that "efficiency" as the goal of antitrust implies disregard of distributional values, it may not be the centerpiece that developing countries would choose.

(2)   Assessing the Local Problems Before Adopting Law

Law-making should come from within, not without. Legislation should respond to contextual problems that need to be solved. Law is not ideally generated by outsiders who say: We have this law and you should, too.[53] Therefore it is important to take stock and to assemble the facts: Who within the country is harmed by what practices? How can the harms be prevented? And at what cost?

Professors Jenny and Evenett, and Consumers Unity & Trust Society under the leadership of Pradeep Mehta, have done noteworthy work to build the databases that answer these questions. The data show:

Seller cartels target basic necessities, including staples of diets. In Peru, poultry farms and their trade association conspired to eliminate competitors and prevent entry. In Zambia, the dominant producer of day-old chickens required the biggest buyer to stay out of the production market, and the buyer agreed to the requirement.

Evidence of buying cartels is rampant. This includes cartels that exploit small farmers and producers such as coffee producers in Kenya and Latin America, cotton, tea and tobacco growers in Malawi, milk processors in Chile, and fish processors near Lake Victoria.

Cartels, boycotts, and non-compete agreements have been detected and prosecuted in the milling and baking, milk and sugar mar-

---

53. The two clauses need a link. Does the outsider claim that the law is needed to solve negative externalities visited on the outsider, as in pollution: Your smokestacks are polluting us? Does the outsider claim that its businesses pay a cost and to be fair the insider's businesses should pay the same costs? Does the outsider claim: If only you will make your laws like ours, our businesses will find it easier to make more money in your backyard? Or is the outsider altruistic; a paternalistic good Samaritan: We know this is good for you; we "offer" it to you.

See Daniel Berkowitz, Katharina Pistor & Jean Francois Richard, *Economic Development, Legality, and the Transplant Effect*, 47 EUR. L. REV. 165 (2003), for a discussion of the problems of legal transplants when the law is not adapted to the country's conditions.

kets. Beer mergers in highly concentrated beer markets threatened to exploit buyers in Namibia, Turkey, Malawi, Kenya and Tanzania.

In Kenya, owners of minivans sought monopolies over lucrative routes and teamed up with criminal gangs, not only overcharging but also terrorizing the population. Also in Kenya, the fertilizer manufacturers organized a secret bidding cartel in their tenders to the government by buying authority, which impoverished the farmers who needed an increasing number of supplies.

In many countries, numerous vertical agreements have tied up scarce channels of distribution.

In Turkey, the two dominant telecommunication firms had sole control of the infrastructure necessary to provide national roaming capability for GSM mobile telephone service and refused to allow access to would-be new entrants. Typically, dominant firms have been found to deny small firms access to essential facilities such as telecom and electricity infrastructure.[54]

Press stories add to the data daily. In Mexico, half of the people live on $4 or less a day, and many survive on tortillas and beans. From December 2006 to January 2007, the price of corn soared, and the price of the tortilla rose by 35 cents a pound. The *New York Times* reported: "The crisis has hit hardest for the poorest Mexicans, who may spend more than a quarter of their daily salaries on tortillas."[55] It has displaced poor tortilla makers, who have lost up to forty percent of their business, since the people are compelled to buy and eat less. While the price shock came first from extraneous causes, the giant Mexican tortilla makers took advantage of the situation, "hoarding

---

54. *See* Frederic Jenny, Anticompetitive Practices in Developing Countries: Lessons from Empirical Evidence (May 23-24, 2005) (unpublished paper presented at First National Competition Seminar, Amman, Jordan) (on file with author); Frederic Jenny, *Anti-Competitive Agreements: Meaning and Examples*, CARIBBEAN DIALOGUE, July-Sept. 2004, at 1 (anticompetitive practices in Trinidad and Tobago, Kenya, Lebanon, Indonesia and other smaller economies; Kovacic, *supra* note 2; Alvarez, Evenett and Wilse-Samson, *supra* note 33. The latter chapter documents numerous other specific restraints in health, education, financial services for low-income earners, infrastructure and housing, and food. *Id.* at 65-77; *see also Pulling Up Our Socks* (Consumer Unity and Trust Society Centre for Competition, Investment & Economic Regulation, Rajasthan, India), Feb. 2003 (report based on the 7-Up Project analyzing competition problems in seven developing countries – Kenya, Tanzania, Zambia, South Africa, Sri Lanka, Pakistan and India); PRADEEP S. MEHTA & NITYA NANDA, COMPETITION POLICY, GROWTH AND POVERTY REDUCTION IN DEVELOPING COUNTRIES, http://www.competition-regulation.org.uk/conferences/southafrica04/mehta&nanda.pdf (last visited June 30, 2007). For examples of abuse of dominance violations in Latin American countries, see Russell W. Pittman & Maria Coppola Tineo, *Abuse of Dominance Enforcement under Latin American Competition Laws*, Mar. 2006, http://ssrn.com/abstract=888186.

55. James C. McKinley Jr., *Cost of Corn Soars, Forcing Mexico to Set Price Limits*, N.Y. TIMES, Jan. 19, 2007, at A12.

supplies to drive prices up even more," according to Mexican officials.[56]

Mexico's monopolies thrive even under the free market regime of President Calderon. Jorge Castañeda, Mexico's former foreign minister, wrote: "The monopolist control of practically every walk of Mexican life is in place . . . ." Huge monopolies that exclude and exploit dominate the country in oil, electricity, telephone (fixed line and mobile), television, cement, banks, bread, and tortilla production.[57]

The case of Mexico is not unique to the developing world. It is typical.

In sum, the people of developing countries are impacted by cartels and monopolistic practices. These practices include those that raise consumer prices and input prices to their businesses, which exclude or build hurdles to their outputs, and foreclose domestic suppliers. They do so by all means: coercive practices such as boycotts, covenants not to compete, price manipulation, and predation. They shore up their power to do so by mergers. Anticompetitive practices are rife in areas of physical and business necessity, such as milk, soft drinks, beer, chicken, sugar, cotton, paper, aluminum, steel, chemicals (for fertilizer), telecommunications including mobile services, cement and other construction materials, transportation including trucking, shipping, and port access, industrial gases, banking, insurance, coal and electricity. Many of the practices are local, many are facilitated by the government, and many others are offshore, resulting in inbound restraints.

(3) A Perspective

Let us suppose that we are policymakers who live and work in a developing country and we have at heart the welfare of our fellow citizens. Half of our fellow citizens live in abject poverty. A third of the citizens are farmers. We have extractive natural resources. We have a thin manufacturing industry with potential for growth. We have cotton and lumber. Our people are extraordinary craftspeople. Most of our people do not have enough food to eat. State-owned monopolies dominate our infrastructure industries. The education system is poor. Disease and corruption are rampant. A decade ago in an expanding economy we glimpsed possibilities to move up the ladder so that at least our children could have a better life. After opening

---

56. *Id.*

57. Jorge Castañeda, *Mexico Needs to be Freed from Unhealthy Monopolies*, FIN. TIMES, Feb. 5, 2007, at 13.

our markets, the richest two percent have yet better lives. A fraction of others who have had sufficient education and training now fortunately participate in opportunities opened by globalization, including opportunities from outsourcing. But the overwhelming majority of our people have seen no gains. They see a bigger wealth gap: no ladder and a wider moat.[58]

What do we want?

Of course, we want more food, medicine, necessities at lower prices, education and training, and infrastructure. We want a better chance to fend for ourselves; to participate in the economic enterprise; to have the opportunity to make a living. Do we need and want antitrust? And if so, what type of antitrust? We want to explore what antitrust can do for us, assuming that we have enough money and trained people to staff the office and enforce the law.

We conclude that antitrust law can help – if we can obtain sufficient funding and access the necessary information to find and prosecute cases; if we can get jurisdiction over the violators, who may be offshore; if we legally and practically have sufficient enforcement power, and if the agency's reasoned decisions will be upheld by courts within a reasonable period of time. Antitrust can deter the practices catalogued above, and in doing so it can empower people to participate in the market on their merits.

Assuming that we want antitrust, what kind of antitrust do we want?

We have looked at the anti-cartel law of industrialized countries. We find it strong and attractive in principle although we worry about our ability to prove cartel agreements even when we are confident they exist.

For monopolization and abuse of dominance, we will look at the United States' recent monopolization cases.[59] We see that U.S. law has a narrow scope for dominant-firm violations: It is not concerned with excluded competitors. It is in theory concerned with consumers who are overcharged. Yet it tends to strike the balance in favor of freedom for dominant firms on the theory that the incentives of domi-

---

58. *See* Lamy, *supra* note 16. There may be gains but they are not perceived by the majority of the poor; and the gains are unequally distributed to the well-off or the otherwise (e.g. educationally) advantaged.

59. *See* Weyerhaeuser Co. v. Ross-Simmons Hardwood Lumber Co., Inc., 127 S. Ct. 1069 (2007); Verizon Commc'ns Inc. v. Law Offices of Curtis V. Trinko, LLP, 540 U.S. 398 (2004).

228   *SOUTHWESTERN JOURNAL OF LAW & TRADE IN THE AMERICAS*   [Vol. 13

nant firms are aligned with consumer interests, and antitrust duties discourage firms from inventing and investing.[60]

Verizon v. Trinko[61] illuminates the perspective that non-intervention against the dominant firm is the best prescription for economic welfare. Verizon was the incumbent local telephone service provider in the northeastern United States, and it owned elements of the local telephone loop, which connected long distance calls to the local area. When competition among local telephone service providers became technologically feasible and economical, the United States deregulated the market and invited local competition into each geographic area. Rivals entered. They needed access to the local loop, which a federal statute required the incumbent to assure. Verizon, however, wanted to keep its own customers from defecting to the new entrants. Therefore it made sure that it would give better service by interrupting its rivals' access to the local loop.[62] The Supreme Court held that this conduct did not violate antitrust laws.[63]

In part, the issue of the case was whether Verizon violated antitrust laws by using the leverage it had over the local loop to gain advantages over its new competitors. Verizon was not likely to re-monopolize this local market, which had just been opened to competition. It was argued on behalf of the plaintiffs that Verizon's strategic manipulations by many "small" acts, such as disrupting local loop connections, "threatened [the rivals] with 'death by a thousand cuts.'"[64] This is a metaphor sometimes used in civil rights cases to describe the thousands of every day slights that keep the marginalized marginalized.

To the invocation of this metaphor, the U.S. Supreme Court replied:

> [T]he identification of [a thousand cuts] would surely be a daunting
> task for a generalist antitrust court. Judicial oversight under the

---

60. See R. Hewitt Pate, *The Common Law Approach and Improving Standards for Analyzing Single Firm Conduct, in* INTERNATIONAL ANTITRUST LAW & POLICY: FORDHAM CORPORATE LAW 2003 195 (Barry Hawk ed., 2004) (supporting the minimalist approach).

61. 540 U.S. 398 (2004).

62. The Court assumed these alleged facts to be true because the case before the Court arose on Verizon's motion to dismiss the complaint.

63. The Court would have preferred to leave the problem to the regulatory agency, and to the regulatory statute, which prohibited the conduct, but the statute declared that antitrust law was not preempted. Therefore, by necessity, the Court's opinion went beyond the regulated industry context. The Court expressed a general principle of non-interference with the monopolist's freedom of action

64. Brief for the State of New York et al. as Amici Curiae, in Support of Respondent at 10, Verizon Commc'ns Inc. v. Law Offices of Curtis V. Trinko, LLP, 540 U.S. 398 (2004) (No. 02-682).

Sherman Act would seem destined to distort investment and lead to a new layer of interminable litigation . . . .[65]

Thus the Court held that a dominant firm's use of leverage to gain advantages in, but not to monopolize, the local telephone market was not an antitrust violation. "Mere" leveraging by a monopolist that will not lead to a new monopoly is not of U.S. antitrust concern.

But for developing countries, the answer might be different. Death by a thousand cuts is a reason *for* antitrust accountability, not against it. "A thousand cuts" by the powerful against the powerless describes the constant fate of the peoples of developing countries.

In formulating antitrust law in our developing country, we may not want *Trinko* law. We want a law against cartels, monopolistic practices, and abuse of dominance that prevents dominant firms from using their power and leverage to fence out powerless firms. We want a law against mergers that create or reinforce the power to exploit and exclude (if we have enough resources to do the job and our enforcement powers reach the mergers that hurt us). Moreover, we want a strong law that reaches restrictive and market-blocking acts and anticompetitive practices that the state sponsors or facilitates – problems that are exponentially greater in developing countries than in, for example, the United States.

Are we not worried that our law will handicap the efficiencies of the dominant firm and thereby harm our own consumers? This was not the problem in the forefront of our minds. Inclusiveness as a value can enhance efficiency. Enforcement that might tend to undermine efficiency can be guarded against by limiting principles.[66]

V.   OBSERVATIONS ON THE DESIGN OF APPROPRIATE LAW

Developing countries face countless dilemmas and opportunities in formulating their substantive principles. Some are telescoped above. Here are six:

1. Developing countries face markets that are much less dynamic and open than markets in developed countries. Moreover the markets are pock-marked by state intervention and control. Whether the in-

65. *Trinko*, 540 U.S. at 414.

66. For example, we might choose a principle that must not harm consumers through antitrust *enforcement*.

Law that protects the openness of markets and access of market players on the merits does not inherently protect inefficiencies; and law that ignores the values of openness and access can protect the power of the dominant firm. *See* Eleanor Fox, *Monopolization, Abuse of Dominance, and the Indeterminacy of Economics: The U.S./E.U. Divide*, 2006 UTAH L. REV. 799 (2006).

230 *SOUTHWESTERN JOURNAL OF LAW & TRADE IN THE AMERICAS* [Vol. 13

tervention is through state measures, state-owned enterprises, or enterprises licensed or privileged by the state, these enterprises are likely to run on principles of privilege, preference, and cronyism.[67] These factors have major implications regarding error costs. If the competition agency is relatively independent, resourced, and capable, more intervention, especially against market-blocking and discriminatory action[68] by state-owned or state-privileged enterprises, might promise more gains and fewer costs than abuse-of-dominance intervention in developed economies.[69]

2. Most developing countries have insufficient resources to run their competition offices. They are short of staff, especially staff members who are economics experts. This suggests that brighter-line rules might be needed, whether they tip in the direction of more or less aggressive enforcement. The kind of analysis suggested, for example, by the U.S. Supreme Court in *California Dental Association*,[70] might be too complex and of uncertain application. Yet the focused analysis suggested by Justice Breyer's dissenting opinion – relying on experience and theory that rules against advertising discounts raise prices – might prove more appropriate.[71]

3. Apart from the observations above, each nation must make important decisions regarding the degree of antitrust intervention. It faces conundrums. For example, excessive pricing, especially after price controls are removed, may be a pressing problem, especially on the price of necessities. But easily-triggered antitrust intervention may lead to price control by another name and undermine the effort to prime markets. Low, especially below-cost, pricing might seriously threaten local firms and undermine their chance to take root. But intervention against low pricing deprives the people of one of the most important benefits of competition. Moreover, whether the low price is truly below cost might be difficult or impossible to ascertain. The nation might want to avoid intervening against low pricing.

---

67. See DUTZ & KHEMANI, *supra* note 6.

68. I refer to discrimination in favor of cronies and against outsiders.

69. *See* John Fingleton, *De-Monopolizing Ireland, in* EUROPEAN COMPETITION LAW ANNUAL 2003: WHAT IS ABUSE OF DOMINANT POSITION? 53, 65 (Claus Dieter Ehlermann & Isabela Atanasiu eds., 2006); *see also* John Vickers, Competition Law and Economics: A Mid-Atlantic Viewpoint, The 10th Burrell Competition Lecture (Mar. 19, 2007) (explaining that historically monopolized economy and weak "self-righting mechanisms" may require more interventionist policies towards abuse of dominance).

70. Cal. Dental Ass'n v. F.T.C., 526 U.S. 756 (1999) (holding that dentists' rules against the advertisement of price discounts and quality do not inevitably lessen the output of dental services and that probability of output limitation must be the subject of detailed inquiry).

71. *Id.* at 782.

4. A legitimate abuse-of-dominance law would be copious enough to prohibit unjustified foreclosing restraints, without the need of a plaintiff to prove output effects across the whole market. But as a corollary, law that seriously respects the right of the underdog to compete on the merits should also seriously respect the right of an alleged violator to prove: My conduct responded to consumers and served the market.

5. While there is high value to a nation in formulating its own law, nations will also appreciate the benefits of following a blazoned path. Anchoring new law in existing jurisprudence promises greater legal certainty and other efficiencies. If one adopts "dominant" law, one need not reinvent the wheel. One can take account of international norms while enhancing the ease of foreign investment. The challenge is to understand when foreign law is appropriate law and when it is not.[72]

6. For efficiency and growth, developing countries need always to adjust to the changing dynamics of markets and competition. All principles and rules should be consistent with the imperative of flexibility and adjustment and should avoid the temptation to try to hold back the tide.

VI. CORRELATIVES

The perspective suggested above concerns antitrust proper – the substantive rules and principles. A number of additional considerations and conditions are necessary to make the law useful and meaningful.[73]

---

72. This is a challenge that South African law explicitly embraces. *See Mondi Ltd. & Kohler Cores and Tubes v. Competition Tribunal, Competition Appeal Court,* 2003 (1) CPLR 25(CAC) (S. Afr.).

Gesner Oliveira and Cinthia Konichi Paulo add the following differences and concerns that developing countries must take into account when implementing competition law: 1) the large informal sector, which does not comply with law and may lead to overestimation of market power; 2) the size of the market, which for Brazil is a medium-sized economy with many prominent multinationals; 3) the magnitude of expected efficiency gains, which often are larger for transitional than developed economies; 4) precariousness of the infrastructure; 5) higher transaction costs, which can prevent new entrants from contesting quasi-monopolies; and 6) more severe political market failure. "In sum, developing countries have more competition problems and fewer resources." Gesner Oliveira & Cinthia Konichi Paulo, The Implementation of Competition Policy in Developing Countries: The Case of Brazil (May 2006) (prepared for the workshop, The Development Dimension of Competition Law and Policy: Economic Perspectives in Cape Town, South Africa).

73. These considerations and conditions have been well articulated by others. *See, e.g.,* William Kovacic, *Getting Started: Creating New Competition Policy Institutions in Transition Economies,* 23 BROOKLYN J. INT'L L. 403 (1997); William Kovacic, *Designing and Implementing*

232 *SOUTHWESTERN JOURNAL OF LAW & TRADE IN THE AMERICAS* [Vol. 13

First, exemptions must not be overly broad. Antitrust operates only within the area carved out for it. Exemptions and immunities, including untouchable market actors who may be favored by the state, can so shrink this area as to lose most of antitrust law's promised benefits. In that spirit, including within the coverage of antitrust law, regulated industries and state enterprises that operate in a commercial capacity can be significantly advantageous to developing countries. Often the industries most important to the people are regulated and each is dominated by a state-owned monopolist. These industries include infrastructure industries such as energy, communications, and transportation. Exclusion of the market actors from antitrust is not only a recipe for cronyism and exploitation;[74] it is a recipe for a tiny antitrust domain.[75]

Second, the competition agency must be as independent as possible, free from political interference, lest the government and its politicians commandeer antitrust and confine it to a not too meaningful realm.

Third, institutions: Ideally, the agency should be well-funded and sufficiently staffed with educated and trained personnel. The leaders and staff should not be corrupt. Appellate channels should be provided. These institutions, too, should be staffed by well-qualified and non-corrupt individuals. Due process should be assured in all proceedings. The workings of the institutions should be transparent and their agents accountable. Indeed, well-functioning institutions are more important to trade and competition than is the convergence of the laws of various nations.[76]

Fourth, advocacy: Competition advocacy is a critical tool. Commonly, the most serious restraints are government measures, often

---

Competition and Consumer Protection Reforms in Transitional Economies: Perspectives from Mongolia, Nepal, Ukraine and Zimbabwe, 44 DePaul L. Rev. 1197 (1995); Clive S. Gray, *Antitrust as a Component of Policy Reform: What Relevance for Economic Development?*, in Reforming Economic Systems in Developing Countries 404 (Dwight H. Perkins & Michael Roemer eds., 1991); R. Shyam Khemani, *Competition Policy and Economic Development*, Policy Options, Oct. 1997, at 23, *available at* http://www.irpp.org/po/archive/oct97/khemani.pdf.

74. *See* Fox, *supra* note 48.

75. Likewise, antitrust should not be crowded out by protectionist measures that serve the entrenched interests. *See* Dennis Davis & Eleanor Fox, *Industrial Policy and Competition – Developing Countries As Victims and Users*, in International Antitrust Law & Policy: Fordham Corporate Law 2003 195 (Barry Hawk ed., forthcoming 2007)

76. *See* Roumeen Islam & Ariell Reshef, *Trade and Harmonization: If Your Institutions Are Good, Does it Matter If They Are Different?* (World Bank, Policy Research Working Paper No. 3907, 2006).

The choice in developing countries, however, is often a grim choice. The quality of institutions cannot be expected to approach the ideal.

procured by vested interests. Moreover, "corporate elites . . . [tend to] resist policy reforms . . . ."[77] The competition agency can play an important role in calling attention to anticompetitive and unproductive state measures and their costs to society. It should probably be the nation's "strongest public voice on promoting competition and articulating the competition perspective."[78]

More generally, education and adequate health care are *sina qua nons* of effective participation in the economic system.

These are difficult requirements to fulfill. If crucial elements are missing, the country might choose not to adopt antitrust at all.

VII. THE DEVELOPED COUNTRY'S DUTY OF COOPERATION

Developing countries are hurt by international cartels and practices and are vulnerable to them. The violators know that developing countries have few resources to devote to antitrust (if any, after they serve other human priorities). Offshore firms direct exploitative practices at developing countries, often by acts taken and agreements made on their home shores.[79]

These anticompetitive practices launched from distant shores are likely to be beyond the practical reach of developing countries. To solve this problem, the European Union ("EU") has proposed a helpful framework,[80] which could be or could have been implemented in the context of the WTO, but could also be implemented as a stand-alone project.

In the spirit of the EU proposal, developed countries with mature antitrust laws can and should help developing countries, especially

---

77. DUTZ & KHEMANI, Competition Law & Policy, *supra* note 6, at 12.

78. *Id.* at 28.

Dutz and Khemani noted:

[E]ffective competition advocacy can help create an environment where, over time, enforcement strengthens the role of markets by reducing government interventions and concomitant regulatory burdens. Thus advocacy may not just be a complement to enforcement, but an essential first step in expediting full, effective competition. Given that competition authorities typically lack sufficient political capital and reputation in their early years, and that policy-generated obstacles to competition are often maintained by support from powerful vested interests, initial advocacy efforts should focus on public restraints whose removal is subject to less debate, or [on projects] that directly benefit entrepreneurs, exporters, and other stakeholders who can be counted on to provide strong backing and support. Special attention should be paid to initiatives that directly or indirectly benefit as broad a base as possible. *Id.* at 28-29.

79. *See* Frederic Jenny, *Globalization, Competition and Trade Policy: Issues and Challenges, in* TOWARDS WTO COMPETITION RULES 3 (Roger Zäch, ed., 1999).

80. Working Group on the Interaction between Trade and Competition Policy, World Trade Organization, *Communication from the European Community and Its Member States*, WT/WGTCP/W/184 (Apr. 22, 2002).

when the developed country's own nationals are the violators of clear and shared principles of antitrust.[81] The developed countries can and should revise their laws, extending jurisdiction so as to make hardcore export cartels illegal.[82]

An environmental convention provides a model. This is the Basel Convention on the Control of Transboundary Movements of Hazardous Wastes and their Disposal,[83] which the United States has signed. Under the Basel Convention, if a signatory country prohibits import of hazardous wastes, all other signatories must make the shipment of hazardous wastes to that country illegal. The United States and other developed countries could and should adopt this model for hardcore export cartels, which are the hazardous wastes of antitrust.

Failing that, the United States and other developed countries should amend their antitrust laws to provide jurisdiction for the discovery of documents and testimony from knowledgeable people. This should include subpoena power when the developed country's citizens are the alleged victimizers of the people of developing countries.[84]

In antitrust law and enforcement, in the absence of international law, the world demands a cosmopolitan vision and a willingness by developed nations to accept responsibility for the harms they cause. The evolving case law of the United States does not demonstrate this vision and it does not reflect generosity of spirit. Instead it shows a retreat and puts the United States on a track towards solipsism and Balkanization.[85]

---

81. It has been estimated that for nineteen selected products, the value of cartel-affected imports to developing countries in 1997 was $51.1 billion and that the price of these imports by reason of the price-fixed overcharge was elevated by at least 10 percent. Margaret Levenstein & Valerie Y. Suslow, *Contemporary International Cartels and Developing Countries: Economic Effects and Implications for Competition Policy*, 71 ANTITRUST L.J. 801, 813-16 (2004).

82. *See* Eleanor Fox, Walter J. Derenberg Professor of Trade Regulation, New York University School of Law, Testimony Before the Antitrust Modernization Commission, Hearing on International Issues in Washington, D.C. (Feb. 15, 2006), *available at* www.AMC.gov; *see also* Special Committee on International Antitrust, ABA Antitrust Section, The Special Committee's Report 83-90 (Sept. 1, 1991).

83. Mar. 22, 1989, 1673 U.N.T.S. 125.

84. Fox, *supra* note 82.

85. *See* F. Hoffmann-La Roche Ltd. v. Empagran, 124 S. Ct. 2359 (2004) (holding that foreign buyers in worldwide conspiracy cannot invoke U.S. antitrust laws unless they are harmed by the effect in the U.S.); Intel Corp. Microprocessor Antitrust Litigation, 452 F. Supp. 2d 555 (D. Del. 2007) (holding that U.S. plaintiff complaining about worldwide anticompetitive strategies of U.S. defendant cannot invoke defendant's foreign acts).

VIII. NETWORKS

Networking is the new world order.[86] Antitrust networks exist.[87] They tend to be dominated by developed nations because the developed nations' experience is deeper and longer; they are likely to be heavier users of networks,[88] and they have more resources – people and money – to devote to the project. As a result, the agendas tend predominantly to reflect the interests of developed countries.[89] Developing nations need their own networks to explore their own interests more centrally. Regional trade groupings can serve as a platform for this objective.[90] And a world-wide developing-country network on competition law would be useful.[91]

Developing nations themselves are diverse. They share certain characteristics and do not share others. The situation and characteristics of India are not the same as those of Benin. Communications and cross-fertilizations through the network can begin to sort out the differences as well as to crystallize the commonalities.

IX. CONCLUSION

Developing countries deserve an antitrust law that fits the facts of their markets and responds to their condition and needs. They deserve a law so designed and so characterized that their peoples will embrace it as sympathetic and legitimate rather than reject it as foreign.

If there is an appropriate symbol for a developing country's antitrust, it is not neo-liberalism, which may imply a widening moat. It is the rising ladder. Antitrust can be seen as the complement to Hernando de Soto's *The Other Path*.

---

86. Anne-Marie Slaughter, *The Real New World Order*, FOREIGN AFFAIRS 183 (Sept.-Oct. 1997).

87. *See* D. Daniel Sokol, *Monopolists Without Borders: The Institutional Challenge of International Antitrust in a Global Gilded Age*, 4 BERKELEY BUS. L.J. 41 (forthcoming 2007), also available as a working paper, Univ. of Wis. Legal Studies Research Paper No. 1034. *See* text at notes 178-94, 287-92.

88. *Id.*, text at notes 226-29.

89. For example, the International Competition Network's first project was convergence of procedures for pre-merger notification – an issue of concern to multinational corporations. Subsequent projects have stressed substantive merger standards and coordination of cartel procedures. Technical assistance for developing countries is, however, also on the agenda. *See* International Competition Network Home Page, http://www.internationalcompetitionnetwork. org (last visited June 30, 2007).

90. *See* U.N., Implementing Competition-Related Provisions in Regional Trade Agreements: Is it possible to obtain development gains? (2007).

91. UNCTAD, which is not a network, has specific regard for the interests of developing countries and competition law is one of many missions.

The antitrust law of developing countries is likely to incorporate the lion's share of the developed country's antitrust principles. In doing so, it will embody a different set of default presumptions about how well markets work while incorporating a mandate and perspective of inclusiveness. Developing countries have a choice.

[2]

LATIN AMERICAN COMPETITION POLICY: FROM NIRVANA ANTITRUST POLICY TO REALITY-BASED INSTITUTIONAL COMPETITION BUILDING

IGNACIO DE LEÓN, PH.D.*

Definitions do not yield any knowledge about the real world,
but they do influence impressions of the world.

—George J. Stigler[1]

[T]he problem that is usually being visualized is how capitalism administers existing structures, whereas the relevant problem is how it creates and destroys them. As long as this is not recognized, the investigator does a meaningless job. As soon as it is recognized, his outlook on capitalist practice and its social results changes considerably.

—Joseph A. Schumpeter[2]

INTRODUCTION

Since the 1990s, several Latin American countries have adopted antitrust policies as part of their economic reform agenda.[3] Often, the policies have been based on an implicit assumption that they would have the beneficial effect of promoting pro-market goals in the region.

Since its inception, however, advocates of antitrust policy in Latin America have insisted on implementing the policies with little to no regard

---

* Dr. Ignacio De León previously served as the founder and President of Venezuela's Competition Authority, Pro-Competencia (1998–2000) and as counsel of the Venezuelan Foreign Trade Institute (1990–1992). Dr. De León received an LL.M. from Queen Mary College, and holds an M. Phil. and a Ph.D. in Law from University College London. He is a professor in the Department of Economics at the Universidad Católica Andrés Bello in Caracas, and is the Executive Director of EconLex Development Strategies. He also serves as a member the Editorial Advisory Board of World Competition Law and Economics Review.

1. GEORGE J. STIGLER, MEMOIRS OF AN UNREGULATED ECONOMIST 94 (1988).

2. JOSEPH A. SCHUMPETER, CAPITALISM, SOCIALISM AND DEMOCRACY 84 (3d. ed. Harper Torchbooks 1962) (1942).

3. Gheventer explores the possible links between economic liberalization and the introduction of antitrust policy; in his view, there is a correlation between the intensity of pro-market reforms and greater autonomy for the antitrust body. Alexandre Gheventer, *Política Antitruste e Credibilidade Regulatória na América Latina* [Antitrust Policies and Regulatory Credibility in Latin America], 47 DADOS 335, 358 (2004) (Braz.), *translated in* 1 DADOS (SPECIAL EDITION) (2005), http://social-sciences.scielo.org/pdf/s_dados/v1nse/scs_a05.pdf.

for the institutional setting for which they are intended.[4] After more than a decade of practical experience, it is time to make an institutional assessment about the real effects of such policies in the region.

Assessing antitrust policy is not easy due to the lack of reliable empirical research about its effects.[5] According to Hylton and Deng, the reason for the scarcity of data lies in the lack of "useful statistical information on the law, enforcement policies and penalties."[6] In my view, however, the failure to measure antitrust effectiveness lies instead in the lack of a unanimously accepted normative yardstick to measure the success of the policy. As we shall see in this article, the notion of competition used in antitrust theory—that is, perfect competition—leads the analyst to make misleading, normative conclusions about the causes and consequences of business practices.

Conventional critiques of antitrust policy have avoided discussing whether the policy stands on a firm intellectual foundation; instead, commentators have engaged in a futile discussion about the particular ethical goal the policy should seek (namely, efficiency or equity). Hence, analysts of antitrust policy have been driven into a fruitless dispute about the completeness and accuracy of empirical evidence collected in support of their preferred normative goal.[7]

---

4. Kovacic notes: "In their enthusiasm for the adoption of antitrust laws in transition economies, international donor groups such as the World Bank and individual Western countries have tended to overlook grave problems that emerging markets have encountered in implementing the new statutes." William E. Kovacic, *Antitrust and Competition Policy in Transition Economies: A Preliminary Assessment*, 2000 FORDHAM CORP. L. INST. 513, 514.

5. From a quantitative perspective, there are few empirical studies on the effectiveness of antitrust policy in attaining its goals. For examples of such studies, see generally Arnold C. Harberger, *Monopoly and Resource Allocation*, 44 AM. ECON. REV. 77 (1954); Richard A. Posner, *A Statistical Study of Antitrust Enforcement*, 13 J.L. & ECON. 365 (1970); George J. Stigler, *The Economic Effects of the Antitrust Laws*, 9 J.L. & ECON. 225 (1966); Keith N. Hylton & Fei Deng, *Antitrust Around the World: An Empirical Analysis of the Scope of Competition Laws and Their Effects* (Boston Univ. Sch. Of Law, Working Paper Series, Law & Econ., Working Paper No. 06-47, 2006); Michael W. Nicholson, *Quantifying Antitrust Regimes* (FTC Bureau of Econ., Working Paper No. 267, 2004).

6. Hylton & Deng, *supra* note 5, at 1.

7. Adams and Brock noted this in sarcastic terms:
Aficionados of the theatre of the absurd would find the character of the [antitrust] debate intimately familiar. There is an absence of communication—a terrifying diversity of utterances, with the actors on stage listening only to snatches and fragments of the dialogue, and responding as if they had not listened at all. At times the dialogue consists of statements that are in and of themselves perfectly lucid and logically constructed but lacking in context and relevance. At other times, absurd ideas are proclaimed as if they were eternal truths. In this dialogue of the deaf, the actors are animated by the certitude and unshakeable nature of their basic assumptions—one side relying on the wisdom of past experience, the other prepared to sweep away the beliefs that have been tested and found wanting, beliefs they consider illusions and self-deceptions.
WALTER ADAMS & JAMES W. BROCK, ANTITRUST ECONOMICS ON TRIAL: A DIALOGUE ON THE NEW LAISSEZ-FAIRE, at xii (1991) (citations omitted).

In view of these empirical limitations, this paper argues that the source of doubt about antitrust policy's effectiveness lies in the policy's internal contradictions. To put it another way, the pursuit of perfect competition as a normative goal leads antitrust policymaking into distorting, not reinforcing, institutional arrangements that are necessary for markets to function. To this extent, antitrust subverts competition rather than promoting it.

My focus in this paper will be different from the conventional discussion of whether transitioning economies should endorse efficiency-oriented competition policies (namely, consumer welfare) or some alternative goal. Instead, I concentrate on how the perfect competition model, upon which all antitrust theory rests, is beset with all sorts of limitations as a model of market dynamics, and why any policy reference to it will undermine policy analysis. In particular, I concentrate on how the model not only misreads the informative role of those institutions necessary for markets to function, but also—and more importantly—how it chastises these institutions as "market imperfections" that policymakers should eliminate from the system, if the system is to perform optimally.

The perfect competition model is the cornerstone of antitrust enforcement.[8] The model supports the appraisal of markets carried out through industrial organization, as well as normative precepts aimed at overcoming perceived "market failures" arising from misallocation of resources caused by anticompetitive business restrictions. Conventional market theory postulates that perfectly competitive industries set prices equal to marginal costs; therefore, they maximize consumers' rent. Under this theory, monopolies are objectionable because the absence of competitors allows monopolists to set prices above marginal costs.[9] From this perspective, it follows that antitrust policymakers assume their role should be to promote policies that align markets closer to perfect competition and further from monopoly. Alternative notions of economic competition employed in antitrust policy, such as "effective competition" or "workable competition," are surrogate forms that share the same conceptual criticisms as the perfect competition model.

---

8. This model depicts a market structure featuring an infinite number of market participants because: (i) entry and exit from the market is assumed to be free, so that any firms outside the industry can move in at any time to take advantage of any above-normal profits; (ii) products are assumed homogeneous, so there is no brand loyalty segmenting the market; (iii) no advertising is assumed to exist; and (iv) all sellers and buyers are assumed to know all information. In other words, the model conveys to the analyst a series of assumptions making up for the results expected from interactions under such markets.

9. *See generally* MASSIMO MOTTA, COMPETITION POLICY: THEORY AND PRACTICE 39–55 (2004); W. KIP VISCUSI, JOHN M. VERNON & JOSEPH E. HARRINGTON, JR., ECONOMICS OF REGULATION AND ANTITRUST 2–5, 73 (MIT Press 2d ed. 1995) (1992).

In this paper, I highlight the misleading normative treatment of market institutions that the perfect competition model encapsulates. Indeed, the perfect competition model leads analysts into condemning institutional arrangements that are necessary for entrepreneurs to display their capabilities—namely, to compete in the market place. I demonstrate that this model is internally contradictory and, as a result, leads policymakers to flawed conclusions.

This paper does not address the economic impact of the flawed policy (as seen in the erosion of the rule of law it creates on the already weak Latin American economic institutions), nor will it address the public choice explanation (for example, that modern antitrust policy arises out of political pressure from domestic industries that, in the wake of economic liberalization, are unable or unwilling to compete with far more resourceful foreign entrepreneurs). I therefore concentrate on the significant missing element of conventional antitrust analysis which underlies the perfect competition model: the role of economic expectations. Decisions are built upon beliefs; hence, expectations are key to understanding how businesses make investment decisions in the real world. From there, I examine what sort of competition policy should be implemented that will align with the alternative theoretical view of competition proposed in this paper.

I. THE AFTERMATH OF ECONOMIC LIBERALIZATION IN LATIN AMERICA

The introduction of antitrust policy in Latin America has been heralded as a mark of the new pro-market ethos brought about by economic liberalization. As Ryan and Faden recently observed:

> [T]he economic benefits of free competition are increasingly recognised and the need for a strong and effective competition law to underpin a competitive economy is now almost taken as a given. Thus many Latin American countries are dedicating increasing government resources, both human and financial, to establishing or developing antitrust laws and policy.[10]

The ultimate purpose of economic liberalization in transitioning and developing countries is promoting entrepreneurial creativity, innovation, and economic growth, all of which were stifled during previous decades of burdensome regulations, trade protectionism, and government dirigisme.[11] Consequently, policymaking should be judged by how effective the poli-

---

10. Alan Ryan & Karine Faden, *Managing Antitrust in Latin America*, 2007 GLOBAL COMPETITION REV. (SPECIAL REPORT: THE ANTITRUST REVIEW OF THE AMERICAS 2007) 61, 62.

11. Norberg provides an excellent empirical account of the welfare benefits accompanying trade and institutional reforms. *See* JOHAN NORBERG, IN DEFENSE OF GLOBAL CAPITALISM 114–20 (Roger Tanner & Julian Sanchez trans., Cato Institute 2003) (2001).

cies are at fostering these goals. As this paper will show, antitrust policy cannot do the job because its underlying logic necessarily results in enforcement decisions that prevent achievement of these goals.

From the economic point of view, under the postulates of the perfect competition model competitive equilibrium leads to an optimal allocation of social resources.[12] Regardless of whether such an allocation seeks Pareto efficiency or some alternative goal, such as the protection of small firms, it entails a departure from the spontaneous market outcomes that would occur without interference. Thus, it is necessary to appraise the logic of antitrust policy more closely before endorsing the conventional belief—that antitrust policy will eradicate economic government dirigisme and consolidate pro-market habits among otherwise anticompetitively-biased businesses.[13] Antitrust policy advocates may have a misconception about the particular nature of markets and the role of entrepreneurs, which could distort (and possibly delay) both genuine initiatives aimed at introducing new markets in Latin America and the real purposes behind antitrust policies.[14]

There is a clear risk that antitrust enforcement could reintroduce discarded government interventionist policies, albeit in a disguised fashion. Consider, for example, a decision to penalize a business for entering into an exclusive distribution contract that is allegedly an abusive or monopolistic attempt to foreclose market access to a downstream competitor. Such penalties represent administrative charges that businesses have to compute as unexpected production costs that undermine their competitiveness. There is no question that pre-merger control, as well as market surveillance that protects against restrictive anticompetitive arrangements and that challenges "excessive," "monopolistic," or "unfair" prices, or prosecutes unpopular dominant firms, has much in common with the old-style

---

12. Optimal efficiency in the allocation of resources, along with a state of equilibrium, would prevail in markets under perfect competition. AMARTYA SEN, ON ETHICS AND ECONOMICS 29–40 (1st paperback ed. 1988); Cento G. Veljanovski, *Wealth Maximization, Law and Ethics—On the Limits of Economic Efficiency*, 1 INT'L REV. L. & ECON. 5, 20 (1981). Under these conditions, market forces would allocate social resources amongst individuals where they would obtain their maximum value. Veljanovski, *supra*, at 20. The whole purpose of allocating such resources where their economic value is highest is to benefit consumer welfare. *See* SEN, *supra*.

13. Consider, for example, the following statement made in reference to the rationale of antitrust policy in Central and Eastern European countries: "The competition policy conducted by CIS Governments is directed at ensuring conditions for effective functioning of markets and promoting private initiative. The appropriate regulatory bodies created in CIS countries exercise State antimonopoly control and promote the development of market relations on the basis of effective competition and entrepreneurship." U.N. Conference on Trade and Development [UNCTAD], *Competition Policy in Countries in Transition—Legal Basis and Practical Experience*, 2, U.N. Doc. UNCTAD/ITCD/CLP/Misc.16 (2000) (*prepared by* Natalya Yacheistova).

14. *See generally* THE CAUSES AND CONSEQUENCES OF ANTITRUST: THE PUBLIC-CHOICE PERSPECTIVE (Fred S. McChesney & William F. Shugart II, eds., 1995).

44   *CHICAGO-KENT LAW REVIEW*   [Vol 83:1

government dirigisme. In this respect, Rajapatirana provides us with an interesting study on the effects of trade liberalization policies in several Latin American countries. She shows how the effectiveness of these policies has been limited by the reintroduction of many trade restrictions under new forms and disguises.[15] My hypothesis is that antitrust policy is one example of such disguised restrictions.

To be sure, my argument is not that competition policy is altogether unnecessary or harmful. Rather, I argue that the meaning of competition is open to alternative economic interpretations, and that such alternatives should define alternative policymaking routes. In my view, the conventional wisdom surrounding notions of competition has framed a sort of policymaking that undermines, rather than reinforces, market mechanisms. To this extent, antitrust policy principles are often oriented toward resurrecting old government customs, which consist of rearranging market outcomes, condemning certain market prices on considerations of fairness, and judging whether certain levels of output are "socially convenient" (or optimally efficient). If anything, this is a renewed form of government dirigisme, rather than a policy to promote effective competition and entrepreneurship.

Rather than being concerned about opening spaces for entrepreneurs to display their talent and creativity, the investigative activity of antitrust agencies usually centers around measuring market size in order to ascertain the proper market share of each market participant and to see if any particular participant's share is extremely large. Moreover, antitrust agencies typically assess the optimal levels of market concentration, establish the proper degree of contestability in suspect industries, count the appropriate number of firms, measure the right size of the relevant market, and undertake similar structural endeavors.[16]

---

15. The study to which I refer, which was conducted in Argentina, Chile, Colombia, Jamaica, Uruguay and Trinidad, gives a School of Public Choice-based explanation for the reasons that these countries slowed the pace of trade reform in different areas and levels of economic activity. The conclusions highlight the real problems that the promotion of competition faces in the region. In particular, Rajapatirana argues that "despite [trade] liberalizations, some sectors have continued to receive protection. . . . [and] there have been attempts to introduce measures to provide relief to activities which have been subject to increased competition from imports, on the grounds of [unfair] trade practices." Sarath Rajapatirana, *Post Trade Liberalization Policy and Institutional Challenges in Latin America and the Caribbean* 17–18 (The World Bank Latin America and the Caribbean Technical Dep't Advisory Group, Policy Research Working Paper No. 1465, 1995). Although the study explains the Latin American rent-seeking behavior in the field of international trade, its conclusions can be easily extended beyond, to trade in general.

16. To show this, one only needs to look at the items evaluated under the U.S. Merger Guidelines, which outline the standard analysis employed internationally to evaluate merger operations. U.S. DEP'T OF JUSTICE & THE FED. TRADE COMM'N, HORIZONTAL MERGER GUIDELINES (rev. ed. 1997), http://www.usdoj.gov/atr/public/guidelines/hmg.pdf.

Notably, none of the guidelines used by antitrust agencies to evaluate whether anticompetitive restraints exist give priority to the innovation of market participants or the intensity of innovation in the industry as a whole. Antitrust scholars' views of these arrangements appear biased inasmuch as they assume that market participants bear some "natural" monopolistic tendencies.

Hence, instead of analyzing competition from the idealized assumption that markets fail to achieve the idealized standard of perfect competition, I propose quite the opposite: due to its reliance on idealized market models that utterly disregard the institutional surrounding where market action takes place, antitrust analysis is inherently biased against any form of market arrangement entailing business coordination (which is viewed as an expression of monopolistic intent). Our problem, then, is not located at the empirical level, but higher, at the epistemological level: we need to explore the way the antitrust mindset operates and its conceptual limitations.

In my opinion, the implicit bias in antitrust thinking stems from a particular understanding of the world—one that misinterprets the arrangements entered into by entrepreneurs in order to solve their lack of certainty about the institutional environment where they must invest. Therefore, a wholesale reappraisal of markets and regulation, which conventional epistemology is unable to deliver, may be necessary before endorsing the optimism of regulatory reform in Latin America.

II. NIRVANA ANTITRUST POLICYMAKING

At the theoretical level, the lure of economic efficiency is rooted in policymakers' quest to achieve utopian social welfare through targeted intervention. This idea stems from the assumption that policymakers can attain a complete picture of the underlying forces that shape social reality and regulate them to attain optimal social welfare.[17]

---

17. *See generally* 1 F.A. HAYEK, *The Fatal Conceit: The Errors of Socialism, in* THE COLLECTED WORKS OF F.A. HAYEK (W.W. Bartley III ed., press ed. 1989); In the field of economic science, see Mario J. Rizzo, *The Mirage of Efficiency*, 8 HOFSTRA L. REV. 641, 641–42 (1980). Policymakers generally acknowledge that this goal is unattainable; hence, they make do with attaining second best objectives, namely, to merely improve market performance by intervening and eliminating market failures. On the theory of second-best, see David P. Baron & Roger B. Myerson, *Regulating a Monopolist with Unknown Costs*, 50 ECONOMETRICA 911 (1982). Rey critiques the second-best theory as applied in the field of antitrust. *See* Patrick Rey, Director of the Industrial Economic Institute, University of Toulouse, Antitrust Policy, Comments at the Economics for an Imperfect World Conference (Oct. 24, 2003), *transcript available at* http://www2.gsb.columbia.edu/faculty/jstiglitz/festschrift/Papers /Stig-Rey.pdf.

This nirvana mindset reproduces in the realm of economic policy what, in social sciences, Epstein has termed "perfect justice."[18] As a goal of policymaking, perfect justice requires rooting out error in every case, regardless of the costs.[19] Similarly, Sowell refers to "cosmic justice," or justice that is cost-free, and takes into account the particular welfare position of each individual in society so as to level his or her condition to that of the rest.[20] Sowell criticizes this endeavor on the grounds that it is impossible to devise an ideal standard of equality that would satisfy the individual condition of everyone, given the costs involved in such efforts. Thus, "[w]ith justice, as with equality, the question is not whether more is better, but whether it is better at all costs."[21]

Similar concerns arise in antitrust policymaking. Those who support economic efficiency and consumer welfare base their views on the welfare properties of the perfect competition model: if the model embodies optimal competitive equilibrium, it follows that policy initiatives should aim to achieve such a state. This is why such thinking has been branded as a "nirvana" mindset: if one takes into account the costs of attaining such optimality, it becomes clear that no such optimal state really exists.[22]

In the 1940s, Clark noted:

> [T]he conception of "perfect competition" has itself for the first time received really specific definition and elaboration. With this has come the realization [sic] that "perfect competition" does not and cannot exist and has presumably never existed . . . . *What we have left is an unreal or ideal standard which may serve as a starting point of analysis and a norm with which to compare actual competitive conditions. It has also served as a standard by which to judge them.*[23]

Indeed, the perfect competition model has been used extensively to develop antitrust policy prescriptions.[24] In the 1970s, Hayek indicated with

---

18. RICHARD A. EPSTEIN, SIMPLE RULES FOR A COMPLEX WORLD 38 (1995).

19. *Id.*

20. THOMAS SOWELL, THE QUEST FOR COSMIC JUSTICE 12 (1999).

21. *Id.* at 27.

22. Harold Demsetz referred to this as the "nirvana fallacy," which is the intellectual error of considering the possibility of perfection, but ignoring how hard it is for the authority to obtain the necessary information to accomplish it. The tendency of anyone falling within this intellectual error is to consider his neighbor's garden always greener. Thus, compared to nirvana, reality always appears full of "market failures." *See* Harold Demsetz, *Information and Efficiency: Another Viewpoint*, 12 J.L. & ECON. 1, 1–3 (1969).

23. J.M. Clark, *Toward a Concept of Workable Competition*, 30 AM. ECON. REV. 241, 241 (1940) (emphasis added).

24. The use of surrogate models such as the workable or effective competition model does not invalidate this conclusion. These models are grounded on the assumption that the perfect competition model cannot be found in "reality"; yet, the epistemological flaws invalidating the latter also apply to the former. Thus, like the perfect competition model, the effective competition model also endorses the mistaken welfare duality between perfect competition and pure monopoly.

regard to the perfect competition model that this "ideal case . . . came to be regarded as the model and was used as a standard by which the achievement of competition in the real world was judged."[25] More recently, Klein confirmed the importance of the perfect competition model for antitrust purposes by indicating that of all the various analytical toolkits that constitute contemporary political economy, "[p]erhaps the most important model for economists is the model of perfect competition."[26]

Naturally, by comparison with optimal idealized perfect competition, real world businesses are subject to a permanent state of failure. As Nobel Prize laureate Stigler commented:

> If only markets with a vast number of traders are perfectly competitive, and if markets with few traders are called oligopolistic (literally, "few sellers"), that suggests that these latter markets are not competitive, as well as not perfectly competitive . . . . This suspicion of small numbers was gradually reinforced by the antitrust cases.[27]

It is no coincidence that Oskar Lange, the most renowned economist to advocate economic socialism, shared the same contempt as antitrust regulators over non-perfect competition markets due to their less-than-optimal allocation properties.[28] Indeed, his conclusion was inescapable: since perfect competition can only be found in the imagery of the ideal world of equilibrium, the capitalist system is, by definition, a less desirable choice than economic socialism.[29]

---

25. 3 FRIEDRICH A. HAYEK, LAW, LEGISLATION AND LIBERTY: THE POLITICAL ORDER OF A FREE PEOPLE 66 (1979).

26. Benjamin Klein, *The Use of Economics in Anti-trust Litigation: Realistic Models of the Competitive Process*, *in* THE LAW AND ECONOMICS OF COMPETITION POLICY 420 (Frank Mathewson et al. eds., 1990).

27. STIGLER, *supra* note 1, at 94.

28. *See* OSKAR LANGE & FRED M. TAYLOR, ON THE ECONOMIC THEORY OF SOCIALISM 106–07 (Benjamin E. Lippincott ed., 1964).

29. In Lange's words:
> The possibility of determining the distribution of incomes so as to maximize social welfare and of taking *all* the alternatives into the economic account makes a socialist economy, from the economist's point of view, superior to a competitive regime with private ownership of the means of production and with private enterprise, but especially superior to a competitive capitalist economy where a large part of the participants in the economic system are deprived of any property of productive resources other than their labor. However, the actual capitalist system is not one of perfect competition; it is one where oligopoly and monopolistic competition prevail. This adds a much more powerful argument to the economist's case for socialism. The wastes of monopolistic competition have received so much attention in recent theoretical literature that there is no need to repeat the argument here. The capitalist system is far removed from the model of a competitive economy as elaborated by economic theory. And even if it conformed to it, it would be, as we have seen, far from maximizing social welfare. Only a socialist economy can fully satisfy the claim made by many economists with regard to the achievements of free competition.

Id. Of course, Lange assumed that in operational terms such a goal could only be achieved by nationalizing production and giving orders to public officials in charge of running state-owned enterprises. In the absence of extreme government intervention, there is no question that he would have seen antitrust

In conclusion, antitrust policy is conceived in terms of nirvana thinking to the extent it employs the ideal perfect competition model as a normative reference for implementing policy recommendations. This policy, also known as "competition policy" in Europe and Latin America, is a government instrument designed to intervene in markets in order to preserve rivalry among independent buyers and sellers in relatively unregulated markets. In other words, antitrust intervention is driven by the need to correct perceived market failures; the role of the authority is primarily to challenge the business conduct that causes such failures. Antitrust enforcement focuses on preserving "independent" business decision-making, and controlling the potential sources of market foreclosure that would otherwise limit the effective number of business operators.[30] In sum, antitrust thinking is grounded on the belief that industrial concentration is bad for competition—but where does that conviction come from?

III. MATHEMATICAL SIMPLIFICATION TRIGGERS AN ILLUSION

The nirvana approach is flawed due to its contrived view of market dynamics. But even more significant than its rejection of any trace of realism are its fundamental contradictions, which deserve further attention.

Under the nirvana approach, the underlying assumption is that the perfectly competitive firm is so small relative to the overall market that it cannot influence the market's course: its impact is negligible or, as economists usually put it, infinitesimally small. Under this logic, naturally, each firm has to behave as a price taker, in the sense that it cannot decide unilaterally what price consumers will pay. Thus, the perfect competition market will be the polar opposite of a pure monopoly market where, through output restrictions, firms unilaterally dictate the terms under which consumers will pay higher prices. This is possible because monopoly firms face a negatively sloped demand curve, so that prices exceed marginal revenues (P >

---

policy as a perfectly logical device to achieve the socialist allocation goals that he advocated, by prosecuting firms unwilling or incapable of behaving as social welfare dictates. Clearly, from a policy viewpoint the underlying logic is similar in both cases: governments must intervene in order to achieve optimal resource allocation because the market is plagued by market failures, such as those arising from monopolistic competition.

30. *See* Roger A. Boner & Reinald Krueger, *The Basics of Antitrust Policy: A Review of Ten Nations and the European Communities* 2–5, 92–93 (World Bank Technical Paper No. 160, 1991). This policy is also referred to as "antitrust policy" because it focuses on the ills of economic concentration arising from the collective action of trusts and cartels. *Id.* at 1. Hence, it condemns any business conduct that aligns competitors and any unilateral behavior that excludes or raises impediments to prevent third parties from joining the market; it strives to control mergers and acquisitions; it focuses on mechanical measurements of market size, based on the cross-elasticity of demand; and it views market power structurally. *Id.* at 1–5.

M_r). Under these conditions, monopoly firms will be able to set prices above the ideal point where consumers would otherwise maximize their income.

In perfect competition, by contrast, no such wealth transfer happens. In such markets prices equal marginal revenues and these are equal to marginal production costs ($P = M_r = M_c$); therefore, firms must yield to the price set by the market. Such prices force firms to produce efficiently so that their marginal revenues will equal their marginal costs ($M_r = M_c$), otherwise they will be expelled from the market (by going out of business). This is why, on paper, perfect competition appears desirable whereas a monopoly does not. The implicit assumption is that, due to their infinitesimal market share, firms placed in perfectly competitive situations must take whatever price they are offered in the market; the effect of their business decisions is therefore negligible.

Naturally, the welfare implications of such polar ends (monopoly versus perfect competition) rest on the assumption that such duality does exist; in particular, they rest on the assumption that at the market price perfectly competitive firms face individual flat demand curves, as displayed in the sequence of Figures 1–4, below:

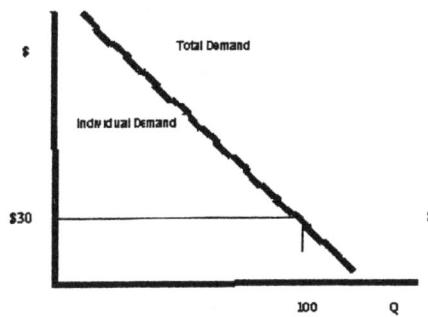

Figure 1
Individual demand of a monopoly firm

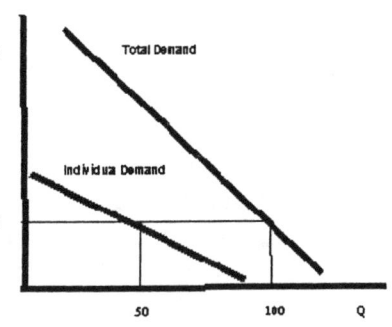

Figure 2
Individual demand of a duopoly

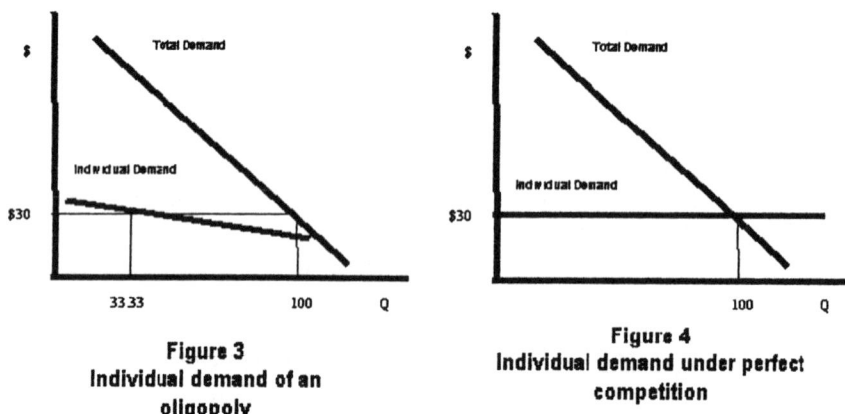

Figure 3
Individual demand of an oligopoly

Figure 4
Individual demand under perfect competition

But are individual demand curves ever really flat?

As the conventional theory postulates, perfectly competitive firms are so small that they do not change their output in response to a change in output by other firms. Therefore, if a single firm happens to increase its output by one unit, the total industry output should also increase by one unit, since other firms will not react. Thus, under the terms of the perfect competition model, individual demand curves can never truly be flat, because an increase in the supply of one firm increases the total market output, causing market prices to fall. The only way individual demand curves could be flat would be if, in the event that one firm increases its supply, all other firms reduced their output by that same amount. Only then would the market supply curve and the price remain constant.

In other words, the two assumptions underlying the perfect competition model are mutually inconsistent: either firms operating in such markets do not face flat demand curves (for the price would then fall, even infinitesimally, in the event of an output increase by another market participant), or prices do not fall in the event of an output increase. Naturally, the latter choice would deny that individuals operating in perfect competition markets act under the same logic of economic behavior that applies to other markets. Hence, we are forced to conclude that the only viable choice is assuming that flat demand curves are as real as unicorns; that is, they exist only in fantasy. Indeed, the perfect competition model assumes that firms do not react to each other's behavior, yet experience and common sense demonstrate this is exactly what businesses do in the real world.

Consider the position faced by a firm such as PepsiCo in the soft drink market. PepsiCo must be as attentive to its competitors' moves as it is to its customers' demands. It must see how Coca-Cola and other competitors perform in the market, what new products they advertise, what control they hold over their distribution networks, what productive capacity they have, how easily they can reach new and existing markets, what level of confidence Coca-Cola's consumers have in Coca-Cola's products, and so forth. As this simple example demonstrates, firms do not act in isolation; rather, they place themselves in a strategic setting, where they make investment decisions after taking into consideration the simultaneous moves of their competitors, suppliers, clients, and customers. From one perspective, these are indeed *competitive* moves, as they are intended to challenge competitors in the market, but from another perspective, they also can be regarded as *coordinative* strategies aimed at avoiding overproduction.

The real economic problem of interacting firms in the market is, then, how do they coordinate their activities in the event of a single firm's decision to change its output? This is not to pretend that coordination does not exist (or that it has been already understood and "worked out" by other firms). We shall come back to the fundamental problem of how economic agents develop their expectations about the conduct of other firms later. The problem I want to emphasize at this point is simply that the perfect competition model is not only unreal, in the sense that it does not consider this aspect of real-life markets, but also that it is internally flawed, since it is based on two mutually inconsistent assumptions: on one hand, it postulates that an increase in the supply by one firm would increase the total market output while the individual demand faced by perfect competitors would remain flat, yet at the same time it contends that prices would fall in the event of a market output increase—a situation in which total demand, no matter how little, would decrease instead of remaining the same.

In short, the demand curve faced by individual firms can never be flat; instead, it is infinitesimally sloped. Mathematically speaking, *infinitesimal* is not equal to *zero*. The addition of infinitesimally negative sloped individual demand curves will result in a negative sloped collective (namely, industry-wide) demand curve. Conversely, if the assumptions of the perfect competition model were true (namely, the slope of an individual demand curve is zero), then the addition of such curves would mathematically result in an industry demand curve with a zero slope. Therefore, the alleged distinction between firms operating in perfect competition markets and those operating in non-perfect competition markets is untenable. All firms will mark their prices at a level which is above the point where marginal revenues and marginal costs are equal. In other words, all firms will behave as monopolists, even if in highly decentralized markets they will do so on an infinitesimally small scale.

It is evident that the drafters of the perfect competition model tried to simplify reality in order to isolate and better examine the market's constitutive forces, but in doing so they created a virtual reality that distorted the forces the analysis was intended to examine. Virtual reality embedded in economic models is useful only insofar as long as it preserves those essential traits of the phenomenon that it purports to analyze.[31] The question is whether the perfect competition model does so. The answer is obviously negative. By assuming that under perfect competition individual firms face flat demand curves, and that firms would become price takers no matter the increase in total output, the drafters of this model took away the most important trait of competition as we know it: the obvious fact that firms do not act in isolation, but take into account what other firms do in the market where they compete. No individual firm would increase its own output without paying due regard to the expected conduct of other firms. Coordination of expectations becomes the key economic problem to be addressed.

Although the coordination problem of economic transactions was identified and discussed by Hayek in 1937,[32] it was not until Richardson's work in 1960 that the contradictions of the perfect competition model were laid bare.[33]

Richardson noted that the very assumptions of the perfect competition model, summarized in the idea of "perfect knowledge," were inherently contradictory.[34] The assumption of perfect knowledge (namely, that knowledge is evenly shared by everyone in the market) denies individuals any chance of reaching the perfect competition state. Why? Because if the knowledge needed for individuals to attain perfect competition is equally and perfectly shared by all individuals in the market, then no one would be able to seize the profit opportunity:

> A general profit opportunity, which is both known to everyone, and equally capable of being exploited by everyone, is, in an important sense,

---

31. Popper contended that it is impossible to verify the perfect competition model, given that models are metaphysical statements. If this is the case, then we will have to accept the implications of the model as a matter of logical deduction and admit that the world may reach a state of perfect competition. In this case, though, it is crucial for the model to replicate the world. However, this is not simple; models in economics are merely tools for expressing certain relationships in mathematical terms. Reality, as Popper has indicated, is a non-verifiable issue—and, therefore, beyond the realm of science. *See* David Papineau, *Philosophy of Science, in* THE BLACKWELL COMPANION TO PHILOSOPHY 291–93 (Nicholas Bunnin & E.P. Tsui-James eds., 1996).

32. *See* F. A. von Hayek, *Economics and Knowledge*, 4 ECONOMICA 33 (1937).

33. G.B. RICHARDSON, INFORMATION AND INVESTMENT 1–2, 36–38 (1960).

34. *Id.* at 36–38.

a profit opportunity for no-one in particular; it will create the incentive to invest only provided some people are less able to discern it, or to respond to it, than others.[35]

So the perfect competition model creates an illusion of business behavior that is never real, for all firms—even those whose influence on price is infinitesimal—behave as monopolists. In other words, there is no distinction between the welfare effects of these firms and those who command large chunks of the market. All firms price their goods above marginal costs in order to obtain profits.

Two questions follow, then: First, what remains of the antitrust admonition against firms who happen to operate in non-perfectly competitive markets? Second, given the lack of theoretical support for contemporary antitrust policy, what are the available alternatives? In other words, how should competition policymaking be redrafted in order to more accurately take into account how firms behave in the real world? Let us address these two problems in turn.

IV. IMPLICATIONS OF FOLLOWING PERFECT COMPETITION'S NORMATIVE INNUENDO

Having demonstrated that the perfect competition model is inherently flawed, what happens if we nevertheless insist on imposing perfect competition standards upon real-world firms? To put it differently, what is wrong with judging real life situations under ideal standards of "perfection"? Let us see how firms operating at perfect competition would fare if we dropped the assumption that they confront a flat demand curve. Let us see how they fare if, as we have already established, they do operate in markets where $P > M_r$.

Again, perfect competition assumes that $M_c = M_r = P$. Individually, perfectly competitive firms produce a level of output that maximizes their profit; but *collectively* such firms produce at a loss, because they will be forced to sell at a price where $P = M_c$, which is lower than the price that would maximize their profits ($M_c = M_r$). Such loss arises from the costs of firms acting without coordination between them. By forcing them to act independently, perfectly competitive firms will be unable to seize profits from market opportunities. These profits would accrue only at the point where prices paid by the market actually exceed marginal cost. Instead, perfectly competitive firms will undercut their competitors by forcing them into a price war, which will force them to sell a higher level of output at the

---

35. *Id.* at 57.

point where supply (marginal cost) and demand (price) intersect—but from the viewpoint of the individual firm (under our realistic assumption that P > M_r), that will yield collective losses for everyone.

To see this more clearly consider Figure 5:[36]

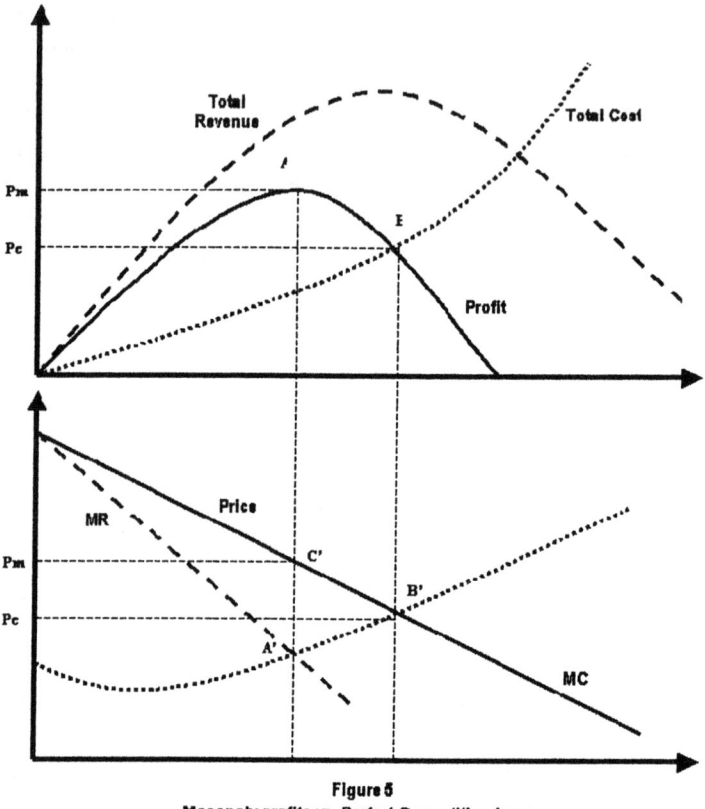

Figure 5
Monopoly profits vs. Perfect Competition losses

As this figure shows, by forcing firms to charge perfect competition prices at point B, where total supply (the sum of M_c) and total demand intersect, the firms individually obtain lower profits than they would if they charged monopoly prices, or prices above marginal revenues (C'- B'). At point A, firms would maximize their profits; past this point, their profits would diminish. Clearly, the addition of losses would lead everyone in the market to a loss (assuming, of course, perfect information).

---

36. This figure was adapted with permission from STEVE KEEN, DEBUNKING ECONOMICS: THE NAKED EMPEROR OF THE SOCIAL SCIENCES 95 fig.4.5 (2001).

As Keen explains, firms in perfect competition would face a loss because in these markets, marginal costs exceeds marginal revenue, unlike monopoly markets where the opposite is true.[37] The only possible explanation for profit-maximizing, where perfectly competitive firms produce at a higher level of output and lower price, is that they are irrational. The only possible way of making a profit is to collectively coordinate their actions in such a way as to avoid losses.

In short, antitrust policy enforcement brings about market losses, as it forces individual firms to sustain individual losses on the false assumption that under perfect competition, they would produce optimally. Antitrust policy thus ignores that, in the real world, firms need to collectively avoid losses (such as costs) that would otherwise impede them from attaining optimal results. These losses would be avoided through collective coordination.

Policymaking needs to address practical questions faced by flesh-and-bone individuals in their ordinary transactions. In order to do so, it needs to rest on sound economic theory. The perfect competition model is a futile imaginary device that does not explain how markets achieve optimality, except by postulating that the information of the system is already known to economic agents—*before* it has, in fact, passed to them. To put it differently, it assumes that collective coordination among economic agents has already occurred without telling us how. Yet knowing how economic agents coordinate their actions is precisely the key to achieving the optimality it seeks: to this extent, the model is totally hapless. The perfect competition model cannot explain this, because it rests on the flawed assumption that firms would maximize their profits individually without being affected by what other firms do in the market; the optimal production level is attained without considering the collective market outcome. For if, along with economic theory, we assume that economic agents are profit-maximizers, there is no reason to expect that, collectively, they would be willing to take losses.

For this reason, analysts end up twisting the motives of market participants. By taking perfect competition as the ideal of how markets should function, policymakers misleadingly look to uneven information coordination such as the "failures" or "costs" of the economic system that enlightened policymaking can easily spot and eliminate. Loasby observes in this connection:

37. *Id.* at 99.

[The competitive equilibrium] program produces misleading prescriptions for policy. Those prescriptions are derived from the study of a system that is fully adjusted [*i.e., perfectly competitive markets*] to existing data and in which there is no expectation that these data could ever change: thus any elements that might be necessary to recognize and respond to change are strictly superfluous. Once everything is agreed—and within the analytical convention, finally agreed—there is no further need for any of the apparatus of enquiry, communication, and control which might have been required to secure agreement. It is all to be condemned as [according to taste] organizational slack, *x*-inefficiency, wastes of competition, or monopolistic misallocation. There is not even any reason for the existence of firms.[38]

In the real world, where equilibrium is not gained by mere analytical postulation but through coordinative actions undertaken by entrepreneurs who lack knowledge about their optimal course of action, these so-called "failures" are in fact essential institutional means whereby they can obtain the necessary knowledge to induce them into action. In other words, these institutional "failures"—from the conventional antitrust viewpoint—are in fact necessary in order to coordinate the market system at all.

Richardson noted the pervasive effect of this model in the construction of a mindset for market analysis:

[The perfect competition model] undoubtedly stood, for many people, as an ideal or model form of organization—strictly speaking only a logical as opposed to an ethical ideal, although this distinction was not always sharply made. It does not seem to have been recognized that the fact that 'imperfections', in some forms and degree of strength, are clearly an obstacle to adjustment, does not entitle one to conclude that it would be best if [market] 'imperfections' were absent altogether. Yet the pedagogic convenience of perfect competition, and its suitability as a base for extensive formal and mathematical elaboration, gave the system a central place in theoretical discussion . . . .[39]

In order to adapt to the conduct of rational firms whose actions are dictated by the premise that prices exceed marginal costs $(P > M_c)$, it is necessary for us to reconsider the notion of competition built upon the false duality of two extreme and idealized market structures, between which firms presumably would command some degree of market power. Further, in order to restate the notion of economic competition, we must focus our attention on the problem of collective knowledge, where firms must coordinate in order to avoid losses.

---

38. Brian J. Loasby, *Economics of Dispersed and Incomplete Information, in* METHOD, PROCESS AND AUSTRIAN ECONOMICS: ESSAYS IN HONOR OF LUDWIG VON MISES 113 (Israel M. Kirzner ed., 1982). In a similar vein, see SCHUMPETER, *supra* note 2.

39. RICHARDSON, *supra* note 33, at 39.

V. THE ONLY GOAL OF COMPETITION POLICY: ENABLING THE SEARCH FOR KNOWLEDGE

A restatement of competition policy, naturally, must reinstate the notion of competition along the lines of market process. In this sense, McNulty argued:

> That perfect competition is an ideal state, incapable of actual realization, is a familiar theme of economic literature. That for various reasons it would be less than altogether desirable, even if it were attainable, is also widely acknowledged. But that perfect competition is a state of affairs quite incompatible with the idea of any and all competition has been insufficiently emphasized.[40]

Perfect competition is no competition at all, for the very simple reason that it is a situation where all potential for exchanges has already been exhausted and all profit opportunities have already been seized.

Instead of assuming that knowledge about the *collective* behavior of firms is readily known to each market, I propose adopting a competition model governed by the opposite assumption—that such knowledge is missing and, therefore, no one in the system knows how others will behave in response to anticipated changes in future demand. This alternative vision of competition assumes individuals would react differently to anticipated events: individuals have differing capacities for awareness about new market information, prejudices and beliefs condition the type and quantity of knowledge which individuals internalize and assimilate, etc. Under this vision, institutions play a crucial role in explaining how market exchanges are brought about via a process whereby knowledge is conveyed to some individuals and denied to others.[41]

Market competition is a dynamic phenomenon whereby alert entrepreneurs seize unfolding profit opportunities that are constantly changing. In this model, labor division, specialization, and differentiation take place thanks to the creativity of entrepreneurs. However, since people are not equally creative, it follows that not all opportunities will be available to all entrepreneurs, as they will interpret market information about new goods,

---

40. Paul J. McNulty, *Economic Theory and the Meaning of Competition, in* THE COMPETITIVE ECONOMY: SELECTED READINGS 65–66 (Yale Brozen ed., 1975).

41. In this respect the institutional paradigm represented in schools of economic thought—such as the Austrian school (begun by Menger in the last century and developed in this century by Mises, Hayek, Lachmann, and Kirzner), the Subjectivist school (Shackle), and the post-Marshallian school (Penrose, Richardson, Earl, and Foss)—has emphasized the need to focus on the institutional restraints that determine trade, rather than on trade itself. Nicolai J. Foss, *Austrian and Post-Marshallian Economics: The Bridging Work of George Richardson, in* ECONOMIC ORGANIZATION, CAPABILITIES AND CO-ORDINATION: ESSAYS IN HONOUR OF G. B. RICHARDSON 138–43, 149–50 (Nicolai J. Foss & Brian J. Loasby eds., 1988).

consumer preferences, tastes, and needs differently according to their subjective perceptions. Indeed, progress is possible if only a few attentive entrepreneurs can spot and/or seize the profit opportunities presented by the changing circumstances in which markets constantly evolve. Only by enabling a few (as opposed to infinite) entrepreneurs to seize the opportunity would investments take place, since a simultaneous attempt by all to seize it would result in collective losses. Some individuals are excluded momentarily from obtaining access to certain social resources, while others are granted exclusivity.

This is the purpose of market institutions such as property rights, contractual devices, arrangements, and even informal collaboration that results, in the eyes of antitrust advocates, in "restrictive behavior." By contrast, Schumpeter, who clearly grasped the dynamic essence of market capitalism, noted the role of such devices thus:

> In analyzing such [restrictive] business strategy ex visu of a given point of time, the investigating economist or government agent sees price policies that seem to him predatory and restrictions of output that seem to him synonymous with loss of opportunities to produce. He does not see that restrictions of this type are, in the conditions of the perennial gale, incidents, often unavoidable incidents, of a long run process of expansion which they protect rather than impede. There is no more of paradox in this than there is in saying that motorcars are travelling [sic] faster than they otherwise would because they are provided with brakes.[42]

Naturally, these devices also interrupt or block outsiders' access to similar opportunities, but in doing so they ensure the effective exploitation of the available opportunity. Thus, "the availability of [the] kind of information related to competitive production depends in particular on the existence of restraints which, in varying degree, reduce the freedom of action of individual entrepreneurs."[43]

It is essential, however, that businesses are free from any other obstacle to their awareness of profit opportunities. Thus, in an evolutionary market setting, policymakers would only prohibit those restrictions that impose a fixed course of action on or exclude third parties (such as boycotts, cartels set up through government legislation, legal monopolies, etc.). In this setting, regulatory reform and the elimination of legal impediments to trade acquire particular relevance to the policy agenda of competition authorities. By the same token, competition authorities should abstain from intervening when third parties are not affected, even if competitors align their conduct

---

42. SCHUMPETER, *supra* note 2, at 84.
43. RICHARDSON, *supra* note 33, at 69.

with respect to prices. Richardson explains how increasing returns[44] are compatible with dynamic competition in evolutionary settings.[45] It is not the purpose of this article to embark on the details of this topic, but merely to visualize how embracing this alternative theory—which calls for abandoning the perfect competition premise—inevitably leads to framing an alternative agenda for competition policymakers.

Clearly, this alternative "market process" vision of competition explains the existence of those institutions that we currently find in real life situations: property rights, contracts, arrangements, practices, routines, business reputations, and similar other means of conveying knowledge across the system. Far from neglecting the role of these institutions in the market or treating them as an anomaly, the market process view of competition clearly explains their existence: these institutions are necessary for market competition to become operational. For example, without property rights, it would not be possible to know who has access to what social resources; without exclusive supply contracts, no entrepreneur would be certain about the conduct of other entrepreneurs in connection with the delivery of complementary inputs for her production, and therefore she would probably not invest in such activity; and in a world without business reputation or advertising, firms would find it extremely difficult to anticipate their own levels of output, given their ignorance about the likely output of other firms, and so on.

Institutionally-based (or market process) competition policy would look into the ease with which market processes evolve, unencumbered from contrived liens and burdens, and focus on attaining optimal outcomes. According to O'Driscoll and Rizzo, it is only possible to do so with reference to the processes of which those outcomes are the result: "There are not competitive results unless there is competition. . . . Without competition, there is no reference point to which comparisons with real-world results can be made. In the absence of competitive markets, economic theory cannot tell us what is optimal."[46] Therefore, "[c]ompetitive values or alloca-

44. In the short term, firms would tend to bear increasing production costs, thereby stimulating decreasing returns: costs will increase together with output levels. In the long run, however, industries usually diminish their costs, thereby increasing returns to all participating firms. Alfred Marshall termed this finding a "law of increasing return." According to this law, long term equilibrium would bring about lower production costs for all the firms participating in an industry—no matter the output increases. 1 ALFRED MARSHALL, PRINCIPLES OF ECONOMICS 318 (9th variorum ed. 1961).

45. G.B. Richardson, *Competition, Innovation and Increasing Returns* (DRUID Working Paper No. 96-10, July 1996), *available at* http://www.druid.dk/uploads/tx_picturedb/wp96-10.pdf.

46. GERALD P. O'DRISCOLL, JR. & MARIO J. RIZZO, THE ECONOMICS OF TIME AND IGNORANCE 143 (1985).

tions do not exist 'out there,' independently ascertainable apart from actual market results."[47]

In fact, "[t]here are a few abstract distinctions that can be posited about the outcomes of monopolistic as compared with competitive markets."[48] In a similar vein, Hayek declared: "[C]ompetition is a sensible procedure to use only if we do not know beforehand who will do best. . . . [I]t will only tell us, however, only who did best on the particular occasion, and not necessarily that each did as well as he could have done . . . ."[49]

Under these guidelines, competition agencies would be called to challenge any restrictions (either business- or government-created) that constrain market growth. As Adam Smith believed, economic progress depends on market size; therefore, competition agencies should encourage division of labor by lifting barriers to trade that would otherwise reduce market size. Competition policymaking will promote dynamic competition inasmuch it is capable of removing barriers that limit market size. In short, competition policymaking should not attempt to devise "optimal" market outcomes or surrogate market allocation; rather, it should direct its endeavors towards eliminating obstacles that artificially reduce market size.

VI. REDEFINING THE COMPETITION POLICY AGENDA

In view of the theoretical considerations already discussed, the alternative, institutionally-based competition policy demands an alternative policy agenda, as follows:

Promotion of regulatory reform and open trade as a means of opening legal bottlenecks to competition. Competition agencies should concentrate on eliminating official barriers to trade through deregulation and privatization on the one hand, and trade liberalization on the other hand. This would create the preconditions for firms to enter the market by reducing transaction costs in the system. Competition agencies also should concentrate on simplifying administrative rules so as to create a level playing field. However, the flexibility needed to adapt to market change should not be sacrificed for clear principles. Competition authorities should lay down clear principles with respect to intellectual property, to avoid deterring research and innovative activities by inappropriately interfering with them.

---

47. *Id.*
48. *Id.* at 144.
49. HAYEK, *supra* note 25, at 67–68.

Differentiating standards from trade restrictions. Competition authorities should promote competition between competing networks and standards. Markets, and not governments, should determine which new features and products should be introduced into the marketplace, which standards should succeed, and whether open standards should achieve general acceptance. Consumers should not be prevented from enjoying the benefits of the network externalities that result from the adoption of common systems and standards, even if this results in the universal acceptance of a single product. Competition agencies should rely on white papers and other means of identifying voluntary business standards for each industry. These instruments could enable the authorities to devise general principles of fair conduct, a necessary element to promote regulatory reform.

Targeting obstacles to potential third-party competitors entering the market. These restrictions include both quasi-legal restraints on those who would want to depart from standardized conventions, as well as corporate rules, such as fixing the professional fees of chartered liberal professions such as the law, medicine, and others.

Facilitating the means for settling disputes. Competition agencies should advocate means of dispute resolution that leave the allocation of rights in dispute to the economic agents involved in the controversy, rather than appealing to the dictum of a government regulatory agency that is potentially less connected with the particulars of the case in dispute. Also, competition authorities and sectorial regulators should improve their institutional cooperation in cases where public policy considerations other than the pursuit of innovation, entrepreneurship, and economic growth dictate legal regulations (such as preservation of labor, market access to less efficient competitors, and so on).

Enforcing pro-competition guidelines in privatization of public assets, by eliminating concessions to legal monopolies during transitional periods, or by requiring privatizing firms to fulfill strict pro-competitive conditions such as industrial restructuring and investment targeting during transitional stages.

In Latin America, these guidelines are seldom pursued consistently.[50] Instead, the bulk of competition agencies' work is devoted to antitrust prosecutions, in which cumbersome measures of market power coupled with an intuitive balancing of economic efficiencies consume most of their

50. *See* IGNACIO DE LEÓN, LATIN AMERICAN COMPETITION LAW AND POLICY: A POLICY IN SEARCH OF IDENTITY 161–65 (2001).

effective time, and ultimately compromise the predictability and stability of the rule of law.[51]

CONCLUSION

Conventional antitrust policy assumptions tell us that business' manipulations through contractual devices, exclusionary conduct, and "misuse" of property rights create market failures that are responsible for the sub-optimal allocation of social resources.[52] From this perspective, restricting monopolistic behavior is necessary if markets are to function properly. Instead of giving names to market arrangements, however, the question policymaking should ask is what would happen if such restrictions were absent altogether. This question is never answered, of course, because under perfect competition models such a problem does not exist: that is, monopolistic behavior is eliminated through antitrust policies, and remaining market participants' knowledge of each other's behavior is postulated by the model; hence analysts are left to grapple with a problem that does not exist in the real world.

As Richardson argues:

> [B]y neglecting the whole problem of information, the perfect competition model condemns itself not only to unrealism but to inadequacy even as a hypothetical system. It is no defence [sic] to appeal, moreover, to the analogy of mechanical statics which, though neglecting friction, can still identify the equilibrium position of a system of forces, for we cannot demonstrate that economic systems have such positions of rest without reference to expectations and information which could not be presumed to be available in the absence of restraints.[53]

The conventional antitrust perspective imposes a contrived view of market function that entirely disregards a fundamental problem: firms do not operate in an institutional vacuum; on the contrary, in order to maximize their profits they must take into account other market players' decisions. The coordination of knowledge among market players is thus the key economic problem in search of policy solutions.

This is a problem that requires an alternative understanding of the economic problems faced by entrepreneurs. Addleson states: "[T]he econo-

---

51. Judging the success of a policy on the basis of its capacity to achieve its goals creates problems because, as Rizzo reminds us, "[a] utilitarian or balancing framework would require us to trace the full effects of each (tentative) judicial decision, and then evaluate it against the particular utilitarian standard adopted," which places an unbearable burden of information on the shoulders of whoever must decide the success of a policy. Mario J. Rizzo, *Rules Versus Cost-Benefit Analysis in the Common Law*, 4 CATO J. 865, 873 (1985).

52. *See* Demsetz, *supra* note 22.

53. RICHARDSON, *supra* note 33, at 69.

mists' meaning[] of competition requires a taxonomy, not a definition; and a taxonomy needs a framework."[54] Wubben is even more assertive when contending that what is needed is a new epistemology.[55] If criticizing antitrust policy must begin at the epistemological level, where the relevant questions are determined and the premises of the analysis are laid down, it is necessary to define an alternative paradigm in order to understand market phenomena and competition.

Competition policy has to adopt an alternative perception of the way in which the market functions, where the knowledge coordination problem becomes central. In this alternative paradigm, one has to look into economic institutions shaping market transactions before condemning them as "anticompetitive," "monopolistic," and so forth. Competition analysis must be enriched with comparative institutional analysis, economic history, and other social sciences in order to gain effectiveness. Exploring the role of culture in competition policy development immediately raises important issues of law and economics that are far from settled. Given its broader perspective, institutional analysis overcomes the constraints of the legal wording of a competition statute that holds competition policy (understood as the development of entrepreneurial ways and promotion of creative innovation) in a very tight grip. Such reliance has driven policy makers away from a more complete understanding of those issues that explain the fundamental role played by institutions.

It follows from the foregoing that the substratum of economic institutions such as culture, learned habits, and ethical values play a fundamental role in shaping competition policymaking. To shape competition policy appropriately one must take into consideration the institutional development of the society, which will allow one to evaluate any potential restrictions on competition that may exist in the form of government policies.

An institutional perspective of competition policy grounds the analysis in the social rules where the policy is actually enforced. Acknowledging this fact reveals several crucial points. First, competition policy, like any human endeavor, is grounded in ideology and normative values, not hard science. This is not necessarily a disadvantage, provided analysts are aware of the nature of the ethical debate entertained by competition policy authorities. In this way, the necessary institutional constraints will be instituted to prevent competition policy from becoming unbridled or

---

54. Mark Addleson, *Competition, in* THE ELGAR COMPANION TO AUSTRIAN ECONOMICS 97 (Peter J. Boettke ed., 1994).

55. Emiel Wubben, *Austrian Economics and Uncertainty: On a Non-Deterministic but Non-Haphazard Future, in* NEW PERSPECTIVES ON AUSTRIAN ECONOMICS 106–07 (Gerrit Meijer ed., 1995).

uncontrolled. Indeed, such constraints are essential to reinforcing the rule of law, predictability of the policy, and transparency of market rules.

Second, the fact that normative standards are ultimately ethical does not necessarily undermine the conclusions drawn from an understanding of market dynamics. For this reason, rather than judging entrepreneurial behavior from a normative standpoint, competition analysts should concentrate on making surrounding institutions more transparent and open to entrepreneurs, so as to draw tentative guidelines about the best possible way to promote market exchanges. By doing away with imaginary constructions of contrived social welfare, and closely inspecting and looking at past business experience, the market exchanges have a greater opportunity to reach their utmost potential.

Third, competition authorities should avoid falling into the intellectual trap of endorsing contrived social welfare standards that essentially contradict market competition. Developing and transitioning countries should be particularly careful to remember that the ultimate goal of competition must be connected to the development of competitiveness, innovation, and economic development.

Fourth, culture is a fundamental factor that policymakers must take into account at the time of a competition policy's development. A central planning tradition perpetuates ways of conceiving policymaking that may run contrary to the logic of introducing markets, thereby making the initial work of competition authorities particularly cumbersome. It is necessary to give them the right tools to devise alternative policy solutions to government interference in the markets.

These fundamental reasons suggest that the competition authorities' policy agenda should address regulatory reform and exercise strong "competition advocacy," thereby challenging government regulations and rules that inhibit innovation and business development. Based on the experience of Latin America and other countries outside the region, this should become a central concern of policymaking for competition authorities. It is essential that professional, independent, and highly motivated officials enforce competition policy. In addition, proper rules should be instituted to ensure that decisions are balanced, carefully drafted, quickly enforced, and above all, always controlled by a well-trained judiciary.

The conventional competition policymaking usually applied in developed countries has suffered evident mutation in the anti-market institutional constraints of Latin American societies; hence, optimal design of competition policy must be crafted to overcome the particular anti-capitalist bias prevailing in the region's economic culture. Instead of blaming the poor market performance and low competitive levels of Latin American firms on the high industrial concentration that prevails among Latin America's domestic markets, competition agencies would fare better if they went one step further and asked themselves about the causes of such concentration. They probably will not find the "invisible hand" of markets which, if anything, has been absent from the region, dominated as it is by mercantilist trade policies and high government dirigisme. More likely, they will find the "visible hand" of governments behind such concentration. Godek has put it very simply: "Worrying about antitrust issues shows an unhealthy anxiety about the imagined ills of capitalism."[56]

---

56. Paul E. Godek, *One U.S. Export Eastern Europe Does Not Need*, REGULATION MAG., Winter 1992, at 20, *available at* http://www.cato.org/pubs/regulation/regv15n1/reg15n1-currents.html#godek.

B
Monopolies and Abuse of Dominant Position

[3]

ABUSE OF DOMINANCE AND ITS EFFECTS ON ECONOMIC DEVELOPMENT

Michael Adam and Simon Alder

Abstract

Rules on abuse of dominance are used to find a balance between three objectives: 1) ensuring enough competition between firms in order to force them to be efficient and to compete on merit, 2) allowing a certain degree of profitability so that companies have incentives to become more efficient, and 3) achieving an equal distribution of wealth and business opportunities among different sectors of society. While the discussion in developed countries focuses on the first two aspects in order to maximize innovation and growth, developing countries may also want to consider the third dimension and include the reduction of inequality and poverty as objectives of abuse of dominance laws. But even the relationship between the first two aspects tends to vary among regions, because investment depends on factors that differ between developing and developed countries. These factors sometimes contradict each other and it is crucial to find a sound balance between them. Firstly, since developing economies often have smaller markets and, therefore, a lower equilibrium number of firms that can exploit economies of scale and operate efficiently, markets in developing countries are more likely to be concentrated. Furthermore, entry barriers tend to be higher and capital markets are often less developed, which causes obstacles for firms trying to compete with a dominant company. Secondly, large firms play a different role regarding their investment activity in developing countries than they do in more developed economies. Established firms can be important for less developed economies to have a sufficiently high level of investment in production. In such countries, the benefits of increased investments may outweigh efficiency losses that can arise from a more lax treatment of dominant firm conduct. Thirdly, distributional aspects may be especially important for developing countries. Smaller firms, which often represent poorer sectors of society, may have to be given better chances to compete against large dominant companies. Competition law can be used for such public interest issues, but it is crucial that the law gives clear guidance on how these objectives should be balanced against other objectives such as efficiency. The comparison of the EU and the US regarding abuse of dominance shows that significant differences exist even among developed countries. One reason for the disparity is differing assumptions about what types of conduct are harmful and how difficult it is to differentiate them from other conduct. The 'access to market principle' of the EU arises from the assumption that restrictions of market access are harmful to the economy and that a harmful conduct can be distinguished from other, not harmful, conduct. On the other hand, the 'non-intervention principle' of the US is based on the assumption that the distinction of such conduct is difficult, that there is great danger of prohibiting behaviour that is efficient and that the unnecessary prohibition of efficient conduct is severe. One conclusion from the comparison is that these assumptions should be analysed and be grounded on the economic reality. How likely and severe errors of competition authorities are can, for example, be assessed in an analysis of past decisions and their effects on the economy. Support of developing countries' competition authorities in analysing their own cases and the impact of their decisions on the economy would therefore be valuable.

1. Introduction

The fundamental goal of competition policy is to increase welfare. Competition policy aims to accomplish this goal by defining appropriate rules for business conduct, but the impact of competition on welfare is complex and may differ between countries. On the one hand, competition can improve the efficiency of firms and consequently increase the welfare of consumers. On the other hand, unfettered competition may augment an unequal distribution of assets, power and business opportunities which exist in many countries and reduce growth. This aspect is particularly important for developing countries, which face poverty and inequality as their most pressing issues.

Laws on abuse of dominance are central to both aspects of competition, i.e. the efficiency of the firms and the equal distribution of opportunities. Outperforming competitors and achieving a position of dominance that allows making profits is the key incentive for firms to do their best in serving their clients and thus to become more efficient: "*It is precisely the prospect of enjoying some market power (i.e. of making profit) that pushes firms to use more efficient technologies, improve their product quality, or introduce new product varieties."*[713]. But welfare is reduced if a firm abuses its dominant position to keep more efficient competitors away or exploit its costumers. Maximizing the efficiency therefore requires a careful trade-off between providing incentives and limiting abuses. Given that market structures are different in developed and developing countries, the outcome from this trade-off is likely to be different across countries and regions. For example, higher barriers to entry, less developed capital markets and asymmetries of information reduce the opportunities of firms and thus the dynamic of competition particularly in developing countries[714]. Authorities in these countries may choose to adopt a stricter approach towards dominant firms. On the other hand, investments in production made by established firms are important for less developed economies, this being an argument for developing countries to be more in favour of dominant firms than developed countries. Laws on abuse of dominance are also crucial for the distributional aspects of competition. Many developing countries may find it important to include rules that focus on reducing the foreclosure of markets. The objective of such an approach can be to give better opportunities to small firms often representing poorer parts of society to engage in the economy and to increase the income of their owners and employers.

The purpose of this study is to link the discussion about the appropriate competition policy for developing and emerging economies to the specific issue of abuse of dominance. To establish this link, we first briefly provide an economic and legal background of abuse of dominance. We then look at the situation of different developed, developing and emerging economies and make recommendations for future cooperation between institutions and organizations to improve the legal framework.

---

[713] Motta (2004: 64).
[714] Anderson and Heimler (2007: 61).

2. The scope of the prohibition of abuse of a dominant position

2.1. The United Nations Set of Principles and Rules on Competition

The abuse of a dominant position is addressed in the United Nations Set of Principles and Rules on Competition and naturally also in individual jurisdictions worldwide.

The United Nations Set of Principles and Rules on Competition – like the majority of national competition authorities – defines dominance in a behavioural way, although many structural criteria are still used in practice: *"Dominant position of market power refers to a situation where an enterprise, either by itself or acting together with a few other enterprises, is in a position to control a relevant market for a particular good or service, or groups of goods or services"*[715]. The set then lists a number of acts from which dominant firms must refrain.

> **Box 1: Section D.4 of The United Nations Set of Principles and Rules on Competition**
>
> Enterprises should refrain from the following acts or behaviour in a relevant market when, through an abuse or acquisition and abuse of a dominant position of market power, they limit access to markets or otherwise unduly restrain competition, having or being likely to have adverse effects on international trade, particularly that of developing countries, and on the economic development of these countries:
>
> (a) Predatory behaviour towards competitors, such as using below-cost pricing to eliminate competitors;
> (b) Discriminatory (i.e. unjustifiably differentiated) pricing or terms or conditions in the supply or purchase of goods and services, including by means of the use of pricing policies in transactions between affiliated enterprises which overcharge or undercharge for goods or services purchased or supplied as compared with prices for similar or comparable transactions outside the affiliated enterprises;
> (c) Mergers, takeovers, joint ventures or other acquisitions of control, whether of a horizontal, vertical or a conglomerate nature;
> (d) Fixing the prices at which goods exported can be resold in importing countries;
> (e) Restrictions on the importation of goods which have been legitimately marked abroad with a trademark identical with or similar to the trademark protected as to identical or similar goods in the importing country where the trademarks in question are of the same origin, i.e. belong to the same owner or are used by enterprises between which there is economic, organizational, managerial or legal interdependence and where the purpose

---

[715] UNCTAD (2000).

of such restrictions is to maintain artificially high prices;
(f) When not for ensuring the achievement of legitimate business purposes, such as quality, safety, adequate distribution or service:
(i) Partial or complete refusals to deal on the enterprise's customary commercial terms;
(ii) Making the supply of particular goods or services dependent upon the acceptance of restrictions on the distribution or manufacture of competing or other goods;
(iii) Imposing restrictions concerning where, or to whom, or in what form or quantities, goods supplied or other goods may be resold or exported;
(iv) Making the supply of particular goods or services dependent upon the purchase of other goods or services from the supplier or his designee.

UNCTAD: *The United Nations Set of Principles and Rules on Competition.* United Nations. Geneva. 2000.

2.2. Different competition laws in developed and developing countries

Most developing countries have adopted laws on abuse of dominance that have been inspired by the rules of the European Union (EU), i.e. Art. 82 of the EC Treaty. According to EU case law, dominant firms have the "special duty" not to exploit consumers and not to exclude competitors by anti-competitive means[716]. The idea of a special responsibility of dominant companies is founded in the view that competition is already weakened when one company dominates the market. The decreased level of competition is balanced by stricter rules on the conduct of the dominant firm, which should not be able to take advantage of this situation. The European concept of special responsibility of dominant firms is in conflict with the rules on dominance in the US, where dominant companies are granted greater freedom.[717] Developing countries often have highly concentrated markets with sometimes only one or two companies offering a certain product or service[718]. Therefore, there is a danger of dominant companies taking advantage of their position by charging higher prices, offering inferior products to consumers and foreclosing potential competitors thus consolidating their dominant position. This explains why it makes sense for many developing countries to opt for strict rules on the behaviour of

---

[716] Case 322/81, *Nederlandsche Banden-Industrie Michelin N.V. v Commission,* 1983 E.C.R. 3461, [1985].
[717] See Section 5.
[718] Lipimile (2004: 199, 201).

dominant companies and to invoke a special responsibility of dominant firms.

2.3. Theoretical concepts of abuse of dominance

There are two tests in the European framework for assessing whether the prohibition of the abuse of dominance applies:
1) the undertaking has to be dominant, and
2) it must be abusing that dominant position.

The first test raises two questions: the definition of the market in which the undertaking is alleged to be dominant, and whether it is actually dominant in this market.

2.3.1. Market definition

Before assessing whether an undertaking is dominant, the relevant market must be determined. This relevant market has two dimensions:
1.   the product market, and
2.   the geographic market.

As to the product market, it is examined if the product offered by the dominant company is interchangeable with other, similar products. If it is found that buyers would be ready to switch to an alternative product if the price of the first product increases slightly, these two products belong to the same product market. If buyers prefer paying a higher price for the first product rather than switching to another product, the two products are offered on different markets.

Box 2: Market definition in the EU

The basic principles for the market definition are for example laid down in the EU Commission Notice on the *Definition of Relevant Market for the Purpose of Community Competition Law* (Official Journal C 371, 09/12/1997 p. 5-13). According to Paragraph 2, market definition is a tool to identify and define the boundaries of competition between firms. Market definition is not an end in itself but is an analytical tool.

Paragraph 13 states that firms are subject to three main competitive constraints:
  1.   demand substitutability
  2.   supply substitutability
  3.   potential competition.

For the purpose of market definition, it is demand substitutability that is significant. One way of making this determination can be viewed as a speculative experiment, postulating a hypothetical small, lasting change in relative prices and evaluating the likely reactions of customers to that increase (the so-called SSNIP Test – **S**mall but **S**ignificant **N**on-transitory **I**ncrease in **P**rice).

Paragraph 25 relates to the evidence to be used in order to define the relevant market. There is a range of evidence permitting an assessment of the extent to which substitution would take place. In individual cases, certain types of evidence will be determinant, depending very much on the characteristics and specificity of the industry and products or services that are being examined. The same type of evidence may be of no importance in other cases. In most cases, a decision will have to be based on the consideration of a number of criteria and different items of evidence. The Commission follows an open approach to empirical evidence, aimed at making an effective use of all available information which may be relevant in individual cases. The Commission does not follow a rigid hierarchy of different sources of information or types of evidence. Evidence of substitution in the recent past, the views of customers and competitors, studies and consumer surveys, barriers and costs associated with switching demand to potential substitutes and the different categories of customers and price discrimination are factors that can be taken into account.

When defining the geographic market, a similar test is carried out: will buyers switch to a product from another geographic region if the price of the first product increases slightly? If transportation costs and other barriers are low, this is likely and the two products could belong to the same geographical market. If goods are perishable and cannot be transported or if transport is very costly, buyers are not able to switch to products from other regions, which therefore are offered on a distinct geographic market.

The outcome of the market definition is crucial in determining dominance. The same firm may be regarded as dominant if the market in which it is active is defined narrowly or it may be considered as not dominant if the market is defined broadly. The key concept for the market definition is substitutability. A market should not simply be defined as a collection of similar goods, but of goods that can be used for the same purpose and thus exercise a competitive constraint on each other[719]. Other factors that have to be considered here are, for example, functional characteristics of the product or transportation costs[720]. All these factors are reflected in the willingness of the customers to switch to other products. It is therefore a straightforward way to define a market by investigating whether customers change to other products when the price of the product they normally purchase increases. This test is used in areas of antitrust such as merger control[721]. However, in the case of abuse of dominance, the test can be misleading, because the consumers' willingness to change supplier can be considerably influenced by the abusive conduct under consideration. If a firm has in the past undertaken abusive conduct such as excluding direct competitors, it is likely to have a dominant position and to be able to set higher prices. The consumers who are faced with this high price may switch to imperfect substitutes if they would have to pay an even higher price (which is hypothetically assumed in the test). This substitute would consequently be included in the market and, on this broadly defined market, the firm under consideration may appear to not even have market power[722]. Consequently, this test will be biased towards defining markets too broadly in abuse of dominance cases[723]. The assessment of dominance in cases of abuses is difficult and authorities will have to rely more than in other cases on the products' characteristics and their interchangeability in the individual case and they will have to take the distortions in observed prices into account. This reflects a more behavioural approach to dominance, which looks at the firm's ability to act to some extent independently from other market

---

[719] Motta (2004: 102).

[720] Anderson *et al.* (1999).

[721] This is referred to as the Hypothetical Monopolist Test or the Small But Significant Non-transitory Increase in Price (SSNIP) Test. See Motta (2004: 102).

[722] This is referred as the Cellophane Fallacy. See also Motta (2004: 105).

[723] However, the test can still be used in a negative way. Evidence that two products are substitutes at current prices does not prove that they are in the same relevant market, but the failure to show that two products are substitutes at current prices does prove that they are not in the same market. See National Economic Research Associates (NERA) (2001: 24).

forces, as opposed to the structural approach, which looks at the market conditions[724].

2.3.2. Existence of a dominant position

Having defined the relevant product, geographical and temporal markets, the next issue is to decide what constitutes dominance. In *United Brands,* the EU Court of Justice defined dominance as "*a position of economic strength enjoyed by an undertaking which enables it to hinder the maintenance of effective competition on the relevant market by allowing it to behave to an appreciable extent independently of its competitors and customers and ultimately of its consumers*".

The question remains, however, how to measure such market power. Market shares may be a useful indicator but there are several other factors that have to be taken into consideration such as market position, buyer power and entry conditions[725]. There are differences between markets regarding at what market share level a firm is dominant, but a lower bound (safe harbour presumption) and an upper bound (dominance presumption) can give guidance and predictability. However, an investigation that takes the characteristics of the case into consideration may be needed in an individual case. The size and market shares of competing firms also have to be considered. Secondly, entry barriers must be analysed, whereby special attention needs to be paid to those barriers that may be an outcome of the firm's abusive conduct itself [726]. Thirdly, buyer power needs to be considered in order to know whether the buyers can put a constraint on the dominant firms.

The more direct assessment of market power uses econometric techniques to estimate the elasticity of demand in response to price changes. Market power then is defined as the ability of a firm to raise prices above its marginal cost[727]. This ability depends on the elasticity of demand and estimating the elasticity therefore allows one to directly assess market power. The econometric analysis can become

---

[724] For the discussion of the behavioural and structural definition of dominance, see Section 4.3.3.
[725] Motta (2004: 117).
[726] Anderson *et al.* (1999: 71).
[727] Motta (2004: 115).

complicated and demands a certain quality and quantity of data. The traditional indirect approach, which focuses more on the market structure (such as concentration), is therefore still widely used in practice[728].

Dominance not only exists if one company holds a paramount market position, but it can also be found with regard to several firms if certain conditions are fulfilled. Cases involving *collective dominance* have emerged in developed and in developing countries and posed significant problems in both.

---

[728] This was shown in International Competition Network (ICN) (2007: 43).

Box 3: Case 1 – Collective dominance in the Zimbabwean cement industry

In December 1998, the Competition Commission commenced a preliminary probe into various allegations of restrictive and unfair trade practices in the cement industry, which were leading to shortages and excessive prices of cement on the local Zimbabwean market. The allegations came from complaints made to the Commission by the cement trade and the general public, as well as from newspaper reports.

Four companies were involved in the production and distribution of cement in Zimbabwe: (i) Portland Holdings Limited (Unicem) of Bulawayo, (ii) Circle Cement Limited of Harare, (iii) Zimbabwe Cement Company (Pvt) Limited (ZimCement) of Norton' and (iv) Techniks (Pvt) Limited of Gweru. Only Unicem and Circle Cement were involved at all stages of cement production, from the quarrying of limestone to the final product. The other two companies were more involved in blending operations. A new cement manufacturing plant, under a joint venture between China and the Industrial Development Corporation (IDC), was nearing completion in Lalapanzi. The cement industry was found to be highly concentrated, with a Herfindahl-Hirschman Index (HHI) of 4,602. The two largest players in the industry (Unichem and Circle Cement) controlled a combined market share of over 90%.

The evidence gathered confirmed some of the allegations levelled against Unicem and Circle Cement, and others which came up during the course of the investigation, such as: (i) restricting the distribution of cement; (ii) enhancing or maintaining the price of cement; and (iii) supporting or promoting the distribution of cement by inefficient and uneconomical means. No evidence was found to support the allegations of: (i) prevention or restriction of entry into the cement industry; (ii) undue refusal to distribute cement; and (iii) collusive arrangements between the cement producers. With regards to allegations of collusion between Unicem and Circle Cement, it was found that the fact that Unicem was a more efficient producer than Circle Cement was clearly reflected in that company's lower retail prices on the market. It was also found that even though the two companies had natural markets in the northern and southern parts of the country, because of high transports costs of distributing their products, the companies' products were sold in either of their 'natural' markets.

The Commission therefore ordered Unicem and Circle Cement, in terms of Section 31 of the Competition Act, to discontinue and terminate the identified restrictive practices.

The Commission's investigation also identified other public interest concerns in the distribution of cement on the local Zimbabwean market, such as lack of transparency in the distribution of the product, lack of distribution outlets in remote rural areas, high import duties on cement raw materials and discriminatory sales tax regime in favour of large buyers. The Commission made appropriate recommendations to the relevant authorities and parties on the alleviation of the concerns.

Quoted from: UNCTAD: *Review of Recent Experiences in the Formulation and Implementation of Competition Law and Policy in Selected Developing Countries: Thailand, Lao, Kenya, Zambia, Zimbabwe.* United Nations. New York and Geneva. 2005.

Defining when a collective dominant position exists is a difficult task. The case law in the EU has developed a rather specific definition that may be helpful for the treatment of collective dominance cases in developing countries as well. According to this definition, collective dominance exists if two independent firms act as a collective entity on the market and are as this entity not subject to substantial competition from other companies. Collective dominance exists mostly in oligopolistic markets and is therefore of special interest for developing countries, where markets are often highly concentrated. However, the existence of an oligopoly in itself is not enough to assume that collective dominance exists[729].

Box 4: EU case law regarding collective dominance

According to the case law of the EU Court of Justice, three conditions have to be met:[1]

1) The market has to be *transparent* enough for every member of the oligopoly to be able to quickly inform itself of the conduct of the other members.

2) There must be an *incentive for tacit and permanent coordination* between the members of the oligopoly. This means that all members must know that unilateral moves of one member with the objective of trying to increase its market shares - e.g. by cutting prices - would immediately provoke the same measure or sanctions by the other members, so that it would make no sense for the individual member to make moves of this kind.

3) The *oligopoly is not faced with substantial competition from outside the group* so that members can be sure that customers will not switch to other providers easily.

[1] ECJ, Judgment of 16 March 2000, Compagnie maritime belge, Joined cases C-395/96 P and C-396/96 P, ECR 2000 Page I-01365.

Substantial market power of few companies can make it especially difficult for small firms to remain in the market and even more to enter new markets. Markets in developing countries are often highly concentrated and dominated by – often foreign – firms that hold strong positions in these markets and are sometimes the only provider of a

---

[729] Another crucial issue is the role of the state, which may allow, facilitate or even create dominant companies. This issue will be discussed in more detail in Section 4.5.

certain good or service[730]. On the other hand, the local economy is often characterized by a large number of small business units that create employment for most of the population but lack economic power. Survival in the markets by these small, often newly created, companies is made difficult if dominant players abuse their dominant position in order to prevent market entry and competition by other players. In order to create a more level playing field and to protect smaller local companies from such abusive practices, rules on abuse of dominance are essential for developing countries.

2.3.3. Abusive conduct

There are two types of abusive unilateral conduct by dominant firms: exploitative abuses and exclusionary abuses[731]. The former refer to cases where firms charge excessively high prices from their customers, pay low prices to suppliers, or discriminate among consumers. The latter refer to cases where firms suppress competition by refusing to deal, engaging in predatory pricing or tying products in order to raise costs of entry and exclude competitors from the market to create or strengthen a dominant position. The difficulty with abusive conducts is that the same conduct can be pro- or anti-competitive, depending on the individual case. For example, refusals to deal may be necessary to ensure quality standards, and lower prices are, in principle, a fundamental goal of competition policy.

---

[730] Lipimile (2004: 199, 201).
[731] Anderson *et al.* (1999: 72).

Box 5: Case 2 – Preliminary investigations into allegations of predatory pricing in the clear beer brewing and distribution industry in Zimbabwe

In December 1999, Nesbitt Brewery (Pvt) Limited of Chiredzi complained to the Competition Commission that National Breweries Limited was engaged in predatory pricing, having drastically reduced the price of its clear beer in Chiredzi to levels that were unprofitable, with the intention of driving Nesbitt Brewery out of the market. The investigations conducted by the Commission revealed that the clear beer industry in Zimbabwe is highly concentrated with an HHI (Hirschman-Herfindahl Index) concentration index in excess of 8,000. Nesbitt Brewery was a new entrant into the clear beer market challenging the long-standing monopoly position of National Breweries, which held a market share of 90%. National Breweries has a national distribution network while Nesbitt Brewery only operates in Chiredzi. The investigations further revealed that the National Breweries had run a beer promotion in Chiredzi from May 1999 to April 2000 when the Competition Commission started gathering information on the case. The promotion included free snacks and T-shirts, lucky-draw tickets, free beers and substantial price reductions. The promotion was only held in Chiredzi where Nesbitt Brewery is based and sells the bulk of its beer. The National Breweries retail prices for its beer in Chiredzi during the promotion period were below its normal landed prices in that town. The Commission found the alleged practices to be predatory within the terms of Section 2 of the *Competition Act*. Although National Breweries stopped the practices as soon as it became aware that the Competition Commission was investigating it, the Commission compelled it to formally undertake that it would desist from future practices aimed at driving Nesbitt Brewery out of the market.

Quoted from: UNCTAD: *Review of Recent Experiences in the Formulation and Implementation of Competition Law and Policy in Selected Developing Countries: Thailand, Lao, Kenya, Zambia, Zimbabwe*. United Nations. New York and Geneva. 2005.

584

Box 6: Case 3 – The Coca-Cola Company (TCCC)/Zambia Bottlers (ZB) exclusive dealing arrangements

ZB notified its exclusive dealing arrangements to the Zambia Competition Commission (ZCC). The Board observed that ZB had in place both distributorship and cooler hire contracts into the trade. It was also found that ZB owned the distribution containers, the Strategic Sales Depots (SSDs), and appointed operators for public service after purchase of merchandise. ZB also had cooler hire contracts with retailers along with conditions not to sell competing products. The Board approved the exclusive dealing arrangements in so far as the SSDs are owned by ZB, on condition that they are devoid of price fixing, abuse of dominant position and that the cost of cooler repairs be met by ZB since maintenance fees are being paid. These conditions have also been made an essential part of the compliance programme regarding the takeover of Cadbury Schweppes (CS) brands by TCCC. The compliance programme will be monitored by ZCC.

Quoted from: Zambia Competition Commission: *Annual Report 1999*. Lusaka. March 2000.

Box 7: Case 4 – Microsoft's abuse of market dominance in the Republic of Korea

The Korea Fair Trade Commission (KFTC) reported to UNCTAD that, in 2000, Microsoft had tied its Windows Media Service (WMS) to the Personal Computers (PC) Server Operating System (OS). The Window Media Player (WMP) was first tied to the PC Operating System Windows 98 Second Edition in 1999, and since then, WMP has been tied to the succeeding PC Operating Systems. Additionally, the company combined MSN Messenger with Windows ME in 2000 and Windows Messenger with Widows XP in 2001. Under the *Monopoly Regulation and Fair Trade Act* (MRFTA) of the Republic of Korea, Microsoft has a dominant position in the market. Its market share of the PC Operating System was 99% in terms of domestic sales, as compared with a 50% threshold stipulated in the Act.

The investigation and analysis of the case revealed three factors. Firstly, the tie-in sales constituted obstruction of competitors' business, which is part of abuse of market dominance. The tie-in sales deprived companies of the opportunity to purchase PC OS without WMS, WMP, and Windows Messenger attached, even when they did not wish to purchase them. Moreover, the tie-in sales had the effect of driving competitors out of business by restricting competition in the market. The market shares of other players in the market, for example RealNetworks, Daum Messenger, Nate-On Messenger and others, continued to decline as Microsoft's market share continued to rise in all aspects of its business.

Secondly, it was feared that the tie-in sales would significantly undermine consumer interest. Using dominance, Microsoft virtually forced consumers to purchase WMS, WMP, and Windows Messenger, even when they did not wish to do so. This is an infringement of the consumer's right to choice. Lastly, in the tied product markets, Microsoft's tie-sales constituted unfair business practices, as they restricted competition from competitors and consequently forced consumers to purchase the PC OS bundled with WMS, WMP or Windows Messenger.

The KFTC concluded that the company's tie-in sales were in violation of Articles 3-2 and 23 of the MRFTA ban on abuse of market dominance and unfair business practices that work against consumer interests and restrict or hinder competition in related markets.

On 7 December 2005, the KFTC imposed a series of corrective measures: (i) a surcharge of 33 billion Won (US$ 31 million); (ii) with regard to the tie-in of WMS, the KFTC ordered the company to strip WMS from the PC Server OS within 180 days from the date when the corrective order was imposed; (iii) for the bundling of WMP and Windows Messenger, the company was ordered to provide two different versions of the PC OS, whereby one version would have WMS and the Messenger programme removed from the PC OS while the other would keep WMP and Windows Messenger and allow customers to download competitors' products; and (iv) to ensure compliance with the decision of this case, the KFTC was to appoint a Supervisory Board composed of members nominated by the KFTC, the Minister of Information and Communication and Microsoft. The board was to be tasked with the responsibility of determining the specifics of the remedies and overseeing their implementation, while Microsoft was to bear all costs associated with the running of the Supervisory Board.

Quoted from: UNCTAD: *Recent important competition cases involving more than one country.* Report by the UNCTAD Secretariat. Geneva. 2007.

2.3.4. The possibility of objective justification

In some cases, an objective justification of an abusive conduct may be invoked. A company has the right to legitimate commercial behaviour and the defence of its legitimate interests. Under which circumstances a justification of otherwise abusive behaviour exists is determined on a case-to-case basis. Examples for such a justification can be efficiency increases or quality improvements that arise from the conduct.

3. Why should developing countries and countries in transition consider abuse of dominance?

3.1. The political economy dimension in developing countries

One of the reasons why rules on abuse of dominance are important for developing countries lies in the challenges many of them face as a result of their political institutions. Most developing countries have had economic systems with a relatively strong degree of command economy until recently. A command economy brings about the inherent existence of concentrated markets and of monopolies, because in many fields of the economy the state is the only actor and will not expose itself to competition. Nowadays, these systems have mostly been subject to the liberalization and privatization efforts of developing countries' economic systems[732]. In this process, the former public monopolies had to be abolished and the markets were supposed to be open to free competition of various private actors. However, what has happened in many cases is that large companies, often from developed countries, have been able to take over the position of the former state monopoly. Privatization has in many cases not led to more competition but simply to a substitution of public monopolies by private ones. This is one of the reasons for high market concentrations in developing countries[733]. Examples for this tendency exist in various sectors, for example in the field of sugar, beer, cement or packaging. These private companies have acquired a key position in many developing countries' markets. If they decide to engage in exploitative conduct – e.g. by charging overly high prices to customers or by offering only inferior products – or exclusionary conduct by excluding their competitors and thus consolidate their dominant position, developing countries' authorities need an instrument to tackle such business behaviour. This instrument is the existence of laws on abuse of dominance. Developing countries can only regulate efficiently the conduct of dominant firms if they create

---

[732] Lipimile (2004: 177).
[733] As to the high market concentrations, e.g. in the beer brewing and distribution and the cement distribution sectors, see the cases cited in Lipimile (2004: 199, 201).

and apply laws on abuse of dominance that allow them to tackle the anti-competitive behaviour of such firms to protect competition in their markets and, as a result of this, consumers. It is in this context that especially the EU approach, which attributes a "special responsibility" to a dominant company, suits rather well the interest of developing countries to gain control over dominant firms and keep their markets open to competition.

Another aspect that is linked to the political economy of developing countries concerns the role of the state. In newly liberalized economies, the role of government in the national economy typically remains strong. Many dominant companies are either state owned or controlled by the government; others are afforded a special protection by government policies. Such phenomena can especially, but not only, be witnessed in many network industries (railways, ports, electricity, telecommunications, etc.). The question of the role of the state in competition policy is delicate and difficult to handle, especially by public authorities that are themselves subject to government control. On the other hand, also, companies protected by governments should not be allowed to exploit consumers or to unduly restrain competition, which may lead to the exclusion of other players that offer better products or lower prices. Competition policy and, more specifically, rules on abuse of dominance are a useful instrument to treat this issue. By laying down general rules that apply to all companies with a paramount market position, a more level playing field can be created and it can be argued that governments also have to respect the basic rules of fair play in the markets which in the end will benefit the overall welfare and consumers.

3.2. Inequality, competition, and growth in developing and emerging economies

Laws against abuse of dominance can influence the distribution of assets, power and business opportunities. This distributional aspect of competition is particularly important for developing countries, where economic power and wealth are not fairly distributed. Competition policy may have to play the dual role of raising the power of underprivileged individuals and enterprises to participate in the process of competition and of creating a sound legal framework for free competition. If these objectives are not met, unfettered competition will simply help the big firms to monopolize domestic markets that are usually protected from foreign competition[734]. The resulting inequality will lead to public dissatisfaction and the excessive market power has the potential to raise prices[735]. Dominance not only leads to an unequal distribution of market power, wealth and business opportunities, but has also a potential negative effect on growth and development if such power is abused. The abuse hampers the good functioning of markets and the efficient allocation of resources so that the economy cannot reach its growth potential. Developing countries with low growth rates are unable to catch up with industrialized economies and are unlikely to experience substantial and sustained poverty reduction. Growth is therefore a central goal of limiting abuse of dominance in developing countries. On the other hand, the possibility of achieving a certain degree of market power is necessary, because it allows firms to make profits and this gives them incentives to become more efficient. If the limits on dominant firms and their conduct are too restrictive, growth may be reduced.

Although the relationship between market structure and economic performance is complex, it is, particularly in developing countries, crucial to consider it in the context of abuse of dominance. The extreme view is "the market will fix it all", which is partly based on the theory of contestable markets[736]. According to this theory, even a firm that enjoys a monopoly position in a market cannot price above the marginal costs because new firms would enter the market as soon as they observe that profits can be made. But this outcome depends on strong assumptions: the monopolist cannot change the prices as a reaction to entry and there are no barriers to and sunk costs of entry. These assumptions obviously do not hold in many markets of developed and developing economies. A third reason why market forces may not be able to reduce market power is anti-competitive practices, which is at the focus of this study.

Even in newly liberalized economies where barriers to entry have been reduced substantially, incumbent monopolists may not be challenged by new entrants and foreign investments may remain low in many cases[737]. This could suggest that a stricter approach to

---

[734] Fox (2003: 163).
[735] Economic theory predicts that the optimal pricing of a monopolist usually is above the welfare maximizing level.
[736] Motta (2004: 73).
[737] This situation has for example been observed lately in Albania.

dominance should be chosen, but it is clearly valuable to understand why there is no entry. Firstly, if the dominant position is unchallenged because of anti-competitive practices by incumbent firms or because obstacles to competition remain even after liberalization, then a stricter approach is appropriate[738]. Secondly, if dominant firms are not challenged simply because not enough profits can be made in the market, it would most likely be counterproductive to restrict incumbent firms and thereby reduce their incentives to invest in the development of the market.

Acemoglu *et al.* (2006) argue that less developed countries rely more on investment by incumbent firms and that less product market competition may be beneficial[739]. The reason is that established firms are important in order to have sufficiently high levels of investment in these countries, even if less intense competition is likely to have a negative impact on innovation. If there was fierce competition with new firms constantly entering the market and established, but less efficient ones leaving it, then the currently existing firms will be able to make smaller investments. Since less developed countries operate in sectors with generally lower levels of technology, they can use existing technologies and do not themselves need to innovate as much. Consequently, it is less important for them to have the most innovative and efficient firms selected by the competitive process, but rather to have large incumbent firms that can make investments in production. In less developed economies, the benefits of increased investments are therefore more likely to outweigh efficiency losses such as higher prices and less innovation that may arise from the dominant position. In developed countries on the other hand, it is more important that the competitive process selects the firms that are the most efficient and innovative, because they compete in sectors where innovation is a key factor of success. For this selection process to work, a fiercer competition policy may be required[740].

---

[738] Related to this issue is the discussion about natural and state-created monopolies and how liberalization should be managed. It is important that the consequences for competition are considered when planning and implementing liberalization. See also Section 4.5.

[739] Acemoglu *et al.* (2006).

[740] It may be difficult to switch out at the right time of the setting that protects dominant firms, because those who have profited from the monopolization will use their economic power to influence the political process. This raises the

A special case of the trade-off between investment and competition is infrastructure. This is particularly relevant for governments with low budget resources, because they may rely on private firms to finance and build infrastructure such as roads and ports. Given that the infrastructure would not come into existence if not financed, owned and used by a private enterprise, it may be a crucial driver for development. But at the same time, the firm can strengthen its dominant position and exclude competitors if the infrastructure is an essential facility that is necessary for all other industry participants and is not easily duplicated[741]. As in the case of intellectual property, governments need to calculate carefully how much ownership they want to transfer to firms in order to give sufficient incentives to invest. It must be assessed for what sectors a monopoly should be allowed, how broad it must be, for what period it is granted, and if concessions can be renegotiated after a certain time or when circumstances have changed.

3.3. Exploitation of producers by dominant buyers

Dominance not only has the potential to exclude competitors or exploit consumers, but can also lead to exploitation of producers if they are faced with a dominant buyer. This is likely to be the case if a large number of small producers supply a relatively homogenous good, such as a commodity, to a small number of large buyers. Producers in developing countries may often find themselves in such a situation, where they have little choice as to which buyer they sell to and at what price because there is only one buyer, they have limited information about other possible buyers or switching to a different buyer involves high costs. It can therefore be important for developing countries to also have rules that apply to the abuse of buyer power.

---

related issue of linkages between political and economic power and we will come back to this in Section 3.3.

[741] Motta (2004: 66). For example, a government can give a logistics enterprise the licence to build and maintain a port on a certain part of the coast. If this port cannot be duplicated nearby and if other firms need the port in order to compete, then the incumbent can exclude competitors by refusing them access to the essential facility.

Box 8: Buyer power of oligopsonistic cocoa traders *vis-à-vis* farmers

Abuse of market power may occur in the upstream market at the farmers' level. Local farmers do not have bargaining power *vis-à-vis* an "oligopsony" of cocoa traders as buyers. The buyers have enough buyer power to set cocoa prices at a level below what would be set under competitive market conditions. Economic analysis has shown that the abusive behaviour of firms with excessive buying power tends to disadvantage sellers while the excessive profit made due to such behaviour is not passed on to consumers in the downstream market to which these firms sell, regardless of the degree of competition in this market.[1] Thus, in the context of cocoa producers, the question would rather be how to deal with the buyer power of cocoa traders and processors.

[1] Peter C. Carstensen, *Competition, Concentration and Agriculture*. Statement to the Senate Committee on Agriculture, Nutrition, and Forestry, Agriculture Concentration and Competition Hearing, 27 April 2000.

Quoted from UNCTAD, *Cocoa Study: Industry Structures and Competition*. United Nations, forthcoming 2008.

3.4. The implementation of inequality considerations in developing countries

Fox (2000) analyses the trade-off between efficiency and distributional aspects of competition in the cases of South Africa and Indonesia[742]. The question that the examination of these two countries helps to answer is whether competition law can be used in practice to foster social and economic equality and if these goals are compatible with the goals of efficiency and growth.

---

[742] The discussion of South Africa and Indonesia in Boxes 9 and 10 is based on Fox (2000).

Box 9: South Africa

During the apartheid regime in South Africa, the white minority had political and economic power. Markets were extremely concentrated and cartels and monopolies largely controlled the economy[1]. When the apartheid regime ended in the mid-nineties, the process of democratization was accompanied by reforms of the competition law in order to reduce discrimination and inequality, but also to foster efficiency. For the most part, the competition law adapted rules and principles that were already successfully applied in developed countries[2]. But besides the common objective of efficiency, the new policy also wanted to *"(...) ensure that small and medium-sized enterprises have an equitable opportunity to participate in the economy; and (to) promote a greater spread of ownership, in particular to increase the ownership stakes of historically disadvantaged persons"*[3]. However, these objectives are balanced against the impact on competitiveness so that the additional clauses are only likely to be decisive in cases where there is doubt as to whether a conduct is efficient.

[1] OECD: *Competition Law and Policy in South Africa. An OECD Peer Review.* OECD. Paris. 2003. at p. 10.
[2] UNCTAD: *Handbook on Competition Legislation.* Note by the UNCTAD Secretariat. Intergovernmental Group of Experts on Competition Law and Policy. 2007.
[3] *Ibid.* p. 6.

Box 10: Indonesia

The International Monetary Fund (IMF) intervened in Indonesia in the late nineties because of the Indonesian financial crisis. This crisis was caused by a political elite, which controlled important parts of the economy and put a large debt burden on the country. One requirement after the intervention was the adoption of a competition law. This law included a large number of rules against certain conducts such as price discrimination and vertical foreclosure. The law generally contained more rules to promote equality than the South African law, but it gave less guidance on how the potential conflict between efficiency and equality should be resolved. There is therefore great responsibility on the courts to find a sound balance between the different goals[1].

[1] Eleanor M. Fox: *Equality, Discrimination, and Competition Law: Lessons from and for South Africa and Indonesia.* Harvard International Law Journal. Vol. 41. 2000. at p. 592.

3.5. The balance between different objectives

What becomes clear from the study of the two countries is that if competition policy should play a role in reducing inequality in developing countries, there needs to be clear guidance on how to balance efficiency and equality[743]. The two cases of South Africa and Indonesia also show that the current political environment strongly influences the competition law. In both countries there was, in the beginning, a politically or economically powerful minority that had every reason to protect its position and to allow its enterprises to dominate the economy and restrict smaller competitors. Once the political situation changed and the links between political and economic power broke, politicians' incentives may have moved towards protecting the smaller businesses of their supporters. Good political institutions are needed to make sure that there are incentives to follow long-term goals in both political environments.

4. Cross-country differences and their implications for developing countries

4.1. Abuse of dominance laws in the general context of unilateral conduct laws

Abuse of dominance refers to cases in which a firm has a dominant position and then engages in harmful conduct. It is related to the concept of unilateral conduct, which focuses on single-firm action and its potential anti-competitive effects, including the creation or strengthening of dominance, but that does not always require a prior existence of a dominant position.

The following section now gives an overview of how abuse of dominance and unilateral conduct are assessed in a number of developing and developed countries. A range of differences persists, and the recent EU Microsoft judgement of 17 September 2007[744] and

---

[743] Fox (2000: 594).
[744] *Microsoft v Commission*, T-201/04 [2007]. Judgement under: http://curia.europa.eu.

the US reaction to it have highlighted again that within the developed world also there are significant differences as to the treatment of dominant market players[745]. On the other hand, there are also areas of convergence. In this context, the International Competition Network (ICN) identified several issues that merit further research and cooperation[746]: objectives of unilateral conduct laws, assessment of dominance, and state-created monopolies.

4.2. Objectives of unilateral conduct laws

The objectives of unilateral conduct laws differ across competition systems. In most unilateral conduct regimes, more than one objective is considered relevant. Objectives include: ensuring an effective competitive process, promoting consumer welfare, maximizing efficiency, ensuring economic freedom, ensuring a level playing field for small and medium-sized companies, promoting fairness and equality, promoting consumer choice, achieving market integration, facilitating privatization and market liberalization, and promoting competitiveness in international markets.

In many countries, ensuring an effective competitive process is considered an objective on its own. The competitive process is seen as a dynamic, self-initiating market phenomenon that requires competition agencies' intervention only when obstructed. In other systems it is seen as a means to achieve other desirable goals such as consumer welfare, economic freedom or efficiency. In some cases it is both an objective and a means to achieve such goals. Apart from ensuring the competitive process itself, the most commonly used goals seem to be the economic goals of promotion of consumer welfare and enhancing efficiency. One example of the difficult relationship between these goals is the discussion about the 'more economic approach' to unilateral conduct rules in the EU[747]. This discussion focuses on whether the European rules of unilateral conduct should be interpreted in a more economic way thus aligning with current US law. This would essentially mean looking at the type of effects of a certain practice on consumers rather

---

[745] Vickers (2007).
[746] Parts of the discussion below are based on International Competition Network (ICN) (2007).
[747] European Commission (2005).

then at the market structure and the abusive behaviour in question, which were relevant criteria in the traditional European approach to unilateral conduct[748].

In developing countries, the objective of competition law and more specifically of unilateral conduct rules is sometimes also to protect domestic firms by seeking to prevent powerful foreign firms from using their power in order to eliminate local competitors[749]. In principle, countries are free to choose the objectives they see appropriate for unilateral conduct rules. This is a political decision that stakeholders in every country have to take, considering the economic realities in their markets. However, different standards across jurisdictions represent obstacles not only for companies with cross-boarder business, but also to the effective enforcement and cooperation in the field of competition policy. A certain degree of harmonization may therefore be desirable[750].

The relationship between the objectives of intellectual property and unilateral conduct rules remains another possible field of conflict, where further work is required. Also, the widespread practice of exemptions from unilateral conduct rules may create a conflict with the very goals of these rules.

4.3. The assessment of dominance

Significant differences exist in the way the surveyed jurisdictions assess dominance and also what the finding of dominance then implies for a dominant firm and its conduct. The following sections give an overview of the differences between countries and illustrate the situation with examples from individual countries.

4.3.1. Finding of dominance as a filter for anti-competitive effects

---

[748] Dreher and Adam (2006: 259 *et seqq.*).
[749] Gerber (2007: 707, 721).
[750] The notion that domestic firms should be protected until they are able to compete against foreign competition leads to an industrial policy that wants to foster national champions. Section 4.5 discusses the relationship of industrial policy and competition policy in greater detail.

In the majority of countries the finding of dominance serves as a first filter for separating conduct that has anti-competitive effects from conduct that does not. However, it is not dominance itself that is prohibited, but the anti-competitive unilateral conduct of dominant firms. The underlying assumption is that such a conduct would not harm competition if exercised by a non-dominant firm or that such a firm cannot even enter into the conduct. Some countries do not use the existence of a dominant position as a filter, but the existence of a dominant position is nonetheless often a criterion in the assessment of the conduct[751].

4.3.2. Interventions against unilateral conduct by firms without strong market power or against the creation of dominance

In total, 15 out of 35 jurisdictions in the ICN report have prohibitions against anti-competitive unilateral behaviour by non-dominant firms or firms that attempt to acquire a dominant position[752]. These standards are also often related to fair trade laws. The examples of intervention against firms that do not have a dominant position show that dominance is not necessarily the decisive test in cases of unilateral conduct. But even in jurisdictions where dominance is not required as a precondition for considering unilateral conduct cases, it still has a role to play as a criterion in the assessment of the conduct and its potential for harm.

Box 11: Examples of interventions against unilateral conduct by firms without strong market power or against the creation of dominance

The Sherman Act in the US prohibits "attempts to monopolize" and "monopolization". The former is the anti-competitive conduct with the specific intent to acquire a dominant position and with the high probability of doing so. The latter is the use of anti-competitive conduct either to acquire or to maintain a dominant market position. The existence of a dominant position prior to the conduct is therefore not required for attempts to monopolize. An example is the US Microsoft case where the Court of Appeals had to investigate whether

---

[751] Marsden (2006: 292).

[752] International Competition Network (ICN) (2007: 60–61).

> **Microsoft had unlawfully harmed Netscape's Internet Navigator browser in order to protect the monopoly position of its Windows operating system (monopolization) or to leverage the monopoly position of Windows to the browser market (attempt to monopolize)[1].**
>
> **Brazil and Chile contain a general prohibition of restrictive trade practices. The French competition law sanctions abuses of economic dependence on the basis of reputation, access to essential facilities or the structure of the business relationship. Similarly, the German law prohibits that one undertaking hinders another without objective justification if it has relatively more market power than the other one. An example would be sales under costs or under acquisition prices. Also, the Japanese law does not require dominance when prohibiting unfair trade practices, e.g. unjust refusals to deal.**
>
> ---
>
> [1] *United States v Microsoft*, 253 F.3d 34 (D.C. Cir. 2001). Section 5.2. will look at the US approach in more detail. For the above also see UNCTAD: *Model Law on Competition*. UNCTAD Series on Issues in Competition Law and Policy. United Nations. New York and Geneva. 2007.

4.3.3. Behaviour vs structural definition of dominance

Twenty-eight out of 35 jurisdictions in the ICN survey use a behaviour definition for dominance that focuses on a firm's appreciable freedom from competitive constraints. This freedom is sometimes referred to as independence (e.g. EU) and in other cases as the ability to profitably raise prices (e.g. Canada, US[753]). Many authorities also consider the durability of this freedom. Only five out of 35 use a structural definition, which means that dominance is primarily defined by structural criteria.

Although most of the countries state that they use a behaviour definition, many of them still use structural criteria for the assessment of dominance. The following section illustrates that many of the most frequently used criteria are structural. The fact that the vast majority of countries name their general definition 'behavioural' consequently loses some significance, because a different – more structural – definition seems to be used for the actual assessment of dominance.

---

[753] See discussion on 'hypothetical monopolist test' in Section 2.1.

There is little doubt that structural criteria have an advantage in the practical application[754]. It seems easier for competition authorities to observe a current situation such as the market structure than to look at the behaviour of actors in the market. This concern of practicability is especially important for competition authorities in developing countries, because their means to assess dominance are more limited. On the other hand, the behaviour approach to defining dominance is theoretically more exact, because it focuses on the target variable, which is the actual and potential behaviour of firms. The downside of this approach is that it requires more case-specific analysis.

4.3.4. The criteria for the assessment of dominance

Table 1 shows that structural criteria are important for the assessment of dominance in most jurisdictions.

Table 1: Criteria for assessment of dominance		
Which of the following criteria do you use?	**Yes**	**No**
- Market share of the firm and its competitors	32	0
- Market position and market behaviour of competitors	32	0
- Barriers to entry or expansion	32	0
- Buyer power	32	0
- Economies of scale and scope/network effects	32	0
- Access to upstream markets/vertical integration	32	0
- Durability of market power	30	2
- Market maturity/vitality	30	2
- Access to essential facilities	29	3
- Financial resources of the firm and its competitors	23	9
- High prices (at absolute or comparative level)	23	9
- Profits of the firm	17	15

Source: ICN (2007).

The first three criteria are also those most often mentioned as being among the most important criteria. However, this is not the case for some large jurisdictions such as the UK, the US and Japan[755].

---

[754] Dreher and Adam (2006: 259 *et seqq.*).

[755] This observation will be discussed further in Section 5, which concerns the US and EU laws.

Market shares:

Market shares are a relevant criterion for the assessment of dominance, because they are a close approximation of how a firm stands *vis-à-vis* its competitors. It is not a perfect approximation for market power because the latter depends on a number of other factors. Even a firm that has more than a 50% market share may have little market power if there is only one buyer or many possible entrants. Therefore, the significance of a certain market share depends on the characteristics of the market.

Market share thresholds are levels of market shares above which market power is assumed and below which it is not assumed. The use of market share thresholds has both advantages and disadvantages. The most obvious advantage is legal certainty and predictability. If the procedure of the competition authorities is sufficiently transparent, firms can to some extent predict how the authorities will define the market and what market share they will assume. A market share threshold then allows them to assess whether they are assumed to be dominant or not and consequently if their conduct could be prohibited. This higher degree of legal certainty allows them to invest more efficiently, because they know when an activity is likely to be profitable. The apparent disadvantage is that market share thresholds are generalizations across a large number of special cases. Consequently, they need to be defined conservatively, i.e. levels for safe harbours must be rather low to take into account that in some instances even firms with relatively low market shares can be dominant, and thresholds to assume dominance must be high in order to consider the possibility that firms with large market shares have no market power. However, when the levels are defined too conservatively, the market share thresholds lose their significance, because few firms can actually use them. It becomes evident from these considerations that the definition of the optimal thresholds is a difficult task. The benefits of thresholds are particularly high for jurisdictions with less experienced competition authorities that profit from a more structured approach. However, the definition of the accurate threshold is likely to be very difficult for these countries as well. Table 2 shows that in our sample less developed countries in terms of gross domestic product (GDP) *per capita* are more likely to have market share thresholds, but they are not necessarily higher or lower than in developed countries[756].

Nineteen out of 35 jurisdictions in the ICN survey use market share thresholds to assume dominance or safe harbours. Interestingly, some countries have a differentiated approach to thresholds for dominance, since they apply a lower benchmark for a rebuttable presumption and a higher mark for a non-rebuttable presumption (South Africa, Ukraine). The majority of jurisdictions that use safe harbours only have 'soft' safe harbours, because their presumption is rebuttable.

---

[756] Our sample consists of countries referred to in the ICN report, the UNCTAD model law, and one additional country. Two identical thresholds do not necessarily imply the same treatment, because some jurisdictions make them dependent on other conditions.

Table 2: Market share dominance

Country	Dominance presumption	Safe harbours	Country	Dominance presumption	Safe harbours
Australia*			Lithuania**	40%	
Brazil*	20%	20%	Mexico*		
Bulgaria*	35%	20%	Mongolia**	50%	
Canada*	80%	35%	Netherlands*		
Chile*			New Zealand*		20%
Croatia***	40%		Pakistan*	33%	
Czech Republic**	40%		Poland**	40%	
Estonia*	40%		Portugal**	40%	
EC*			Romania*	40%	
France*			Russia*	50%	20%
Germany*	33%		Singapore*		
Hungary*		20%	Slovakia*		
India*			South Africa*	45%	n.a.
Indonesia**	50%		Spain*		
Ireland*			Sweden*	40%	
Israel*	50%		Switzerland*		
Italy*			Turkey*		
Jamaica*	50%		Ukraine*	35%	35%
Japan*			United Kingdom*		
Republic of Korea*	50%	10%	United States*	70%	50%
Latvia*		40%	Zambia**		40%

Data: *ICN (2007), **UNCTAD (2007), ***country legislation.

Barriers to entry:

Apart from market shares, dominance is also linked to the ease of entry and thus to the existence of entry barriers. Entry barriers make it more difficult for potential competitors, i.e. new firms or firms that are currently active in other markets, to enter the market under consideration. Entry barriers can for example be legal barriers in the form of licences or structural in the form of high sunk costs that make entry either more costly or more risky[757]. If such barriers exist, the firms already in the market are protected from potential competition and thus enjoy more market power. Most agencies look not only at the theoretical possibility of entry, but also at whether entry is likely, timely and sufficient. Some respondents stated that barriers must be put into a dynamic perspective, where the changes in barriers are observed over time.

Buyer power:
The profitability of a firm is not only threatened by its competitors who take away its costumers, but also by the costumers themselves, because buyers bargain with the sellers to get lower prices. If the bargaining power of a buyer is high, for instance if there is only one buyer but many potential sellers, the sellers have to lower the price until it only covers costs[758].

The ICN survey shows that buyer power is one of the most important criteria for competition authorities in the assessment of dominance. The EC stressed that strong buyers can discipline the dominant seller if they actually switch to new entrants when the incumbent offers bad deals. In doing so, they ease the entry of new firms that are willing to sell at lower prices and therefore also benefit other, smaller, buyers. Competition authorities in developing countries should pay special attention to this, because small and poor buyers are likely to suffer from the abusive conduct by dominant firms.

4.3.5. Market size and economies of scale

Developing countries, and especially the least developed countries, are mostly characterized by a low GDP, which has important implications for competition policy. Due to economies of scale, firms must be of a certain size to be cost-efficient. Small markets naturally

---

[757] Sunk costs can arise when a firm must make an investment, e.g. in infrastructure, to enter a market, but cannot recoup the investment if the market entry fails. This is especially the case if the investment cannot be used for other purposes.
[758] This is conceptualized in Porter's five forces analysis. See Besanko (2003).

enable fewer firms to be large enough to produce at the efficient scale and consequently there will be higher levels of concentration in small economies.

For some industries the domestic markets may be too small to allow even one firm to be efficient and if it does, the resulting monopoly is likely to be inefficient exactly because it is a monopoly[759]. Openness to trade is therefore crucial for such countries in order to enlarge their markets and allow their firms to exploit economies of scale[760]. It is argued that due to this need of openness to trade, small economies are likely to have lower barriers to entry and that higher levels of concentration on domestic markets should be tolerated[761]. However, small economies are not always open, and it is therefore necessary to make a distinction between open and isolated small economies. This also becomes clear in the ICN survey: "*There was a general consensus among the respondents that if an economy is small and isolated from external trade, this may result in higher barriers to entry which could facilitate a finding of dominance or substantial market power. On the other hand, the presence of free-trade agreements can be seen as lowering an economy's entry barriers to new or potential competition, and thus making the exercise of market power in the economy's markets less likely.*"[762].

Most respondents agreed that in small economies the same type of criteria for the assessment of dominance is appropriate, but that the size of the economy significantly influences the outcome. They didn't agree on the question of whether small economies should generally assume dominance at lower or higher levels of concentration, which is not surprising in view of the argument made above that countries are not equally open to trade and therefore have different entry barriers. The necessity to take into account openness to trade when defining tolerable concentration levels shows that the appropriate level of concentration needs to be defined by each country individually and that the markets are defined correctly.

---

[759] Monopolies can for example be inefficient because they set prices too high or do not innovate enough.
[760] Alesina *et al.* (2000).
[761] The definition of the market is crucial here. When economies are open and their markets expand beyond their political borders, the market should be defined accordingly and concentration levels will be lower.
[762] International Competition Network (ICN) (2007: 58).

4.3.6. Examples of dominance assessment in developed and developing countries and countries in transition

---

Box 12: Examples of dominance assessment in developed and developing countries and countries in transition

The presumption contained in the 1991 Law of the Czech Republic is **40%**, which is also the case in Portugal and Poland. In the Czech Republic, provided that the **other indicators** mentioned in the Act do not show otherwise, a competitor or competitors with joint dominance that have not achieved the 40% market share in a given period are **considered not to have a dominant position** on a market.

In Estonia, an undertaking in a dominant position is one that accounts for at least **40%** of the turnover in the relevant market or whose position enables the undertaking to operate in the market to an appreciable extent independently of competitors, suppliers and buyers. Undertakings with special or exclusive rights or in control of essential facilities are also undertakings in a dominant position.

Under Lithuanian law, a **40%** market share establishes a presumption of dominance; in addition, the new law creates a presumption of joint dominance when the three largest firms in a market have a collective market share of 70%.

Under Canadian law, it must be shown that the practice has had, is having or is likely to have the effect of preventing or lessening competition substantially.

In Germany, the legislation contains several presumptions, namely: at least one enterprise has **one-third** of a certain type of goods or commercial service; three or fewer enterprises have a combined market share of 50% or more; five or fewer enterprises have a combined market share of two-thirds or over.

In the *"Akzo" Judgement*, the Court of Justice of the European Communities considered **that highly important parts (of the market)** are by themselves, except for extraordinary circumstances, the sole proof of the existence of a dominant position. In the *Michelin Judgement*, the Court of Justice of the European Communities stated that under Article *82* of the EEC Treaty a dominant position refers to a situation of economic strength that gives the enterprise the power to obstruct the maintenance of effective competition in the market concerned because it allows the enterprise to conduct itself in a way that is independent from its competitors, clients and, finally, consumers. **In addition to market shares**, the **structural advantages** possessed by enterprises can be of decisive importance. For example, the Court of Justice of the European Communities in the *United Brands Judgement* took into account the fact that the undertaking possessed a high degree of vertical integration, that its advertising policy hinged on a specific brand (Chiquita), guaranteeing it a steady supply of customers and that it controlled every stage of the distribution process, which together gave the corporation a considerable advantage over its competitors. In consequence, dominance can derive from a **combination of a number of factors,** which, if taken separately, would not necessarily be determinative.

In the United States, monopoly power is not defined by statute but courts have traditionally defined it as being *"the power to control market prices or exclude*

---

competition." (*United States v E.I. du Pont de Nemours & Co.*, 351 US 377, 391 (1956)). **The market share** is not the only factor considered in determining whether monopoly power exists. **Other factors**, such as the absence of entry barriers, may indicate that a firm does not have monopoly power even if it does account for a large share of the relevant market.

The Indian *Competition Act* 2002 defines, 'dominant position' as a position of strength, enjoyed by an enterprise, in the relevant market, in India, which enables it to: (i) operate independently of competitive forces prevailing in the relevant market; or (ii) affect in its favour its competitors or consumers or the relevant market. The Competition Commission of India, while inquiring whether an enterprise enjoys a dominant position or not, has due regard to all or any of these factors.

The legislations of Mongolia and the Ukraine consider that dominance exists when a single entity acting alone or a group of economic entities acting together account constantly for **over 50% of supply** to the market of a certain good or similar goods, products or carried out works and provided services.

In Zambia, under Section 7 (2) of the Act, an enterprise is considered to be dominant if it has a level of market power that allows it to behave independently of competitive pressures (e.g. pricing and distribution strategies). An **important but not conclusive factor** in determining dominance is the **share of the market** that the undertaking has. An undertaking is **unlikely** to be dominant if its market share is **less than 40%** – although this rule will largely depend on the circumstances of the case.

The Saudi Arabian Implementing Regulations on Competition Law state in Article 1 that dominance exists where an entity or group of entities are in a position to influence the prevailing price through controlling a specific percentage of the total supply. A specific **threshold is not mentioned**.

The Indonesian *Competition Law* (Law No. 5) defines dominance in Article 25 as a situation in which one business actor or a group of business actors controls over **50%** of the market segment of a certain type of goods or services; or if two or three business actors or groups of business actors control over 75% of the market segment.

The *Competition Act* of Trinidad and Tobago defines in Section 20 monopoly power in a market as a situation in which an enterprise, by itself or together with an interconnected body corporate, occupies a position of economic strength that will enable it to operate in the market without effective constraints from its competitors or potential competitors. The Act contains **no threshold for the positive presumption** of dominance, but states in Section 22 (2) that the Commission should not investigate cases unless it is satisfied that the enterprise controls 40% of the market or more or such percentage as the Minister may by order prescribe. This can be labelled as a **"negative presumption"**.

Source: UNCTAD: *Model Law on Competition*. UNCTAD Series on Issues in Competition Law and Policy. United Nations. New York and Geneva. 2007.

4.4. Examples of abusive practices

Once dominance has been found, authorities need to investigate whether a certain conduct should be prohibited. The following are some examples from both developing and developed countries of practices that are considered abusive.

4.4.1. Predatory pricing

Box 13: Some examples of rules on predatory pricing from country legislations

Hungary prohibits the setting of extremely low prices that are not based on greater efficiency in comparison with that of competitors and that are likely to drive out competitors from the relevant market or to hinder their market entry.

The *Law for Countering Unfair Competition* in the People's Republic of China states that an operator (i.e. enterprises or individuals) may not sell its or his or her goods at a price that is below the cost for the purpose of excluding its or his or her competitors.

In the United States, the Supreme Court has held that two elements must be present in order to establish predatory pricing. First, the prices complained of must be *"below an appropriate measure of cost"*, and second, the competitor charging low prices must have a *"dangerous probability"* of recouping its investment in below-cost prices.[1] The US Supreme Court has stated that it is important to distinguish between pro-competitive price cutting and anti-competitive predatory pricing because *"cutting prices in order to increase business often is the very essence of competition"*[2].

Predatory pricing is also prohibited in the European Community. The European Court of Justice defined in TetraPak[3] that pricing is predatory if the price is set below the average variable costs[4].

[1] *Brooke Group Ltd. v Brown & Williamson Tobacco Corp.*, 509 U.S. (1993). See also *Cargill Inc. v Monfort of Colo., Inc.,* 479 U.S. 104, 117 (1986).
[2] *Matsushita Elec. Indus. Co. v Zenith Radio Corp.*, 475 U.S. 574, 594 (1986).
[3] *Tetra Pak v Commission*, [1996] ECR I-5951 (ECJ).
[4] For the above see also UNCTAD: *Model Law on Competition*. UNCTAD Series on Issues in Competition Law and Policy. United Nations. New York and Geneva. 2007.

607

Box 14: Case 5 – Predatory pricing in the Zambian beer brewing industry

On 8th June 2001, the Official agents of the Zambian Breweries lodged a complaint, with the Commission alleging that MetPress Zambia Limited, t/a Metro Wholesalers was wholesaling the Zambian Breweries "Mosi" and "Castle" clear beers at prices lower than the manufacturer's, i.e. predatory pricing. This conduct was allegedly forcing members out of business. It was observed that the firm was actually taking over business in various parts of Lusaka. The complainants alleged further that the local distributors did not have the financial power to compete with such pricing strategies from Metro. Metro is part of the Metro Cash & Carry, which operates in at least 15 countries. The conduct by Metro appeared to be in breach of Section 7(2)(a) of the *Competition and Fair Trading Act* (the Act), which requires enterprises to refrain from predatory behaviour towards competition including the use of cost pricing to eliminate competitors.

Metro was a new entrant in the market and was growing at a fast rate aided by its below-cost pricing (which was used as a market penetration strategy). It purchased its clear beer from Zambian Breweries as did other distributors. However, it appeared that its selling price was below the purchase price and there appeared to be no objective justification for the conduct. Zambian Breweries confirmed that they had no unique "trade arrangement" with Metro. The selling price from Zambian Breweries was uniform.

The Commission considered that while Metro was not a dominant player, its pricing strategies had an effect on the smaller distributors, hence the intervention. Although the *Competition and Fair Trading Act* provides that any form of price resale maintenance is anti-competitive it was in this situation found to be special to justify its continuity. A resale price maintenance was proposed (the "minimum price") to avoid future breaches. As noted already, the business relies heavily on volume sales and small disparities in price can and do have significant effects on other players. The favourable credit period awarded to Metro by Zambian Breweries was ordered to be discontinued and or be extended to all the other distributors.

Quoted from: UNCTAD: *Review of Recent Experiences in the Formulation and Implementation of Competition Law and Policy in Selected Developing Countries: Thailand, Lao, Kenya, Zambia, Zimbabwe*. United Nations. New York and Geneva. 2005.

608

Box 15: Case 6 – Abuse of dominance cases in Jamaica

The FTC (…) considered, under the abuse of dominance provisions, three complaints regarding predatory pricing. In its decision regarding price reductions of Super Plus Food Store, it found that the list of items for promotion was limited and the duration of the sale was short such that predation did not occur. With regard to the allegation that Tank-Weld Metals Limited (TWM) was selling nails at predatory prices, it concluded that TWM was dominant but, except for one month, its prices were above average variable costs. It thus found there was no evidence of predation. The last case involves an advertisement by Telstar Cable Ltd. for three months of free cable service to subscribers who switch from another cable company within the month of December 1999. The FTC found that the pricing was not below costs and the duration of the offer was not long enough to have an appreciable effect on competition.

Quoted from: UNCTAD: *Voluntary Peer Review on Competition Policy: Jamaica*. United Nations. New York and Geneva. 2005.
FTC, Fair Trading Commission.

4.4.2. Resale price maintenance

Box 16: Some examples of rules on resale price maintenance from country legislations

In the Swedish Competition Act, setting minimum prices that have an appreciable effect on competition is prevented through the prohibition of anti-competitive cooperation. An economic approach has been chosen concerning resale price maintenance

In the United States, the Supreme Court has held that minimum resale price maintenance is *per se* illegal under Section 1 of the Sherman Act, but there must be an actual agreement requiring the distributor to adhere to specific prices[1]. Because maximum resale price maintenance may lead to low prices, the Supreme Court has recently ruled that maximum resale price maintenance is not *per se* an offence.

Resale price maintenance is also prohibited for example in India, New Zealand, the Republic of Korea, and the United Kingdom.

In the European Community, fixing the resale price of goods is normally

---

609

prohibited if competition between Member States is affected.[2]

[1] See *Business Elecs. Corp. v Sharp Elecs. Corp.*, 485 U.S. 717, 720, 724 (1988).

[2] For the above see UNCTAD: *Model Law on Competition*. UNCTAD Series on Issues in Competition Law and Policy. United Nations. New York and Geneva. 2007.

Box 17: Case 7 – Carbonated soft drinks sector in Kenya

The Minister of Finance directed the Commission to investigate the carbonated soft drinks sector, believing that it might feature one or more factors relating to unwarranted concentrations of economic power. The Minister had received complaints from other companies and was aware of the dominance of Coca Cola and its vertical integration with its bottling operations and its distributors. The Commission conducted an investigation that included interviews with the major players in the industry and a sample of 85 distributors.

The investigation found that Section 23(1)(a) of the Act, which deals with the control of a chain of distributing units, the value of whose sales exceeds a third of the relevant market, was relevant to the activities of Coca Cola East Africa Limited. Section 23(1)(b), which concerns companies that control two or more physically distinct units that manufacture substantially similar products and that supply more than one-third of the value at ex-factory prices of the domestic market, applied to Coca Cola Holdings Limited. Finally, Section 23(1)(c), which applies to a person who has a beneficial interest exceeding 20% in a manufacturing enterprise and simultaneously has a beneficial interest in one or more wholesale or retail enterprises that distribute products of the manufacturing enterprise, is relevant to ICDC and Softa Bottling Company.

During the investigation, several potential restrictive trade practices came to light and were addressed in a draft consent order. These included possible resale price maintenance, territorial allocation, exclusive dealership arrangements and tied selling. However, the Commission suspended its investigation under Section 23 when some of the complainants took the matter to the High Court. The High Court proceedings have not been concluded.

Quoted from: UNCTAD: *Voluntary Peer Review on Competition Policy: Kenya*. New York and Geneva. 2005.

4.4.3. Exclusive dealing

Box 18: Case 8 – Exclusive dealing arrangements in the poultry sector in Zambia

During investigations into alleged cartel activities in the poultry industry in Zambia in 1998, the Commission became aware that there existed restrictive business arrangements involving Hybrid Poultry Farm (HPF – a day-old chicks (DOCs) rearer with 60% market share then), Galunia Holdings Limited (GH – a commercial chicken broiler rearer), and Tamba Chicks (Tamba – a (DOCs) rearer with 30% market share then). ZCC advised the parties to notify the said exclusive agreements as required under the *Competition and Fair Trading Act* Cap 417 of the laws of Zambia. At the time, parallel investigations were launched on the sale of Tamba Chicks. GH management was interviewed.

During the investigations it was revealed that in the sale of Mariandale Farm, which specializes in the raising of DOCs into table birds, HPF required GH to only purchase DOCs from itself. Further, GH was also required to consider HPF's right of first refusal should it intend to resell Mariandale Farm. GH was also not allowed to raise any type of poultry, at the farm, apart from broiler chickens, including the provision not to go into the business of a chicken hatchery. The parties also agreed that GH should be accorded the right of first refusal should HPF intend to sell some of its shares and that HPF should be given the first right of refusal to participate in an outgrowers scheme should GH come up with one. The ZCC noted that the parties to this transaction are the two leading players in the poultry sector's upstream (HPF) and downstream (GH) subsectors. HPF is the dominant producer of DOCs in Zambia with a 60% market share. GH with its Mariandale and Diamondale Farms has an uptake of 48,000 DOC per week and hence is the largest buyer in the poultry sector.

The exclusive dealing arrangements appear to have been over and above the offers each party made and hence the considerations made by the other. The excesses hinge on the ulterior motives of the parties in as far as the poultry sector is concerned. The parties seem to have taken advantage of their dominant market positions upstream and downstream – where each party was dominant. The parties were, both by motive and concerted practices, foreclosing competition both in the DOCs, table birds (broiler) and frozen chicken markets.

These practices were in direct contravention of Section 7 of the Act and have the tenets of distractive cartel behaviour. The Board of Commissioners found all the exclusive dealing provisions in the sale and purchase agreements by the parties anti-competitive and nullified them.

UNCTAD: *Review of Recent Experiences in the Formulation and Implementation of Competition Law and Policy in Selected Developing Countries: Thailand, Lao, Kenya, Zambia, Zimbabwe.* United Nations. New York and Geneva. 2005.

4.5. State-created monopolies and national champions

4.5.1. Sectors with state-created monopolies

In many countries certain companies derive their dominant position from government support or are even publicly owned enterprises. The ICN report identified postal services, lottery, airports, and commodities as the most frequent sectors where monopolies have been created by the government[763]. Table 3 shows that both developing and developed countries have such sectors[764].

Table 3: Sectors with state-created monopolies	
Sector	**Countries**
Postal services	Australia, Brazil, Bulgaria, Canada, Czech Republic, Germany, Hungary, Italy, Jamaica, Japan, Jersey, Republic of Korea, New Zealand, Slovak Republic, Spain, Switzerland, Turkey, UK, US
Lottery	Brazil, France, Germany, Hungary, New Zealand, Slovak Republic, Spain, Sweden, Turkey
Airports/Airport infrastructure	Australia, Canada, Czech Republic, Jersey, Spain, UK
Commodity	Australia (rice, wheat, sugar, barley), Canada (wheat), Pakistan (rice), Turkey (opium)
Ports	Jamaica, Jersey, Israel, Pakistan, Spain, UK, Turkey
Insurance	France (insurance companies in social services), Germany (social insurances), New Zealand (accident), Pakistan
Airlines	Jamaica, Israel, Pakistan, Spain, Turkey
Public transport	Australia, Chile, France, Jamaica
Highways	Brazil, France, Russia
Tobacco	France (retail trade), Spain, Turkey
Mining	Chile, Serbia, Turkey
Alcohol retailing	Sweden
Alcohol products	Turkey

[763] International Competition Network (ICN) (2007: 64). This report only covers state-created monopolies, not natural monopolies.
[764] The table provides a non-exhaustive list of sectors where state-created monopolies existed or still exist.

Table 3: Sectors with state-created monopolies	
Sector	Countries
Hospitals	Germany
Pharmaceuticals	Sweden
TV/Radio centres	Russia
Motor industry/automobile production	Serbia
Table from ICN (2007).	

4.5.2. Objectives of creating monopolies by the state

These monopolies were usually created by governments in order to fulfil a public service mission or to play an active role in coordinating the economy instead of relying on free markets. Table 4 provides a non-exhaustive list of the objectives that the various jurisdictions stated.

Table 4: Objectives of creating monopolies by the state	
Objective	Country
Public service obligations ensuring citizens have access to important/essential services	Australia, Czech Republic, France, Germany, Hungary, Japan, Republic of Korea, Serbia, UK, US
The state made necessary investments in infrastructure and important sectors as part of a previous economic policy based on import substitution	Brazil, Turkey
Safety standards	Switzerland
In order to align with the recommendations of the European Commission	Czech Republic
Prevent illegal gambling and ban excessive gaming incentives and exclude commercial profit-making purposes	Germany, Hungary
Marketing in an orderly manner grain grown and leveraging the size to obtain the highest price	Canada
Operation of state liquor monopolies in order to prevent over-consumption by limiting economic incentives for liquor sales	US
Public safety in taxi cab monopolies	US

613

Table 4: Objectives of creating monopolies by the state	
Objective	Country
Public interest: government intervention is warranted if the private sector fails to produce the desired outcome	Netherlands
Insuring traffic security in air, space, naval transportation; meteorological service, including its satellite component	Russia
Table from ICN (2007).	

Public service missions may be particularly important in developing countries that face problems of severe poverty and lack of infrastructure. Governments in such situations may find it more often necessary to create or hold ownership of firms that fulfil these public service missions, but at the same they should keep restrictions on competition as low as possible.

4.5.3. Natural monopolies and state-created monopolies

In some industries, state intervention is due to natural monopolies that arise because the market size and the cost structure of production allow a monopoly to produce more efficiently than if production was split among several firms. The market failure is evident in this case because the resulting monopoly position will lead to inefficiencies and therefore regulation is needed. Where a monopoly is accepted (and possibly regulated) for such reasons, it is crucial to define the market correctly in the vertical dimension. For example, if economies of scale are highly important in the distribution, but not so much so in the production, then it has to be ensured that a distribution monopoly is not allowed to vertically integrate into production. A possible solution is the approach of the European Commission that intends to split the production and distribution of energy[765].

4.5.4. National champions

Section 4.5.2 has shown that there are also industries without a natural monopoly justification, but where the state still intervenes and

---

[765] European Commission (2007a).

creates a monopoly in order to reach other political or economic goals. One such goal can be the creation or protection of 'national champions'. This is subject to a lot of debate and is often related to the infant-industry argument for developing countries. Those in favour of such protection argue that certain national firms must – at least for a certain period – be protected in order to become internationally competitive. It is often suggested that firms with small domestic markets have a disadvantage because they cannot exploit economies of scale and that they should be protected until they reach the critical size that allows them to compete globally against firms with larger home markets. A second argument is that some sectors are strategically important or that they produce positive externalities – such as innovation spillovers or supply capacities – on other sectors. One counter-argument is that competition on domestic markets is the best condition for firms to become internationally competitive, because they are forced to be innovative in order to succeed. Having incentives to become competitive is likely to be more important for productivity and growth than only having the ability to do so based on government protection. Secondly, it is difficult for governments to choose the sectors and firms that may deserve protection. In particular those firms that already receive support are likely to use their influence to get government assistance. Thirdly, the support that one country gives to its national champions generates pressure on other countries to also support their businesses. If every national champion receives support from its government, the relative positions between these firms remain the same, but resources are lost at the expense of private citizens and consumers. When all this is taken together, it becomes clear that the risks and costs that the support of national champions involves are often greater than the benefits[766].

4.5.5. Competition policy in sectors with state-created monopolies

In some jurisdictions actions of public companies are exempted under a state action doctrine, others treat public companies as they would privately owned entities. The special treatment of public enterprises is usually justified by the 'public service mission'. In these cases, the powers of competition authorities are often limited to advocacy activities and other 'soft' enforcement tools[767].

---

[766] Paul A. Geroski: *Competition Policy and National Champions*. March 2005.
[767] International Competition Network (ICN) (2007: 87).

Box 19: Case 9 – Preliminary probe into allegation of abuse of dominant position in the steel sheet industry in Thailand

In 2002, there was a complaint lodged by end-users of steel sheet products that the alleged party and its wholesalers raised the price of their hot-rolled steel sheet every week and certain hot-rolled steel sheet products were not available on the market. Those end-users who tried to import such products were threatened by the alleged party that the supply would be cut off. The investigations conducted by the officials at the office of the Competition Commission revealed that the alleged party distributed its steel sheet through three channels. The first one was through its distributors (12%). The second one was through wholesalers (26%) and the third one was the direct sale to end-users (62%). During August 2002-December 2000, the alleged party adjusted its price up and down below the controlled-price ceiling (steel sheet is a "controlled product" under the *Price Control Act* of 1999). The price adjustment of the alleged party led its distributors, wholesalers, to do the same thing. The officials concluded that the price adjustment conduct of the alleged party did not violate the *Price Control Act* of 1999 because the price was below the controlled-price ceiling for steel sheet. Also, there was no evidence to support the allegation of abuse of market dominance by setting an unjustly high price.

Quoted from: UNCTAD: *Review of Recent Experiences in the Formulation and Implementation of Competition Law and Policy in Selected Developing Countries: Thailand, Lao, Kenya, Zambia, Zimbabwe.* United Nations. New York and Geneva. 2005.

Most agencies stated that they determine dominance in the same way as for privately owned and managed firms. The past has shown a tendency towards privatization and liberalization to foster efficiency and competition, which is implemented either by a general privatization law or by a sector-specific law. During privatization, competition authorities should have an advocacy role to ensure that the markets work properly after the privatization. For this advocacy to be effective, the competition authorities should be in a position to give binding recommendations in defined areas.

5. Best practices from the US–EU discussion regarding abuse of dominance

While other areas of competition law have experienced significant convergence, rules on unilateral conduct differ considerably across jurisdictions[768]. The EU and the US are good examples of this as is illustrated by the diverging Microsoft rulings in the two jurisdictions[769].

5.1. Objectives and criteria of unilateral conduct laws in the US and the EU

Almost all countries in the ICN report agree that ensuring an effective competitive process is an important goal or means to achieve other goals[770]. The survey also showed that the EU and the US have almost the same objectives (the EU has the additional objective to 'achieve market integration'). Even the list of criteria used for assessing dominance seems similar, with the EU using two additional criteria 'high prices' and 'profits of the firm' which the US does not use. However, when asked what the most important criteria are, significant differences are revealed between the US and the EU In the EU, 'market share', 'barriers to entry', 'market position and behaviour of competitors' and 'buyer power' are very important, but the US authorities mention none of these criteria as the most important one and focus instead on consumer harm. The first conclusion therefore is that both jurisdictions say that they pursue the same goals but use different approaches to reach them. These differences may be justified not only due to the historic and political context, but also because of different business environments[771].

---

[768] Vickers (2007).

[769] *United States v Microsoft*, 253 F.3d 34 (D.C. Cir. 2001) and *Microsoft v Commission*, T-201/04 [2007].

[770] International Competition Network (ICN) (2007). See also Section 4.3, which concerns the assessment of dominance.

[771] Well-developed capital markets provide an example for this. It is more accurate to trust in the well functioning of competition if access to capital is relatively easy because it enables the creation and expansion of firms that can enter into the market. See Anderson and Heimler (2007: 71).

Table 5 illustrates the features that the US and EU laws have in common and where they differ:[772]

Table 5: Differing features of US and EU unilateral conduct laws	
EU (Article 82 EC)	**US (Sherman Act Section 2)**
"Access-to-markets principle" • Contestability of monopolized markets • Fear of blockage of markets	"Non-intervention principle" • Privilege to single-firm action • Fear of false positives

5.2. Harm to competition vs harm to competitors

Article 82 of the EC Treaty prohibits the abuse of a dominant position. The authorities have to establish that a dominant position exists and that there is anti-competitive conduct. The counterpart in the US is Section 2 of the Sherman Act, which prohibits the monopolization and attempts to monopolize. There is a different approach to dominance in the US, because it is not the existence of dominance that requires the dominant firm to refrain from an anti-competitive conduct, but the anti-competitive attempt to create or maintain this position, which is forbidden by Section 2 of the Sherman Act. Hence, there must be a causal link from the anti-competitive conduct to market power[773].

The legal standards in the two jurisdictions differ considerably, but how much their approaches differ in practice depends crucially on how the terms are defined and interpreted. Harm to the competitive process for example is prohibited in the EU because it is assumed that the outcome of a sound competitive process is generally favourable to consumers. But harm to the competition process such as from foreclosure may also involve a strengthening or creation of a dominant position and consumers may be hurt directly, which are the necessary conditions in the US, so that the two standards may overlap in many respects.

---

[772] The following discussion is based on Fox (2003: 149 *et seqq.*, 2006a).
[773] Vickers (2005: 247).

5.2.1. The US view

The US Supreme Court followed the view of the US Department of Justice and the Federal Trade Commission that Section 2 of the Sherman Act is not an abuse of dominance law. Even monopolists who control a facility that competitors need have no duty other than to refrain from increasing their monopoly power by anti-competitive means. They have no duty of refraining from leveraging their market power in other markets, of fair dealing, or of providing a level playing field to competitors[774]. The framework that the US authorities follow is based on the harm to consumers and this harm is only expected when either prices increase or output decreases. If this is not the case, the unilateral conduct by a firm is said to only hurt competitors, not competition. Behaviour that increases efficiency and thereby benefits consumers is not prohibited by Section 2 even if that behaviour harms the competition process[775]. In the US Microsoft case, the Court of Appeals had to decide whether Microsoft had unlawfully tied its web browser to its operation system[776]. The Court of Appeals rejected the ruling of the lower court that had found the tying *per se* illegal and it demanded from the lower court a rule of reason evaluation that shows the anti-competitive effect. The Court of Appeals would probably require a showing that the tying increased or maintained the monopoly in the operating system market or that it decreased output and therefore directly harmed consumers[777]. This illustrates that even if a monopolist significantly suppresses the chances of competitors, the conduct is not necessarily illegal in the US The next section will show that in the EU, on the other hand, such conduct is likely to be illegal.

---

[774] Fox (2006b: 69). Leveraging market power means that the dominant position in one market is used to exercise power in a related market. For example, a firm that has market power in one market can tie its product for this market to a product that it sells in another market where it initially does not have market power.
[775] Bloch *et al.* (2005: 331).
[776] *United States v Microsoft*, 253 F.3d 34 (D.C. Cir. 2001). For a description of the case, see Motta (2004: 511). The case not only involved tying, but also monopolization and attempted monopolization.
[777] Fox (2006a: 737).

5.2.2. The EU view

Article 82 EC prohibits all conduct that is covered by the Sherman Act Section 2 and in addition covers conduct by dominant firms that is not increasing market power. In the EU, dominant firms have the special duty not to exclude competitors by anti-competitive means, because it is assumed that a conduct that excludes firms from competing may harm the competition process[778]. This can be explained by the 'access-to-markets principle' mentioned above and is illustrated in Table 6. Harm to the competition process refers to situations where the behaviour of a firm reduces the intensity of competition, for example by putting constraints on the entry of new competitors, but does not have an immediate effect on consumers by limiting output or raising prices.

Table 6: The EU *vs.* US view		
Harm to Competition		**Harm to Competitors**
(Outcome) Business conduct limits output, raises prices	(Process) Business conduct unnecessarily blocks competition on the merits	Efficient business conduct hurts competitors. Enforcement against this conduct will protect competitors and harm consumers.
Table based on Fox (2006b).		

In a recent ruling, the European Court of First Instance considered the tying of the Windows Media Player to the Windows operating software[779]. The court found that Microsoft had foreclosed competition because other providers of media players could not compete on the merits and that Microsoft had tied the two products without objective justification. The diverse decision of the Microsoft case

---

[778] This is expressed in the case law of the European courts, but there is currently a discussion about a re-orientation of the European rules in the sense of a 'more economic approach'. See Dreher and Adam (2006: 259 *et seqq.*, 2007).
[779] *Microsoft v Commission*, T-201/04 [2007]. The case also involved the refusal to supply interoperability information.

in the US and the EU are illustrated in Table 6. The US authorities tend to assume that if a conduct does not directly harm consumers, it is only harmful to competitors, not to competition. Harm to the competition process is not investigated if there is no harm to consumers. The European authorities on the other hand are concerned with the foreclosure of markets and thus harm to the competition process. But harm to the competition process is difficult to distinguish from harm to competitors and there is a risk that they unnecessarily prohibit a conduct that is not harmful.

5.2.3. Identifying harmful conduct

The US courts and agencies assume that this probability of error is high because they consider it to be difficult to distinguish conduct that is harmful to the competition process from conduct that only hurts competitors. Furthermore, they assume the damage of over-enforcement to be greater than that of under-enforcement and are more sceptical towards the capabilities of enforcement agencies[780]. Their approach is therefore mainly a fear of false positives (incorrectly prohibiting conduct that belongs to the right-hand column of Table 6) and they do not consider harm to the competition process (i.e. assume it to be within the right-hand column of Table 6). The follow-up question is whether this leads to too many false negatives, because if cases of harm to the competition process are frequent, firms are allowed to behave anti-competitively. This shows the differences between the approaches in the two jurisdictions. The US law gives preference to single-firm action and not to possible harm to the competition process, because it considers it difficult to distinguish it from not harmful conduct. The EU law privileges the contestability of markets and thus investigates cases where markets are blocked. As pointed out above, the divide between the two jurisdictions is also due to differing assumptions about the consequences of considering or not considering a conduct. A possible answer would be a more detailed analysis of cases in the middle column of Table 6, i.e. those that concern the competition process[781]. Empirical work should be done to assess the effects of

---

[780] Kovacic (2007: 70).
[781] Fox (2006b: 76).

exclusionary practices and to quantify the dynamic losses from harm to the competition process[782].

Other competition authorities are more likely to be successful in the implementation and application of abuse of dominance laws when they are aware of the various possible conducts and their impacts in their country-specific context. Instead of following one of the approaches discussed above, competition authorities in developing countries should assess the consequences of, for example, considering or not considering harm to the competition process. If they choose to consider such cases, it will need more resources and may in some cases result in the prohibition of conduct that is not harmful. On the other hand, not considering them will allow certain dominant firms to foreclose the market and thus increase inequality, which may have particularly negative consequences in developing countries. Knowing the actual impact of these cases on the economy helps to find the optimal balance between the advantages and disadvantages of different approaches and legal standards.

5.3. Assessing error costs of competition enforcement

A possible approach to analyse the impact on the economy is an empirical assessment that estimates the error costs and the probability of errors based on the analysis of past cases[783]. Table 7 illustrates schematically the types of errors that can be made. One type of error is to declare a practice that is actually not harmful to competition to be illegal (dark grey). The other type is to declare a conduct that is harmful to competition as legal (light grey).

---

[782] This is another question addressed by a study on the quantitative effects of anti-competitive practices in developing countries, which is currently being undertaken by UNCTAD.

[783] Kovacic (2007: 71). Such an error-cost framework must constantly be updated to take into account that the investigation techniques of the authorities are improving and the economic environment changing.

Table 7: Error costs of competition enforcement		
	Harm to Competition (should be illegal)	**Harm to Competitors (should be legal)**
Declared illegal	**Correctly prohibit** conduct that harms competition	**Incorrectly prohibit** conduct that does not harm competition, but only competitors
Declared legal	**Incorrectly allow** conduct that harms competition	**Correctly allow** conduct that doesn't harm competition, but only competitors
Table based on Evans and Padilla (2004)[784]		

Evidence about the probability that a certain conduct is assessed incorrectly should be provided. Together with the costs of each incorrectly decided case, these probabilities provide evidence on the accuracy of the present law and can give guidance on what changes should be made, because it will give competition authorities as well as policy makers a better picture of the economic reality in their jurisdiction. An illustrative example is the use of market share thresholds. Once authorities know how likely and costly it is to incorrectly find or not find dominance with the current standard, they know if they should change the threshold or use more behavioural criteria. Other costs, such as increased inequality, social instability, etc., should also be given a weight and be included in the framework. This will allow basing the legal standards on empirical evidence, but it will also increase the capacity of less experienced authorities and courts to use economic analysis in the decision making in future cases and therefore advance their competence and lead to convergence in the approaches between countries. It is clearly a demanding exercise and the lack of accurate data will form an obstacle to many jurisdictions, especially in developing countries. However, the discussion above showed that the benefits are likely to be significant and competence in the application of economic analysis is increasingly an essential skill for the competition authorities.

---

[784]Evans and Padilla (2004).

6. Recommendations

Abuse of dominance refers to cases in which a firm has a dominant position and then engages in a harmful conduct. It is related to the concept of unilateral conduct, which focuses on single-firm action and its potential anti-competitive effects, including the creation or strengthening of dominance, but does not require a prior existence of a dominant position. Abuse of dominance can be seen as an approach that uses the criterion of dominance as a filter to only analyse cases in which harmful effects are likely, because it is assumed that only dominant firms can engage in such conduct or that the conduct is only harmful if entered into by a dominant firm.

To find dominance, the relevant market first has to be defined. One problem here is that the often-used criterion 'willingness of the consumer to switch to other products' (substitution) is biased by the firm's conduct, which has already taken place and possibly allowed the sellers to set prices above the competitive level. Consumers who are then faced with an even further price increase might easily be willing to switch to other suppliers. When this criterion is used for the market definition, then the suppliers to which consumers switch are included in the relevant market under consideration because it is assumed that these producers sell close substitutes. But actually the switch to other suppliers is due to the fact that the price of the original product is already too high. The relevant market is then defined too broadly and other criteria, which focus more on product characteristics, have to be given more weight. On the basis of the market definition, it needs to be established that a dominant position exists. This assessment includes the analysis of market shares, entry barriers, position of competitors, vertical integration, economies of scale, buyer power, and access to infrastructure.

The second element of abuse of dominance is the abusive conduct. There are generally two types of abusive conduct: exploitive conduct and exclusionary conduct. The former refers to cases where firms charge excessively high prices from its customers, pay low prices to suppliers, or discriminate among consumers. The latter refers to cases where firms suppress competition by refusing to deal, engaging in predatory pricing or raising costs of entry in order to exclude competitors from the market and thus to create or strengthen a dominant position.

624

The difficulty here is that the same conduct may be harmful or efficient, depending on the individual case.

After looking at what abuse of dominance is and how it is approached in theory, we turned to the role of laws on abuse of dominance in developing countries. Such laws have to find a balance between three objectives: ensuring enough competition between firms in order to force them to be efficient, allowing a certain degree of profitability so that they have incentives to invest and innovate, and achieving an equal distribution of wealth and business opportunities among different parts of the society. While the discussion in developed countries focuses on the first two aspects in order to maximize innovation and growth, developing countries may also want to consider the third dimension and include the reduction of inequality and poverty in their objectives. But even the relationship between the first two aspects tends to be different in developing countries than in other regions, because they depend on factors that differ between developing and developed countries.

Firstly, since developing economies often have smaller markets and therefore a lower equilibrium number of firms that can exploit economies of scale and operate efficiently, it is more likely that one finds more concentrated national markets. One argument is that smaller markets allow fewer firms to operate efficiently and that higher concentration should therefore be accepted. The opposite view is that since small economies are more vulnerable to abuse of dominance, a stricter approach should be followed. The optimal solution differs from one country to another, because it depends on a number of individual characteristics such as barriers to entry. A stricter approach prevents high levels of concentration and this may be more accurate in cases where barriers to entry are high and where the economies are isolated from international trade. But this approach would have significant disadvantages for open economies with low barriers to entry if the market was not defined accordingly, because it can prevent firms from reaching an efficient size. Each country therefore must choose the optimal approach and define the relevant markets according to its situation. In general, in developing countries there are higher barriers to entry, less developed capital markets and more information asymmetry, which make the good functioning of competition more difficult than in developed countries.

625

Secondly, large firms play a different role regarding their investment activity in developing countries than they do in more developed economies. Established and possibly dominant firms can be important for less developed economies to have a sufficiently high level of investment in production. Long-term relationships and profitability make it easier for incumbent firms to invest. If there was fierce competition with constantly new firms entering the market and established, but less efficient ones leaving it, then the currently existing firms would not be able or willing to make sufficient investments. The dominant positions may have a negative impact on innovation, but since less developed countries generally operate in sectors with less advanced technology, they can use existing technology and innovation is not as important for them. Therefore, it may be less important for them to have the most innovative and efficient firms, but rather to have large incumbent firms that can make investments more easily. In less developed economies, the benefits of increased investments are more likely to outweigh efficiency losses that arise from a dominant position, because investments in production are relatively more important. As economies become more developed, it is increasingly crucial that the competition process selects those firms that are the most efficient and innovative. Countries therefore need to switch out of the more protective setting at the right time and expose their firms to more competition.

A related issue concerns investment in infrastructure. A government may not have sufficient resources to make investments in infrastructure and therefore may allow private firms to exercise a monopoly position in markets such as port, airport, or even road infrastructure. If the infrastructure is an essential facility for other enterprises, this firm has the power to exclude competitors or demand high prices. There needs to be a balance between the firm's incentives to invest and efficiency losses. It must be carefully assessed for what sectors the monopoly is allowed, how broad it needs to be, for what period it should be granted, and if concessions can be renegotiated after a certain time or situation.

Thirdly, distributional aspects may be important for developing countries. Smaller firms, which often represent poorer parts of society, may have to be given a better chance to compete against large dominant firms. Enforcement against exclusionary practices of dominant firms may therefore have to be fiercer. Competition law can be used for such public interest issues, but it is crucial that the law gives clear guidance on how these objectives should be balanced against other objectives such as efficiency. Comparing this to the investment argument above shows that there are justifications for more but also for less strict standards in developing countries. These justifications naturally contradict each other and therefore necessitate a sound balance.

After analysing the role of abuse of dominance laws in developing countries, we took a broader perspective and compared the approaches to abuse of dominance across a number of developed and developing countries. A survey by the ICN investigated the differences between countries regarding the objectives of unilateral conduct laws and the assessment of dominance. It found that 'effective competitive process' and 'consumer welfare' are objectives that almost all jurisdictions share. There are, however, considerable differences in other objectives such as 'ensuring a level playing field' and 'promote fairness and equality'.

The assessment of dominance is very much based on the criteria mentioned above. Most countries rank 'market shares of the firm and its competitors' and 'barriers to entry or expansion' among the most important criteria. These criteria are structural criteria, because they do not directly look at the firms' behaviour, but at the market structures that influence their behaviour. The use of more structural criteria has the advantage of giving more clear-cut rules, which may be important particularly for developing countries and less experienced competition authorities. But even apparently clear rules such as market share thresholds for the assessment of dominance can make demanding case-specific analysis such as market definition necessary.

Developing countries often look at the situation in developed countries for possible ways to design their own competition laws. Examples could be the US or the EU, but particularly in the area of abuse of dominance, these two jurisdictions differ significantly. It is therefore beneficial to look at the differences in the two approaches in order to derive some lessons for developing countries. The first difference is that in the US Section 2 of the Sherman Act is not regarded as an abuse of dominance law, but as a unilateral conduct law. It does not always require a prior existence of a dominant position, but there has to be a causal link from the conduct to the creation or maintenance of a dominant position. A second difference is that the EU law wants to protect the competition process, while the US law only intervenes when

627

there is direct harm to consumers. The legal standards in the two jurisdictions differ considerably, but how much their approaches differ in practice depends crucially on how the above-mentioned terms are defined and interpreted. Harm to the competition process for example is prohibited in the EU because it is assumed that the outcome of a sound competition process is generally favourable to consumers. But the harm to the competition process may also involve a strengthening or creation of a dominant position and consumers may be hurt directly, which are the necessary conditions in the US, so that the two standards overlap in many respects. A reason for the disparity are differing assumptions about what types of conduct are harmful and how difficult it is to differentiate them from other conduct. The 'access to market principle' of the EU probably arises from the assumption that impediment to this access is severe and that it can be distinguished from other, not harmful, conduct. On the other hand, the 'non intervention principle' of the US is rather based on the assumption that the distinction of such conduct is difficult, that there is great danger of prohibiting behaviour that is not harmful, and that the unnecessary prohibition of efficient conduct is severe. One conclusion from the comparison is that such assumptions should be analysed and be grounded on the economic reality. How likely and severe errors of competition authorities are can, for example, be assessed in an analysis of past decisions and their effects on the economy. The impact of decisions should be assessed *ex post* in order to know if the rules need to be revised. The resulting country-specific error-cost framework can be an important input for competition authorities in developing countries, because it allows basing the rules on empirical evidence. Support of competition authorities in analysing their own cases and their impacts would therefore be valuable.

The insights from quantitative analysis are also crucial for finding a sound balance between the different objectives of competition policy. For example, incentives to innovate arise from the possibility to make profit and therefore depend to some extent on dominance, but this must be weighted *inter alia* against price increases by dominant firms. A second example is that developing countries often also have to consider distributional aspects of laws on abuse of dominance and therefore need to assess whether there exists a trade-off with efficiency considerations. Quantitative analysis will help competition authorities to understand the economic and political context in which their decisions and rules take place.

References

Acemoglu, D., Aghion, P. and Zilibotti, F., 2006: *Distance to Frontier, Selection and Economic Growth.* Journal of the European Economic Association. Vol. 4, No. 1.

Alesina, A., Spolaore, E. and Wacziarg, R., 2000: *Economic Integration and Political Disintegration.* The American Economic Review. Vol. 90, No. 5.

Anderson, R. and Heimler, A., 2007: "Abuse of Dominant Position: Enforcement Issues and Approaches for Developing Countries." In: Vinod Dhall (ed.): *Competition Law Today: Concepts, Issues, and the Law in Practice.* Oxford University Press, New Delhi.

Anderson, R., Daniel, T. and Heimler, A., 1999: "Abuse of Dominance". In: *A Framework for the Design and Implementation of Competition Law and Policy.* The World Bank and OECD. Washington and Paris.

Besanko, D., Dranove, D., Shanley, M. and Schaefer, S., 2003: *Economics of Strategy.* John Wiley. New York.

Bloch, R., Kamann, H.-G., Brown, J. and Schmidt, J., 2005: *A Comparative Analysis of Art. 82 of the EC Treaty and Section 2 of the Sherman Act.* Journal of Competition Law (ZWeR). No. 4.

Dreher, M. and Adam, M., 2006: *The more economic approach to Article 82 EC and the legal process.* Journal of Competition Law (ZWeR). No.3.

Dreher, M. and Adam, M., 2007: *Abuse of Dominance Under Reform – Sound Economics and Established Case Law.* European Competition Law Review. Issue 4.

EAGCP, 2005: Report by the EAGC: *An economic approach to Article 82.*

Easterly, W., 2007: *Inequality does cause Underdevelopment: Evidence from a New Instrument.* Journal of Development Economics. Vol. 84.

European Commission, 2005: *DC Competition discussion paper on the application of Art 82 of the Treaty to exclusionary abuses.*
European Commission, 2007a: *More competitive energy markets: building on the findings of the sector inquiry to shape the right policy solutions.* Speech by Neelie Kroes on 19 September 2007.

629

European Commission, 2007b: *DG Competition Report on Energy Sector Inquiry*. 10 January 2007.

Evans, D. and Padilla, J., 2004: *Designing Antitrust Rules For Assessing Unilateral Practices: A Neo-Chicago Approach*. CEMFI Working Paper No. 0417. September 2004.

Fox, E., 2000: *Equality, Discrimination, and Competition Law: Lessons from and for South Africa and Indonesia*. Harvard International Law Journal. Vol. 41.

Fox, E., 2002: *What is Harm to Competition?* Antitrust Law Journal. Vol. 70.

Fox, E., 2003: *We Protect Competition, You Protect Competitors*. World Competition. Vol. 26, No. 2.

Fox, E., 2006a: *Monopolization, Abuse of Dominance, and the Indeterminacy of Economics: The U.S./E.U. Divide*. Utah Law Review. No. 3.

Fox, E., 2006b: "Abuse of Dominance and Monopolisation: How to Protect Competition Without Protecting Competitors". In: Claus-Dieter Ehlermann and Isabela Atanasiu (eds). European Competition Law Annual 2005: *What Is An Abuse of A Dominant Position?* Hart Publishing.

Fox, E., 2007: *Economic Development, Poverty and Antitrust: The Other Path*. Southwestern Journal of Law and Trade in the Americas. Vol. 13.

Gerber, D., 2007: *Competition Law and the WTO*. Journal of International Economic Law. Vol. 10, No. 3.

Geroski, P., 2005: *Competition Policy and National Champions*. March 2005.

International Competition Network (ICN), 2007. *Report by the Unilateral Conduct Working Group*. Presented at the 6th Annual Conference of the ICN in Moscow. May 2007.

Kovacic, W., 2007: *Intellectual DNA of Modern U.S. Competition Law for Dominant Firm Conduct: The Chicago/Harvard Double Helix*. Columbia Business Law Review. No. 1.

Lipimile, G., 2004: "Competition Policy as a Stimulus for Enterprise Development". In: *UNCTAD, Competition, Competitiveness and Development: Lessons from Developing Countries*. pp. 199, 201.

Marsden, P., 2006: *Handbook of Research in Trans-Atlantic Antitrust.* Edward Elgar Publishing, Cheltenham.

Motta, M., 2004: *Competition Policy: Theory and Practice.* Cambridge University Press, Cambridge.

National Economic Research Associates (NERA), 2001: *The role of market definition in monopoly and dominance inquiries.* Economic Discussion Paper 2. Office of Fair Trading.

OECD, 2003: *Competition Law and Policy in South Africa.* An OECD Peer Review. OECD. Paris.

UNCTAD, 2000: *The United Nations Set of Principles and Rules on Competition.* United Nations. Geneva.

UNCTAD, 2004: *Competition, Competitiveness and Development: Lessons from Developing Countries.* United Nations. New York and Geneva.

UNCTAD, 2005: *Review of Recent Experiences in the Formulation and Implementation of Competition Law and Policy in Selected Developing Countries: Thailand, Lao, Kenya, Zambia, Zimbabwe.* United Nations. New York and Geneva.

UNCTAD, 2007a: *Handbook on Competition Legislation.* Trade and Development Board. Intergovernmental Group of Experts on Competition Law and Policy.
UNCTAD, 2007b: *Model Law on Competition.* UNCTAD Series on Issues in Competition Law and Policy. United Nations. New York and Geneva. 2007.

UNCTAD, 2007c: *Recent important competition cases involving more than one country.* Report by the UNCTAD Secretariat. Geneva.
Vickers, J., 2005: *Abuse of Market Power.* The Economic Journal. Vol. 115.

UNCTAD, *Cocoa Study: Industry Structures and Competition.* United Nations, forthcoming 2008.

Vickers, J., 2007: *Competition and Economics: A Mid-Atlantic Viewpoint.* European Competition Journal. Vol. 3, No. 1.

Zambia Competition Commission, 2000: *Annual Report 1999.* Lusaka. March 2000.

[4]

SHOULD DEVELOPING COUNTRIES WORRY ABOUT ABUSE OF DOMINANT POWER?

PHILIPPE BRUSICK *
SIMON J. EVENETT**

This Paper suggests that in developing countries, especially where small and poor markets prevail, abuse of dominant power—or monopolization, as it is known in the United States—can be much more damaging to the economy than in developed countries. It pays special attention to the abuses that state-owned firms and recently privatized monopolies can inflict on developing economies and suggests that collusion between the state and dominant enterprises can seriously hamper the economy and stifle development. This Paper analyzes the main concerns of developing countries in this respect and provides a list of examples of concrete cases of abuse of dominance affecting developing-country economies. This Paper recommends that far from challenging only price-fixing cartels, as is sometimes advocated by representatives from developed countries, competition authorities in developing countries should devote increased attention to abuse of dominance, and their powers in this respect should be strengthened when they must challenge abuses by dominant firms, which are sometimes protected by their own government.

* Former Chief, Competition and Consumer Protection Branch, United Nations Conference on Trade and Development (UNCTAD).

** Professor of International Trade and Economic Development, Department of Economics, University of St. Gallen, Switzerland. For contact information and other writings, see http://www.evenett.com.

270   WISCONSIN LAW REVIEW

INTRODUCTION

Since the fall of the Berlin Wall, a rapidly rising number of countries have realized the importance of deterring and punishing price-fixing cartels and abuses of dominance, the latter term being typically referred to as *monopolization* in U.S. antitrust law. While antitrust laws were first introduced in Canada and the United States in the late nineteenth century, subsequently so-called fair-trade laws—later renamed competition laws—were adopted in many jurisdictions. Today, all of the members of the Organisation for Economic Co-operation and Development (OECD) have enacted such legislation.[1] More developing countries have adopted such laws, and, most recently, in September 2007, China enacted a new antitrust statute.[2] According to the International Competition Network (ICN) and other sources, at present more than one hundred national jurisdictions from all over the world have enacted some form of competition law.[3] Many countries seek to actively enforce such laws to improve associated knowledge and implementation capacities and to exchange views in many different fora, ranging from the OECD to the United Nations Conference on Trade and Development (UNCTAD) and including ICN and numerous regional and subregional meetings of experts. In addition, many countries have established sectoral regulators to investigate, punish, and deter firms with market power operating in the network industries that supply numerous essential services to consumers, producers, and the government.[4]

---

1. *See* OECD, OECD ANNUAL REPORT (2007), *available at* http://www.oecd.org/dataoecd/34/33/38528123.pdf; OECD.org, OECD Country Web Sites, http://www.oecd.org/infobycountry (last visited Mar. 18, 2008).

2. The Anti-Monopoly Law of the People's Republic of China was passed by National People's Congress on August 31, 2007, and comes into effect on August 1, 2008. Antimonopolychina.com, Anti-Monopoly Law of the People's Republic of China Has Passed!!!, http://www.antimonopolychina.com (last visited Mar. 18, 2008).

3. *See* InternationalCompetitionNetwork.org, Members, http://www.international competitionnetwork.org/index.php/en/members (last visited Mar. 18, 2008); *see also* UNCTD, DIRECTORY OF COMPETITION AUTHORITIES (2007), *available at* http://www.unctad.org/en/docs/c2clpd56_en.pdf.

4. *See* SIMON J. EVENETT & MICHAL S. GAL, A REPORT ON THE THIRD ANNUAL CONFERENCE OF THE INTERNATIONAL COMPETITION NETWORK (2004) 16–22 (Antitrust Enforcement in Regulated Sectors Working Group), *available at* http://

While competition laws are far from being all alike, they typically have provisions prohibiting price fixing and other forms of cartels, as well as measures to tackle abuses of market power by so-called dominant enterprises or attempts by firms to monopolize markets. In recent years, partly as a result of frequent discussions and exchanges of experience by competition-law experts from around the world, a certain degree of consensus has emerged concerning the enforcement priorities of nascent competition authorities, which are mainly found in the developing world. Much advice from industrialized-country experts recommends giving preference to action against cartels and so-called competition advocacy over measures to tackle monopolization or abuses of dominance.[5] Moreover, some scholars, in particular from the Chicago school of thought,[6] consider the abuse of a dominant position as transitory.[7] On this view, such dominance rewards technological and product innovation, and measures to constrain dominance are unnecessary so long as incentives to enter profitable lines of business are not unduly diminished.[8] Other experts draw attention to the fact that some famous antitrust cases against alleged abuses of a dominant position, such as the European Commission's enforcement action against Microsoft, took so long to be decided that, by the time the ultimate decision was rendered, technological developments had made many of the circumstances of the initial alleged violations of competition law irrelevant to the future of interfirm rivalry in the sector concerned.[9] On both conceptual and practical grounds, then, there are doubts about the wisdom of enforcement actions against abuses of a dominant position.

The purpose of this Paper is to revisit the question, should governments and proponents of competition law in developing countries

---

www.internationalcompetitionnetwork.org/media/library/conference_3rd_seoul_2004/se oul_icn_final.pdf.

    5.   *Id.* at 9–11, 18–21.

    6.   *See, e.g.*, Richard A. Posner, *The Chicago School of Antitrust Analysis*, 127 U. PA. L. REV. 925 (1979).

    7.   *See, e.g.*, Michael S. Jacobs, *Introduction: Hail or Farewell? The Aspen Case 20 Years Later*, 73 ANTITRUST L.J. 59, 67, 70–72 (2005) (discussing some scholars' views of dominant corporations and antitrust interventions).

    8.   *Id.* at 67.

    9.   Michael Yeh, Senior Att'y, Microsoft Corp., Characteristics of a Sound Competition Law—A Global Perspective, Presentation at Third Asian Competition Law Conference at Hong Kong Polytechnic University (Dec. 10, 2007), *available at* http://64.233.167.104/search?q=cache:hkcTpXvVLHwJ:www.asiancompetitionforum. org/3rd%2520ACF%2520Conference%25202007/3rd%2520ACF%2520Conference%2 5202007%2520Schedule%2520(Website%2520Purpose).doc+Ningrum+Sirait+Indone sia+Retail+in+Indonesia&hl=en&ct=clnk&cd=1&gl=us&client=firefox-a (follow hyperlink).

272   WISCONSIN LAW REVIEW

seek to tackle abuses of dominant position by public and private firms in their respective economies? To that end, the available evidence and its implications for the design of competition law and for postenactment enforcement priorities are considered.

In the effort to formulate a substantial response to this question, a review of recently compiled statistics on alleged anticompetitive practices collected by Professor Simon Evenett, Professor Frédéric Jenny, and their research collaborators in sub-Saharan Africa and Latin America was undertaken. Such evidence, which is reported in the following Part, suggests that it is unwise to dismiss out-of-hand concerns about abuses of a dominant position in many developing countries (in these two regions, at the very least). The fraction of allegations concerning such practices, including dominance-creating mergers and acquisitions, reaches close to half of the total allegations and sometimes exceeds the total number of accusations concerning cartels and bid rigging. Subsequent Parts give further attention to the characteristics of developing countries that tend to make them more susceptible to harm caused by abuses of a dominant position by firms and to a number of cases that highlight the deleterious effects of such abuses. The Paper concludes with a summary of the main findings and their practical implications for policy makers and others concerned with tackling abuses of a dominant position in developing countries.

I. Review of Allegations of Abuse of Dominance in Latin America and Sub-Saharan Africa

Eighteen different types of allegations concerning anticompetitive practices can be identified on the basis of statistics in newspaper articles collected by Julian Clarke, Simon Evenett, and Krista Lucenti that report allegations of anticompetitive behavior and information concerning the relationship between competition-related factors and the effects of market-liberalization reforms in Latin American and Caribbean countries.[10] A comparable exercise was conducted for sub-Saharan Africa in 2004 by Evenett and Jenny.[11] In the Latin American and Caribbean sample, 17 percent of the total number of allegations related to "monopolistic" practices, and another 11.7 percent of all the allegations concerned specific accusations of abuse of a dominant

---

        10.   Julian L. Clarke, Simon J. Evenett & Krista Lucenti, *Anti-competitive Practices and Liberalizing Markets in Latin America and the Caribbean*, 28 WORLD ECON. 1029 (2005).

        11.   Simon J. Evenett & Frédéric Jenny, *An Inventory of Allegations of Anti-competitive Practices in Sub-Saharan Africa* (Working Paper, Sept. 5, 2004), *available at* http://www.evenett.com/working/evenettjennycapetownsummary.pdf.

2008:269   *Abuse of Dominant Power*   273

position.[12] Very few allegations were made of anticompetitive mergers or acquisitions.[13] However, monopolization and abuse-of-dominance allegations combined to yield 28.7 percent of all allegations, which compares with allegations of cartelization that accounted for approximately 40 percent of the total.[14] Such evidence is hard to reconcile with the view that monopolization and abuses of dominance do not happen in developing countries and, by implication, that these anticompetitive acts are clearly not an enforcement priority for competition authorities. Analysis of allegations of anticompetitive practices in sub-Saharan Africa yielded similar findings (see figure 1).[15] Although cartel allegations amounted to approximately 38 percent of the total number, alleged monopolistic practices accounted for 2.9 percent of the total and allegations of specific forms of abuse of a dominant position accounted for a further 7.9 percent of the total.

Figure 1
Distribution of alleged anticompetitive acts in sub-Saharan Africa.

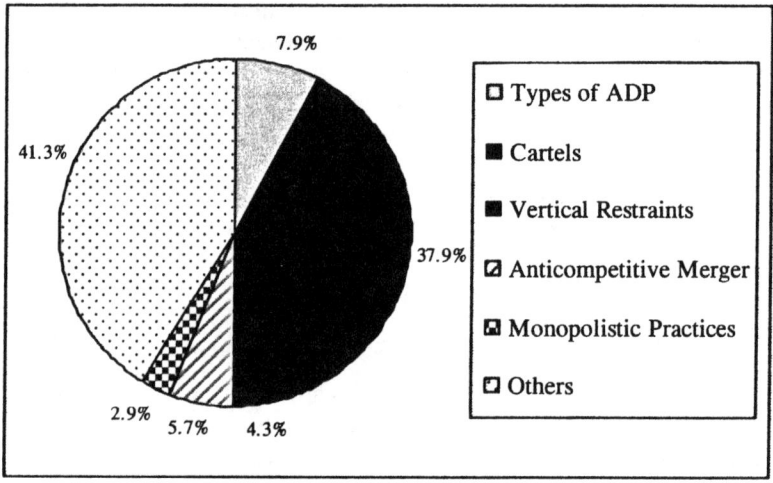

The African dataset also shows an increase in the first half of this decade in the average number of annual allegations of abuse of a dominant position (see figure 2).[16] While this is suggestive of abuses of a dominant position being more prevalent in sub-Saharan Africa during

---

12. Clarke, Evenett & Lucenti *supra* note 10, at 1040 tbl.4.
13. *Id.*
14. *Id.*
15. *Id.*
16. Evenett & Jenny, *supra* note 11, at 2 tbl.1. Note, the information is current through September 5, 2004.

274   WISCONSIN LAW REVIEW

this period, it may also be the result of more extensive reporting on these matters by the media. It may also be the result of an improved ability and willingness to identify and tackle anticompetitive practices in general, or abuses of a dominant position in particular, by national competition authorities, relevant sector regulators, and other elected or state officials. It should also be noted that sub-Saharan countries may differ in the degree to which national newspapers with significant coverage of commercial matters are available electronically and therefore accessible by researchers in other countries. Even so, the statistics presented in this Part suggest that it would be imprudent to automatically discount abuses of a dominant position as a priority for competition authorities in developing countries and associated government agencies.

Figure 2
Allegations of anticompetitive acts in sub-Saharan Africa.

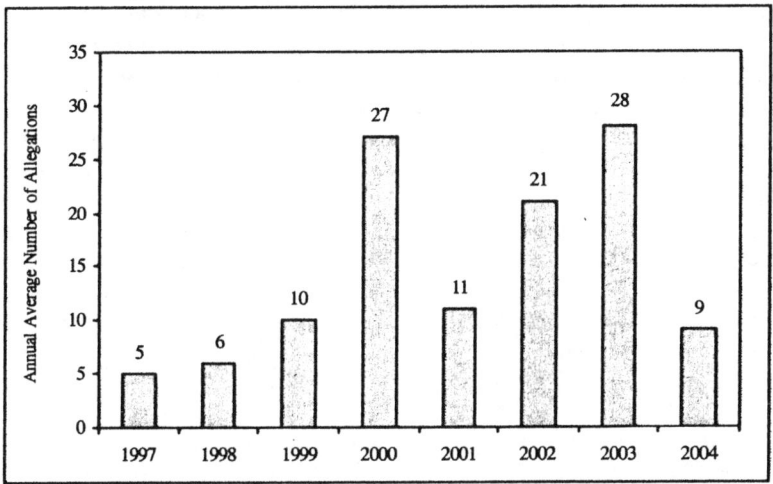

II. The Characteristics of Developing Countries That Make Them Prone to Monopoly and Abuse of Dominance

This Part identifies certain characteristics of developing economies that make them particularly susceptible to abuses of a dominant position. These arguments seek to counter the point of view that even if abuses of a dominant position happen in market economies, they are inherently self-defeating, perhaps because the entry of other firms is spurred on by large economic profits.

Most developing countries have transportation and communication infrastructures whose performance is far from best practice, and this affects the degree of interfirm rivalry in national markets.[17] For a start, many poor countries are either island or landlocked countries, and efficient transportation infrastructures are a prerequisite for the inexpensive distribution of domestic- and foreign-produced goods and for fast exportation, both of which foster economic development. Examples of two representative African countries illustrate the effect of abuses of a dominant position and other anticompetitive practices on the performance of national transportation infrastructures.

The first example involves a three-island country where deep-port infrastructure only exists on one island, which happened to be the native island of the president at the time the port was built. As a result of the cargo shipping lines controlling the freight routes to that port by fixing prices, the cost of shipping doubled between the deep-water port and the other, less-well-equipped islands. When not controlled by the shippers' price-fixing "conference," the remaining markets are divided among shipping lines, which have exclusive rights, and are free to abuse their market power since no other line has found it attractive to serve a route that has been awarded to one of the incumbent lines. In sum, then, small freight ports are served by a single shipping line, while the bigger ports are served by a few carriers who impose uniform freight charges and conditions. This, in turn, raises prices of shipped products and reduces the purchasing power of what is already a low-income country.[18]

The second all-too-typical example is that of a land-locked country in central Africa that relies for its imports and exports on a single port on the Atlantic Ocean that is located in a neighboring country. Transportation between the land-locked country and the port is controlled by truck-drivers' unions that fix prices on the merchandise that they transport. The foreign port is congested and requires excessive handling and storage tariffs for merchandise. The merchandise is often stranded at the docks for weeks, sometimes months, at excessive stevedoring charges. Moreover, the port authority enjoys a full monopoly and has a free hand to abuse its dominant position concerning traders from the landlocked neighboring country, significantly affecting both import prices for merchandise finding its way to that country and taking a toll on exports, in particular for time- and price-sensitive perishable farm products.[19] These problems were publicized a decade ago when the European Union fined shipping lines between Europe and

---

17.   Bernard Hoekman & Aaditya Mattoo, *Services Trade and Growth* 18–20 (World Bank Policy Research Working Paper, Working Paper No. 4461, 2008).

18.   Findings by Philippe Brusick in UNDP Country Study on competition (Confidential, unpublished).

19.   *Id.*

Africa for excessive freight costs as a result of a price-fixing cartel agreement.[20]

More generally, inside many poor countries, the roads are often impassable for commerce-carrying trucks and are often seasonally blocked. In the case of the island countries, regular boat services between the islands may not exist either. Foodstuff produced on one island might not be distributed to the other islands, although their qualities and production capacities differ widely. As a result, markets are fragmented and small, often leading to all sorts of anticompetitive practices by a single or a few local operators.[21]

Difficulties in securing financial capital in poor countries typically result in some industries being characterized by a few large enterprises that enjoy a de facto monopolistic position.[22] Such firms can use their profits to amass financial resources that might deter entry by other firms. This effect reinforces any tendency toward natural monopolization that is found in certain sectors—utilities, for instance. Worse still, privatization programs, where they take place, often result in state-owned monopolies being sold to the highest bidder, so as to make the greatest contribution to national treasuries, a step that often transforms a public monopoly into a private one with little or no serious regulatory oversight.[23]

In the case of essential facilities, such as banking and financial services, it is interesting to note that many poor countries still depend on a small number of banks. The banks argue that the small size of the national market prevents the viable operation of many financial institutions. In one case examined, the decade-long existence of a banking monopoly had resulted in very limited banking services being offered, in addition to high costs. For example, long-term mortgages were unavailable, and clients had to get short-term loans both for housing and business and pay heavy penalties when they were unable to repay the loan upon maturity. In addition, it was found that the single bank acted in a discriminatory manner, refusing loans to certain traders and offering them to others, allegedly giving consideration to noncommercial considerations.[24]

In sum, there are a number of reasons why dominant firms arise in poorer countries with smaller economies and certain sectoral and

---

20.   *See French West-African Shipowners' Committees*, 1992 O.J. (L134/1) 446 (Commission Decision Relating to a Proceeding Pursuant to Articles 85 and 86 of the EEC Treaty).

21.   Brusick, *supra* note 18.

22.   *Id.*

23.   *Id.*

24.   *Id.*

geographic characteristics. This is not to say that every poor country suffers from the same abuses of a dominant position or that these factors are only found in developing countries. Rather, it is a statement about the manner in which certain underlying characteristics of societies, especially poorer societies, affect the propensity for dominant firms to arise and to abuse their dominant positions. Such experience implies that it cannot be assumed that new firms will enter markets when incumbents exercise market power. Access to finance, distribution networks, information about customers, and the necessary approvals from state bodies often frustrate the extent to which dominant firms will be disciplined in this manner. The following Part contains further information about specific types of abuse of dominance that prevail in developing countries.

III. COMMON TYPES OF ABUSE OF DOMINANCE IN DEVELOPING COUNTRIES

It is useful to distinguish between a number of different types of abuse of dominance found in developing countries, and the material in this Part is organized accordingly.

A. Abuse of Dominance by the State

Given the importance of the state as an investor and regulator, it is necessary to examine in detail the conduct of the state in developing economies and trace out a number of fundamental ways in which state officials stifle economic development. First, the dominance of the state over infrastructure utilities such as telecommunications, public transportation, electricity, water supply, and the ever-bankrupt situation of the public budget, typically results in a situation in which the state never pays for the public services it utilizes.[25] A dominant state often receives electricity and water for free and consumes a large proportion of public services without contributing for them. As a result, these utilities are always undercapitalized and in a situation of near bankruptcy.[26] When such utilities are privatized, old habits often do not die: new incumbents find to their dismay that they are expected to continue serving the state for free, perpetuating unwritten rules.[27] There have been many cases of newly privatized utilities where the incumbent has broken the contract and left because it could not run the firm as

---

25.   *Id.*
26.   *Id.*
27.   *Id.*

initially planned.[28] Sometimes, the state colludes politically with the informal sector, which also used to benefit from tolerated or illegal free service, to pressure the private incumbent firm to continue providing generous terms to the poor and the informal sector.[29]

The state also often intervenes heavily in the competitive process, distorting free competition for political or other more opaque reasons.[30] This may be in the selection process of bidding for public works or in the awarding of contracts. Moreover, in cases of awarded public-works contracts, the state often finds itself unable to pay its dues, and many contractors then find themselves with large arrears.[31] Cases have been reported of public-works contractors being obliged to pay taxes and thus being unable to compensate for overdue payments that the state was unable to pay.[32]

Two examples are provided by the Suharto administration in Indonesia and could easily be applied to other developing countries. The first example was reported by Emanuele Lobina and David Hall of the Public Services International Research Unit:

> In 1997, while the country was still under the control of President Suharto, Jakarta's water supply was privatized under the auspices of a World Bank program. One concession went to a consortium led by Thames Water and another to a consortium led by Lyonnaise des Eaux. Both consortia included partners which were owned by friends of the president. After Suharto's fall, these contracts were deemed to be corrupt and the two companies moved rapidly to negotiate new contracts with Jakarta City Council to run from February 1999. However, these contracts were also the subject of bitter criticism on the grounds that they were never properly advertised, that the prices involved were excessive, and that Suharto's son continued to hold a 5 percent equity stake in the new Thames Water venture. Court action was taken to have the contracts declared void, and a trade union of water workers demanded that the contracts be rescinded.[33]

---

28.   *Id.*
29.   *Id.*
30.   *Id.*
31.   *Id.*
32.   *Id.*
33.   EMANUELE LOBINA & DAVID HALL, PROBLEMS WITH PRIVATE WATER CONCESSIONS: A REVIEW OF EXPERIENCE 20 (2003), *available at* http://www.psiru.org/reports/2003-06-W-over.doc.

Another example from Indonesia is provided by a Consumers International report. Indonesia only recently enacted the Prohibition of Monopoly and Unfair Business Competition Practices legislation of 2000 and the Consumer Protection Law after a long period of heavy government intervention and restricted opportunities for foreign investment. The Consumers International Report notes,

> These government measures included marketing controls, pricing regulations, industrial licensing requirements, dominance of state-owned enterprises (SOEs) in certain sectors, officially sanctioned cartels, ad hoc measures in certain industries (for example, the preferential tax privileges accorded to the "national car" firm), and controls and "taxes" on intracountry trade.[34]

The report adds that enforcing laws is as important as enacting them. Honest and effective investigators and courts are necessary if competition laws are to work. Corruption in the civil service is commonplace in many developing countries, often simply because poorly paid officials feel they need to supplement their earnings. Therefore, in addition to adopting a law, senior leaders in government have to find it in their interest to fight corruption and to provide the resources necessary to ensure compliance.[35]

It should be noted that in many developing countries effective independence of the competition authority from the executive political powers may not exist.[36] And even if the competition law provides for a certain degree of independence for the competition officials, there can be a de facto dependence on the wishes of politicians who might want to favor certain enterprises including state firms, firms owned by relatives, or foreign multinationals with strong links to the political elite.[37]

Another important matter is the flawed interpretation of competition laws by judges who are not specialized in such matters, and this runs the risk of using the large discretion given by such laws in a counterproductive or definitely anticompetitive manner. Judicial

---

34.   CONSUMERS INTERNATIONAL, CONSUMERS AND COMPETITION 17 (2001), *available at* http://www.consumersinternational.org/Shared_ASP_Files/UploadedFiles/31EA343D-63B6-4221-8A75-49326FD47AA8_Doc319.pdf.

35.   *Id.* at 18.

36.   Deunden Nikomborirak, *Thailand, in* COMPETITION POLICY AND DEVELOPMENT IN ASIA 243 (Douglas H. Brooks & Simon J. Evenett eds., 2005).

37.   For a discussion on the facets and importance of regulatory agencies, see GESNER OLIVERIA ET AL., ASPECTS OF THE INDEPENDENCE OF REGULATORY AGENCIES AND COMPETITION ADVOCACY (2005).

WISCONSIN LAW REVIEW

mistakes are more frequent in delicate decisions relating to abuse of dominance, where laws might attribute a too-strict meaning to the market share as a criterion to determine the existence of dominance.[38]

It is interesting to note in this respect that the West African Economic and Monetary Union (WAEMU) rules on competition[39] cover "anti-competitive practices by member States, to avoid distortions to competition resulting from action of member State governments protecting or subsidizing their 'national champions' to the detriment of other firms from other WAEMU member States."[40] Centralizing competition policy in the hands of regional organizations might be a way to resolve the difficulties listed above, provided, of course, that the regional authority is afforded the necessary powers and expertise.

Finally, abuses of dominance have been frequently alleged against large state-infrastructure-providing firms, such as those in the energy, telecommunications, banking, and transportation sectors.[41] It is not difficult to appreciate that abuses of dominance in such sectors result in higher prices and lower quality, negatively affecting the efficiency of producers and exporters downstream and hence acting as a break to development. The solution to this concern, however, is not merely to privatize the large state enterprise, as the examples in the following Section make clear.

B. Abuse of Dominance by Privatized Monopolies

Abuses of dominance may be triggered or exacerbated when state-owned utilities are privatized. At first, it can be expected that privatization should bring with it much-needed capital investment and modern technology, improving the quality of the service and having a favorable impact on development. However, if privatization has been accorded on the basis of granting a long-term monopoly to the acquiring or concession-obtaining firm, as was often the case in the 1990s,[42] then it is likely that prices and conditions of sale are not going

---

38.   *See* CAPACITY BLDG. & COMPETITION POLICY IMPLEMENTATION WORKING GROUP, ICN, COMPETITION ADVOCACY IN REGULATED SECTORS: EXAMPLES OF SUCCESS (2004).

39.   *See* U.N. CONF. ON TRADE AND DEV., VOLUNTARY PEER REVIEW OF COMPETITION POLICIES OF WAEMU, BENIN AND SENEGAL (2008), *available at* http://www.unctad.org/en/docs/ditcclp20071_en.pdf.

40.   *Id.*

41.   *See generally* CUTS Institute for Regulation and Competition, http://www.circ.in/ (last visited Mar. 18, 2008).

42.   *See, e.g.*, DAVID HALL & EMANUELE LOBINA, WATER PRIVATIZATION IN LATIN AMERICA, 2002 (2002), *available at* http://www.psiru.org/reports/2002-06-W-Latam.doc; Andrew Nickson, *The Córdoba Water Concession in Argentina* (DFID Knowledge and Research Project, Working Paper No. 442 05, 2001).

to be competitive for long, if at all. In order to remedy such a problem, the state often regulates the privatized natural-monopoly sectors,[43] creating a regulatory authority with powers to oversee that the privatized utility functions competitively. In short, the state requires that the privatized utility refrain from abusing its dominant power on customers downstream. Unfortunately, one of the main problems of regulators around the world, and indeed in developing countries, is that they become captive to the utility they are expected to control.[44] This captivity occurs either because the regulators were previous civil servants working in the utility before privatization or because they do not accord necessary priority to competition issues over other pressing concerns of the utility, such as maintaining high-employment aims and profit objectives.

1. ABUSE IN PRIVATIZED INFRASTRUCTURE

Zambia provides an example of abuse of dominance in privatized infrastructure. As part of a privatization program there, "the Government decided to concession the Mpulungu Harbor and Port for the purpose of increasing the productivity and efficiency of the harbor, freight, transportation, and associated services."[45] In 2000, the Zambia Privatization Agency awarded a twenty-five-year concession for the port management to Mpulungu Harbor Management Ltd. (MHML) after a competitive-bidding process. The concession was subject to review every five years. Following complaints by port customers against MHML, the Zambian Competition Commission investigated the case and found that MHML was abusing its dominant position as port operator because of its discrimination in favor of its subsidiary, Agro-Fuel Investments Ltd., making MHML port user, port operator, and port manager. Hence, it gave Agro-Fuel an unfair advantage over other port users in its management of shipping space, especially with respect to limited cargo facilities operating between Mpulungu and the Great Lakes region. MHML was also found to abuse its position by chartering vessels and choosing the type of cargo to be loaded in a way that its subsidiary Agro-Fuel would get the largest share of the most

---

43.   *See, e.g.*, COMPETITION POLICY IMPLEMENTATION WORKING GROUP, ICN, COMPETITION ADVOCACY IN REGULATED SECTORS (2005), *available at* http://www.internationalcompetitionnetwork.org/media/library/conference_4th_bonn_2005/Competition_Advocacy_Review.pdf.

44.   *Id.*

45.   ORG. FOR ECON. CO-OPERATION AND DEV., GLOBAL FORUM ON COMPETITION: ABUSE OF DOMINANCE IN REGULATED SECTORS, MPULUNGU HARBOUR AND PORT: A SUMMARY OF COMPETITION ISSUES 3 (2005), *available at* http://www.oecd.org/dataoecd/50/9/34285468.pdf.

lucrative markets. Moreover, it was forcing customers to transport their cargo exclusively through Agro-Fuel truckers or haulers. Finally, only two weeks after having taken over the port management, MHML unilaterally increased its tariffs by 46 percent. Hence, the Zambia Competition Commission constituted a Port Regulatory Review Committee in January 2003, composed of various national ministries and the Zambia Privatization Agency in order to remedy the situation. A Memorandum of Understanding was drafted, realizing that the port was an essential facility requiring all its customers to be able to use its facilities in a fully transparent and nondiscriminatory manner. MHML nevertheless rejected the Memorandum of Understanding, arguing that section 3(f) of the Competition and Fair Trading Act of Zambia exempts all matters of which the government is a party from the application of the law. In this case, the Government was a party to the concession. Hence, the case was postponed until the first five-year review of the concession, due in 2005.[46]

This example shows how major anticompetitive practices can result from the privatization process of essential facilities, the extent to which abuses of dominance by the holder of a concession can affect competition and harm the economy of a poor country as well as its neighbors, and the difficulties in remedying the situation when government-related acts are exempted from the competition law.

Also in relation to port facilities, a Latin American study conducted by the Economic Commission for Latin America and the Caribbean (ECLAC) notes that "[t]he liberalization of Maritime Transport is one important element to increase the export competitiveness of a country."[47] For some countries, the effective rate of protection by the cost of transportation is much higher than that of tariffs.[48] The study noted that one of the most relevant elements of the cost of maritime transport concerns the degree of efficiency in the management of ports.[49] The study adds that one of the most important conditions for port regulation is the existence of competition or potential competition among port operators.[50]

---

    46.   *Id.* at 3–7.
    47.   José Carlos S. Mattos & María José Acosta, Maritime Transport Liberalization and the Challenges to Further its Implementation in Chile 5 (2003), *available at* http://www.eclac.org/publicaciones/xml/4/14814/lcl2051i.pdf.
    48.   *Id.* at 10.
    49.   *Id.* at 13.
    50.   *Id.* at 15.

2. ABUSE BY FOREIGN-OWNED MONOPOLIES

In Peru, Telefónica of Spain was granted a monopoly in fixed telephony when it was awarded the public concession in 1993. In addition, Telefónica obtained the concession to operate the mobile-telephony net in Lima when it took over CPT and in the rest of the country when it acquired ENTEL. CPT had one competitor, TELE 2000, in the Lima area of mobile telephony, and ENTEL was the sole provider of mobile telephony outside Lima. After Telefónica bought CPT and ENTEL, it decided to merge them in 1994, and, by 1995, it developed an automatic-national-roaming system (ANR).[51]

Hence, with Telefónica's ANR, its clients were able to communicate everywhere in Peru while TELE 2000 was unable to offer the same facility since it was limited to the Lima area. When TELE 2000, which benefited from a manual-national-roaming facility agreement with ENTEL, requested Telefónica to offer it the same facility, Telefónica refused.[52]

TELE 2000 sued Telefónica arguing that the ANR was a telecommunications public service that should be made available to the general public for a nondiscriminatory fee. TELE 2000 also stated that Telefónica dominated the market for mobile telephony outside Lima because it was the sole operator and that its refusal to share network and service interconnection amounted to an abuse of a dominant position. Accordingly, it requested that the Organismo Supervisor de la Inversión Privada en Telecomunicaciones (OSIPTEL), Peru's telecommunications regulator, which is in charge of competition issues in the telecommunications sector, order Telefónica to grant access to its ANR services for TELE 2000's clients.[53]

Telefónica argued that ANR was not a public service and that TELE 2000 was really aiming to indirectly enlarge its concession rights and gain indirect benefits. As it had been awarded the concession for mobile telephony outside Lima and no other concession had been granted in this case, Telefónica could not therefore be considered to be abusing its dominant position in that market. While OSIPTEL found that Telefónica did not have a dominant position in the Lima market, which it considered as the relevant market, OSIPTEL considered that Telefónica did have a dominant position in the market outside Lima and

---

51.   ORG. FOR ECON. CO–OPERATION AND DEV., GLOBAL FORUM ON COMPETITION: ABUSE OF DOMINANCE IN REGULATED SECTORS, TELE 2000 VS. TELEFONICA DEL PERU 2 (2005), *available at* http://www.oecd.org/dataoecd/49/57/34286241.pdf.

52.   *Id.*

53.   *Id.* at 3.

used that power to generate advantages in the Lima market. As a result, OSIPTEL ordered Telefónica to give TELE 2000 clients access to the ANR under the following conditions: First, both companies were given a period of seven days to negotiate the terms of access to ANR for TELE 2000's clients. Second, the compensation to use Telefónica's net would be established taking into account the magnitude of ANR coverage, installation costs, traffic, and additional investment Telefónica had to make to enable TELE 2000's clients to use the ANR. Finally, OSIPTEL indicated it would impose mandatory terms and conditions should the two firms not find an agreement after the seven-day delay had lapsed.[54]

Similar cases of incumbent telecommunications firms refusing to allow competitors to use essential facilities or imposing excessive fares for such services are commonplace in both developed and developing countries.[55] As such, it often becomes necessary for such countries to enforce competition legislation, either by the central competition authority or, such as the case in Peru, through the sector regulator's powers to enforce competition rules. In the latter system, the regulator might be too willing to support the views of the incumbent ex–state monopoly and to disregard competition rules.

3. ABUSE BY OTHER PRIVATE-SECTOR FIRMS, INCLUDING MULTINATIONAL FIRMS

Even when foreign firms are not monopolies, they may easily become dominant players in developing countries simply as a result of their large turnover and deep pockets compared to domestic competitors. And having power means it is very tempting to abuse such power in order to quash competition. Many types of complaints have been made in developing countries in this respect. These include, for example, local dairy- and farm-products suppliers to large multinational retail chains, such as Carrefour and Tesco, that were accused of abusing their dominant power to impose excessively restrictive conditions on local suppliers.[56] Alerted by this situation, competition authorities in these countries have often been unable to take any decisive action to remedy such concerns.[57] When authorities have tried

---

54.   *Id.* at 3–4.

55.   ORG. FOR ECON. CO-OPERATION AND DEV., COMPETITION AND REGULATION ISSUES IN TELECOMMUNICATIONS 8 (2001).

56.   *See, e.g., New Code Won't Break British Chains' Armlock on Farmers,* HOMETOWN ADVANTAGE, Mar. 2, 2002, http://www.newrules.org/retail/news_archive.php?browseby=slug&slugid=102.

57.   They have resorted to other means than competition policy. *See infra* notes 79–80 and accompanying text.

to protect suppliers, such action has been frowned on by international experts arguing that "competition policy should be to protect competition—not competitors."[58]

Another major source of discontent in developing countries is the excessive prices imposed by large pharmaceutical firms on essential medicines. Patent owners can usually prohibit to one country imports of its products that are sold abroad. Patent owners can fix different prices according to their interest, keeping higher prices, for example, in small markets or higher-income countries, whereas their prices could be lower in lower-income markets or larger markets where competition may be stronger. Usually, the patent holders, pharmaceutical firms, or other beneficiaries of intellectual-property rights such as patents or trademarks can invoke their property rights to foreclose the market from parallel imports. Parallel importers would purchase the goods where they are sold at lower prices to import them in the higher-priced country. The question that arises, then, is whether the importing country recognizes international or only national exhaustion of property rights. Most countries only accept national exhaustion of rights. In other words, if the goods have been purchased on the national market, the owner can sell them without any restriction; while if the goods are bought abroad and imported, the owner still cannot resell them without authorization from the patent (or trademark) owner.[59]

In developing countries, and in some developed countries, the question of limiting excessive prices when identical goods are sold at consistently lower prices can lead to the adoption of international exhaustion and authorization of parallel imports. The issue took a highly political turn in South Africa with respect to HIV medicines and other drugs that could be imported from generic-medicine-producing countries, such as India, at considerably lower prices, enabling the government's social security to save many more lives.[60] In the end, the antiretroviral-drug-producing laboratories agreed to offer substantial rebates before the South African Supreme Court's ruling, which might

---

58.   Gerald F. Masoudi, Deputy Assistant Att'y Gen., Antitrust Div., U.S. Dept. of Justice, Promoting Economic Development through Sound Competition Policy, Presentation at TAIWAN 2006 International Conference on Competition Policies/Laws (June 20, 2006), *available at* http://149.101.1.32/atr/public/speeches/217616.pdf.

59.   *The Concept of Exhaustion of Rights for Industrial Property*, IPR HELPDESK (IPR Helpdesk, Univ. Alicante, Alicante, Spain), *available at* http://www.ipr-helpdesk.org/documentos/docsPublicacion/pdf_xml/8_ES_ExhaustionIP%5B0000006554_00%5D.booklet.pdf.

60.   *See, e.g.,* John Donnelly, *Deal Paves Way for Generic HIV Drugs,* BOSTON GLOBE, Dec. 11, 2003, at A8.

have authorized parallel imports of essential medicines.[61] In the pharmaceutical sector, similar situations may also arise, especially in times of emergency. When faced with the prospect of saving lives, governments often agree to authorize parallel imports. This was the case recently in Thailand, where imports of low-cost generics were authorized.[62]

Another type of abuse, which is found in developed countries but affects poor countries most often, is the practice of pharmaceutical companies using repackaging or nonessential formula changes to extend their patents and to increase prices at the same time.[63]

Obviously, some of these developments are reflected in the waiver to the Trade-Related Aspects of Intellectual Property Rights (TRIPS) agreement of the World Trade Organization (WTO), decided on August 30, 2003. According to the WTO,

> That waiver made it easier for poorer countries to obtain cheaper generic versions of patented medicines by setting aside a provision of the TRIPS Agreement that could hinder exports of pharmaceuticals manufactured under compulsory licenses to countries that are unable to produce them.[64]

IV. MERGERS AND TAKEOVERS RESULTING IN CONCENTRATION OF MARKET POWER

Although not abuses of dominant power as such, mergers and acquisitions that may lead to the creation of monopolies or dominant firms are closely monitored in most countries having competition legislation because of the potential for abuse that such concentrations of market power carry with them. Some developing countries, however,

---

61.   *See, e.g.*, Desa Sri Hartamas, *Thailand to Import Plavix Generics from India*, THIRD WORLD NETWORK, http://www.twnside.org.sg/title2/intellectual_property/info.service/twn.ipr.info.080701.htm.

62.   *See, e.g.*, Nicholas Zamiska, *Thai Move to Trim Drug Costs Highlights Growing Patent Rift*, WALL ST. J., Jan. 30, 2007, at A8.

63.   *See, e.g.*, Press Release, Cong. Comm. on Oversight & Gov't Reform, Medical Drug Price Manipulation (Feb. 16, 2000), *available at* http://oversight.house.gov/story.asp?ID=573; Andrew Pollack, *New Drug, New Price, Old Results*, INT'L HERALD TRIB., June 30, 2006, at 15.

64.   Press Release, World Trade Org., Members OK Amendment to Make Health Flexibility Permanent (Dec. 6, 2005), *available at* http://www.wto.org/english/news_e/pres05_e/pr426_e.htm. On December 6, 2005, the WTO members decided to make permanent the waiver to the TRIPS Agreement on patents and public health for poorer countries originally adopted in 2003. *Id.* So far, however, the 2005 decision, which depends on a two-thirds ratification, has not been implemented, which means that the 2003 temporary waiver is still in force. *Id.*

have refrained from adopting merger-control provisions when adopting competition legislation. This is the case, for example, in Jamaica, which was followed by a series of developing countries that decided to adopt competition or antitrust legislation but stopped short of granting oversight agencies the powers to address anticompetitive mergers and takeovers. The alleged reasoning for this omission was often that small markets of developing countries necessitated large companies in order to perform economies of scale and that dominant firms might be necessary in order for national firms to compete with foreign giants.[65] This reasoning, however, does not take into account the need to counter practices by dominant foreign companies that are willing to acquire local firms in order to expand their control of the domestic market until they achieve a monopolistic position, or until they are in a position to abuse their power to the detriment of the domestic market.

Among the developing countries that have competition laws that include merger-control power, Zambia has been able to successfully monitor a foreign takeover in the telecommunications sector. On June 15, 2005, the Zambian Competition Commission (ZCC) received a formal notification from the MTN Group Limited of South Africa that it was purchasing 100 percent of the capital of Telcel Zambia Limited. The Board of Commissioners considered that the acquisition was more likely to bring procompetitive benefits to the Zambian mobile-telecommunications sector by increasing investment and employment and by upgrading technology. As a result, the Board granted final authorization for the takeover, subject to the following conditions: First, 10 percent of the capital of Telcel Zambia Limited must be blocked in a Special Purpose Vehicle (SPV) for Zambian public ownership, to be released to the public within fifteen to eighteen months, with the establishment of an effective mechanism to this effect by MTN. Second, "MTN shall, within six months after taking over, identify a senior management official to be a Trade Practices Compliance Officer . . . in constant touch with the [ZCC] as regards implementation of the undertakings and compliance with the Competition and Fair Trading Act . . . of Zambia."[66] By so doing, the Zambia Competition Commission ensured that the competitive process would be protected in the telecommunications sector, which is an essential infrastructure sector for the country's economic development.

---

65.   For a detailed account and assessment of related arguments, see Simon J. Evenett, *The Return of Industrial Policy—A Threat to Competition Law?*, in COMPETITION LAW TODAY: CONCEPTS, ISSUES, AND THE LAW IN PRACTICE (Vinod Dhall ed., 2007).

66.   U.N. CONF. ON TRADE & DEV., RECENT IMPORTANT CASES INVOLVING MORE THAN ONE COUNTRY 13 (2006), *available at* http://www.unctad.org/en/docs/tdrbpconf6d5rev1_en.pdf.

In a similar case in the petroleum sector, Malawi's Fair Trading Commission authorized a takeover in the petroleum sector of Mobil Malawi Limited by Total Malawi Limited. The mergers between the overseas parent companies, Total Outre-mer S.A. and Mobil Holdings (Europe and Africa), had already taken place, and the parties were seeking authorization for a similar merger of their subsidiaries in Malawi. The Malawi Fair Trading Commission, which is empowered by the Competition and Fair Trading Act to control concentrations, found that the combined final market share of the combined entities would be 32 percent. Before the merger, the petroleum market was considered to be highly concentrated, as the top three players in Malawi—Total, Mobil, and BP (39 percent)—controlled more than 70 percent of the relevant market, defined as the importation, supply, and distribution of petroleum products in Malawi. However, as there was no oil refinery in Malawi at the time (October 2005), all petroleum products were imported into the country, and neither the merged entity, Total-Mobil, nor the market leader, BP, had a market share that could be considered dominant. Moreover, market entry was free, as evidenced by the recent entry into the market of other operators, such as Niot, Injena, and Energem. Accordingly, the board of the Malawi Competition Commission authorized the merger on economic efficiency grounds, subject to certain conditions in accordance with section 39(2) of the Competition and Fair Trading Act of Malawi. Consequently, Malawi, which is a Least Developed Country, was able to monitor the effects on its territory of an international merger. This would have been impossible if the Competition Act did not exist or if it did not include powers to control mergers and takeovers.[67]

V. EXAMPLES OF SPECIFIC ENFORCEMENT CASES IN DEVELOPING COUNTRIES

This Part uses specific enforcement cases to describe the challenges faced and the requirements for successful prosecution of abuses of a dominant position in developing countries.

A. Relationships with Suppliers

Provisions of competition laws on abuses of dominance in developing countries often miss the point when, for the sake of legal certainty, they place too much or exclusive emphasis on market share as the only threshold to decide whether a company has a dominant position of market power. Moreover, in their application, competition

---

67.   *Id.* at 15–16.

laws give much discretion to the decisions of the competition authority. Accordingly, in cases where the law is unclear or where the authority is not sufficiently trained, results can miss the point or simply be anticompetitive. The examples described below are illustrative of possible divergences of views in this respect.

In a case in India going back to 1975, Bata Shoes was alleged to have abused its dominant position by imposing tied-purchasing practices in its contracts with small-scale manufacturers. The agreement, which was passed with small firms, mostly poor cobblers and leather workmen engaged in the manufacture of leather and rubber canvas, imposed that the small manufacturers purchase their raw material and components exclusively from suppliers specifically approved by Bata. In addition, the small manufacturers were required to use molds sold or supplied by Bata for manufacturing footwear.[68]

This agreement was challenged and prohibited by the Monopolies and Restrictive Trade Practices Commission (MRTPC) of India,[69] as the Commission observed that the small manufacturers were "by and large impecunious and survived on leather footwear manufacture for their livelihood" and that the restrictive conditions contravened the provisions of the MRTP Act.[70]

The other case relates to the National Competition Commission of Senegal, which received a complaint from the Union of Senegalese Travel and Tourism Agents, alleging that Air France had unilaterally decided to reduce the commission it offered travel agents from 9 percent, as was the case for more than a decade for agents selling international tickets for the twenty-one carriers serving Senegal, to 7 percent, explaining that it was "adapting its distribution costs to new global economic realities."[71]

In their letter of complaint dated May 29, 2001, the travel agents alleged that the practice in question was likely to infringe Senegal's rules on competition, in particular Article 27 of Act 94-63 of August 22, 1994, as "various companies were believed to have consulted each

---

68. CONSUMER UNITY AND TRUST SOCIETY, INSTITUTE FOR REGULATION AND COMPETITION, COMPETITION AND REGULATION IN INDIA 104–05 (Pradeep S. Mehta ed., 2007).

69. The old MRTP Commission has now been replaced by a new Competition Commission, and the MRTP Act has been replaced by the new Competition Act of 2007. *See* The Competition Bill, No. 70 (2007) (India).

70. CONSUMER UNITY AND TRUST SOCIETY, *supra* note 68, at 104–05.

71. ORG. FOR ECON. CO-OPERATION & DEV., GLOBAL FORUM ON COMPETITION: ABUSE OF DOMINANCE IN REGULATED SECTORS, UNION OF SENEGALESE TRAVEL AND TOURISM AGENTS VS. AIR FRANCE 2 (2005), *available at* http://www.oecd.org/dataoecd/49/57/34286241.pdf.

other before Air France cleared the way as the most powerful company in the market, . . . which was flights between Senegal and France."[72]

In response to the complaint, the Commission set up an inquiry and entered investigations, including hearings of the parties, and ruled as follows: "Air France occupied a dominant position in the relevant market, not only because Air Afrique was no longer in business, but for other, psychological and historical, reasons."[73] France was the main destination for traffic from Senegal, and Air France enjoyed strong demand on this segment, having increased its flights from six to seven days per week. Also, "[t]he travel agencies were in a state of economic dependence on Air France, which accounted for 50.72% of their combined turnover and for between 54.79% and 86.98% of the turnover of five of the ten agencies covered by the investigation."[74] In addition, the travel agencies had no equivalent alternative, and Air France was found to have abused the state of economic dependence of the travel agents by unilaterally imposing a rate that the agents "would not have accepted if they had enjoyed full independence."[75]

In this case, the issue of abuse of dominance was considered through the lenses of the economic-dependence theory,[76] which is found in the competition laws of some countries, including France. Under this theory, the law protects not only the interests of consumers but also, to a certain extent, the interests of dependent firms, such as distributors, where competition is absent or insufficient to allow distributors to switch to other companies without incurring irremediable damages.

B. Large Distribution Chains

The case of large supermarket chains, often multinational distribution chains abusing their dominant power to extract ever-lower prices from their domestic suppliers, including farmers and agricultural producers, has often been complained of in many parts of the world, developing and developed countries alike. While the prevailing consensus view in developed countries seems to be that competition laws seek to defend the interests of consumers and not to protect producers or competitors, complaints about such abuses, especially on impoverished farmers, are common in less developed countries. Complaints have emanated from Thailand, with the arrival of

---

72.   *Id.*
73.   *Id.* at 3.
74.   *Id.*
75.   *Id.*
76.   See Part 3 (Analysis of Jurisprudence), Chapter IV (La Notion de Dependence Économique) of FRENCH COMPETITION COUNCIL, ANNUAL REPORT (2001).

international distribution chains such as Carrefour of France and Wal-Mart of the United States; from Peru, where agricultural producers are demanding measures to defend their income; and, perhaps most surprisingly, from French President Nicolas Sarkozy on French television TF1 on November 28, 2007, where he expressed alarm in defense of French farmers who are losing ever more purchasing power as a result of increasing pressure from distributors. Prices at the supply end of the chain are ever more compressed, he said, while consumer prices, at the other end of the distribution chain, are increasing constantly.

It is important to note that this is a universal concern, which if stressed in industrialized countries such as France, is all the more damaging in developing countries, where agriculture counts for a much-higher proportion of GDP and employment and where the poor are mainly occupied in farming. A similar situation arose in Indonesia, where the competition authority, KPPU, dealt with a case in 2005 involving abuse of purchasing power by the French retailer Carrefour against wholesalers, producers, and suppliers.[77]

In another case involving Carrefour in Hong Kong, the French supermarket was allegedly blocked entry on the local market because the two dominant local retailers, which are owned by two large conglomerates that together control the real-estate market of the territory, refused to let Carrefour obtain prime locations for establishing its retail supermarkets.[78]

In Thailand, the cabinet is said to be considering a draft bill that would oblige foreign-owned retailers, such as Carrefour, Tesco, and others, to apply for prior authorization from the government before opening new outlets in the country.[79] In Indonesia, local-zoning laws and regulations of business hours are applied to limit entry and restrict the "undue" competition of retail chains in order to protect traditional local stores.[80]

---

77. Ningrum Sirait, Professor, Univ. N. Sumatra, Overview of Retail Business in Indonesia, Presentation at Third Asian Competition Law Conference at Hong Kong Polytechnic University (Dec. 10, 2007), *available at* http://64.233.167.104/search?q=cache:hkcTpXvVLHwJ:www.asiancompetitionforum. org/3rd%2520ACF%2520Conference%25202007/3rd%2520ACF%2520Conference%2 5202007%2520Schedule%2520(Website%2520Purpose).doc+Ningrum+Sirait+Indone sia+Retail+in+Indonesia&hl=en&ct=clnk&cd=1&gl=us&client=firefox-a (follow hyperlink).

78. Information received at the Third Competition Law Conference, H.K. Polytechnic Univ., Dec. 10–11, 2007.

79. *Thailand Approves "Stopgap" Limits on Retail Chain Expansion*, INT'L HERALD TRIB., May, 8, 2007.

80. *See* Sirait, *supra* note 77.

C. Computer Software Tie-in

In 2000, Microsoft was accused of tying its Windows Media Services (WMS) to its personal-computer operating system in Korea. Additionally, the company combined its Windows Microsoft Network (MSN) Messenger service with other services. The Korean Fair Trade Commission (KFTC) found that Microsoft's tie-in sales were an abuse of dominant position and had the effect of driving competitors out of business by restricting competition in the relevant market. On December 7, 2005, KFTC imposed a series of corrective measures on Microsoft, including the following: (1) a fine of 33 billion Won ($31 million); (2) an order to drop the tie-in of WMS within 180 days; and (3) an order to provide two different versions of the personal-computer operating system, allowing customers to download competing products. In addition, KFTC established a supervisory board to monitor implementation of the conditions set, at the expense of the company.[81] This is an important case of abuse of dominance by a foreign multinational because it was settled by a developing-country authority after similar cases were brought against the same company in developed countries including the United States and Europe.

CONCLUSION

This Paper examines the different forms and prevalence of abuse of dominant positions by commercial entities in developing countries, with an eye toward assessing the advice given to these jurisdictions concerning the priorities for their competition-law enforcement regimes. Both case-study evidence and statistics on the number of alleged anticompetitive practices were employed to advance the position that abuses of a dominant position ought not to be discounted as a priority for action by state bodies in developing countries. The available evidence pointed to important nuances as well. For example, tackling abuse of dominance is not merely a matter of targeting foreign multinationals as the state itself. State-owned firms or private firms with strong ties to—amounting in some cases to strong protection from—national policy makers are a significant source of abuse of dominance in developing countries. Mergers and acquisitions can also result in dominant positions that may be abused. A comprehensive view of the various forms and origins of abuse of dominance in poorer countries is recommended.

---

81.   U.N. CONF. ON TRADE AND DEV., RECENT IMPORTANT COMPETITION CASES INVOLVING MORE THAN ONE COUNTRY 5-6 (2007), *available at* http://www.unctad.org/en/docs/c2clpd62_en.pdf.

Abuses of dominant market power by single firms are a significant type of anticompetitive practice that affects both industrialized and developing countries alike. Cases brought by nascent competition authorities in developing countries increasingly concern abuses of dominance. This fact alone calls for a reexamination of the widely held view that competition law in poorer countries should have priorities of cartel enforcement actions and competition advocacy.

While there is no doubt that cartels, including international cartels, can have a damaging impact on the trade and well being of developing countries' trade, this does not imply that there is little or no harm done by abuses of dominance in developing countries. The description given earlier of the relevant characteristics of poor countries, showing their vulnerability to various types of abuses of dominance by public and private firms, sheds light on the ultimate sources of this policy problem. No doubt, future research and enforcement experience could enrich and potentially qualify the findings and inferences presented here.

Many developing economies are dominated by the state, acting directly as the owner of state monopolies or indirectly through the close links it entertains with national champions, which the state often seeks to promote. The dominance of the state can be at the expense of other domestic or foreign firms and can result in heavy-handed anticompetitive practices, damaging the very economy that it purports to nurture and safeguard.

As a result of their size, relative financial power, and access to foreign markets, multinational corporations are naturally prone to be dominant in many markets in smaller economies and could abuse their dominant position if not deterred effectively by a competition authority. However, such corporations are not the only relevant firms in this regard, as the actions of local monopolies and dominant firms can inflict considerable harm on their host societies too.

As to enforcement capacity, all too often the difficulty facing poor countries is that their officials are often ill equipped for the difficult task of tackling abuses of dominance. This task is much more challenging if the abuse comes from the state. But even when private firms have to be challenged, any lack of credibility and relevant expertise of the competition authority risks erroneous enforcement decisions and underenforcement. Similarly, lack of familiarity with abuse of dominance among judges can frustrate effective enforcement action.

In sum, given the various forms of abuse of dominance in developing countries and the experiences of state bodies in attempting to tackle such abuses, particular attention needs to be given to the following technocratic matters: the types of business practices deemed to be abuses in competition statutes, the inclusion of state-owned and privatized firms in the scope of application of the competition law, the resources (including expertise) and independence of the competition-law enforcement body, and the assistance and cooperation that can be provided by other competition authorities and relevant international agencies. Having said this, injecting the discipline of competition and limiting the exercise of market power into economies where vested interests have strong links to policy makers is unlikely to be easy in developing countries (and in industrialized countries for that matter). Like many other types of competition-law provisions, the effective enforcement of measures on abuses of a dominant position will redraw the boundaries within a jurisdiction between business, the state, and customers. Proponents of such measures ought to marshal a wide base of support within society and not solely focus on the important technocratic details that these measures entail.

[5]

CHILLING COMPETITION

David Lewis*

The anxiety that errors committed by antitrust enforcers may give rise to business decisions that forego pro competitive conduct for fear that it will be erroneously found to contravene antitrust rules ("chilling competition"), may arise as a result of merger regulation or through the prosecution of horizontal and vertical agreements and unilateral conduct or, as it is termed in the South African and many other statutes, abuse of dominance. However the prospect of chilling competition is most powerfully asserted and most strenuously cautioned against in the context of enforcement action against unilateral conduct. The proffered reason is that it is in the unilateral actions of dominant firms that the line between conduct that has procompetitive impact or anticompetitive impact is said to be most blurred.

Erroneous antitrust enforcement action that inadvertently discourages a dominant firm from pursuing vigorous procompetitive conduct may not only punish success — and so may even discourage a firm from striving for dominance — but, in discouraging procompetitive conduct, will negatively impact on welfare across a broad front, one that extends way beyond the markets implicated in the original sin, in the initial erroneous decision. These latter are the ex ante costs of erroneous enforcement — the costs imposed as a result of restraining the conduct of all dominant firms who may otherwise have engaged in the procompetitive conduct that has been erroneously impeached — as opposed to the ex post costs, the costs imposed on the firm whose actual conduct has been impeached in consequence of an erroneous enforcement decision.

The errors referred to here are of course Type 1 errors, false positives reflected as "over-enforcement" of the proscriptions that apply to unilateral conduct. Errors may also be of the Type 2 variety, false negatives, where anticompetitive conduct is erroneously permitted and is thus reflected as "under-enforcement" of the strictures against abusive unilateral conduct. These will also potentially incur both ex post and ex ante costs. However the prospect of Type 2 error receives little more than lip service in the literature.

---

* Chairperson, South African Competition Tribunal, Pretoria. I am indebted to Londiwe Xaba for her assistance in preparing this paper and to Simon Robert for his valuable comments.

A report commissioned by the Office of Fair Trading on the erroneous enforcement of Article 82 asserts that there is a "higher probability that some conducts normally investigated by competition authorities are competitive rather than abusive."[1] It appears that the basis for this claim is the rather anodyne observation that more vertical restraints investigated by antitrust authorities are likely to be procompetitive than anticompetitive, a conclusion which, in part, appears to be based on the low number of successful prosecutions of abuse of dominance.[2] We will argue that there are a range of more compelling reasons why there is a low rate of prosecution, let alone of proven contravention, of abuse of dominance.

On the other hand, it is widely held that to the extent that Type 1 error can be reduced to a single general source this is to be found in the alleged proclivity of antitrust enforcers and courts to apply legal rules rather than economic standards in their assessment of unilateral conduct. In other words, despite the well established influence of economic analysis in the assessment of unilateral conduct, the fact that the economics has ultimately to find expression in statutory rules and in judicial or quasi-judicial decisions, is, it appears, implicitly assumed to predispose the analytical and interpretative approach in favour of legal over economic disciplines and principles and is, for this reason, prone to Type 1 error. The adoption of legal rules as the decisionmaking basis relies upon the identification of pre-determined triggering facts, and, so it is argued, uniquely risks the prospect of the triggering facts being found to be present, when, in fact, the conduct may not be abusive. This too is thought to make enforcement based on legal rules more prone to "over-inclusiveness" or "over-enforcement," than when enforcement decisions are based on economic standards which are, per definition, not triggered by the breach of pre-determined rules, but whose economic effects are evaluated on a case-by-case basis.[3] So not only is the rate of prosecution likely to be low (because vertical restraints tend to be procompetitive) but, within the universe of those vertical restraints that are actually prosecuted, the rate of Type 1 error or false positives is likely to be high.

I am however going to argue that not only is the likelihood and consequence of Type 1 error in the enforcement of unilateral conduct vastly exaggerated but that the likelihood and consequence of Type 2 error are significantly understated. Indeed I will argue that, at least in South Africa and in a great many economies characterised by broadly similar historical and structural features, the likelihood of Type 2 error in the

---

[1] Office of Fair Trading, The Cost of Inappropriate Interventions/Non-Interventions Under Article 82 (A report prepared for the Office of Fair Trading by Lear, Economic Discussion Paper September 2006, OFT 864) para. 6.84.

[2] Id. at para. 6.46.

[3] Id. at para. 5.15ff.

enforcement of unilateral conduct rules is almost certainly greater than that of Type 1 error.

Surely any economic analysis worthy of the name must begin an assessment of the likelihood of the direction of error in antitrust enforcement with an attempt to specify the pertinent features of the actual economy in which the enforcement is carried out, rather than with the application of industrial organisation theories to abstracted generic conduct in abstracted generic economies. The strong tendency towards a "black box" treatment of the broader economic context within which antitrust is enforced precisely privileges form over content, or, more accurately, privileges the application of general theoretical propositions to a widely divergent and pertinent range of concrete circumstances whose actual general features can in fact be easily ascertained. It's my strongly held view that much of the microeconomic theory that dominates thinking about firm conduct and its consequences has tunnelled so deep into the entrails of the conduct that it has lost sight of the features of the actual economies in which the rules are being applied, economies of vastly differing sizes, structures and histories. This is particularly pertinent in the analysis of errors in application, that is to say in the application of theories where it is explicitly acknowledged — for why, after all, the concern with likely error — that actual outcomes may go either way. My contention is that the likelihood, direction and cost of the error — and so the approach towards enforcement — will be significantly influenced by history and structure of the economy in which unilateral conduct rules are being enforced.[4]

Take South Africa for example. A wide range of key markets are highly concentrated with single firm dominance in the 60%-plus market share range not uncommon.[5] This is particularly true of markets in key intermediate industrial products and services such as steel, basic chemical feedstocks, various forms of transport, energy and telecommunications characterised by high entry barriers and a history of state ownership. And it is also true of significant consumer goods markets — beer, cigarettes, detergents, magazine publishing and glass to list but a few important random examples that have recently come to the attention of South African antitrust enforcers.

Moreover many of these dominant positions clearly do not originate in the superior competitiveness of the products and services of the firms in

---

[4] A similar point has been made with reference to differences in unilateral conduct enforcement between the U.S. and Europe: "arguably there should be transatlantic differences in policies towards abuse of dominance. The European economy has historically been more monopolized than that of the U.S., and its competitive self-righting mechanisms may be more robust." J. Vickers, Competition Law and Economics: a Mid-Atlantic Viewpoint, 3 Eur. Competition J.

[5] See also L. Nncube – What Are the Implications of the 'Post-Chicago' Synthesis For Competition Policy in South Africa? Competition Commission of South Africa Research Brief (March 2003).

question. Historically poor antitrust enforcement, protectionism, geographic isolation, state ownership and privatisation combined with weak regulatory structures are major contributors to single firm dominance in key markets. Hence, and merely by way of several pertinent examples, the structure of the country's beer and wine and spirits markets have their origins in a public market allocation agreement which, though contested by an earlier, and significantly weaker, incarnation of the contemporary antitrust agencies, was nevertheless approved on blatantly political grounds by the then government. Autarkic industrial policies characterised by high levels of tariff and other forms of protection in the post-World War II period, subsequently bolstered by the isolating effect of economic sanctions, have contributed to high levels of concentration in many markets for both key intermediate products and consumers goods. Key markets are dominated by firms that were privatised or partially privatised into unregulated or weakly regulated markets. Steel, basic chemical feedstocks and fixed line telephony exemplify these markets. Defective licensing regimes coupled with weak regulation account for dominated markets in, inter alia, mobile telephony, commercial radio and pay television. Markets in important segments of transport, energy, broadcasting and telecommunications are still dominated by state controlled enterprises many of which persistently attempt to leverage the dominance achieved through license into related, unlicensed markets.[6]

Under these actual economic circumstances, those charged with promoting competition in South Africa should be forgiven for fearing the direct consequences of abusive conduct by dominant firms and the chilling effect that this will have on potential new entry rather more than the possible competition chilling consequences of restricting, albeit occasionally erroneously, the freedom of action of these dominant firms. And if this assessment is applicable to the South African economy, how much more does it apply to a transition economy in which in the recent past every market had been subjected to dominant SOEs and in which, to this day, dominance cannot remotely be ascribed to procompetitive conduct? And I suspect that the chickens will come home to roost for the developed economies when Chinese and Indian competition law enforcers start soft-pedalling enforcement of the abuse of dominance provisions in their laws, all no doubt in the name of extending to their dominant domestic firms the right to compete vigorously. The first to feel the shoe pinching will be very large north American and European firms who will struggle to penetrate the vast and growing domestic Chinese and Indian markets and will wish to invoke abuse of dominance allegations against alleged exclusionary conduct by dominant Chinese and Indian firms just as Phillip Morris and JTI, with their powerful Marlboro and Camel brands, have sought to invoke them in our dominated domestic cigarette market.

---

[6] Telkom SA & Business Connexion Group Ltd, Case No: 51/LM (June 2006).

So we begin in our country with a historical and structural predisposition — fully justified I would contend — that apprehends the likelihood of abuse of dominance. And we then move to our statute, in which both the definition of dominance itself, as well as the identification of potentially abusive conduct, is articulated in the form of elaborate rules.

To start with the definition of dominance, a firm found to have a market share of 45% or greater is irrebuttably presumed dominant. At market shares of 35% or more but less than 45% a firm will be dominant unless it can show that it does not possess market power. And below 35% a finding of dominance requires a showing from the Competition Commission or the private complainant that the firm has market power.

Potentially abusive conducts are described in some detail in the statute. Two of these practices are subject to a form of per se prohibition at least to the extent that the statute does not provide for a procompetitive defence once the elements of the conducts have been established. These are excessive pricing and denial of access to an essential facility. Then there is a general prohibition of an "exclusionary act" in respect of which the complainant, in addition to proving the conduct, is required to establish the absence of countervailing procompetitive gains. And then several conducts are described including a refusal to deal, tying and bundling and predatory pricing, in which the complainant has the onus of establishing the conduct while the onus of establishing the existence of procompetitive gains shifts to the respondent. Price discrimination practiced by a dominant firm is also, under very highly specified circumstances, proscribed.

So our economic circumstances predispose towards vigorous attention directed at the prospect of abuse of dominance and our statute, at least according to the wisdom received from those who live in fear of "false positives," appears to make proof of dominance as well as proof of abusive conduct a simple matter of establishing a breach of pre-determined rules. If the literature on unilateral conduct enforcement is to be believed, one would, under these circumstances, expect significant over-enforcement, particularly from an authority that has developed a reputation for robust enforcement of the merger provisions of the Act and, more recently, for aggressive pursuit of cartels.

In fact it is manifestly clear that over-enforcement of unilateral conduct has *not* occurred. The Tribunal has, in the nine years of its existence, decided five abuse of dominance cases.[7] One case was brought

---

[7] In the early days of the Tribunal's existence several more abuse of dominance cases were decided in applications for interim relief that were not taken through to the trial stage. The reasons why these cases were not pursued further is varied and, while these definitely include a change in the offending practice – and so the possibility of erroneous chilling or effective deterrence - in other cases they unquestionably revealed to the plaintiffs just how difficult it was from both a substantive perspective and from the perspective of the prosecutorial resources required, to pursue an abuse of dominance complaint.

against the dominant producer of steel which was previously state owned and is now part of the Arcelor Mittal group;[8] another was brought against the dominant producer of chemical feedstocks (and also previously state owned);[9] a third case involved a large international print media group;[10] a fourth case involved the bottler of a multinational carbonated soft drink bottler;[11] and the fifth case involved the dominant passenger air travel carrier which is still owned by the state.[12] Of these only one was actually brought by the Commission while the others were brought by private parties after the Commission declined to prosecute. Three of the five adjudicated complaints were upheld by the Tribunal and two were dismissed. Two of the Tribunal's affirmative findings of abuse were appealed. One of these appeals was upheld by the Appeal Court, while the appeal on the second is pending. Needless to say even if we had erred in every one of our affirmative findings — and that is certainly not the case — the direct or ex post cost of these errors would be trivial.

We have no evidence regarding the ex ante consequence of this enforcement — in fact despite the confident assertions of those antitrust practitioners who apprehend likely Type 1 error, and fear, in particular, their ex ante costs, I have yet to see actual evidence of unilateral firm conduct being restrained for fear of erroneous prosecution. Although, as elaborated below in our discussion of deterrence, I would like to believe that the high profile nature of our affirmative findings in the pricing and discounting practices that have come before us has indeed generated some degree of internal appraisal of the conduct of dominant firms engaged in practices similar to those that were impeached and more attention to our abuse of dominance provisions in general, I have no evidence to support this.

Why, in what appears to be an intensely rule-focused unilateral conduct enforcement regime, and contrary to the predictions of some economic theory, has over-enforcement clearly not occurred?

The simple answer is that abuse of dominance allegations are extremely difficult and resource consuming to investigate and to prosecute. First, a complainant in a unilateral conduct matter is, per definition, inevitably up against an extremely well resourced opponent — a dominant firm. Inevitably what is at issue is a widespread and long standing practice across a large group of companies and so will be vigorously defended. There is little imperative to settle — not all of the first-time unilateral conduct offences even carry the prospect of a fine and so it is highly likely that after a massive trial involving years of litigation

---

[8] Harmony Gold Mining Limited Durban Roodepoort Deep Ltd. & Mittal Steel SA Ltd. Macsteel Int'l Holdings BV, CT Case No.: 13/CR (Feb. 2004).

[9] Nationwide Poles v Sasol (Oil) Pty Ltd., CT Case No.: 72/CR (Dec. 2003).

[10] Mandla-Matla Publ'g (Pty) Ltd. v Indep. Newspapers (Pty) Ltd., CT Case No.: 48/CR (June 2004).

[11] Mapula Restaurant v Coca-Cola Fortune (Pty) Ltd., CT Case No.: 91/CR (Aug. 2007).

[12] Competition Comm'n v S. Afr. Airways (Pty) Ltd., CT Case No.: 18/CR (Mar. 2001).

all that may be imposed on the guilty party is a behavioural direction.[13] Private damages claims are not easy to make — in fact in only one of our abuse of dominance cases has the complainant proceeded to the high court on the basis of our finding and instituted a claim for damages. We do not have standing for class action suits to recover damages. Accordingly prudent advice to the Commission or, more especially, to a prospective private plaintiff in an abuse of dominance suit, would counsel a long, hard look at the consequences of proceeding even with a prosecution that is prima facie strong. It will tie up huge resources merely in dealing with the range of interlocutory and invasive discovery applications that inevitably precede a trial. And then the trial itself will, of necessity, presuppose the retention of expensive counsel and economic experts. Note that our statute only gives a private plaintiff the right to proceed once the Commission has elected not to proceed and if unsuccessful an adverse costs order almost inevitably follows. And then, even if successful, the retribution is limited particularly in the form of recompense to the direct victims.

In short then, whatever high economic theory suggests about the likelihood of over-enforcement in a rule-based enforcement regime, the more prosaic incentives to proceed against a firm for abuse of dominance all suggest the likelihood that these conducts will be under-enforced. It is conceivable that a unilateral conduct enforcement regime, even one putatively based on economic standards rather than legal rules, in which potential retribution and recompense incentivises private abuse of dominance actions may have greater reason to apprehend the prospect of frivolous, adventurous unilateral conduct litigation. In fact given the frequency with which the spectre of frivolous litigation is invoked by the U.S. courts as the basis for the a priori scepticism directed at unilateral conduct cases, it is clear that the incentive given to private complainants by the prospect of treble private damages plays a significant role in explaining the excessive caution of U.S. courts in relation to claims of monopolisation.[14] However this is not a problem that we, or, to my

---

[13] Note that in *South African Airways* the complaint was initially filed with the Commission in October 2000 and the (affirmative) decision of the Tribunal was finally handed down by the Tribunal in July 2005, slightly under five years later. In *Arcelor-Mittal* the complaint was filed with the Commission in September 2002 and the Tribunal's affirmative decision was handed down in March 2007. The appeal before the Competition Appeal Court in the latter case will be heard later this year and, should the CAC uphold the Tribunal's appeal, there is the further possibility of appeal to the Supreme Court of Appeal. These extraordinary time frames appear to be mirrored in many other jurisdictions and reflect the complexity of these cases and the endless opportunity for extensive pre-trial litigation rather than the tardiness of the competition authorities. They certainly suggest that complainants who elect to prosecute unilateral conduct cases require high levels of commitment and extremely deep pockets.

[14] Note Competition and Monopoly: Single-Firm Conduct Under Section 2 of the Sherman Act (U.S. Dep't of Justice, September 2008), at page 15: "The Court's concern about overly inclusive or unclear legal standards may well be driven in significant part

knowledge, any other jurisdiction, faces. Clearly the first-best solution is to reduce the incentives for vexatious competitor-driven litigation rather than to adopt an approach that would effectively treat most unilateral conduct as per se legal or, at best, as potentially frivolous or vexatious.

Secondly, the substantive hurdles that have to be cleared in proving abuse of dominance are formidable. Hence the provision in our legislation of an irrebuttable presumption of dominance based upon market share has occasioned much hand-wringing in antitrust circles. The impression that critics of this provision create is that dominance is established on the basis of a cursory arithmetic exercise. Of course nothing could be further from the truth. It is rather rooted in a rigorous identification of the relevant market a requirement which, as the DOJ report on single firm conduct acknowledges,

> ...brings discipline and structure to the monopoly-power enquiry, thereby reducing the risks and costs of error.[15]

Market definition would include an analysis of supply-side substitution which has the potential to greatly influence our definition of the boundaries of the relevant market and hence the finding of dominance within that market. We would also require evidence of the durability of the market share — we would never make a finding of dominance on the market share of a single year particularly if that share was at or close to the 45% threshold. I should add that even though our test of dominance is satisfied by proof of a market share of 45% or higher we have generally, in order to bolster our conclusions, gone beyond our legal requirement and shown evidence of the existence of market power. Note too that the lowest market share on which we have actually found an <u>abuse</u> of dominance is 56% - the abuse of dominance cases that have actually come before the Tribunal for final adjudication involved market shares of 56%, 57%, 66% and 81%. In fact I can't recall many allegations of abuse that are filed when

---

by the particularly strong chilling effects created by the specter of treble damages and class-action cases." See also Chairman W. Kovacic, Fed. Trade Comm'n, Modern U.S. Competition Law and the Treatment of Dominant Firms: Comments on the Department of Justice and Federal Trade Commission Proceedings Relating to Section 2 of the Sherman Act, at page 4 "Judicial Concerns about over-deterrence also appear to stem from perceptions that the existing system of private rights of action is unduly expansive. Fears about unduly expansive private enforcement are driving doctrine in an increasingly non-intervention minded direction that encumbers public agencies as well. In their efforts to correct what they believe to be overreaching by private litigants, courts are embracing liability standards that inevitably curb public enforcement bodies" and further, at page 8: "If, as I believe, judicial perceptions of overreaching by private suits are narrowing the zone of substantive liability, public agencies may eventually be unable to do their job. This consideration points to the need for a deeper empirical examination of how the operation of private rights actually affects business decision making and how public agencies can prosecute cases without carrying burdens that courts have imposed on private litigations to cure perceived deficiencies in the system of private rights."

[15] Competition and Monopoly, at p. 25.

dominance is at or even near the threshold 45%. What our Act achieves is to explicitly put in place a somewhat lower hurdle for proving dominance than that involved in proving a significantly more elusive and less settled concept like market power. Market power, I should add, can rarely be proved by direct evidence but involves the use of proxies and indicia and much inferential reasoning. Our Act simply cuts to the chase and provides for proof of dominance on the basis of the most commonly used proxy or index for market power, namely, market share.

And then, of course, proof of dominance has no direct bearing on the question of whether or not an <u>abuse</u> of that dominance has occurred. For that much more is required. As already noted, our Act describes in terms that are fairly elaborate the conduct that <u>may</u> qualify as an abuse. However, in respect of most of the described conduct the elements that are required to be proved require crossing some significant hurdles by way of the economic evidence that is explicitly demanded. Indeed our statute effectively imports economic standards into an assessment of its stated rules, the contravention of which may trigger a finding of abuse. Hence in respect of the two contraventions which do not permit an efficiency defence, the charging of an excessive price and denial of access to an essential facility, the elements that have to be proved in order for a price to be defined as excessive or for a facility to be deemed essential are formidable.[16] As noted, in respect of the other abusive conducts described in the statute an efficiency defence is expressly provided for. Hence, as already noted, for the general category of exclusionary acts to constitute an abuse the complainant has to establish that "the anticompetitive effect of that act outweighs its technological, efficiency or other procompetitive gains," a clear economic effects based approach.[17] In respect of the named abuses — predatory pricing, tying and bundling, refusal to supply, etc – the respondent is invited to present an effects-based defence by establishing that the procompetitive gains outweigh the anticompetitive effects that are proved to arise from the conduct described.[18] Moreover, the necessity to prove economic effects has been strongly emphasised in the Tribunal's jurisprudence on unilateral conduct. The Tribunal's approach to a decisionmaking process that requires both the application of legal rules and economic standards in exclusionary unilateral conduct cases is summarised in *South African Airways:*

> In summary, we find that the Act sets out the following approach to exclusionary standards. In the first place we

---

[16] Section 1(ix) defines an "excessive price" as "a price for a good or service which (a) bears no reasonable relation to the economic value of that good or service, and (b) is higher than the value referred to in paragraph (a)." Section 1(viii) defines an "essential facility" as "an infrastructure or resource that cannot reasonably be duplicated, and without access to which competitors cannot reasonably provide goods or services to its customers."

[17] Section 8(c).

[18] Section 8(d).

examine whether the conduct in question is exclusionary in nature. In terms of Section 8(c) that would be conduct that fits the definition of the Act for what constitutes an <u>exclusionary</u> act. In terms of 8(d) it is conduct that meets the definition set out in the sub-paragraphs of that section. If the conduct meets the requirement of the definition, we then enquire whether the <u>exclusionary act</u> has an anticompetitive effect. The question will be answered in the affirmative if there is (i) evidence of actual harm to consumer welfare or (ii) if the exclusionary act is substantial or significant in terms of its effect in foreclosing the market to rivals. This latter conclusion is partly factual and partly based on reasonable inferences drawn from proven facts. If the answer to that question is yes, we conclude that the conduct will have an anticompetitive effect. Whichever species of anticompetitive effect we have, consumer welfare or likely foreclosure, we have evidence of a quantitative nature and hence we can return to the scales with a concept capable of being measured against the alleged efficiency gain.[19]

There is thus no robotic or mechanistic "box-ticking" approach to the application of the rules and standards that have to be proved in order to sustain an allegation of abuse of dominance. Instead experienced antitrust enforcers and adjudicators, bolstered by access to many years of scholarly reflection and international jurisprudence (which Section 1(3) of the Act specifically directs us to consider), are required to exercise their judgement in investigating and deciding a case brought before them. Indeed it would seem that the open-ended and vague wording of the Sherman Act is more likely to lend itself to the vicissitudes and caprices of intellectual fashion — and so potentially to alternating bouts of over- and under-enforcement — than is an Act such as the South African Competition Act relatively elaborately crafted on the basis of long-standing international experience.

So, in summary, the investigation and prosecution of abuse of dominance is a resource consuming exercise, with limited prospect of success and remedies that are not particularly dis-incentivising. Moreover, the substantive hurdles that have to be cleared in the form of onerous legal and economic tests are formidable. And so, as might be expected, under-enforcement, or Type 2 error, is the likely upshot even in an economy whose history and structure suggests the strong likelihood of anticompetitive unilateral conduct and whose enforcement agencies are strongly committed to enforcing the rules proscribing this type of conduct.

Given then the caveats, the economic standards, with which our Act and our jurisprudence qualify our rule-based approach, why not merely opt for a pure economics standard? Why not replace our elaborate rules

---

[19] *S. Afr. Airways,* at para. 132.

that describe dominance and abusive conducts with a pure economic standard that simply provides that firms possessed of market power are prohibited from engaging in conduct likely to cause harm to competition. This would seem to best capture an abuse of dominance proscription that would find favour with those intent upon reducing the prospective chill on competition arising from over-enforcement of unilateral conduct.

Note that our view is not simply that over-enforcement is unlikely to occur, but that everything points to under-enforcement occurring. Under these circumstances it appears that the correct approach to take is one that provides the prospect of an antidote to the likelihood of Type 2 error. The approach adopted by our law — an approach that essentially interfaces legal rules and economic standards — provides, I would contend, for greater deterrence, certainty and administrability than an approach based on economic standards alone.

First, regarding deterrence, it should be acknowledged that antitrust enforcement is law enforcement and, in common with other law enforcement activity must, for the most part, rely upon deterrence rather than prosecution. We use market share as a proxy for market power and while, given the uncertainties that often surround the precise location of the boundaries of a relevant market, precise market shares cannot always be known in advance; a firm whose market share significantly exceeds a chosen proxy — in our case 45% — will generally know that it is likely to be found to be dominant. As for the potentially abusive conducts described in our law, these represent the most frequently identified and prosecuted abusive conducts. What is then achieved is to signal to a firm that is likely to be found to be dominant that, before engaging in the well known forms of potentially abusive conduct enumerated in our statute, it should take a view based on well established jurisprudence and much scholarly writing of the likelihood that its conduct will actually be found to be abusive. If it is so advised it will either refrain from such conduct or undertake it fully cognisant of the risk, which we would describe as low, that it will be successfully prosecuted for abuse of dominance.[20] As already

---

[20] I have not found data on the success rate of abuse of dominance prosecutions. However note the following comment on the U.S. DOJ's success rate in securing convictions in criminal antitrust trials:

> The antitrust arena is a notable exception to the government's dominance in criminal trials, with conviction rates in criminal antitrust trials consistently falling well short of overall success rates. Since 1996 not even half of all criminal antitrust defendants who have gone to trial have been convicted. Although the sample set from a statistical point of view is relatively small, the numbers over the years do provide an undeniable trend – despite dedicated and skillful prosecution by DOJ lawyers, defendants in criminal antitrust cases fare far better at trial than other criminal defendants.

F. Warin, D. Burns &J.F. Chesley, To Plead or Not to Plead? Reviewing a Decade of Criminal Antitrust Trials, The Antitrust Source (July 2006), available at www.antitrustsource.com.

noted, we have no evidence on the extent to which there is effective deterrence, however the prospect of deterrence is clearly promoted by the use of clear rules and standards.

The need to provide <u>certainty</u> traverses similar issues. While it is widely accepted that abusive conduct should always be analysed by a rule of reason standard and judged on the factual matrix applicable to each case, this does not reduce the analysis of abusive conduct to some sort of post-modernist relativism where no outcomes can possibly be known, with a reasonable degree of certainty, in advance. Resort to pure economic reasoning provides little by way of certainty and so cannot effectively guide the actions of firms. This observation is not intended to imply that uncertainty can ever be comprehensively eliminated from fact-based antitrust analysis. However lawyers advise clients who take important decisions on the basis of this advice. In these circumstances it would not be at all surprising if both lawyer and client were willing to accept the possibility of a degree of error as a result of the application of well-established rules as a trade-off for the certainty that the latter brings to the business of providing legal advice and guiding business decisions.

Thirdly, there is the question of <u>administration</u>. Antitrust enforcement does not have the luxury of indulging perpetually in the inconclusive analysis that is found in much of the scholarly work on abusive conduct and reproduced in the evidence of economic "experts" — who are, in reality, better described as economic advocates — testifying in antitrust trials. Anyone who has adjudicated an antitrust trial alleging anticompetitive unilateral conduct or even an anticompetitive merger will testify to the extraordinary range of theories presented by expert economic witnesses, and, worse, to the extraordinary range of outcomes predicted on the basis of broadly similar theoretical positions advanced by these experts. We are not here dealing with the relative certainties of physical science, but with the uncertain predictions of social science. Moreover antitrust enforcers are obliged to arrive at decisions based upon statutory language and reflected in the decisions of courts of law. If antitrust laws are to be successfully administered while taking account of economic standards, administrable proxies have to be sought for these economic standards. Most antitrust literature that has enforcement in mind has to have recourse to proxies. This includes the use of market shares as proxies for market power.

The authoritative Antitrust Law Developments published by the American Bar Association clearly establishes that market shares have been used as proxies for monopoly or market power in the U.S. since at least *Alcoa*.[21] The Antitrust Law Developments state categorically that

---

[21] See Antitrust Law Developments (Fifth), A.B.A (2002), at p. 234ff.

courts generally regard the alleged monopolist's market share as the most important factor in determining the existence of monopoly power.[22]

This approach is affirmed in the recent DOJ report on unilateral conduct, which, though admittedly hedged, certainly indicates that the enforcement agency too makes use of presumptions when determining monopoly power:

> Where courts have found monopoly power — as opposed to market power — the defendant's market share has been at least 50% and typically substantially higher.

> When a firm has maintained a market share in excess of two-thirds for a significant period and the Department concludes that market conditions likely would prevent the erosion of its market position in the near future, the Department will presume that the firm possesses monopoly power absent convincing evidence to the contrary.[23]

This is followed by reference to literally dozens of U.S. court decisions that clearly affirm that market share is, to this very day, widely and explicitly used as a proxy for monopoly power. The disparate variety of positions taken by U.S. courts regarding market share and monopoly power is also outlined in the DOJ report.[24]

A trawl through EU guidelines and jurisprudence reveals a strikingly elaborate use of market share as a proxy for market power.[25] The European

---

[22] Id. at p. 234.

[23] Competition and Monopoly, at p. viii. See also in the main body of the report, at pp. 23, 30.

[24] Id. at pp. 21-22.

[25] From a variety of EC guidelines and court decisions I have been able to glean the following:

90% is usually conclusive of dominance as stated in the *Hoffman-La Roche* case. However in the EC merger case of *Tetra Pak v Alfa-Laval* 90% did not confer dominance;

— 75% is indicative of dominance (cf *Hoffman-La Roche* case);

— 50% strong evidence of dominance, where held for three years except in exceptional circumstances (*Akzo v Commission*; <u>NB</u> other factors were also taken into account);

— 40% or more indicate that there is evidence of dominance which has to be considered with other factors

— 25-40% show that single dominance is unlikely unless a fragmented market and significant other factors;

— 20% the possibility of dominance is left open.

— To be considered in the context of other factors. The relative size is also considered. Where a firm with a 45 % market share is in a market with the shares of the three firms operating in the market in a 45:35:20 ratio, the largest

Court has explicitly endorsed the use of markets shares as a proxy for determining dominance:

With regard to market shares the Court has held that very large shares are in themselves, and save in exceptional circumstances, evidence of the existence of a dominant position (judgment in Hoffman-La Roche v Comm'n, Case 85/76, 1979 ECR 461 , at para. 41). That is the situation where there is a market share of 50% such as that found to exist in this case.[26]

Indeed U.S. and EU jurisprudence reveal not only the importance of proxy rules based upon market share in the determination of market power, they also demonstrate that when the precise proxy is left unspecified and, particularly, when it is formally unacknowledged and even eschewed by influential scholars and even enforcers, then the range of decisionmakers, commonly burdened with the task of administering a legal instrument, will be obliged to select a proxy themselves, in the process undermining certainty that could be easily established by means of a simple stated rule judiciously applied.[27]

Effective administration also dictates that familiar proxies be employed in identifying abusive conduct. Hence the OFT-commissioned report already cited is predicated on the by-now familiar argument that economic standards rather than legal rules constitute the analytically correct basis for describing and analysing alleged abuses of dominance. And so the report commences with debunking the old rule-based categories — exclusive dealing, tying and bundling, refusal to supply, predatory pricing, price discrimination, etc — in favour of a new effects-based taxonomy designated "output conducts" and "structural conducts"

---

firm would probably not be considered to be dominant whereas if the ration was 45:15:10 it would probably be considered dominant.

[26] Akzo Chemie BV v Commission of the European Communities – Judgement of the Court (5th Chamber) of 3 July 1991- Case C-62/86

[27] What the actual U.S. and EU practice also reveals is that the recently adopted International Competition Network's (ICN's) "recommended practice" on market power which strongly qualifies the use of market share proxies in the determination of market power is substantially at odds with actual practice in the two leading antitrust jurisdictions and would erect substantially greater barriers to enforcement actions against unilateral conduct. See ICN Unilateral Conduct Working Group, Dominance/Substantial Market Power Analysis Pursuant to Unilateral Conduct Laws, ICN Recommended practice. Available at, www.inc-kyoto.org/documents/index.html. In their response to the DOJ report three members of the Federal Trade Commission describe the report as "a blue print for radically weakened enforcement of Section 2 of the Sherman Act." (Statement of Commissioners Harbour, Leibowitz and Rosch on the issuance of the Section 2 report of the Department of Justice, at p. 1). To emphasize, if not belabor, my point: the recent DOJ report is considered by no less than three members of the FTC to be a higher hurdle for Section 2 prosecutor than established U.S .enforcement practice and jurisprudence while the standards recommended by the ICN are at least as onerous as those set out in the DOJ report and possibly more so. The conclusion then must be that the ICN recommended practice prescribe a more onerous regime for unilateral conduct enforcement than that reflected in current U.S. practice.

with the latter further categorised as "raising rivals costs" and "lowering rivals demand." But no sooner has this new taxonomy been formulated then it is immediately re-cast in the familiar old language of legal rules. So "raising rivals cost" conducts are re-cast in strikingly familiar terms as, inter alia, "margin squeeze from above non linear pricing," "refusal to supply" and "exclusive contracts" while "lowering rivals demand" is described as, inter alia, "fidelity rebates" and "tying and bundling." Output conducts for their part are characterised as "predatory pricing" and "price discrimination." The effects-based taxonomy proposed by the authors will doubtlessly assist in a rigorous identification of the economic consequences of selected conduct but, equally, in order to effectively administer an antitrust statute, proxies drawn from enforcement experience and established jurisprudence have still to be relied upon even by the proponents of an economic standards-based approach.

The dissenting judgement of Justice Breyer in *Leegin* provides an instructive outline of the role and importance of proxies in the administration of antitrust rules. Here the Court is examining the administrative importance of using proxies in deciding whether a specific form of conduct should be judged by per se rules as opposed to rule of reason; however the judge's reasoning is apposite, possibly more apposite, to the issue under discussion here. Justice Breyer argues:

> The upshot is as many economists suggest, sometimes resale price maintenance can prove harmful; sometimes it can bring benefits. But before concluding that courts should consequently apply a rule of reason, I would ask such questions as, how often are harms or benefits likely to occur? How easy is it to separate the beneficial sheep from antitrust goats?

> Economic studies such as the studies the Court relies upon, can help provide answers to these questions, and in doing so, economics can and should, inform antitrust law. But antitrust law cannot, and should not, precisely replicate economists' (sometimes conflicting) views. That is because the law, unlike economics, is an administrative system the effects of which depend upon the content of rules and precedents only as they are applied by judges and juries in courts and by lawyers advising their clients. And that fact means that courts will sometimes bring their own administrative judgements to bear, sometimes applying rules of per se unlawfulness to business practices even when those practices sometimes produce benefits.[28]

---

[28] Leegin Creative Prods., Inc. v. PSKS Inc., 551 U.S._, 7-8 (2007).

And further, Justice Breyer identifies the prospect of error implicit in the absence of reasonably clear rules:

> Are there special advantages to a bright-line rule? Without such a rule, it is often unfair, and consequently impractical, for enforcement officials to bring criminal proceedings. And since enforcement resources are limited, that loss may tempt some producers or dealers to enter into agreements that are, on balance, anticompetitive.[29]

Expressed otherwise, Justice Breyer is cautioning against the prospect of ex ante costs that derive from Type 2 errors that in turn result from the absence of clearly formulated rules.

Nor, by any means, is it only those who are concerned with Type 2 error who rely on proxy rules. It seems that even those who are exclusively concerned with Type 1 error rely on proxies despite their assertion of the superiority of economic reasoning over legal rules. Note the oft-cited passage from Justice Scalia's judgement in *Trinko:*

> The mere possession of monopoly power, and the concomitant charging of monopoly prices, is not only not unlawful; it is an important element of the free-market system. The opportunity to charge monopoly prices — at least for a short period — is what attracts "business acumen" in the first place; it induces risk taking that produces innovation and economic growth. To safeguard the incentive to innovate, the possession of monopoly power will not be found unlawful unless it is accompanied by an element of anticompetitive conduct.[30]

Certainly South African practice would support Justice Scalia to the extent that the "mere possession of monopoly power (is) not unlawful." But to ascribe "risk taking, innovation and economic growth" to the

---

[29] Id. at 11. Note that the assumed superiority – from a competition perspective – of inter-brand competition over intra-brand and the willingness to sacrifice less of the latter for more of the former, is one bright line accepted without question by the majority in *Leegin*. While this economic standard – that has achieved the status of a rule - may indeed be well-established and useful for the effective administration of competition law, it may also be a somewhat outdated "rule" of economics in a contemporary world where the distribution of goods and services is ubiquitously separated from their production and is an important arena of competition in its own right. In these circumstances should one not take care when adopting too easily the mantra that holds that inter-brand competition is more important than intra-brand competition? Certainly the manner in which this view of the relative importance of the two forms of competition is accepted is a clear example of the adoption of competition rules and proxies even by those who decry the application of bright line rules in antitrust analysis.

[30] Verizon Commc'ns Inc. v Law Offices of Curtis V. Trinko. LLP, 124 S. Ct. 872 (2004).

possession of monopoly power seems little distant from asserting that the freedom of a dominant firm to conduct itself unfettered is, in Justice Scalia's view at any rate, a proxy for consumer welfare![31] And this despite the powerful evidence accumulated over decades of antitrust enforcement that dominance lends itself not merely to the charging of monopoly prices, but enables conduct (the general features of which are well documented in scholarly literature and jurisprudence) the effect of which is precisely to exclude those who, despite Justice Scalia's bold assertions, would wish to enter a market whose structure has enabled the dominant incumbent to extract monopoly rents.[32]

A final word on innovation: those most concerned with Type 1 error commonly assert that the ex ante costs are likely to be most severe in dynamic economies "where firms achieve a dominant position mainly through the adoption of innovative and efficient conducts. The same type of error is much less costly in those markets with heavy-handed regulations that make rent-seeking a suitable means to gain privileged positions and market power."[33] In particular, it is feared that remedies imposed in refusal to deal or essential facilities claims may effectively undermine intellectual property rights and so dis-incentivise innovation. This argument — which has also assumed mantra-like proportions — requires much closer examination.

First, there are many economies which exhibit the less dynamic features alluded to and who may thus justifiably be more concerned with the positive consequences of limiting rent-seeking than with the prospect of chilling innovation, who may, in other words, derive more gain from protecting static efficiencies than from promoting dynamic efficiencies .

Indeed it should be borne in mind that in the vast majority of national economies, patentable innovation based on laboratory-type research is not a common source of dynamism. Despite a proclivity on the part of those who assert the imperative of innovation most strenuously to

---

[31] This is precisely the conclusion that the Federal trade Commissioners arrived at in their response to the DOJ report: "The Department's report is chiefly concerned with the firms that enjoy monopoly-power, or near monopoly power, and prescribes a legal regime that places firms' interests ahead of the interests of consumers. At almost every turn, the Department would place a thumb on the scales in favour of firms with monopoly or near-monopoly power and against other equally significant shareholders." (Statement of Commissioners, at p. 1). See E. Fox "The Efficiency Paradox" forthcoming in ...for an analysis of how conservative economic theory has superceded fact and effectively established rule bound proxies for the analysis of unilateral conduct in important recent U.S. antitrust enforcement practice including court decisions.

[32] As the Federal Trade Commissioners note in their response to the DOJ report: "For one reason or another, it may take a long time for rivals to surmount entry barriers or other impediments to effective competition. Indeed, the monopolist's own deliberate conduct may further delay a market correction and prolong the duration of consumer harm.". (Statement of Commissioners, at p. 4. Our emphasis).

[33] OFT report, at para. 6.84.

conflate innovation with intellectual property rights, process innovation and incremental, on-the-job adaptations of technologies and processes, innovations that drive down costs of production and improve existing products, are certainly more prevalent than those that produce new products and move out the technological frontiers and which commonly invoke intellectual property rights. Process and incremental innovation is precisely driven by rivalry from new entrants with low overhead costs and a handful of entrepreneurial engineers who challenge established incumbents by introducing lower cost production techniques and small improvements to existing products. This is, for the most part, the form that innovation takes in developing and middle-income countries and may well be the most important source of dynamism even in the developed economies which are also engaged in the development of new products and services. Process and incremental innovation is precisely the sort of innovation that is positively promoted by robust unilateral conduct enforcement that promotes accessible markets by guarding against exclusionary conduct on the part of incumbents.

Secondly, it should be acknowledged that the sources of even patentable product innovation are many and complex. It is widely acknowledged that successful innovation is rooted in considerable public support, including direct and indirect state subsidy. Indeed even critics of industrial policy are hard-pressed to deny the productive and necessary role of public investment in the process of innovation. Given this, those who boldly predict the end of innovation based on the disincentives alleged to flow from the possibility of Type 1 errors in a small number of antitrust cases should be required to provide more evidence of the putative link between unilateral conduct prosecution and innovation before throwing out the proverbial baby with the bathwater. To the extent that innovation is the product of public rather than private investment, there is no warrant for believing that antitrust enforcement, erroneous or otherwise, will sound the death knell on innovation.

Third, one should not lose sight of the fact that — the obvious interface between competition and innovation notwithstanding — the principal legal instruments underpinning new product innovation are the rules governing the acquisition and exercise of intellectual property rights. If those rules are "under-protecting" innovation or, indeed if they are "over-protecting" innovation, and, hence, coming into systemic and regular conflict with competition rules and standards, then surely the first-best solution is to fix the intellectual property rules rather than to demand compensatory action from competition enforcers, which action carries with it the distinct possibility of the under-enforcement of competition rules and standards.[34]

---

[34] See T. Brennan 'Should Innovation Rationalise Supra-Competitive Prices? A Skeptical Speculation' Swedish Competition Authority J. (2007).

C
Cartels

[6]

World Competition **29(1)**: 109–137, 2006.

Cartels and Collusion in Developing Countries: Lessons from Empirical Evidence

Frédéric JENNY*

During the course of the debate at the WTO on the Singapore issues, a number of government officials from developing countries have suggested that their countries would derive little benefit from competition law enforcement. Some even argued that competition law enforcement would actually hinder the development of their country. To a large extent these views were based on the idea that domestic anticompetitive practices are not prevalent on developing economies or do not impose a large cost on their economies. This discussion on the relationship between trade competition and development, however, has remained fairly abstract in multilateral fora. This article attempts to look at the reality of anticompetitive practices around the turn of the century in developing countries by drawing from numerous public sources to identify the types of anticompetitive practices most frequently observed or alleged by type and sectors. The analysis shows that the economies of developing countries are subject to a wide array of anticompetitive practices, that such practices not only hurt consumers in developing countries but also affect the competitivity of the economies of these countries, and that they are often similar across countries. The policy implications of such findings are discussed in the last section.

The relationships linking competition policy and law and economic development have been the subject of an intense controversy in recent years. This controversy arose, in particular, in the context of debate on the "Singapore Issues" during the Doha round of discussion at the WTO. As is well known, the Singapore issues (competition, investment, government procurement, and trade facilitation) were ultimately dropped from the agenda of the WTO Doha round of negotiation. The two most controversial topics were competition and investment.

The many reasons behind the failure of the WTO Cancun conference and why competition was, together with the other Singapore issues, dropped from the agenda of this multilateral trade negotiation are beyond the scope of this article. Today we will rather focus on a narrower set of issues dealing with the interactions between competition law enforcement or competition policy and economic development.

Among the various reasons a number of developing countries strongly favoured the elimination of competition as a topic of negotiation during the Doha round was the fear, expressed both by many officials and by some development economists, that the adoption and enforcement of competition law would work against the interests of developing countries.

* Professor of Economics, ESSEC This article is based on research that is part of an ongoing project involving the creation and maintenance of a data base on competition cases, allegations and issues in developing countries. It was presented as a paper at the fifth UNCTAD Conference to Review All Aspects of the Mutually Agreed Equitable Principles and Rules for the Control of Restrictive Business Practices. The author wishes to thank Med Rezzouk for extremely valuable research assistantship, Professor Patrick Rey and the members of the economic seminar at CREST (University of Toulouse) where a prior version of this article was presented and Simon Evenett with whom the author is co-operating on a related project.

Some argued that competition law enforcement would make the domestic markets of developing countries more vulnerable to imports from developed countries because public authorities in developing countries would be obliged to enforce their domestic competition law against private anticompetitive practices preventing market access.

There was a similar fear that competition law enforcement would prevent the protection of national champions.

It is also often argued that the enforcement of competition law would inevitably contribute to the decrease of profit rates in developing countries, thereby deterring investment and, in particular, foreign direct investment which is badly needed in countries which have an insufficient capital base.

The theoretical arguments about why there should be (or should not be) a relationship between competition and economic development are commonly known, so will not be repeated here in detail. It should be sufficient to say that the existence of substantial scale economies in various industries and of externalities, the possibility of incomplete markets, the lack of domestic capital, the need to facilitate the acquisition of a technological base, the need to facilitate reallocation of resources and simultaneously to alleviate transition costs, argue in favour of the idea that market mechanisms should be complemented, at least in the first phases of economic development, by government intervention and industrial policy measures. However, it is also clear that competition plays a useful role in forcing firms to become more efficient and to better supply the needs of consumers because no economy can thrive in the long run without the challenge of a competitive environment.

While both approaches have merits from a logical point of view, economists have yet to come up with a model defining the optimal mix of government intervention and competitive pressure as a function of the level of economic development and other determinants. As a result, ideological warfare tends to pollute the debate.

I.   COMPETITION AND ECONOMIC DEVELOPMENT: MACRO ANALYSIS

Rather than speculating further on the theoretical relationship between competition and economic development, and perhaps as WTO discussions focused on whether developing countries should commit themselves to having a competition law enforcement capacity, a small number of economists have recently begun to focus on a narrower, more pragmatic set of questions: Is there any empirical evidence that competition law enforcement contributes to economic development? Is there any empirical evidence that anticompetitive practices impair economic growth? A complementary and more recent development is an attempt on the part of economists to measure the direct and indirect cost of law enforcement in developing countries against the costs of anticompetitive practices in these countries.

Much to the chagrin of competition law enforcement officials, it must be said that there are no convincing macroeconomic studies demonstrating the existence of a positive and strong correlation between the intensity of competition law enforcement and the rate of economic growth (in developed or developing countries). However, there is a fair amount of evidence that countries which engage in proactive competition policies designed to increase the intensity of competitive pressures (open trade and investment policies, regulatory reform etc.) tend to fare better than other countries.

There are several possible explanations for these results.

The first one, of course, is that the effect of competition law enforcement is rather small or even negligible compared to the effect of other elements of competition policy. If this is the case, competition law is not necessarily disqualified as a policy instrument (indeed its marginal cost could be smaller than its marginal revenue even if the latter is small), but it would buttress the case of the adversaries of competition law enforcement in developing countries who argue that there is not much for them to gain from such an instrument (and that the relative cost of enforcement is likely to be higher in their countries than in larger, more developed economies).

A second explanation is that it is difficult to measure the intensity of competition law enforcement. Indeed, competition authorities have many different means of intervention: investigating and prosecuting cases of anticompetitive practices, obtaining commitments as a condition for allowing mergers and engaging in advocacy work. In addition, because the scope of exemptions from competition law enforcement activities varies widely across countries it is difficult to rely on indicators of the activity of the competition enforcement agency to get a clear picture of their real scope and the possible impact of competition law enforcement at the macroeconomic level. It is thus possible that indicators of the intensity of competition law enforcement (such as statistics on the budget of the competition agency, or the number of cases dealt with each year, etc.) are poor proxies for the actual level and scope of competition law enforcement efforts.

It must be emphasised that competition law enforcement does not function the same way as sectoral regulations do. Sectoral regulations (such as, for example, a price cap) apply throughout the regulated sector from the moment the regulation comes into force. Competition law enforcement can show results only in the long term. This means that it is only through the accumulation of cases in which anticompetitive practices are sanctioned that the credibility of the competition authority as an enforcement agency can be built up and that the dissuasive effect of competition law enforcement can develop. This process, which is part of the development of a competition culture, and is as important as the dissemination of a proper understanding of the goals and provisions of the competition law through competition advocacy, takes time. How long is difficult to say but if one uses as a reference the experience of developed economies having a well established competition law enforcement system, it is likely that several decades must elapse before the full effect of competition law enforcement is felt. Such a time frame is consistent with experience in the United States, Canada, Japan, the European Union, etc. Some have argued that as late comers new competition institutions can benefit in part from the mistakes of older agencies, but nobody disputes the fact that building a competition culture is a slow process.

In short, quite aside from possible difficulties with assessment or measurement, in most developing countries having active enforcement of a competition law, legislation has not been enforced long enough to have made measurable macroeconomic impact.

Thus, the lack of correlation between the intensity of competition law enforcement efforts and indicators of economic development in developing countries (such as growth rates or indexes of competitivity) means they cannot tell us much about whether competition law enforcement is a useful tool for developing countries.

Another line of enquiry may thus shed more light on the issue. Rather than asking whether competition law enforcement contributes to economic growth one may instead ask whether anticompetitive practices are prevalent in developing countries and try to assess the cost they impose on those countries. A major advantage of this method is that, because it starts from actual instances of anticompetitive practices, it is less abstract and more graphic than correlation analysis.

This line of reasoning was initiated by the pioneering study of international cartels by Levenstein, Suslow and Evenett in Margaret C. Levenstein, Lynda Oswald and Valerie Surlow, Contemporary International Price-Fixing Cartels and Developing Countries: A discussion of effects and policy remedies, PERI Working Paper No. 53, William Davidson Institute Working Paper No. 538. In that study, which drove home the point that international cartels were imposing a huge cost on developing economies, the authors started from a sample of nineteen international cartels which had been prosecuted during the 1990s and asked the simple question of what quantities of products subjected to a cartel agreement had been imported in a typical year by developing countries. As was well known, these nineteen cartels were only the tip of the iceberg since there is no systematic detection and prosecution of international cartels for reasons related to the difficulty of gathering proof of such cartels which are often disseminated in a number of countries (or in countries which do not have a domestic competition law) and because other private international cartels were known to have existed during the period studied (such as the East of Burma agreement on steel which was exposed at the OECD, but never prosecuted, or the heavy electrical equipment cartel). It was, however, a stunningly heavy tip of an iceberg since the results showed that developing countries imported about $51,000,000,000 a year of such products, representing nearly 5.2 percent of their total imports and 1.2 percent of their GDP. Further research estimated the magnitude of the annual overcharge for those imports by developing countries to be amount to between 15 and 25 billion dollars or between $\frac{1}{3}$ and $\frac{1}{2}$ of the annual aid to economic development provided by developed countries.

II.   COMPETITION AND ECONOMIC DEVELOPMENT: EMPIRICAL EVIDENCE

This approach prompted further research of the same nature, not on international cartels but on documented domestic anticompetitive practices reported either by the press or by competition authorities when they exist in developing countries.

Several data bases have been developed to systematically gather indications of such anticompetitive practices. One of these data bases, which I developed with Simon Evenett deals with African countries; another one covering Asia and parts of Latin America is being developed by Evenett and Julian Clark in the context of a major project. A third source is one I developed from OECD peer reviews of non-member countries.

Again the results are stunning with respect to the scope and importance of anticompetitive practices revealed in developing countries.

The results can be assessed in several ways. One is to draw up statistical tables showing the type of practices, the sectors in which they are alleged to take place, the frequency of these practices and various indicators concerning the firms involved. An advantage of such a presentation is that it reveals the frequency with which the same practices or types of practices are encountered in the same sectors in different developing countries. When the same type of practice is alleged or prosecuted in a number of developing countries, it can be assumed that this practice is fairly typical of the situation of such countries.

Grouping the anticompetitive practices most frequently alleged or documented (and providing some precise references to bring home the reality of these practices), I will sketch the situation of a typical developing country.

To begin with, concentration in the trade of a number of agricultural products and price fixing agreements among traders in their purchasing activities often limit the income of small farmers in developing countries below what it would be if there was more competition among such traders. This is, for example, a real problem for coffee producers in Kenya[1] and in Latin America or cotton farmers and tea and tobacco growers in Malawi,[2] fish processors and exporters in the Lake Victoria region,[3] milk processors in Chile[4] (where two cartels among the same milk processors were being investigated in 1997, and in 2001 and where the main point of the complaints was that the milk processors had set the prices paid to milk producers too low).

It also sometimes true that farmers pay inflated prices for their inputs, due to anticompetitive practices among their suppliers, particularly those in the chemical industry.

For example,[5] in 2003, the Kenya Tea Development Authority (KTDA) claimed that a group of suppliers had organised themselves into a cartel to control fertiliser tenders. The KTDA claimed that suppliers were colluding to minimise competition amongst themselves by pre-determining who would supply KTDA each year. KTDA said that over the last two decades, as the quantities of fertiliser used by the farmers

---

[1] *Africa Analysis*, 19 April 2002.
[2] *Spine chilling experiences of anti-competitive practices in Malawi*, CUTS and Consumer Association of Malawi (CAMA), 2003.
[3] Panafrican News Agency, 26 June 2001.
[4] OECD, *Competition Law and Policy in Chile, A Peer Review*, April 2003.
[5] *The East African Standard*, Nairobi, 3 July 2003.

increased, only a small group of fertiliser manufacturers were able to supply the Authority with the input required, due to the restrictive specifications of NPKS and more specifically to the inclusion of sulphur which has few manufacturers. Allegations were made that a group of suppliers then emerged which colluded and formed a ring to minimise competition. "Indeed, there is evidence that the fertiliser was not necessarily manufactured by the winning bidder", said Mr Kimani, KTDA Managing Director, in a statement. He also said the Board was then compelled to re-advertise the supply tenders to break the monopolistic tendency that had sprung up and denied farmers the benefits of lower prices.

Consumers in developing countries are also frequently the victims of antic-ompetitive practices due to price fixing either in the production or the distribution of basic food products.

The market for chicken, a basic staple in many countries, is frequently affected by anticompetitive practices. This was, for example, the case in Peru[6] where poultry firms and their association engaged in what amounted to price fixing by agreeing to prevent new entry, exclude some existing competitors, and limit the availability of live poultry for sale in order to raise or maintain prices. It was also the case in Zambia[7] where the dominant producer of day old chicks (60 percent market share) Hybrid Poultry Farm (HPF) and Galaunia Holdings Limited (GH), the largest buyer in the poultry sector, entered into sales and purchase agreements which included provisions foreclosing competition on day old chicks, table birds (broilers) and frozen chicken as well as an agreement that GH could not begin to sell day old chicks in competition with HPF. In Turkey,[8] during the mid 1990s, the General Directorate of Consumer and Competition Protection prosecuted a cartel case again in the poultry industry.

The milling industry is also frequently cartelized resulting in high prices for basic staples. For example, in Peru,[9] Indecopi's first important cartel case was the 1996 "Bread Case" against wheat flour producers and their association. Eleven producers were found to have ended a price war through a price fixing agreement and the association had made price recommendations about the price of bread. In Malawi,[10] where the industry consists of a few giants (notably Press Bakeries and Portuguese Bakeries) and many small baking firms, the Master Bakers Association fixed prices, and hence there was no competition until consumer organisations started a boycott and the Minister of Trade intervened to prohibit price fixing among the bakeries. In Zimbabwe,[11] in 1999, there were allegations that the country's three major millers were "operating as a cartel". In Turkey,[12] several price fixing cases among bakers were investigated by the General Directorate of Consumer and Competition Protection

---

[6] OECD, *Competition Law and Policy in Peru, A Peer Review*, 2004.
[7] Zambian Competition Commission Press Release.
[8] OECD, as note 4 above.
[9] OECD, as note 6 above.
[10] CUTS and Consumer Association of Malawi (CAMA), as note 2 above.
[11] *Comtex News*, 30 June 1999
[12] OECD, *Competition Law and Policy in Turkey, A Peer Review*, 2005.

before 1997 and since then by the Competition Board with respect to bakeries (Ankara, Gaziantep, Kütahya). In Zambia,[13] labour unions have taken the government to task for having a soft approach to the problem posed by the lack of competition among millers resulting in high prices of mealie meal, a staple food.

Other markets for foodstuff are sometimes affected by monopolistic situations (see for example the situation of the milk market in Malawi[14] where Dairiboard, a company from Zimbabwe and a supplier of the domestic market, bought Malawi Dairy Industries (MDI), Malawi's major domestic company in this sector, thereby substantially reducing competition in the Malawian milk market. Also in Malawi,[15] the sugar market is alleged to be controlled by a cartel formed by several politicians and sugar is expensive and difficult to find in Malawi because of this monopoly situation. In Turkey,[16] the dominant firm in the salty snacks market was barred in May 2004 from including non-compete clauses in its distribution agreements with retail outlets. The Turkish Competition Board concluded that the restrictive clauses yielded no significant efficiencies and served principally as a barrier to entry by competing suppliers.

A worrisome situation from the standpoint of competition is also frequently be encountered in the popular drinks sector, which includes beer and carbonated soft drinks.

The beer sector is very concentrated in a number of African and Latin American countries (for example in Zambia, South Africa, Kenya, Tanzania, Namibia, and most countries in Latin America) and there is convincing evidence that mergers in this sector are sometimes motivated by a desire to limit competition (for example, the case of beer mergers in Namibia,[17] Turkey[18] and the case of merger in the traditional beer sector in Malawi). A good example of possibly anticompetitive mergers comes from Kenya and Tanzania[19] where, in 2002, East African Breweries and South African Breweries exchanged their stakes in subsidiaries in Kenya and Tanzania thus allowing South African Breweries to take control of the Tanzania market and East African Breweries to retain its hold on the market in Kenya.

Additionally, it is often the case that, in addition to being heavily concentrated, the beer sector is also rife with vertical restrictive agreements which limit the scope for competition at the retail level through a variety of devices such as quantity forcing (a practice involving a specified minimum quantity the retailer is required to distribute), the placement of coolers in a retail outlet by dominant firms on condition that competing brands will not be placed in the coolers (see, for example, the case of Zambian Breweries limited in Zambia[20] and Kenyan Breweries in Kenya), exclusive

---

[13] *The Post*, Zambia, 23 January 2002.
[14] CUTS and Consumer Association of Malawi (CAMA), as note 2 above.
[15] Id.
[16] OECD, as note 12 above.
[17] Southern Africa Business Intelligence, 28 March 1994.
[18] OECD, as note 12 above.
[19] *The Nation*, Nairobi, 15 May 2002.
[20] Zambian Competition Commission, *Annual Report 1999*.

dealing, resale price maintenance, and exclusive distribution (see, for example, the case of Kenyan Breweries in Kenya[21]).

Similar practices that result in diminished competition, possibly higher prices for consumers and limited opportunities of growth for retailers are also frequent in the soft drink sector. The acquisition of local bottlers by multinational firms frequently results in high structural concentration.

For example, in 1997, the Kenyan subsidiary of Coca Cola, M/s Coca Cola SABCO, acquired M/s Flamingo Bottlers of Nakuru, which bottled Coca Cola.[22] It had already acquired Nairobi Bottlers (the most important bottler in the country) in 1995. Coca Cola had a dominant position in the market for carbonated soft drinks in Kenya and the merger seemed to be part of a strategy for strengthening and sustaining its dominance in the market. The Competition Authority, while allowing the merger, decided that the plan of taking over all the other bottling companies and consolidating them into one entity to be run by SABCO would lead to both horizontal and vertical concentration of market power and likely abuse of dominance. Thus the Minister prevented Coca Cola from taking over any of the remaining bottling companies.

In Chile,[23] acting on a complaint by Pepsi Cola and certain soft drink bottlers, the Prosecutor's Office conducted an investigation on the acquisition by Coca Cola of Cadbury Schweppes' soft drink brands and made a report that noted risks to competition but did not contain a *"requerimiento"*—a formal charge seeking a fine or other remedy. In the carbonated soft drink market, Coca Cola already had a 73 per cent market share, which the acquisition would raise to 82 per cent (nearly 100 per cent of orange flavoured soft drinks and mixers).

Furthermore the soft drink market is also frequently beset by anticompetitive vertical restraints. For example, according to some sources the market for cola based drinks in Kenya is characterised by quantity forcing, retail price maintenance or suggested retail price.[24]

In Zambia,[25] the franchise arrangements of Coca Cola and Schweppes included provisions barring distributors from dealing in similar products as those put out by Coca Cola and Schweppes, price fixing, and territorial restrictions.

In Turkey,[26] certain firms in the soft drinks market, included non compete clauses in agreements with retail outlets.

More generally, both vertical and horizontal anticompetitive practices are reported in many developing countries in the retailing sector.

For example, the South African Competition Commission launched an investigation in 2002 into the business practices of two franchisors, Seven Eleven

---

[21] David Ong'olo, *Distribution Restraints: Experiences in the Beer and Soft Drink Industries in Africa*, 2004.
[22] David Ong'olo, as note 21 above.
[23] OECD, as note 4 above.
[24] David Ong'olo, as note 21 above.
[25] *Times of Zambia*, 23 September 1999.
[26] OECD, as note 12 above.

Corporation and Seven Eleven Africa, following complaints lodged against them by a large body of Seven Eleven franchisees.[27] The franchisees were alleging that Seven Eleven Corporation and Seven Eleven Africa were engaged in price-fixing and exclusionary business practices relating to rental agreements, forced purchases, shop fittings and insurance, among other issues. One Seven Eleven franchisee said the interim relief application referred to the practice whereby franchisees were bound to purchase from approved suppliers and sell at recommended prices rather than being allowed to buy and sell to their best advantage. The relief order application also related to alleged incidents of intimidation by the franchisors involving suppliers, particularly in Gauteng, the franchisee said. Seven Eleven, a mini-supermarket/convenience store retail concept, has about 240 stores throughout South Africa, of which about 180 are owned by franchisees. Seven Eleven Corporation and Seven Eleven Africa, between them, own a handful of in-house supply companies (such as bakery operations), have a number of associate companies (for example cigarette merchants and ice suppliers), as well as direct suppliers. The franchisees complaint was that the prices of some of the products from the in-house operations and associate companies from which they were obliged to buy, were not competitive, resulting in Seven Eleven stores operating at a price disadvantage to the rapidly expanding network of competing convenience store brands, as well as "cafs".

An important percentage of the budget of individual consumers in any developing country is devoted to services such as transportation and communications. However, the passenger transportation sector (buses, taxis, airlines etc.) is also rife with anticompetitive practices resulting in high prices for consumers, low quality of service and occasionally exposure to physical danger.

This deadly combination was illustrated, for example, in Kenya in November 2003,[28] when two members of the Matutu Owners Association (MOA) gave an insight into the operations of the cartel. According to them, "the cartel comprises a group of city matutu owners who want monopoly over lucrative routes, the police and militia gangs. Mungiki, an outlawed sect and Kamjesh, a band of thugs for hire, make up the vicious, more criminal side of the cartels".

Along the same lines, a report from South Africa in 2001[29] indicates that in the Cape Town area "taxi associations are organised into territories the same way that gangs cut up the town and rule by fear over the bits of turf they claim. Because taxis are mobile, competition for turf involves routes. (. . .) The taxi associations have come to "own" the routes they serve. Huge profits were made in the beginning. As the number of taxis grew, so profits fell. There is now over-trading and owners have become ruthless. Meanwhile, passengers are left with no choice, are at risk and remain voiceless. They have to transfer at the dangerous boundaries between taxi territories. Many are

---

[27] Business Day, South Africa, 20 January 2000.
[28] Douglas Okwatch and Otsieno Namwaya Monday 3 November 2003.
[29] *Business Day*, Cape Town, 17 October 2001.

compelled to take from two to four taxis on every trip to work and back, with long waits at points between association boundaries.(. . .)".

In Peru, taxi firms and their association were found by Indecopi to have agreed to increase their fares.[30]

Cartels and other anticompetitive practices in passenger road transportation are not limited to taxis and matutus. For example, in Turkey[31] the competition authorities prosecuted cartel cases against bus companies.

In 2000, it was alleged that South African Airways (SAA)[32] was using predatory pricing techniques to force competitors out of key routes. Nationwide, a competitor, claimed that despite fuel price increases of about 50 percent in four months, SAA had not increased fares on routes where it faced competition, but had increased prices on routes where there was no competition. Nationwide also alleged that SAA had signed deals with travel agents, which provide rebates according to the volume of tickets sold. These agency over-rides provide selected travel agents with rebates over their current commissions, which are typically 7 percent of the ticket price, if they channelled business to SAA. Nationwide claimed that SAA abused its dominant position by implementing these rebates, which it could not afford to match due to its smaller size.

Also in the air transport sector, the Brazilian competition watchdog, CADE, ruled that carriers Varig, TAM, Vasp and now-defunct Transbrasil formed an illegal cartel in the mid 1990s covering the Sao Paulo-Rio de Janeiro market, the country's most important sector.[33]

Owning a car in a developing country is often a costly luxury as car owners may have to buy their cars from price fixing car dealers and are all the more likely to be hit by a lack of competition in the petroleum retail sector because, in developing countries, this sector is usually highly concentrated and in the hands a few oligopolists who do not necessarily need to collude explicitly to keep prices high or prevent them from falling.

For example, in Kenya[34] in December 1998, the Permanent Secretary for Energy publicly denounced what he considered to be a cartel-like behaviour by major oil companies which resulted in high retail prices of oil products in the country and a refusal by oil companies with truck loading facilities to extend the hospitality to new entrants at a fee, thus making it difficult for new entrants to set up business. In 2000, the Kenya Transporters Association resolved to import oil for its members to counter what it termed as: "unjustified hikes of fuel prices by a cartel of companies in Kenya" and called on the Commissioner of Monopolies in the Tourism, Trade and Industry Ministry to investigate the local oil firms and find ways to break the cartel: "to save the ailing economy from being destroyed altogether by the constant price hikes."

---

[30] OECD, as note 6 above.
[31] OECD, as note 12 above.
[32] *Business Day*, South Africa, December 2000.
[33] Cade press release.
[34] *The Nation*, Nairobi, 21 December 1998.

In Tanzania,[35] in 2000, the Minister for Energy and Minerals threatened to withdraw the licences of oil marketing companies if they operated like a cartel and colluded to hike fuel prices. His remarks were prompted by the government fear that the multiplier effect of the increase in petrol prices over the previous twelve months was likely to harm the economy.

In Uganda,[36] also in 2000, legislators urged the government to find ways of breaking the monopolistic cartel of oil companies. Threats of possible mass civil disobedience were voiced if appropriate measures were not taken to address popular anger over skyrocketing fuel prices.

In Zambia,[37] in 1999, nine oil marketing companies were prosecuted for participating in a price fixing conspiracy involving the supply of refined petroleum products. The companies had acted collectively in making price adjustments since 1997. They selected one company to apply for a price adjustment to the Sector regulator which sets a price cap. They held regular meetings where exchanges of information regarding sales volumes and prices took place. The cartel leaders also forced other companies to comply with standard behaviour on prices.

In Ghana,[38] in 2004, politicians expressed fears that deregulation of the country's petroleum sector might lead to the creation of cartel by Oil Marketing Companies (OMCs) if caution were not taken during its implementation. A professor of economics from Ghana suggested that deregulation would be feasible and prices of fuel products might see a downward decline if there were no cartel to hike prices.

In Malawi,[39] when the government eliminated price controls on petroleum products, all or most of the oil companies concerned formed a joint company called Petroleum Importers Limited, through which they jointly monopolised the importation of all oil products into Malawi, and colluded on prices. When a new petroleum importer emerged on the market and introduced new fuel prices different from (and lower than) those of the cartel it was persuaded to join the cartel.

In South Africa[40] during the mid 1990s, evidence surfaced that oil companies providing jet fuel to airlines had refused to compete on prices and would not make a quote to their competitors' customers. As a result, the contract price for jet fuel at Jan Smuts airport was more expensive than at Cape Town and nearly 30 percent more than at Heathrow airport in London.

In Chile,[41] the market for petroleum products at the turn of the century was very concentrated at the wholesale level and increasingly concentrated at the retail level as well, with little price competition, and it was generally perceived that prices were quick to rise and slow to fall. The Prosecutor's Office initiated a proceeding against four firms

---

[35] *The Guardian*, Tanzania, 28 April 2000.
[36] *New Vision*, Kampala, 13 July 2000.
[37] Zambian Competition Commission, press release.
[38] *Ghanaian Chronicle*, 18 March 2004.
[39] CUTS and Consumer Association of Malawi (CAMA), as note 2 above.
[40] *Southern Africa Business Intelligence*, 21 April 1995.
[41] OECD, as note 4 above.

without specifically alleging collusion. By way of relief, the Office sought mainly structural remedies. For example, the Office asked the Antitrust Commission to recommend that the government modify two laws that create entry barriers (one preventing the installation of new gas tanks in some areas and the other preventing all but a government-owned firm from laying pipelines). It also sought an order requiring one firm to grant access to its pipeline, and an order directing all four firms to agree not to fix prices.

After having seen food and beverage products, transportation services and fuel, we can now move to construction materials, particularly cement which is a major input for low cost housing. Major competition problems are reported in the sector in a large number of developing countries either because there is a monopolistic situation (such as in Malawi where Lafarge has a controlling stake in Commonwealth Development Corporation) or because of anticompetitive cartels.

For example, in Egypt in December 2002,[42] Al Arham newspaper reported that representatives of almost all local cement producers had met and set a price range for cement between LE167 and LE176 per ton. Just hours before the meeting, the price had been as low as LE125 per ton. According to the press report, the cement manufacturers involved had considered the possibility of entering a market sharing agreement if the price fixing agreement did not succeed in keeping the prices up.

In South Africa,[43] the largest cement companies in South Africa at the time (PPC, Anglo-Alpha and Blue Circle) operated as an officially sanctioned cartel until 1996, when the Competition Board forced the companies to discontinue the practice.

The Commonwealth Development Corporation (CDC) and Pan African Cement (PAC) notified the Zambian Competition Commission,[44] under Section 8 of the Zambian Competition Act, of their intention to sell their 50.1 percent shareholding of Chilanga Cement PLC to Lafarge SA of France, pursuant to a Sale and Purchase Agreement entered into by the parties on 4th December 2000. Chilanga Cement is the sole producer of cement in Zambia with substantial upstream and downstream integrations to SMEs. Information gathered by the Commission pointed to the fact that with Lafarge (which also owns plants in the neighbouring countries of Tanzania, Malawi and Zimbabwe), Chilanga Cement appeared to be engaged in production and pricing strategies that made Zambian export cement less competitive when compared to cement produced by the plant in Mbeya, Tanzania. Chilanga Cement wanted to divide the regional market (through market allocation and territorial restrictions) so that Zambian exports would be targeted to the DR Congo, while the Burundi and Rwandese markets would be supplied from its Tanzanian plant. Such conduct was likely to make the Zambian plant less competitive by restricting its production capacity. The Board of Commissioners reviewed the submission from Lafarge and conditionally

---

[42] *Al Arham*, Cairo, December 2002.
[43] *Business Day*, South Africa, 4 August 2000.
[44] *Pulling up our socks*, CUTS.

authorised the transaction after Lafarge gave substantive undertakings to the ZCC including a commitment not to restrict the growth potential of Chilanga Cement. Chilanga has since ceased its anticompetitive conduct and cement exports to the Great Lakes region have continued.

In Turkey,[45] between 1997 and 2002, the Competition Board rendered decisions against anticompetitive agreements among cement producers, including a 1999 case in which five cement companies were fined nearly 900 billion Turkish Lira ("TRL") (USD 603,000) for a price fixing and market division agreement in the Aegean region. Since 2002, an additional cement case involving the Ankara and South Marmara markets resulted in fines against 18 firms, totalling TRL 4.88 trillion (USD 3.3 million).

Cement cartels have been alleged or prosecuted in many other developing countries such as the Philippines, Indonesia, Pakistan etc.

Other types of construction materials are also occasionally cartelized.

For example, in July 2003, the first dawn raid in the history of Brazil[46] was carried out by the Secretariat of Economic Law of the Ministry of Justice (SDE). Targeted were the premises of the State of São Paulo Crushed Rock Mining Industries Association (Sindipedras) in pursuit of hard evidence of alleged cartel behaviour among competitors in the market for crushed rock (one of the most essential raw materials in the civil construction industry). The mining companies concerned accounted for 70 percent of the crushed rock produced in São Paulo, and the alleged cartel had purportedly been in operation for over two years, increasing prices to the detriment of the civil construction industry, including public works.

During this raid, documents, reports, tapes, textbooks, slide transparencies, software to monitor the alleged cartel, receipts and notices of invitations were seized. According to the SDE, an initial examination of the documents seized indicated that: (a) price quotes were fed by the companies into a computer program, and the data were kept in a central file at Sindipedras; (b) alleged cartel decisions were made at meetings known as "course" meetings held on Association premises; (c) software carried information on the daily sales figures of 17 companies and was designed to monitor the activities of the alleged cartel; (d) a fine was levied on whomever failed to comply with decisions made by the group; (e) cartel members divided up customers, and each company was given a certain sales quota, including for bids to be tendered in public competitive bidding processes; and (f) each company's list of customers was saved on a file known as the "Bible", and a cartel member could only sell to another cartel member's customers at a premium (generally R$2.00 over the price charged by the respective member).

---

[45] OECD, as note 12 above.
[46] United Nations Conference on Trade and Development, Recent Competition Cases, Intergovernmental Group of Experts on Competition Law and Policy, Sixth session, 8–10 November 2004.

Let us now move on to the service sector and begin with the type of professional services which consumers as well as business firms might use, such as services offered by lawyers, architects, surveyors, public notaries etc. The record shows that those well organised professions often make sure, in developing countries as well as in developed countries, that their members do not compete with one other, which is detrimental to their customers.

For example, in 2002 there were reports in Kenya[47] of buyers complaining that cartels had taken over dealings at Mombasa Port Customs Department auctions.

In early 2002, the Turkish Competition Board fined the Turkish Architects' and Engineers' Chambers Association (TAECA)[48] and ordered it to abolish its by-law provisions setting minimum fees. The Association's authorising statute entailed no price setting power. By contrast, in late 2003, the Board decided that no prosecution was possible against minimum fee schedules promulgated by the Turkish Medical Association, the Turkish Dental Association, and the Turkish Bar Association, because the foundation laws for those associations clearly articulated their authority to establish fee minimums. The Board also imposed fines on a group of mechanical engineers in Konya, who were found to have created a "revenue pool" through which they equally shared income from their various jobs.

In 2003 in South Africa,[49] the Competition Tribunal confirmed the Competition Commission's order prohibiting the Pretoria Association of Attorneys from issuing guidelines for recommended fees (which had the indirect effect of fixing prices) and imposed administrative penalties on the Association. The tribunal found that Association guidelines, setting tariffs that members should charge clients, amounted to price-fixing and contravened the Competition Act. The tribunal's order was expected to have far reaching implications for other professional associations which also provide tariff guidelines.

That same year in South Africa,[50] a probe into the private health-care industry revealed that the South African Medical Association, the Hospital Association of SA and the Board of Health Care Funders had all contravened Section 4(1)(b)(i) of the Competition Act of 1998 by recommending and publishing benchmark tariffs annually.

In Peru,[51] in a 2003 case, the Lima association of public notaries was found to have engaged in illegal price fixing by negotiating an agreement with the Urban Estate Registry that the latter would pay notaries a specified fee.

In Zambia,[52] it was reported in 2004 that the surveyors' cartels artificially restricted the number of surveyors who could practice, leading to backlogs of up to seven years.

---

[47] *The Nation*, Kenya, 20 December 2000.
[48] OECD, as note 12 above.
[49] *Business Day*, Johannesburg, 31 July 2003.
[50] *Business Day*, Johannesburg, 31 July 2003, and 21 August 2003.
[51] OECD, as note 6 above.
[52] *Breathing life into dead capital*, The Economist, 17 January 2004.

Banking services are important both to consumers who need personal financial services and to business firms because the availability and the affordability of financing are crucial determinants of their ability to grow. Yet there is evidence that in many developing countries competition in the banking sector is weak, either because of anticompetitive practices or because of anticompetitive mergers and that this lack of competition leads to a greater spread between borrowing and lending rates than would be observed if there were more competition. This hinders the prospect for economic development of firms that are too small to have easy access to international capital markets.

For example, in South Africa[53] in July 2000, the competition authority blocked a proposed merger between Nedcor and Standard Bank Investment. M Simelane said concentration in South Africa's banking sector was already way above safe harbour thresholds applied in the United States, Canada and Australia, and that the merger would have led to further concentration. The merged bank would have had 52 percent of all South African small business customers, giving it a market share advantage of more than 26 percent over its nearest competitor.

That same year the Deputy Governor of the Bank of Uganda[54] regretted the lack of competition in the banking sector in his country and called for more competition in the sector in order to increase the quality of banking services and reduce profit margins. He stated: "for our markets to become sophisticated, the sector has to develop new products. An efficient and developed market is key to market competition, which would lead to lowering margins in the sector. The Bank of Uganda is of a view that the sector should not have cartels where margins remain fixed for long time otherwise the public will agitate for intervention from the central bank".

In Turkey,[55] the competition authority moved in August 2003 against a leading bank that required retail outlets to honour only the bank's brand of credit card and prohibited the practice.

Insurance services are also important for consumers and business firms, but in many developing countries the insurance sector is also characterised by anticompetitive practices which lead to higher prices than necessary being charged both to individual customers and to business firms.

For example in Turkey[56] a 2003 proceeding found an agreement between 11 insurance companies and one reinsurance company to set prices for fire insurance, as well as a separate scheme orchestrated by the Turkish Union of Insurance Companies to set tariffs and conditions for various forms of insurance coverage.

In Kenya in 2001[57] it was reported that following an agreement by companies to fix prices instead of undercutting one another in the fierce competition that had seen industry profits plunge in previous years, insurance premiums were to increase sharply.

---

[53] *Business Day*, South Africa, 8 July 2000.
[54] *New Vision*, Kampala, 11 December 2000.
[55] OECD, as note 12 above.
[56] Id.
[57] *The East African*, Nairobi, 3 December 2001.

Motor vehicle insurance was to be the most affected, with cost of coverage rising by at least 50 percent. These increases were passed on to consumers by bus operators. For example, when the insurance premiums increased, operators on the route between Nairobi and Mombasa immediately decided that they would increase fares by Ksh100 ($1.3) per passenger and fares for distances under 200 kms would rise by Ksh50 (US cents 65).

In 2003, the Kenya insurance sector[58] was again embroiled in a public controversy over the issuance by the Association of Kenya Insurers (AKI) of minimum premium rates for a number of non-life classes of insurance in order to raise premiums. AKI was accused of prompting an illegal price-fixing cartel in contravention of the Restrictive Trade Practices, Monopolies and Price Control Act and the Commissioner of the Monopolies and Prices Commission opened an investigation.

In 2002, in Peru,[59] the National Institute for the Defense of Competition and Protection of Intellectual Property Rights (INDECOPI) ruled against nine Peruvian insurance companies and their professional association after an investigation regarding the pricing of Mandatory Traffic Accident Insurance (SOAT). In its conclusion, the Commission stated that, during the period under investigation (July 2001 to April 2002), the insurance companies were involved in price-fixing practices, and it sanctioned the association and all the companies involved.

Consumers and business firms are also heavily dependent on other services such as telecommunications. In many developing countries, as in many developed countries, the incumbent telecom operators, usually having a large market share, try to drive new entrants out of the market so as to counter the effects of the opening up of the telecommunications sector to competition.

For example, in South Africa, in 2002,[60] in a case initiated by a complaint from the South African Value Added Network Services Association (SAVA), and various value added network service providers, the Competition Commission found that Telkom, the *de facto* monopoly provider of telecom facilities required by VANS providers to enable them to provide services to their customers and, in addition, their competitor in the market for value-added services had abused its dominant position as the monopoly provider of telecom facilities by engaging in a number of anticompetitive practices (tied selling, refusal to deal and discriminatory pricing) in the market for value added network services.

Many similar claims of anticompetitive practices by Telkom have been voiced over the years by Internet Service Providers or by mobile telephone operators.

In Uganda[61] in 2001 the scenario was different but competition was still rare. The government realised that while the promotion of competition was one of the main goals of the privatisation and the liberalisation process, some privatised mobile phone

---

[58] *The Nation*, Nairobi, 21 April 2003.
[59] United Nations Conference on Trade and Development, as note 46 above.
[60] Id.
[61] *New Vision*, Kampala, 27 December 2001.

operators, such as MTN Uganda, UTL telecel and Celtel Uganda were engaging in price fixing with their competitors thus "denying customers the full benefits of competition". This moved the government to prepare an antitrust bill to deter these firms from pursuing this kind of activity.

A year earlier, in Zambia,[62] the Zambian Competition Commission was prompted to initiate an investigation of two private cell phone providers—Telcel and Zamcell—for alleged cartel practices of excessive pricing, following customer complaints that cellular phone service firms were working in league to charge excessive prices.

In 2002,[63] the Romanian Competition Council concluded an investigation into Romtelecom, the national dominant fixed-line telephone operator, and Global One Communications for undertaking non-competition clauses on the data transmission market (X25, Frame Relay, TCP/IP, ATM) and ISP (Internet Service Protocol) services market. These companies entered into a joint venture, Global One Communications Romania ("GOCR"), whose articles of association prevented the parties from creating or participating in any way, directly or indirectly, in Romanian companies competing with GOCR, and from competing with GOCR, directly or indirectly, as long as they had an interest in GOCR, and for a period of five years from the date when they ceased to be shareholders. Romtelecom argued that the non-competition clause represented an anti-competitive practice, as defined in art. 5(1) and 5(6) of the Romanian Competition Law preventing it from undertaking on its own any activity in the data transmission or ISP markets. The Council concluded that the non-competition clause produced harmful effects only during the years 1999 and 2000, when GOCR had 78 percent market share of the data transmission market, and Romtelecom had the financial and logistical means to enter this market. As a mitigating circumstance, the Competition Council noted that the non-competition clause was entered into when the competition law was not in force and therefore the parties had no intention of breaching any legal provisions.

One learns from the OECD report on Turkey[64] that the telecommunications sector has been a fertile field for proceedings under the Turkish competition law. For example, in a March 2002 decision against Turkcell and Telsim, the Board concluded that the two firms exercised joint dominance over the "essential facility" infrastructure necessary to provide national roaming capability for GSM mobile telephone services and had denied a prospective service provider use of their infrastructure without a legitimate basis, in violation of competition law.

Other Article 6 cases have involved Turk Telekom ("TTAS"), the state-owned monopoly provider of land line telephone infrastructure. In late 2002, a fine of TRL 1.1 trillion (USD 737,000) was imposed on TTAS for excluding competition in the dial-up internet services provider ("ISP") market. The Board found that independent

---

[62] Panafrican News Agency (PANA) Daily Newswire, 11 August 2000.
[63] OECD, Jont Group on Trade and Competition, *Anti-competitive Practices in the Telecom Sector in Romania*, 15 September 2004.
[64] OECD, as note 12 above.

ISPs could not effectively compete for retail customers because of the spread between the low prices charged by TTAS to its own retail customers and the high prices charged to the competing ISPs.

In Nigeria in 2001[65] Mobile Telecommunications Services Limited (MTS) called on the Nigerian Communications Commission (NCC) to apply sanctions against MTN Nigerian Communications Limited for "its anti-competitive actions and pronouncements" in the conducts of its business in the country. According to a high level MTS executive: "MTN is asking that operators like Multilinks and Intercellular, who began to offer limited mobility services must be stopped for MTN to have no threat to its business case." He said: "we believe this is an orchestrated attempt by MTN to derail our roll-out plans in December while it continues to attract more subscribers."

In Cambodia,[66] at the end of September 2000, there were complaints from users of Mobitel, a major mobile phone service provider that had an 85 percent share of the Cambodian mobile phone service market, that they could not reply to the SMS sent to them by users of Camshin, another mobile phone provider. It was subsequently found that Mobitel had deliberately blocked customers of Camshin from reaching the Mobitel phones. The problem was later solved through the intervention of the Ministry of Post and Telecommunications of Cambodia; however interconnection rates between different lines remain high.

In Chile,[67] the Competition Commission issued the maximum fine against Telefonica for using its power in the fixed local telephony market to gain a competitive advantage in the mobile telephony market. Telefonica owns a number of mobile firms, which offered a subscription to mobile users under which there was in effect no charge for the network services.

Those are but a few of the numerous competition problems which affect the telecommunication sector in a number of developing countries.

Similar problems where an incumbent with an essential facility tries to drive small competitors out of the market by denying them the possibility to interconnect are also typical in the electricity sector. Needless to say, reducing competition in the supply of electricity can be particularly damaging for the development of an industrial sector in a developing economy.

For example, in Turkey a 2003 decision[68] involved ÇEAS, a company holding a monopoly concession for the distribution and transmission of electric power in one of Turkey's 33 designated distribution areas. The Board found that refusals by ÇEAS to provide system interconnections for independent electric generation facilities were unjustified and fined it TRL 9.5 trillion (USD 6.4 million).

---

[65] *Financial Standard*, Lagos, 22 October 2001.
[66] *Cambodia Daily*, 18 October 2000, quoted in *Competition Scenario in Cambodia* prepared for Cuts International, *Advocacy and Capacity Building on Competition Policy and Law in Asia*, CUTS International, 2005.
[67] OECD, as note 4 above.
[68] OECD, as note 12 above.

Another service which is of considerable importance for the competitivity of business firms in developing countries is freight transportation. In addition to poor infrastructure, business firms in developing countries are often also victims of price-gouging by unscrupulous freight transportation operators engaging in anticompetitive practices or abusing their market power.

For example, in Malawi,[69] although the government liberalised the trucking sector, and in spite of the fact that industry consists of a few large firms, such as Trans African Transport (TAT), Central African Road Services (CARS), Zagaf, Welsons, Fersons, etc and many small ones, rates are not set competitively. The Road Transport Operators Association which includes among its members foreign trucking firms operating in Malawi (mainly South African and Zimbabwean firms) sets the rates for the industry at large.

In addition, there was not much possibility for businesses to avoid anticompetitive practices by using alternative means of transportation. Indeed, the railway company, which has a 25 year concession, enjoys a complete monopoly of rail services, without any form of regulation of rates or quality of service and there is only one shipping company that operates a monopoly service on Lake Malawi.

In 1999 in Zambia,[70] the Zambia Competition Commission (ZCC) rejected an application from Zambia Export Growers Association (Zega) to take over National Air Charters (NAC) because the acquisition would stifle competition in the cargo and service market.

In 2004,[71] the Union of African Shippers Council voiced opposition to tariff increases for North–South shipping services that went into effect 1 March 2004, arguing that the measure penalised its members and the economies of the region. The Europe-West Africa Trade Agreement (EWATA) (EWAC) conference had agreed to increase freight rates, and shipping agencies that were members of the cartel were required to implement the decision. Prominent among the shipping lines concerned are Delmas, Maersk Sealand, Nlle Dutch Africa Line, OT Africa Line, P&O Nedlloyd, Safmarine and West Afrika Linien Dienste.

In 2001, in Peru,[72] the 36 individuals licensed to pilot ships in Lima's Callao harbour (which is the most important harbour in Peru) and who until then had operated as individual competitors or 1-2 person firms, decided to eliminate competition among them. To do so they created three corporations (fearing that a single corporation might be considered a monopoly), and decided that one firm would "hire" all 36 pilots and the others would hire one or two pilots each. All 36 pilots considered themselves as working for the first corporation, but there was no real integration of their operations; they merely charged the same price. The other two corporations existed only on paper. A few months later, a new firm decided to enter the

---

[69] CUTS and Consumer Association of Malawi (CAMA), as note 2 above.
[70] *Times of Zambia*, 8 October 1999.
[71] *PANA*, Libreville, Gabon, 2 March 2004.
[72] OECD, as note 6 above.

market, and persuaded two of the pilots to join it. The other 34 pilots and their association sought to prevent this by engaging in various forms of harassment, including making a criminal charge of inducing a breach of contract.

In another case in Peru, a harbour administrator was charged with abusing its dominant position by forbidding other companies to offer towing services.

In 1995,[73] the Mexican Constitution was amended to allow private participation in the railroad sector, the RSL was enacted and guidelines for the privatisation process were issued. The government decided that the best option was a geographical or territorial separation of the network as follows: Northeast Railroad (FNE), North Pacific Railroad (FPN), South East Railroad (FSE), Railroad Terminal of the Valley of Mexico and several short lines. Territorial separation sought to enhance intra-railroad competition by ensuring that the main cities and ports were served by more than one railroad and to strengthen competition for freight traffic among points of origin and destination. The concessionaires have repeatedly accused one another of setting excessive, unfavourable and discriminatory rates, access conditions and even refusing to provide interconnection and right of way. The result has severely affected interline traffic, especially on long-distance routes, which has become an inefficient and non-competitive service that has lost market share to the trucking sector even though railroads have a natural competitive advantage in this segment of the market. The net consequence of these practices has been higher prices, delays and longer transport times, which make Mexican manufacturers less efficient and competitive.

Until 1990, Brazilian ports were controlled by a State owned company, giving no opportunity for competition.[74] In 1993, a law was passed that enabled the government to grant concessions to private enterprises for the exploitation of port infrastructures. A number of concessions have been granted over the past last decade, introducing competition on the cargo handling and storage market. Besides granting concessions for terminal operations to private enterprises, the port administration also control a public terminal, which is used by companies that do not own a terminal concession to load and unload their clients' cargo.

However, the privatisation of ports opened opportunities for anticompetitive practices on the part of the concessionaries. One such practice is the creation of "extra tariffs" by Port Operators. Most concession contracts only regulate the tariff for cargo handling. Other tariffs can be freely set. Concessionaries have therefore created various different tariffs that often do not represent a real service. The consequence is an artificial increase in the cost of cargo handling. Another type of anticompetitive conduct that has been observed in some Brazilian ports is the fact that concessionaries compete for space in the public terminals, even when space in their own terminal is available. This artificially increases costs and lowers the quality of other port operators who do not

---

[73] OECD Joint group on Trade and Competition, *Anticompetitive Practices in the Railroad Sector in Mexico*, 30 September 2004.
[74] OECD Joint Group on Trade and Competition, *Privatization and Competition in the Port Sector in Brazil*, February 2005.

own a terminal. Cases have been opened by the Secretariat of Economic Law (SDE) to investigate such conduct in the ports of Salvador, Santos, and Rio Grande.

Because of an inadequate rail system and the high costs, uncertainty and risks of inland trucking, Turkish importers and exporters depend heavily on maritime transport services[75] to distribute their goods into foreign markets. However, anticompetitive practices in this sector can raise maritime transport costs, increasing the overall price of final goods and thus, Turkish manufacturers become less competitive than foreign firms paying lower prices for, and having alternative and more efficient, transport services. Currently, RO-RO ship transportation in Turkey is carried by four lines: two Black Sea lines (the Western Black Sea line to Ukraine and the Eastern Black Sea line to Russia) and two Mediterranean lines (the Izmir-Trieste line and the Istanbul-Trieste Line, operated by UN). Only one firm currently operates the Izmir-Trieste line and another firm operates the Istanbul-Trieste line. Two firms compete on the Western Black Sea line, and a monopolistic situation exists on the Eastern Black Sea line (UT). In 2004 the Turkish Competition Authority initiated an investigation against UT and UN for allegedly entering into a price-fixing agreement. During 2004, both companies increased their prices three times, at the same time and in the same proportion (by 5 percent each time). Thus, pursuant to the Turkish Competition Act, these parties must prove that they acted independently or that their conduct was based on economic and commercial grounds. In addition, there are allegations of a pooling agreements between all the operators and attempts to prevent entry through predatory excess capacity reallocation of ships.

In Cambodia,[76] boat transportation services from Phnom Phen to Siem Reap are provided by eight private companies. The price for one-way travel was about US$ 10 for Cambodian nationals and around US$ 25 for foreigners. Competition between boat companies, however, drove down the prices. In 2005, the boat companies have entered into an agreement to fix their services prices to the above mentioned levels. The eight companies further agreed that they would not compete with each other anymore and would share departure schedules. According to their verbal agreement, only one boat may provide boat transportation service in a day by taking turn from one company to another. The bigger companies can have more quotas to provide the services.

To finish this survey of anticompetitive practices in various sectors of developing countries, let me now turn to practices in the industrial sector. We have already seen in the previous section that businesses in developing countries tended to suffer from artificially inflated prices for a number of the services they depend on such as freight transportation or telecommunications. We saw that they may also suffer from anticompetitive practices in the provision of their product inputs; for example, it is clear that anticompetitive practices in the cement industry lead to higher costs for

---

[75] OECD Joint Group on Trade and Competition, *Anticompetitive Practices in the Maritime Transport Sector in Turkey*, October 2004
[76] Competition Scenario in Cambodia, *Advocacy and Capacity Building on Competition law and Policy in Asia*, CUTS International, Economic Institute of Cambodia, 2005.

construction firms. But there are other clear examples of domestic anticompetitive practices transactions which penalise domestic manufacturing industries in developing countries.

For example, in October 1999,[77] the Zambian Competition Commission turned down an application by BOC Gases (formerly Zamox) to take over Industrial Gases. BOC Gases currently controls 80 percent of the local industrial gases markets while Industrial Gases controls approximately 19 percent of the market. The final 1 percent market share of the industrial gases market is controlled by the major consumers of industrial gases: ZCCM, Nitrogen Chemicals of Zambia (NCZ) and Tazara. According to the Board, the acquisition of Industrial Gases by BOC Gases would eliminate the small amount of competition in the sector and place control of 99 percent of the industrial gases market under one firm.

In 2000 it was reported in South Africa[78] that industrial sugar users had accused South Africa's sugar industry of operating as a cartel that abused an antiquated piece of legislation to fix local sugar prices. South African Federation of Soft Drink Manufacturers spokesman Liz Farquharson said that the outdated Sugar Act allowed the Sugar Association of South Africa to act as a cartel by setting a maximum price for sugar. This meant South Africa's mills all sold sugar at the same price. The association represents producers and South Africa's three sugar mills, Illovo, Tongaat-Hulett and Transvaal Suiker. Import duties and local prices of sugar were still centrally controlled. According to Farquharson, this was the last piece of outdated legislation similar to that of the country's old agricultural laws. Government efforts to change the law has met resistance from the sugar association. The move to import sugar gained momentum after the association increased prices by 6.25 percent in 2000. In reaction, users decided to import sugar. As a result of high duties and the depreciation of the rand, the price advantage was, however, marginal. In 1998/99 South Africa produced 2.6 million tons of sugar, of which an estimated 1.3 million tons was exported. The confectionery and soft drink manufacturers bought about 80 percent of domestically produced sugar. Sugar users were considering alternatives to remain competitive in the global market and soft-drink manufacturers were investigating a switch from cane to maize-based sweeteners. Confectioners were considering importing sweets as it was cheaper than producing them locally.

Also in South Africa,[79] the Competition Commission recommended that the South African Fine Paper division of pulp and paper giant Sappi be fined more than R500m for anti-competitive practices. This followed a case brought by paper wholesaler Papercor, which claimed it had found it impossible to get bulk supplies from Sappi or its merchants at the same price offered to other customers, and that Sappi was thus trying to squeeze Papercor out of the market. Sappi, in turn, argued that Papercor was unable to satisfy standard customer trading criteria, which included

---

[77] *Times of Zambia*, 8 October 1999.
[78] *Business Day*, South Africa, 27 March 2000.
[79] *Business Day*, South Africa, 30 November 2001.

creditworthiness. The commission declared Sappi to be in breach of the Competition Act, by abusing its dominant position in the local market. Papercor CE Geoff Saks said that Sappi: "just won't supply us with paper. They have ganged up with our opposition to try and put us out of business." He stated that Sappi had a powerful influence over the local market because: "in SA, you have to do business with Sappi." He added: "We are now forced to import from overseas suppliers it's ludicrous".

The South African Competition Tribunal also decided to reject as anticompetitive the plans of MONDI, an Anglo American paper subsidiary to acquire Kohler Cores & Tubes on the basis that it would reinforce a domestic duopoly.[80] The commission and the tribunal both said the merger of the two companies would mean there would only be one vertically integrated maker, which might lead to a conflict in the market as it would be both a supplier of paper and core board.

The Jordanian aluminium cartel is a particularly telling example.[81] Four aluminium producers cover Jordanian market consumption, namely: Modern Aluminium Industrial Co. (MODAL), Arabic Aluminium Industrial Co. (AALU), National Aluminium Industrial Co. (NALCO) and Universal Metal Extrusion Co. (UMEX). In April 2000, the above-mentioned companies entered into a joint agreement (the Jordanian Company for Aluminium Marketing Industry Agreement, JAMC) to regulate domestic production and marketing operations as follows: 1) to share the domestic market on the following basis: MODAL 40 percent; AALU 21 percent; NALCO 21 percent; UMEX 18 percent; 2) to fix prices and profit margins of aluminium products; 3) to prohibit direct sales by the Parties on the domestic market other than via JAMC. In 2003, the aluminium cartel was reported by MODAL Co. The Competition Directorate therefore initiated an investigation analysing the agreement in light of the new Competition Law for the industry and trade sector. It concluded that the loss of competition led to increases in aluminium prices by JD 400–500 per ton, limited consumers' range of choices and locally produced products. Regarding NALCO's experience, the General Manager notes that terminating the above-mentioned agreement increased competition within the sector as the four companies battled to dominate the market, leading prices to fall by 22–27 percent,

In Brazil,[82] during the 1990s, the market for flat rolled steel was characterised by high concentration (CSN, 40 percent; UNIMINAS, 35 percent; and COSIPA, 25 percent), high entry barriers and lack of competitive imports. Concerned with price control attribution by the Ministry of Finance during prior years, representatives of the companies and the steel association went to SEAÉs offices on 30 July 1996 to say that they would increase prices by a specific amount on a specific date. This event started the process of a cartel investigation against the companies involved. In 1999, CADE

---

[80] *Business Day*, Johannesburg, 1 July 2002.
[81] OECD, Joint Group On Trade and Competition, *Anti-Competitive Practice in the Aluminium Industry in Jordan*, February 2005.
[82] OECD, Joint Group on Trade and Competition, *Anticompetitive Practice in the Brazilian Steel Industry*, February 2005.

decided to condemn the companies, based on the "parallelism plus doctrine", for a combination of structural factors favourable to collusion (i.e. few players, high entry barriers) and the 1996 SEAE meeting, which demonstrated that the companies had previously discussed price increases. The fines were set at 1 percent of the companies' 1996 gross income (CSN: R$ 22 million, Usiminas: R$ 16 million, Cosipa: R$ 13 million. The decision was appealed and was confirmed by the first instance court, based on the parallelism behaviour, but not considering the SEAE meeting.

Finally in the industrial sector, it may also be the case that domestic industries in developing countries are not only the potential victims of anticompetitive practices but also the seat of such practices.

In South Africa[83] in 2003, the Competition Commission advised against a merger which involved a major producer of bottle tops. Coleus Packaging, a subsidiary of South African Breweries (SAB), wanted to acquire Highveld Steel's Rheem crown plant which manufactures metal crown bottle tops used in the liquor and soft beverage industry. Highveld was disposing of its non-core packaging assets, which included the Rheem bottle top plant, having already disposed of its beverage can plant. The transaction was seen as a vertical merger because it would link the production of bottle tops to a major customer. For this reason, the Commission recommended to the Competition Tribunal that the merger be blocked. The Commission worried that the merger would result in SAB owning the country's largest crown manufacturing plant and felt that this could lessen competition in the downstream market. Rheem's only competitor and a new entrant to the market, Metal Closure Group, a Cape Town based manufacturer of crowns, made submissions to the Commission arguing that the merger should be prohibited. Metal Closure alleged the takeover would result in the possible loss of an important customer, Amalgamated Beverages Industries, a soft drinks producer whose controlling shareholder is SAB. SAB's competitors, Distell and Guinness, also opposed the proposed merger, on the grounds that SAB could potentially reduce competition in the crown market, which might raise bottle top prices.

That same year, the Zambian Board of Commissioners[84] rejected the application of Dunavant Zambia Limited to take over Amaka Cotton ginnery assets. The Board of Commissioners felt that this acquisition was likely to prevent, restrict and distort competition in the relevant market. They further stated that allowing another new entrant, other than Dunavant Zambia Limited, in the cotton ginning market would enhance effective competition

III. LESSONS FROM EMPIRICAL EVIDENCE

I would now like to draw some lessons from all these cases.

---

[83] *Business Day*, Johannesburg, 17 January 2003.
[84] Press release on 19th Zambia Competition Commission Board meeting decisions, 31 October 2003.

CARTELS AND COLLUSION   133

1) Clearly, the scope for anticompetitive activity in developing countries is staggering in terms of the type of practices (cartels, abuses of dominance, vertical restrictions to competition or anticompetitive mergers), the sectors affected (bread, chicken, beer, retail distribution, cement, aluminium, steel, telecommunications, railways, bus services, freight, professional services) and potential harm to economies (as we saw in several instances where price surcharges of up to 25 to 30 percent are not uncommon in some sectors). In addition, as previously mentioned, the documented practices referred to are only a sample of actual practices. As a matter of fact, this sample can be seen as an indicator of competition problems existing in most developing countries because we saw that the same practices are often encountered in the same sectors in many countries and there is no reason to believe that they are limited only to the countries where they have so far been observed. For example, it is highly likely that some of the practices observed in East African countries could also be observed in West Africa. A number of developing countries have small concentrated economies with regionally or locally segmented markets within the country characterised by high barriers (due, among other things, to poor communications infrastructure, mono-polistic behaviour by the operators of essential facilities, trade barriers etc.), a weak industrial base, and limited consumer demand. Economic theory predicts that such economies would be prone to anticompetitive structures, transactions and practices. Firms in developing countries, whether large or small, behave no differently from firms in developed countries. When they can increase their profits to the detriment of consumers through an agreement with their competitors, they do. When they can eliminate competitors they do. When they can increase prices to the detriment of consumers, they do.

2) One must then ask why it is that there is such a gap between economic reality and political scepticism regarding competition law and competition law enforcement in some of the countries concerned by the sample we worked from. It seems remarkable, for example, that many instances of anticompetitive practices or transactions were observed in countries such as Kenya, Zambia and Zimbabwe, where there is very little political support for existing (vibrant) competition institutions and where government officials routinely assert that competition law enforcement is neither useful nor necessary for developing their country. A number of hypothesis can be offered to explain why this is so. One hypothesis is that public debate on competition has relied too much on theoretical arguments (often too abstract or too general to be very persuasive from a public policy standpoint) and that there has not been enough emphasis on a systematic exploration and presentation of facts that would raise public awareness of the problems. This article is an attempt to reverse that trend.

3) As mentioned above, many anticompetitive practices or transactions which affect developing countries emanate from local firms, sometimes very small local firms (for example in the retail sector), sometimes from sizeable developing countries firms implanted in several countries located in a particular region (such as in the beer sector in Africa and in Latin America). Thus, although we know from previous research that

multinational firms based in developed countries can also engage in anticompetitive practices or transactions and can impose considerable harm on the economy of developing countries, they are not, by a long shot, the only source of anticompetitive practices affecting developing countries. Thus competition problems in developing countries should not be seen as an issue of "them" (firms from developed countries) against "us" (firms or consumers in developing countries). Because of this, it is difficult to adhere to the views occasionally expressed in international fora that competition law and competition law enforcement are not a useful tool for economic development or that interest for competition law enforcement in developing countries reflects mainly a desire to facilitate the penetration of multinational firms in developing economy markets.

4) The fact that a number of potentially anticompetitive mergers involve firms based in developing countries that are simultaneously present in several neighbouring countries and the fact that such firms pursue regional strategies in terms of investment, marketing, production, employment and competition (for example, the production and the distribution of beer, the production of cement etc.) suggests that developing countries would indeed benefit greatly from regional agreements on competition law enforcement, whether such agreements are part of trade agreements or are stand alone agreements between national competition agencies. It is therefore encouraging, that an increasing number of regional groups (Mercosur and the Andean Community in South America, Caricom in the Caribbean, Comesa, Cemac, UEMOA in Africa) have begun to consider the development of regional competition law enforcement systems. One can only wish that the speed of development in this area would accelerate.

5) Aside from their potential impact on economic development, anticompetitive practices or transactions such as price fixing in the retail sector or in the consumer goods sector clearly impose a large cost on consumers, and in particular the poorest consumers, by artificially increasing the price of basic necessities (such as chicken, bread, milk, beer, cement, bus transportation) and therefore reducing the real income of poorer consumers. Poor consumers consume a comparatively high proportion of locally produced goods and services, for which there is little competition even at the local level. If a sizeable portion of these goods and services are beset by competition problems and subject to overcharges of 10 to 15 percent, the problems of the poor will be compounded and their lives made even worse. Thus, the fight against extortionary anticompetitive strategies should rightly be a part of pro-poor policies.

6) It is also clear from the data we have presented that poor farmers are often victimized, on the one hand, by large firms which supply their inputs (chemical firms for fertilisers, petroleum firms providing fuel for tractors, banking or insurance etc.) by intermediaries (trading in tea, coffee, tobacco, fish etc.) who, because they are concentrated, wield a lot of buying power and are occasionally able to conspire with one other to keep the prices paid to farmers artificially low, and finally by the operators of freight transport (for example, the cases of railways in Mexico or Malawi and ports in Peru or Brazil). Because poor farmers are often also poor consumers, they can be

doubly the victims of anticompetitive practices and the social dimension of that problem cannot be ignored.

7) We have also seen that anticompetitive practices involving key industrial inputs for manufacturing processes (such as steel for the automobile industry in Brazil, aluminium for the building industry in Jordan or sugar or metal crown for the beer and soft drink industries in South Africa) together with abusively high transport costs and high capital costs decrease the competitivity of local industries and directly hamper industrial growth, thereby compounding the problems of economic underdevelopment and unemployment. Fighting anticompetitive practices which limit economic opportunities for industrial development should also rightly be part of a pro-growth policy agenda.

This is not to say that competition law enforcement should be the only policy tool of economic development. There are market failures, incomplete markets, externalities, possibly a trade off between accelerated growth and allocation of resources, a necessity to alleviate the cost of transition and to facilitate this process due to the process of reallocation of resources. Even if one believes in the usefulness of competition, there is a role for government intervention in a number of areas. Also, competition law enforcement is not the only means of promoting competition. Trade policy and deregulation are other crucial elements of a development policy. However, what clearly emerges from our case studies is that competition law enforcement is a necessary complement to market oriented reforms.

What have we now learned about the challenges to competition law enforcement in developing countries?

8) Changing the mindset of politicians, the bureaucracy, the business community, and the public, in other words developing a competition culture, is necessary to diminish the cost of enforcing competition laws. However, this is an exceedingly slow process. We have seen examples that underline the challenge of developing a competition culture, for example in Brazil where steelmakers chose to report their price cartel because they thought that prices were still controlled in their country. Even if, in some rare cases, the lack of understanding of competition laws can facilitate the work of a competition authority by making the gathering of proof of anticompetitive practices easier, in many countries it does not help the competition authority to build the constituency it needs to be immune from pressure and to have a stable source of revenues.

9) Cartel enforcement is a highly promising field for a new competition authority with limited staff resources because, as we have seen, there are a large number of horizontal anticompetitive agreements in a number of countries and because many cases concern products (retail, bread, chicken, cement, etc.) which are important to the daily life of the general public. It therefore comes as no surprise that the most famous Peruvian case dealt with by Indecopi was a chicken case or that the most controversial merger case in Zambia was the Cilanga cement merger. Furthermore, if the prosecution of cartels requires wide ranging investigatory powers, it does not

require as much economic expertise as the prosecution of other types of anticompetitive practices.

However cartel enforcement can be a challenge, particularly in small developing countries or in countries with comparatively concentrated industrial structures, because in such countries horizontal anticompetitive restraints can be achieved through tacit collusion among a small number of players who know each other well and understand each other rather than through explicit agreements. Whenever this is the case, the competition authority will face difficulties gathering proofs of a competition law violation that will stand in court. In order to overcome this problem a number of developing countries have shown a great deal of interest for learning from competition authorities in countries with more experience than they have in the area of competition law enforcement what kind of evidence, besides proof of parallel conduct, one needs to be able to establish the proof of tacit horizontal agreements. In some other developing countries, the competition law includes a provision allowing the competition authority to infer an anticompetitive agreement from parallel behaviour.

For example, the 1999 CADE decision in Brazil concerning the steel cartel which we referred to earlier[85] was appealed and was confirmed in the first instance court based on the parallel behavior of the firms. The court first considered a number of structural factor of the market for steel: the small number of enterprises, the homogeneity of the product, the existence of high barriers to entry, the low monitoring costs of the cartel, the lack of incentives to desertion, the similarity of cost structures, the similarity of the production technology used by the different firms and the stability in the market shares. The court then remarked that as a consequence of these market conditions, similar prices in the industry and their readjustments in amount and time could be expected, even in the absence of cartel and then noted, however, that in the particular case of the steel market the economic explanations invoked by the litigants were fragile and not sufficient to explain the readjustment of prices that happened in 1996. In particular it noted that the alternation of enterprises in the leadership of price increases made it difficult to believe in non-collusive leadership process.

In Turkey, Article 4 of the Competition law gives a non-exclusive list of anticompetitive practices including price fixing, market division, concerted control of outputs or inputs, boycotts, and entry deterrence. A unique feature of Article 4, however, is language providing that the existence of unlawful collusion among competitors may be inferred if market conduct or conditions are similar to those that would arise in a market where competition is artificially distorted. The Board's approach to this presumption has been a topic of considerable controversy.

10) There is a fair amount of controversy over the importance and the usefulness of merger control in developing countries. Some suggest that merger control is too complex for a young competition authority with limited experience and few resources. Others, and in particular David Lewis who heads the South African Competition

---

[85] OECD, Joint Group on Trade and Competition, as note 82 above.

tribunal, have suggested that merger control is particularly important for developing countries both because anticompetitive mergers in such countries are frequent and potentially very damaging and because young competition authorities can develop a reputation of strength and relevance faster and more easily through merger control cases (because in merger cases notifying parties have the duty to provide the information required by the competition authority) than through cases of anticompetitive practices (because in such cases there is no compulsory notification and competition authorities have to use whatever investigatory powers they have to try to get the evidence necessary to characterise a violation). What we learn from the cases we reviewed is that, potentially anticompetitive mergers, whether purely domestic or transnational, are frequent in developing countries (for example bottlers of soft drinks in Kenya, traditional beer manufacturers in Malawi, bottlers of soft drinks, cement plants or cotton ginning plants in Zambia, tobacco manufacturers in Zimbabwe, bottle tops, paper manufacturers, banks in South Africa, banks in Chile etc.) and that for the reasons discussed when dealing with tacit agreements, it is often extremely difficult to remedy situations in which oligopolistic interdependence has been reinforced by mergers.

11) Privatisation and the granting of concessions have led to recurring problems of abuse of dominance in a number of sectors, such as rail transportation, telecommunications, electricity, water distribution, ports etc. in many developing countries. These problems have occasionally led to a severe socio-political crisis. Clearly the problem of organising the regulation of privatised monopolies has not been easy to solve in a number of countries.

[7]

Latin America and the Control of International Cartels

JOHN M CONNOR[*]

I. Introduction

Despite the evident antitrust successes in sanctioning international cartels since 1990, many remain skeptical about whether current enforcement regimes are capable of serving the aims of antitrust. A narrow construction on the purpose of antitrust laws limits it to maximizing consumer welfare and efficiency; a broader interpretation gives some weight to income redistribution, small business protection, or dispersion of political and economic power. However, under either stance the aims of antitrust are served by competition policies that deter recidivism. Deterrence is the most commonly accepted legal-economic theory that justifies the passage of antitrust laws, but its role as a practical guide to imposing anti-cartel sanctions across world jurisdictions is doubtful.

While deterrence may have improved marginally in the 1990s, scholars of modern international cartels believe that current competition policies cannot fully deter them because they are 'oriented towards addressing harm done in domestic markets ... [or] merely prohibit cartels without [sufficiently strong] sanctions'.[1] Connor and Lande[2] find that cartel overcharges are so high and conspiracies so durable that current US public and private monetary sanctions provide inadequate deterrence. International cartels—those with international participation—are more difficult to convict yet as a group are even more harmful to customer welfare than domestic collusion. *Global* cartels—those that operate across multi-continental markets—typically reap above-average monopoly profits in jurisdictions with weak anti-cartel enforcement. Moreover, empirical evidence from recent years demonstrates a significant degree of continued cartel formation

---

[*] Professor of Industrial Economics, Purdue University.

[1] Simon J Evenett, Margaret C Levenstein and Valerie Y Suslow, 'International Cartel Enforcement: Lessons from the 1990s' 24 *The World Economy* 1221–45 (2001).

[2] John M Connor and Robert H Lande, 'How High Do Cartels Raise Prices? Implications for Optimal Cartel Fines' 80 *Tulane Law Review* 513–70 (2005).

and multiple corporate convictions for price fixing. It would appear that either greater sanctions ought to be applied, or that a multilateral approach should be implemented or both, in order to approach optimal deterrence of international price fixing.[3]

Although studies exist of prosecutions of individual cartels and of anti-cartel efforts in single jurisdictions, few have examined the global effort to deter cartels. The purpose of this chapter is to describe the magnitude of and trends in global antitrust sanctions imposed on modern international cartels, paying special attention to Latin America's anti-cartel efforts. By doing so, this chapter can contribute critical information for the ongoing debate about the effectiveness of global antitrust sanctions in deterring international price-fixing conduct.

The focus of this chapter is on monetary antitrust sanctions that have been imposed on detected private hard-core international cartels between January 1990 and December 2007, and the impact upon Latin America. Monetary sanctions include:

a) *fines* imposed by antitrust authorities on both corporations and individuals; and

b) *payments* made by defendants in private suits to direct and indirect buyers of cartelized products. Payments made by defendants to settle private class action suits usually include the legal fees and costs incurred by plaintiffs in prosecuting their cases.

International cartels are those that have participants from two or more countries; the qualifier does not refer to the geographic scope of the cartel's agreement. *Private* cartels are those that operate without the active involvement of governments or legal protection of national sovereignty. Thus, mandatory agricultural marketing orders are not private, neither are cartels which parliamentary statutes establish (eg, the East India Company), or by treaties among nations (eg, OPEC).

The next section of this chapter presents a broad historical summary of anti-cartel enforcement, followed by a brief literature review and descriptions of anti-cartel laws and policies. The remaining sections lay out the cartel data set, actual enforcement patterns 1990–2007, and measures of effectiveness of sanctions.

---

[3] One way of increasing sanctions without changing statutes is to extend standing to foreign buyers to permit them to sue for private damages in US courts. On the *Empagram* case, see W Davis, 'US Antitrust Treatment of International Cartels' 17 *Antitrust* 31–35 (2003); John M Connor and Darren Bush, 'How to Block Cartel Formation and Price Fixing: Using Extraterritorial Application of the Antitrust Laws as a Deterrent' 122 *Pennsylvania State University Law Review* 813 (2008).

II. Historical Sketch of Anti-Cartel Enforcement

Nations in nearly every corner of the world have adopted antitrust laws, and virtually all of these laws make price fixing illegal in most circumstances.[4] Prior to World War II, only the United States had an effectively enforced antitrust law, the Sherman Act,[5] but there were few significant US prosecutions of international cartels until the mid-1940s.[6] By the mid-1960s, at least two dozen countries had antitrust laws and 'were engaged in serious efforts to control restrictive practices'.[7] By 1996, 70 countries had adopted competition laws; these countries comprised about 78 per cent of world output and 86 per cent of the value of world trade.[8] With the adoption of an antitrust law in China in 2007, virtually all the world's leading economies have made cartels illegal.[9] Of course, the effectiveness of enforcement of these laws varies widely, as do the legal standards and sanctions available.

Attempts to collude on market prices or output are as old as markets themselves.[10] Most pre-modern cartels were associations whose rules were supported by national courts or the active participation of governments. Formal *private* international cartels, on the other hand, are more recent historical phenomena. The first wave of international cartels began as a consequence of an economic downturn in Germany in the 1870s; the potash syndicate is one of the better studied cartels of this era.[11] Many of the first US-based international cartels began about the same time.[12] Very few if any of these pioneering schemes survived the economic disruptions spawned by World War I, but many were re-established in the early 1920s only to disband again in 1939. Most of these 'interwar cartels' were organized by European companies or national associations allocating exclusive territories to its members—monopolies for domestic commerce and market quotas for international trade to the rest of the world. In the 1930s, nearly 200 private cartels were estimated to have controlled 40 per cent of world commodity

---

[4] Wyatt Wells, *Antitrust and the Formation of the Postwar World* (New York, Columbia University Press, 2002); ABA, *Competition Laws Outside the United States*, vols I and II (Chicago, American Bar Association, 2002 and 2005 Supplement).

[5] 15 USC § 1–7.

[6] Wendell Berge, *Cartels: Challenge to a Free World* (Washington, DC, Public Affairs Press, 1944); George W Stocking and Myron W Watkins, *Cartels or Competition?* (New York, Twentieth Century Fund, 1948).

[7] Corwin D Edwards, *Control of Cartels and Monopolies: An International Comparison* (Dobbs Ferry, NY, Oceana Publications, 1967).

[8] Mark R A Palim, 'The Worldwide Growth of Competition Law: An Empirical Analysis' 43 *Antitrust Bulletin* 105–45 (1998).

[9] China's new law was passed on Aug 30, 2007 and came into force Aug 1, 2008.

[10] Roman Piotrowski, *Cartels and Trusts* (London, George Allen & Unwin, 1933).

[11] Harm G Schröter, 'The International Potash Syndicate' in Dominique Barjot (ed), *International Cartels Revisited, 1880–1980* (Caen, France, Editions-diffusion du Lys, 1994); Philip C Newman, 'Key German Cartels under the Nazi Regime' 62 *Quarterly Journal of Economics* 576–95 (1948).

[12] Elliot Jones, *The Trust Problem in the United States* (New York, Macmillan, 1900, 1921); William Yandell Elliott *et al*, *International Control in the Non-Ferrous Metals* (New York, Macmillan, 1937).

trade.[13] Participation by Latin American firms in interwar international cartels was confined to a few agricultural and mining schemes.

From 1943 to 1949, the US Department of Justice (DOJ) convicted dozens of international cartels and won nearly all of the criminal cases.[14] From 1950 until 1995, the DOJ launched few cases against alleged international cartels, and the few that it brought to trial mostly resulted in embarrassing losses.[15] The EU began imposing fines on cartels in 1969, with substantial and accelerating fines beginning in the mid-1980s; it principally tended to target intra-EU cartels until about 2000.[16]

Modern international cartels—those detected since 1990—have some distinct characteristics. In recognition of the key industry positions attained by East Asian manufacturers in many lines of business since 1960, most modern cartels have had to include Asian corporations as members. Similarly, a large number of international cartels have sought to control markets in what business marketers call the Triad—North America, Western Europe, and the most industrialized nations of East Asia. Another unique feature is that they were formed by companies that were aware of the antitrust risks. Since the beginning of serious anti-cartel enforcement by the European Union in the late 1980s, international cartelists have had to weigh the benefits of monopoly profits against some probability of being apprehended and punished for collusion in multiple jurisdictions.[17] The antitrust authorities of Canada, the EU and the United States implemented new policies and procedures in the 1990s that are widely believed to have significantly increased the probability of detection. Most obviously, the severity of penalties directed at international cartels has soared compared with the preceding decades. These authorities reallocated enforcement resources toward prosecution of such cartels, increased cross-authority coordination, adopted more effective automatic leniency and 'amnesty plus' programs, imposed higher corporate

---

[13] Corwin D Edwards, *Economic and Political Aspects of International Cartels* (Washington, DC, US Gov't Printing Office, 1944).

[14] Wells, above n 4, at 96–116, 125–36.

[15] During 1980–94, the DOJ brought only four cases (out of 1,025 criminal price-fixing suits) against international cartels (Joseph C Gallo *et al*, 'Department of Justice Antitrust Enforcement 1955–1997' 17 *Review of Industrial Organization* 75–133 (2000)). See also, John M. Connor, Global Price Fixing, 2nd edition. (Heidelberg, Springer, 2007).

[16] The EU's first two decisions (*Quinine* and *Dyestuffs*) in 1969 involved global cartels, but there were few such convictions until the *Lysine* decision was announced in 2000 (Christopher Harding and Julian Joshua, *Regulating Cartels in Europe: A Study of Legal Control of Corporate Delinquency* (New York, Oxford University Press, 2003), 121–24). See *Amino Acids* (Case COMP 36.545/F3) Commission Decision 2001/418/EC (June 7, 2000) OJ L 152/24; *Quinine Cartel* (Case IV/26.623) Commission Decision 69/240 EEC (1969) OJ L 192/5 (1969); *Dyestuffs Cartel* (1969) OJ L 195/11; *In Re Amino Acid Antitrust Litigation*, 1996 WL 164434 (ND Ill, Apr 2, 1996).

[17] The story of the increasingly effective EU prosecution of cartelists is told in Harding and Joshua, above n 16. Canada, Australia and South Korea have aggressively pursued international cartels since 1990. Opinions vary about the dedication of Japan's FTC to fighting cartels (Harry First, 'Antitrust Enforcement in Japan' 64 *Antitrust Law Journal* 137 (1995); Stuart M Chemtob, 'Antitrust Deterrence in the United States and Japan' Remarks at Competition Policy in the Global Trading System Conference, Washington, DC, June 23, 2000).

fines, and in some jurisdictions applied individual criminal penalties.[18] As the decade of the 1990s progressed, rather than concerned calls for reform in the face of an alarming onslaught of cartels, the speeches of top antitrust officials began to acquire a tone of triumphalism.[19]

III. Literature Review

Analyses of US antitrust prosecutions and convictions of cartels are commonplace, but similar analyses for other jurisdictions are uncommon. Gallo *et al*[20] review the enforcement of the Sherman Act by the US DOJ for the period 1955–97. They describe the number of antitrust cases by type and outcome over time. For per se horizontal violations (a category that corresponds closely to cartels), Gallo *et al* find a total of only 34 international cases during 1955 to 1989, merely 2.3 per cent of all such cases. During 1990–2002, the international rate dropped to 0.4 per cent, but from the late 1990s the rate exceeded 50 per cent.[21] Gallo *et al* find that the average number of defendants per cartel was about four, and that the average size of a cartel's affected sales was 870 million 1982 dollars (about 1,700 million 2007 dollars).[22] The average duration of these US conspiracies was 5.4 years, with no trend over time. Finally, this study determines that the total fines imposed on 2,908 companies during 1955–97 was $305 million (approximately 839 million in 2007 dollars), two-thirds of which was imposed after 1989. In addition, 143 individuals were fined a total of $30 million (83 million in 2007 dollars).

---

[18] John M Connor, *Global Price Fixing*, 2nd edn (Heidelberg, Springer, 2007); OECD, *Report on the Nature and Impact of Hard Core Cartels and Sanctions against Cartels under National Competition Laws* (DAFFE/COMP (2002) 7), Paris, Organization for Economic Co-operation and Development (April 9, 2002); Wouter P J Wils, 'The Commission's New Method for Calculating Fines in Antitrust Cases' 23 *European Law Review* 252–63 (1998); *Final Report of the International Competition Policy Advisory Committee to the Attorney General*, Washington, DC, US DOJ (2000) (herein 'ICPAC'); Gary R Spratling, 'International Cartels', Speech before the American Conference Institute's 7th National Conference on the Foreign Corrupt Practices Act, Washington, DC (Dec 9, 1999); Donald Klawiter, 'After the Deluge: The Powerful Effect of Substantial Criminal Fines, Imprisonment, and Other Penalties in the Age of International Criminal Enforcement' (2001) 69 *George Washington Law Review* 745–65; William J Kolasky, 'Antitrust Compliance Programs: The Government Perspective', Address at the Corporate Compliance 2002 Conference, Practicing Law Institute, San Francisco, CA (July 12, 2002).

[19] Anthony V Nanni, 'Squeezing the Cartels: Criminal Enforcement Gets Tough' *Legal Times*, April 20, 2002, at 30–35; Scott D Hammond, 'From Hollywood to Hong Kong—Criminal Antitrust Enforcement is Coming to a City Near You', Address at Antitrust Beyond Borders Conference, Chicago, IL (Nov 9, 2001); Mario Monti, 'The Fight against Cartels' Address before EMAC, Brussels, Belgium (Sept 11, 2002), <http://europa.eu.int/rapid...>; R Hewitt Pate, 'The DOJ International Antitrust Program—Gaining Momentum', Speech before the American Bar Association, New York City (Feb 6, 2003); Joel I Klein, Address at the International Anti-Cartel Enforcement Conference, Washington, DC (Sept 30, 1999).

[20] Gallo *et al*, above n 15.

[21] John M Connor, *Price-Fixing Overcharges: Legal and Economic Evidence* ch 4, pp 59–153 in John B Kirkwood (ed), Jan 2007 *Research in Law and Economics* Vol 22 (Oxford, Amsterdam and San Diego, Elsevier).

[22] Gallo *et al*, above n 15.

Russo *et al*[23] compile lists of all cartel decisions taken by the EC from the beginning in 1969 to Spring 2007; Guersent summarizes cartel conduct and EC sanctions taken against 19 international cartels from July 2001 to December 2003[24]; and Harding and Joshua offer an admirable narrative of the evolution of EU cartel enforcement.[25] Levenstein and Suslow survey the economics of cartels, but do not cover legal treatment of cartels.[26]

The Organization for Economic Co-operation and Development (OECD) has an active program for the consideration of a common policy approach towards international cartels. Its report *Hard Core Cartels* presents a unique survey of its member countries' experiences in sanctioning such cartels.[27] In addition, the OECD organizes voluntary annual reporting on competition law developments and enforcement by both its members and non-members; comparable annual reports are available for Argentina, Brazil and Mexico.[28] Particularly valuable are occasional *Peer Reviews* conducted by the OECD upon the request of antitrust authorities; four such reviews have recently been conducted for Argentina, Brazil, Chile and Mexico.[29] The limited literature on Latin American cartel enforcement will be discussed below.

IV. Anti-Cartel Laws and Policies

This section describes the legal basis for antitrust enforcement, the sanctions that can be imposed on cartels, and reasons for successful prosecution in the world's

---

[23] Francesco Russo *et al*, 'European Commission Decisions on Competition' (ACLE Working Paper 2007–04, Amsterdam Center for Law and Economics, Aug 23, 2007), at 34–96.

[24] O Guersent (ed), 'The Fight Against International Cartels of the European Commission: 19 Decisions in 19 Months between July 2001 and December 2003', Brussels: EC Directorate for Competition (2001) <http://europa.eu.int/indus/competition/antitrust>.

[25] Harding and Joshua, above n 16.

[26] Margaret C Levenstein and Valerie Y Suslow, 'Cartel Contract Duration: Empirical Evidence from International Cartels, in Grossman' in Z Peter (ed), *How Cartels Endure and How They Fail: Studies of Industrial Collusion* (Cheltenham, UK, Edward Elgar, 2004).

[27] OECD (2002), above n 18.

[28] OECD, *Annual Report on Competition Policy Developments in Argentina* (DAF/COMP(2005)33), Paris, OECD (Oct 17, 2005a and previous), <http://www.oecd.org/countrylist/0,3349,en_2649_37463_28325800_1_1_1_37463,00.html>; OECD, *Annual Report on Competition Policy Developments in Brazil* (DAF/COMP(2007)15), Paris, OECD (May 25, 2007a and previous), <http://www.oecd.org/countrylist/0,3349,en_2649_37463_28325800_1_1_1_37463,00.html>; OECD, *Annual Report on Competition Policy Developments in Mexico* (DAF/COMP(2007)14/25), Paris, OECD (May 21, 2007b and previous), <http://www.oecd.org/countrylist/0,3349,en_2649_37463_28325800_1_1_1_37463,00.html>.

[29] OECD, *Competition Law and Policy in Chile: A Peer Review* (Paris, OECD, 2004a)); OECD, *Competition Law and Policy in Mexico: A Peer Review* Paris, OECD, 2004b); OECD, *Competition Law and Policy in Brazil: A PeerReview* (Paris, OECD, 2005b); OECD, *Competition Law and Policy in Argentina: A Peer Review* (Paris, OECD, 2006).

three most active antitrust jurisdictions: the United States, the EU, and Canada.[30] With these three institutions as benchmarks, I then outline the major features of competition-law enforcement in four of Latin America's most active national authorities—Argentina, Brazil, Chile and Mexico.[31]

The choice of these four authorities is not arbitrary. When I last surveyed the antitrust landscape of Europe and the New World in the late 1990s, Argentina, Brazil, Chile and Mexico were already at the forefront in adopting the 'Antitrust Idea'.[32] Since the early 1990s, limitations to effective enforcement were diagnosed by the four nations, several appropriate amendments have been made to national competition laws, and new enforcement policies (many inspired by successes of foreign antitrust authorities) have become standard operating procedures. Public interest in anti-competitive acts still remains highest in these four Latin American nations. Clarke *et al*[32a] show that up through January 2005, the top four nations in Latin America ranked by the number of allegations of anti-competitive activities were Brazil, Mexico, Argentina and Chile; they account for 69 per cent of all such allegations. Moreover, data presented in this chapter confirm that these countries have the continent's strongest record of international cartel enforcement.

A. The United States

'Naked' cartels, those arranged through direct explicit communications between independent firms, are per se violations of US law; no amount of evidence concerning circumstances in the industry or effects of the agreement on markets will be considered evidentiary in determining guilt.[33] More than 90 per cent of detected conspiracies are serious enough and the evidence of intent strong enough that corporations and individuals will be charged by the Antitrust Division of the DOJ as a criminal matter. Unless an investigation is closed, nearly all indicted cartel participants

---

[30] A Working Paper authored by OECD economist Jens Hoj, 'Competition Law and Policy Indicators for the OECD Countries' (Economics Department Working Paper No 586 (ECO/WKP(2007)28), Paris, OECD, Aug 8, 2007), at 13–16, confirms the leading status of these three jurisdictions in overall competition law enforcement.

[31] In Brazil and Chile, as in the United States, the work of the national competition authorities is supplemented by provincial or State-level competition law authorities; these sub-national authorities are beyond the scope of this chapter.

[32] John M Connor, 'International Convergence of Antitrust Laws and Enforcement (I)' 28 *Law and Economics Review* 17–30 (1997a); John M Connor, 'International Convergence of Antitrust Laws and Enforcement (II)' 28 *Antitrust Law and Economics Review* 73–94 (1997b). See also Jaime Fernandez, 'Antitrust Regulation in Latin America' 30 *The International Lawyer* 521–53 (1996); and Clive S Gray and Anthony A Davis, 'Competition Policy in Developing Countries Pursuing Structural Adjustment' 38 *Antitrust Bulletin* 425–67 (1993). Since then, antitrust activities have begun in earnest in Peru, Columbia, El Salvador and Venezuela. About 10 other Latin American jurisdictions have price-fixing laws.

[32a] Julian L Clarke *et al*, *Anti-Competitive Practices and Liberalizing Markets in Latin America and the Caribbean*. World Economy 28 (2005) 1029–1056.

[33] Herbert Hovenkamp, *Federal Antitrust Policy*, 2nd edn (St Paul, MN, West Group, 1999).

agree to plead guilty.[34] Although the DOJ has a panoply of sanctions that can be imposed on guilty cartelists, by far the most common US Government sanctions are corporate fines, individual fines and incarceration of responsible managers.

The DOJ's notable success in prosecuting international cartels after 1995 may be traced to several amendments to the law and improved investigatory techniques.[35] The Sherman Act's maximum penalties were steadily increased by amendments in 1955, 1974, 1987, 1990 and 2004.[36] In 1974, cartel conduct was made a *felony* for corporations, and prison sentences for individuals were raised from a maximum of one year to three years. To summarize, from 1974 to 1990, the maximum corporate liability from government fines rose from $50,000 to potentially *six times* the cartel's overcharge.

Since 1987, corporate fine calculation has begun with applying the Federal Sentencing Guidelines to the particular defendant's antitrust offense. First, a base fine is calculated by finding 20 per cent of the company's sales of the cartelized product during the conspiracy; in principle the affected commerce could be global in scope, but in practice only US sales are used.[37] Secondly, a pair of culpability multipliers is determined by reference to tabulated values in the Guidelines. Various aggravating factors raise the multipliers (size of company, whether bid rigging was alleged, involvement of top officers, a previous conviction for a similar offense, etc), while mitigating factors lower them (cooperation with the DOJ's investigation, acceptance of responsibility, and the existence of a good antitrust training program). The highest possible multiplier is 4.0, and the lowest is 0.75, which means that a company can be fined as much as 80 per cent of affected commerce. Thirdly, in return for cooperation, a company can request leniency: under DOJ policy the first qualified applicant can receive a 100 per cent discount (ie, amnesty), while the second and third to apply get substantial but progressively smaller discounts. In practice, the cooperation discounts for international cartels average 70 per cent of the maximum fine specified by the Guidelines.[38]

Around 1993 an enforcement policy shift took place in the DOJ that placed a higher priority on investigating international antitrust violations and that instructed the FBI to employ all the tools of their trade to collect evidence. The

---

[34] About 95% of all formal investigations of international cartels opened by the DOJ end in guilty pleas by at least one company (John M Connor and Gustav Helmers, 'Statistics on Modern Private International Cartels' (Working Paper 07-01, Washington, DC, American Antitrust Institute, Jan 2006), <http://www.antitrustinstitute.org/recent2/567.pdf>). Typically this process takes less than six months. Convictions of companies at trial are rare—less than one per year—but one or two trials of individual managers of cartels do occur each year.

[35] John M Connor, 'Price-Fixing Overcharges: Legal and Economic Evidence' in John B Kirkwood (ed), Jan 2007 *Research in Law and Economics* Vol 22 (Oxford, Amsterdam and San Diego, Elsevier), 59–153; Connor, above n 18; Donald I Baker, 'The Use of Criminal Law Remedies to Deter and Punish Cartels and Bid-Rigging' 69 *George Washington Law Review* 693–720 (2001).

[36] Connor (2007b), above n 18.

[37] Connor and Lande, above n 2, at 559–64.

[38] See John M Connor, *A Critique of Cartel Fine Discounting by the US Department of Justice* (Working Paper), available at SSRN, <http://ssrn.com/abstract=977772>, at 31.

1993 revision of the DOJ Corporate Leniency Program described below was a particularly important investigative innovation. In addition, the DOJ has introduced a number of methods of cooperating with other jurisdictions.[39] Protocols and treaties permit sharing of information on cartel investigations or enforcement actions, subject to restrictions set by national laws on confidentiality. Regular international meetings of enforcement officials have fostered the exchange of effective investigatory techniques.[40]

The Sherman Act authorizes private suits by direct buyers for treble damages and reasonable legal costs in federal court.[41] Besanko and Spulber show that treble damages generally lead to positive welfare increases if the probability of conviction and the multiple of damages recovered is high enough.[42] Since the late 1970s, the largest private cartel cases have been organized initially as class actions and have ended with judicially approved negotiated settlements. Moreover, in about half of the states of the United States indirect purchasers can sue for damages; alternatively, indirect buyers of cartelized products can also receive compensation through suits initiated in federal court by state attorneys general. Therefore, the (theoretical) maximum US liability facing corporate price fixers from government and private prosecutions after 1990 approaches *10 times* its overcharge.

B. The European Union

The European Commission's Directorate General for Competition (DG-COMP) is the world's second most powerful antitrust authority.[43] EU law treats antitrust violations solely as civil infractions by business entities.[44] Individual conspirators are not personally liable for monetary penalties or prison sentences.[45] Corporate members of cartels are subject to maximum fines of 10 per cent of sales in the year prior to the year in which the EC makes its decision. The EC's fines can be based on the *global* sales of an offending firm in *all* its lines of business.

The EU first adopted detailed guidelines in 1998 for calculating firm-by-firm cartel fines.[46] First, the EC considers the 'gravity' of the offense. Although a matter of discretion, cartels are usually placed in the 'very serious' category, which

---

[39] ICPAC (2000), above n 18; Pate, above n 19.

[40] ICN, International Competition Network Web Page (2007), <www.icn.org>.

[41] Hovenkamp, above n 33.

[42] David Besanko and Daniel F Spulber, 'Are Treble Damages Neutral?' 80 *American Economic Review* 870–87 (1990).

[43] John M Connor, 'Effectiveness of Sanctions on Modern International Cartels' 6 *Journal of Industry, Competition, and Trade* 195–223 (2006).

[44] Besides the USA and Canada, eight other countries provide for criminal sanctions: Austria, Germany, France, Norway, Ireland, Slovakia, Japan and South Korea (Scott D Hammond, 'A Review of Recent Cases and Developments in the Antitrust Division's Criminal Enforcement Program', speech at the Conference Board's 2002 Antitrust Conference, New York City, March 7, 2002). The UK criminalized antitrust in 2005.

[45] Connor, above n 18.

[46] Harding and Joshua, above n 16, at 240–52.

is the highest of three levels of antitrust infringements. Large damages that are geographically widespread add to the gravity. Secondly, to account for disparities in the power of fines to deter, relatively large companies are fined more than smaller participants. Thirdly, fines are increased by 10 percentage points per year for each year the cartel is effective. Fourthly, these three factors result in a base fine (called a 'basic amount') for each company, which is adjusted for culpability—upwards for cartel leaders and downwards for various mitigating factors. Fifthly, under the EU's Leniency Notice, violators are given 10 per cent to 50 per cent discounts for their degrees of cooperation. Since 1996, amnesty has been granted, with a 2001 improved program attracting large numbers of applicants. Lastly, the Commission ensures that the amount of the fine does not exceed 10 per cent of global sales. In late 2006, revised EU fining guidelines were adopted that may double average fines.[47]

There is no provision for private compensatory suits under EU law. However, changes are afoot in the UK, Germany and France.[48] In the UK, which liberalized its rules for launching private suits, at least 21 such actions against cartels resulted in settlements for monetary damages in 2000–05.[49] A handful of EU nations (UK, France, Ireland, Norway) have criminalized price fixing, and the EU seems to be moving slowly in that direction, but instances of incarceration are apparently unknown.[50]

A notable shift in EU enforcement is the devolution of anti-cartel enforcement away from Brussels toward the National Competition Authorities (NCAs) in the 27 Member States. Around 2000, obviously cross-national coordination of cartel investigations began, probably as the result of bilateral sharing of information. As the number of international cartels being detected in the EU outpaced the ability of the EC's DG-COMP to process the decisions, a higher and higher proportion of cartel decisions emanated from the EU's NCAs. The regionalization of antitrust in the EU, already a *fait accompli*, was formalized by the creation in November 2002 of the European Competition Network.[51]

C. Canada

The Canadian Competition Bureau (CCB), together with the Ministry of Justice, enforces criminal laws similar to those in the United States, and its prosecutions of international cartels tend to follow those in the United States by six months to

---

[47] Cento Veljanovski, 'European Commission Cartel Prosecutions and Fines, 1998–2007: A Statistical Analysis' (London, Case Associates, Sept 2007), <http://papers.ssrn.com/sol3/papers.cfm?abstract_id=1016014>.

[48] Alan Wiseman *et al*, 'Bring On the Private Suits', *Legal Times*, March 19, 2007, at 36.

[49] Barry J Rodger, '*Private Enforcement of Competition Law: The Hidden Story*' (2007), unpublished manuscript.

[50] Harding and Joshua, above n 16.

[51] First reported in *European Report 2002*.

a year.[52] The CCB is a small agency that cooperates closely with the US DOJ on cartels. Hard-core cartel violations are crimes treated in effect as per se illegal acts. Persons can be fined and imprisoned, but this power is used quite sparingly. The CCB imposes antitrust penalties typically close to 20 per cent of Canadian sales during the affected period.

Canada is one of the few jurisdictions outside the United States with effective private antitrust remedies.[53] Private actions usually follow upon government indictments. Introduced in 1976, private suits were little used until Ontario issued formal class action rules in 1992. Now at least four other provinces have such laws, but plaintiffs from any part of Canada may join a provincial suit.

> The situation in Canada increasingly reflects that of the United States and, in the event of a conviction of an international price fixing case in the United States ... the commencement of one or more class actions in Canada ... is now a virtual certainty.[54]

D. Four Latin American Competition Authorities

The antitrust authorities of Latin America are quite diverse in terms of their histories, legal foundations, and institutional arrangements.[55] In their modern forms, some of the same external conditions in the 1980s and early 1990s seem to account for their births: a return to democracy after a period of dictatorship, the abandonment of formal centralized economic planning and price controls, high rates of inflation, realization of the inefficiencies of many State-owned enterprises, abuse of dominance associated with privatized former monopolies, relaxation of import and foreign-investment restrictions, and the formation of customs unions.[56] In general, they also share a tendency for increasingly intensive and effective cartel prosecutions that dates from the late 1990s. These anti-cartel efforts are pursued in environments where there is little or no popular or business support for antitrust principles, where merger cases or consumer protection vie for agency resources, and where political interference has historically been a concern.

1. *Brazil*

Although antitrust law can be traced to 1962, Law 8884 (passed in 1994) is the principal legislation that forms the basis of modern Brazilian competition law.[57]

---

[52] Connor (2006), above n 43, at 195–223.

[53] Calvin S Goldman *et al*, 'Private Access to Antitrust Remedies: The Canadian Experience', Address before the Section of Antitrust Law, American Bar Association, April 2–4, 2003.

[54] *Ibid*, at 7.

[55] Ignacio De Leon, *Latin American Competition Law: A Policy in Search of Identity* (The Hague, Kluwer Law 2001).

[56] Connor (1997a), above n 32, at 26–30.

[57] Dallal Stevens, 'Framing Competition Law within an Emerging Economy: The Case of Brazil' (1995) 40 *Antitrust Bulletin* 929–71; John W Clark, 'Competition Policy and Regulatory Reform in Brazil' 2 *OECD Journal of Competition Law and Policy* 193 (2000).

Article 21 of this Law prohibits price fixing, allocation of markets, and other horizontal market restraints.[58] Abuse of market power (private control of prices) can be prosecuted as a criminal or as a civil infraction. In cartel cases, two tests are required for proof: the existence of collective market power from a case-specific analysis, and an agreement to collude in that market.[59] While mention is made of possible efficiency benefits of cartelization, this potentially exculpatory factor is ignored in practice. Unlike many other jurisdictions, Brazil's law has no exemptions for export cartels, 'crisis' cartels, or agricultural cooperatives.

Enforcement is split among three government agencies. Investigations are carried out by the Economic Law Office (SDE) of the Ministry of Justice. If probable cause is established by the SDE, it refers the case to the Administrative Council for Defense of the Economy (CADE), an independent agency reporting to the Prime Minister's office. A third agency, the Secretariat of Economic Monitoring (SEAE) in the Ministry of Finance, contributes non-binding economic analyses of the case to CADE. CADE then decides whether to initiate an administrative law proceeding, decides the case, and announces penalties or other remedies. CADE administrative decisions may be appealed to as many as four levels of federal court, which has created great delays in final outcomes.[60]

In general, practitioners judge Brazil's anti-cartel enforcement to be relatively and increasingly successful,[61] though some critics fault CADE for choosing cases that are the easiest to prove and that have small effects on the economy.[62] In 2000, amendments granted the SDE the power to obtain and serve search warrants at short notice, a change that made 'dawn raids' possible for the first time.[63] In addition, a leniency program similar to the 1993 US program was authorized. Applicants can expect corporate and individual fine reductions of from about 33 per cent to 100 per cent. Both techniques were first implemented in 2003. The SDE and the federal police exercise full powers to search premises, compel oral interviews, and retain evidence. Together with a redeployment of merger specialists, these changes permitted CADE to issue an increasing number of cartel decisions. As of 2007, at least seven cartel investigations are known to have been initiated as a result of leniency applications.[64]

While a few price-fixing defendants have allegations against them dismissed, most cartel decisions result in corporate and individual fines. The former must be in the range of 1 per cent to 30 per cent of a company's total (national and foreign) sales revenues in the year prior to a decision; if indicted, a manager pays

---

[58] OECD (2005a), above n 28.

[59] Roberto A C Pfeiffer, 'Recent Aspects of Hard Core Prosecution in Brazil' (presented at the Third Latin American Competition Forum, Madrid, 2005), at 2.

[60] Mauro Grinberg, 'Cartels: The Brazilian Experience' (paper at the Global Competition Forum, Toronto, May 2006), at 2.

[61] Barbara Rosenberg and Jose da Matta Berardo, 'Brazil: Cartels and Leniency' *Global Competition Review, Antitrust Review of the Americas*, Special Issue, 2008, at 1.

[62] Grinberg, above n 60.

[63] OECD (2005a), above n 28.

[64] Rosenberg and da Matta Berardo, above n 61, at 2.

from 10 per cent to 50 per cent of his company's fine. There are no specific fining guidelines, but general principles from Law 8884 include:

a) market overcharges or illegal gains to violators as aggravating factors; and
b) cooperation of defendants and their ability to pay as mitigating factors.

Prosecutors appear to be guided by the principle of specific deterrence in setting fines.[65] The first true cartel case, *Flat Rolled Steel*,[66] was filed in 1999 and decided in 2005. Around 1999–2002, most cartel fines tended to be close to the 1 per cent minimum, but by 2005 a few cases (*Liquid Petroleum Gas*[67] and *Crushed Stone*[68]) had concluded with fines in the 10 per cent to 15 per cent range.[69] Several managers have been required to pay personal fines of 0.1 per cent to 1.5 per cent of their company's annual revenues.

The industrial distribution of the 45 cartel convictions made during 1999–2005 is quite different from that in the EU or United States, which tend to be dominated by manufactured industrial material inputs and construction.[70] In Brazil, 69 per cent of the decisions involved localized collusion in the service sector, predominantly bid rigging against medical institutions; only 13 per cent were directed at manufacturing, mining or construction.[71]

A May 2007 proposed amendment (Law 11482) to Brazil's antitrust law will permit cartelists to plea bargain with CADE, ie to receive a reduced fine, immunity for managers, and closure of the investigation in return for inculpatory information about the other cartelists. Like US plea bargaining, this new process of partial leniency will permit rapid disposition of cases because trials and other judicial hearings are avoided. Brazilian antitrust authorities prefer to term this process 'direct settlement'.[72] Indeed, CADE began direct settlements prior to this amendment; the first leniency accord occurred in 2005, followed by six in 2006.[73] The sizes of the fine discounts are not known, but some instances of partial leniency have resulted in substantial fines. In late 2007, a large French company negotiated a fine of $24 million in return for cooperation with CADE and cessation of cartel conduct.[74] In August 2006, CADE announced a leniency accord with orange processors for US $45.9 million to settle allegations of collusion that

---

[65] Pfeiffer, above n 59; Ana Paula Martinez, Interview, *Global Competition Review* (Sept 7, 2007).

[66] 'Three Brazil steel makers guilty of price fixing', *Globe and Mail* (Canada), Sept 24, 2005, p B7.

[67] *Brazil Liquid Petroleum Gas*—Administrative Proceeding 08012.004860, May 10, 2004.

[68] Juliano Basile, 'SDE julga formacao de carteis no Brasil nos setores industriales; Julgamento do "cartel de britas" marca nova leva de decisoes da SDE', *Valor Economico* (Brazil), Nov 26, 2004.

[69] Pfeiffer, above n 59; OECD (2005a), above n 28, at 50–52.

[70] Connor and Helmers, above n 34.

[71] Grinberg, above n 60.

[72] Martinez, above n 65.

[73] Lorenna Rodriguez, 'Government Closing Circle against Price Fixing'. *Gazeta Mercantil* (Jan 30, 2007) at 1.

[74] 'Lafarge to pay $24USmn in fines', *Business News Americas* (Nov 29, 2007).

304   *John M Connor*

depressed fresh orange prices.[75] Because direct settlements substitute for normal judicial findings of guilt, the latter began to decline after 2005.

Several cartel managers have been required to pay substantial personal fines. Criminal proceedings against managers are possible, resulting in up to five years in prison, but no such penalties are known to have been imposed. Private compensatory suits are theoretically possible in Brazil's courts, but few if any have been filed. Legal discussions of Brazil's antitrust scene rarely bother to mention them.

Brazil's antitrust authorities show signs of being overburdened.[76] The federal budget was declining in US dollar terms in 2000–04, employee turnover was high, and there were signs of a chronic shortage of qualified personnel. However, in 2005–06 the budget and number of personnel rose. CADE had a backlog of 738 antitrust cases of all types in 2004. In early 2007, CADE had more than 300 cartel suits underway.[77]

2. *Argentina*

Argentina's antitrust authority began active prosecutions of cartels a few years later than Brazil's, and seemed to be making up for lost time around 2005, but more recently has run out of steam.

Argentina adopted a law similar to the US Sherman Act in 1923, but it was seldom used.[78] Argentina's modern competition law (22,262/1980) was consciously modeled on the EU's law, and established the National Commission for the Defense of the Economy (CNDC). The CNDC can present only advisory opinions to the ministry to which it is attached. To remedy the lack of independence, Law 25,156/1999 created a truly independent oversight Tribunal for the CNDC, but for political reasons the Tribunal was, as of 2008, never constituted. The 1980 law and decisions through 1999 remain the dominant antitrust law in Argentina for horizontal restraints.

Price fixing is unlawful if it harms 'the general economic interest', a legal term that the CNDC interprets as equivalent to consumer welfare. This rule implies that the burden of proof for the CNDC is to show market price effects. Cartel fines cannot exceed AR $150 million (in 2008 about US $49 million) per company and are to be calculated on the basis of the harm caused to victims or the illegal gain to the cartelist. Recidivism can double fines, but cannot exceed the cap, which has not been adjusted since 1999. Argentine law accepts the principle of extraterritoriality and in theory (but not in practice) can impose prison sentences.[79]

The CNDC can participate in dawn raids, but has refrained from many in recent years. Argentina has no leniency program. Merger enforcement takes precedence over anti-cartel activity. While the CNDC opened almost 100 formal

---

[75] *Tendencias Data* (Aug 1, 2006).
[76] OECD (2005a), above n 28.
[77] Rodriguez, above n 73.
[78] OECD (2006), above n 29.
[79] Ismael Malis *et al*, 'Anti-Cartel Activity in Argentina' (paper at the Third Latin American Competition Forum, Madrid, 2005), at 5.

conduct investigations per year during 2000–05, it closed only 30 per year, leading to a large backlog of cases. An alternative to fines are cease-and-desist orders, of which 35 were issued in 2000–05.[80]

Cartel enforcement began in 2003 with small fines imposed on two municipal conspiracies (LPG distribution and sand).[81] By 2005, 12 cases had been judged, four defendants found guilty, and 30 more cases were under investigation.[82] The two biggest cartel cases (*Cement*[83] and *Liquid Oxygen*[84]) culminated in fines of US $130 million after investigations lasting six and three years, respectively. These decisions and more than 100 others have been appealed; most appeals are brought to a quasi-specialized Commercial Court.[85] In 2006–07, confusion erupted about the proper forum for antitrust appeals.[86]

The absence of an appointed Tribunal makes the CNDC more sensitive to the policies of the national President and the Ministry of the Economy than most other antitrust authorities. Political pressure is most evident in interventions concerning the choice of investigatory targets.[87] The national government's attempts to suppress inflationary tendencies through persuasion prompted several recent CNDC investigations of particular industries.[88]

3. Chile

Chile is widely recognized as the Latin American pioneer in implementing an active antitrust law regime.[89] Its first law (13,305) was adopted in 1959 at about the same time the country abandoned centralized price controls. The current competition law (Decree 211) was implemented in 1973 as part of a comprehensive plan to reorganize the economy on laissez-faire principles. It is a criminal statute widely recognized as being modeled on the Sherman Act. Consequently, cartel conduct is viewed by the national antitrust authority as illegal per se. A major amendment (Law 19,610) was enacted in 1999. The current institutional structure was implemented in 2004.

The law is enforced by an independent National Economic Prosecutor (FNE) and 11 non-professional provincial commissions. By the early 1990s, the FNE was recognized

---

[80] *Ibid*, at 18.

[81] *Ibid*, at 11.

[82] *Ibid*, at 1.

[83] *CNDC v Loma Negra and Others* (2005), Resolution 124/05 from the Secretary of Technical Coordination.

[84] *CNDC v Air Liquide and Others* (2005), Resolution 119/05 from the Secretary of Technical Coordination.

[85] Malis *et al*, above n 79, at 35.

[86] GCR, 'Argentina's Main Appeal Court Is Refusing to Accept Competition Cases', *Global Competition Review* (Feb 9, 2007a).

[87] *Ibid*, at 32.

[88] EIU, Argentina: Competition and Price Regulations, *Economist Intelligence Unit* (July 24, 2007); GCR, 'Argentina Appoints New Antitrust Chief', *Global Competition Review* (May 3, 2006).

[89] OECD (2004a), above n 29.

for its consistency and professionalism.[90] Until May 2004, FNE's recommendations were reviewed by the quasi-judicial, unpaid Antitrust Commission, loosely supervised by the Supreme Court.[91] This Commission met about four hours each week and had no staff or budget. Until 2004 the absence of a staff or budget for the Commission meant that its decisions received little elaboration or justification. The Chilean Supreme Court has overturned a high proportion of these decisions.

The statutory goals of antitrust are economic efficiency and consumer welfare, but in the last decade or so somewhat broader goals, such as economic freedom and non-discrimination, have been enunciated.[92] The FNE and the Commission are extremely reluctant to find antitrust violations, and even more reluctant to assess sanctions. An analysis of 260 FNE decisions during 1974–93 found that the vast majority dealt with monopolization matters; only 37 hard-core cartels were investigated, and only 30 per cent were found to be violations—an extremely small share by international standards. In 2001, out of 55 Commission decisions, only one was a cartel case. In 2004, the FNE had a total backlog of four cartel cases.[93]

In May 2004, because of its 'erratic rulings', the Antitrust Commission was replaced by the Free-Competition Defense Tribunal (TDLC), a competition court that can appeal directly to the Supreme Court.[94] As from 2008, the TDLC will be staffed with full-time, professional commissioners with antitrust expertise who serve six-year terms. It rules on decisions of the FNE or initiates investigations requested by private citizens.

The Antitrust Commission and its successor, the TLDC, have a broad array of remedies at their disposal: fines, cease-and-desist orders, issuing industry rules, restructuring firms, and disbarring individuals or trade associations. Consent decrees and plea negotiations are not employed.

Up through 1998, the FNE had only about 30 employees, but the number doubled in 1999. A parallel budget increase allowed FNE to attract better-qualified professional staff in the early 2000s.[95] In 2003, the maximum antitrust fine was $230,000.[96] There were no fining guidelines and no leniency program. Fines were few and very small. Out of more than 2000 decisions of the Commission during 1973–2002, only 73 carried fines. Of those decisions with fines, only nine referred to horizontal agreements.[97] The average cartel fine per case was $51,000. Many antitrust decisions are overturned by the courts or the fines greatly reduced. *Oxygen*, the country's greatest international cartel case, with $7 million in fines, was dismissed by the Supreme Court in January 2007.[98]

---

[90] Connor (1997b), above n 32, at 74.
[91] OECD (2004a), above n 29.
[92] *Ibid*, at 18–24.
[93] *Ibid*, at 70.
[94] EIU, 'Chile: Competition and Price Regulation', *Economist Intelligence Unit* (Jan 23, 2008), at 1.
[95] OECD (2004b), above n 29, at 26–27.
[96] *Ibid*, at 30.
[97] OECD (2004a), above n 29, at 71.
[98] GCR, 'Chilean Supreme Court Quashes Antitrust Fine', *Global Competition Review* (Jan 23, 2007).

Chilean antitrust enforcement is, on the whole, weak. A noted analysis of anti-trust enforcement in Chile finds four causes:

a) there is little concern by members of the Antitrust Commission for 'white-collar' economic crimes that have such diffuse social harms;
b) Commissioners have strong laissez-faire biases;
c) the FNE is underfunded; and
d) the Commission is composed of part-time amateurs with little economic literacy.[99]

The OECD also seems to be of the opinion that the Chilean criminal antitrust law has not been grafted successfully on to a civil law system.[100]

There have been several positive changes in the law since 2003. Beginning in 2004 the maximum fine was raised to about $17 million, and Congress is likely to pass higher limits in 2008.[101] A leniency program is also being considered. Nevertheless, few high-profile cartel cases have been pursued since the 2004 amendments.

4. Mexico

Mexico has the newest antitrust law among the four Latin American authorities covered in this chapter. In the mid-1980s, the Mexican Government began to priva-tize State-owned corporations, eliminate tariff protections for domestic industry, and end most price controls.[102] Mexico's competition law (the Federal Law of Economic Competition—FLEC) was introduced in 1993, as a condition of its entry into the NAFTA free-trade zone in 1994. At the same time the Federal Competition Commission (CFC) was created to enforce the law. The fundamental purpose of the FLEC is to promote economic efficiency. Petroleum, postal services and a few other 'strategic' industries are exempt from FCC regulation, as is direct price regulation of a few consumer necessities by the Ministry of Commerce. Numerous decisions of the Supreme Court have supported the constitutionality of the FLEC, and the Congress has repeatedly resisted expanding antitrust exemptions for designated industries, yet obtaining effective remedies in the lower courts often eludes the CFC.

The CFC has demonstrated a great deal of independence since about 2000 by attacking some of the country's most powerful business interests. Although nominally part of the Ministry of Commerce, the CFC is guaranteed indepen-dence by statute. Importantly, the five Commissioners are appointed by the national President to staggered 10-year terms. A client survey gave the CFC very high marks for its professionalism, honesty, independence and commitment to improving competitiveness.[103]

---

[99] P Serra, 'La Politica de Competencia en Chile' 10 *Revista de Analisis Economico* 63–88 (1995).
[100] OECD (2004a), above n 29.
[101] EIU (2008), above n 94, at 2.
[102] OECD (2004b), above n 29.
[103] *Ibid*, at 55.

Conduct that creates or maintains monopoly power, such as hard-core cartel behavior, is illegal per se under the FLEC. There are no efficiency or small-business defenses. The CFC maximum cartel fine is tied to the level of wages; in 2004 the maximum corporate fine was $1.6 million, but in egregious cases the upper limit is 10 per cent of a company's annual sales or assets. There are no explicit fining guidelines, but section 38 of the FLEC says that the CFC must take into consideration the size of the market, amount of damage, recidivism, and ability to pay.[104] Individual criminal charges may be imposed if a cartel affects markets for consumer necessities, or for obstruction of justice. 'In practice ... the CFC has not typically imposed severe sanctions in horizontal conduct cases.'[105]

From 1993 to 2002, the CFC handled 428 monopoly or horizontal restraint cases (39 per year), of which 59 per cent resulted in sanctions, recommendations or settlements.[106] Only about 40 of these cases dealt with hard-core cartels.[107] During 1993–2002, the CFC imposed fines on 493 violators totaling $31 million, ie an average of $2.8 million per year or $63,000 per company.[108] The number of such decisions is rising over time, but merger decisions are four times as numerous.[109]

Much of the CFC's enforcement in the 1990s was directed at industry associations. Prior the mid-1980s, these associations had negotiated prices with the Ministry of the Economy, and these habits proved difficult to change. Other CFC cases involved small businesses that had colluded to cope with the power of large firms. In the late 1990s, extraterritorial conduct by the global lysine and citric acid cartels was punished.

The OECD *Peer Review* contained a number of recommendations regarding CFC procedures.[110] Bi-partisan proposals in the Congress in 2005 led to major amendments of the FLEC which became effective in June 2006.[111] The CFC is now empowered to make dawn raids without prior notification. Also, the CFC now has a US/EU-style corporate amnesty program for the first whistleblower to come forward in a hard-core cartel case; later arrivals can receive discounts of 50 per cent, 30 per cent, and 20 per cent on their fines for their additional, significant cooperation. Finally, the upper limit on fines was raised by 400 per cent to $62 million, and for recidivists to 10 per cent of annual sales or assets (whichever is larger).

---

[104] *Ibid*, at 65.
[105] ABA, above n 4, at 4.
[106] OECD (2004b), above n 29, at 41.
[107] *Ibid*, at 51–52.
[108] *Ibid*, at 47.
[109] *Ibid*, at 49.
[110] *Ibid*.
[111] Jorge A Sanchez-Davila, 'Mexico Takes Important Steps Forward in the Combat of Cartels and Implementation of Leniency Programs' (2008) *Global Competition Review: Antitrust Review of the Americas: Special Issue* 1.

V. Global Antitrust Enforcement Patterns

The previous section discussed the legal authority and procedures to control cartels in general in seven jurisdictions. This section presents original data specifically on prosecutions of *international* cartels, many of them global in scope, in the same seven jurisdictions. The focus is on the actual pattern of anti-cartel enforcement by both government agencies and private suits. These data help to develop a fuller understanding of the potential for effective cartel deterrence in the long run, and of Latin America's role in assisting in that deterrence.

A. Modern Private International Cartels Data

In common with nearly all other empirical studies on cartels, this chapter considers only *detected* cartels. These cartels were clandestine, and their members typically attempted to cover up or destroy evidence of their meetings and communications.[112] Cartel studies generally conclude that only about 10 per cent to 30 per cent of all such conspiracies are detected and punished.[113] Studies that depend on detected cartels may suffer from sample selection bias.[114] Undetected cartels are probably more durable than detected cartels and may differ in some other economic characteristics.

The sample consists of 433 cartels.[115] Seventy-four per cent of these cartels have had several participants indicted or found guilty[116]; the greatest amount of information is available for these cases. Ten per cent of the cartels' investigations have been closed (in some cases because of a statute of limitations), and 16 per cent are still being investigated. All private cartels with international membership that were detected between January 1990 and December 2007 are included in the sample.[117]

The number of companies that have participated in international cartels exceeds 4,800.[118] By far the largest number (3,433 or 72 per cent) are headquartered in Europe. The Netherlands is the world leader, followed by Germany, France, the UK, and Italy. Despite its long history as an antitrust jurisdiction, nearly 500 US companies have been suspected or convicted of price fixing. Next in order of importance are Japan and Korea. Companies from Africa, Latin

---

[112] Spratling, above n 18.

[113] John M Connor, 'Optimal Deterrence and International Cartels' (paper at the 4th International Industrial Organization Conference, April 15, 2007c), at Table 1.

[114] Andrew R Dick, 'When Are Cartels Stable Contracts?' 39 *Journal of Law and Economics* 241–83 (1996).

[115] John M Connor, 'Latin America and the Control of International Cartels' (SSRN Working Paper, April 14, 2008), at Table 1 (available from the author).

[116] *Ibid*, at Table 2.

[117] John M Connor, 'Private International Cartels' (Spreadsheet, December 2007d).

[118] John M Connor (2008), above n 115, at Table 10.

310   *John M Connor*

America and low-income economies seldom participate in international price collusion. More than 200 companies have been participants in multiple international cartels: 53 were convicted in *five* or more, and 17 in *10* or more separate violations.[119]

Approximately 275 executives have been accused or convicted of illegal involvement in international cartels. A large number (180 or 72 per cent) are citizens of countries that have criminal price-fixing laws, ie Australia, Canada, Germany, and the United States; most were cited for national price-fixing violations. Almost all the remaining individuals hail from Japan, Korea, The Netherlands, and the UK; a majority of these persons were convicted because of their involvement in global cartels. In total, cartel managers have paid $192 million in fines and have been sentenced to 764 months in prison; 98 per cent of these penalties were imposed in the United States.

B. General Trends in Enforcement

The acceleration in annual rates of detection of international cartels is quite impressive. Recall that 'detection' is the first date that a formal investigation becomes publicly known, which in some cases is also the date that sanctions are levied. Almost 33 international cartels were detected each year during 2004–07, a rate five times higher than 1990–95.[120] As this chapter will show, Latin American antitrust authorities have also launched an era of notable anti-cartel activism since 2003.

Another trend is the decline in the duration of detected international cartels.[121] In the early 1990s, the average cartels endured for more than 100 months, but longevity has declined steadily to a time barely half as long in 2004–07. The duration of international cartels averages 4.5 years.[122] The longevity of global cartels is much higher, but that of Latin American cartels is particularly brief. With very few exceptions, Latin American authorities have avoided prosecuting global cartels.

The prosecutorial success of the US DOJ and the EC's DG-COMP appears to have encouraged other national agencies to focus more resources on anti-cartel enforcement, to adopt new laws strengthening investigatory powers or raising sanctions, and to reorganize the antitrust authorities. Antitrust authorities have been goaded into action by the disrespect shown by cartelists to competition laws and those who enforce them. Speech after speech by top antitrust officials betrays a visceral antipathy for global price-fixers. The global conspirators are consistently described in highly emotive language as brazen, cold-blooded, contemptuous of the law, disdainful of their customers, and eager to ignore company antitrust compliance policies.[123]

---

[119] *Ibid*, at Table 14.
[120] *Ibid*, at Fig 1.
[121] *Ibid*, at Figs 5–8.
[122] *Ibid*, at Table 9.
[123] Hammond (2002), above n 44; Spratling, above n 18; Monti, above n 19.

C. The US Department of Justice

Once the newly-appointed head of the Antitrust Division in 1992–93 recognized the threat of global conspiracies, the agency reordered its priorities fairly quickly. Beginning in the late 1990s, about four-fifths of the DOJ's fines for criminal price fixing have been imposed on non-US firms. The use of personal fines and prison sentences has also escalated, many of them applied to non-US citizens.

During 1990–2007, the Antitrust Division convicted 67 international price-fixing crimes.[124] Starting with *Lysine* in September 1996, the most important US price-fixing convictions have been global conspiracies.[125] Thirty-six such cartels were fully or partially prosecuted during 1996–2007. About 200 companies have been fined by the DOJ for international price fixing since 1995. The DOJ has obtained corporate fines totaling $4.1 billion, of which 90 per cent was from participants in global cartels.[126] It is likely that the future number of international cartel cases will continue to be high. In the early 2000s the DOJ had about 100 grand juries empanelled on price-fixing allegations, of which half were examining international cartels[127]; in 2007 there were 130 such investigations.[128]

In general, the fines collected from individual criminal conspirators are modest compared with their corporate salaries, but prison sentences are becoming more severe. Historically, the DOJ sought prison sentences for individuals in a minority of price-fixing cases; the rate was 23 per cent of all price-fixing cases during 1970–99.[129] But in the case of *global* cartels, the DOJ has obtained prison sentences in about 50 per cent of the cases since 1995. Since 1990, for all types of cartels, more than 300 individuals have been given criminal fines and 260 received prison sentences.[130] During 2000–07, prison sentences averaged 16 months per individual, and half of the prison sentences exceed the felony level of more than 12 months. On average, about three executives plead guilty or are indicted per global cartel, but the number and severity of prison sentences has been increasing since the mid-1990s. This policy reflects an oft-repeated belief by DOJ prosecutors that prison sentences are the most effective tool for deterring cartels.

The conviction and imprisonment of non-US executives for criminal price fixing by US authorities is an extraordinary development in antitrust enforcement history. The US DOJ has arranged guilty pleas from more than 50 top

---

[124] Connor (2008), above n 115, at Table 5.

[125] *In re Amino Acid Lysine Antitrust Litigation*, 918 F Supp 1190 (ND Ill 1996).

[126] Connor (2008), above n 115, at Table 6.

[127] Pate, above n 19.

[128] Gerald F Masoudi, 'Cartel Enforcement in the United States (and Beyond)' (Speech at the Cartel Conference, Budapest, Hungary, Feb 16, 2007).

[129] Connor (2007b), above n 18.

[130] John M Connor *et al*, 'DOJ Cartel Enforcement: Appraisal and Proposals' in Albert Foer (ed), *The Antitrust Transition* (forthcoming, 2008), at Table 1.

executives who were nationals of about 20 foreign countries.[131] Many of these executives worked in the United States, but some traveled from their residences abroad to submit to the jurisdiction of the US court, plead guilty and pay fines. One reason for foreigners' willingness to serve time in US prisons is that if they reside or even *pass through* countries that have criminal statutes for price fixing, they may be extradited to the United States.[132] The United States has explicit treaties with Canada, Ireland and Japan that permit extradition for antitrust violations, though none of these has yet been invoked.[133] In 2002, Interpol added US antitrust fugitives to its 'Red Notice' watch list for the first time. When foreign executives plead guilty for price fixing, they are frequently granted the right of free passage across US borders for their cooperation.

In summary, the financial penalties applied by the US DOJ to global price fixers in the late 1990s were unprecedented in their severity. Despite an increasing number of amnesties, average corporate fines for members of global cartels after the mid-1990s were many times higher than the fines collected earlier. While individual fines remained modest on the whole, managers of global conspiracies were more than twice as likely to receive prison sentences as managers of domestic conspiracies, and the length of the sentences has risen markedly. The main reasons for the escalation in fines in the late 1990s were the extraordinary rise in the maximum fine levels allowed, the expanded size of the markets affected, the high overcharge rates, the longevity of many of the conspiracies, and, if truth be told, the rising intolerance of the judicial system for 'thieves dressed in expensive suits'. This rise is especially notable in light of the fact that, correcting for inflation, average corporate fines were essentially unchanged for the first 90 years of the 20th century.

D. Canadian Competition Bureau

Canadian cartel-enforcement policy shifted in the mid-1990s. Prosecution of large global cartels began in 1998 with the lysine and citric acid cases.[134] The fines imposed on these two cartels were almost double the amount the Canadian Competition Bureau (CCB) had collected from all other cases in 1990–97. By mid-2007 Canada had collected US $167 million in fines from 20 global cartels, most of which followed quickly after parallel US convictions. In addition, five other international cartel convictions brought the Canadian total to $199 million.

---

[131] Scott D Hammond, 'When Calculating the Costs and Benefits of Applying for Corporate Amnesty, How Do You Put a Price Tag on an Individual's Freedom?', speech at the 15th Annual National Institute on White Collar Crime, San Francisco, CA, March 8, 2001a; Masoudi, above n 128.

[132] Nanni, above n 19.

[133] In 2004 the first Japanese manager was indicted for a criminal cartel offense.

[134] Connor, above n 18.

Only one person, the CEO of a Canadian vitamin manufacturer, has been incarcerated. This sentence of 90 days was the first such punishment in many years. Three more cartel managers, from Germany, Switzerland and Japan, have paid fines for their roles in the citric acid, vitamins and sorbates cartels.[135]

Although Canada has a relatively small national market and many of the convicted firms sold cartelized products only through exporting (thus owning few, if any, assets in Canada that could have been seized in the event of non-payment of fines), it has been able to mount a surprisingly effective anti-cartel campaign using modest enforcement resources and simple rules for fines. Canada is a model for many smaller industrialized countries that have tough anti-cartel laws on their books yet have small enforcement resources. Unlike many other areas of law enforcement, the returns to Canada's treasury far exceed the CCB's budget.

E. European Commission

In 2005, the European Commission surpassed the DOJ in the amount of fines imposed on international cartels. It fined 89 international cartels US $15 billion during 1990–2007, of which 53 were intra-EU and 36 global.[136] Lysine was the first global cartel fined in the 1990s. This fine, of US $110 million, was the fifth largest ever imposed by the Commission. In 2001, decisions were reached in four huge cartel cases with total fines of $1.115 billion—a record amount for any antitrust authority. In 2007 the Commission had a backlog of over 100 amnesty applications, which makes it likely that large fines will continue for the next few years. To handle the backlog, the Commission is about to institute a process of 'direct settlement' with corporate cartelists that is similar to the DOJ's practice of plea bargaining, which exchanges inculpatory information for partial leniency.

F. National Competition Authorities of Europe

This section examines the recent but accelerating number of prosecutions of international cartels by national competition authorities (NCAs) in Europe that are members of the EU-27. Since 1990, each of the members of the EU has enacted competition laws that are compatible with the EU Treaty. All new members have had to have effective NCAs before joining. Some NCAs pre-date the Treaty, but all NCAs have developed increasingly convergent anti-cartel laws and policies. For many years the dividing line between Brussels' anti-cartel activities and those of the NCAs was unclear. Before 1999, an investigation by an NCA that involved some non-domestic firms could be pre-empted by the Commission.

---

[135] *Ibid.*
[136] Connor (2008), above n 115, at Tables 5 and 6.

The devolution of the Commission's cartel-prosecution activities to its Member States began in 1999, and became formalized in 2003 with the establishment of the European Competition Network (ECN). Now the NCAs can investigate cartels with significant, but not predominantly cross-Member State sales. Brussels retains jurisdiction over global cartels and those with large cross-national EU market effects.

These NCAs have fined a total of 112 international cartels, issued six cease-and-desist orders and, as of late 2007, were investigating another 20 international cartels.[137] These 138 cartels comprise about one-fourth of the Private International Cartels spreadsheet data set. The NCAs' total fines amount to $6.8 billion.[138] The total amount of fines imposed is larger than in the United States—an impressive amount given the restricted size of these national economies and the relatively few years of active enforcement.

The first international cartel to be fined by a Member State was that in *Glass Containers*, a case reported by the national antitrust authority of Italy in July 1997.[139] Italy has been the most aggressive Member State in prosecuting international cartels—29 in all. The national antitrust authorities in The Netherlands, France, Hungary and Germany have also become energetic in prosecuting international cartels—42 cases with fines. All of The Netherlands authority's cases have been launched since mid-2001, shortly after its investigative powers were strengthened. Much of its work is consumed by a major scandal involving bid rigging by more than 2,000 construction companies.

G. Latin American Cartels and Penalties

In a global context, the antitrust authorities of Latin America are small players in prosecuting international cartels. During 1990–2007, Latin American antitrust agencies investigated or penalized a total of 21 international cartels, most of them in markets for intermediate industrial inputs or services.[140] Of those 21, 16 operated in Latin America proper; they were investigated or prosecuted by Brazil (eight cartels), Argentina (three), Chile (two), and Mexico, Columbia and El Salvador (one cartel each). In addition, two global cartels were fined by Brazil and Mexico (*Vitamins* and *Lysine*).[141] The *Vitamins* conviction by Brazil was the result of a long and difficult investigation.[142] The affected sales of these 21 cartels exceed US $20 billion. As of late 2007, at least three more global cartels were under investigation by CADE: the *Lysine* cartel had global sales of US $1.9 billion and

---

[137] *Ibid*, at Table 5.
[138] *Ibid*, at Table 6.
[139] AGCM, *Produttori di vetro cavo*, 12 June 1997.
[140] Connor (2008), above n 115, at Table 11.
[141] See Connor (2007a) above n 6, at pp 379 and 390, respectively.
[142] Jorge Nemr, 'Brazil Government Censures Vitamin Cartel' (June 2007) *International Enforcement Law Reporter*.

sales of about US $160 million in Latin America; the *Air-Insulated Switchgear*[143] cartel had about US $1.8 billion in Latin American affected sales; and the huge *Air Cargo*[144] case generated US $30 to US $40 billion in Latin American affected commerce.

In addition to these 21 cartels, another 80 or more global cartels have been detected by other jurisdictions outside Latin America, most of which fixed prices in Latin America. Affected sales in Latin America from global conspiracies were probably $100 to $150 billion. Thus, a total of $150 to $210 billion in affected sales in Latin America can be attributed to *known* international cartels with either regional or global scope. Detection rates are 10 per cent to 33 per cent, so total Latin American affected sales of all cartels is somewhere between $0.5 and $2 trillion.

VI. Assessing Latin American Cartel Enforcement

To assess the enforcement efforts of the four leading antitrust authorities of Latin America, I collected information on the resources available and the enforcement outcomes. Like Hoj,[145] I examined such resources as the budgets and employees assigned to antitrust law activities, the availability of cartel leniency programs and variations on them, and the size of potential and actual monetary and penal sanctions on corporations and individuals convicted of hard-core cartel conduct. In addition, I assembled cross-country data on the number of cartel cases processed annually (with special attention to international cartels), the backlogs of such cases, cartel fines imposed, and the composition of the authorities' professional staffs.[146]

A. Brazil

By nearly all measures, Brazil has the largest and most effective anti-cartel authority in Latin America. Antitrust authorities employ almost 400 persons and have by far the largest budgets. However, the proportion of employees with advanced education is relatively low by Latin American norms, and the budgets are quite low relative to Brazil's huge GDP.

CADE and its allied agencies operate under a 1994 law that has frequently been amended to give wider powers and other improvements. Moreover, recently it has overtly emphasized an increased focus on cartel cases rather than merger

---

[143] See Connor, above n 118.
[144] *Ibid.*
[145] Hoj, above n 30.
[146] Connor (2008), above n 115, at Table 13.

control.[147] Dawn raids have been permitted as of 2003, and Brazil was the first jurisdiction to implement an amnesty program (2003) and a partial leniency program (2007). In general, Brazil fines the largest number of hard-core cartels annually, imposes the highest average corporate cartel fines in Latin America, and is the only one regularly to fine cartel managers.[148] Fines are rising over time. Imprisonment is a possible sanction (up to five years), but this option appears never to have been used.

The great majority of cartel cases pursued by CADE consist of highly localized markets, such as gasoline or LPG in one city, or bid rigging on medical services.[149] However, CADE is clearly in the forefront of prosecuting large-scale international cartels organized within Brazil, and is nearly unique in Latin America in prosecuting global cartels.[149a] The highly injurious *Generic Pharmaceuticals, Toy Manufacturers, Industrial Gasses, Blood Products*, and *Sao Paulo Crushed Rock*[150] cases each involved large numbers of well-defended multinational companies; fines in the two decided cases amounted to $120 million. Brazil is the only antitrust authority on the continent to have investigated and convicted members of the vast global *Vitamins* cartel.[151] CADE has also been investigating the global *Lysine* cartel for the past five years or more. In 2007, CADE staged raids on companies suspected of price fixing in two global cartels that are believed to have very large affected sales: *Air-Insulated High-Voltage Switchgear* and *Air Cargo*.[152] Despite a high probability of injuries to their economies, no other Latin American antitrust authority has been reported to have commenced investigations into these two global cartels.

B. Argentina

In terms of budget and employees, Argentina's CNDC is the smallest antitrust authority of the four Latin American countries selected. Even accounting for increases in personnel in the 2000s, the CNDC has the slimmest resources relative to its GDP. It has the ability to launch dawn raids, but has no leniency program.[153] Most of its activities are devoted to merger control. Consequently, the CNDC typically prosecutes only one or two hard-core cartels each year, and imposes negligible cartel fines or sentences of imprisonment.

The year 2005 was a notable exception to Argentina's normally relaxed approach to cartel enforcement. In that year, two vast international cartels—*Cement*

---

[147] OECD (2007a), above n 28, at 2.
[148] Connor (2008), above n 115, at Table 13.
[149] OECD (2007a), above n 28.
[149a] Connor (2008), above n 115, at Table 11.
[150] See Connor, above n 118.
[151] Nemr, above n 142.
[152] Connor (2008), above n 115, at Table 11.
[153] OECD (2005a), above n 28.

and *Medical Oxygen*[154]—were fined a total of $133 million.[155] These cartels incorporated several powerful multinational companies with long histories of price-fixing convictions in these industries in other jurisdictions. The CNDC expert in charge of these cases was subsequently transferred to another ministry, so comparable high-profile prosecutions may be unique for some time.

C. Chile

Chile's current Competition Law was passed in 1973, making it the oldest in the region. Chile's antitrust authority (FNE) has the second smallest resources of the four Latin American cases examined in this chapter.[156] It is also the only one of the four agencies that does not participate in the OECD's Competition Committee. Yet for the size of its economy, Chile's FNE is almost three times the size of Brazil's three federal agencies.[157] In general, FNE appears to spend the greatest share of its time on merger control rather than cartel activity. A very large proportion of allegations of price fixing result in cases concluded without sanctions, suggesting that there is a high burden of proof on prosecutors in Chile.

The number of decisions on horizontal restraint cases averages two per year, and the average annual cartel fine is a very low $50,000. Until the maximum fine was increased in 2004, Chile's cap was unlikely to provide even minimal deterrence for the typical large-scale international cartel. Without the modern tools of cartel investigation common in other jurisdictions, the FNE is not equipped to uncover or punish international cartels. The one such cartel that was fined was *Medical Oxygen*; participants were fined about $300,000.[158] The only other international case, *Gasoline Distribution*, was closed after many years of investigation.[159] Chile has neither investigated nor punished any global cartels.

D. Mexico

By Latin American norms, Mexico has the largest and best-funded antitrust authority. Relative to national GDP, the CFC's budget is more than four times as high as Brazil's. The CFC appears to have no authority to perform dawn raids. Until 2004, the maximum fine for corporate cartel members was low by international antitrust

---

[154] *CNDC v Loma Negra and others* (2005), Resolution 124/05 from the Secretary of Technical Coordination; *CNDC v Air Liquide and Others* (2005), Resolution 119/05 from the Secretary of Technical Coordination.

[155] Connor (2008), above n 115, at Table 11.

[156] *Ibid*, at Table 13.

[157] Note that the resources of Chile's extensive regional competition commissions are not included.

[158] *Medical Oxygen Case*; Connor (2008), above n 115, at Table 11.

[159] OECD 'Competition Law and Policy in Chile. A Peer Review (Paris, Organization of Economic Co-Operation and Devlopment, 2004), at 38–40.

standards ($1.6 million), as was the maximum fine for managers ($30,000). Cartel managers have no fear of imprisonment.

Both political parties in the Mexican Congress appear to be prodding the CFC to be more aggressive in fighting cartels; in 2004 the maximum cartel fine was raised to $6.2 million, and in 2006 an amnesty program was authorized. Despite these increased powers, the CFC penalized only 10 hard-core cartels in 2004–06.[160] Rather, the authority seems to be preoccupied with mergers and time-consuming monopoly cases.[161]

For all these reasons, the CFC has done little to attack hard-core cartels in general, or international cartels in particular. It has rendered only four cartel decisions per year since it was founded, and there is no upward trend. The CFC does not publish the level of fines imposed for antitrust violations—the only one of the four authorities that does not. The sole known fine imposed on an international cartelist is about $200,000 for ADM's leading role in *Lysine*.

E. Private Suits

Settlements in private antitrust damages suits are the major form of monetary penalties on international cartels in Canada and the United States. Despite the higher government fines imposed by the EC and the EU's NCAs, because of the near absence of private rights of action, the EU has not been as successful as North America in imposing high monetary penalties on international cartels operating in Western Europe. In the rest of the world antitrust penalties are negligible. Even from an *ex post* point of view, no international cartel has been required to disgorge 100 per cent of its illegal profits.[162] Therefore, absent government fines far in excess of the current legal maximums, private rights of action are essential to achieving optimal (*ex ante*) deterrence of international cartels. This statement applies with even greater force to global price-fixing schemes.

Information on the results of private suits is especially difficult to assemble, because most suits end in out-of-court settlements, many of which are not fully reported; very few involve trials with final published judgments.[163] As a result, relative to government fines, antitrust settlement amounts are significantly

---

[160] OECD (2007b), above n 29.

[161] David Luhnow, 'The Secrets of the World's Richest Man—Mexico's Carlos Slim Makes his Billions the Old-Fashioned Way: Monopolies', *The Wall Street Journal*, August 4, 2007; Dow Jones, 'Mexico's Anti-Trust Agency Starts Mobile Telephony Mkt Probe', *Dow Jones International News*, Nov 30, 2007.

[162] Connor (2006), above n 43, at 195–223; John M Connor, 'The Great Global Price-Fixing Conspiracy: Sanctions and Deterrence' (Oct 2006a), 4 *Concurrences: Revue des Droits de la Concurrences* 17–20; Connor (2007c), above n 113.

[163] Most large settlements do get reported in the business press or in company financial reports. If the private suit is a class action, there is some information available because many of the opinions of the supervising judges are published on Web-based search engines. The results of suits threatened or launched by firms that opt out of class actions are often unreported in any public source. On the difficulties of gathering information on private antitrust suits, see Robert H Lande and Joshua P Davis,

under-reported. Nevertheless, thorough searches of business and legal news sources turned up satisfactory information on most of the 114 private damages suits against members of international cartels from 1990 to 2007.[163a] All but four of the 114 suits in the sample were filed in US and Canadian courts. Of the 72 US suits, 22 concerned global and 48 regional (NAFTA area) cartels. In Canada, at least 21 global cartels were prosecuted by affected customers, and 13 more international cartels that were regional in geographic scope were prosecuted by Canadian customers. One private price-fixing suit was won by Australian buyers of animal-grade bulk vitamins in 2006—the first such case in Australia's legal history.

Information on settlement amounts is available for 92 of the 114 suits, but a score are still being negotiated. In the United States, private parties have recovered at least $19.7 billion from international cartel defendants.[164] That includes $13.6 billion in the global cartel cases (of which $3 to $5 billion is from *Vitamins* manufacturers) and $6.0 billion to US plaintiffs injured by North American cartels. In Canada the respective amounts are US $164 and $8.7 million. An amazing fact is that private plaintiffs in North America were awarded *about five times* the amount collected in fines by the US and Canadian Governments.

The contrast with international cartel penalties in Europe is stark. In the European Economic Area, the EU and its Member States imposed an impressive $21.3 billion in fines on intra-EU international cartels ($15.8 billion) or on global cartels that affected EEA markets ($5.4 billion). In contrast, restitution or private recoveries in Europe amounted to a paltry $200 million or less.

There is virtually no information about the number or outcomes of private cartel suits outside North America. Private suits are permitted in Japan, Taiwan, Mexico, Australia and several EU Member States, but are rare in practice.[165] These jurisdictions typically permit only single damages, do not allow discovery, disallow class actions and make the plaintiffs pay court costs, have high burdens of proof, and award puny damages to plaintiffs. The absence of private suits outside of North America has a negative effect on deterrence of global cartels, because only 40 per cent of the global injuries caused by such cartels occur there.[166] At present, buyers in nearly all other parts of the world have no recourse to private compensation in their local court systems.

Private suits are legally permitted in two of the four Latin American jurisdictions that are the subjects of this chapter.[167] Except for a small number of cases

---

'Benefits From Private Antitrust Enforcement: An Analysis of Forty Cases' *University of San Francisco Law Review* (2008).

   [163a] Connor (2008), above n 115, at Table 5.
   [164] *Ibid*, at Table 6.
   [165] Connor (2007b), above n 18.
   [166] Connor (2008), above n 115, at Table 10.
   [167] *Ibid*, at Table 13.

320   *John M Connor*

in Brazil, private antitrust suits are practically unknown in Latin America.[168] The principal barriers to launching such suits are the absence of legal traditions and mechanisms for aggregating large numbers of small claims and of something akin to pre-trial discovery.[169]

F. Empirical Analysis of Cartel Deterrence

Even from an *ex post* perspective, penalties on international cartels are sub-optimal. Because of positive skewness, we focus on the medians of three ratios.[170] The general findings for all regions are: *damages* represented by the price overcharge averaged 19 per cent of affected sales of the cartel in all the jurisdictions in which they functioned; monetary antitrust *penalties* typically represented 3.3 per cent of sales; and penalties recouped 34 per cent of cartel damages.

Three subgroups are of interest. First, let us consider the effectiveness of anti-trust penalties imposed in North America, which is widely regarded as having the most effective antitrust enforcement in the world. The median degree of harm (ratio of damages to affected sales) of North American regional cartels was 30 per cent. Private and government monetary penalties accrued to 9.1 per cent of affected sales, which is interesting to some perhaps, but irrelevant for deterrence analysis. The key finding is that the typical penalty recouped only 47.5 per cent of damages in the United States and Canada. On average, cartelization was profitable in the region with the most severe laws and penalty structures in the world.

Secondly, the fines imposed by Latin American antitrust authorities are pitifully low relative to either affected sales (4.9 per cent on average) or to damages (less than 1 per cent). This sub-sample is quite small, but even the highest penalty/damages ratio was only 8 per cent.

Thirdly, the penalties on the sample of global cartels are quite revealing. In general, it was global cartels that were the most severely penalized in 1990–2007, US and Canadian fines alone disgorged 42–49 per cent of jurisdictional damages on average. But then one must add the generally larger settlements obtained by private plaintiffs; for global cartels, North American courts approved median recoveries that amounted to about 103 per cent of Canadian and US overcharges. All told, global cartelists paid penalties that averaged 150 per cent of North American damages. Recovery of greater than single damages is impressive, and from an *ex post* vantage point would appear to provide specific and general deterrence. However, when one considers that global cartels make the great majority of their illegal profits outside of North America, this 'deterrence'

---

[168] Daniel A Crane, 'Private Enforcement Against International Cartels in Latin America: A US Perspective', ch XV in this book.

[169] *Ibid.*

[170] Connor (2008), above n 115, at Table 8.

is no longer supra-deterrent: only 61 per cent of global cartel profits were disgorged.[171] Moreover, if the probability of detection is indeed in the 13 per cent to 17 per cent range, as most scholars believe, then *ex ante* deterrence is far below optimal.

The absence of high fines or private damages suits outside North America and Europe contributes to the inability of contemporary antitrust regimes to deter international cartels. Although discussions continue, access to treble damages suits in US courts by injured buyers abroad is far off.[172] Improvements in this regard among Asian and Latin American jurisdictions will not only benefit local populations, but also will help discourage the harmful effects of global cartels.

VII. Conclusion

International cartelists face investigations, possible fines, and other monetary penalties in a score of national and supranational jurisdictions. Brazil, South Korea, Australia and several Member States of the EU have increasingly active anti-cartel agencies. However, the world still depends largely on the three jurisdictions with the greatest experience in combating international cartels: the United States, Canada, and the EU. Latin American antitrust authorities play a small role in punishing international cartels, particularly those with a global reach. This is a pity, because international cartels have had large sales in Latin America and cause great economic harm on the continent. Optimal cartel deterrence cannot be achieved without active anti-cartel enforcement in Latin America.

By all measures, of the four Latin American antitrust authorities examined in this chapter, Brazil's CADE has been far and away the most effective in dealing with international price fixing since 1990, and Chile's FNE has been the least effective. The relative success of Brazil is not explained by its age or the quality of its enforcement resources (Chile's and Mexico's authorities rank higher in these regards). Factors that appear to differentiate CADE from the other Latin American competition law authorities are:

— A high degree of independence from ministries that support business.
— Government support for making cartels the highest enforcement priority.
— A critical mass of trained lawyers and economists.

---

[171] In the absence of pre-judgment interest, the forces of inflation and the time value of money further work against deterrence. For an illustration, see John M Connor 'The Great Global Price-Fixing Conspiracy: Sanctions and Deterrence', *Concurrences: Revue des droit de la concurrences* (Oct 2006) 4: 17–20.
[172] Connor and Bush, above n 3.

— Adherence to the goal of specific deterrence.
— A high limit and objective but flexible rules for setting corporate fines.
— A commitment to punishing individual cartel managers.
— Adoption of modern amnesty, leniency, and other proven cartel-discovery methods.
— A willingness to give weight to domestic harm caused by foreign firms in choosing cases to investigate for cartel conduct.

Continuing high rates of cartel discoveries and evidence of rising cartel recidivism suggest that the need for aggressive cartel enforcement is as high as ever. The phenomenon of historically high and highly-touted monetary sanctions imposed on international cartels in the past decade is obscuring major deficiencies in world anti-cartel efforts. While Brazil's anti-cartel enforcement is on balance the most effective in Latin America, future modifications must be considered to ensure that its goal of optimal deterrence can be reached.

First, CADE is rapidly approaching the maximum permissible price-fixing fine. In any case, by limiting corporate fines to 30 per cent of a company's annual sales, CADE cannot hope to recover all of a cartelist's illegal profits, even in a typical international cartel.[173]

Consideration ought to be given to altering the way in which fines can be calculated, particularly for egregiously harmful cartels. For example, a flexible cap of either 30 per cent of a cartel's affected sales or of treble damages would provide for fines with greater deterrence power. Secondly, increases in the maximum corporate penalties by governments alone may be insufficient to deter cartel formation. The failure of compensatory private suits to take hold outside of North America, and the near absence of large fines in most Latin American jurisdictions, also casts doubt on the power of current penalties to deter recidivism by international cartels. Like the European Union, CADE and other Latin American antitrust authorities should be advocating changes in local court rules that would facilitate private rights of action by the victims of cartels. In order to get the greatest discovery effects, private suits should be allowed to proceed independently from government prosecutions. Thirdly, CADE and its sister agencies can expand the list of available incentives for destabilizing operating cartels. Techniques include

---

[173] A typical international cartel historically has had a median average overcharge of 31% in the cartelized market and a duration of about six years (Levenstein and Suslow (2004), above n 26; at 59–153). Modern cartels have similar characteristics (Connor and Helmers (2006), above n 34). Therefore, a specialized (single product) participant in a typical international cartel tends to generate illegal monopoly profits equal to 186% (31% × 6) of a single year's total revenues. A maximum Brazilian fine would recoup only one-eighth of the company's cartel profits. Of course, if the cartelist has many lines of business in Brazil or large sales outside Brazil's borders, then the maximum fine rule will not constrain a compensatory fine. On the other hand, one can argue that Brazil's fining rule discriminates against small, specialized firms.

fine surcharges for recidivism and duration, 'Amnesty Plus' fine discounts, and whistleblower payments.[174]

Without significant increases in cartel detection, in the levels of expected fines or civil settlements, or expansion in the standing of buyers to seek compensation, international price fixing will remain rational business conduct for decades to come.

---

[174] William E Kovacic, 'Private Monitoring and Antitrust Enforcement: Paying Informants to Reveal Cartels' 69 *George Washington Law Review* 766–97 (2001).

Part II
Institutions

[8]

INSTITUTIONAL FOUNDATIONS FOR ECONOMIC LEGAL REFORM IN TRANSITION ECONOMIES: THE CASE OF COMPETITION POLICY AND ANTITRUST ENFORCEMENT

WILLIAM E. KOVACIC*

INTRODUCTION

The modern progression toward market processes in nations once committed to comprehensive central economic planning is one of the most extraordinary events of our time. Since the mid-1970s, many communist or socialist nations have undertaken market-oriented reforms of varied intensity and scope.[1] There is no assurance that this attempted transformation will succeed in all or most cases, as economic and political turmoil today besets many countries seeking to rely more extensively on market systems.[2] Yet, despite enormous uncertainty and upheaval in the transition from planning to markets, economic liberalization still remains the strategy of choice for boosting growth.[3]

Competition policy laws that prohibit various restraints of trade and create public or private rights of action to enforce such prohibitions have become remarkably common elements of market-

* General Counsel, Federal Trade Commission. Professor Kovacic is on leave from the George Washington University Law School. The views expressed in this Article are the author's and not necessarily the views of the Federal Trade Commission or any of its individual members. The author thanks Kathryn Fenton, Geraldine Foster, Michal Gal, Michael Trebilcock, and Frederic Vissi, and participants in conferences or workshops at the University of Canterbury, Chicago-Kent College of Law, Fordham University, George Washington University, and the University of Toronto for many useful comments and discussions. The author owes a special debt to the editorial staff of the Chicago-Kent Law Review.

1. Extensive treatments of modern economic reform in communist and socialist countries include THE EMERGENCE OF MARKET ECONOMIES IN EASTERN EUROPE (Christopher Clague & Gordon C. Rausser eds., 1992); FOREIGN ECONOMIC LIBERALIZATION (Andras Koves & Paul Marer eds., 1991); INSTITUTIONS AND ECONOMIC DEVELOPMENT (Christopher Clague ed., 1997).

2. See, e.g., Stephen Fidler, World Bank Lifts Growth Forecasts, FIN. TIMES, Dec. 8, 1999, at 19 (describing economic vulnerabilities of emerging market economies).

3. See Joseph E. Stiglitz, Knowledge for Development: Economic Science, Economic Policy, and Economic Advice, in ANNUAL WORLD BANK CONFERENCE ON DEVELOPMENT ECONOMICS 1998, at 9, 14 (Boris Pleskovic & Joseph E. Stiglitz eds., 1999) ("In most countries, there is almost universal agreement that markets should be at the center of any vital economy.").

oriented, economic law reform in the transition environment.[4] Over forty formerly communist or socialist states have enacted new competition laws or augmented older competition statutes since 1975.[5] Considerable additional activity in the competition policy field is underway. Within the next decade, as many as twenty additional transition economies are likely to establish competition policy systems.[6] The adoption of new laws in transition countries is a vital element in a process of competition policy globalization that has seen the number of nations with antitrust systems grow to over ninety.[7]

The proliferation of new systems raises questions about the proper scope and form of competition policy in transition economies and, more generally, about the design of legal reforms in emerging markets.[8] Individual Western countries and multinational bodies actively have encouraged emerging markets to establish new competition laws.[9] Western advisors sometimes have pressed

---

4. *See* Clive S. Gray & Anthony A. Davis, *Competition Policy in Developing Countries Undergoing Structural Adjustment*, 38 ANTITRUST BULL. 425, 427–28 (1993) (describing adoption of antitrust legislation as a component of structural adjustment programs in developing economies); William E. Kovacic, *Getting Started: Creating New Competition Policy Institutions in Transition Economies*, 23 BROOK. J. INT'L L. 403, 403–08 (1997) (describing creation of competition policy systems as a component of economic law reform).

This Article uses the term "competition law" to describe a statute of general national applicability that prohibits specific forms of anticompetitive conduct and creates public or private rights of action to redress misconduct. This definition omits laws adopted by local or regional government authorities that do not apply to the nation as a whole. This definition excludes countries that have general antimonopoly provisions in their constitutions but have yet to adopt legislation that translates these general provisions into operation principles and creates a mechanism for their enforcement. It also omits consumer protection measures that broadly forbid "unfair competition"—a term that could be interpreted to proscribe price fixing among competitors.

5. *See* Kovacic, *supra* note 4, at 403–04 (discussing the adoption of new competition systems since the late 1970s).

6. *See* William E. Kovacic, *Developing Competition Policy in Transition Economies: Milestones in 2000*, 4 INT'L ANTITRUST BULL. 40, 41 (2000) (discussing perspectives for new competition systems).

7. *Id.* Identifying nations with competition laws in the transition environment can be an uncertain process. In some instances, the collection of information is relatively easy. The competition regimes of a number of countries have been the subject of extensive study and published commentary. A growing collection of transition economies maintains highly informative web sites about their competition systems. In many cases, however, current, reliable information is difficult to come by, if only because new competition laws are being adopted at a relatively rapid pace. The best source of information sometimes will be an advisor who by word of mouth reports the establishment of a new system.

8. *See* Jean-Jacques Laffont, *Competition, Information, and Development*, in ANNUAL WORLD BANK CONFERENCE ON DEVELOPMENT ECONOMICS 1998, *supra* note 3, at 237 (analyzing hazards associated with transplanting sophisticated Western antitrust systems into a transition economy environment).

9. *See* United Nations Conference on Trade and Development, *Report by the UNCTAD Secretariat, Empirical Evidence of the Benefits from Applying Competition Law and Policy Principles to Economic Development in Order to Attain Greater Efficiency in International Trade*

transition governments to adopt close replicas of competition laws typically found in mature market economies.[10]   In the field of medicine, the bases for prescribing a sound regime of care include formulating an accurate diagnosis, selecting the correct treatment, monitoring results, and making adjustments over time.   Only in extreme circumstances would a physician treat a complex affliction with a standardized, off-the-shelf solution on the basis of a snap diagnosis.

The development of new competition policy systems and the promulgation of other economic legal reforms have important consequences reaching beyond the borders of the emerging markets that have enacted new laws. For business managers accustomed to focusing on the competition systems of a few Western nations, the new transition economy competition systems will require ever greater attention in the preparation of business plans that affect commerce in such economies.   Many emerging market antitrust systems require pre-merger notification of certain transactions.[11]   Such mechanisms are common elements of modern antitrust practice in Western economies, and they reflect a consensus that, in principle, meaningful remedies frequently will be unattainable if antitrust intervention occurs after a transaction is completed and the operations of the merging parties are combined. Though the application of pre-merger oversight in Western countries is not lacking for controversy, such

---

and Development 2, TD/B/COM.2/EM/10/Rev.1 (May 25, 1998) (finding that "there would be substantial benefits to be obtained from strengthening the application of competition law and policy principles in developing and least developed countries in transition in terms of greater production, allocative and dynamic efficiency, welfare and growth").

10. *See* JOHN FINGLETON ET AL., COMPETITION POLICY AND THE TRANSFORMATION OF CENTRAL EUROPE 54–57 (1996) (discussing the EU's influence on antitrust laws in the Czech Republic, Hungary, Poland, and Romania); Mark R.A. Palim, *The Worldwide Growth of Competition Law*, 43 ANTITRUST BULL. 105 (1998) (documenting how the EU has induced countries in Central and Eastern Europe to modify their antitrust laws to copy the EU model); Carolyn Brzezinski, *Competition and Antitrust Law in Central Europe: Poland, the Czech Republic, Slovakia, and Hungary*, 15 MICH. J. INT'L L. 1129, 1149–56 (1994) (describing how the prospect of EU membership has reshaped competition laws in Central Europe); Eleanor M. Fox, *The Central European Nations and the EU Waiting Room—Why Must the Central European Nations Adopt the Competition Law of the European Union?*, 23 BROOK. J. INT'L L. 351, 352–56 (1997) (describing how the European Union requires candidates for accession to the EU from Central and Eastern Europe to approximate EU law, including competition law).

11. *See* Roger Alan Boner, *Competition Policy and Institutions in Reforming Economies*, in REGULATORY POLICIES AND REFORM: A COMPARATIVE PERSPECTIVE 38, 45 (Claudio R. Frischtak ed., 1995) (discussing merger notification requirements in transition economy antitrust laws); Michael J. Cicero, *Overview: International Merger Control*, 15 ANTITRUST 15 (2001) (summarizing national merger control systems); WHITE & CASE LLP, SURVEY OF WORLDWIDE ANTITRUST MERGER NOTIFICATION REQUIREMENTS (2001) (reviewing merger control regimes).

mechanisms are noticeably harder to design and administer in transition economies than in the Western environments in which the concepts were first devised. Transition economy enforcement actions in applying mechanisms modeled on Western practice show that new competition laws can have a substantial impact on specific transactions in emerging markets and can dictate adjustments in the way firms plan arrangements such as mergers and joint ventures.[12]

This Article uses the development of competition systems to examine economic law reform in transition economies. The Article provides a context for the development of transition economy competition policy by presenting the modern debate about the proper approach to economic development and law reform in emerging markets. Part II defines the concept of "competition policy" and emphasizes how nations can achieve important competition policy goals by a mix of strategies that includes antitrust enforcement. Part III addresses conceptual rationales for and against making competition policy a component of reform efforts. Part IV discusses the initial conditions that typically confront a transition economy seeking to develop a competition policy system and identifies the implications of such initial conditions for designing and implementing a new system of law. Part V considers the implications of modern experience for the proper design of technical assistance programs.

I. COMPETITION POLICY, ANTITRUST ENFORCEMENT, AND LAW REFORM

The decision to adopt a competition law, or promote the adoption of a competition law, as an element of economic development raises a number of issues about the appropriate approach to law reform in transition environments and the possible contributions of competition policy to economic progress. Since the mid-1980s, multinational donors and individual Western countries have expended substantial resources advising countries with centralized economic and political systems about legal reforms designed to promote economic and political liberalization.[13] The principal targets

---

12. *See* William E. Kovacic, *Merger Enforcement in Transition: Antitrust Controls on Acquisitions in Emerging Economies*, 66 U. CIN. L. REV. 1075, 1106–08 (1998) (discussing a challenge in 1996 by Venezuela's competition authority, Pro Competencia, to Coca-Cola's joint venture with the Cisneros Group).

13. For an overview of contributions of foreign donors to economic development, see WORLD BANK, ASSESSING AID: WHAT WORKS, WHAT DOESN'T, AND WHY (1998).

of assistance have been the countries of the former Soviet Union and the socialist states of Central and Eastern Europe, although donors have undertaken significant projects in Africa, Asia, and Latin America as well. Recent technical assistance programs are the latest chapter of post–World War II efforts by Western countries with democratic political structures and market systems to export their institutions to states with totalitarian governments and planned economies.[14] The most recent period of technical assistance has inspired extensive discussion about the appropriate design and phasing of law reforms to promote economic and political liberalization.[15] This Section summarizes some major focal points of recent debate about transition economy law reform initiatives.

A.   Setting Priorities for Economic and Legal Reforms

Efforts to establish market systems in planned economies confront a number of difficult choices. The choices are forced by three basic conditions of scarcity. One form of scarcity involves human capital. Transition economies ordinarily feature a comparatively small number of individuals with formal training in disciplines relevant to a market economy or experience in market-oriented institutions. The second condition of scarcity involves political capital. A government committed to reform does not enjoy infinite good will or political power as it undertakes departures from past practices that endanger beneficiaries of the status quo. A third form of scarcity involves the level of foreign assistance. Donor assistance programs have limited resources and cannot support the full range of possible reform initiatives.

Scarcity dictates that advocates of economic law reform rank specific measures by their importance and choose assistance strategies that focus chiefly on the greatest needs. Modern commentary on economic reform has tended to emphasize five law reform prerequisites for economic development:[16]

---

14. Post–World War II trends in development work and the philosophy that animated specific foreign assistance programs are traced in Vernon Ruttan, *Participation and Development, in* INSTITUTIONS AND ECONOMIC DEVELOPMENT, *supra* note 1, at 217, 217–20.

15. *See* Jeffrey Sachs, *Poland and Eastern Europe: What Is to Be Done?, in* FOREIGN ECONOMIC LIBERALIZATION, *supra* note 1, at 235, 235 ("The main debate in economic reform should ... be about the means of transition, not the ends.").

16. *See* Charles Cadwell, *Implementing Legal Reform in Transition Economies, in* INSTITUTIONS AND ECONOMIC DEVELOPMENT, *supra* note 1, at 251, 260 ("The key institutions of a market economy are property rights, mechanisms for enforcement of contracts, and reliable and peaceful ways of organizing political debate."); Christopher Clague et al., *Institutions and*

1. Creating and defining private property rights and creating systems for recording and transferring such rights.

2. Establishing contract principles and enforcement mechanisms to facilitate exchange.

3. Recognizing the formation of business enterprises in the form of partnerships, corporations, and sole proprietorships and specifying the means for governing such bodies.

4. Promoting capital formation through the sale of securities, issuance of debt, and pledging of assets.

5. Facilitating the exit of assets and their redeployment through bankruptcy procedures.

Pursuit of these aims would not come at the exclusion of other measures, such as adopting laws to control pollution, prohibiting restrictive business practices, and addressing other market failures.

B.   *The Importance of Supporting Institutions*

The recent literature on law and economic development shows a growing recognition that the effectiveness of economic and legal reforms depends on the quality of numerous supporting institutions inside and outside the government.[17] Much of the modern emphasis

---

Economic Performance: Property Rights and Contract Enforcement, in INSTITUTIONS AND ECONOMIC DEVELOPMENT *supra* note 1, at 67, 74 ("[P]oorer countries as a group have grown somewhat less rapidly than rich countries, not because they are inevitably doomed to fall further behind but because the majority of them have failed to establish mechanisms for securing rights to property, for enforcing contracts, and for establishing efficient public bureaucracies."); Peter Murrell, *Evolution in Economics and in the Economic Reform of Centrally Planned Economies, in* THE EMERGENCE OF MARKET ECONOMIES IN EASTERN EUROPE, *supra* note 1, at 35, 49 (describing key legal institutions underpinning market systems); Mancur Olson, *The Hidden Path to a Successful Economy, in* THE EMERGENCE OF MARKET ECONOMIES IN EASTERN EUROPE, *supra* note 1, at 55, 65. Olson writes:

> To realize all the gains from trade, . . . there has to be a legal system and political order that enforces contracts, protects property rights, carries out mortgage agreements, provides for limited liability corporations, and facilitates a lasting and widely used capital market that makes the investments and loans more liquid than they would otherwise be. These arrangements must also be thought likely to last for some time.

Id. See also Gordon C. Rausser, *Lessons from Emerging Market Economies in Eastern Europe, in* THE EMERGENCE OF MARKET ECONOMIES IN EASTERN EUROPE, *supra* note 1, at 311, 318–21 (describing essential elements of the "legal and regulatory infrastructure" for a market economy in transition economies).

17. *See* Bernard Black et al., *Russian Privatization and Corporate Governance: What Went Wrong?*, 52 STAN. L. REV. 1731, 1797 (2000).

> We have learned that Western-style capitalism is more fragile than we thought. It will not emerge—certainly not quickly, perhaps not at all—if seeds are simply scattered widely through mass privatization, to grow in the thin soil of an institutionally impoverished country. Instead, the institutions that control theft in its myriad forms,

on institutions results from the work of scholars, such as Douglass North, who have contributed to what is known as the New Institutional Economics ("NIE") and applied its insights to explain the process of economic development.[18]   "Institutions" in the NIE literature encompass a broad collection of "socially devised constraints on individual action."[19]   Christopher Clague suggests the wide range of phenomena that might be characterized as institutions:

> They can be organizations or sets of rules within organizations. They can be markets or particular rules about the way a market operates.   They can refer to the set of property rights and rules governing exchanges in a society. They may include cultural norms of behavior.   The rules can be either formally written down and enforced by government officials or unwritten and informally sanctioned.[20]

In the field of law reform, among the most important government institutions are a well-functioning judiciary and other mechanisms for resolving disputes arising from the enforcement of the law. To some degree, private parties can rely on nongovernment dispute resolution methods, such as arbitration, to compensate for weaknesses in the judicial process.   For the longer term, a country's inability to create courts that are regarded as competent, impartial fora for resolving commercial disputes will seriously restrict growth. A second essential government institution consists of principles of

---

especially self-dealing by managers and controlling shareholders, are an essential fertilizer.
Id.   See also Paul L. Joskow, *Regulatory Priorities for Infrastructure Sector Reform in Developing Countries*, in ANNUAL WORLD BANK CONFERENCE ON DEVELOPMENT ECONOMICS 1998, *supra* note 3, at 69 ("These regulatory institutions should be created as an integral component of the entire reform program, not as an afterthought."); Steven Knack & Philip Keefer, *Institutions and Economic Performance: Cross-Country Tests Using Alternative Institutional Measures*, 7 ECON. & POL. 207 (1995) (demonstrating links between institutional quality and economic growth in emerging markets); Laffont, *supra* note 8, at 30 ("[L]ittle can be expected in countries where the political willingness is lacking and that in others international aid for institution building is essential to exit vicious circles of underdevelopment."); Mancur Olson, *Why Are Differences in Per Capita Incomes So Large and Persistent?*, in ECONOMIC GROWTH IN THE WORLD ECONOMY 193 (Horst Siebert ed., 1993) (describing the value of institutional improvements in raising living standards); Stiglitz, *supra* note 3, at 10 (identifying, as a flaw of some economic reform proposals for transition economies, "the lack of emphasis on institutional infrastructure, including not only competition policy, but also legal structures that enforce contracts, implement bankruptcy, and ensure sound financial institutions"); WORLD BANK, *supra* note 13, at 3 ("Improvements in economic institutions and policies in the developing world are the key to a quantum leap in poverty reduction.").

    18. *See* DOUGLASS C. NORTH, INSTITUTIONS, INSTITUTIONAL CHANGE, AND ECONOMIC PERFORMANCE (1990); Douglass C. North, *Economic Performance Through Time*, 84 AM. ECON. REV. 359 (1994).

    19. Chrisopher Clague, *The New Institutional Economics and Economic Development*, in INSTITUTIONS AND ECONOMIC DEVELOPMENT, *supra* note 1, at 13, 17.

    20. *Id.* at 18.

public administration that compel government bodies to operate honestly and transparently. Achieving economic growth in transition economies often demands simultaneous efforts to weaken the state's capacity to control economic activity and to increase its ability to execute public functions necessary to the operation of a market system. The latter category of activities includes the honest administration of mechanisms to dispense justice, to raise revenue by taxing individuals and businesses, and to execute proper regulatory responsibilities.

The effectiveness of government bodies in turn rests upon the vitality of a number of supporting institutions, both public and private, that provide resources essential to the operation of the law.[21] Prominent among these are universities, which contribute major inputs to the process of economic and political liberalization. Universities train specialists in business administration, economics, law, and public administration. Graduates from such programs take positions in the government agencies that carry out the new laws or work outside the government advising those whose interests are affected by the legal regime. University faculties also conduct research that informs judgments about existing public policies and the need for further adjustments. Building a self-sustaining indigenous capacity in universities and other institutions to collect data and perform policy research is a key step toward improving the quality of public policy.[22]

Most legal regimes also rely on a variety of nongovernmental organizations to explain the content of various laws to affected groups.[23] Professional associations provide networks through which lawyers and others who advise business operators can learn about new policy developments. Media organizations disseminate information about rights and responsibilities created by law, report on economic trends and the activities of individual business operators, and monitor the performance of government bodies responsible for

---

21. *See* Kovacic, *supra* note 4, at 440–41 (describing how "collateral institutions" influence the effectiveness of new competition policy systems).

22. *See* Peter Murrell, *Missed Policy Opportunities During Mongolian Privatization: Should Aid Target Policy Research Institutions?*, *in* INSTITUTIONS AND ECONOMIC DEVELOPMENT, *supra* note 1, at 235, 236 (recommending that foreign assistance programs "aim to create a capacity for information gathering, research, and analysis").

23. *See* William E. Kovacic, *Creating Competition Policy: Betty Bock and the Development of Antitrust Institutions*, 66 ANTITRUST L.J. 231, 234–45 (1997) (describing Betty Bock's role in building nongovernment institutions that facilitate antitrust enforcement in the United States).

enforcing legal commands. Consumer groups inform citizens about their legal rights and collect complaints about alleged violations.

C.   The Sequence of Economic, Legal, and Institutional Reforms

Studies of the interaction between economic reforms, new laws, and implementing institutions demonstrate the importance of ensuring that the development of implementing institutions receives careful attention at the beginning of the economic liberalization and law reform processes.   Liberalization measures are prone to fail unless preceded (or at least accompanied) by the creation of appropriate regulatory frameworks.[24]   The massive privatization of assets without the creation of mechanisms for ensuring competition and effective shareholder governance may enable company managers during the era of planning to loot the productive core of the newly private enterprises.[25]   Institutional improvements—such as the establishment of effective judicial systems—must precede or be undertaken in parallel with substantive law reforms, such as the establishment of a company's law or the creation of private property rights in land.

D.   Pre-reform Study of Initial Conditions

It has become increasingly apparent to Western donors that the selection of law reform priorities and the design of a process for their implementation are prone to fail unless it emerges from a careful initial assessment of existing conditions.   One recent assessment of privatization in Russia suggests that a careful, pre-reform evaluation of initial conditions might have raised serious doubts about the wisdom of adopting a strategy that immediately transferred vast amounts of state holdings into private hands. The study observes:

> [I]n the early 1990s, Russia wholly lacked the institutional infra-structure to control self-dealing by managers of private firms.

---

24. *See* Jean-Jacques Laffont, *Regulation, Privatization and Incentives in Developing Countries, in* CURRENT ISSUES IN ECONOMIC DEVELOPMENT 164 (M.G. Quibria & J. Malcolm Dowling eds., 1996) (explaining how decontrol of natural monopolies requires establishment of regulatory framework).

25. *See* Black et al., *supra* note 17, at 1735 (stating that to prevent business managers from stealing the assets of their firms, "development of a decent legal and enforcement infrastructure must precede or at least accompany privatization of large firms"); Stiglitz, *supra* note 3, at 10 ("The experience in Russia shows that, without the appropriate institutional infrastructure, privatization provides incentives for asset stripping—and shipping wealth abroad—rather than for wealth creation.").

Prosecutors, judges, and lawyers had no experience in untangling complex corporate transactions or understanding of the indirect ways in which company insiders can siphon off profits. Legal concepts of fiduciary duty and proscriptions against self-dealing didn't exist.[26]

The requisite initial assessment is unlikely to succeed if undertaken by outsiders alone. Early and continuing participation by host country specialists and indigenous research institutions is vital to develop an understanding of the status quo and to formulate a strategy for changes.[27]

E.   *Determining the Rate of Change*

A focus of extensive debate within the reform community is the appropriate rate of change.[28] Many donor-supported efforts at law reform in the early 1990s emphasized a "big bang" or "shock therapy" approach involving, among other measures, rapid decontrol of prices, trade liberalization, and swift privatization of government-owned assets.[29] The essential logic of shock therapy is that the swift divestiture of the state's economic holdings and relinquishment of other forms of economic control would best stimulate the development of market processes and create a constituency for the establishment of a legal regime to ensure its growth over time. The urgency to

26. *See* Black et al., *supra* note 17, at 1752.

27. *See* Murrell, *supra* note 22, at 237:

Each new institution interacts with a larger preexisting structure. Therefore, the effectiveness of each new institutional brick crucially depends on its fit with the existing institutional foundation. As a consequence, if it is to be effective, the generation of information on the effects of existing policies and the formulation of new policies needs to reflect the deep characteristics of a society. To know how a policy will work, one must understand the concurrent processes occurring in the economy. A model imported from the West is useful only to the extent that it provides a disciplining pedagogical device, not a magic key that will fit any door.

Id. at 237. *See also* Georges Korsun & Peter Murrell, *Ownership and Governance on the Morning After: The Initial Results of Privatization in Mongolia* (Univ. of Md. Ctr. for Institutional Reform and the Informal Sector (IRIS), Working Paper No. 95, Jan. 1994) (reviewing effects of the failure, in drafting Mongolia's Economic Entities Act, to account for the existing Mongolian economic environment).

28. *See* Paul Starobin, *What Went Wrong*, 31 NAT'L J. 3450 (1999) (describing the debate in the economic reform community about the causes of failed efforts to promote capitalism in the former Soviet Union).

29. For an extensive discussion of the rationale for shock therapy by one of its leading architects, see JEFFREY SACHS, POLAND'S JUMP TO THE MARKET ECONOMY (1994). *See also* Armeane M. Choksi et al., *The Design of Successful Trade Liberalization Policies*, in FOREIGN ECONOMIC LIBERALIZATION, *supra* note 1, at 37, 55 (proposing that a transition economy's trade liberalization program "should be bold and it should start with a bang"); Sachs, *supra* note 15, at 236 (explaining the need for "rapid transformation" and quoting a Polish economist as saying, "'You don't try to cross a chasm in two jumps'").

implement broad-based adjustments swiftly reflected the concern that reformers faced only a narrow window of opportunity and that an incremental process of reform would falter as political opposition to market liberalization mobilized.

Other commentators proposed evolutionary approaches that would introduce market-oriented economic reforms and related laws more gradually.[30] The evolutionary model cautions that some big bang strategies—such as the immediate, large-scale privatization of state-owned firms—may retard the growth of a vital private sector in ways that actually extend the length of the transition from planning to markets. Advocates of the more gradual, evolutionary approach offer two specific recommendations about the content and timing of law reform efforts. The first is that the design of wise reform measures demands extensive preliminary study of initial conditions. The second is that technical assistance programs should promote the establishment of implementing institutions as precursors or complements to adopting new legal commands. In a number of national settings, these measures may provide a more effective path to durable reforms.

F.   Popularizing Reforms

To have positive long-lived effects, reforms ultimately must command the assent and support of the general public.[31] Gaining public acceptance for market-oriented legal reforms is a tremendous challenge in countries accustomed to comprehensive government intervention and conditioned to view private institutions with suspicion. The common path of reform efforts is to engage the host country's elites—public sector and private sector professionals who often have gained formal training in Western universities or held positions that provide extensive contact with Western market institutions.

Extending participation in and support for the reform process beyond the elites, to the larger body of citizens who live in extreme poverty or are politically disaffected, requires conscious efforts to increase public awareness of the rationales for reform and the

---

30. *See* Murrell, *supra* note 16, at 37–40 (describing the evolutionary model of law reform in transition economies); Peter Murrell, *What is Shock Therapy? What Did It Do in Poland and Russia?*, 9 POST-SOVIET AFF. 111 (1993) (analyzing early results of rapid privatization).

31. *See* Clague et al., *supra* note 16, at 88 ("[S]ociety has to accept the new [economic reform] policies, and this is not simply a matter of changing directions at the top.").

encouragement of public participation in the design and implementation of specific measures.[32] Where specific structural adjustment initiatives (such as the removal of price controls) can cause short-term upheaval, sustaining broad public support may require the expansion of social insurance programs and recourse to other redistribution measures.[33]

G. *Introducing Democracy*

There is a substantial debate among commentators about the relationship between economic reform and political liberalization.[34] A number of American foreign assistance programs have sought to spur the development of democratic institutions by, among other means, supporting free and honest elections, building political institutions such as constitutions, courts, and legislatures, and stimulating the creation of nongovernment civic bodies such as professional societies.[35]

Programs to promote political liberalization have stimulated debate about whether the promotion of democracy is a necessary or desirable element of efforts to increase reliance on market processes. The literature on development emphasizes that generalizations about links between autocracy or democracy and economic growth are especially difficult.[36] It is nonetheless possible to identify a number of distinct perspectives in the commentary. One perspective suggests

---

32. *See* WORLD BANK, *supra* note 13, at 86–87 (discussing the value of "beneficiary participation" in ensuring the success of economic reform projects); Elinor Ostrom, *Investing in Capital, Institutions, and Incentives, in* INSTITUTIONS AND ECONOMIC DEVELOPMENT, *supra* note 1, at 153, 177 (analyzing investments in local health and irrigation projects; observing that foreign assistance programs that "build little at the ground level are a poor investment from the donor's perspective").

33. *See* David M. Newbery, *The Safety Net During Transformation: Hungary, in* THE EMERGENCE OF MARKET ECONOMIES IN EASTERN EUROPE, *supra* note 1, at 197 (describing strategies for protecting vulnerable groups during the transition process).

34. A valuable starting point for analyzing the impact of different forms of political organization on economic growth is Mancur Olson, *The New Institutional Economics: The Collective Choice Approach to Economic Development, in* INSTITUTIONS AND ECONOMIC DEVELOPMENT, *supra* note 1, at 37.

35. *See* THOMAS CAROTHERS, AIDING DEMOCRACY ABROAD (2000) (examining modern US efforts to promote development of democratic institutions).

36. *See, e.g.,* Christopher Clague et al., *Democracy, Autocracy, and the Institutions Supportive of Economic Growth, in* INSTITUTIONS AND ECONOMIC DEVELOPMENT, *supra* note 1, at 91, 111 (observing that "democratic regimes differ in their economic effectiveness"); Stephan Haggard, *Democratic Institutions, Economic Policy, and Development, in* INSTITUTIONS AND ECONOMIC DEVELOPMENT, *supra* note 1, at 121, 121 ("Cross-national empirical evidence on the relationship between regime type and economic performance remains highly contested.").

that economic reform progresses most swiftly in countries with comparatively authoritarian structures. By this view, one needs a strong national leader to design and impose the package of reforms. Some commentators point to modern experience in Chile, China, Peru, South Korea, and Taiwan to support this interpretation. At least in the short- to middle-term, a durable autocracy may have greater success in establishing conditions conducive to growth than an unstable democracy.[37] A corollary point is that market decentralization eventually will create social conditions that foster political liberalization. From this perspective, measures to promote growth by the decentralization of economic decision making tend to require a decentralization of political power and the establishment of a more politically astute and active middle class.[38]

A number of scholars have concluded that, compared to a condition of anarchy, autocratic forms of government increase the possibilities for growth.[39] These observers caution that autocratic systems ultimately provide comparatively weak assurance that mechanisms necessary for long-term prosperity—such as the protecting of property and contract rights—will be sustained. Research on the long-term stabilizing influence of democracy has generated a second perspective on the role of democracy in economic development—namely, that the adoption of democratic political institutions ultimately is necessary to ensure that economic reforms are enduring.[40] Without a broad perception that rules affecting

---

37. *See* Clague et al., *supra* note 36, at 114 ("For a country for which stable democracy is not a feasible option, a durable autocracy with a leader who is rationally maximizing his long-term tax extraction may be, among the available political arrangements, the one most favorable to property rights.").

38. An early influential statement of this thesis appears in Seymour Martin Lipset, *Some Social Requisites of Democracy: Economic Development and Political Legitimacy*, 53 AM. POL. SCI. REV. 69 (1959). Later empirical verifications of Lipset's thesis include Robert Barro, *Democracy and Growth*, 1 J. ECON. GROWTH 1 (Mar. 1996), *available at* http://kapis.wkap.nl/ oasis.htm/10643; Ross E. Burkhart & Michael S. Lewis-Beck, *Comparative Democracy: The Economic Development Thesis*, 88 AM. POL. SCI. REV. 903 (1994); *see also* Ruttan, *supra* note 14, at 229 ("[P]olitical liberalization is more sustainable when it is preceded by a successful program of economic liberalization.").

39. *See* Olson, *supra* note 34, at 42–54 (describing how "roving bandits" and "stationary bandits" have different incentives to establish an environment that induces individuals to create wealth).

40. *See* Clague et al., *supra* note 36, at 114 (reporting empirical evidence that "long-lasting democracies provide better property rights than long-duration autocracies or short-duration regimes of either type"); Olson, *supra* note 34, at 60 ("It is no accident that the only societies that have enjoyed high levels of capital accumulation across successive generations are the durable democracies. Every society with autocratic rulers sooner or later is victimized by roving banditry from the top. Thus, there are compelling and normally neglected practical as well as moral reasons why the United States should make the promotion of democracy a priority.").

economic activity are legitimate and without political safeguards against arbitrary state interference in the economy, the impact of economic reforms may be short-lived. A corollary proposition is that a commitment to protect civil liberties is necessary to attract and sustain investment from domestic and foreign sources.[41]

Commentators who have endorsed the development of democracy as an element of foreign assistance have cautioned that establishing democratic institutions and cultures will require a sustained, substantial commitment of foreign support and cannot be done with short-term intervention or external political pressure alone.[42] Though democratic systems tend to ensure the emergence of a superior environment for economic growth in the longer term, new democracies may feature significant periods of instability that impede investment and growth.[43] Experience with individual democracies also may vary considerably according to the specific design of the country's democratic institutions, such as the choice between parliamentary and presidential rule, the definition of executive authority, and the establishment of rules that affect the level of fragmentation in a party system.[44]

A third noteworthy perspective is that the effect of adopting democratic reforms depends heavily on initial economic, political, and social conditions. Some observers have warned that the adoption of democratic reforms in countries with strongly disfavored ethnic

---

41. *See* WORLD BANK, *supra* note 13, at 87 (describing the positive impact on investment projects of a political environment in which citizens enjoy civil liberties, particularly those related to free expression); Jonathan Isham et al., *Civil Liberties, Democracy, and the Performance of Government Projects*, in 11 WORLD BANK ECON. REV. 219 (1997).

42. Olson comments that, in promoting democracy in transition environments, the United States "should either devote the considerable investment of resources and patience needed to make the effort succeed, or else not intervene at all." Olson, *supra* note 34, at 61. Olson adds that "the promotion of democracy is in large part an educational problem: it requires giving elites in countries without democracy an appreciation of the extraordinary practical value of the secure contract, property, and other individual rights that lasting democracies provide." *Id.*

43. *See* Clague et al., *supra* note 36:
   [N]ewly established democracies may require time to consolidate the mosaic of institutions that characterize successful democratic polities. Executive branch adherence to the rulings of a supreme court, the education of voters, and the modalities of transparent administrative procedures do not emerge instantly. Rather, the multiple sources of authority that underpin successful democracies might in the early years, when decision-making procedures are underdeveloped and not well understood or accepted, create substantial uncertainties regarding property rights.
Id. at 94.

44. *See* Cadwell, *supra* note 16, at 255–60 (describing implications for executing law reforms of the distribution of authority between national and local authorities and within the executive branch of the national government); Haggard, *supra* note 36, at 129–41 (analyzing implications of various models of democratic governance).

minorities may increase the ability of majority groups to oppress minority interests, particularly where the disfavored minority accounts for a disproportionate share of economic activity.[45]

A fourth perspective emphasizes the importance of decentralizing political power from central government authorities to political subdivisions such as regional and local administrations. Democracy development programs sponsored by the United States and other foreign donors have attempted to strengthen the capacity of local and regional government institutions.[46] Among other effects, political decentralization is seen as a partial antidote to unprincipled decision making and corruption by central government authorities, which otherwise are shielded from effective monitoring by nontransparent administrative processes.[47] An unresolved issue is whether decentralization of power diminishes the ability of interest groups to manipulate government processes and allocate the state's resources in ways that disadvantage the public as a whole.

H. Role of the Government in Carrying Out Reforms

The move from centralized power to dispersed authority requires a basic decision about what role the government should play in executing reforms. Two basic models of government involvement have received attention in commentary about economic development. The first is what Robert Cooter calls "political modernization" of the law.[48] In this model, the state plays the leading role in law reform by enacting comprehensive statutes and regulations. Foreign advisors make significant contributions to this process by drafting models,

---

45. *See* Amy L. Chua, *Markets, Democracy, and Ethnicity: Toward a New Paradigm for Law and Development*, 108 YALE L.J. 1 (1998) (considering how market liberalization and democratic reforms in transition economies can increase ethnic tensions).

46. *See* Ruttan, *supra* note 14, at 220 ("An important theme in the democratization agenda has been the design of local institutions of governance to empower communities to mobilize their own resources for development.").

47. Transition economies often have resisted decentralization measures that would give political subdivisions more control over economic and political resources. Vernon Ruttan observes that "the strengthening of local governance is often viewed as a threat to political stability rather than as a resource for development by the national political leadership and the central bureaucracies." *Id.* at 228. Ruttan adds that national government attitudes disfavoring political decentralization "have sometimes been reinforced by the staffs of development assistance agencies, who often have little historical insight into the evolution of rural development institutions in the currently developed countries." *Id.*

48. *See* Robert D. Cooter, *Market Modernization of Law: Economic Development Through Decentralized Law, in* ECONOMIC DIMENSIONS IN INTERNATIONAL LAW 275, 276 (Jagdeep S. Bhandari & Alan O. Sykes eds., 1997).

which draw principally upon Western solutions and rely on variants of Western institutions for their implementation.

The chief alternative to this approach is what Cooter terms "market modernization" of the law.[49] In this framework, the state establishes initial conditions, such as recognizing private property rights and liberalizing trade, necessary to promote the evolution of a market economy, but it looks mainly to private individuals, firms, and institutions (e.g., trade associations) to devise specific legal principles that the state ultimately will embrace. The market modernization approach de-emphasizes state efforts to conceive comprehensive legal frameworks at the beginning of the reform process and stresses gradual, piecemeal approval by courts and legislatures of privately created norms.

Compared to a political modernization approach, the market modernization model channels more effort by host country reformers and their foreign advisors to studying indigenous economic and social conditions as a predicate for the state's recognition of new legal rules. Unlike "top-down" law reform, "bottom-up" initiatives place a premium on identifying and understanding customs and norms that promote market processes. The bottom up orientation would discourage rote application of Western legal models in ways that fail to account for crucial differences in local circumstances and would force host country policy makers and foreign advisors to study more carefully, and improve, the apparatus for translating widely accepted norms into binding legal rules.

Executing a market modernization strategy can raise special problems of its own.[50] The first obstacle concerns the state's role in creating the initial conditions that permit the emergence and evolution of private norms, which form the basis of future legal rules. One cannot underestimate the difficulty of accomplishing these foundational tasks, which include creating and defining private property rights, lifting price controls, liberalizing trade, and removing unnecessary legal barriers to the entry of new firms. These reforms will not emerge spontaneously and will demand extensive effort by the national government (and close monitoring by external donors) to ensure their implementation.

---

49. *See id.*

50. *See* William E. Kovacic, *Comments on Chapter 7, in* ECONOMIC DIMENSIONS IN INTERNATIONAL LAW, *supra* note 48, at 317 (reviewing limitations of Robert Cooter's market modernization model).

A second problem involves the process by which courts and legislatures ultimately endorse private norms. This requires that judges and legislators have the ability and incentive to identify private norms that enhance efficiency and forms that reduce it. For example, a court must be able to make distinctions between a variety of contractual restrictions—to approve a restrictive covenant because such covenants enhance efficiency by increasing an employer's incentive to share proprietary data and commercial know-how with her employees, but to forbid an agreement among direct competitors not to make sales in the traditional home market of each. Both types of restrictions might be widely used, customary norms, but each type has significantly different efficiency effects. Judges must have the expertise to tell the difference, and the judicial system must have sufficient integrity to ensure that parties cannot purchase the outcome they wish.

The third problem deals with the proper residual role of the state in addressing market failures. Even a system that relies heavily on the government's approval of privately generated norms will find instances in which the operation of the private norms reduces economic welfare. At least some regulatory apparatus may be necessary to identify and address such market failures.

II. FORMS OF COMPETITION POLICY: ANTITRUST AND OTHER POLICY INSTRUMENTS

In discussions among Western commentators about economic law reform, there is a tendency to equate "competition policy" with enforcing prohibitions against restrictive business practices. This might be called an antitrust-centric view of competition policy. Properly understood, competition policy encompasses a large collection of policy instruments by which a country can promote business rivalry.[51] A sound competition policy program need not invariably place antitrust enforcement at the top of its agenda. A transition economy might use a variety of techniques to increase the role of competition as a means for governing economic activity. In the full set of possible competition policy tools, antitrust enforcement might not always be the principal instrument.

---

51. *See* R. Shyam Khemani & Mark A. Dutz, *The Instruments of Competition Policy and Their Relevance for Economic Development, in* REGULATORY POLICIES AND REFORM: A COMPARATIVE PERSPECTIVE, *supra* note 11, at 16 (describing policy tools by which countries can achieve competition aims).

282   *CHICAGO-KENT LAW REVIEW*   [Vol 77:265

A. Advocacy

There is widespread recognition that one of the most important contributions of a competition policy system is to serve as an advocate within the government and the country at large for reliance on market processes and business rivalry to organize economy activity.[52] Government regulations that restrict entry, pricing, and trade often curb new business development and distort the competitive process. Though most countries feature such phenomena, the dangers of government regulation assume special significance in emerging markets where public policies and cultural perceptions often reflect a basic suspicion of capitalism and a preference for statist solutions to economic problems. In emerging markets, the competition agency can discourage the adoption or maintenance of competition-suppressing measures by unmasking their social costs and pressing public officials to justify the restriction of business rivalry.

B. Education and Constituency Development

One important role for a competition agency is to educate business officials, consumers, and government policymakers about the merits of market processes.[53] The competition policy authority can be a catalyst for debate about the appropriate role of government intervention in the economy and the correct choice of strategies for promoting growth.[54] Performing the education function can help the

---

52. *See* Malcolm B. Coate et al., *Antitrust in Latin America: Regulating Government and Business*, 24 U. MIAMI INTER-AM. L. REV. 37, 58 (1992) ("In any economy, the antitrust agency can act as a useful watchdog to protect the market economy from excessive regulation. In effect, the antitrust agency should attempt to regulate bureaucracy and minimize the burden of government on society."); Ana Julia Jatar, *Comment on "Competition, Information, and Development" by Jean-Jacques Laffont*, in ANNUAL WORLD BANK CONFERENCE ON DEVELOPMENT ECONOMICS 1998, *supra* note 3, at 258, 259 ("A competition agency should have the legal authority to challenge other government agencies' decisions that conflict with competitive principles."); Ben Slay, *Industrial De-monopolization and Competition Policy in Poland*, in DE-MONOPOLIZATION AND COMPETITION POLICY IN POST-COMMUNIST ECONOMIES 123, 143 (Ben Slay ed., 1996) ("Perhaps the [Polish] Antimonopoly Office's most important (and least-discussed) function has been the advocacy of liberal, pro-competitive solutions to economic policy problems during the Polish transition.").

53. *See* Ana Julia Jatar, Competition Policy in Latin-America: The Promotion of a Social Change 13 (1995) (paper presented at the Annual Meeting of the American Economic Association) (on file with author) (observing that "[c]hanges in conduct and attitudes must be considered one of the major goals in competition policy" in transition economies). Ana Julia Jatar is the former head of Venezuela's competition authority.

54. A focus of donor assistance can be to assist competition authorities in stimulating public discussion of economic organization. *Cf.* Cadwell, *supra* note 16, at 263 ("[D]onors can

competition agency can build a political constituency for market-oriented policies. Building a political constituency for competition and other market-oriented solutions may be as vital to the competition system's effectiveness as "technocratic" measures (such as raising salaries and increasing expertise through training) that seek to build the system's stature and influence.[55]

C.   Research and Studies

A competition agency can establish a research capability that permits it to analyze impediments to competition. The results of the competition agency's research can inform its competition advocacy activities and the selection of possible subjects for law enforcement. Publication of studies can help educate government agencies and the public generally about the sources of poor economic performance. One model for such research is Hernando de Soto's formative study of the informal sector in Peru.[56] De Soto and a team of researchers examined the impact of public regulations involving housing, transportation, and retailing in Lima. The study suggested how adjustments in various government regulatory policies discouraged entrepreneurs from making the type of "sunk" investments that often are instrumental in spurring growth. De Soto and his colleagues documented how a more austere regulatory regime would reduce entry barriers and improve public administration by reducing the number of opportunities for public officials to accept bribes for giving necessary approvals.

Similar work by competition authorities in other countries would provide highly informative perspectives on domestic obstacles to competition. In many instances, the barriers to rivalry might not be immediately apparent. A number of transition economies have taxation mechanisms that feature high marginal rates, poor success in making collections, and extraordinarily complex codes that confer tremendous   discretion   on   individual   tax   officials   and   create

---

contribute to broadening of public debate, especially among the idea elites who lead opinion in democracies: journalists, academics and researchers, and officials in competing centers of power."); WORLD BANK, *supra* note 13, at 57 ("Stimulating debate in civil society about policy is an intangible way for development assistance to influence policy reform.").

55. *See* Haggard, *supra* note 36, at 144 ("For agencies to sustain themselves over time, they must also build on bases of constituent support.").

56. HERNANDO DE SOTO, THE OTHER PATH: THE INVISIBLE REVOLUTION IN THE THIRD WORLD (1989).

compelling temptations for corruption.[57]   The operation of such systems deters new business entry and expansion by existing entrepreneurs. As identified by a competition agency's study, reform of the taxation system—reducing rates, improving collections, and imposing integrity-related administrative safeguards—could enhance competition by encouraging entry.[58]

A second possible focal point for attention could be preferences that some economies confer upon state-owned enterprises ("SOEs"). In a number of countries, SOEs have special access to cheap land and favorable credit.   Private entrepreneurs can face substantial cost disadvantages in seeking to compete with public enterprises. Foreign investors sometimes cannot purchase land directly but must engage in joint ventures with SOEs to build and operate facilities.

In many countries, deficiencies in the financial services market discourage entry.   Where the state prevents the establishment or growth of private commercial banks, individual entrepreneurs often must raise capital by saving net revenues and seeking loans from customers, family members, and friends.   Such loans might enable a small business operator to amass modest amounts of money, but recourse to these devices precludes assembling the sums needed to undertake a significant expansion of operations.

In other settings, frailties in the mechanism for registering and recognizing business enterprises can discourage entry.[59]   In Vietnam, entrepreneurs must prepare a registration form that requires them, among other information, to specify their business plan.   Various government officials review the application and have authority to reject the applicant if they believe the business plan is deficient. One possible deficiency is that the applicant seeks to enter a field already occupied by an SOE or otherwise wishes to do business in a sector with "excess" capacity. Simplification of the registration process and elimination of reviews of business plans as elements of the reforming Vietnam's companies law would promote entry.

---

57. *See infra* notes 115–17 and accompanying text (describing difficulties with taxation systems in transition economies).

58. *See* Vito Tanzi & Anthony Pellechio, *The Reform of Tax Administration, in* INSTITUTIONS AND ECONOMIC DEVELOPMENT, *supra* note 1, at 273 (describing recent experience with technical assistance programs to improve tax administration in transition economies).

59. *See Report on Recommendations on Building and Improving Economic Legal Framework in Vietnam,* U.N. Development Programme, at 155–58, U.N. Doc. VIE/94/110 (1998) (recommending reducing legal obstacles to the creation of new enterprises).

D. Antitrust Enforcement

A fourth component of competition policy is the one that appears most prominently in discussions about competition and law reform: the enforcement of prohibitions against restrictive business practices. There is considerable room for variation in determining which commands a transition country should adopt and in deciding the sequence of efforts to apply them. A country reasonably could choose a strategy that begins with enacting basic prohibitions on hard core horizontal restraints, such as collusive tendering, and gradually adds a fuller collection of prohibitions.[60] Alternatively, a country could adopt a more elaborate set of antitrust measures, but with an express commitment to focus on simpler enforcement tasks at first and expand its operations to apply more conceptually complex and resource-intensive commands over time as the institution's capability grows.

A good case can be made for including some level of law enforcement in the competition agency's initial package of responsibilities. It will be impossible for the competition agency to become proficient in antitrust enforcement if it does not gain experience in investigating and prosecuting cases.[61] Yet a decision to undertake some enforcement measures does not mean that a nation must attempt everything. There is no principle of sound implementation that compels a country to make law enforcement the central component of its early competition policy strategy or to adopt a full collection of Western-style prohibitions as part of its initial competition policy regime.

E. Implications

Discussions about the desirability of competition policy as a component of economic development need not automatically assume that a competition policy system will consist exclusively, or even chiefly, of enforcing antitrust prohibitions. Nations can tailor

---

60. *See* Coate et al., *supra* note 52, at 81–82 (recommending that in Latin American countries "prohibitions on price fixing should represent the core antitrust policy"; concluding that enforcement priorities should not include non-price horizontal agreements, vertical restraints, or price discrimination); Jatar, *supra* note 52, at 259 (observing that competition rules in recently liberalized economies "should prohibit horizontal agreements among competitors, including price cartels").

61. *Cf.* Black et al., *supra* note 17, at 1735 (observing, in the context of discussing privatization and corporate governance in Russia, that "to learn to prosecute fraud and self-dealing, regulators need some fraud and self-dealing to practice on").

competition policy systems to suit their unique needs and capabilities through their initial choice of tools (e.g., advocacy, education, research, and law enforcement) for promoting market rivalry, through the relative emphasis that the new competition agency gives to these tools as it begins operations and matures, and through adjustments to the agency's powers over time to alter the initial collection of policy tools. There is considerable room to account for specific national circumstances and changing capabilities through the initial definition of responsibilities and creation of policymaking instruments, the sequencing of activities, and the adjustment of powers over time.

III. COMPETITION POLICY AS AN ELEMENT OF LAW REFORM

The design of a competition policy program can follow various approaches that involve different combinations of policy instruments. Despite the widely acclaimed benefits of competition in promoting economic progress, the inclusion of competition policy on the transition economy reform agenda has stimulated controversy. This Section examines arguments for and against making competition policy an ingredient of reform and offers a synthesis of these views that emphasizes possibilities for varying the content of competition policy according to the institutional capabilities of the transition economy.

A. The Critique of Competition Policy as an Element of Reform

The widespread adoption of new competition policy systems in transition economies has not attracted unqualified praise. A number of commentators have criticized efforts by Western governments and multinational donors to adopt competition statutes or make competition laws a high priority for law reform.[62] The major themes of this literature are presented below.

---

62. Notable contributions to the critical literature include: Cooter, *supra* note 48; Paul E. Godek, *A Chicago-School Approach to Antitrust for Developing Economies*, 43 ANTITRUST BULL. 261 (1998); Paul E. Godek, *One U.S. Export Eastern Europe Does Not Need*, 15 REGULATION 20 (1992) [hereinafter Godek, *One U.S. Export*]; Laffont, *supra* note 8; A.E. Rodriguez & Mark D. Williams, *The Effectiveness of Proposed Antitrust Programs for Developing Economies*, 19 N.C. J. INT'L L. & COM. REG. 209 (1994); Armando E. Rodriguez & Malcolm B. Coate, *Limits to Antitrust Policy for Reforming Economies*, 18 HOUS. J. INT'L L. 311 (1996); Paul H. Rubin, *Growing a Legal System in the Post-Communist Economies*, 27 CORNELL INT'L L.J. 1, 45–46 (1994).

1. The Foreign Trade Liberalization Alternative

Some commentators address the competition policy issue by arguing that transition economies seeking to improve competition will achieve far more by liberalizing trade than by creating laws to attack private trade restraints. The core of such a policy would be to dismantle tariff and nontariff barriers to imports of foreign goods. The trade liberalization advocates suggest that removing obstacles to imports will supply an effective means for disciplining domestic producers of tradable goods, particularly in smaller economies.[63]

2. Facilitating Domestic Trade

A second criticism of creating programs to challenge trade restraints is that a transition economy's public resources are better invested in initiatives to improve the flow of goods and the provision of services within its own borders. One focus of such a program would be to eliminate government regulations that restrict the shipment of goods outside of specific regions or otherwise induce producers to sell their output to local purchasers only.[64] A second strategy would be to invest more public funds in airports, communications systems, highways, port facilities, railroads, and other infrastructure assets whose improvement could give consumers access to a wider range of potential sellers.[65]

3. Dangers of Misguided Competition Law Enforcement

Critics of antimonopoly enforcement as a law reform element contend that transition economy officials too often will misapply competition policy commands and retard the development of free

---

63. *See* Cooter, *supra* note 48, at 306 ("The pressure of international competition is more reliable and relentlessly procompetitive than the activities of antitrust officials. Developing nations can accomplish many goals of antitrust policy through free trade without the state creating an enforcement bureaucracy. . . . Free trade is, consequently, the best antitrust policy."); Godek, *One U.S. Export, supra* note 62, at 20 ("Free trade stimulates wealth creation and development, and in a small country it makes antitrust concerns largely irrelevant.").

64. *See* ANNETTE W. BROWN ET AL., THE MYTH OF MONOPOLY: A NEW VIEW OF INDUSTRIAL STRUCTURE IN RUSSIA 38–39 (World Bank, Policy Research Paper No. 1331, 1993) (discussing how reducing regional and local limits on entry and shipments of goods could improve Russia's distribution system).

65. *See* Laffont, *supra* note 8, at 245 ("Beyond institutional weaknesses, competition is weak in developing countries because transactions are localized as a result of poor communications systems and inefficient trading organizations. Focusing attention on these areas should be useful, but these problems call even more for investments in infrastructure than for better competition policy.").

markets and the decentralization of political power.[66]   In this perspective, antitrust is excessively prone to become another instrument of central government control that hinders the growth of a relatively fragile private sector. Excesses in enforcement that might be acceptable in wealthy Western countries can be especially damaging in emerging markets.   In countries with a deep-seated culture of rent-seeking and weak or corrupt systems of public administration, well-established political and economic interests may readily subvert the competition policy system to protect the existing distribution of wealth and privilege in society. Possibilities for faulty enforcement increase where transition economy competition agencies lack adequate expertise and physical resources.[67]   In nations where disfavored ethnic minorities account for an especially high share of activity in certain industries or functional areas (such as distribution), antimonopoly prohibitions on "abusive" conduct by "dominant" firms might serve as tools by which the majority oppresses the minority.

4.   High Opportunity Costs in the Reform Process

Nations undertaking the transition from central planning to reliance on markets typically face a daunting collection of reform needs. These include enhancing the protection of private property rights, privatizing publicly owned enterprises, building a regime of contract enforcement, creating a legal framework for the founding and dissolution of business entities, and forming legal institutions

---

66. *See* Godek, *One U.S. Export, supra* note 62, at 21 ("The potential harm of misguided antitrust policy to newly emerging economies should not be discounted."); Laffont, *supra* note 8, at 252 ("Poorly designed and applied competition laws can even discourage trade and foreign investment."); Rubin, *supra* note 62, at 45–46 (describing ineffectiveness and frailties of antitrust enforcement in developing economies).

67. Some commentators who approve transition economies' adoption of antimonopoly statutes point out how some controls—particularly those designed to address the abuse of a dominant market position—are particularly vulnerable to misuse. *See* Robert D. Willig, *Anti-Monopoly Policies and Institutions, in* THE EMERGENCE OF MARKET ECONOMIES IN EASTERN EUROPE, *supra* note 1, at 187, 195 ("Anti-monopoly laws with broad provisions permitting intervention against dominant-firm behavior and 'price gouging' pose the danger of chilling the very investment and entrepreneurship that emerging economies sorely need."). *But see* Ross C. Singleton, *Competition Policy for Developing Countries: A Long-Run, Entry-Based Approach,* 15 CONTEMP. ECON. POL'Y 1, 7 (1997) (maintaining that transition economy antitrust systems should give competition authorities "substantial discretion in challenging the business practices of dominant firms"; law should treat various practices as prima facie evidence of violation and require dominant firms to offer efficiency justifications; behavior that "could be specified and scrutinized in this manner likely would include exclusive dealing arrangements, refusal to deal, predation, access to essential facilities, vertical mergers, and perhaps horizontal and even conglomerate mergers").

(such as laws allowing securing lending) to promote the formation of capital.[68] Some scholars observe that establishing competition policy and antitrust enforcement mechanisms can divert scarce transition economy resources away from achieving higher reform priorities.[69] In this view, competition policy and antitrust enforcement warrant attention only after a transition economy has made considerable progress toward laying other foundations for a market system.

Concerns about the sequencing of reforms rest partly on the awareness that many transition economies have a relatively small pool of public officials with expertise in market-related economics available to administer economic law reform efforts.[70] The limited number of officials with such expertise often must manage demanding, diverse portfolios of economic reform initiatives. Time consumed in overseeing the pursuit of one reform initiative—drafting laws, meeting with foreign advisors, consulting with government and nongovernmental constituencies inside the country, and participating in the creation of new government bodies—comes at the expense of completing other projects. The opportunity costs in the transition environment of allocating scarce resources to inferior priorities are substantial.

5.   Summary: A Skeptics' Consensus for a Modest Competition System?

Many commentators who have criticized efforts to transplant elaborate replicas of Western antimonopoly systems into transition economies appear to see benefits in establishing properly limited competition policy mechanisms and giving a government agency at least some enforcement powers. Critics of elaborate Western-based

---

68. *See* William E. Kovacic, *Designing and Implementing Competition and Consumer Protection Reforms in Transitional Economies: Perspectives from Mongolia, Nepal, Ukraine, and Zimbabwe*, 44 DEPAUL L. REV. 1197, 1200–01 (1995) (describing obstacles to entrepreneurship in Ukraine due to a lack of well-defined property rights and a reliable contract enforcement mechanism).

69. Paul Godek casts the argument in these terms:

> East Europeans have limited resources and much more important things to worry about at this precarious stage in their development. Worrying about antitrust issues shows an unhealthy anxiety about the imagined ills of capitalism. Exporting antitrust to Eastern Europe is like giving a silk tie to a starving man. It is superfluous; a starving man has much more immediate needs. And if the tie is knotted too tightly he won't be able to eat what little there is available to him.

Godek, *One U.S. Export, supra* note 62, at 21.

70. *See* Kovacic, *supra* note 68, at 1213 (discussing limited availability in many transition economies of indigenous expertise in market-oriented economics or law).

transplants appear to see a useful role for a national competition agency to perform advocacy and education functions.[71] Some skeptics also seem to endorse the establishment and enforcement of antitrust controls on cartels and perhaps other forms of trade restraints.[72] To sum up their views, the critics would accept a competition policy system that emphasized advocacy and enforced prohibitions on naked trade restraints. They would not establish competition laws that prohibit the full range of behavior—abuse of a dominant position, mergers, vertical restraints, and price discrimination—commonly subject to antitrust oversight in older Western competition systems.[73] While acknowledging a potentially useful role for competition policy programs that entail advocacy, education, and carefully delimited enforcement duties, these observers predict that the immediate gains to transition economies are likely to be modest, at best, and warn against efforts by Western advisors to make heroic claims about the impact of adopting new systems.[74]

B.   Rationales for Competition Policy and Antitrust Enforcement

Many participants in the debate about economic law reform take a sanguine view about the contributions of competition policy, including enforcement of prohibitions against trade restraints, to economic growth.[75] Commentators who favor making competition

---

71. *See* Laffont, *supra* note 8, at 245 (noting that "a competition agency can play a valuable educational role in advocating the social benefits of fair competition.").

72. *See* Cooter, *supra* note 48, at 309 ("Free trade . . . may not be enough to destabilize cartels created by overt agreements. Courts should not enforce such agreements and the antitrust authorities should undermine them."); Laffont, *supra* note 8, at 244–45 ("[D]esigning simple and transparent rules for developing countries, particularly to prevent horizontal collusion and abuse of dominant position, remains a worthy task.").

73. *See* Laffont, *supra* note 8, at 244 (concluding that "U.S.-style competition policy—with its armada of lawyers and economists—is neither affordable nor implementable").

74. Laffont offers a representative statement of this assessment:
[T]he benefits that can be expected from competition policy in very poor countries will be quite small for the foreseeable future, for several reasons. Complexities and ambiguities remain in the economic analysis of predatory behavior and vertical restraints. Emerging industries will necessarily be highly monopolistic, yet competition agencies lack expertise and information, and interest groups have considerable discretion and potential for interference.
Id. at 245.

75. *See* Black et al., *supra* note 17, at 1800 (calling competition policy one of the "essential accompaniments" in the privatization process); James Langenfeld & Marsha W. Blitzer, *Is Competition Policy the Last Thing Central and Eastern Europe Need?*, 6 AM. U. INT'L L. REV. 347, 367–76 (1991) (discussing the impact of antitrust laws in creating competition in Central and Eastern Europe); Sachs, *supra* note 15, at 238 (stating that state-owned enterprises in transition economies "must be subjected to real market disciplines" by, among other means, "antitrust policies to break up industrial giants"); Richard Schmalensee, *Comment on*

policy a central element of law reform in transition economies offer the following justifications.

1.   Catalyst for Market Reforms

Many reforms proposed as alternatives to antimonopoly enforcement—including trade liberalization and other forms of deregulation—require government institutions to surrender power and contradict the preferences of powerful economic interests that benefit from the regulatory status quo.   There is little reason to believe, either, that reform measures will arise spontaneously within government institutions that have spawned and profited from competition-suppressing policies.   Beneficiaries of the *ancien regime* are unlikely to surrender power passively.[76] Even when donors elicit reform commitments as conditions for approving financial assistance, governments have proven themselves adept at subverting the impact of nominal reforms through outright neglect or subtle forms of resistance in implementation.[77]

A competition policy agency can supply an institutional counterweight within the government to promote liberalization measures and resist overt or subtle efforts to sabotage market-oriented reforms. Through a variety of advocacy and education activities, the competition agency can provide valuable support for policy measures, such as trade liberalization, that some observers have advanced as alternatives to antitrust enforcement.   Specific focal points of activity

---

"Competition, Information, and Development," by Jean-Jacques Laffont, *in* ANNUAL WORLD BANK CONFERENCE ON DEVELOPMENT ECONOMICS 1998, *supra* note 3, at 262, 265 ("I contend that a competition policy focused on blatant cartel behavior and mergers to monopoly would be relatively cheap and could have substantial benefits in developing countries."); Spencer Weber Waller & Rafael Muente, *Competition Law for Developing Countries: A Proposal for an Antitrust Regime in Peru*, 21 CASE W. RES. J. INT'L L. 159 (1989) (maintaining that competition law can be vital to developing an effective national economy); Willig, *supra* note 67, at 195 (stating that emerging markets correctly recognize that "anti-monopoly policy is integral to the process of transition").

76.   *See* Jeffrey Sachs, *In Defense of Russia's Reformers*, WALL ST. J., Dec. 30, 1993, at A8 (describing "hand-to-hand political combat" between economic reformers and the "communist old guard" in Russia).

77.   *See* Ana Julia Jatar, *supra* note 53, at 2–3 (discussing how despite nominal programs to encourage economic liberalization, Latin American governments continue to restrict competition through use of price controls, limits on entry, and public ownership of various industries); PETER MURRELL ET AL., THE CULTURE OF POLICYMAKING IN THE TRANSITION FROM SOCIALISM: PRICE POLICY IN MONGOLIA 7 (Univ. of Md. Ctr. for Institutional Reform and the Informal Sector (IRIS), Working Paper No. 32, 1992) (examining how, despite economic liberalization measures, the Mongolian government continued to implement earlier centralization policies, including price controls).

include participation in developing privatization programs,[78] advising legislators on drafting economic reform legislation,[79] and participating in regulatory proceedings conducted by other government institutions (such as public utility regulatory commissions) with authority to determine competition policy in specific economic sectors.

2.　Preserving the Benefits of Privatization

Foreign assistance programs commonly emphasize the need for transition economies to privatize a wide range of state-owned assets. Privatization programs often raise significant competition policy issues.　Without adequate attention to competition concerns, the strategy and methods chosen to alienate assets may simply reincarnate obdurate state-owned monopolies as durable privately held monopolies.[80]　A number of commentators have concluded that measures designed to promote competition are a vital predicate to the success of privatization.[81]

As part of a competition policy program, the host country might design the privatization process to transform the state enterprise monopolist into two or more viable successor firms.　A competition policy agency—either acting solely in an advocacy capacity within the government or exercising authority to veto certain privatization plans—can promote the achievement of privatization results that increase future prospects for competition.[82]

Competition policy oversight in the post-privatization period also can serve to ensure that the public reaps the benefits of creating private property rights.[83]　Where the government dissolves a

---

78. *See infra* notes 80–84 and accompanying text (reviewing possible contributions of a competition policy program to the privatization process).

79. *See* Kovacic, *supra* note 68, at 1204–05 (describing possible contributions of a competition agency in reforming the legal structure governing the regulation of natural monopolies).

80. *See* Stiglitz, *supra* note 3, at 10 ("Turning a state monopoly into a private monopoly . . . is unlikely to help create a more dynamic market economy.").

81. *See* Laffont, *supra* note 8, at 253 ("Privatization and formal liberalization are likely to lead to private monopolies, which will generate resources for interest groups apt to resist further development of authentic competition.　Efforts to impose these reforms before a credible set of institutions—for regulation, competition policy, financial regulation—has been designed will yield disappointing results."); Stiglitz, *supra* note 3, at 10 ("[C]ompetition remains thwarted in many of the former socialist economies that pursued privatization first.").

82. *See* Vladimir Capelik & Ben Slay, *Antimonopoly Policy and Monopoly Regulation in Russia, in* DE-MONOPOLIZATION AND COMPETITION POLICY IN POST-COMMUNIST ECONOMIES, *supra* note 52, at 57 (describing the role of Russia's antimonopoly authority in promoting disaggregation of the construction industry as part of the privatization process).

83. *See* Black et al., *supra* note 17, at 1800 ("Just as it helps to install controls on self-

monolithic public enterprise into a number of privately-owned successor firms, the successors may seek to use mergers, holding companies, or other institutional arrangements to re-establish the monopoly structure of the public ownership era. Some forms of consolidation or cooperation will increase efficiency by enabling the participants, for example, to realize scale economies or link complementary assets. Competition policy oversight of outright consolidations or cooperation by contract can help ensure that such measures are not mere efforts to create a private variant of the predecessor public monopoly.[84]

3.   Redressing Private Trade Restraints

Even with extensive efforts to liberalize foreign and domestic trade, transition economies still may remain vulnerable to harmful private trade restraints.[85]   Consider four scenarios involving horizontal collusion. Trade liberalization may do little to improve competition in various services and local goods markets.[86] In many developed and developing countries, service sectors feature collusive efforts by incumbent sellers to raise prices by setting fees, allocating sales opportunities, and restricting entry. Although entry into some services might seem relatively easy and capable of destroying cartel discipline,[87] incumbent suppliers nonetheless may succeed in jointly restricting output. This is particularly true where incumbents coordinate their affairs through trade associations or other institutions that the government previously has recognized as legitimate

dealing together with privatization, lest the managers of privatized firms defeat subsequent efforts to install these controls, so too with competition and trade policy, lest the private owners defeat efforts to reduce their monopoly rents.").

84. *See* Rausser, *supra* note 16, at 329–30 (describing the rationale for antitrust oversight of holding companies that may take shape in the wake of privatization measures).

85. For an extensive overview of possibilities for harmful private trade restraints in developing nations, see PATRICK REY, COMPETITION POLICY AND DEVELOPMENT (1997) (on file with author).

86. *See* Jatar, *supra* note 52, at 259 (reporting on experience with competition systems in transition economies and finding that "many competition agencies have found it useful to give high priority to nontradable sectors and quasi-nontradable products such as perishables and those with low price-volume ratios (paints, beverages), since potential foreign competition will have little or no impact on local firm behavior"); Anne O. Krueger, *Institutions for the New Private Sector, in* THE EMERGENCE OF MARKET ECONOMIES IN EASTERN EUROPE, *supra* note 1, at 219, 223 (stating that "preventing anti-competitive practices among domestic producers of nontradable goods" poses "major challenges" to "the governments of Eastern European countries"); Willig, *supra* note 67, at 190–91 (describing limited capacity of free trade to stimulate competition in local goods and services markets).

87. Godek points to ease of entry as a reason for emerging markets to forego establishing statutory prohibitions on cartels. Godek, *One U.S. Export, supra* note 62, at 21.

294   *CHICAGO-KENT LAW REVIEW*   [Vol 77:265

fora for orchestrating sectoral activity.[88] A statutory prohibition on cartels could include a clear statement forbidding output restrictions through trade associations or similar instrumentalities and withholding immunity where the government previously has acquiesced in the private ordering of output.

A second rationale for anti-cartel enforcement is to prevent the continuation of patterns of inter-firm relationships that flourished during the period of planning. Central planning, with its regime of production quotas and price controls, ingrained in the managers of individual firms an ethic of cooperation that may persist even when an emerging market has formally liberalized the economy.[89] Even when a government enacts laws that allow enterprises to set their own production levels and choose their own prices, the cooperation ethic will not disappear instantaneously. Business operators might continue privately to abide by conduct norms that the state once mandated.[90] An anticollusion measure in a competition law could serve a useful purpose by making clear that the government will not tolerate private efforts to recreate collective planning techniques that the country has abandoned.

The third scenario concerns public procurement. Public purchasing authorities are common targets for collusive schemes throughout the world.[91] Collusive tendering poses especially grave dangers in transition economies where public purchasing accounts for a substantial part of national economic activity and public projects, such as transportation infrastructure development, are vital to economic growth. An anti-cartel measure in a competition law could

---

88. *See* Kovacic, *supra* note 68, at 1206 (discussing the use of trade associations to set prices and control bidding for construction projects in Zimbabwe).

89. *See* Paul L. Joskow et al., *Competition Policy in Russia During and After Privatization*, *in* BROOKINGS PAPERS ON ECONOMIC ACTIVITY: MICROECONOMICS 301, 306–24 (Martin N. Baily et al. eds., 1994) (reviewing the extent and methods of state oversight of business units in Russia during the Soviet era).

90. *See* Karen Turner Dunn et al., *The Meat Processing Sector in Mongolia, in* DE-MONOPOLIZATION AND COMPETITION POLICY IN POST-COMMUNIST ECONOMIES, *supra* note 52, at 107, 110 (finding that despite economic liberalization measures, Mongolian meat producers continued to use private agreements to determine what prices they would bid for livestock and to delineate territories in which their meat would be sold).

91. *See* ORGANIZATION FOR ECONOMIC COOPERATION AND DEVELOPMENT, COMPETITION POLICY AND PROCUREMENT MARKETS 7 (1999) (on file with author) ("There is general agreement, though it is not unanimous, that certain characteristics of public buyers render them to become more likely to be the victims of collusion."); Kara L. Haberbush, Note, *Limiting the Government's Exposure to Bid-Rigging Schemes: A Critical Look at the Sealed Bidding Regime*, 30 PUB. CONT. L.J. 97, 98 (2000) ("[C]ertain aspects of the government procurement process may be particularly vulnerable to antitrust abuses, especially bid-rigging.").

provide a valuable tool for punishing and deterring efforts to rig public tenders.

The fourth possible setting for anti-cartel enforcement involves international collusive schemes. In recent years, the exposure of international price-fixing cartels involving food additives and vitamins has demonstrated the ability of multinational enterprises to carry out global schemes to allocate territories and curb production.[92] It is likely that the cartels in question have raised prices to consumers and industrial purchasers in transition economies. An anti-cartel mechanism would enable the transition economy to seek redress for injuries imposed by international cartels and to cooperate with foreign competition authorities in prosecuting cross-border collusive arrangements.[93]

The emphasis upon collusion enforcement scenarios above reflects a general view among those who favor antitrust intervention as an element of transition economy competition policy that "clear and tough" rules against hard-core horizontal restraints supply the appropriate core of law enforcement.[94] Anti-cartel enforcement, however, does not necessarily exhaust the range of desirable applications of antitrust enforcement in the transition process. Scrutiny of exclusionary behavior by dominant incumbent firms may

---

92. The prosecution of the international food additives and vitamins cartels is discussed in Harry First, *The Vitamins Case: Cartel Prosecutions and the Coming of International Competition Law*, 68 ANTITRUST L.J. 711 (2001).

93. Laffont describes the threat that international producer cartels pose to economic growth in transition economies:

> In developing countries lacking technical, management, and government expertise, it may be that only foreign investment can help development, because it brings new technologies and the credibility needed to borrow on international capital markets. Such investments should be welcomed if they help build local capacity. But when international cartels engage in anticompetitive practices, foreign investment can undermine economic development in developing countries. For this reason it is clearly desirable to make progress in global competition policy to discipline international cartels.

Laffont, *supra* note 8, at 245–46 (citation omitted). The establishment of a competition policy authority could provide the transition economy government with a necessary platform for cooperating with foreign competition agencies in policing international cartels.

94. *See* Willig, *supra* note 67, at 195; *see also* Jatar, *supra* note 52, at 259 (competition rules in transition economies "must be simple and straightforward" and "should prohibit horizontal agreements among competitors, including price cartels"). *But see* Singleton, *supra* note 67, at 6–8 (discouraging reliance on per se rules to address horizontal restraints in transition economies and suggesting that antitrust statutes simply deny enforcement of "naked price fixing provisions" due to doubtful persistence and adverse consequences of such arrangements and "limited judicial and bureaucratic abilities that characterize most developing countries"; proposing that transition economy statutes instead emphasize control of dominant firm exclusionary behavior by giving the competition agency broad power to challenge a wide array of entry-deterring conduct).

be necessary where, for example, the state previously has created or permitted monopolies to control the distribution of goods. The operation of a distribution monopoly will retard expansion of trade within the country and diminish the capacity of imported goods to press domestic producers to improve performance.[95]

4. Deterring Corruption

The corruption of government officials is a serious problem in many transition economies, especially in nations that have relied heavily on central economic planning.[96] In transition economies, government bodies have tremendous power to affect the competitive process when they issue licenses, permits, franchises, and subsidies. For poorly paid and weakly monitored civil servants, the authority to dispense entitlements and privileges creates countless opportunities to solicit bribes.[97] Where traditional safeguards to ensure transparency and integrity in public administration are feeble, individual business operators may enjoy great success in bribing public officials to obtain special benefits or deny privileges to their opponents.

A competition policy system could help undermine corrupt agreements between government officials and business managers.[98] A number of transition economy competition laws directly limit the ability of government agencies to diminish competition.[99] Some measures forbid government bodies to restrict entry by, for example,

---

95. *See* Black et al., *supra* note 17, at 1764 (discussing impediments to successful privatization in the former Soviet Union and observing that "poor transportation and state-owned local distribution monopolies often limited import and interregional competition"); Jatar, *supra* note 52, at 259 ("In Latin America the enforcement of competition since liberalization has been instrumental in lowering entry barriers to foreign competition, particularly where dominant local firms have used vertical mechanisms to control distribution channels.").

96. *See* Rick Stapenhurst & Shahrzad Sedigh, *Introduction: An Overview of the Costs of Corruption and Strategies to Deal with It, in* CURBING CORRUPTION 1 (Rick Stapenhurst & Sahr J. Kpundeh eds., 1999) (describing the pervasiveness of corruption in many transition economies); Samantha Marshall, *Vietnam Puts a Price Tag on Corruption*, ASIAN WALL ST. J., May 27, 1999, at 1 (describing the results of a Vietnamese government study that documents massive corruption by public officials).

97. *See* Daniel Kaufmann, *Economic Reforms: Necessary but Not Sufficient to Curb Corruption?, in* CURBING CORRUPTION, *supra* note 96, at 89, 94–95 (describing regulatory and entitlement-related functions that create opportunities for corruption in transition environments).

98. *See* Kovacic, *supra* note 4, at 442 (discussing the use of a competition policy system as an anticorruption device).

99. *See* Roger Alan Boner & William E. Kovacic, *Antitrust Policy in Ukraine*, 31 GEO. WASH. J. INT'L L. & ECON. 1, 23–25 (1997) (discussing limits in Ukraine's antitrust system upon anticompetitive government intervention).

imposing licensing requirements, unless the national legislation expressly grants such authority. Other provisions bar public officials from granting exclusive franchise rights or otherwise discriminating improperly against entrepreneurs that seek access to the market.

Enforcement of these and similar measures can complicate the formation and execution of corrupt agreements between public officials and private individuals. The competition policy mechanism essentially prevents the public official (the seller) from fulfilling her promise to the payer of the bribe (the buyer) to provide an illicit economic privilege. The competition law does not directly sanction the payer or recipient of the bribe by subjecting them to civil or criminal punishment. Rather, it diminishes the gains from improper bargains by impeding the execution of the promises that form the core of any single corrupt agreement and diminishes the maintenance of stable buyer-seller relationships that characterize corruption in many settings.[100] By raising the costs of conceiving and executing corrupt arrangements, the competition policy system can help prevent their creation.

C. *Facilitating the Transition from Planning to Markets*

Extensive, long-lived reliance on central planning can create a pervasive suspicion of capitalism. Comprehensive planning limits the exposure of citizens to market mechanisms, and government policies continually reinforce the notion that the state is the sole appropriate conservator and manager of the nation's economic resources. In many countries, efforts to decentralize the economy take place in a political and social context that is wary of markets and fearful that the state's retreat from its traditional role as producer and protector will endanger consumer interests.

In such environments, it may be unrealistic to expect that the government will commit itself to economic liberalization without establishing a mechanism to address market failures.[101] Without the creation of a competition policy system (and other measures such as a

---

100. *See* Susan Rose-Ackerman, *Corruption and the Global Economy*, in CORRUPTION AND INTEGRITY IMPROVEMENT INITIATIVES IN DEVELOPING COUNTRIES 25, 25 (1998) (analyzing patterns in corruption and noting how "[c]orrupt buyers and sellers frequently develop systems that are mutually reinforcing and persist over time").

101. *See* William E. Kovacic & Robert S. Thorpe, *Antitrust and the Evolution of a Market Economy in Mongolia*, in DE-MONOPOLIZATION AND COMPETITION POLICY IN POST-COMMUNIST ECONOMIES, *supra* note 52, at 89, 92 (describing the role of an antitrust system in facilitating the political transition to a market system).

consumer protection regime and environmental protection mechanisms), a nation may choose not to undertake measures such as decontrolling prices or privatizing state-owned enterprises. Viewed in this light, a competition policy system can facilitate the transition from planning to markets by demonstrating the government's commitment to address serious market failures. The competition policy system becomes an outward symbol of a basic change in the government's role from planner and producer to referee.

D. Synthesis: The Link between Competition Policy and Capability

Discussions about competition policy in emerging markets sometimes suggest that the policy choice confronting transition governments and their foreign advisors is between establishing no competition statute or competition policy bureau on the one hand, or immediately adopting a competition law with the full array of provisions found in wealthy market economies. Posing the question this way ignores a host of intermediate options that might be desirable for a number of countries. The "do nothing" and "do everything" solutions are neither the exclusive competition policy options nor, in most countries, are they sensible formulas.

1. Phasing Reforms

The all-or-nothing solution set obscures important intermediate possibilities. One alternative is to vary the initial design of a competition policy system according to the host country's existing capabilities and resources and the strength of commitments by foreign advisors to provide implementation assistance.[102] A country with weak initial capabilities and uncertain assurances of foreign assistance sensibly might choose to begin with a more austere

---

102. In the context of discussing possible strategies for pollution control in transition environments, Laffont addresses the importance of accounting for institutional capabilities in designing policy commands:

> [W]hat if the agency in charge of the environment is nonexistent, poorly staffed, or captured by the industry, or if the pollution is diffuse and cannot be measured at the individual level? A barrier to entry, such as a license to operate, may then be the only way to limit production and therefore pollution, at least if this policy can· be implemented and is not a pretext for rent seeking. The right policy answer should take into consideration many aspects of the problem that are not easily measured or even modeled. Thus it is not surprising that the right answers may differ by industry or country, particularly between industrial and developing countries.

Laffont, *supra* note 8, at 238–39; *see also* William E. Kovacic, *Capitalism, Socialism, and Competition Policy in Vietnam*, ANTITRUST, Summer 1999, at 59, 61 (arguing for the use of strategies that gradually phase in competition policy as implementation capacity increases).

competition policy system that emphasized advocacy and education and forbade a narrow range of behavior, such as hard-core horizontal restraints. As capabilities and implementation resources increase, the host country could augment its law. An alternative is to enact a relatively elaborate law but expressly phase in the implementation of certain operative provisions over time as the country's capabilities grow. There are many examples from the history of competition law in transition economies and mature market systems to rebut the notion that a nation gets a single chance to formulate a competition law and therefore must pack every conceivable power or responsibility into the original statute.[103]

It would also be reasonable to begin with a more ambitious competition policy system—with fuller advocacy and law enforcement powers—in emerging markets with strong institutional foundations and substantial resource commitments from foreign advisors. Countries with greater capabilities and resources stand a stronger chance of making good use of an ambitious competition policy system than countries with weak institutions and few resources. There is a great difference between Jamaica, which appears to have received $9 million in the early 1990s from the US Agency for International Development to create its competition mechanism,[104] and many other transition economies that will be fortunate to receive even a tenth of that amount from foreign sources to build their own systems. The point to keep in mind is that a decision to move from a more austere competition policy system to a more complex design should be justified by showing that there are measures in place to ensure effective implementation.

Two examples from other areas of law reform suggest how the design of a reform strategy and the emphasis of different reform elements might vary from country to country, depending upon one's evaluation of initial conditions. The first example involves privatization in Russia in the 1990s. Privatization reformers had to decide the relative importance to be given to privatizing small firms and large firms, respectively, and to building the institutional framework for ensuring sound corporate governance.[105] The strategy actually

---

103. Examples in mature antitrust systems include Australia, Canada, and the United States. Transition economy examples include Brazil, South Africa, and South Korea.

104. *See* Geraldine Foster, *Antitrust in Transition Economies, in* 2000 FORDHAM CORP. L. INST. 563, 564 (B. Hawk ed.) (containing remarks made at the Fordham Corporate Law Institute on International Antitrust Law & Policy in New York City on October 14–15, 1999).

105. Black et al., *supra* note 17, at 1797–1800.

chosen gave primary emphasis to rapidly privatizing small and large firms and to making the establishment of the legal framework, in effect, a secondary priority. A more effective approach might have involved rapidly privatizing small enterprises, undertaking a slower "staged privatization" of large firms, reallocating some of the efforts actually devoted to large firm privatization into creating the supporting institutional infrastructure, and focusing greater attention to establishing a "friendlier business climate," mainly through reforms in the tax system. Such an approach does not dispute the elements of the reform agenda pursued by the "big bang" privatization advocates, but it suggests changes in the relative emphasis given to specific elements.[106]

The second example involves the choice of policies for reforming infrastructure sectors such as energy and telecommunications in transition economies. As described by Paul Joskow, one reform model is a "'big bang' approach" in which "privatization, restructuring, and the introduction of competition occur at the same time."[107] The alternative "gradualism" approach "is to provide for a relatively long transition period, during which the industrial organization and associated regulatory institutions are allowed to evolve according to a planned transition program."[108] Joskow concludes that the suitability of either approach—big bang or gradualism—depends on six factors:

> [T]he performance of the existing system, the complexity of implementing a big bang approach given pricing and other imperfections that cannot be fixed instantly, the capacity of legal and political institutions to support competitive markets for infrastructure services, the speed with which reasonably competitive markets can evolve, the time required to create effective regulatory institutions, and the government's ability to credibly commit to a restructuring framework that supports private investment and competitive entry.[109]

Among other considerations, Joskow's factors directly account for the quality of institutions whose efficacy will determine the impact of the infrastructure privatization and deregulation program. Differences in such conditions across countries would dictate different strategies in the continuum of approaches between an immediate big bang and protracted gradualism. Joskow concludes that infrastructure "regulatory agencies may do best by starting with simple regulatory

---

106. *Id.* at 1778 (describing the content of introducing privatization in stages).
107. Joskow, *supra* note 17, at 198.
108. *Id.*
109. *Id.*

rules and procedures and refining them as they gain information and experience."[110]

The framework for analyzing the timing and content of privatization and infrastructure reforms can be applied to competition policy as well. The correct dosage of individual competition policy reform elements would depend on a country's initial conditions and the need for donors and the host country to make choices in how to use scarce technical assistance resources. There is no particular reason to think that the competition policy reform strategy for each nation would be identical in its content or the timing of its implementation.

2.   Shared Tasks

A second basis for variation is to consider possibilities for multinational regional cooperation in building competition policy institutions. Consider the case of neighboring states whose institutions are weak and whose prospects for obtaining substantial foreign assistance for implementing new measures are poor. Rather than individually attempting to construct elaborate competition policy institutions, such countries might seek to develop regional alliances through which members delegate certain functions (such as the adjudication of disputes) to a common instrumentality.[111]

IV. COMMON INITIAL CONDITIONS AND THEIR IMPLICATION FOR LAW DESIGN AND IMPLEMENTATION

A common theme in the foregoing analysis of competition system design possibilities is the centrality of initial conditions and implementation. To be effective, competition policy law reform strategies require careful pre-reform analysis of existing conditions in the host country and rigorous attention to how the host country will implement nominal competition policy commands. Accounting properly for these concerns is a vital ingredient of effective reforms.

Transition economy antitrust agencies confront implementation challenges that are largely alien to their Western counterparts. Decisions about the appropriate design of antitrust systems in emerging economies must acknowledge the distinctive features of the

---

110. *Id.* at 220.

111. *See* Kovacic, *supra* note 6, at 42–43 (describing possibilities for regional cooperation in the "Caribbean Community").

transition environment. Western antitrust systems benefit from a number of favorable circumstances, including access to substantial financial resources, wide availability of expertise in antitrust economics and law, broad acceptance of administrative safeguards to restrict the discretion of public decision makers, and reliance on well-established market processes. These conditions rarely characterize the transition economy experience. Approaches that have proven effective in Western countries are hardly assured of success when transplanted into a transition economy setting.

A. Durability of Public Policies That Impede Competition

Despite adoption of various economic liberalization measures, many transition economies continue to feature substantial resistance to market-oriented reforms inside and outside the government. Such resistance often is manifest in the maintenance of substantial government-imposed barriers to entry and exit. In many instances, competition-suppressing policies persist at all levels of government despite nominal measures by the national legislature to encourage private entrepreneurship and new business development.[112]

1. Barriers to Imports and Foreign Investment

A number of transition economies maintain significant barriers to participation by foreign companies in their domestic market. In some cases, obstacles to trade take the form of substantial tariffs and quotas. Countries that formally have reduced tariffs and quotas sometimes replace these measures with nontariff trade barriers that eliminate or severely curb competition from imports.[113] National regulatory regimes also place cumbersome limits on the ability of foreign firms to enter the market directly by constructing new facilities or investing in existing domestic enterprises.

---

112. *See* Irina Starodubrovskaya, *The Nature of Monopoly and Barriers to Entry in Russia*, 6 COMMUNIST ECON. & ECON. TRANSFORMATION 3, 13 (1994) (discussing techniques used by local government authorities in Russia to control commercial activity and limit competition despite efforts by the national government to promote economic liberalization).

113. *See* Andras Nagy, *Institutions and the Transition to a Market Economy*, in THE EMERGENCE OF MARKET ECONOMIES IN EASTERN EUROPE, *supra* note 1, at 301, 305 ("It is luckily difficult for the new [transition economy] governments formally to resist formal trade liberalization, but—under the influence of the big lobbies behind them—they learn quickly how to build non-tariff barriers.").

2.   Restrictions on New Business Development

Transition economy governments maintain a variety of barriers to entry and exit.   Some transition economies impede entry by imposing significant burdens on firms seeking to incorporate or otherwise register to do business.   In Vietnam, firms seeking to register must satisfy formidable initial capital requirements and must present a business plan that is subject to review and approval by government officials.[114]   In reviewing business plans, government overseers often take account of whether there is "sufficient capacity" in the business sector into which the business operator wants to enter. This screen is a frequently used tool to deny approvals to private firms whose operations might threaten sales of incumbent state-owned enterprises.

3.   Complex and Arbitrary Taxation Systems

A second common impediment to entry and expansion by private firms is the tax system.   Tax codes in many transition economies discourage legitimate private sector development.   One pathology is to set rates at extraordinarily high levels and closely monitor the bank accounts of business operators to determine whether taxable cash balances are available for confiscation.   The use of high marginal tax rates and the monitoring of bank account or balance sheet surpluses as taxation points create a host of perverse incentives for small and large enterprises alike.   Many entrepreneurs choose to forego ordinary registration requirements and operate outside the bounds of the law as "informal" enterprises, denying the state any tax revenues from their operations and precluding the informal firms from availing themselves of mechanisms, such as judicial enforcement of contracts, that properly registered enterprises can use to undertake substantial investments and reduce operating costs.   Companies may refuse to pay workers or suppliers to avoid giving tax authorities the impression that they have funds available to pay additional taxes.[115]   Other

114.   *See* NGUYEN DINH CUNG, SOME REMARKS OF THE MARKET STATE IN VIETNAM (1997) (on file with author) (describing how business formation and registration formalities curb competition by raising barriers to entry by new firms).

115.   One study describes how the tax system induces company managers in Russia to hide income and engage in barter transactions. Black et al., *supra* note 17, at 1757–60. In evaluating the causes of failure for the Russian privatization program in the 1990s, the study concludes that "perhaps the single most important regulatory obstacle to earning an honest profit is the Russian tax system." Tax rules all but compelled managers to hide profits from tax inspectors and shareholders alike. *Id.* at 1758.

enterprises refuse to deposit significant amounts of cash in banks. Instead they take costly precautions to keep cash in private safes or increase reliance on barter transactions.[116] The fear of revealing liquidity also induces companies to publish untruthful financial statements, thus impeding efforts by investors to make well-informed judgments about the firm's condition.[117]

Transition economy tax codes also tend to be extremely complex and subject to continuous, selective adjustment. One form of ad hoc adjustment consists of conceiving special assessments, sometimes applied retroactively, to business operators who appear to be profitable. The details of the codes seldom are widely available to affected business operators, and many operational provisions are promulgated in the form of regulations or interpretations held exclusively within the offices of the taxation authority. Governments frequently delegate enforcement of these measures to public officials, who use their expansive enforcement discretion to "discover" violations and gather bribes under the guise of "settling" tax claims. Taxpayers rarely have recourse to an appeals mechanism, much less a system of review that affords swift, impartial analysis of tax claims.

4. Price Controls

The abandonment of price controls is a common element of economic liberalization in the transition environment. Multinational financial institutions such as the International Monetary Fund and the World Bank often insist on price decontrol as a condition for providing loans or other forms of assistance. Researchers have documented a number of instances where price control regimes persist despite a government's formal adoption of decontrol measures. Reforms undertaken at the national level lack significance when individual national ministries, regional government bodies, or local public officials establish surrogate mechanisms whose operation is more difficult for external institutions to monitor.[118]

---

116. *See* Clifford G. Gaddy & Barry W. Ickes, *Russia's Virtual Economy*, 77 FOREIGN AFF. 53 (1998) (describing an increased reliance in Russia on cashless barter transactions because maintenance of cash in bank accounts attracts the attention of tax authorities).

117. *See* Black et al., *supra* note 17, at 1758 ("Companies that can't report income honestly to the tax inspectors also can't report honestly to investors. Investors therefore can't use a company's financial statements to check on management honesty and skill.").

118. *See* MURRELL ET AL., *supra* note 77, at 7 (discussing how local governments in Mongolia regulated prices despite the national government's abandonment of price controls).

5.   Restrictive Labor Laws

A number of transition economies have labor laws that severely restrict the ability of an employer to adjust the size of its workforce.[119] One common form of control is to forbid layoffs or make termination decisions very costly. By limiting the firm's flexibility to reduce employment when demand for its products sags, the labor regime can discourage companies from expanding capacity. The adoption of more flexible retention and termination policies could encourage new business development.

B.   Fragile Political Foundations

New competition authorities often begin with weak political foundations. In some countries, the new agencies represent institutional innovations, such as the creation of an independent regulatory body in a country that has no history of such agencies. In other nations, the new competition authority has been given a familiar, widely accepted institutional form. Even if the agency is created within an existing ministry or established as a new entity similar in form to other government bodies, it usually will begin operating without the political ties and power base that its adversaries inside and outside the government will enjoy. New competition bodies continually must ask whether the exercise of nominally significant powers will arouse debilitating political opposition.

C.   Weak Indigenous Competition Policy Expertise

Most transition economies begin implementing new competition policy systems and other types of market-oriented legal reforms with relatively little indigenous expertise in competition law or industrial organization economics.[120] This condition is one dimension of a general deficiency that afflicts economic law reform programs in transition economies. In examining reform efforts in former command economies, Michael Trebilcock points to "the critical

---

119. *See* Black et al., *supra* note 17, at 1761–62 (describing restricting labor laws in Russia).

120. *See* James Langenfeld & Dennis A. Yao, *Competition Policy and Privatization: An Organizational Perspective, in* GOVERNMENTS AND MARKETS 195, 205–07 (Hendrikus J. Blommestein & Bernard Steunenberg eds., 1994) (discussing human resource problems confronting new antitrust agencies); William E. Kovacic, *The Competition Policy Entrepreneur and Law Reform in Formerly Communist and Socialist Countries,* 11 AM. U. INT'L L. REV. 437, 452–60 (1996) (discussing the limited pool of transition economy individuals who are expert in antitrust economics or law).

shortage of what might be called 'the human capital of capitalism'—legal, managerial, economic, accounting, statistical, and so on—required to effectuate and operate a market economy and, from a public sector perspective, to regulate or otherwise address its dysfunctions or limitations effectively."[121] Laffont warns that human capital "shortcomings are usually underestimated, despite their dramatic implications for many areas of public policy."[122]

In the short term, antitrust agencies and other government agents of market reform must rely heavily on a handful of individuals who either have studied or worked in Western universities, or have participated extensively in training programs through which foreign experts provide instruction in the fundamental economic and legal underpinnings on competition policy. Over time, the pool of indigenous experts may expand as university programs in business, economics, law, and public administration reformulate their curricula to teach courses relevant to developing a market economy. Transition economy agencies often find that professionals who have become expert in antitrust economics or law become extremely attractive to private sector employers. Rapid turnover in personnel is common.

D. *Dysfunctional Courts*

In many transition economies, the courts are ill suited to adjudicate antitrust disputes, either as tribunals of the first instance or as appellate overseers of administrative competition policy bureaus. Few judges have even a rudimentary understanding of market processes, let alone comprehension of the basic rationale for and elements of an antitrust system. Corruption and delay deeply infect many transition economy court systems, denying the judiciary legitimacy as a forum for resolving business disputes.[123]

---

121. Michael J. Trebilcock, *What Makes Poor Countries Poor?: The Role of Institutional Capital in Economic Development, in* THE LAW AND ECONOMICS OF DEVELOPMENT 15, 50 (Edgardo Buscaglia et al. eds., 1997).

122. Laffont, *supra* note 8, at 242.

123. *See* Edgardo Buscaglia, *Corruption and Judicial Reform in Latin America,* 17 POL'Y STUD. J. 273 (1996); Sergio Garcia-Rodriguez, *Mexico's New Institutional Framework for Antitrust Enforcement,* 44 DEPAUL L. REV. 1149, 1177 (1995) (stating that Mexico's "judicial system is perceived by many as plagued with considerable delays, institutional corruption and a lack of independence"). One recent study describes how weaknesses in the Russian judicial system prevent effective enforcement of laws designed to ensure honest corporate governance:

[A] shareholder who sues a major company will usually lose at trial and first-level appeal, because of home-court bias, judicial corruption, or both. A shareholder with a strong case has a decent chance of getting an honest decision on further appeal, but

E. Frail Transparency Safeguards and Vulnerability to Corruption

Few transition economies have adopted mechanisms for ensuring transparency in operations of government ministries, including competition authorities. Most countries lack basic controls on bureaucratic discretion, such as requirements that policy adjustments be promptly and widely publicized (or subject to comment and debate before their enactment). Procedures for ensuring the confidentiality of business records or preserving the integrity of settlements of disputes are uncommon. Effective mechanisms for obtaining expeditious review of agency decisions are rare. The lack of transparency creates frequent opportunities for corruption and deprives the legal system of the clarity needed to provide meaningful guidance for business operators.[124]

A number of transition economies recognize that developing new competition agencies presents an opportunity to establish models for improving public administration. In transition economies such as Mexico and Ukraine, for example, the new competition agencies present possibilities for significant improvements over existing administrative structures. Means to this end include the promulgation of rules that insulate competition authorities from political interference, compel disclosure of the content of and rationale for agency decisions, and permit affected parties to challenge deviations from procedural requirements.

F. Resource Shortages

Most transition economy competition agencies labor under oppressive resource shortages. Civil servants often are paid minuscule wages, making it difficult for the competition agency to retain capable professional staff and creating temptations for employees to accept bribes in return for relaxing nominal regulatory

---

that will take years. And judgments must be enforced (or, often, not enforced) by the same biased or corrupt lower court where the case began.

Black et al., *supra* note 17, at 1755.

124. *See* Clague et al., *supra* note 16, at 80 ("Fair and transparent procedures for property, contracts, and government regulation of business facilitate the entry of low- and middle-income people into many areas of economic life. They also promote the accumulation of physical and human capital, which raises wages."); Garcia-Rodriguez, *supra* note 123, at 1178 ("In the not-too-distant past, Mexican administrative entities enjoyed unbridled discretionary power selectively to enforce legal requirements against individuals or firms. The bureaucratic structure for administrative enforcement in Mexico was tailor-made for the extension of political favors and other forms of corruption.").

requirements. Many agencies struggle with little success to obtain minimally adequate quarters, office equipment, and reference materials.

G. Data Shortcomings

Transition economy antitrust agencies typically must operate with limited access to data that offers an accurate view of existing market conditions and the competitive significance of individual firms.[125] Competition authorities often rely on official government statistical records that use classification schemes that correspond poorly with the economic concept of an antitrust relevant market.[126] Government data sets also may fail to reflect important categories of activity, such as imports, or the contributions of important groups of market participants, such as operators in the informal sector who do not formally register as business enterprises.[127] Calculating market shares without accurate data on the identity of market participants and the size of their activities is treacherous.

Gaining direct access to company records may be difficult or fruitless, at least for some period of time. Especially in the early period of a new competition agency's operations, business managers may resist requests for records until the country's courts have validated the agency's authority to obtain data and demonstrated their willingness to enforce compulsory process. Where public law enforcement institutions are weak, business managers may threaten government antitrust officials with violence if such officials insist on collecting company documents or interviewing employees. Even where competition authorities obtain company records, such data may provide an uninformative view of the firm's significance. Many firms in formerly planned economies maintain data that reveals little about the true economic value of their assets, the size of their sales, or their profitability.

---

125. *See* Ben Slay, *From Monopoly Socialism to Market Capitalism*, in DE-MONOPOLIZATION AND COMPETITION POLICY IN POST-COMMUNIST ECONOMIES, *supra* note 52, at 1, 8–9 (describing methodological difficulties in defining markets and measuring concentration in transition economies).

126. *See* Adam Torok, *Competition Policy and De-monopolization in Hungary After 1990*, in DE-MONOPOLIZATION AND COMPETITION POLICY IN POST-COMMUNIST ECONOMIES, *supra* note 52, at 24, 31 (discussing problems with official government statistical records in Hungary).

127. Georges Korsun and I traveled to Benin in March 1998 to perform research on competition policy under a project sponsored by the US Agency for International Development. In interviews with participants in the trucking industry, we discovered that roughly 80 percent of all trucking industry operators in Benin are "informals."

Official records and internal company data also may fail to give a clear view of ownership patterns. Privatization and economic liberalization blur the boundaries of individual firms and complicate the analysis of inter-firm relations as existing companies are bought and sold, as firms form joint ventures, and as new enterprises are created. In some countries, government and company records may not account for inter-firm connections that take shape through family relationships or personal friendships. Such relationships have great economic significance in some settings, as they serve to unify the operation of seemingly independent economic entities.[128]

H. Implications

The design of a competition policy system must account for initial conditions that will determine the effects of enforcement. A thoughtful assessment of initial conditions not only will influence decisions about the content of the statute but also will force foreign advisors to identify weaknesses in supporting institutions and offer plans to enhance their capability. It should be clear to donors that the real measure of a law reform initiative is not simply the quality of the original statutes but the strength of programs to build the institutional capacity to apply them effectively.[129]

The interplay between initial conditions and institutional design is evident in two illustrations. The first concerns the decision about whether to create private rights of action to enforce a competition law. In principle, decentralizing enforcement authority to private citizens can act as a valuable safeguard against default—for reasons of inadequate resources, sloth, or corruption—by a public prosecutor. In practice, the value of a private right of action depends crucially on the quality of the tribunal that will adjudicate cases initiated by private parties. In a country with dysfunctional courts, it makes little sense to create a private right of action and do nothing more than channel lawsuits through the existing judicial process.[130] A decision to create a private right of action requires an immediate commitment of

---

128. *See* Jatar, *supra* note 53, at 19–20 (describing the significance for competition policy of family relationships in Latin America).

129. *See* Laffont, *supra* note 8, at 253 ("Because competition is not an automatic outcome of deregulation, simply conditioning loans on the existence of competition laws will not ensure the creation of proper institutions for effective competition. Only a strong state can implement competition.").

130. *See* Coate et al., *supra* note 52, at 53 ("Unless a well-developed and experienced court system exists, [private] civil suits would not be advisable.").

resources to rehabilitate existing tribunals or create new judicial bodies to hear the cases that private entities invoking the competition law are likely to file. The second illustration involves merger control. One element of establishing a merger control regime is to determine the thresholds of activity that will trigger the obligation of merging firms to report their transactions to the competition authority.[131] The wisdom of a specific threshold for any single competition agency depends heavily on the agency's resources. Merger analysis has proven to be the most resource-intensive activity for new competition agencies. Agencies that set reporting thresholds too low will find themselves swamped with reviewable transactions, including a substantial number of mergers with no conceivable competitive significance. Establishing comparatively high thresholds may be the only means that impoverished agencies can use to focus scarce resources on matters of the highest importance.

V. IMPLICATIONS FOR TECHNICAL ASSISTANCE

A careful assessment of the predicates for successful competition law reforms and of the initial conditions in transition economies has basic implications for how countries with older antitrust systems provide technical assistance. Perhaps the most fundamental lesson is that the successful development of competition policy institutions in transition environments will require extensive, sustained contributions from foreign governments in the form of human and physical capital. It is irresponsible for Western governments and multinational donors to promote the establishment of antitrust laws or the adoption of other economic law reforms without providing extensive assistance in preparing and implementing the new legal mechanisms.[132]

A. Building Foundations for Creating New Competition Systems

The possibilities for success in preparing new legislation or designing new institutions are likely to increase if such initiatives are

---

131. *See* Boner & Kovacic, *supra* note 99, at 37–40 (discussing the importance of defining reporting requirements in the context of Ukraine's antimonopoly law); Kovacic, *supra* note 12, at 1097–99 (describing the selection of reporting thresholds).

132. *See* Laffont, *supra* note 8, at 250 (discussing economic liberalization and financial services reform and observing that "the most effective aid is aid that helps to design those regulatory institutions"; concluding that "it is irresponsible to advocate liberalization without providing such aid").

informed by careful study of the host country's existing conditions. This involves analyzing the economic, legal, political, and social context in which reforms will take place. An accurate diagnosis of initial conditions requires collaboration by foreign advisors with host country specialists.

A thoughtful pre-reform analysis serves four major purposes. The first is to guide the assessment of how to draft the original competition policy statute. The pre-reform assessment will help identify the types of public and private competitive restraints that warrant attention and indicate what types of institutions the competition law should create or augment. No sensible system of law reform would try to draft legal commands or design institutions without such an evaluation of initial conditions.

The second purpose is to formulate possible priorities and competition policy strategies for the new competition policy institution. The initial assessment can assist in diagnosing the obstacles to effective competition and proposing their cures. Case studies of specific industry sectors might reveal that the chief impediment to new business development is a government policy that would be an appropriate target for advocacy efforts (or direct prohibition in the competition statute). Industry analysis also might reveal common practices—such as the tendency of various trade associations to adopt bylaws that set fee levels or control bidding—which the competition agency might challenge.

The third objective is to identify implementation needs and formulate a plan for building the competition agency and enhancing the capability of institutions—such as courts and universities—on which the agency will depend to function effectively.

The fourth reason to perform an extensive pre-reform assessment is to identify existing institutions that the competition authority can draw upon or adapt to execute its responsibilities.[133] For example, an existing social network might provide a conduit for communicating information about the operation of the new competition policy regime and performing educational programs. Indigenous organizations might play a role in detecting deviations from competition policy norms or assist in resolving community-level disputes.

---

133. *See* Melinda Smale & Vernon Ruttan, *Social Capital and Technical Change: The Groupements Naam of Burkina Faso, in* INSTITUTIONS AND ECONOMIC DEVELOPMENT, *supra* note 1, at 182, 183 (describing how existing indigenous cultural and social endowments can facilitate the development process).

B. Sustained Assistance During Implementation

The best assistance programs are anchored by the presence of long-term advisors who reside within the country and work directly with the host country's competition policy officials. There is a growing recognition that short-term initiatives, while useful in limited respects, do little to improve conditions for the longer term.[134] Charles Cadwell makes this point in reflecting upon his experiences as one of the principal managers of the University of Maryland's Center for Institutional Reform and the Informal Sector, a major technical assistance provider:

> While assistance such as short-term training and study tours are helpful if conducted as part of a longer term interaction, IRIS experience in Russia, Poland, Nepal, Chad, and Mongolia suggests that, absent sustained interaction, one ought to have limited expectations about the effect of such activities. As frustrating as it is for us to host study tours that generate much interest but only a brief exchange without a chance to plumb the details of issues, it is similarly frustrating for local officials and others to host a series of short-term "development tourists."[135]

The cost of supporting such operations is trivial compared to the potential gains in the form of improved institutional capability and sensible policy making.

C. Regional Cooperation

For many transition economies, regional cooperation can supply a valuable means for developing new implementation capabilities and reducing the cost of building new competition policy institutions. Multinational initiatives such as Mercosur and the Andean Pact provide opportunities for transition economies to cooperate in developing enforcement strategies, to harmonize procedures and substantive standards, and to share best practices.[136] In some instances, regional alliances may permit transition economies to

---

134. *See* Robert Picciotto, *Putting Institutional Economics to Work: From Participation to Governance, in* INSTITUTIONS AND ECONOMIC DEVELOPMENT, *supra* note 1, at 343, 363 ("It is no accident that, where development has failed, basic governance and institutions have usually been weak. Enhancement of domestic capacities simply cannot be handled within reasonable time frames without sustained international cooperation and development assistance.").

135. Cadwell, *supra* note 16, at 267.

136. *See* Jose Tavares de Araujo, Jr. & Luis Tineo, The Harmonization of Competition Policies Among the Mercosur Countries (June 1997) (paper presented to the Organization of American States Trade Unit) (on file with author) (discussing possible use of Mercosur competition policy protocol to achieve common competition policy approaches).

reduce the costs of implementation by consolidating certain functions, such as the investigation of region-wide trade restraints or the adjudication of cases, in the regional authority. Multinational bodies whose members include developed and developing economies, such as ASEAN, APEC, and NAFTA, also can provide useful conduits for transferring information and know-how from well-established Western competition systems to newer regimes.[137]

D. Transferring Knowledge and Investing in Human Capital

In most transition environments, the long-term success of new competition policy institutions will require considerable effort to transfer information and expand the pool of individuals with professional training in market-oriented economics and law.[138] Donors can and must provide some of this training on a short-term basis in the form of seminars for competition agency enforcement officials, judges, academics, and members of the private sector. The more important task is to build a self-sustaining intellectual infrastructure.[139] Constructing the requisite infrastructure will require longer-term investments that may not have an immediate tangible payoff. Such investments include improving university departments of business administration, economics, law, and public administration and providing assistance for promising students to obtain graduate training in Western universities.[140]

E. Continuing Efforts to Evaluate Results

The successful execution of competition policy programs re-quires a continuing commitment by donor agencies and host country competition authorities to assess the impact of efforts to design and

---

137. *See* Garcia-Rodriguez, *supra* note 123, at 1193–95 (discussing the use of NAFTA to coordinate the antitrust policies of Canada, Mexico, and the United States).

138. *See* WORLD BANK, *supra* note 13, at 5 (stating that "[foreign assistance] projects need to focus on creating and transmitting knowledge and capacity").

139. *See id.* at 83 ("Creating knowledge does not mean that donor agencies (or the experts they hire) have chunks of technical or engineering information that they simply transmit to aid recipients"; observing that the knowledge that matters "must be created locally and internalized").

140. *See* Black et al., *supra* note 17, at 1801–02 (discussing the possible value to market reforms in Russia of foreign aid investments in building Russian business and law schools and paying for Russian students to study in foreign graduate programs); WORLD BANK, *supra* note 13, at 17, 55 (describing the positive impact of donor funding for future transition economy policy makers' overseas study).

implement the competition policy system.[141] Continuing assessment of implementation experience is a necessary ingredient of any competition policy program.[142]

CONCLUSION

The extraordinary pace of creation of competition policy systems in emerging markets raises a series of interrelated issues about law reform. The first issue is whether competition policy deserves a high priority on the agenda of economic reform measures. The answer that commentators give to this question depends on how we define competition policy. There seems to be a universal consensus that transition economies should take affirmative measures to increase business rivalry as a tool for promoting growth. Most observers appear to agree that creating an institution to advocate pro-market solutions, to educate business leaders, public officials, and citizens about the merits of a market system, to perform industrial organization research, and to undertake an antitrust enforcement program against collusion among competitors is appropriate. The sharpest point of disagreement involves the wisdom of establishing the full panoply of antitrust commands found in mature competition policy systems.

In encouraging transition economies to create competition policy systems, Western nations and multinational bodies have tended to slight grave problems that emerging markets will encounter in implementing the new statutes. In most transition countries, there is a significant mismatch between national implementation capabilities and the demands of new competition laws, especially where statutes dictate enforcement of the elaborate commands found in experienced Western antitrust systems.

To decide about the correct measure of completeness and complexity in transition economy competition policy systems, one must confront the mismatch between well-developed conceptions from Western experience about the optimal design of laws and the existing institutional capacity of emerging markets to implement them. As Jean-Jacques Laffont has observed, the potential mismatch between

---

141. *See* WORLD BANK, *supra* note 13, at 27 ("[Donor] agencies should be asking themselves continually: Why do we do what we do? And what is the impact?").

142. *See* William E. Kovacic, *Evaluating Antitrust Experiments: Using Ex Post Assessments of Government Enforcement Decisions to Inform Competition Policy*, 9 GEO. MASON L. REV. 843 (2001) (making a case for evaluating the outcomes of competition policy programs).

legal commands and institutional capabilities forces one to make a fundamental choice: "Do we take a purely normative view or do we take into account political and administrative constraints?"[143] Many modern law reform programs, including competition policy projects, have tended to begin by creating the conceptually ideal legal regime on the assumption that political and administrative constraints that will influence the application of the law can be resolved later. There is a growing awareness among commentators, including many participants in the foreign assistance process, that issues of institutional capability deserve far greater attention in designing laws and timing their application. The modern literature identifies a number of possibilities for adjusting the sequence of law reforms to ensure that host countries attain the institutional capacity to implement nominal legal commands.

The expanded emphasis on institutional capability has significant implications for technical assistance. Law reform projects are more likely to succeed in promoting economic development when donors satisfy certain conditions. Law drafting and institutional design should build upon careful pre-reform analysis of economic, political, and social conditions conducted by indigenous specialists and foreign advisors. Successful reform measures require close attention to enhancing the capacity of a wide variety of institutions—among them, universities, research institutions, professional societies, and courts—whose effectiveness is vital to the operation of the legal regime. The key to setting the proper institutional foundation and encouraging sensible application of new laws is a durable commitment to provide assistance, anchored by a sustained, in-country presence of foreign advisors.

143. Laffont, *supra* note 8, at 238.

[9]

Competition and Development: Towards an Institutional Foundation for Competition Enforcement

Abel M. Mateus[*,**]

We bring together three strands of contributions to the study of institutions in the development process in order to lay down the foundations for an economic approach to the formulation of competition policies and competition law. Competition policies need to be complemented by trade, industrial, and procurement policies that provide the context for the operation of any policy regime in developing countries, laying down the foundations of a competitive market economy. First, models of the political economy of development that incorporate interest groups and their influence in the political process show that when a small group of vested interests dominate economic policy there is little room for competition policy. Second, based on the decision theory and the theory of torts of Glaeser and Shleifer we define the different regimes of competition law according to the capability to avoid subversion, elicit the optimal precaution of damages, and minimize information costs. This shows that competition regimes should be graduated by the level of institutional development. Third, we characterize the level of institutional development with a composite index of governance and government capture. Bringing together these three strands of research, we stress the need that the competition policy regime should fit each institutional level of development. We thus propose a research agenda to help policy makers and advisers better ground competition regimes and laws. This type of approach of policy, paying particular attention to the institutional background, could be applied to most areas of policy and law.

1. INTRODUCTION

The road of economic development is littered with advice of consultants and officials that transpose their recipes for policies without regard for the institutional development of the particular country. However, when we talk about institutions, a 'catch all' word, we need to be specific: what institutions and what policies? The foremost important institution in every country is the political system, political structure, and how economic policies are chosen and implemented. Other important institutions are the capacity of the public administration, structure of the constitutional and other basic legal institutions, structure of the judiciary, regulatory framework, and the environment to do business.

There is hardly any policy more influenced than competition policy by vested interests, because it touches their rents. Sometimes governments oppose the introduction

---

[*] I would like to thank Bill Kovacic, Daniel Sokol, Eleanor Fox, Frederic van Papp, Ioannis Lianos, Philip Marsden, Valentine Korah, Wolfgang Kerber, and participants at seminars at NYU in New York, and UCL, London and Santorini, for helpful comments.

[**] New University of Lisbon, former President of the Portuguese Competition Authority and Visiting Professor at New York University and University College of London.

Mateus, Abel M. 'Competition and Development: Towards an Institutional Foundation for Competition Enforcement'. *World Competition* 33, no. 2 (2010): 275–300.

of a competition law because it may curtail the economic power of groups to whom they cater. Even if ultimately the law is adopted, its implementation remains quite muted. Other governments establish a competition agency to implement the law, but it remains under tight control of the government and sometimes without 'real teeth'. However, there are also other development policies, like trade, industrial, and tax policies where the level, structure of policy, and type of implementation are essential to build a competitive market economy but can also be subject to a high level of state capture.

The main tenet of this article is that the choice of competition law, which is one of the main components of competition policy, should be largely determined by the institutional development of the country. After showing that the antitrust regime can be largely derived by a combination of decision theory and the theory of regulation and torts built by Glaser and Shleifer, we define the main traits of the competition regime for each level of development.

How do we determine the level of institutional development? The concrete level can only be determined case by case. However, some general criteria could help approach the case. We use survey indicators collected by Kaufman and his team on governance to build an indicator of institutional development. It combines information about the level of capture of the state, voice and accountability of the state, the rating of the judicial system, and control of corruption.

This is an example of application of theoretical and empirical work to define a concrete policy for a developing country that can also be used in other policy areas. However, for each policy area we need to define an enforcement model and the relevant institutional context.

Section 2 of this article will summarize some recent theoretical and empirical research that establishes the importance of competition for development in developing countries. It also shows the proper place of competition policy as a way to establish competitive markets. However, competition policy is defined and implemented by a concrete state and to a less or higher degree influenced by vested interests. Thus, in section 3 we investigate to what extent the theory of 'captured state' is important for the context in which policies are defined and implemented. Section 4 discusses the broad economic policies like trade, industrial, and procurement policies that are the prerequisite of any competition law regime. Section 5 builds a theory of implementation of competition law based on the institutional level of development as an example of 'adaptive institutions'. Section 6 exemplifies the criteria that could be used in practice with clinical analysis in order to define the proper level of institutional development. Finally, section 7 concludes.

2.   The Role of Competition Policy in Development Policies

First, we need to establish the proper role of competition policy and competition law and enforcement in the development process. In this article, competition policy, also known as markets policy, is a set of policies directed at promoting competitive markets. Besides setting the rules of the game of competition among firms, it promotes entry, growth, and exit in the dynamic process of an economy as well as innovation and technical progress.[1] Naturally, competitive markets require a broad set of well-functioning market as a pre-requisite. The ultimate goal of competition policy is to contribute in the short and long runs to an improvement in social welfare through an efficient economy. Competition law and enforcement, also known as antitrust, is a subset of competition policy that regulates mergers and practices that restrict the competitive process.

The basis of the market economy is the operation of the markets and the process of rivalry that sets markets in motion (competition). The new microeconomics of develop-ment has shown the central role of the mechanism discovered by Adam Smith regarding the link between labour division and market dimension. Yang and Borland have shown the importance of multiplication of markets for growth – the process of development is characterized by specialization and productivity increase associated with the division of labour that is only possible with market expansion and multiplication.[2] The second strand of the recent literature is the dynamics of firms that shows the importance of the turnover of firms, entry and exit, and the growth and success of these firms in successive waves of technological growth. This is, only to some extent, the Schumpeterian process of 'destruc-tive creation'. There are two processes operating at the microlevel: the shift of resources from less productive to more productive firms, and the expansion of the more productive firms by technological improvements, as in the work of Haltiwanger[3] and others. These two mechanisms: the division of labour with market expansion and the dynamics of firms that lead to productivity increase are largely driven by competition.

The main link in today's Industrial Organization models is between competition and dynamic efficiency as in Spence's seminal paper.[4] There are generally four channels that have been corroborated empirically. First, competition creates a larger number of oppor-tunities for benchmarking, so the market can monitor firm management.[5] Second, innova-tions tend to increase productivity and reduce costs generating a higher level of profits in a competitive environment, where demand price elasticities are higher.[6] Third, higher levels of competition increase the probability of failure, which is an incentive for management to be more efficient.[7] Fourth, workers share in rents, so higher competition leads also to a higher effort.[8]

---

[1] Competition policy interfaces and encompasses trade, licensing, procurement, R&D, and firm's entry and exit polices.

[2] See Y. Yang & J. Borland, 'A Microeconomic Mechanism for Economic Growth', *Journal of Political Economy* 99, no. 3 (1991): 460–482.

[3] J. Haltiwanger, 'Aggregate Growth: What Have We Learned from Microeconomic Evidence, OECD Econom-ics Department Working Paper 267' (2000).

[4] M. Spence, 'Cost Reduction, Competition and Industry Performance', *Econometrica* 51, no.1 (1984): 101–121.

[5] Important contributions are E. Lazear & S. Rosen, 'Rank-Order Tournaments as Optimal Labor Contracts', *Journal of Political Economy* 89 (1981): 841–864; and B. Nalebuff & J. Stiglitz, 'Information, Competition and Markets', *American Economic Review* 73 (1983): 278–293.

[6] S. Nickel, D. Nickolitsas & N. Dryden, 'What Makes Firms Perform Well?', *European Economic Review* 41 (1997): 783–796.

[7] P. Aghion, M. Dewatripoint & P. Rey, 'Corporate Governance, Competition Policy and Industrial Policy', *European Economic Review* 41 (1997): 797–805.

[8] J. Haskel, 'Imperfect Competition, Work Practices and Productivity Growth', *Oxford Bulletin of Economics and Statistics* 53, no. 3 (1991), 265–279.

The Schumpeterian models that dominated the 1990s, arguing that in order to generate innovation we need monopolies,[9] are not only misleading but are also subject to contradictions, as in the seminal models of endogenous growth of Aghion and Howitt[10] and Grossman and Helpman.[11] For example, how can the entrants that had no profits use large amounts of financial resources to finance Research and development (R&D), before entering the market?[12]

Focusing on the different channels through which competition influences innovation, we could distinguish, among others: (i) The Darwinian effect introduced by Aghion[13] and Portes,[14] (ii) the 'neck-and-neck' effect,[15] (iii) the Arrow effect,[16] and (iv) the mobility effect (skilled workers become more adaptable and will switch to more productive industries faster[17,18]). Second, competition may lower the pre-innovation rents by more than post-innovation rents so it increases the after innovation profits, eliminating the Schumpeterian effect. Third, empirical evidence on patents and other Intellectual Property Rights (IPRs) shows that the impact of patenting is only beneficial in some intensive R&D subsectors, like pharmaceuticals or heavy chemicals. Only in these cases the Schumpeterian effect is important. These two cases may lead to the empirical finding of a U curve by Aghion,[19] with empirical data relating market structure to innovation.[20]

There is now important empirical evidence that competition is linked to growth in developed countries. Disney et al.[21] concludes that competition increases productivity levels and the rate of growth of productivity. Recently, Bloom and van Reenen[22] show that good management practices are strongly associated with productivity and those are better when product market competition is higher. Finally, an efficient market for

---

[9] There are a lot of variants of this doctrine from the stricter that we need big firms to generate innovation to the broader that industrial policies should take precedence to competition polices or that too much competition is bad for development.

[10] P. Aghion & P. Howitt, 'A Model of Growth through Creative Destruction', *Econometrica* 60 (1992): 323–351 and P. Aghion & P. Howitt, *Endogenous Growth Theory* (Cambridge, MA: MIT Press, 1998).

[11] G. Grossman & E. Helpman, *Innovation and Growth in the Global Economy* (Cambridge, MA: MIT Press, 1991).

[12] In fact, narrowing down the link between competition and R&D as the core of dynamic efficiency, as in recent controversies mainly about IPRs, is erroneous and deceptive.

[13] P. Aghion et al., 'Competition, Imitation and Growth in a Step-by-Step Innovation', *The Review of Economics Studies* 68 (2001): 467–492.

[14] M. Porter, *The Competitive Advantage of Nations* (London: Macmillan Press, 2000).

[15] P. Aghion & R. Griffith, *Competition and Growth: Reconciling Theory and Evidence* (Cambridge, MA: MIT Press, 2005).

[16] K. Arrow, 'Economic Welfare and the Allocation of Resources for Inventions', in *The Rate and Direction of Inventive Activity: Economic and Social Factors*, ed. R. Nelson (Princeton: Princeton University Press, 1962).

[17] R. E. Lucas, 'On the Mechanics of Economic Development', *Journal of Monetary Economics* 22 (1988): 3–42.

[18] See Aghion & Howitt, n. 12.

[19] P. Aghion et al., 'Entry and Productivity Growth: Evidence from Micro-level Panel Data', *Journal of the European Economic Association, Papers and Proceedings* 2 (2003): 265–276.

[20] However, these empirical models narrow immediately the problem. They relate some measure of market concentration to the number of patents, citations, or any other related measure related with R&D. The empirical work has been carried out for the UK, a developed country.

[21] R. Disney, J. Haskel & Y. Heden, 'Restructuring and Productivity Growth in UK Manufacturing', *Economic Journal* 113 (2003): 666–694.

[22] N Bloom & J. van Reenen, 'Measuring and Explaining Management Practices across Firms and across Countries, CEP Discussion Paper 716' (2006).

corporate control with open rules for takeovers reinforces the impact of competition on productivity.[23] Other studies by Blundell et al.[24] and Aghion and Griffith[25] also confirm the above results. A study for Australia shows that competition enhancing reforms in the 1990s contributed to an increase in GDP.[26]

Research in developing countries has also shown the importance of the link between competition and development. Dutz and Hairy[27] find that competition policy has a positive impact on growth, even after taking into consideration the contribution of trade and institutional policies. Reviewing a large number of studies in the 1990s, Tybout[28] concludes that there is evidence that protection increases price-cost margins and reduce efficiency at the margin, and that exporters (firms that succeed in the international market) are more efficient than non-exporters. Using a new data set for Latin America, Haltiwanger et al.[29] confirm that trade liberalization and competition leads to higher levels of efficiency at the firm level and also to reallocation of resources to more productive sectors. Using data for Colombia, Eslava et al.[30] (2004) show that trade and financial reforms of the 1990s were associated with productivity increases resulting of reallocation from low to high productivity firms. Similar evidence has been shown for Chile[31] and Brazil[32] due to trade liberalization and for India due to the elimination of the Raj licensing scheme.[33] Aghion et al.[34] show evidence that increasing competition in South Africa manufacturing should have 'large productivity effects'.

Aghion and Schenkerman[35] even found situations where countries can find themselves in a competition trap that blocks growth. Those most vulnerable are when the initial level of competition is low, the initial degree of cost asymmetry among firms is low, and politicians are less driven by social welfare concerns.

---

[23] S. Nickel, D. Nickolitsas & N. Dryden, 'What Makes Firms Perform Well?', *European Economic Review* 41 (1997): 783–796 and S. Januszewski, J. Koke & J. Winter, 'Product Market Competition, Corporate Governance and Firm Performance: an Empirical Analysis for Germany, Mimeo' (2001).

[24] R. Blundell, R. Griffith & J. van Reenen, 'Market Share, Market Value and Innovation in a Panel of British Manufacturing Sector', *Review of Economic Studies* 66, no. 3 (1999): 529–554.

[25] See Porter, n. 16.

[26] OECD, *Sources of Economic Growth* (Paris, 2003).

[27] M. Dutz & H. Hayri, 'Does More Intense Competition Lead to Higher Growth? World Bank Policy Research Working Paper 2320' (2000).

[28] J. Tybout, 'Manufacturing Firms in Developing Countries: How Well They Do and Why?, World Bank Policy Research Working Paper 1965' (1998).

[29] J. Haltiwanger et al., 'Effects of Tariffs and Real Exchange Rates on Job Reallocation: Evidence from Latin America, Mimeo' (August 2004).

[30] M. Eslava et al., 'The Effects of Structural Reforms on Productivity and Profitability Enhancing Reallocation: Evidence from Colombia', *Journal of Development Economics* 75 (2004): 333–371.

[31] P. Ferreira & J. Rossi, 'New Evidence from Brazil on Trade Liberalization and Productivity Growth', *International Economic Review* 44, no. 4 (2003): 1383–1405.

[32] N. Pacvnick, 'Trade Liberalization, Exit and Productivity Improvements: Evidence form Chilean Firms', *The Review of Economic Studies* 69 (2002): 245–272.

[33] P. Aghion et al., 'Entry Liberalization and Inequality in Industrial Performance, Mimeo' (Harvard University, 2004).

[34] P. Aghion, M. Braun & J. Fedderk, 'Competition and Productivity Growth in South Africa, Mimeo' (2007).

[35] P. Aghion & M. Schankerman, 'On the Welfare Effects and Political Economy of Competition-Enhancing Policies', *Economic Journal* 114 (October 2004): 800–824.

3. POLITICAL ECONOMY MODELS OF DEVELOPMENT

Major determinants of economic development are the economic policies undertaken by governments. Those economic policies, and in particular, competition policies, cannot be explained simply using a benevolent government that maximizes intertemporal welfare, like most of the formal theoretical models assume. They are influenced by the structure of the society and in particular by the power of different socio-economic groups. This section will give evidence that vested interests have a major influence in formulating and implementing competition polices and competition law. However, what is relevant for development is the actual impact of those policies in resource allocation and innovation. Moreover, competition policy is about control and prevention of abuse of market power. Thus, in order to define a competition regime we have to take in consideration the level of concentration of economic and political power.

In the recent theory of political economy models of development, Olson[36] is a prominent contribution. His theory of collective action offers an explanation why some countries grow and others stagnate. He uses the concept of distributional coalition, a group whose collective action can secure a larger share of the resources generated by the economy to its members, at the expense of the population at large. An important topic that Olson has left unproven is how important are these distortions to economic development.

Olson also addresses the important issue of the time dimension. How can a prospering country fall into a phase of stagnation? In a stable society, distributional coalitions gradually find way to solve their collective action problems. Once they are formed and established, they prefer the status quo and are likely to oppose innovations that would increase the economic growth rate. Thus, coalitions can trap a society into a stagnant economic state. In fact, Parente and Prescott[37] build a formal model that captures the idea that insider groups that operate with a given technology may oppose the introduction of innovations and thus block economic growth.

Grossman and Helpman[38] build a simpler, but very insightful model, to explain why there are different protection rates in external trade by industries and sectors.[39] In their model, special-interest groups, organized in lobbies, make contributions in order to bias the government choice of trade policy in their favour. Politicians maximize a two-part welfare function that depends on those contributions collected and the welfare of voters at large, because they need them for re-election. The need for party financing and particularly campaign financing in a democratic state leads politicians to put 'protection for sale'. The model generates a set of protection rates that obey a Ramsey modified rule. This is

---

[36] M. Olson, *The Rise and Decline of Nations: Economic Growth, Stagflation, and Social Rigidities* (New Haven, CT: Yale University Press, 1982).
[37] S. Parente & E. Prescott, 'Monopoly Rights: Barriers to Riches', *American Economic Review* 89, no. 5 (1999): 1216–1232.
[38] G. Grossman & E. Helpman, 'Protection for Sale', *American Economic Review* 84, no. 4 (1994): 833–850.
[39] The model is generalized to all types of taxation and subsidies by A. Dixit, 'Special-Interest Lobbying and Endogenous Commodity Taxation', *Eastern Economic Journal* 22, no. 4 (1996): 375–388.

a type of common agency problem where an agent (the government or political party) acts in the name of several principals (interest groups), while bearing a cost for the implementation of the policy in terms of welfare costs of protection.[40]

Mitra[41] extends the work of Grossman and Helpman to show that greater inequality in income or wealth distribution leads to a higher rate of rent extraction from lobbies and thus lowers social welfare. He also shows that industries with higher capital intensity, more concentrated and with inelastic demand, have stronger lobbies.[42] A test of the 'protection for sale' model by Gawande and Bandyopadhyay[43] for the United States gives high marks to that theory.

Acemoglu, Aghion, and Zilibotti[44] also tackle an issue in the line of Parente-Prescott: a change in policy by the government against vested interests would increase the level of development, because societies can be trapped with the 'inappropriate institutions' and relatively backward technologies. In their model, the authors prove the existence of a dynamic equilibrium and the possible occurrence of a *political economy trap* where capitalists bribe the government in order to maintain a regime of monopoly rents with low competition that ends up blocking growth over the long term. Such trap is more likely in societies with weak institutions (more corruptible).

Another strand of the literature that is relevant to this article links competition, rents, and corruption. Andes and di Tela[45] built a model of compensation and corruption for government agencies.[46] They claim that when the principal (the people) pursues multiple and diffuse objectives, state contingent contracts with the agent (government) are hard to write and rents have to be allocated to enhance performance, in the spirit of Gary Becker and George Stigler. A similar agency problem may occur between another principal (government) and the agent being the bureaucracy. They use an efficiency wage theory to determine the optimal level of corruption. When a firm under the influence of a bureaucrat enjoys rents, the value of his control rights is high. Bureaucrats can trade part of this control in exchange for bribes. Then, in a regime of monopolies, with higher rents, there would be higher level of corruption compared with a more competitive world. In fact, their empirical analysis corroborates this view. The problem is particularly acute in

---

[40] These are largely consumer surplus costs and may also be producer surplus in industries that have to pay a higher price for their inputs. These costs may translate in lower votes to the government.

[41] D. Mitra, 'Endogenous Lobbying Formation and Endogenous Protection: A Long-Run Model of Policy Determination', *American Economic Review* 89, no. 5 (1999): 1116–1134.

[42] Infrastructure sectors satisfy these conditions. They also benefit from high natural protection.

[43] K. Gawande & U. Bandyopadhyay, 'Is Protection for Sale? Evidence on the Grossman-Helpman Theory of Endogenous Protection', *Review of Economics and Statistics* 82, no. 1 (2000): 139–152.

[44] D. Acemoglu, P. Aghion & F. Zilibotti, 'Distance to Frontier, Selection and Economic Growth, NBER Working Paper 9066' (2002).

[45] A. Andes & R. di Tela, 'Rents, Competition and Corruption', *American Economic Review* 89, no. 4 (1999): 982–993

[46] There is a large literature on corruption and non-directly productive activities that deal with 'petty' corruption in public administration and bureaucracies and which is only lateral to our analysis. Unless corruption at all levels of administration is rampant, this type of corruption is dwarfed by capture of governments by vested interests.

an oligarchy and when those vested interests represent small groups, like traditionally powerful family groups.[47,48]

As we will discuss below, anti-competitive policies influence the economy in multiple ways:

(a)   Create distortions in the economy with static and dynamic effects.
(b)   Appropriate resources or increase rents to these groups increasing inequality and may decrease productivity of the economy.
(c)   Deviate resources from more productive to less productive sectors or industries.
(d)   Prevent the process of creative destruction to take place.
(e)   Block the entry of new firms.

These problems lead the economy to produce inside the Production Possibility Frontier due to the misallocation of resources, which has static and dynamic effects, and may lead to political economy traps and generate growth collapses.

The first empirical work that tried to measure these effects directly around the world has been undertaken at the World Bank by Kaufman and others under the umbrella of 'governance and capture'. Kaufman calls this type of behaviour 'legal corruption', in the sense that corporations can lobby or obtain certain policy measures that may not be illegal but increase their rents at the cost of social welfare.[49] He has also suggested the term 'the privatization of public policy'. Transparency International that collects data on corruption does not cover this type of behaviour and has proposed the concept of 'misuse of entrusted power for private gains'.[50] One of the pioneering works on state capture by firms and its implications was carried out by the World Bank on Transition economies at the end of the

---

[47] According to the Financial Times of 5 Aug. 2000, in an article signed by John Lloyd, 'The oligarchs were so called because they had real power, state power. They wrote laws. They appointed ministers, often entire cabinets, and made sure that their interests were served. They corrupted the new governing, legislative and bureaucratic class of Russia, in the centre, in the regions and abroad . . .'. Cited in D. Kaufman, 'Governance, Crisis and the Longer View: Unorthodox Reflections on the New Reality, Mimeo' (2008), available at the site on Governance of the World Bank. The same author also cites the Chef of the Pink House of the Presidents of Argentina. ' "Have dinner menus here always been the same?," asked a key aide to Menem's to his chef. "The menus change, the presidents change. What never changes are the dinner guests," retorted the presidential chef, referring to the cadre of businessmen who frequented the residence. In El Octavo Circulo, by Cerruti and Ciancaglini'.

[48] The problem is acute in small countries with a short tradition of democracy.

[49] Sometimes those methods are illegal, like the recent case of Siemens that was condemned in December 2008, by the SEC and the Office of Public Prosecutor in Munich, because of several practices of bribing government officials around the world in order to obtain contracts. This was the largest settlement under the US Foreign Corrupt Practices Act, since it became law in 1977, with a fine of USD 1.4 billion paid in part to the SEC, DoJ, and the Prosecutor in Munich. The act prohibits American companies from bribing foreign government officials. According to the SEC, the company also used bribes to develop mobile telephone networks in Bangladesh, develop national identity cards in Argentina, and medical devices in Vietnam, China, and Russia (<CNNMoney.com>, 15 Dec. 2008). We are not aware that this case has triggered investigations in the relevant countries. The Volcker report on the UN Food for Oil programme also refers several cases of bribing. On the positive side, we should cite the case of the government of Singapore that banned Siemens for entering in any bidding contracts for five years after a after a public official was accused of receiving millions of dollars in bribes from the company (news available in <www.againstcorruption.org/BriefingsItem.asp?id=13595>).

[50] See <www.transparency.org/news_room/faq/corruption_faq>.

1990s.[51] According to the authors, the 'leviathan' state is being replaced by the oligarchs who 'capture the state', the policy and law environment is moulded to the captor firm's advantage, at considerable social cost.

Based on the Business Environment and Enterprise Performance Survey, they study three potential interactions between firms and state in twenty-one transition countries: (i) *administrative corruption*: when firms make illicit and non-transparent private payments to public officials to alter administrative regulations; (ii) *state capture*: when firms make illicit and non-transparent private payments to public officials in order to influence the formation of laws, rules, regulations, or decrees by state institutions, including the courts; and (iii) *influence*: extent to which firms influence the formation of those laws or decrees without recourse to payments. The private gains to capture are quite substantial. They find that captor firms grew about four times more than other firms in high capture countries, but in the regression results it seems that capture does not lead to higher levels of investment.[52] In addition, it is not only incumbent firms that engage in capture, there is a sample of de novo firms that also engages in capturing in order to get more secure property rights and contractual advantages, which is also consistent with a 'grabbing hand' state.

These are some of the most important issues in developing countries' political economy and have been clearly neglected for a long time.[53] They explain certain phenomena of stagnation and growth debacles witnessed in developing countries.

The challenge is how to structure institutions to limit the influence of vested interests in policy formulation, limit their rent extraction, and give a major voice to the interests that embody social welfare. Most of the existing literature in competition policy and competition law takes for granted that socio-political institutions control excess economic and political power and the role of vested interests. This may be true in the vast majority of democratic societies. Particularly important is the constitutional regime that establishes the independence and balance of power between the three branches of the state: executive, parliamentarian, and judiciary. An analysis of this issue is beyond the limits of the paper. Let us then concentrate on competition policies and policies that interface with competition and show how they can establish the foundations for the competition regimes and contribute ultimately to development.

4.   COMPETITION POLICIES AS FOUNDATION FOR COMPETITION LAW REGIMES

As defined above, competition policies give the framework for markets and thus largely influence resource allocation required for economic development. In fact, a discussion of competition policies and other policies that are related with the functioning of the market

---

[51] See J. Hellman, G. Jones & D. Kaufman, 'Seize the State, Seize the Day, World Bank Policy Research Working Paper' (2000).

[52] This would be consistent with the hypothesis that the additional rents are not always used productively.

[53] The phenomenon that resource-rich developing countries have usually very poor performance in economic development is mainly explained by this type of model. The traditional 'Dutch disease' explanation is only a small part of the story.

should precede any discussion of competition law regimes. They are the context in which competition law and enforcement takes place. For example, can we discuss, in a small developing country, abuses of dominance if there are high barriers to external trade? In addition, if large parts of the economy are monopolized? Otherwise, what is the purpose of having a competition authority if government favours the formation and protects national champions?

The policies that are more directly related with the functioning of the market and that can promote more competitive outcomes are market infrastructure policies, external trade policies, entry and exit of firms policies, licensing, privatization, investment policies, procurement, regulation, and innovation policies. It is also important to emphasize that in developing countries structural policies regarding the formation and functioning of markets are more important and are the precondition for any policy regime.

In developed countries, we take for granted that most of the markets exist,[54] and that markets' infrastructures function. However, in developing countries quite a number of markets do not exist or do not function with a minimum efficiency. In order for a market of a certain good or service to operate, there has to be supply and demand but also a way for both to match and establish equilibrium. Physical infrastructure like transportation and information networks may not exist or function properly or there might be too much market fragmentation. For example, a well-functioning market for an agricultural commodity requires an articulated system of producer, wholesale, and export markets. It requires the physical infrastructure for trade, storage, and handling. It requires a well-functioning system of price information from the world level up to the local level. It also requires financing and insurance by-markets.[55]

Adam Smith and the work of Yang and Borland[56] have identified that for development to occur markets have to multiply and generate specialization. Few economists would contest the major role that creating infrastructure and markets that link up the agriculture hinterland with the coastal urban areas is a precondition for growth (market multiplication), or to give a historical example in Europe, that the Zollverein had a major role in the development of Germany (integration of fragmented markets). In addition, as the geography of development shows,[57] we have to think in terms of local, national, regional, and global markets. Thus, as a precondition for any competition or market policy the country needs to build its markets and market infrastructure.

The second most important policy in developing countries for competition is external trade policy. In fact, reducing the level of protection and exposing the tradable sector to

---

[54] We do not enter here into the discussion of private versus public goods.

[55] The experience in several African countries has also shown the need of complementary markets. For example, the export of cashew nuts in the North of Mozambique did not take off before there were manufactured goods available in local markets in order for the farmers to trade their agricultural surplus with clothing, shoes, bicycles, and other goods that they needed. On a larger scale, in the old socialist countries there were not enough consumer goods for workers to buy. This fact limited the value of their wages and affected the incentive to work and innovate.

[56] See Yang & Borland, n. 4.

[57] The World Bank has surveyed the literature in this area in World Bank, 'Reshaping Economic Geography, World Development Report' (2009).

external competition increases the level of rivalry in domestic markets. It has been shown both theoretically and in practice that reducing tariffs and quantitative restrictions leads to resource reallocation in favour of more productive sectors, specialization, and to increases in productivity as firms both import more technological advanced capital and improve their methods of operation to compete either with imports or in external markets.[58]

The opening of economies is particularly important for small economies, and the exposure to foreign competition may reduce substantially market concentration in the tradable goods sector. Moreover, the expansion of markets due to the access to world markets, and particularly developed countries' markets that are much larger, allows domestic firms to reap significantly economies of scale.

However, developing countries still use external protection and industrial policies. Besides the traditional 'infant industry argument' due to learning-by-doing,[59] there is the national champions justification: the argument is the need to create powerful national business groups in order to locate in the country 'the centre of decision' of their industry or service sector (energy and banking are some of the sectors widely used).[60] Another argument is the need to strengthen a particular group because it has accumulated management expertise, with specific human capital that is scarce in the country. A third reason is that the country needs to build a large national champion in order to have access to finance and have the scale to expand into the international market. These are examples of industrial and other policies that are in conflict with competition policies and may contribute to build the 'competition traps' identified above. Sometimes they are strengthened by having tight rules against takeovers.

Using the Grossman–Helpman model, we can say that the higher the role of vested interests and the more they are concentrated, the higher the level of protection. Moreover, Andes and di Tela also find evidence that corruption is higher in countries where domestic firms are sheltered from foreign competition by natural or policy-induced barriers to trade, with economies dominated by a few number of firms, or where antitrust regulations are not effective in preventing anti-competitive practices. The size of the effect is rather large: almost a third of the corruption gap between Italy and Austria can be explained by Italy's lower exposure to foreign competition. They also find some evidence, using indicators from the World Competitiveness Report that the degree of concentration in the economy increases the level of corruption and that antitrust laws decrease that level.

In our opinion, the external trade policy is a core policy for promoting competition in developing countries and is the prerequisite for any antitrust law regimes. Thus, in order to improve market functioning in the tradable sector, governments need to eliminate quantitative restrictions and reduce tariffs to a low level (trade liberalization), avoid major

---

[58] For empirical evidence, see the empirical studies for Latin America, Asia, and South Africa cited in s. 2 above.
[59] As is well known, a production subsidy is a superior policy. However, if there are scarce budget resources a third best policy is temporary and regressive protection.
[60] Governments defend that when major decisions will come up to the shareholders or management like locating a new factory or closing a given operation they will take into consideration their own 'nationality'.

differences in the rates of protection across all sectors, and pay particular attention to policies for technology transfer.

Countries that are rich in natural resources and have their major exports dependent on a single or a few commodities also need to pay particular attention to the integration of that sector with the rest of the economy. For example, most of the countries dependent on a major mineral commodity tend to exploit that resource by monopoly.[61] However, in the presence of weak institutions it may lead to the phenomena of the 'natural resource trap' studied by P. Collier in some African countries.[62] Large amounts of resources may be appropriated by the state and vested interests, without proper accountability. Collier has proposed codes of conduct and transparency with a major contribute from multinationals cooperating in the exploitation of those resources and national governments involved.

However, external trade policies do not inject competition in the non-tradables sector, comprising telecommunications, energy, construction, distribution, and financial and business services, among others. Thus, governments need to promote the functioning of efficient markets in those sectors. In developing countries, more important and previous to any antitrust are structural policies directed first at building efficient and competitive market structures in those sectors. Let us look at some of the sector policies that are required.

Licensing, procurement, and privatization policies are the most important instruments to shape these markets. For example, offering through a simple decree or a 'beauty contest' a public enterprise, or a license for a given infrastructure, will create a private monopoly, a clearly inefficient market structure with major negative impact on social welfare. The way governments use to give out such privilege may be from an outright 'legal monopoly',[63] using concessions biased towards the firm and sometimes with costly clauses to the economy,[64] or camouflaged in 'universal service' clauses.[65] When structuring privatization or licensing, governments should take into consideration the market structure that they are creating and in particular their impact on competition.[66] This need should be balanced against the need to solve the agency problem in the corporation of providing a stable and strong shareholder nucleus. In particular, ministries of finance are often interested in

---

[61] This structure may have been inherited from the colonial times, where a mineral or agriculture enclave was often isolated from the rest of the economy and integrated into the imperial power.

[62] P. Collier, *The Bottom Billion* (Oxford University Press, 2008), 38 and following.

[63] In the nineteenth century in several European countries, the tobacco monopoly was a source of acquisition of major wealth.

[64] In Portugal, the concession of all the bridges that cross the Tagus River in Lisbon was awarded to a single consortium. The Audit Court raised serious doubts about the clauses contained in the contract that were in favour of the private firm. According to our estimates, the clauses led to a real rate of return to capital of about 19%. See A. Mateus & M. Mateus, *Microeconomia: Aplicações e Casos*, vol. II (Editorial Verbo, 2002).

[65] A case in point is the Telmex case – the Mexican government argued that it needed to charge high tariffs to users in the United States to finance services in the rural poor areas.

[66] A very important example is the privatization of telecom companies that in some countries led to the break-up of the state monopoly along companies with different networks that can compete among each other, or the break-up of a state electricity firm by unbundling their activities. A recent case with much success was the privatization of the telecom state monopoly in Turkey.

maximizing the financial intake of the sale in order to reduce public debt, but that objective should be traded-off against concerns for building a competitive market.

In fact, infrastructure sectors like telecommunications, energy, banking, large-scale construction, water, and transportation have been the favoured sectors for vested interests to establish their monopoly or quasi-monopoly positions. Monopolies in infrastructure sectors that produce goods or services used widely by other firms in the economy can produce a great damage to the competitiveness and growth of the overall economy. In some economies, those overcharges in terms of the excess costs paid for inputs by the rest of the economy can amount to 3% to 6% of GDP.[67] Sectors that are particularly affected are the small and medium enterprises, usually the most important for employment and exports. Cross-ownership or bargaining power sometimes lowers the costs of large enterprises elsewhere in the economy, but consumers at large have no alternative but to pay the cost of those services.

Theoretically, the way to solve the problem of natural monopolies is to regulate them. However, quite often sector regulators in developing countries with weak institutions are captured by the firms that are regulated.[68] Abuses of dominant position, overpricing, and other behaviour are usually tolerated with justifications that 'play well:' need for additional investments, need to 'expand abroad', and high profits show that it is an 'efficient firm' with good performance in capital markets.

Thus, the most important way to solve these problems is by injecting competition in the infrastructure markets. One way is to unbundle market structure, separating the natural monopoly components, like telecom and electricity or gas networks from production, and import from distribution. Simultaneously, the government should impose an open access policy to the natural monopoly components, like in the European Community directives.

Large investment projects and state procurement are also very important to promote competitive markets. Building a country's infrastructure (motorways, railways, airports, large bridges, urban complexes) mobilizes a large amount of the country's resources. Thus, in order to promote an efficient resource allocation they need to be subject to a rigorous project evaluation, be implemented in a timely fashion, and be financed by adequate means. Sometimes these projects are oversized or run into large over costs, as the well-known 'white elephants'.[69] In addition, they need to be subject to competitive bidding, so the execution is awarded to the least cost contractor, and works need to be properly and independently supervised. By introducing competitive bidding in project execution and

---

[67] Assume that the non-tradables in quasi-monopoly situations represent about 20% of GDP and that they overcharge 20%–30%, which is not extraordinary, as price data collected by OECD for utilities show. Then just the direct impact would be 4%–6% of GDP.

[68] The problem is aggravated by the lack of human capital. For example, when in the early 1990s the government of Portugal decided to set up regulators for telecommunications and energy went to the recently privatized state monopolies to get the experts to staff those regulators. In most of the cases, they have retained their old employment links. These problems were not specific to Portugal but affected quite a number of countries where there is a shortage of specialists in a given sector.

[69] Social costs may be higher when recurrent costs cannot be covered by revenues, leading to large current subsidies by the state.

supplies of goods and services to the state, governments are contributing to the reduction of bribing and preventing bid rigging at the expense of taxpayers.

There are a number of other important policies required for the functioning of efficient competitive markets that we cannot dwell on for lack of space. Policies related with entry and exit of firms and market mobility in general are also very important. When there are costly regulations to set up business or to operate it, the phenomena of informality takes large chunks of the economy, with clear inefficiency.[70] In addition, even fiscal and monetary policies can have important competitive market implications. When the law stipulates fiscal loopholes and tax evasion is tolerated, firms in dominant positions may acquire an unfair advantage vis-à-vis their smaller competitors. Otherwise, when firms in a dominant position have access to credit or capital markets beyond what a proper risk analysis would dictate.

These are all policies that have to be taken into account when defining a competition law regime. They constitute the foundation in which a competition law regime operates. They should also be used in defining, on a case-by-case analysis, the different thresholds for defining the above regimes, together with other institutional elements. We now turn to the analysis of the other institutional elements required to define the competition law and enforcement regime.

5.   Competition Law Enforcement Models Conditioned by the Level
      of Institutional Development

The theory of the design of optimal competition rules is still largely undeveloped, when compared with regulation, fiscal, or monetary policies. This is the result of the multivariate characteristic of most competition policy problems. For example, the problem of coordinating strategies (cartels) is fundamentally different from the one of exclusionary practices (abuses of dominance). However, we could raise the bar of abstraction and consider that all competition law decisions are taken in a world of uncertainty and asymmetric information and apply decision theory. Although all decisions are about individual cases, a rule-based approach is preferable. This is in line with general insights from the theory of economic policy concerning the superiority of policies based upon rules rather than on discretionary decisions.

We see at least three advantages. First, rules anchor expectations, reducing legal uncertainty and informing firms' behaviour. Uncertainty can lead both to over- or under-deterrence and cause long lags in decision making with pernicious effects on efficiency and welfare. Second, rules reduce rent-seeking, as emphasized by Buchanan and the constitutional law and economics approach. Third, rules mitigate knowledge problems by benevolent governments, agencies, and courts, if we take into account that a rule-based system uses much less information than a case-by-case approach and thus

---

[70] De Sotto has contributed to this analysis. See H. De Sotto, *The Other Path: The Economic Answer to Terrorism* (Basic Books, 2002).

reduces decision errors. The 'much more economic approach' has led some economists[71] to sketch a proposal of an optimal differentiated competition rule, which is determined by minimizing error costs and regulation costs. In fact, legal decisions are taken in a world of uncertainty and imperfect information. Joskow[72] has called attention to the need to take into consideration that competition law regulates agents' market decisions, involving always transaction costs. One of the concerns of policy should be to minimize those costs. Another approach is the decision theoretical model that minimizes type I and type II errors. In both cases, we are led to a general formulation of the law as a 'structured rule of reason'.

In the same regard, differentiation of competition rules can also involve a sequential multi-stage process of assessment and screening. For example, by using simple low-cost information, like 'safe harbour rules' at an initial stage, a number of unproblematic cases can be filtered out, whereas for the remaining cases, in a second step, more information gathering and additional assessment methods are applied.[73]

Avoiding discretionary behaviour by the state is very important. Research on the quality of regulation by Levy and Spiller[74] is relevant for antitrust enforcement. These authors try to see how political institutions interact with regulatory processes and economic conditions in determining the potential for administrative manipulation, and hence the economic performance of the particular sector. They show that what is important is that institutions and mechanisms restrict the degree of arbitrariness and administrative discretion. This means that regulatory systems should be clear and stable. In fact, they show that a large variety of regulatory rules may all lead to an efficient outcome (e.g., price caps, incentive schemes, and use of competition), if those conditions are satisfied. They also found that the political and social infrastructure is very important to limit arbitrariness and administrative discretion.

As Christiansen and Kerber show,[75] the optimal differentiation rule is equal to the marginal benefits deriving from reducing type I and type II errors with the marginal costs of regulation, that is, acquiring more information, more transaction costs, and further delays. Therefore, it is worthwhile to increase the fineness of the rules, by establishing additional criteria and analysis of pro-competitive and anti-competitive factors, up to the point that the additional regulation costs are equal to the reduction in decision errors.[76] For weaker institutional levels, the information and transaction costs become larger, as information is not easily available and weak institutions, like protection of contracts, lead to higher transaction costs. As a result, rules have to be less sophisticated and more errors have inevitably to be tolerated.

---

[71] For example, A. Christiansen & W. Kerber, 'Competition Policy with Optimal Differentiated Rules instead of "Per Se Rules versus Rule of Reason," University of Marburg Working Paper 6-2006'.

[72] P. Joskow, 'Transaction Cost Economics, Antitrust Rules and Remedies', *Journal of Law, Economics and Organization* 18, no. 1 (2002): 95–116.

[73] As C. Beckner III & S. Salop, 'Decision Theory and Antitrust Rules', *Antitrust Law Journal* 67 (1999): 41–76, have proposed.

[74] B. Levy & P. Spiller, 'The Institutional Foundations of Regulatory Commitment: A Comparative Study of Telecommunications Regulation', *Journal of Law, Economics and Organization* 10, no. 2 (1994).

[75] See Mateus & Mateus, n. 66.

[76] This follows from the important insight by Easterbrook that applying more general rules instead of a case-by-case investigation can economize on information and decision costs. See F. Easterbrook, 'Ignorance and Antitrust', in *Antitrust, Innovation and Competitiveness*, ed. T. Jorde & D. Teece (New York: Oxford University Press, 1992), 119–136.

We now introduce a theory of competition enforcement based on the theory of law enforcement in regulation developed by Glaeser and Shleifer[77] to explain the 'rise of regulatory state'. Their theory is based on the theory of torts of Posner and Becker: the goal of social control of torts is to elicit the optimal precaution of damages. Fundamental to the analysis is the introduction of the possibility of subversion and limitations of law enforcement according to the level of development of institutions in the country. There are two levels of precaution: low (Q1) and high (Q2) and two associated probabilities of causing harm P1>P2. In antitrust, precaution means the actions that firms take to prevent antitrust behaviour. Let D be the harm (damage) caused by the practice, C the opportunity cost of the firm by not adopting the anti-competitive practice in state 2, which is zero in state 1. S is a scale variable. There are two types of firms: type A 'good firms' (like small and medium enterprises) and type B 'bad firms', with PA<P1. It is not socially optimal for firm A to invest in precaution. We assume that precaution (not carrying the practice) is socially valuable so (P1-P2)D>C, and that regulation is useful: p>P1, where p is the probability that the regulator learns that firms chose a low level of precaution. This means that it is inexpensive (certain) to detect lack of precaution. We designate by X the payment the firm has to make in order to avoid paying a fine, either in legal fees, lobbying, or political protection. It can also be interpreted as the maximum fine that can be enforced without subversion.

There are three law enforcement rules: (1) Strict liability: in case harm occurs and is detected, then the firm has to pay a fine. Because it uses less information, it requires higher fine; (2) Negligence: harm occurs and the firm took a low level of precaution; (3) Regulation: requires that high level of precaution be taken, if not, the firm pays a low fine, F. It uses a low level of information. The regulator cannot distinguish between type A or B firms. Everybody is going to avoid antitrust if pF>SC, or F>SC/p (minimum fine). Now let us introduce subversion, which is the sum of lobbying costs and 'buying' political protection. This cost is paid after detection but before a fine is finely hand down by a court, without any additional appeal allowed.

Thus, central to this stage theory of enforcement is the fact that higher levels of enforcement require more information and higher fines and those are more subject to extortion. So, enforcement runs a race neck and neck to extortion by vested interests. The next figure summarizes the results in an axis that orders the different regimes for different levels of subversion by vested interests (for PA<P1).

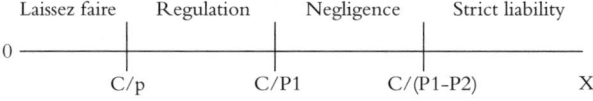

[77] E. Glaeser & A. Schleifer, 'The Rise of the Regulatory State', *Journal of Economic Literature* 41, no. 2 (2003): 401–425.

For high levels of subversion (low level of law enforcement), $pX<CS$, which means that the costs of subversion are lower than the cost of precaution for Q2, then laissez faire is best (in the figure above would be $X<(CS/P)$, with $S=1$, the left segment). For intermediate levels of law enforcement, then regulation (high powered tests, 'bright lines') is best, with lower fines, but general prevention of harm. It requires low levels because it prevents generally antitrust, with a low level of discretion by the law enforcement system. However, it is never efficient because it requires also that type A firms invest in precaution. For higher levels of enforcement, only strict liability or negligence can achieve first best. Strict liability requires high barriers to the subversion of justice (high X) and has no distortions.

Proposition: For each level of institutional development, there is an optimal degree of differentiation in the competition rule that minimizes costs of information and transaction. However, those rules also vary with the level of institutional development. If the level of capture of the government is high, or the costs of subversion of the legal system are low, then there should not be any competition statute. As subversion costs increase and is optimal to introduce a competition statute, individual fines imposed by law and actually enforced have to be higher than per case subversion costs (legal costs, bribing, lobbying costs plus political costs).[78] Negligence is the first best regime when the probability of being detected to violate a more common practice times unit costs of subversion (or fine) is higher than the opportunity cost to the firm (profits lost) restricting competition.[79] Both negligence and strict liability are first best if the unit costs of subversion (or fine) are higher than the opportunity cost to the firm (profits lost) restricting competition, weighted by the cost of an increased level of precaution (P1-P2).

It is easy to see from the proposition that countries that have a low cost of subversion, that is, that have weak institutions, should have a low fine. However, the problem is that a low fine is not dissuasive. The country is caught in a 'law enforcement trap'. Moreover, in general for these countries information costs are high and it is costly for competition authorities or a private firm to make a case, so the best system is to have a simple system of competition rules that can be easily verifiable. As the level of institutional capacity increases, then the country can afford to increase fines (to dissuade unlawful antitrust behaviour) and to impose more sophisticated rules to define damages and causation, which require a higher level of information.

The tragedy is that antitrust instruments can even be used for favouring interest groups and extortion as is evidenced by several cases. Merger control might be used to stop mergers among firms that may reduce the market power of a dominant firm that is part of a vested interest group, but mergers by dominant firms that absorb (predate) smaller ones are authorized. Anti-cartel laws may be used to prosecute agreements among small firms that may pose a threat to the market power of dominant firms. Vertical restraints may block

---

[78] Otherwise, the firm chooses to subvert the system, which is less expensive.
[79] Otherwise, the firm chooses to undertake the restrictive practice. If caught, then it subverts the system and these costs are lower than what it gains from the profit increase due to the practice.

use of franchising or other arrangements that may be a threat to a domestic dominant firm. Glasear and Shleifer[80] refer the case of Russia that introduced an anti-monopoly law and Commission in 1992 to address the problems of industrial consolidation. It is interesting that the oligarchy supported the introduction of regulation but not an anti-monopoly authority. In the beginning, this authority, instead of regulating mergers involving large firms, compiled lists of small firms, like bakeries, arguing that they could abuse their dominant power in local markets. Small firms had sometimes to pay bribes to be lifted of these lists.[81] This is not an isolated case. There are countries with weak institutional development where competition law has been used to block major acquisitions from foreign firms or to protect domestic firms from foreign competition. In others, the law is simply not enforced, like countries where no merger has been effectively blocked, sometimes despite the efforts of the competition authorities. This evidence shows that competition law should only be introduced above a certain level of institutional capacity, as our theory predicts.

Let us now translate the above model from the theory of torts to competition enforcement. We define, similarly, three regimes and indicate the main characteristic of the competition law and enforcement that should fit the regime. However, we should be clear that the same core of competition law should apply everywhere. The core should comprehend prohibition of cartels and monopolization or attempts to monopolize,[82] and also include control of mergers that may have significant impact on social welfare.[83] Merger control should prohibit mergers that impose a substantial lessening of competition. In most of developing countries, there are monopolies in infrastructure sectors, preventing abuses of dominance, regulating prices, and ensuring open access is also essential.

In *Regime I*, there is an environment of weak law and order, so doing nothing is superior to imposing legal and regulatory rules that would only elicit extortion at a higher social cost.[84] The implications for antitrust are quite clear: it is too early to have an antitrust law.[85] What are the alternatives? First, emphasis should be put in building institutions for law and order, and there is no easy substitute for this requirement. Second, governments need to pursue the general policies identified in section 4 in order to build and improve competitive markets.[86] Reduction of tariffs and in particular quantitative restrictions can

---

[80] E. Glaeser & A. Schleifer, 'Legal Origins', *Quarterly Journal of Economics* 117, no. 4 (2002): 1193–1294.

[81] M. Boycko, A. Schleifer & R. Vishny, *Privatizing Russia* (MIT Press, 1995), 54.

[82] Here the most serious practices are exclusionary price and non-price behaviour by dominant firms. Vertical restraints by non-dominant firms may wait for a more sophisticated system.

[83] J. Fingleton et al., 'Competition Policy and the Transformation of Central Europe' (CEPR, 1995), present in Ch. 3 of a proposal for a minimum set of rules for a competition statute.

[84] However, we do not agree with Glaeser and Schleifer that laissez faire reduces extortion, because private groups may organize themselves and impose their own interests (rule of the strongest).

[85] Laffont was one of the first economists to call attention to the fact that a country should have a minimum of development in order to introduce a competition authority. However, reasoning is based on the scarcity of qualified personnel and the superiority of opening up to foreign trade. We have pointed out the limitations of such approach in s. 4. See J. J. Laffont, 'Competition, Information and Development', Annual World Bank Conference on Development Economics, 20–21 Apr. 1998.

[86] The advice of international organizations is also very important, like showing the welfare enhancement impact of trade liberalization.

increase competition in the tradable sector, by subjecting exportables and importables to a higher level of competition from international trade. Another important policy is to eliminate export and import monopolies that sometimes control the most important commodities in developing countries and extract high rents. Sometimes the problem is excessive buyer power.[87] The main result from our model is that contextual competition policies and other policies to build competitive markets are crucial in Regime I and no competition law regime should be introduced before they reach a given level of effectiveness in the country.[88] Finally, international law and international institutions should be used to protect consumers of developing countries from international cartels.

A country should only introduce a competition statute if it is committed to building a competitive market economy. The level of such commitment is given by the policies pursued as defined in section 4, like market development and infrastructure for market integration, openness of the economy to foreign competition, licensing and procurement systems that favour a competitive structure and create a minimum regulatory system. Business environment in terms of entry and exit and contractual laws also need to be in place.[89]

Regime II corresponds to a lower intermediate level of institutional development where the country adopts a simplified system of law enforcement. The country may start by enacting a simplified competition law with low fines to avoid subversion and establish an independent Competition Authority.[90] High-powered incentives, using less detailed information, are best as regulation of competition. One possibility is to use simple 'per se rules' covering the following core areas: (a) prohibition of cartels and (b) prohibition of refusals to supply by large firms, especially essential facilities.[91] Simultaneously, 'bright lines' for merger control should be established: high levels of turnover for merger notification and prohibition of mergers above a set of extreme criteria.[92,93] 'Safe harbour rules' like legality of distribution agreements when 'market share in the relevant market is below 30%' or no existence of dominance if 'market share in the relevant market is below 30%' may be crude but facilitate enforcement.

---

[87] In fact, we have witnessed lately the concentration in the distribution of the final goods (e.g., chocolate or coffee) and manufacturing in developed countries, leaving an ever lower value added in the production chain mainly to farmers in developing countries that are dispersed, confronting high transaction costs and costs of infrastructure. See the case study on cocoa beans in Part C in H. Qaqaya & G. Lipimile (eds), *The Effects of Anti-Competitive Business Practices on Developing Countries and Their Prospects for Development* (UNCTAD, 2008).

[88] This condition needs to be included in the criteria defined in the next section regarding institutional development.

[89] More details on the rule of law will be studied in s. 6.

[90] Sometimes governments are reluctant to delegate the required level of regulatory power to an independent authority. In that case, a compromise may be to set up a competition department in the ministry of economy.

[91] This is an area with very few consensus among jurists and economists. See E. Fox, *Economic Development, Poverty and Antitrust*, SW J. Law and Trade in Americas (2007): 211 and P. Rey, 'Competition Policy and Economic Development, Mimeo' (1997) that address some of these issues. Rey defends that vertical restraints have a higher anti-competitive power in developing countries and capital market imperfections should also lead to a tougher approach to vertical mergers.

[92] This criteria should depend on the market structures of the country and what are the major concerns about monopolization.

[93] Major political pressure always appears in the case of large mergers, concerning vested interests. Those rules would prevent firms to propose those mergers (or acquisitions) or reduce that pressure on authorities.

On broader competition policy issues, the country should also establish a competitive system for procurement with clear rules, supervised by a National Auditing Court. In addition, based on the historical experience of the United States in the Progressive Era, other regulatory legal systems are important for consumer protection. More important than antitrust and probably easier to implement is regulation of natural monopolies with high-powered incentives (for example a price cap is preferable to cost-based systems), as well as imposing interoperability and open access to infrastructures in basic infrastructures: telecommunications, electricity, gas, water, and transportation. Price regulation should avoid high infrastructure service prices. It is also very important to introduce regulation of the financial sector to avoid systemic problems like supervision of depository institutions, insurance, and capital markets.[94]

Once the country has climbed up in the institutional development ladder to an upper middle level, it enters into the first window of *Regime III* where it can attempt to resolve more disputes based on private litigation. The antitrust regime should, first of all, raise the amount of the fines up to an intermediate level. Leniency programmes can start to play an important role.[95] Second, some of the simpler 'per se' rules should give away to more sophisticated 'rules of reason' in a number of clauses of the competition law. However, basic principles like 'per se' prohibition of cartels and refusals of access to essential infra-structures should still be prohibited. However, 'structured rules of reason' for predatory practices using prices[96] or non-price vertical restraints practiced by dominant firms should be introduced. The merger control regime should move towards the principle of 'lessening the competition' but still with some 'bright lines' like per se prohibition in extreme cases of concentration.

Finally, we arrive at the last window of Regime III, where the country has strength-ened institutions in such a way that the political, administrative, and judicial systems are largely immune to extortions. In this case, the country can introduce a mix of private litigation and administrative rule as the main instrument of law enforcement, with high fines for dissuading anti-competitive behaviour. As the competition regime, and competi-tion culture, becomes more widely accepted in society, it is then time to introduce criminal sanctions.[97] In this regime, the economy can reap all the benefits of modern competition law enforcement. If it does not have an independent Competition Authority, with

---

[94] Sometimes governments are tempted to introduce price regulation in any monopoly or quasi-monopoly markets. This is not a policy consistent with the functioning of a market economy. Except for cases of natural monopoly studied above, a superior policy would be to break up the monopoly like in the first stages of the Sherman Act.

[95] Leniency programmes are only effective when participants in the cartel have a benefit of avoiding the fine that compensates the cost of losing the cartel profits times the probability of getting caught. Only with the increase in fines (upheld by courts) and the increase in the probability of getting caught, which depends on the effectiveness of the enforcement system, it becomes effective. There is a kind of vicious circle.

[96] For example, in the case of predatory pricing, a simplified rule of exclusion, sacrifice, and recoupment should be established. Fidelity rebates and exclusivity clauses, like the black clauses in EU law, may be incorporated into the competition law of the country. For non-price exclusionary behaviour, it may be more difficult to define these rules.

[97] When criminal sanctions are introduced too early, it can paralyse the judicial system. Courts are not yet fully knowledgeable about evidence and due process in competition law and tend to apply penal procedures from criminal law, making it difficult to enforce competition law. In fact, according to our model, since criminal sanctions are considered harsher than fines, they should be introduced only in countries with high-quality institutions.

appropriate human resources and a major profile among regulatory institutions, should do so. The Competition Authority should be entrusted with prosecuting violations under administrative law, like the Federal Trade Commission (FTC) or Department of Justice (DoJ) in the United States or the Office of Fair Trading and Competition Commission in the UK.[98] It should entrust it with enough investigative powers and set high fines, enforcing them in real cases, when practices violate the law. The model of law to follow, at this high level of institutional development, will necessarily draw on the standard antitrust law of the United States and EU.

The best regime, for countries with this higher level of rule of law, is to combine administrative and litigation systems. Private enforcement is also essential to redress damages between parties and to make antitrust more 'democratic' and understood by citizens.

6.   INSTITUTIONAL DEVELOPMENT AND CRITERIA FOR ESTABLISHING
     REGIMES OF COMPETITION ENFORCEMENT

What is the social infrastructure required to have a competition law? What are the levels of institutional development required to graduate a country for each of the three regimes presented above? Those are questions of major importance in designing a competition law regime, but they cannot be answered in abstract and need a clinical analysis of each country. However, we can identify certain dimensions and scales in order to assess the country. This is the task of this section. We certainly have to take as granted that we are in a reasonably working market economy. If the dominant economic ideology of the government is socialist or corporatist, it is not even possible to discuss the introduction of a competition policy.

The social infrastructure required to have a regime of competition law involves the following dimensions:

> (i)   State and political system with a minimum functioning democratic regime, with a separation of powers and checks and balances among the three branches of the State, periodic general elections with political parties representing the spectrum of society and government with minimum quality. We distinguish three sub-dimensions:
>
> (1)   State subject to checks and balances.
> (2)   Government policies that take into consideration social welfare and not be dominated by vested interests.
> (3)   Political stability and peace and order. Otherwise it is not even possible to conduct orderly economic activity.
>
> (ii) Public administration and regulatory system with a minimum of efficiency, control (non-discretionary) and not with a high level of corruption. This is

---

[98] There are a number of efficiency reasons for having a unified competition authority subject to control by a specialized court, like Spain and France. This is also the model of the European Commission.

required for the business environment to operate in terms of licensing, taxes, and subsidies. Bureaucratic interferences and control of business activity should be fair and in the conduct of public interest.

(iii)   Rule of law establishing the following institutions:

(1)   Protection of property rights. Required for a firm to operate in a market economy

(2)   Contractual enforcement. All transactions in the market are based on formal or informal contracts.

(3)   Judicial system with a minimum level of efficiency and being able to enforce (i) and (ii) with a minimum of predictability and in a timely process, respecting the due process. Obviously, the judicial system has to be complemented by a police and sanction system that is able to sustain order and carry out decisions of the judicial system.

The first dimension of the social infrastructure is a general requisite for the functioning of a society and the basic system for the economy. A stable and peaceful environment is essential for the functioning of the economy. Although a democratic regime may not be a sine qua non for development, we think that the exceptions only confirm the rule that a democracy with the three branches of government and checks and balances among them are the basis of a well-functioning market economy with rule of law. It would be difficult to implement the other two dimensions of the social infrastructure without this constitutional basis on a sustainable basis.

Since antitrust law enforcement is only a part, and sometimes a small part, of the economic law and also embedded in the regulatory framework, it requires a minimum of efficiency of public administration and regulatory quality. One part of the law is usually enforced through administrative bodies and law, so it is intrinsically part of the public administration. The other major role is played by courts that control decisions of these administrative bodies and also by private litigation, so the judicial system also plays a major part of law enforcement.

Besides the judicial system, the institutions of rule of law that are central to the enforcement of competition law are property rights that are the foundation of a market economy and contract enforcement that encompass formally or informally the majority of transactions.

No regime of antitrust can be enforced without the involvement of the judicial system. Even decisions adopted by the competition authority are subjected to control and appeal by courts. In addition, private litigation takes place in the court system. So, the most important institution for the functioning of the antitrust system is the type of judicial system. What criteria of development of the judicial system should be taken into account? The literature is still quite scarce.[99] An efficient

---

[99] See M. Trebilcock & R. Daniels, *Rule of Law Reform and Development Charting the Fragile Path of Progress* (Edward Elgar, 2008).

judicial system is the set of laws, procedures, and courts that delivers justice to citizens in a cost-effective and timely manner. Djankov et al.[100] are among the economists to have studied the traits of judicial systems, but they do not touch on the question of outcomes and characteristics in the broader view that we require. In a survey conducted in 130 countries, the authors study two types of cases: evicting a tenant and check collection. Based on the answers to the survey, they build an index of formalism. One of the conclusions is that an increased rate of formalism leads to a lengthier process but not necessarily to a better outcome (as perceived by survey respondents). Common law and Scandinavian law systems are more efficient in eviction and the German system in enforcement of credit contracts. The civil law system is always the less efficient. Another interesting conclusion is that legal structure and not the level of development shapes judicial efficiency and that 'bright lines' are more important when the judicial systems are weak and inefficient. Finally, because of the legal transplants that are so common nowadays, they caution that transplanting a given law system of a developed country to a country with weak institutional development (with 'bad government') may lead to an inefficient judicial system.

We finally proceed to build an Index of Institutional Development required to identify the regime for the competition law structure and enforcement. Given the three dimensions of the social infrastructure identified above, we look for indicators in the large number of surveys already available under the Governance Project at the World Bank. To measure the level of government capture by corporations, we take the Corporate Ethics Index[101] built by Daniel Kaufman and his collaborators, which is an average of the corporate legal and illegal corruption indexes. Still included in the first dimension of the social infrastructure, we include the Voice and Accountability Index of the Governance Matters database of the World Bank. The level of efficiency of the public administration is measured by an overall index of Control of Corruption. In addition, the rule of law is measured by the Index of Judicial and Legal Effectiveness.

These four indicators are all taken for 2004 and then averaged to build the Index of Institutional Development. All indicators are scaled from 0 to 100% with 0 representing the worst and 100% the best institution.

When plotted against the GDP per capita in Purchasing Power Parities, the Index shows a high and positive correlation, although we do not try to identify any causality.

---

[100] S. Djankov et al., 'Courts', *Quarterly Journal of Economics* 118, no. 2 (2003): 453–517.
[101] Table drawn from Appendix 2 of D. Kaufmann, 'Corruption, Governance and Security: Challenges for the Rich Countries and the World, Global Competitiveness Report 2004/2005', <www.worldbank.org/wbi/governance/pubs/gcr2004.html>, September 2004.

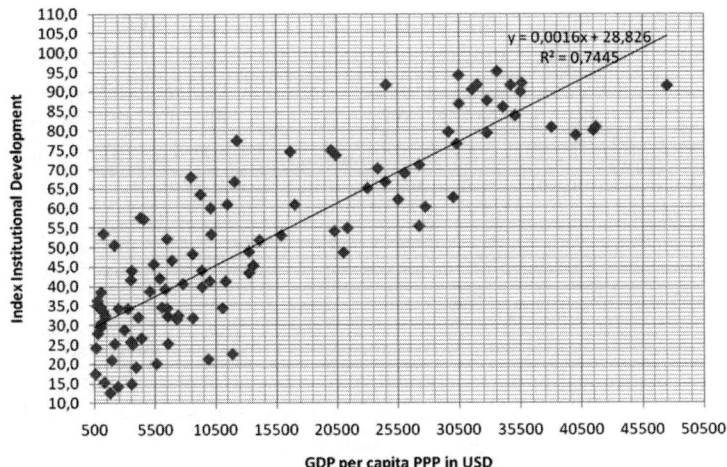

Source: Author's computations. GDP per capita for 2005 from World Bank, Main Economic Indicators.

Ideally, we should use this Index to establish the regime of competition law and enforcement. However, it is not an easy task since we do not have clusters of countries well specified. Thus, we need to use information about specific countries to define the cut-off points for each regime. These should be complemented in practice with a detailed clinical analysis of each country.[102]

The first group of countries, which corresponds to a full developed system of antitrust, is a large part of the countries of the EU, as well as most of the Organization for Economic Cooperation and development (OECD) countries. They are all high-income countries and have a GDP per capita above USD 20,000, except for Estonia, Chile, Botswana, and South Africa that have a lower income per capita but higher institutional development indices.

At the other end of the scale are the countries in Regime I that do not have the institutional level of development appropriate for an antitrust regime. Several EU countries are in Regime III but not in the highest level like Lithuania, Slovak Republic, Czech Republic, Italy, and Greece. Further down are Romania and Bulgaria.

Notice that countries like Indonesia, Egypt, and Peru do not have the institutional development level yet, according to the above indicator, to adopt a fully blown regime of antitrust. In fact, among about hundred countries that have considered or already have a competition law, there are about forty that still belong to Regime I or are in transition to Regime II.

---

[102] In future research, we are planning to also use indicators relative to s. 4 like the level of opening of the economy and dimension of the market economy for defining the context in which competition law regimes operate.

One final remark, Glaeser and Shleifer[103] also draw important conclusions in terms of social policies in developing countries, in particular the importance of promoting a more equal income and wealth distribution. They point out that economic inequality exacerbates the problem of 'inequality of weapons', which has been central to the discussions of legal design. They also point out that growth in inequality, as observed in Russia in the 1990s is accompanied by deterioration of institutions, raising political demand for reform in order to improve law and order.

7. CONCLUSIONS

We start by surveying several studies that show the importance of competition to development at the theoretical and empirical levels, with particular emphasis to developing countries. The causal link that competition is essential for development and that higher competition leads to a higher level and growth rate of GDP is by now reasonably established, at least in theoretical terms. We then turn to the political economy models of development and show that development can be trapped by vested interests through a set of policy instruments that attribute rents to those small groups, distort growth, and may desincentivize investment and innovation.

In order to lay the foundation of any competition law regime, several policies need to be implemented to build a competitive market economy. One important insight is that in most developing countries markets either do not exist, they are fragmented and lack integration. Building physical, informational, and transactional infrastructures to make those markets operate efficiently is the priority. Other important policies are external trade and investment policies to open the economy to foreign competition and integrate the national economy in larger global markets. Procurement, privatization, licensing, and industrial policies are also particularly important in shaping the competitive structure of the markets, most of the times a requisite for the appearance of antitrust in order to sanction behaviour ex post.

If the country is committed to a competitive market structure, then it is ready to establish a competition law regime, given its institutional level of development. The rest of this article presents a decision theory with law enforcement model in order to define a sequence of policy regimes for antitrust laws. In order to operationalize those regimes, we have to define the institutional level of development that is coherent with those regimes. By building an Institutional Development Index based on (i) the level of democracy and checks and balances in the political system, (ii) the efficiency of public administration and regulation, and (iii) rule of law, we show the importance of these institutional aspects for choosing the law enforcement regime.

---

[103] See n. 71.

The issues raised in this article, in the interface between development and law and economics, are certainly among some of the most important aspects for building a fully functional market economy. They clearly show that 'one rule fits all' in competition law and enforcement is not appropriate. We hope that our contribution establishes a research agenda for improving competition regimes around the world and contribute to shed light on some important issues in world competition.

Part III
International Architecture

[10]

Competition policy, economic development and the possible role of a multilateral framework on competition policy: insights from the WTO working group on trade and competition policy

Robert Anderson and Frédéric Jenny

INTRODUCTION

The relationship between competition policy and economic development has been a central theme in the work of the World Trade Organisation's Working Group on the Interaction between Trade and Competition Policy and of related technical assistance activities undertaken by the WTO Secretariat over the past several years. This work has identified a number of ways in which anticompetitive practices of firms can impede economic development, and in which national competition policies that are appropriately adapted to the circumstances of developing countries can support development. These findings are independent of questions regarding the pros and cons of a possible WTO agreement on competition policy, which has also been extensively discussed in the working group but on which a consensus has been lacking.

This chapter examines the links between competition policy, development and trade liberalisation. It begins with a review of the role and importance of competition policy and its relationship to economic reform in developing countries. Account is also taken of the role of such policy in addressing international anticompetitive practices. The chapter outlines some of the arguments that have been put forward in the WTO working group regarding the potential benefits for developing countries of a WTO framework on competition policy. It also outlines the principal elements that have been proposed for inclusion should negotiations on such a framework be launched, which has now been ruled out for the duration of the Doha Round (see discussion below). The purpose is not to defend or advocate a particular approach toward future WTO work (if any) on trade and competition policy, but to facilitate informed discussion in the international community.

The central theme of this chapter is the fundamental complementarity of competition policy, trade liberalisation and domestic economic reform, and their importance for development. In debates on development, poverty alleviation and the WTO, it is sometimes argued that a WTO initiative on competition policy would deplete scarce human and institutional resources that would be

62 *Robert Anderson and Frédéric Jenny*

better applied in the pursuit of external liberalisation (see, e.g., Winters 2002). This reflects a false dichotomy. As important as external liberalisation is, it is unlikely to achieve its objectives absent internal market reforms to facilitate an appropriate supply-side response. Furthermore, absent effective competition policies, the economic welfare gains expected to materialise from the reduction of government-imposed barriers to trade can be undercut by the operation of international anticompetitive practices such as cartels. Ample evidence now exists that such cartels are a recurring feature of markets that lack effective competition rules and institutions, and that appropriate enforcement actions by developed countries, while of vital importance, do not adequately protect the interests of developing countries in this area.

In addition to addressing the above concerns, competition policy can itself contribute to continuing external liberalisation, through the advocacy activities of competition agencies. In particular, competition agencies can become an important source of analytical support for continuing market-oriented reforms, both internal and external. For these reasons, appropriate investments in national competition policies are more likely to contribute to than detract from external liberalisation efforts. Nonetheless, in order to be effective, it is important that competition law and institutions are adapted to national economic circumstances and institutional constraints.

The possible role and content of a WTO agreement in this area has been widely misunderstood, including in learned journals and by otherwise well-informed authors. For example, in the run-up to the 2004 Cancun Ministerial, an article in *Foreign Affairs* (Evans 2002) reiterated the concern that WTO rules on competition policy 'could be administered through a supranational agency', notwithstanding that this possibility figured nowhere in any of the recent or earlier proposals that have been made in the context of the WTO and has been explicitly disavowed by the proponents of WTO negotiations on various occasions (see, e.g., Garcia-Bercero and Amarasinha 2001). Also, extensive references were made to the possibility of a WTO antitrust code – implying a comprehensive set of substantive rules. As elaborated below, the proposals for a WTO agreement in this area indicate that any such agreement (if negotiations were eventually to be launched) is likely to be a good deal more modest in its content and aspirations. In particular, such an agreement would likely focus on the promotion of voluntary cooperation and technical assistance, in addition to modest commitments to action against hardcore cartels and to adherence to core principles of transparency, non-discrimination and procedural fairness that are widely recognised as being central to the effective implementation of competition policy.[1] It would not involve the harmonisation of competition laws, where this term is understood as implying the enforcement of uniform approaches to competition policy at the national level (Garcia-Bercero and Amarasinha 2001).

This chapter discusses the role of competition policy in developing countries, drawing on, among other sources, work completed in the WTO Working Group on the Interaction between Trade and Competition Policy, and considers the domestic and international applications of competition law in addition to the advocacy function of competition institutions. Some of the arguments that have been made in favour of action on competition policy in the framework of the WTO are discussed, in addition to the major reservation that has been voiced by developing countries with regard to a possible WTO agreement in this area – namely, the concern that such an agreement would limit their policy options and development strategies. To carry the discussion forward, some key aspects of the recent proposals for a multilateral framework on competition policy are outlined.

THE RELEVANCE OF COMPETITION POLICY FOR DEVELOPING ECONOMIES

Competition law and/or policy[2] is important to protect consumers and industrial users from anticompetitive practices that raise prices and reduce output. This is no less true in developing countries than in developed ones. In fact, there are reasons for believing that less mature markets tend to be more, rather than less, vulnerable to anticompetitive practices. The reasons include: (a) high 'natural' entry barriers due to inadequate business infrastructure, including distribution channels, and (sometimes) intrusive regulatory regimes; (b) asymmetries of information in both product and credit markets; and (c) a greater proportion of local (non-tradable) markets. For these reasons, consumers in developing countries are more vulnerable to anticompetitive practices and have a particularly compelling need to be protected against cartels, monopoly abuses and the creation of new monopolies through mergers. The competition agency can also play a useful role in making the case for related policy and legal reforms (e.g., property rights, contract enforcement and corporate governance) that are necessary to create a healthy market economy (see, for useful elaboration, Dutz 2002).

A specific role of competition policy which may be of particular importance in developing countries (although it is important in all economies) relates to the prevention of bid rigging in public procurement processes. Empirical evidence suggests that the costs of bid rigging to public treasuries substantially exceed the costs of establishing a competition office to investigate and deter such activities (see discussion and references cited below). The possibility of rigged bids cannot be prevented merely by opening procurement processes to foreign competitors, since the latter may be party to any bid-rigging conspiracies (see, e.g., US Department of Justice 2000).

The argument is sometimes made that competition policy is irrelevant in circumstances of extreme poverty. However, where incomes are severely limited, it would seem even more important than otherwise that the purchasing power of consumers not be further diminished through anticompetitive practices. There is growing evidence that anticompetitive practices are particularly prevalent in regard to goods for which there are limited substitutes available in developing country markets, for example foodstuffs. Many of the major international cartels disclosed in the mid- to late 1990s were believed to have been active in developing country markets, for example those relating to the sale of vitamins, lysine and citric acid, all important inputs to agrifood production (Levenstein and Suslow 2001; Evenett et al. 2001; Jenny 2001; Anderson and Holmes 2002). Similarly, the effective prevention of bid rigging would seem to be particularly important where, as in many developing countries, governments are subject to severe fiscal constraints.

Fortunately, the evidence is also growing that, with appropriate resources and training, developing countries can take steps to deal effectively with anticompetitive practices that affect their consumers. A recent comparative study of the role of competition policy in Africa and South Asia initiated by the Consumer Unity and Trust Society with participation from numerous outside researchers found important parallels between the experiences of developing and transition economies (Consumer Unity and Trust Society 2003). The countries studied were India, Sri Lanka, Pakistan, Zambia, Kenya, Tanzania and South Africa, all of which have taken steps to reduce protectionism, reliance on state-owned enterprises and bureaucratic control of the private sector, and have seen fit to implement competition laws in one form or another. In addition, in a few cases, advanced developing countries such as Mexico, Brazil and Korea have initiated successful enforcement actions in relation to international cartels (Working Group on the Interaction between Trade and Competition Policy 2003a; Hur 2002; Mexico 2002). Moreover, evidence regarding the implementation of competition policy as tool of economic transformation in Central and Eastern Europe suggests that in the majority of countries in that region competition law provisions (in particular, provisions relating to abuses of a dominant position) have not, contrary to concerns expressed by some Western analysts at the time the laws were enacted, been overused or used in ways that are counterproductive (see Pittman 2004).

Work in the WTO working group in addition to other venues has highlighted the need for a pragmatic approach to the introduction of competition policies in developing countries, focusing on the most blatantly harmful practices and avoiding overly elaborate institutional structures. The inappropriateness of a one-size-fits-all approach and the necessity of adapting competition policy to the economic circumstances and institutional endowments of individual countries have been repeatedly stressed, including by the proponents of a WTO agreement in this area (WTO Working Group on the Interaction between Trade and Competition Policy 2001, paragraph 15; WTO Working Group on the Interaction between Trade and Competition Policy 2003b, paragraph 16). Under one possible approach discussed in the working group, a national competition authority would first focus on the suppression of horizontal cartels (the most unambiguously harmful type of enterprise practice) and on basic competition advocacy activities relating to essential market reforms. After gaining adequate experience in these areas, it would then take on additional responsibilities for matters such as merger review and anticompetitive vertical restraints. In the last stage, it would take on more sweeping responsibilities for competition advocacy activities relating to all aspects of the interplay between competition policy and regulation (WTO Working Group on the Interaction between Trade and Competition Policy 1998, paragraph 51). Noteworthy here are both the non-insistence on immediate adoption of comprehensive competition laws and the emphasis placed on the advocacy function (for elaboration, see below).

Facilitating a supply-side response to trade liberalisation and reinforcing domestic reforms

As Osakwe (2001) emphasises, in many cases failures of trade liberalisation to generate sustained development and growth can be traced to a failure to introduce complementary domestic policy reforms. In most cases, countries will not be well poised to take advantage of the potential benefits of trade liberalisation unless they simultaneously take steps to reduce costs and enhance the efficiency of infrastructure sectors such as telecommunications and transportation; to promote flexibility by eliminating artificial restrictions on entry, exit and pricing in manufacturing and other industries; and to establish and strengthen incentives for investment, innovation, the creation of efficient management structures and productivity improvement. Competition policy has a role to play in all of these areas. A failure to implement competition policy and related reforms will prevent countries from realising the potential gains from external liberalisation, by inhibiting an appropriate supply response (see also Krueger 1984).

The point has also been made in the WTO Working Group on the Interaction between Trade and Competition Policy that the implementation of a transparent and effective competition policy can be an important factor both in enhancing the attractiveness of an economy to foreign investment and in maximising the benefits of such investment. Competition policy can make an economy attractive to foreign investors by providing a transparent dispute-settlement mechanism that is consistent with international norms. Vigorous competition in markets, reinforced by competition policy, encourages foreign firms to construct state-of-the-art production facilities in host countries, transfer modern technology and undertake training programs, and also prevents the exploitation of consumers. These effects may be particularly important in developing countries, in view of the crucial importance of technology transfer to economic development (WTO Working Group on the Interaction between Trade and Competition Policy 1998).

In the WTO working group, the point has also been stressed that competition policy can reinforce, and may be essential to realising, the potential benefits of privatisation programs and initiatives. The argument here is that, unless appropriate measures are taken to prevent the continuation and/or re-establishment of monopolistic market structures, privatisation will not result in any fundamental change in the incentives facing firms that will improve their behaviour and performance. Supporting the importance of this concern, there

66   *Robert Anderson and Frédéric Jenny*

has been a frank acknowledgement in the working group that, in many cases, privatisation and deregulation in the developing world have failed to deliver their vaunted benefits owing precisely to a failure to engage in procompetitive restructuring and related market reforms (WTO Working Group on the Interaction between Trade and Competition Policy 1998).

The advocacy function of competition agencies

Apart from the potential benefits for developing countries of appropriate competition law enforcement activities, discussions in the WTO Working Group on the Interaction between Trade and Competition Policy and other relevant forums such as the OECD Global Forum on Competition Policy and the UNCTAD Expert Group on Competition Law and Policy have also called attention to the importance of the advocacy activities of competition agencies, particularly in regard to the implementation of procompetitive regulatory reforms. Such activities may include public education activities, studies and research undertaken to document the need for market-opening measures, formal appearances before legislative committees or other government bodies in public proceedings, or behind-the-scenes lobbying within government. These, it has been suggested in the working group, may be among the most useful and high-payoff activities undertaken by competition agencies (WTO Working Group on the Interaction between Trade and Competition Policy 1998, paragraphs 34 and 229).

A particularly important focus of competition advocacy activities is in relation to regulation. To be sure, in both developed and developing economies, regulation can serve valid efficiency-related public purposes. For example, it is well established that regulation can be an efficient response to market failures such as imperfect information, the existence of a natural monopoly (a situation in which a market is most efficiently supplied by a single firm) and other such problems. Nonetheless, it is important to recognise that, notwithstanding its avowed aims, regulation often thwarts rather than promotes efficiency and economic welfare. This is likely to be the case, for example, where it imposes restrictions on entry, exit and/or pricing in non-natural monopoly industries. Experience in both developed and developing countries shows that, in many cases, rather than having regulation imposed on them for the public benefit, incumbent firms have sought regulation for their own benefit, for the purpose of limiting entry into the industry and helping them to enjoy higher prices for their products (the classic diagnoses of this problem are presented in Stigler 1971 and Jordan 1972). Recognition of the significance of such conduct as a barrier to economic development dates back at least to Krueger (1974), and is affirmed in recent analyses by the World Bank and other development-related agencies (see, e.g., World Bank 1997; UNCTAD 1998). In the light of this, efforts to remove inefficient regulatory restrictions and related interventions are central to the establishment of healthy market economies in developing and transition economies (World Bank 1997; World Bank 2000; Frischtak 1995).

In the discussion in the WTO Working Group on the Interaction between Trade and Competition Policy, important links have been made between competition advocacy, successful efforts at regulatory reform and external trade liberalisation. The following examples of regulatory situations having adverse effects on competition and trade have been noted: outmoded or unnecessary regulations; a failure by countries to recognise each others' technical standards; state zoning laws or sanitary and phytosanitary requirements that limit entry unnecessarily or serve as disguised tools for excluding competing suppliers; legal systems that facilitate strategic use of courts by firms to harass competitors; and discriminatory research and development funding. The following additional categories of regulation have been mentioned as warranting appropriate reforms: regulations that openly discriminate in favour of domestic suppliers; regulations that are non-discriminatory on the surface but subtly discriminatory in their substantive requirements; regulations that simply are no longer needed; and poorly designed regulations that are desirable in principle but unnecessarily intrusive. The potential contribution of competition advocacy in addressing these measures has been emphasised (WTO Working Group on the Interaction between Trade and Competition Policy 1998, paragraphs 110 and 111).

The foregoing clearly points to the important contribution that competition advocacy activities can make to both the internal efficiency of markets and to trade liberalisation. As noted, competition agencies in both the developed and (in some cases) the developing world attach high priority to such activities which aim at minimising unnecessary regulatory intervention and ensuring that, where it is used, regulation serves genuinely procompetitive purposes (for the experience of Canada, see Anderson et al. 1998). In doing so, the agencies advance goals that are closely related to those of international trade liberalisation – a further and little-noted but important example of why the proliferation of strong competition agencies is in the broad interest of the multilateral trading system (see also Anderson and Holmes 2002).

THE ROLE OF COMPETITION POLICY IN ADDRESSING INTERNATIONAL ANTICOMPETITIVE PRACTICES

In the 1990s, extensive evidence surfaced that international cartels are alive and flourishing in the 'globalising' economic environment. Investigations conducted by the US Department of Justice, the European Commission, the Canadian Competition Bureau and authorities in other jurisdictions revealed the existence of major cartels in (to cite but a few of many examples) the following industries: graphite electrodes (an essential input to steel mini-mill production); bromine (a flame retardant and fumigant); citric acid (a major industrial food additive); lysine (an agricultural feed additive); seamless steel pipes (an input to oil production); and vitamins (for details, see Levenstein and Suslow 2001). In many such cases, the cartels are known to have operated extensively throughout the developing world, substantially raising the costs of developing

68   *Robert Anderson and Frédéric Jenny*

countries' imports of the affected products (Levenstein and Suslow 2001; Evenett et al. 2001; Anderson and Holmes 2002; Jenny 2003).

The costs imposed by such cartels on the world economy, and specifically on developing countries, have been shown to be in the multi-billions of dollars annually. Levenstein and Suslow (2001) note that many examples of international cartels involve firms headquartered in the developed world with substantial exports to developing countries. Looking at sixteen 'cartelised' products, they note that:

> Examining these sixteen products – which were cartelised at some point during the 1990s and for which we were able to obtain reasonably reliable trade data – the total value of such 'cartel-affected' imports to developing countries was $81.1 billion. This made up 6.7% of all imports to developing countries. It is equal to 1.2% of their combined GDP.

The price impact of cartels supplying these products appears to have been in the range of 20–30 per cent on average – implying a total overpayment by developing countries for their imports of something in the order of US$10–24 billion annually in respect of these cases alone. It is also noteworthy that in many or perhaps most cases, the immediate impact of cartels is on other firms using the products as industrial inputs. This underscores the detrimental impact of cartels on the development prospects of poor countries.

The available evidence suggests that the benefits for developing countries of the implementation of effective measures to tackle international hardcore cartels may exceed the welfare gains for these countries from agricultural liberalisation. An article in the September 2002 edition of the IMF's *World Economic Outlook* suggests that the increase in the welfare of developing countries that would result from a 50 per cent liberalisation of the agricultural policies of industrialised economies would be approximately US$8 billion per annum (International Monetary Fund 2002). While this is unquestionably a significant gain, it is less than the above-noted costs imposed on developing economies by international cartels – implying that the gains from the implementation of effective competition regimes and related cooperation arrangements to tackle the operations of such cartels in developing countries could be even greater (see, for related discussion and additional supporting references, WTO Working Group on the Interaction between Trade and Competition Policy 2003a).

International cartels are not only more numerous and durable, but also impair the process of development in developing countries more significantly than has previously been thought. This is true for at least three reasons (Jenny 2001):

1) In the early stages of their industrialisation, and given their narrow domestic industrial base, developing countries have to rely on imports. To the extent that such imports are subject to anticompetitive practices either by domestic

firms (e.g., an import cartel) or by foreign suppliers of these imports (e.g., an export or international cartel), the importing country will be penalised by higher-than-necessary import prices.

2) To achieve economic development, and in view of the fact that narrowly based domestic markets lead them to rely on export markets, developing countries will be penalised by international cartels, or by import cartels, and by abuses of dominant positions in the countries of export.

3) Foreign firms are more likely to engage in across-the-border anticompetitive behaviour when the countries to which they export do not have a domestic competition law and can neither individually nor through cooperation with foreign competition authorities challenge the firms' market behaviour. Thus, countries that do not have a domestic competition law will be the prime victims of transnational anticompetitive practices.

The implications of international cartels for the gains from trade are also clear: to the extent that they raise prices and reduce output in transnational markets and, in some cases, limit cross-trading by one country's suppliers into markets assigned to other countries' suppliers, they directly inhibit realisation of the gains that should accrue to participating countries. This is not to suggest that the international trading system should itself carry the primary responsibility for investigating and prosecuting cartels – clearly, this will continue to be done primarily at the national level and through the work of specialised agencies – but that ensuring that measures are in place to deal appropriately with such arrangements is a legitimate concern of the system (Anderson and Holmes 2002). Over time a failure to respond adequately to the costs imposed by international cartels on developing countries is likely to subvert confidence in the market economy on the part of the citizens of such countries (Jenny 2003).

To be sure, international cartels are not the only example of anticompetitive practices with an international dimension that can have an impact on trade and development. Access to markets by foreign suppliers can be directly undermined by exclusionary vertical market restraints (contractual linkages between manufacturers and their suppliers or distributors), import cartels and other forms of anticompetitive conduct (Wolff 1994). The empirical significance of such practices and the appropriate policy response have been much debated in relevant literature and official proceedings. In its comprehensive 2000 assessment of the available evidence and commentaries on this issue, the US International Competition Policy Advisory Committee concluded that, although uneven, the record is sufficient to show that private, governmental and mixed public–private restraints that inhibit market access are a problem worthy of the attention of policymakers in both national and international contexts (US International Competition Policy Advisory Committee 2000; see also Marsden 2003 for useful commentary on this issue).[3]

70   *Robert Anderson and Frédéric Jenny*

Competition policy, dynamic efficiency and the 'policy space' available to developing countries

An important consideration in discussions on the importance of competition policy for economic development in the WTO working group has been the implications of such policy for dynamic as opposed to static efficiency. The point has been made that dynamic efficiency gains are likely to be even more important for development than static efficiency considerations. Developing country representatives have expressed concerns that conventional approaches to competition policy may undervalue or possibly even represent an obstacle to the realisation of dynamic efficiency gains (WTO Working Group on the Interaction between Trade and Competition Policy 2001, 2002b; Singh 1999, 2002).

In response, the point has been made that modern approaches to competition policy are by no means concerned only with the achievement of static efficiency; rather, dynamic efficiency is increasingly an explicit goal of such policy.[4] Indeed, much attention has been given in recent years to appropriate ways of supporting and factoring dynamic efficiency gains into competition policy analysis (see, e.g., Gilbert and Sunshine 1995; Gilbert and Tom 2001; Anderson and Gallini 1998). The consensus among scholars is that this has not involved a radical realignment of competition policy principles; rather, it has been a question of adapting well-founded principles to the subject matter of the 'new economy' (see, e.g., Posner 2001). On the whole, competition and competition policy are more likely to contribute to than detract from the attainment of dynamic efficiency gains and other developmental objectives, in that inter-firm rivalry provides a key incentive for firms to lower their costs; to provide better service and expanded choices for consumers; and to innovate and/or adopt the best available technologies (WTO Working Group on the Interaction between Trade and Competition Policy 2003b, paragraph 67). As one particular dimension of its role in promoting dynamic efficiency, competition policy in many jurisdictions is employed to ensure that intellectual property rights are used in ways that support rather than restrict innovation and technology transfer (US Federal Trade Commission 2003; Anderson and Gallini 1998; Anderson 2002).

A closely related argument has been that, even recognising that competition is one important determinant of dynamic efficiency, it is by no means the only determinant, perhaps particularly in the context of developing countries (Singh 1999, 2002). In pursuing development, developing countries may need to have access to a range of tools, possibly including sectoral initiatives and forms of intervention that are at variance with competition policy tools and objectives. In this regard, it is important that their 'policy space' not be unduly restricted (WTO Working Group on the Interaction between Trade and Competition Policy 2001, 2002b).

In responding to this concern, the point has been made that the efficacy of sectoral initiatives and interventions such as the promotion of national champions is a matter of debate. Interventions by relevant WTO members in the working group and related scholarly analyses suggest that, at least to an extent, the success of the various East Asian economies which have undergone periods of rapid growth and development in recent decades has been despite, rather than because of, efforts to promote national champions and other forms of industrial policy intervention (see WTO Working Group on the Interaction between Trade and Competition Policy 2003a and other studies referenced therein). Nonetheless, it has been acknowledged that all governments have employed such measures from time to time and it is understandable that developing countries would not wish their recourse to such tools to be restricted. In this regard, a study prepared for the WTO working group in 2003 identified five ways in which potential conflicts between competition policy and national industrial policy have historically been managed, and the policy space of countries thereby preserved. These are: (1) the use of industrial policy instruments which, even where they tended to restrict competition in markets, are not actionable under the competition laws of most countries (e.g., tariffs, subsidies, training programs and public ownership); (2) the explicit incorporation of goals such as dynamic efficiency gains in national competition laws; (3) the explicit taking into account, by responsible officials, of dynamic as well as static efficiency considerations in the application of national laws; (4) where necessary, the provision for exemptions, exceptions and exclusions from competition law; and (5) allowing for a governmental body to overrule a decision made by the competition enforcement agency in the event that national development priorities might be compromised (WTO Working Group on the Interaction between Trade and Competition Policy 2003a).

The study also found that, by and large, the adoption of a multilateral framework on competition policy along the lines that have been proposed by some WTO members is consistent with and would not jeopardise the ability of members to continue to use these five tools (WTO Working Group on the Interaction between Trade and Competition Policy 2003a, 2003b, paragraph 67). This is not to suggest that such derogations necessarily constitute good policy in all cases, but only that they have been widely used and would continue to be available under the terms of a multilateral framework on competition policy as they have been put forward by the proponents.

Beyond the perceived potential for intrusion on the domestic policy space, developing countries expressed a further concern about the cost of setting up and operating a national competition agency. The 2003 study prepared for the working group suggested, however, that the direct operating costs of national competition agencies in developing countries may be smaller than has been feared and, in any case, pale in comparison to the potential benefits. For example, data assembled by the Consumer Unity and Trust Society indicate that the annual budget of competition enforcement agencies in seven countries, namely India, Kenya, Pakistan, South Africa, Sri Lanka, Tanzania and Zambia, in 2000 was in all cases less than 0.06 per cent of the total budget for the central government – that is, less than one-thousandth of the total government budget

72   *Robert Anderson and Frédéric Jenny*

(in several cases, much less) (Consumer Unity and Trust Society 2003: 54; reprinted in WTO Working Group on the Interaction between Trade and Competition Policy 2003a: 64).[5] Clarke and Evenett (2003:127) estimate that the resource saving that would be generated by only a 1 per cent reduction of bid rigging on government contracts would be greater than the operating budget of the competition agency in these countries, in most cases by a factor of several times over.

Summary: why external liberalisation is not, by itself, sufficient to ensure the efficient functioning of markets

A strong case can be made that the implementation of well-adapted competition policies in developing countries will help to advance development-related goals, both by contributing to and complementing domestic reform processes and by tackling domestic and transnational anticompetitive practices that reduce the welfare of consumers and raise business input costs. With appropriate care, such policies need not restrict countries' access to other tools through which they can promote their development.

In debates on the role of competition policy in the WTO, the argument is sometimes made that competition policy, and especially competition law, may be an inferior instrument for achieving satisfactory economic performance – rather, competition may be more efficiently induced through external market-opening measures such as the reduction of tariffs (Winters 2002; see also Blackhurst 1991). Indeed, the elimination of barriers to international trade and investment can be a powerful instrument in promoting competition and the efficient functioning of markets – there is no disagreement on this point. However, it is a fallacy to conclude from this that competition policy itself is unimportant. The reasons for this follow directly from the foregoing description of the role of competition policy and competition authorities in developing countries.

First, depending on the natural configuration of industries as well as a variety of policy-related factors, markets for many goods and services (particularly the latter) may be largely insulated from external sources of competition. This problem is likely to be particularly prevalent in developing or least-developed countries, due for example to inefficient infrastructure sectors that can impede trade and investment flows.

Second, in many cases, the potential benefits of market-opening measures will not be realised unless countries simultaneously take steps to address anticompetitive practices/structural barriers to development such as private and public monopolies in infrastructure sectors, domestic and international cartels that raise business input costs, and restrictions on entry, exit and pricing in manufacturing and other industries.

Third, experience shows clearly that certain manifestly harmful anticompetitive practices (e.g., international cartels) cannot be remedied by external (or internal) liberalisation alone, where the relevant arrangements cover the main foreign firms in addition to any domestic firms operating in the relevant market(s). Similarly, the possibility of rigged bids cannot be prevented merely by opening procurement processes to foreign competitors (since such competitors may also be party to bid-rigging conspiracies).

Competition law can be important for other reasons as well. For example, in many jurisdictions it is recognised that competition law has a role to play in preventing abusive practices relating to intellectual property rights in the domestic economy. It is unlikely that the mere absence of tariffs, quotas or other traditional trade barriers can suffice to prevent such practices – particularly since patents or copyrights can themselves affect the ability to supply domestic markets through imports.

Finally, the existence of vibrant competition agencies in developing countries can itself be an important factor contributing to the adoption of external and internal market-opening policies, through the agencies' advocacy function. Numerous interventions in the WTO Working Group on the Interaction between Trade and Competition Policy, including by developing country representatives, have stressed the importance of such activities and their contribution to the process of economic reform and development (WTO Working Group on the Interaction between Trade and Competition Policy 1998, paragraphs 36, 45, 51, 53 and 109).

POSSIBLE RATIONALES FOR INTERNATIONAL COMMITMENTS ON COMPETITION POLICY

The subject of international cooperation in the field of competition law and policy is not new. A number of developed countries and a few developing countries are party to bilateral cooperation agreements regarding competition law enforcement. Such agreements have been a key factor in the progressive strengthening of competition law enforcement in various countries over the past two decades, particularly in developed countries (Evenett et al. 2000). Limited cooperation arrangements also feature in a large and growing number of regional trade agreements (World Trade Organisation 1997). The benefits of such arrangements include not only the obtaining of information and sharing of insights relevant to specific investigations but also the resulting learning process for the participating officials (WTO Working Group on the Interaction between Trade and Competition Policy 2002a).

Nonetheless, much evidence suggests that the actual extent of international cooperation in competition law enforcement is less than is optimal in light of what is known about the extent and frequency of anticompetitive practices with an international dimension (see, e.g., Jenny 2002). In this context, a key focus of the exploratory work of the WTO Working Group on the Interaction between Trade and Competition Policy has been on the scope for and potential benefits of new approaches to cooperation in the field of competition law enforcement, particularly at the multilateral level.

A number of rationales for international collective action on competition policy, including at the multilateral level, have been put forward in the economic literature and by delegates in the WTO working group. Clarke and Evenett (2003) postulate two sources of positive spillovers that provide rationales for international action in this area. First, public announcements of cartel enforcement actions in one country tend to stimulate enforcement efforts in other countries, particularly where there is an established relationship between the relevant enforcement authorities. In this way, trading partners benefit from active enforcement abroad. Second, the investigation and prosecution of arrangements such as international cartels can be greatly facilitated by accessing information about the nature and organisation of the arrangement from another jurisdiction that has successfully completed such an investigation. Conversely, a failure to take action against cartels headquartered in a particular jurisdiction may create 'safe havens' that make it more difficult for other affected jurisdictions to take such action. These considerations point to the potential benefits of some form of international accord committing the participating countries to take action in this area (Clarke and Evenett 2003: 117–18).

An important related argument is that the field of competition policy may be subject to 'political market failures' that result in systematic under-investment in related institutions in many countries, owing to the diffuse nature of the interests whose welfare is promoted by such institutions (i.e., consumers). In the work of the WTO Working Group on the Interaction between Trade and Competition Policy, the view has been expressed that cooperation at the multilateral level could be particularly helpful in generating political support for the implementation of effective competition policies at the national level; in ensuring that such policies are applied in a non-discriminatory and transparent manner; in promoting common approaches to particular practices where this seems feasible and warranted; and in promoting educational exchanges regarding the content and sound application of competition policy.

In a recent contribution to the theory of international economic policymaking, Birdsall and Lawrence (1999) state that a principal benefit of trade agreements aimed at measures beyond the border can be to facilitate domestic policy reforms, by providing a tool for overcoming domestic constituencies that could otherwise block the reform process. They refer specifically to the case of competition policy, observing that:

> When developing countries enter into modern trade agreements, they often make certain commitments to particular domestic policies – for example, to antitrust or other competition policy. Agreeing to such policies can be in the interests of developing countries (beyond the trade benefits directly obtained) because the commitment can reinforce the internal reform process. Indeed, participation in an international agreement can make feasible internal reforms that are beneficial for the country as a whole that might otherwise be successfully resisted by interest groups. (Birdsall and Lawrence 1999: 136)

The foregoing are by no means the only rationales that have been advanced by proponents of a multilateral framework on competition policy. Specific objectives that have been advanced include promoting the growth of strong competition agencies in developing countries to protect them from anticompetitive practices that impact on their consumers and businesses; promoting (voluntary) cooperation between the competition agencies of participating countries to assist them in investigating particular cases; and contributing to a greater degree of 'balance' in the WTO system between the rights of producers and the protection provided for consumers and other members of society.

The argument has also been made in the WTO working group that a multilateral framework could reinforce the effectiveness of institution-building programs in the area of competition policy by providing hands-on exposure to best practices in dealing with cross-border cases. Within such a framework, technical assistance programs could receive higher priority and be better focused on the needs of recipient countries (WTO Working Group on the Interaction between Trade and Competition Policy 2001, paragraph 57). A cooperation framework might also contribute to the promotion of a culture of competition (WTO Working Group on the Interaction between Trade and Competition Policy 1999, paragraph 61).

The view has also been expressed that the introduction of appropriate peer review mechanisms could reinforce and enhance the effectiveness of capacity building through technical assistance (WTO Working Group on the Interaction between Trade and Competition Policy 2000, paragraph 61). Peer reviews, which would be voluntary in nature, would be an instrument through which enforcement issues could be discussed in an open and constructive manner. For example, in the case of developing countries, peer review could identify capacity constraints as well as examine enforcement policies being followed in individual countries. Peer review provides an opportunity for countries to learn from others with similar experiences or similar problems. If done well, it promotes convergence and builds confidence among agencies as well as credibility and support. It has been suggested that a peer review process would help to establish benchmarks or guidelines to evaluate the implementation process. However, peer review needs to exist side-by-side with capacity building since they both have a role to play (WTO Working Group on the Interaction between Trade and Competition Policy 1999, paragraph 43; WTO Working Group on the Interaction between Trade and Competition Policy 2000, paragraphs 23 and 47).

The foregoing is not intended to resolve the debate as to whether there is a need for a multilateral framework on competition policy in the WTO and, if so, what would be the appropriate content of such a framework. A range of concerns have been advanced about the implications of such a framework, including that it might not yield sufficient benefits for developing countries. As already mentioned, a key related concern of developing countries relates to the perceived potential for a multilateral framework on competition policy to intrude

76   *Robert Anderson and Frédéric Jenny*

on their 'policy space'. Clearly, much would depend on the terms of such a framework. As an initial step toward further evaluation of this question, some aspects of the past proposals for a multilateral framework for competition policy are discussed below.

A MULTILATERAL FRAMEWORK FOR COMPETITION POLICY?

At the WTO Ministerial Conference in Cancun, Mexico, in September 2003, the majority of developing countries rejected the launching of negotiations on a multilateral framework on competition policy as had been proposed by the European Union and various other countries in the lead-up to the conference. This seemingly reflected a range of tactical and more fundamental concerns, including concerns about a perceived lack of negotiating capacity in this area, the costs that might be involved in setting up a national competition authority, the perceived risk that a multilateral framework in this area might intrude on industrial policy goals, and other considerations. Subsequently, the General Council of the WTO decided, as part of the 'July Package' of 2004, that no further work would be undertaken toward negotiations on competition policy (or on the separate issues of investment and transparency of government procurement) as part of the Doha Round. Still, it is useful to review the nature and content of recent proposals for such a framework to the extent that a number of WTO members remain committed to the long-run goal of developing an agreement to integrate better the implementation of competition policy with the goals and instruments of the multilateral trading system (see, e.g., Lamy 2004a).

As noted in the introduction to this chapter, there have been extensive misconceptions regarding the nature and scope of a possible WTO agreement on competition policy. Such misconceptions may, in some cases, have reflected a confusion between the proposals that were put forward in the WTO and the considerably more far-reaching proposal that was put forward by the Munich Group in the early 1990s (Draft International Antitrust Code 1993).[6] In addition, they may reflect the continuing influence of commentaries made by leading representatives of the antitrust community during the early stages of the WTO's exploratory work in this area, before the likely parameters of a possible agreement became clear. These commentaries (perhaps motivated, in part, by the excesses of the Munich Group proposal) called attention to certain risks posed by the prospect of WTO negotiations in this area, including: (1) a suppression of the scope for innovation in national competition policies, owing to the premature locking in of detailed substantive standards; and (2) an undermining of the scope for the exercise of prosecutorial discretion in antitrust enforcement, which of course is central to current approaches to competition law enforcement in the United States and other common law countries (see, in particular, Klein 1996; Melamed 1997; Tarullo 2000). Furthermore, the concern was voiced that a WTO agreement on competition policy would likely have an undue focus on market access objectives and that this would inevitably distort the principles of competition policy and/or be inimical to the interests of developing countries in this area (Tarullo 2000; Hoekman and Holmes 1999).

These commentaries served a useful purpose in highlighting the potential downsides of an overly rigid or sweeping approach to the implementation of international norms in this area. What is perhaps less well known is the extent to which the early commentaries influenced the debate in the WTO and were even taken on board in the proposals put forward in the run-up to Cancun. This is not to imply that the approach proposed by the proponents of a multilateral framework was necessarily 'right' but only that it was a good deal more modest than has sometimes been pictured and that it deliberately sought to avoid some of the pitfalls identified in the early commentaries.

The main elements of the proposal for a multilateral framework on competition policy are described in the relevant paragraphs of the Doha Ministerial Declaration (see Box 4.1, especially paragraph 25).[7]

Further insights are provided in relevant submissions to the WTO working group by members favouring the development of such a framework. Broadly speaking, these sources indicate that, in the view of those members, a multilateral framework on competition policy would embody the following five elements:

1) A commitment by WTO members to a set of core principles relating to the application of competition law and policy, including transparency, non-discrimination and procedural fairness.
2) A parallel commitment by member governments to the taking of measures against hardcore cartels.
3) The development of modalities for cooperation between member states on competition policy issues. These would be of a voluntary nature, and could encompass cooperation on national legislation, the exchange of national experience by competition authorities and aspects of enforcement.
4) A commitment to ongoing support for the introduction and strengthening of competition institutions in developing countries through technical assistance and capacity building, in the framework of the WTO but in cooperation with other interested organisations and national governments.
5) The establishment of a WTO standing committee on competition policy that would administer the agreement and act as a forum for the ongoing exchange of national experiences, the identification of technical assistance needs and sources for such assistance, and so on. The committee could also provide a forum for discussion of policy issues such as market access barriers arising out of a combination of government policies (or tolerance of anticompetitive conduct) and private actions.

Without attempting a comprehensive assessment of these proposals, the following observations are offered for reflection.[8] First, as already noted, the recent proposals had little in common with earlier calls for a detailed multilateral

78   *Robert Anderson and Frédéric Jenny*

Box 4.1 Relevant paragraphs of the Doha Ministerial Declaration

Interaction between trade and competition policy

23.Recognizing the case for a multilateral framework to enhance the contribution of competition policy to international trade and development, and the need for enhanced technical assistance and capacity-building in this area as referred to in paragraph 24, we agree that negotiations will take place after the Fifth Session of the Ministerial Conference on the basis of a decision to be taken, by explicit consensus, at that Session on modalities of negotiations.

24.We recognize the needs of developing and least-developed countries for enhanced support for technical assistance and capacity-building in this area, including policy analysis and development so that they may better evaluate the implications of closer multilateral cooperation for their development policies and objectives, and human and institutional development. To this end, we shall work in cooperation with other relevant intergovernmental organizations, including UNCTAD, and through appropriate regional and bilateral channels, to provide strengthened and adequately resourced assistance to respond to these needs.

25.In the period until the Fifth Session, further work in the Working Group on the Interaction between Trade and Competition Policy will focus on the clarification of: core principles, including transparency, non-discrimination and procedural fairness, and provisions on hardcore cartels; modalities for voluntary cooperation; and support for progressive reinforcement of competition institutions in developing countries through capacity-building. Full account shall be taken of the needs of developing and least-developed country participants and appropriate flexibility provided to address them.

Source: World Trade Organisation, Ministerial Declaration, Fourth Session of the Ministerial Conference, Doha, WT/MIN(01)/DEC/1, 9–14 November 2001.

---

code on competition policy as proposed by the Munich Group. Certainly, the idea of establishing an international competition law enforcement agency figured nowhere in the proposals. Clearly, the proposals also did not aim at a comprehensive harmonisation of competition law (Garcia-Bercero and Amarasinha 2001). Rather, they were framed in terms of adherence to certain core principles and other elements that embody fundamental values of both competition policy and the multilateral trading system (i.e., non-discrimination, transparency and the suppression of hardcore cartels). As such, these approaches seem unlikely to undermine the scope for continuing adaptation of national approaches to competition policy in response to economic learning and national circumstances (one of the concerns raised in the early commentaries); arguably, they might encourage accelerated learning in this area.[9]

Second, the approaches to hardcore cartels and modalities for cooperation that were called for under the recent proposals were extensively informed by cooperative approaches favoured in other forums, for example the OECD Recommendations on Hardcore Cartels and Cooperation, and were less ambitious than elements that were proposed in the past. For example, an early proposal for the introduction of 'compulsory positive comity' (i.e., a legal obligation for national authorities to undertake investigations into activities allegedly affecting other countries' national interests, when requested to do so by such countries) was dropped some time ago. The proponents of negotiations also made it clear that, as they envisaged it, a WTO framework would not require the exchange of confidential information (WTO Working Group on the Interaction between Trade and Competition Policy 2002b, paragraph 76) – although it also would not preclude individual countries from exchanging such information to the extent it is provided for in relevant bilateral arrangements. Much emphasis would be placed on voluntary cooperation in the development of national legislation and the exchange of national experience, in addition to the enforcement process.

Third, the proposals (and the Doha Ministerial Declaration) placed considerable emphasis on support for technical assistance and capacity building in this area, responding to a key concern of developing countries. This represented a clear recognition that simply mandating the adoption of relevant laws without long-term support for institution building is unlikely to yield satisfactory or appropriate results. Moreover, the expectation was that the required capacity-building activities would be undertaken not principally by the WTO itself; rather, it would be a cooperative effort in which the support and cooperation of other organisations would be essential (although the WTO would play a catalytic role).[10]

Fourth, by relying on broad principles, measures to strengthen cooperation and support for institution building, rather than on detailed legal prescriptions, the recent proposals sought to avoid problems that would have been inherent in a more detailed, intrusive approach. For the most part (and contrary to the way in which the proposals were sometimes characterised in academic commentaries), it would have been left for individual countries to define the details of their national legislation.

Fifth, and notwithstanding concerns expressed previously by some commentators, the recent proposals were not geared inordinately toward market access objectives. Rather, the focus of the proposals was on promoting the development of effective national competition institutions and expanded international cooperation to address anticompetitive practices as they are generally recognised in the competition policy community. In the work of the WTO working group, the value of competition advocacy activities has also been stressed. This approach would undoubtedly yield significant benefits for market access, in that robust competition policies and institutions are supportive of market access objectives in various ways (including through both advocacy and enforcement activities).

80   *Robert Anderson and Frédéric Jenny*

Notwithstanding any of the foregoing, this chapter is not suggesting that the case for a multilateral agreement on competition policy is or was self-evident. As noted, at Cancun the initiation of negotiations leading to the development of such a framework was rejected by the majority of developing countries. In addition to possible tactical considerations, the reasons underlying this rejection included the above-noted concern regarding a perceived intrusion on developing countries' 'policy space', concerns about a lack of negotiating capacity in this area and, for some, a sense that the proponents' proposals were unbalanced and might not, in the end, yield tangible benefits in the form of cooperation for developing countries.[11] It remains to be seen if these concerns can be resolved through some combination of: (a) further educational work and capacity-building activities, particularly to address the perceived deficit in negotiating capacity;[12] and (b) clarification or possible adjustments to the proponents' proposals.[13]

Much is at stake for developing countries and for the success of the multilateral trading system. The empirical record shows clearly that anticompetitive practices impose heavy costs on developing countries. Furthermore, where present, practices such as international cartels directly undermine the goals that the system is intended to serve – including not only access to markets but the continual improvement of living standards and the optimal use of the world's resources in accordance with the objective of sustainable development (as set out in the Marrakesh Agreement Establishing the World Trade Organisation). Unless measures are put in place to counteract such practices (whether at the multilateral or some other level), the realisation of these benefits will continue to be impeded. This, in turn, may contribute to an erosion of confidence in the benefits of the market economy and a liberalised trading order.[14]

NOTES

The authors are, respectively, Counsellor, Intellectual Property Division, WTO Secretariat and Professor, ESSEC (Paris). Professor Jenny is also Vice-Chair, Conseil de la Concurrence, France and has served as Chairman of the WTO Working Group on the Interaction between Trade and Competition Policy since 1997. This chapter draws on material in the various annual reports of the WTO Working Group on the Interaction between Trade and Competition Policy, in Anderson and Holmes (2002), in Anderson and Jenny (2003) and in Jenny (2003). A preliminary version of the first part of the chapter was published in Korea Fair Trade Commission (2002). The views expressed are the personal responsibility of the authors and should not be attributed to the WTO, its Secretariat or any of its members. Helpful discussions with Simon Evenett, Peter Holmes and Adrian Otten are gratefully acknowledged.
1   In August 2004, the General Council of the WTO ruled out the possiblility of négotiations on a multilateral framework on competition policy within the 'single undertaking' of the Doha Development Agenda. The concept of a single undertaking outlined in paragraph 47 of the Doha Ministerial Declaration, recognises that all agreements and instruments contained therein are accepted as elements of a package. Prior to this decision, the European Community had raised the possibility of negotiations that would be conducted outside the single

undertaking of the Doha Development Agenda and on a plurilateral or 'opt-in/opt-out' basis (see Lamy 2004a and related discussion, below).

2   In this chapter, 'competition policy' refers to all measures through which governments seek to promote the efficient and competitive operation of markets. 'Competition law' refers to legislation that prohibits or otherwise deals with specific anticompetitive practices of firms such as cartels, abuses of a dominant position or monopolisation and mergers that create a dominant position or otherwise stifle competition.

3   Notwithstanding the acknowledged importance of these practices, they have not been the main focus of work in the WTO on a possible multilateral framework on competition policy. As discussed below, the focus of that work has been on the development of provisions to deal with cartels, on the promotion of voluntary cooperation and related capacity-building activities, and on 'core principles' (transparency, non-discrimination and procedural fairness) to guide the application of legislation in this area. The reason for the lack of any proposal focused specifically on vertical market restraints relates to the complexity of this area of competition law enforcement and the reluctance of many authorities to reduce the role of prosecutorial discretion and case-by-case analysis in this area. Nonetheless, to the extent that it would play a role in strengthening competition regimes in various respects (including by providing greater political legitimacy and guarantees of independence, transparency and non-discrimination), a multilateral framework could assist in the implementation of this aspect of competition law as well.

4   A related discussion can be found in Working Group on the Interaction between Trade and Competition Policy (2003a) and a useful typology of relevant efficiencies is provided in Kolasky and Dick (2003).

5   This is not to suggest that funding for the competition agency in these countries was necessarily optimal.

6   The draft code was a detailed, ambitious proposal for a binding international agreement on competition law that was put forward by a private group of academics and practitioners.

7   In a statement made prior to the adoption of the declaration, the Chairman of the WTO Ministerial Conference, Mr Youssef Kamal, expressed his understanding that the requirement in paragraph 25 for a decision to be taken, by explicit consensus, on the modalities for negotiations before negotiations on competition policy and other 'Singapore issues' could proceed gave 'each Member the right to take a position on modalities that would prevent negotiations from proceeding after the Fifth Session until that Member was prepared to join in an explicit consensus' (WTO Ministerial Conference, Fourth Session 2001: 2). At the Cancun Ministerial Conference, such a consensus proved elusive.

8   These observations draw on material in Anderson and Jenny (2001), Anderson and Holmes (2002), Anderson and Jenny (2003) and Jenny (2003).

9   The importance of transparency in the formulation of competition policy and its contribution to the evolution of sound enforcement norms in this field is emphasised in the thoughtful analysis in Kovacic (2004), who also stresses the importance of broad scope for experimentation and risk taking in policy formulation in this area.

10 Paragraph 24 of the Doha Ministerial Declaration specified that assistance mandated by the declaration will be provided 'in cooperation with other relevant intergovernmental organisations, including UNCTAD, and through appropriate regional and bilateral channels'.

11 As noted, for some, a further concern was the cost of setting up a national competition agency.

82   *Robert Anderson and Frédéric Jenny*

12   Since the Doha Ministerial Conference, the WTO Secretariat has undertaken an extensive program of technical assistance in the area of trade and competition policy (WTO Working Group on the Interaction between Trade and Competition Policy 2003c).

13   As an alternative to development of a multilateral framework on competition policy as foreseen in relevant provisions of the Doha Ministerial Declaration (but rejected by developing countries at Cancun), the European Community raised the possibility of negotiations that would be conducted outside the single undertaking of the Doha Development Agenda and on a plurilateral or 'opt-in/opt-out' basis (Lamy 2004a and Lamy 2004b).

14   There is no doubt that such concerns were in the minds of the system's founders. Provisions to address 'restrictions imposed by private combines and cartels' were a key element of the US proposal for an International Trade Organisation at the conclusion of World War II. Although this proposal was not, in the end, incorporated into the General Agreement on Tariffs and Trade (GATT) in 1947, its rationale remains instructive: 'when a private agreement divides the markets of the world among the members of a cartel, none of [the goods affected] can move between the zones while the contract is in force. Clearly, if trade is to increase as a result of the lightening of government restrictions, the governments concerned must make sure that it is not restrained by private combinations' (US Department of State 1945: 4; also quoted in Jackson 1969: 522, which provides related context). In a related vein, in 1944 President Franklin Delano Roosevelt had written to Secretary of State Cordell Hull, observing that 'Cartel practices which restrict the free flow of goods in foreign commerce will have to be curbed' (see also Wolff 1994).

REFERENCES

Anderson, Robert D. (2002) 'Intellectual property rights, competition policy and international trade: reflections on the work of the WTO Working Group on the Interaction between Trade and Competition Policy', in Thomas Cottier and Petros Mavroidis (eds) *Intellectual Property: Trade, Competition and Sustainable Development*, Ann Arbor: University of Michigan Press, December.

Anderson, Robert D. and Nancy T. Gallini (1998) *Competition Policy and Intellectual Property Rights in the Knowledge-based Economy*, Calgary: University of Calgary Press for the Industry Canada Research Series.

Anderson, Robert D., Abraham Hollander, Joseph Monteiro and William Stanbury (1998) 'Competition policy and regulatory reform in Canada, 1986–1997', *Review of Industrial Organization* 13(1–2): 177–204.

Anderson, Robert D. and Peter Holmes (2002) 'Competition policy and the future of the multilateral trading system', *Journal of International Economic Law* 5(2): 531–63.

Anderson, Robert D. and Frédéric Jenny (2001) 'Current developments on competition policy in the World Trade Organization', *Antitrust* 16(1): 40–4.

—— (2003) 'The current proposals for WTO negotiations on competition policy: background and overview', paper presented at the Conference on Antitrust Issues in Today's Economy, Conference Board, New York, March.

Birdsall, Nancy and Robert Z. Lawrence (1999) 'Deep integration and trade agreements: good for developing countries?', in Inge Kaul, Isabelle Grunberg and Marc A. Stern (eds) *Global Public Goods: International Cooperation in the 21st Century*, New York: Oxford University Press for the United Nations Development Program.

Blackhurst, Richard (1991) 'Trade policy is competition policy', in *Competition and Economic Development*, Paris: OECD.

Clarke, Julian and Simon J. Evenett (2003) 'A multilateral framework for competition policy?', in State Secretariat of Economic Affairs and Simon Evenett, *The Singapore Issues and the World Trading System: the Road to Cancun and Beyond*, Bern: State Secretariat for Economic Affairs.

Consumer Unity and Trust Society (2003) *Pulling Up Our Socks* (Report based on the 7-Up Project), Jaipur: Consumer Unity and Trust Society, February.

Draft International Antitrust Code (1993) 5 *World Trade Materials*, September, 126–96.

Dutz, Mark A. (2002) 'Competition policy issues in developing and transition markets', presentation at the OECD Global Forum on Competition, Paris, 14–15 February.

Evans, David S. (2002) 'The new trustbusters', *Foreign Affairs* 81(1): 1–19.

Evenett, Simon J., Alexander Lehmann and Benn Steil (eds) (2000) *Antitrust Goes Global: What Future for Transatlantic Co-operation?*, Washington DC: The Brookings Institution.

Evenett, Simon J., Margaret Levenstein and Valerie Suslow (2001) 'International cartel enforcement: lessons from the 1990s', *The World Economy* 24(9): 1221–45.

Frischtak, Claudio C. (1995) *Regulatory Policies and Reform in Industrializing Countries*, Washington DC: The World Bank.

Garcia-Bercero, Ignacio and Stefan Amarasinha (2001) 'Moving the trade and competition debate forward', *Journal of International Economic Law*, 4(3): 481–506.

Gilbert, R. and S. Sunshine (1995) 'Incorporating dynamic efficiency into merger analysis: the use of innovation markets', *Antitrust Law Journal* 63(2): 569–602.

Gilbert, R. and W.K. Tom (2001) 'Is innovation king at the antitrust agencies? The intellectual property guidelines five years later', *Antitrust Law Journal* 69(1): 43–86.

Hoekman, Bernard and Peter Holmes (1999) 'Competition policy, developing countries and the WTO', *The World Economy* 22(6): 875–93.

Hur, J.S. (2002) 'Theories and case study of extraterritorial application of international cartel cases: the international graphite electrodes cartel', mimeo, October.

International Monetary Fund (2002) *World Economic Outlook*, September.

Jackson, John H. (1969) *World Trade and the Law of GATT*, Indianapolis: Bobbs-Merrill.

Jenny, Frédéric (2001) 'Globalization, competition and trade policy: convergence, divergence and cooperation', in Yang-Ching Chao Gee San, Changfa Lo and Jiming Ho (eds) *International and Comparative Competition Law and Policies*, The Hague: Kluwer Law International.

—— (2002) 'International co-operation on competition: myth, reality and perspective', paper presented at the University of Minnesota Law School Conference on Global Antitrust Law and Policy, Minneapolis, 20–21 September.

—— (2003) 'Competition law and policy: global governance issues', *World Competition* 26(4): 609–24, December.

Jordan, W.A. (1972) 'Producer protection, prior market structure and the effects of government regulation', *Journal of Law and Economics* XV(1): 151–76.

Klein, Joel (1996) 'A note of caution with respect to the WTO agenda on competition policy', remarks to the Royal Institute of International Affairs, Chatham House, London, November.

Kolasky, W. and A. Dick (2003) 'The merger guidelines and the integration of efficiencies into antitrust reviews of horizontal mergers', *Antitrust Law Journal* 71(1): 207–51.

Korea Fair Trade Commission (2002) *Seoul Competition Forum 2002*, Seoul: Korea Fair Trade Commission, December.

Kovacic, William E. (2004) 'The modern evolution of U.S. competition policy enforcement norms', *Antitrust Law Journal* 71(2): 377–478.

84   *Robert Anderson and Frédéric Jenny*

Krueger, Anne O. (1974) 'The political economy of the rent-seeking society', *American Economic Review* 64(3): 291–303.

—— (1984) 'The problems of trade liberalization', in A.C. Harberger (ed.) *World Economic Growth*, San Francisco: International Centre for Economic Growth.

Lamy, Pascal (Trade Commissioner for the European Communities) (2004a) 'The relaunching of negotiations under the Doha Development Agenda', Strasbourg, 13 January.

—— (2004b) 'Moving the Doha Development Agenda Forward', speech to the European–American Business Council, Washington DC, 26 February.

Levenstein, Margaret and Valerie Suslow (2001) 'Private international cartels and their effect on developing countries', background paper for the World Bank's *World Development Report 2001*, 9 January, available at http://www-unix.oit.umass.edu/~maggiel/WDR2001.pdf.

Marsden, Philip (2003) *A Competition Policy for the WTO*, London: Cameron.

Melamed, Douglas A. (1997) 'International antitrust in an age of international deregulation', remarks to the George Mason Law Review Symposium on Antitrust in the Global Economy, Washington DC, October 10.

Mexico (2002) 'Communication to the Working Group on the Interaction between Trade and Competition Policy: hardcore cartels', WT/WGTCP/W/196, issued 14 August 2002.

Osakwe, Chiedu (2001) 'Poverty reduction and development: the interaction of trade, macroeconomic and regulatory policies', Tenth Joseph Mubiru Memorial Lecture, organised by the Bank of Uganda, 14 December.

Pittman, Russell (2004) 'Abuse-of-dominance provisions of Central and Eastern European competition laws: have fears of over-enforcement been borne out?', Department of Justice (Antitrust Division), Economic Analysis Group, Working Paper 04–1, January.

Posner, Richard (2001) 'Antitrust in the new economy', *Antitrust Law Journal* 68(3): 925–43.

Singh, A. (1999) 'Competition policy, development and developing countries', Working Paper No. 50, Indian Council for Research on International Economic Relations, New Delhi, November.

—— (2002) 'Competition and competition policy in emerging markets: international and development dimensions', Paper No. 18, G-24 Discussion Paper Series, New York: United Nations, September.

Stigler, G.J. (1971) 'The theory of economic regulation', *Bell Journal of Economics and Management Science* 2(1): 3–21, Spring.

Tarullo, Daniel K. (2000) 'Norms and institutions in global competition policy', *American Journal of International Law* 94(3): 478–504, July.

United Nations Conference on Trade and Development (UNCTAD) (1998) *Empirical Evidence of the Benefits from Applying Competition Law and Policy Principles to Economic Development in order to Attain Greater Efficiency in International Trade and Development*, Geneva: UNCTAD, document TD/B/COM.2/EM/10.

US Department of Justice (2000) 'German company pleads guilty to rigging bids on USAID construction contracts in Egypt', press release, 18 August.

US Department of State (1945) 'U.S. proposals for an international trade organization', Publication No. 2411, Washington DC: Department of State.

US Federal Trade Commission (2003) *To Promote Innovation: The Proper Balance of Competition and Patent Law and Policy*, Washington DC: Federal Trade Commission, October.

US International Competition Policy Advisory Committee to the Attorney General and Assistant Attorney General for Antitrust (2000) *Final Report*, Washington DC: Department of Justice, February.

Winters, Alan (2002) 'Doha and world poverty targets', New York: World Bank, mimeo.

Wolff, Alan W. (1994) 'The problems of market access in the global economy: trade and competition policy', Contribution to the OECD Roundtable on Market Access, 30 June.

World Bank (1997) 'Fostering markets: liberalization, regulation and industrial policy', in *World Development Report*, New York: World Bank, chapter 4.

—— (2000) 'Making markets work better for poor people', in *World Development Report*, New York: World Bank, chapter 4.

World Trade Organisation (1997) 'Special study on trade and competition policy', in *Annual Report of the World Trade Organization for 1997*, Geneva: WTO, chapter IV.

WTO Ministerial Conference, Fourth Session (2001) *Summary Record of the Ninth Meeting, Doha*, Geneva: WTO, WT/MIN(01)/SR/9.

WTO Working Group on the Interaction between Trade and Competition Policy (1998) *Report (1998) of the Working Group on the Interaction between Trade and Competition Policy to the General Council*, Geneva: WTO, WT/WGTCP/2.

—— (1999) *Report (1999) of the Working Group on the Interaction between Trade and Competition Policy to the General Council*, Geneva: WTO, WT/WGTCP/3.

—— (2000) *Report (2000) of the Working Group on the Interaction between Trade and Competition Policy to the General Council*, Geneva: WTO, WT/WGTCP/4.

—— (2001) *Report (2001) of the Working Group on the Interaction between Trade and Competition Policy to the General Council*, Geneva: WTO, WT/WGTCP/5.

—— (2002a) *Background Note by the Secretariat on Modalities for Voluntary Co-operation*, Geneva: WTO, WT/WGTCP/W/192.

—— (2002b) *Report (2002) of the Working Group on the Interaction between Trade and Competition Policy to the General Council*, Geneva: WTO, WT/WGTCP/6.

—— (2003a) *Study on Issues Relating to a Possible Multilateral Framework on Competition Policy* (principal author: Simon Evenett), Geneva: WTO, WT/WGTCP/W/228.

—— (2003b) *Report (2003) of the Working Group on the Interaction between Trade and Competition Policy to the General Council*, Geneva: WTO, WT/WGTCP/7.

—— (2003c) *Secretariat Technical Assistance Activities Pursuant to Paragraph 24 of the Doha Ministerial Declaration*, Geneva: WTO, WT/WGTCP/W/230.

[11]

Linked-In: Antitrust and the Virtues of a Virtual Network

Eleanor M. Fox*

I. Introduction

If networking is the new world order,[1] antitrust law is a provocative example.

Antitrust law is part of a genre. The genre is economic law that is national in origin, that has been adopted in scores of countries, and that addresses conduct that increasingly transcends national borders. Within this genre, cooperation is needed to carry out tasks that lie at the core of the law; commonality in rules, standards, and modes of analysis is desirable to facilitate a linked world system and to soften system clashes; and rules of priority and modes for respect are needed to intermediate differences. Moreover, nations that have recently adopted the law, and especially developing countries, appreciate guidance from more experienced jurisdictions, and the guidance itself is part of a feedback loop that generates soft norms. Finally, the area of law has been resistant to becoming international law. In this genre, networking fills a real need in a globalized world.

This article contains four parts. Part one explores the internationalization of markets and the stalled attempt to achieve an international law of antitrust. Part two explores the rise of the International Competition Network (ICN), which is a unique, virtual network of competition law officials.[2] Part three explores the functioning of the ICN, its benefits, and its limitations. Part four contains an assessment and conclusions.

* Eleanor Fox is the Walter J. Derenberg Professor of Law at New York University School of Law. The author thanks John Fingleton, Barry Hawk, Alberto Heimler, Merit Janow, David Lewis, Daniel Sokol, Maria Coppola Tineo, and Randy Tritell for extremely helpful conversations and comments. She acknowledges research assistance from the Filomen D'Agostino and Max E. Greenberg Faculty Research Fund.

1. *See* Anne-Marie Slaughter, A New World Order (2004). Slaughter conceptualizes networking across borders, and particularly networks of government officials, as a key feature of the new world order and a phenomenon that is "underappreciated, undersupported, and underused to address the central problems of global governance." *Id.* at 1.

2. The ICN differs from networks in other fields of law, which often are engaged in explicit rule-making and standard-setting. *See* Slaughter, *supra* note 1; Kal Raustiala, *The Architecture of International Cooperation: Transgovernmental Networks and the Future of International Law*, 43 Va. J. Int'l L. 1 (2002); Pierre-Hugues Verdier, *Transnational Regulatory Networks and Their Limits*, 34 Yale J. Int'l L. 113 (2009) (comparing the Basel Committee on Banking Supervision, the International Organization of Securities Commissions, and the International Competition Network).

This article argues that the ICN provides an outstanding example of a vehicle for inter-action and cross-fertilization among national authorities, producing some convergences of law, procedures, and policy; increasing knowledge and understanding; and facilitating mentoring and other collaborative relationships. It observes that, in spite of great efforts of inclusiveness, the ICN agenda is principally set and the norms principally forged by the developed world, although consensus when reached involves give-and-take on all sides. The article explores whether the ICN, in spite of its founding concept of "no power," *has* power deriving from the soft-norm formation that it generates. The article ends with an assessment of the ICN as it is and might be. It concludes that the ICN has exceeded expectations of effectiveness to accomplish its circumscribed mission and that it can be credited with a high degree of legitimacy. By its nature, it is not sufficient (and not in-tended) to accomplish tasks that could create more nearly seamless antitrust governance. For the future, the ICN has surprisingly strong (virtual) roots, but it needs continued leadership and new momentum, some of which can be supplied by mining the depths of controversial issues that it has thus far chosen to avoid.[3]

II. Antitrust, the World, and the Stalled Possibility of a Global System

A. What Is Antitrust Law?

The ICN is a network that arose somewhat serendipitously to fill a void. It arose in the absence of an international law of antitrust. To begin this description and assessment of the ICN, antitrust itself needs an introduction in order to identify the seeds of national divergences as well as the space for commonalities.

Antitrust is law designed for market-based economies to control creation and uses of economic power and thus to help markets work for the benefit of the people (buyers, sellers, and firms competing on the merits) rather than for the benefit of a privileged and powerful few. The definition of antitrust law and the articulation of its goals change from time to time and are sensitive to the context of each particular country, its state of devel-opment, and its economic conditions. In the United States for some ninety years, begin-ning in the Industrial Revolution, antitrust was conceptualized as law against power in the marketplace. In the 1960s, this concept was broadened. Antitrust became synonymous with marketplace pluralism and empowerment for the underdog. In the 1980s, in view of lowered trade barriers and a new quest for competitiveness, U.S. antitrust was recon-ceived. It became and is now a tool for efficiency, usually interpreted as a tool to prevent consumer loss through creation or abuse of market power.

In Europe, competition law was defined at the outset of the European Economic Com-munity in 1957 as a vehicle for three goals: market integration; control of abuses of eco-nomic power, often state-granted power; and leveling the playing field for business actors across the Member States of the Community. Especially since the mid-1990s, European competition law has emphasized consumers and efficiency, while still conceiving of com-petition law as a valuable tool to help carry out the agenda of Europe for innovation, integration, and competitiveness.

---

3. For example, inclusive growth as an antitrust guide for developing countries, industrial policy as an unshakeable reality for not only China and India but the whole world.

In Asia, antitrust law was slower in development because business by consensus was the norm, such as in Japan under the umbrella of administrative guidance. Industrial policy and fairness to business were priorities. Eventually in Asia, as well as most of the rest of the world, markets and competition became accepted as a norm. The embrace of markets was especially palpable after the fall of the Berlin Wall in late 1989 and in recognition of the failures of Russian communism and other totalitarian regimes to deliver an acceptable standard of living for the people. In many Asian countries and many other communities that have adopted competition laws, equity and industrial policy objectives—fairness to small and indigenous businesses and the creation of national champions—were built into the law and remain goals. The national-policy mandate is clear on the face of the new antitrust law of China. Even in the supposedly market–friendly West, industrial policy and protectionism are not unknown, as is evident in the current financial crisis; but to the U.S. and the EU competition authorities, protectionism is an unwelcome intrusion into competition policy, while in Asian nations it may be an inseparable part.

Developing countries historically favored a restrictive-practices law, which was meant to proscribe restraints, especially by multinational enterprises, that coerced, foreclosed, or squeezed domestic competitors or restricted their export opportunities. Much of the restrictive business practices (RBP) law addressed concerns with the gapingly unequal distribution of wealth and power. Eventually, most developing countries allowed "reasonableness" defenses to charges of restraints of trade and demanded that their law be friendly to consumers. Moreover, in the modern age of globalization wherein integration into the global economy is seen as the best hope for economic growth and alleviation of poverty, developing countries also desire a competition law likely to produce efficiencies and competitiveness for their firms.

Within each of these divergent conceptions there lie more differences, albeit less dramatic ones. For example, in modern times, although U.S. antitrust law and European competition law are by many measures congruent, they employ modes for reaching efficiency and serving consumers that sometimes differ from one another. U.S. authorities and courts are more likely to assume that the unfettered market will work to produce efficiency; that efficiencies gained by even a monopoly firm will inure to the benefit of the public; and that antitrust intervention tends to compromise efficiency and protect inefficient competitors, raising prices for consumers (except for cartels, which fix prices, divide markets, or rig bids and are clearly inefficient).[4] Therefore, non-cartel conduct must reach a high threshold before it is labeled anticompetitive.

The European Commission and European courts are more likely to pursue the same goal (an efficient system that serves its consumers) by protecting dynamic rivalry, market access, and the competitive structure of the market. Moreover, European antitrust is sometimes proactive and is used, along with other tools, to liberalize markets such as telecommunications, whereas U.S. antitrust is defensive; the place of U.S. antitrust is to prevent obstructive acts that harm consumers but not to *create* environments or duties that might help them.

---

4. Eleanor Fox, *The Efficiency Paradox, in* HOW THE CHICAGO SCHOOL OVERSHOT THE MARK: THE EFFECT OF CONSERVATIVE ECONOMIC ANALYSIS ON U.S. ANTITRUST 77, 79 (R. Pitofsky ed., Oxford 2008).

Despite the differences of the now 100 antitrust regimes, however, the generic characterization above works as a general description of antitrust.

B. Why Antitrust Needs a Global Framework

Antitrust needs a global framework, both because markets are global and because nations are strategic.[5] Conduct launched in one nation can harm people around the world. Without a framework that rises above national boundaries, vision is impaired and coherence is lacking. Full costs and benefits of transactions are obscured. Firms in one nation may squeeze out competitors and harm consumers in another. Culprits may escape detection and punishment.

A piece of this problem—negative externalities—can in theory be handled by norms of extraterritorial jurisdiction embodied in the effects doctrine, by which victim nations can call foreigners to account. But often the victim nation does not have the resources or power to catch the offshore perpetrators. It may not even be able to obtain personal jurisdiction over them. Recourse is often more theoretical than real. These difficulties are experienced especially by developing countries, which almost by definition do not have the resources to catch and deter violations that originate beyond their borders.[6] Therefore, ironically, in the case of a detected cartel that harms the whole world, victims in developed countries may be well compensated, while developing country victims of the same conduct, who may need recompense much more, are left to suffer their wounds.

Second, for businesses (and therefore their customers), maneuvering a balkanized antitrust terrain is costly. A business firm may be forced to deal with twenty or fifty or more jurisdictions, all with different laws, to accomplish one transaction or to implement one business strategy. Being subject to the laws of 100 jurisdictions is disruptive and expensive. The costs are even greater when some nations' laws condemn what others allow, and especially if host laws handicap cost-saving or innovative conduct or impose divergent remedies.[7] Therefore, one hears the business plea in developed country fora: adopt *our* law. Converge to us.

Third, by national level law alone, we cannot achieve global coherence. Neither can we appreciate the full costs and benefits of a multinational merger, nor devise and enforce optimal and congruent penalties for world cartels or monopolistic conduct. Nor can we assure adequate compensation for antitrust victims or appropriately constrain state-authored restraints that privilege private or nationalistic interests.

C. The Agenda for World Antitrust Law and Why It Has Failed

In modern times, the Europeans were the first to articulate and promote a world antitrust agenda.[8] Europe has spent half a century studying and implementing modes of es-

---

5. *See* Eleanor M. Fox, *International Antitrust and the Doha Dome*, 43 VA. J. INT'L L. 911 (2003).

6. *See* Eleanor M. Fox, *Antitrust and Regulatory Federalism: Races Up, Down, and Sideways*, 75 N.Y.U. L. REV. 1781 (2000).

7. *See* A. Neil Campbell & J. William Rowley, *The Internationalization of Unilateral Conduct Laws–Conflict, Comity, Cooperation and/or Convergence?*, 75 ANTITRUST L. J. 267 (2008).

8. For a useful account of the development of international competition policy as launched by the European Commission, see also Alberto Heimler, *Competition Policy as a Tool of EU Foreign Policy: Multilateralism,*

tablishing community among nations, having in mind the benefits of community-wide vision while being mindful of the realm preserved to the non-parochial sovereignty interests of each Member State. It is not surprising, therefore, that the European Community was the first jurisdiction to study the need for global vision in competition policy and to make recommendations to achieve it.

A "Committee of Wise Men" convened, opined, and sketched a model of a competition law for the world, which they placed institutionally within the World Trade Organization (WTO). Under this proposal, designed for transactions or conduct with cross-border effects, the project for a world antitrust framework would begin slowly and from the ground up. It would start with building blocks of cooperation among nations' antitrust authorities, principles of transparency, non-discrimination and due process, and a program for capacity building and technical assistance to developing countries. It would multilateralize existing bilateral cooperation agreements. The system would advance to the adoption of common substantive principles against abuse of dominance and cartels, eventually encompassing the substantive law common to antitrust systems, and would put into place a process for dispute resolution within the WTO framework.[9]

The proposal was vetted within the Competition Directorate of the European Commission and then within the European Commission and European Council. It was aired and refined and became the basis for the Singapore antitrust initiative adopted by the WTO in December 1996, which established the WTO Working Group on the Interaction between Trade and Competition Policy.[10] The Working Group, which met many times over the course of seven years, became a vehicle for discussions and submissions from scores of nations, developed and developing, on the benefits and drawbacks of a world competition-policy initiative, as well as submissions on the various discrete subjects of antitrust.[11] Reactions of jurisdictions to an antitrust competence in the WTO differed widely. The United States expressed strong skepticism toward a world initiative for fear that developing and other countries' protectionist goals would be enshrined, that consensus principles would be reduced to the lowest common denominator, that disputes would be resolved by uninformed bureaucrats), and that independent agencies would lose their prerogative of

---

Bilateralism and Soft Convergence, in THE EUROPEAN UNION FOREIGN POLICY: MYTH OR REALITY? (F. Bindi ed., Brookings 2009).

9. *Commission of the European Communities, Report of the Group of Experts, Competition Policy in the new Trade Order: Strengthening International Cooperation and Rules,* COM (1995) 359 final (Dec. 7, 1995) [hereinafter Van Miert Report]. *See European Commission, XXVIth Report on Competition Policy,* at 95, COM (1997) 628 final (1996), *available at* http://ec.europa.eu/competition/annual_reports/rap96_en.html.

10. *See European Commission, XXVIth Report on Competition Policy, supra* note 9, at 95.

11. *See* World Trade Organization, *Annual Report 1997. Trade and Competition Policy,* Vol. 1, Ch. 4, 29-91 [hereinafter WTO 1997 Report]. For more information, *see* also the annual reports of the working group and the underlying documents, *available at* http://www.wto.org/english/tratop_e/comp_e/wgtcp_docs_e.htm. For the history and early evolution of the WTO initiative, *see* Clifford A. Jones, *Come the Millennium (Round)? Competing Visions of International Antitrust Policy in the European Union and the United States, in* INTERNATIONAL ANTITRUST LAW & POLICY: 2001 FORDHAM CORPORATE LAW ch. 3 (Barry Hawk ed., 2001). For reflections on the work of the WTO Working Group, see Robert D. Anderson & Frédéric Jenny, *Competition Policy, Economic Development and the Possible Role of a Multilateral Framework on Competition Policy: Insights from the WTO Working Group on Trade and Competition Policy, in* COMPETITION POLICY IN EAST ASIA (E. Medalla ed., 2005).

prosecutorial discretion.[12] Europe, Japan, Korea, and Canada favored a WTO framework for antitrust as the natural next step. Hong Kong would support only a regime against state restraints of trade, while India and various developing countries stood against a world antitrust initiative for fear that resulting rules would favor the West and further colonize and marginalize developing countries. Developing countries feared also that they lacked the technical knowledge and sophistication to protect their interests in the course of negotiations and that they lacked the resources and other capacities to establish and carry on the work of a competing agency.[13]

Despite the doubts, the idea of a competition initiative within the WTO gained traction and held its grip for some years. Reactively, the United States introduced a different idea. U.S. officials proposed a recommendation against cartels in the Organization for Economic Development and Cooperation (OECD). The OECD is an organization of developed nations with no dispute resolution powers. While the Europeans had prioritized abuse of dominance, and vertical restraints at national boundaries, as the most heinous of antitrust offenses, Americans prioritized cartels. Americans regarded single firm (non-conspiratorial) acts and vertical restraints as usually efficient and good. They wanted to shift focus away from abuse of dominance and vertical restraints.[14]

They were not pleased with the WTO as an antitrust forum, for the WTO caters to the trade community. Results are negotiated among more than 140 (now 155) nations, including many developing countries, many of which were seen to prefer protection to competition. The virtues of a recommendation against cartels in the OECD were three-fold: it would prioritize hard core cartels (price fixing and market division among competitors); it would mute the stress on abuse of dominance and vertical restraints; and it would move the forum from the WTO to one comprised of more nearly like-minded countries and one without enforcement powers. At the OECD, no nation would risk being disciplined by a remote world organization and by decision-makers who might dislike multinationals, lack understanding of economics, and distrust free markets.[15]

The two initiatives—the focused one in the OECD and the broad one in the WTO—proceeded side by side. The OECD nations adopted the Hard Core Cartel Recommendation.[16] The Hard Core Cartel Recommendation urges that nations adopt and maintain an anti-cartel law. It does not forbid derogations from the anti-cartel principle, but it urges that nations limit and review their derogations. The signatory nations undertake to report new derogations to the OECD.

---

12. *See* Joel Klein, *Anticipating the Millennium: International Antitrust Enforcement at the End of the Twentieth Century, in* INTERNATIONAL ANTITRUST LAW & POLICY: FORDHAM CORPORATE LAW INSTITUTE ch. 1 (Barry Hawk ed., 1998).

13. *See* World Trade Organization [WTO], Documents of the Working Group on the Interaction Between Trade and Competition Policy, Countries' Submission, http://www.wto.org/english/tratop_e/comp_e/wgtcp_docs_e.htm (last visited Apr. 5, 2009).

14. Vertical restraints are restraints in the course of distributing a product, such as exclusive dealing and exclusive directories.

15. *See* Daniel Tarullo, *Norms and Institutions in Global Competition Policy,* 94 AM. J. INT'L L. 478 (2000) (recommending that the OECD, not the WTO, be the forum for antitrust convergence).

16. Organisation for Economic Co-operation and Development [OECD], *Recommendation of the Council Concerning Effective Action Against Hard Core Cartels,* C(98)35/Final (Mar. 25, 1998), *available at* http://strategis.ic.gc.ca/pics/ct/1998oecd_hccrec.pdf.

Meanwhile, in the face of U.S. criticism of its WTO initiative, the European Commission streamlined its proposal, limiting the substantive undertaking of states to adopting and maintaining an anti-cartel law,[17] and all but eliminating dispute resolution. Dispute resolution would be available only for certain objective defaults such as failing to maintain an anti-cartel law. Left unmodified were the recommendations that nations cooperate in matters of common interest, ensure transparency and procedural fairness in application of their competition laws, and support capacity building and technical assistance for developing countries. This slimmed-down proposal became a part of the provisional agenda of the round of the WTO introduced at the ministerial meeting at Doha, Qatar, in 2001—a round dubbed the Doha Development Round in recognition of the fact that the developed countries had been the big winners of the recent trade rounds, and the developing nations had not received a fair share of the gains. The Doha Agenda was meant to focus on measures that would especially help developing countries, perhaps ironically.

At the ministerial meeting in Cancun in fall 2003, however, Europe and the United States came forward with insufficient offers to reduce agricultural tariffs and subsidies, and the whole round faltered.[18] The negotiators considered it necessary to jettison the more tangential aspirations, and the antitrust agenda was sacrificed to the hoped-for success of the round, which has now substantially failed.[19]

At present, there is no active agenda for world antitrust law, and the enterprise is not likely to be revived in the near future. While ongoing research, roundtables, and peer review activity continue in the OECD and United Nations Conference on Trade and Development (UNCTAD), much attention has shifted to the ICN. The work of these older organizations is important, and they continue to make significant contributions to the progress and coherence of antitrust in a globalized world, sometimes in collaboration with one another and with the ICN. The focus of this article on the ICN is not meant to minimize their continuing contributions.

III. The Rise of the Network

A. THE BIRTH OF THE ICN

By the late 1990s, in the wake of the successfully completed Uruguay Trade Round, heightened global business activity exposed the need for deeper transnational coordination in vetting mergers and rooting out cartels. In 1997, President Clinton's Attorney General

---

17. This change effected a sharp shift of focus from vertical restraints and abuses by dominant firms to cartels. *See* THE SINGAPORE ISSUES AND THE WORLD TRADING SYSTEM: THE ROAD TO CANCUN AND BEYOND (State Secretariat of Economic Affairs & Simon Evenett, eds., WTI 2003); Heimler, *supra* note 8. The shift was a U.S. victory

18. *See* Joseph Stiglitz & Andrew Charlton, FAIR TRADE FOR ALL: HOW TRADE CAN PROMOTE DEVELOPMENT 1-6 (2005).

19. In the wake of the Cancun Ministerial Meeting, the European Commission issued a Communication considering how the EU could contribute to a revival of negotiations on competition and the other Singapore issues (investment, trade facilitation, and government procurement). As to the development dimension of the Doha Development Agenda, it said: "The integration of developing countries into the world economy is a necessary condition for development. Such integration will be deeper and fairer if anchored in the multilateral trading system." Communication from the Commission to the Council, to the European Parliament, and to the Economic and Social Committee, at 15, 26 Nov. 2003.

Janet Reno convened the International Competition Policy Advisory Committee (ICPAC) to the U.S. Attorney General and Assistant Attorney General for Antitrust to study the implications of globalization on antitrust cooperation and enforcement. The Committee was co-chaired by James Rill, former Assistant Attorney General for Antitrust, and Paula Stern, former Chair of the International Trade Commission. Its executive director was Professor Merit Janow of Columbia University. The Committee was comprised of ten other members, including seven business or foundation executives and three professors (including the author) of law, business, and economics. At the time, the debate about a competition initiative in the WTO was active and gaining traction, and the U.S. Assistant Attorney General in charge of Antitrust, Joel Klein, had expressed strong opposition.[20]

The Committee held hearings, received submissions, and deliberated. In 2000, it issued a report containing numerous recommendations for increased coordination and cooperation and modes for convergence of law and process, in particular regarding multinational mergers and world cartels. It recommended also a Global Competition Initiative (GCI).[21] The GCI was envisioned as a virtual, voluntary forum with no ground address or secretariat, no power to make binding rules, and no power of adjudication. The idea for the enterprise stemmed from the realization that antitrust authorities, business people, and experts lacked a forum for the sharing of views and experiences, for close cooperation, and for exploration of common issues that could lead to convergence or harmonization. Although competition problems were increasingly global, these issues had no logical antitrust home.

No existing organization filled the need.[22] The OECD was and is an organization of developed nations and is therefore—despite its outreach efforts—exclusive or limited. The UNCTAD caters to developing countries and was not satisfactory to developed countries. The WTO is a trade organization at which trade representatives have the seat at the table. Moreover, success at the WTO entails bargaining and trade-offs, in contrast to (what some antitrust officials saw as) the "purer" antitrust rule-of-law. Antitrust authorities lacked a table of their own. Further, in the WTO the mere prospect of committing their nations seemed to make the representatives reluctant to talk freely about solutions to common problems.

The GCI would by-pass the limits of each of these organizations. It would be a roots-up forum. It would include developing as well as developed countries. It would be purely voluntary, with no binding action. The logic of GCI, said the ICPAC Report, "stems in part from a recognition that countries may be prepared to cooperate in meaningful ways but are not necessarily prepared to be legally bound under international law."[23]

The ICPAC submitted its report to Attorney General Reno and Assistant Attorney General Klein in February 2000. In September 2000, at the Tenth Anniversary Conference for European Merger Control, Assistant Attorney General Joel Klein made a proposal to the international group present:

---

20. *See* Klein, *supra* note 12.

21. U.S. DEP'T OF JUSTICE, ANTITRUST DIV., REPORT OF THE INTERNATIONAL COMPETITION POLICY ADVISORY COMMITTEE TO THE ATTORNEY GENERAL AND ASSISTANT ATTORNEY GENERAL FOR ANTITRUST 281-85 (2000), *available at* http://www.usdoj.gov/atr/icpac/chapter6.htm [hereinafter ICPAC Report].

22. *See* Eleanor M. Fox, *Competition Law and the Millennium Round*, 2 J. INTL. ECON. L. 665, 677 (1999) (proposing a World Competition Forum).

23. ICPAC Report, *supra* note 21, at 284.

[W]e all realize that bilateral efforts, while absolutely essential, are not a complete answer. . . . There is still a lot of work to be done without an obvious unifying forum in which to do it. Our Advisory Committee recognized the problem and called for a Global Competition Initiative. I have been giving this considerable thought and believe that, whatever happens on antitrust at the WTO . . . we should move in the direction of a Global Competition Initiative, cautiously and on an exploratory basis, but in the end I think such a development is almost inevitable.[24]

Klein's proposal came as a surprise to his counterparts, for until this moment unilateralism had held sway. European Competition Commissioner Mario Monti almost immediately welcomed the idea as a positive move towards multilateralism. But Klein's proposal was met with skepticism. Why yet another forum? Would the GCI only tread on the toes of the OECD, the UNCTAD, and to some extent the World Bank? Was the GCI an empty vessel, a "headless horseman," only meant to take the wind out of antitrust sails in the WTO?[25]

Gradually, however, the idea of a virtual global antitrust initiative gained acceptance. In February 2001, the International Bar Association, with support from the American Bar Association Antitrust Law Section and the Fordham Corporate Law Institute, convened a meeting at Ditchley Park near London, under the leadership of William Rowley. The meeting resulted in support for an international competition initiative, which was to be useful to "multiple audiences: government, business, legal and other communities,"[26] inclusive of developing as well as developed jurisdictions, and a forum in which participants could speak in their individual capacities. Rationalizing the merger process was to be high on the agenda. Indeed, rationalizing the burdensome, uncoordinated premerger filing processes of scores of jurisdictions seemed to be business lawyers' motivating passion for their support. The bar associations offered resources and analytical support and offered to host an initial meeting to consider how to proceed.[27] This offer was not accepted by the antitrust authorities, who envisioned government agency control, but the Ditchley meeting and the support it engendered was to be a crucial factor in the eventual launch of the ICN.

The increasing but still tentative enthusiasm for the global forum coincided with the change in presidential administrations in the United States, from Bill Clinton to George W. Bush. U.S. support was crucial to the project. But "in early 2001 it was . . . not yet clear how the incoming U.S. [Bush] administration would view the proposed initiative."[28]

---

24. *See* Joel Klein, Assistant Attorney Gen., Antitrust Div., Dep't of Justice, Address at the EC Merger Control 10th Anniversary Conference: Time for a Global Competition Initiative? (Sept. 14, 2000), *available at* http://www.usdoj.gov/atr/public/speeches/6486.pdf. *See also* Merit Janow, *Observations on Two Multilateral Venues: The International Competition Network (ICN) and the WTO, in* INTERNATIONAL ANTITRUST LAW & POLICY: 2002 FORDHAM CORPORATE LAW INSTITUTE 49 (Barry Hawk ed., 2003); Jones, *supra* note 11.

25. *See* Lawson Hunter & Susan Hutton, *Global Competition Initiative: A "Headless Horseman?," in* INTERNATIONAL ANTITRUST LAW & POLICY: 2000 FORDHAM CORPORATE LAW INSTITUTE ch. 3 (Barry Hawk ed., 2001); *U.S. and Canadian Antitrust (Panel Discussion), in* INTERNATIONAL ANTITRUST LAW & POLICY: 2000 FORDHAM CORPORATE LAW INSTITUTE 45-59 (Barry Hawk ed., 2001).

26. Janow, *supra* note 24, at. 51.

27. *Id.* at 52-53.

28. *Id.* at 53.

Charles James was confirmed by the Senate as Assistant Attorney General in Charge of Antitrust in June 2001. He consulted with Timothy Muris, newly appointed Chairman of the Federal Trade Commission, and both gave their support to the project. James was especially attracted to the idea that the initiative would be "all antitrust, all of the time"[29] (i.e., not trade), and that the initiative would focus on practical tasks where solutions were achievable (i.e., ICN was not to be or to auger a lofty antitrust code for the world). The collaborators in the new initiative would pick the "low-hanging fruit" that touched no raw nerves. For example, they would seek consensus as to the earliest date on which jurisdictions would receive pre-merger notifications, thus eliminating the inefficiencies of multiple uncoordinated filing requirements and waiting periods for multinational mergers.

By fall 2001, sufficient consensus had been achieved, and at the annual Fordham International Antitrust Conference, representatives of fourteen jurisdictions[30] came on stage and announced the launching of the initiative. As for the name of the enterprise, the word "global" was dropped. In the wake of the rioting at the G-8 summit in Genoa, "global" was feared to be a red flag to anti-globalization activists. "International" was a less-charged descriptor. "Network" added an interactive, non-hierarchical flavor. Thus: International Competition Network.

By the time of the announcement of the launching at Fordham, some contours of the enterprise were clear, and others soon became clear. The members of the ICN were to be the government antitrust (competition law) authorities. Representatives of international organizations such as the OECD, the UNCTAD and the World Bank were to be invited to participate in the work and meetings (but not the voting) as non-governmental advisors (NGAs). NGAs were to be drawn, also, from the legal, business, academic, and consumer communities. The latter would be designated by the antitrust authorities of their nation. There would be a steering group, with a chair and vice, who would facilitate activities including the annual conference and telephone conference calls on issues and procedures, and who would manage a web site. The work was to be project-based. Working groups would do research, draft memos, formulate proposed best practices, guidelines and recommendations for consideration at the annual meetings, and engage in other projects such as (as it developed) informal technical assistance. The ICN would facilitate the sharing of information and experience, facilitate cooperation, and work towards consensus rules, principles, methodologies, and procedures.

Thus, the ICN was born. As events took their course in Cancun,[31] the WTO initiative dissolved into the background, and the ICN emerged center stage.

B. The Functioning and Evolution of the ICN

One of the first tasks of the ICN steering group was to launch a work plan. Projects were to be prepared for the first annual meeting, which, it was decided, would be held in Naples in September 2002. To qualify, the subject matter of the project was to be of

---

29. *See* Charles James, *Reconciling Divergent Enforcement Policies: Where Do We Go From Here?, in* INTERNATIONAL ANTITRUST LAW & POLICY: 2001 FORDHAM CORPORATE LAW INSTITUTE 1, 5 (Barry Hawk ed., 2002).

30. Australia, Canada, European Union, France, Germany, Israel, Italy, Japan, Korea, Mexico, South Africa, United Kingdom, United States, and Zambia.

31. *See* Stiglitz & Charlton, *supra* note 18.

broad general interest and likely to engage a large portion of the membership, and the project was to be capable of achieving practical outcomes that would make a difference. A project on merger process was inevitable.

The project work would be carried out by working groups. Each working group would be guided by a chair or by co-chairs, often pairing (as it later developed) a developed and a less developed nation. All interested members of the ICN and the NGAs would be invited to participate in the work of the working groups.

In the initial stages of the ICN, working groups were formed: on multijurisdictional mergers and advocacy. The project of the Advocacy Working Group was designed to highlight the important but daunting work competition authorities can do within their own governments: supporting pro-market policies where the market can work, advocating against unnecessary regulation and statism, and helping to develop a culture of competition.

The working group devised and distributed questionnaires to all members, synthesized the answers, and wrote a report, which was distributed at the first annual conference in Naples and posted on the ICN's website. The report addressed the role of advocacy, the fruits of advocacy in terms of tangible benefits for consumers and respect for the competition authority, political influences on advocacy, and the importance of institutional settings in either facilitating or obstructing the authority's advocacy efforts. This work has been, reportedly, of significant aid to competition authorities.

The Merger Working Group was divided into three subgroups: notification and procedures, the analytical framework of merger review, and investigation techniques in merger review. In the first year, the investigative techniques subgroup planned and soon thereafter held a workshop. The analytical framework subgroup sent questionnaires to all members, with a view to comparing the substantive tests for merger prohibition of each jurisdiction. The subgroup compiled the information for each jurisdiction and wrote a discussion paper on the objectives of analytical frameworks. This subgroup was later to compile an extremely helpful handbook consolidating the analytical methodologies of all responding jurisdictions, with case examples.

The subgroup on notifications and procedures was charged with the subject at the core of the defense bar's support for ICN. Leading members of the bar had been decrying chaos in merger control.[32] At the time, approximately sixty-five nations required merger review, and the jurisdictions had different timing, different informational requirements, arbitrary filing deadlines, and often a long-arm reach to mergers with little relationship with the regulating jurisdiction.

The subgroup included leading merger lawyers from the private sector, who were active and indeed essential participants and became the reliable backbone of the work. The subgroup studied merger notification requirements in all member jurisdictions. It deliberated on practical possibilities for coherence. For the first annual meeting, it proposed that the ICN members adopt eight guiding principles to make the process more transparent, fair, and efficient, and it proposed three recommended practices to address needs for

---

32. *See* Global Forum for Competition and Trade Policy, Special Report, *Policy Directions for Global Merger Review* (1999) (organized by J. William Rowley, then Chairman of the International Bar Association's Section on Business Law and Director of the Global Forum on Competition and Trade Policy) [hereinafter Global Competition Review 1999].

clarity, efficiency, and limits on excessive jurisdiction. It organized a "weblinks" project that posted links to the merger laws and guidelines of all members; it prepared a report on the costs and burdens of merger notification and review; and it later published a report on confidentiality waivers with a model form and a survey and report on merger filing fees. Also, the subgroup devised and facilitated a common template for the presentation of information about merger review procedures from the various jurisdictions. The group requested the member authorities to fill out the template with their own information for posting on the ICN website. More than fifty jurisdictions have now posted their information in template form, which is a form very friendly to practitioners and other users.[33]

The eight guiding principles proposed were: recognition of each jurisdiction's sovereignty; transparency; non-discrimination on the basis of nationality; procedural fairness; efficient, timely and effective review; coordination among agencies reviewing the same transaction; convergence of processes to agreed best practices; and protection of confidential information. The three recommended practices were: an appropriate nexus with the reviewing jurisdiction; clear and understandable notification thresholds based on objectively quantifiable criteria such as sales and assets (not market share); and a recommendation on the timing of merger notifications. The latter has two aspects: flexibility as to the earliest date of notification so as to permit parties to coordinate multijurisdictional filings, and elimination of filing deadlines.

The guiding principles were adopted, after discussion, at the first annual conference. The recommended practices were discussed, and later amended and adopted, along with others, at the second annual conference.

Thereafter, more working groups were formed. A Working Group on Competition Policy Implementation studied technical assistance by more mature to younger agencies and wrote a detailed report on what types and character of technical assistance tends to work and what does not work. The same working group devised and implemented an informal program of technical assistance. Under one model, the consultation model, more mature agencies were invited to offer assistance (usually answering questions and having dialogues by telephone) in whatever area of competition law and they chose, and younger agencies were invited to make inquiries of designated persons. Under the second form, the partnership model, more mature and younger agencies were paired, and they developed a mentoring/mentored relationship for the give-and- take in answering inquiries and addressing problems.

A Cartel Working Group was formed. Its members are currently preparing a manual on Anti-Cartel Enforcement Techniques. The working group has thus far posted three chapters on the website. It produced an anti-cartel enforcement template, available on the website, providing a common format for organizing the information of rules and procedures of the various jurisdictions' anti-cartel enforcement regimes. It assists host nations in organizing cartel workshops in many places in the world, attempting to make the training geographically available.

Also formed was a Working Group on Antitrust Enforcement in Regulated Sectors. This group studied the role of antitrust in banking and produced a report on the appropriate interaction between competition and regulations in the banking sector. It developed

---

33. *See* International Competition Network [ICN], *Merger Working Group 2008-2009 Work Plan, available at* http://www.internationalcompetitionnetwork.org/media/library/mergers/Merger_WG_3.pdf.

ten best practices, such as an open competitive environment without unnecessary restrictions. A Working Group on Telecommunications Services produced best practices of a similar sort on the respective roles for antitrust and regulation in the telecommunications sector.

In the earliest years of the ICN, the projects undertaken were chosen in part for their essentially noncontroversial and practical nature in line with the formulation expressed by Charles James and echoed by the steering group's first chair, Konrad von Finckenstein of Canada, that the ICN would be devoted to getting practical tasks done. It became apparent, however, that some of the major issues of coherence were not about the nuts and bolts of practice.

A proposal was made to study legal standards for abuse of dominance, with a view towards proposing recommended practices. Abuse of dominance was potentially a "lightning rod" subject. In the United States, the scope of the law (the prohibition against monopolization) had been increasingly narrowed.[34] Indeed, many American jurists and policy-makers had expressed the view that almost all strategies of dominant firms, acting alone and not with competitors, are pro-competitive and help consumers, and that most antitrust challenges to dominant firm conduct merely protect competitors from efficient conduct.[35] Many jurisdictions, and probably most developing countries, have a different perspective. In their experience, abusive use of power by dominant firms is a principal obstacle to achieving a competitive market. After discussion and debate, the steering group authorized the study of abuse of dominance.

Accordingly, a Working Group on Unilateral Conduct[36] was formed. It is co-chaired by the German Bundeskartellamt and the U.S. Federal Trade Commission. An unprecedented number of members signed up to participate in the Working Group on Unilateral Conduct, and a very large number of NGAs joined the group as well. The initial subjects studied were: what are the objectives of unilateral conduct rules?, and what is substantial market power,[37] and how is it proved? Questionnaires were formulated and distributed, answered by scores of members and NGAs, and analyzed. Memoranda were drafted, summarizing and describing the result and were vetted in telephone conference calls with contributions from participants around the world, and by email. The working group co-chairs and other interested participants then drafted recommended practices, which again were vetted by participants around the world. The work product was submitted to the steering group and eventually submitted to the membership, debated, and adopted.

The Working Group on Unilateral Conduct is also addressing specific practices that may be anticompetitive. It studied or is studying exclusive dealing, tying and bundling, discounts and rebates, and predatory pricing. It designs and distributes questionnaires to the members to obtain information about their rules and methodologies. It is in the process of assimilating answers regarding certain practices. In doing so, the co-chairs pay particular attention to what the various authorities mean when they use words such as

---

34. *E.g.*, Verizon Commc'ns Inc. v. Law Offices of Curtis V. Trinko, 540 U.S. 398 (2004).

35. *See* U.S. DEP'T OF JUSTICE, COMPETITION AND MONOPOLY: REPORT ON SINGLE-FIRM CONDUCT UNDER SECTION 2 OF THE SHERMAN ACT (2008), *available at* http://www.usdoj.gov/atr/public/reports/236681.pdf.

36. Essentially, this means the law of abuse of dominance and its U.S. counterpart, monopolization.

37. This would include dominant firm or monopoly power.

"anticompetitive," "effect," "foreclosure," and "intent" in order to understand divergences—often concealed by a superficially common language.

The above description gives a sense of the work of the working groups. There is much more.

In addition to the work of the working groups, the ICN (as noted) sponsors workshops on merger and cartel analysis, detection, and enforcement. Most recently, it held a workshop on unilateral conduct, which focused on implementation of the recommended practices thus far adopted and analytical techniques for identifying significant market power and abuses.

The annual conferences are the culminating event of each year's work and a focal point for completing promised work product. They provide a platform for the recommendations of the working groups, and other proposals, which are presented, debated, and normally adopted. The programming is designed to be inclusive of a large range of participants, including individuals from developing countries. For the first years, the annual conference programmers shied away from controversial issues. At the last annual conference (Kyoto 2008), however, there was at last lively debate. Issues of unilateral market power and abuse of superior bargaining position were addressed. All annual conferences feature a number of break-out sessions, at which participants explore issues more deeply and personally in small discussion groups.

After recommended practices are adopted, the working group that originated them normally gives guidance on how to implement them.[38] It may hold workshops to do so. For the recommended practices on merger process in particular, the ICN keeps track of their implementation, including which members change their legislation or rules to bring their systems into conformity. At least thirty-five ICN members, which is approximately half of all members with a merger notification system, have amended their laws, regulations, or procedures, bringing them into closer conformity with the ICN recommendations.[39]

Do members have any (soft) obligations to adopt the ICN recommended practices? On this point there is some difference of opinion or nuance. Konrad von Finkelstein , while chair of the Steering Group, said:

> [T]he ICN is aspirational in nature. It makes best practice proposals. These practices are the product of the best minds in both the private and public sectors. While there is no obligation to adopt any of the best practices endorsed by the ICN, implementation will result from the persuasiveness of our work products, peer pressure among Members and the advocacy and support of NGAs.[40]

---

38. *See* ICN, *Implementation Handbook, Examples of Legislative Text, Rules, and Practices that Conform to Selected ICN Guiding Principles and Recommended Practices for Merger Notification and Review Procedures* (April 2006), *available at* http://www.internationalcompetitionnetwork.org/media/archive0611/conforminglangdraft handbkfinal.pdf, Fifth Annual ICN Conference, Cape Town, South Africa (May 2006). *See also* Randy Tritell, U.S. Federal Commission, Presentation, Panel II: Notification and Procedures, Third Annual ICN Conference, Seoul, Korea (April 2004), *available at* http://www.internationalcompetitionnetwork.org/media/library/conference_3rd_seoul_2004/notiproctritell.pdf.

39. E-mail from Randy Tritell, Director, Office of International Affairs, U.S. Federal Trade Commission, to Eleanor Fox (Dec. 12, 2008) (on file with author).

40. Konrad von Finckenstein, *International Antitrust Policy and the International Competition Network*, in INTERNATIONAL ANTITRUST LAW & POLICY: 2002 FORDHAM CORPORATE LAW INSTITUTE 38 (Barry Hawk ed., 2003).

William Rowley has suggested that ICN's success is directly related to implementation of the merger recommendations. He has expressed concern that "the implementation effort to date has not found sufficient traction to make a material difference with many of those agencies or regimes where implementation is most needed."[41] The ICN Steering Group issued a news release at the close of the 2008 Kyoto meeting entitled "Competition authorities from around the world send clear message on convergence"—implying that greater conformity of the ICN members with the ICN recommendations is a measure of the ICN's success.[42]

IV. Assessment: Effectiveness, Legitimacy, Sufficiency

In this section we ask: is the ICN effective? Is it legitimate? Is it sufficient? Then we turn to a question that has bearing on all three inquiries: does the ICN have power or influence, and if so, what are the implications?

A. EFFECTIVENESS: IS THE ICN EFFECTIVE?

To assess effectiveness, we revert to the ICN's ambitions. The ICN's stated ambitions are modest. It aspires to provide "competition authorities with a specialized yet informal venue for maintaining regular contacts and addressing practical competition concerns,"[43] with a view also to facilitating consensus on issues of law and procedure, thereby bringing antitrust enforcement practices, techniques, and interpretations into greater alignment. The ICN also works to facilitate mentoring of newer and less experienced antitrust authorities.

The ICN was designed to be informal, to have no ground location, and to make no binding rules. The ICN was meant to have no power. The ICN was designed *not* to be antitrust governance.

Recall that the question at the outset was not whether the ICN would fulfill tasks of governance but whether it would do anything at all; whether it would be a "headless horseman;"[44] whether it would be redundant; whether it could and would have any momentum given its humble virtual aspirations; and whether, even if it got traction, it would quickly wither away.

Judged by its own aspirations and against a chorus of skeptics, the ICN has been an enormous success. It appears to be stable and (virtually) rooted. It has leadership and

---

41. *See* William Rowley & Omar Wakil, *The ICN Five Years On*, GLOBAL COMPETITION REVIEW May 2007, at 29, *available at* http://www.mcmillan.ca/Upload/Publication/WRowley_OWakil_TheICN_five_years_on.pdf. The authors decry the fact that "the merger review provisions of a considerable number of ICN member regimes do not conform with, or even fall below, the ICN's recommended practices." They list non-conforming jurisdictions and their thresholds. *Id.* at 30-31. *See also* Ron Stern, General Electric, ICN Implementation Panel: Implementation Is the Goal of the ICN, Fourth Annual ICN Conference, Bonn, Germany, June 2005, *available at* http://www.internationalcompetitionnetwork.org/index.php/en/library/conference/4.

42. ICN, Newsroom 2008, http://www.internationalcompetitionnetwork.org/index.php/en/newsroom/2008 (last visited Mar. 18, 2009).

43. ICN, About the ICN, http://www.internationalcompetitionnetwork.org/index.php/en/about-icn (last visited Mar. 18, 2009).

44. *See* Hunter & Hutton, *supra* note 25.

momentum. It is a unique connector of people around the world committed to a common task. It inspires hard work and devotion. It provides information, perspective, and contacts. It provides guidance and moral support to newer and more vulnerable agencies pursuing the lonely and often resisted task within their nation of creating a competition culture. It provides a blueprint or referent for agencies in drafting or revising their rules or regulations.[45] And it gives anchor to the officials of the newer agencies appearing before legislators and jurists. "This is the way it is done in the world" or "This is the international standard of good practice" is powerful testimony.

The ICN has created a unique work product. Its leaders and cadre of volunteer workers are continually adding to the work product, virtually all of which is posted on the website. The templates for merger analysis and cartel enforcement convey important information about each jurisdiction in a common form, and the merger guidelines handbook of principles, analysis, and methodologies is both an informative comparative document and a guidance document. The competition advocacy toolkit and the cartel handbook, including methods of detection and enforcement, are deeply informational and useful sources for knowledge and skills. The various authorities' answers to questionnaires, for example, on the objectives of their law and on their framework for analyzing unilateral practices, are all posted on the website and form a unique trove of information for research and understanding of comparative antitrust law. The guiding principles and recommended practices in merger review are a particular achievement. Nations' implementation of the recommended practices and use of the guiding principles have rationalized the global merger process, reducing costs, eliminating conflicts, and facilitating transactions. The annual workshops on cartels and periodic workshops on mergers and, more recently, unilateral practices, educate and facilitate convergence. Close professional relationships are forged in the working groups, in the course of the informal mentoring and technical assistance, and at the annual meetings. These networks of relationships deepen understanding, respect, and trust; build community; and provide ready-made avenues for mutual assistance and cooperation.

It appears to this observer that, as a result of the ICN, merger process in the world has improved; cartel enforcement in the world has improved; and the mutual understanding of laws, policies, and cultures among the myriad participants has reached a new level.

One may also assess the effectiveness of the ICN in relation to other organizations. Recall that skeptics argued that existing organizations were already performing or could easily perform the tasks targeted by the ICN. From the vantage of eight years later, what are the merits of this claim of redundancy? The answer to the question is clear. The ICN is doing work that neither the OECD, nor the UNCTAD, nor the WTO could do or could do as well, given the nature, the constituency, and the orientation of each of these bodies.[46] Moreover, a WTO antitrust regime never materialized. The very informality of the ICN, with its lack of secretariat, antitrust-only agenda, noncontroversial initial agenda

---

45. The ICN has, for example, given advice to officials of the new antitrust regimes in China and India. The American Bar Association Antitrust and International Law Sections and the International Bar Association have likewise given advice to China and India based in the ICN recommendations. India has explicitly linked revisions to its draft merger rules to the ICN recommendations.

46. The ICN's unique networking approach, which harnesses immense energy of private stakeholders, is a distinguishing feature. Also, there is a complementarity among the organizations. The ICN's active and dynamic work has acted as a competitive spur to enliven the competition policy work of the OECD.

(merger filing rules and modes of advocacy), and lack of power to make rules or enforce them, has conduced to the fruitful interchange that characterizes the ICN.

Should the ICN's effectiveness be assessed also in terms of the extent to which its recommended practices have been adopted and implemented? Some argue that implementation is the measure of the ICN's success.[47] This author disagrees, but observes nonetheless that there has been a substantial degree of implementation of the ICN's merger process recommendations.

B. Legitimacy: Is the ICN legitimate?

The ICN is built around notions of participation and transparency.[48] All antitrust jurisdictions of the world are invited to belong to the ICN. Representatives of all authorities are invited to attend the annual meetings and workshops and to take part in all working groups. A substantial number of non-governmental advisors (predominantly from the defense bar and business but also some academics and others) actively participate, although consumer groups and representatives of the private plaintiffs' bar are noticeably underrepresented. Attendance at the annual meetings is high. More than 500 delegates, representing more than seventy agencies, NGAs, observers, and guests, took part in the Seventh Annual Conference in Kyoto in April 2008. The ICN prides itself on its open, inviting, inclusive, and transparent process.

The degree of participation by other than a central core of mature antitrust jurisdictions is predictably limited by lack of funds (despite some funding by the ICN), lack of time, sometimes by lack of expertise, and sometimes by language. (The lingua franca of the meetings is, most often, the language of the host plus English).[49] The numerous round-the-world telephone conferences are scheduled for times that will be not inconvenient for most of the world, but this often means 8:00 a.m. eastern time, disadvantaging Australia, New Zealand, and the Far East. Less well-resourced authorities have constraints against aspiring to be chair of the steering group and even serving as a member of the steering group. This means that authorities from resource-strained nations have less opportunity to participate in setting the agenda and to write first drafts of recommendations. Individuals not confident of their English language abilities or their level of technical knowledge are reluctant to speak and often remain silent. These practical considerations may produce effective underrepresentation of developing countries, and (at least by default)

---

47. *See* Rowley & Wakil, *supra* note 34; ICN, Newsroom 2008, *supra* note 40; ICN, Newsroom 2008, *supra* note 41.

48. *See* Eleanor M Fox, Report on the First Annual Conference of the ICN 11 (Naples, Italy, Sept. 2002) (summarizing the remarks of William Kovacic regarding efforts of the ICN fund-raising committee to attract sufficient funds to enable the attendance of representatives of the developing countries), *available at* http://www.internationalcompetitionnetwork.org/media/library/conference_1st_naples_2002/icn_naples_report.pdf. Most systems, however, do not follow the United States procedure but limit challenges to notifiable mergers. For the importance, generally, of transparency, *see* William Kovacic, Remarks Before the Seoul Competition Forum: Achieving Better Practices in the Design of Competition Policy Institutions (April 20, 2004), *available at* http://www.ftc.gov/speeches/other/040420comppolicyinst.pdf. *See also* Slaughter, *supra* note 1; Raustiala, *supra* note 2.

49. Sometimes an additional option, such as German, Italian, French, or Spanish, is available, but translation is expensive. The documents are almost all in English. The merger recommended practices are posted also in French and Spanish.

greater voice of the two antitrust leading models in the world—the United States and the European Union.[50]

These observations would make less difference if the ICN had no power. But does the ICN have power, in spite of its proclaimed nature? This is a question to which we shall come.

C. SUFFICIENCY: IS THE ICN SUFFICIENT?

By definition, the ICN is not sufficient as antitrust global governance; it was never meant to be. It is not sufficient to solve world competition problems that arise from the internationalization of markets such as the disconnect between anti-dumping laws and predatory pricing, jurisdictional gaps allowing export cartels, parochial uses of state measures that immunize private action, and the lack of a coherent view of world competition and trade-and-competition problems.[51] The ICN limits itself to facilitating dialogue, mentoring, and nudging applications of national laws to be more alike.

By facilitating convergence of procedures and legal principles, the ICN could pave the way towards a future international antitrust system.[52] Perhaps more likely, the ICN and the work of the sister institutions, think tanks, and international conferences and training programs, will fill enough of the gap, softening rough edges, to alleviate a felt need for an international law of antitrust. The work of the ICN may tend to confirm the perspective that only an open, informal, and notionally non-consequential process can achieve as much trust, respect, sharing, and consensus as the ICN has done and is likely to do.[53]

D. DOES THE ICN HAVE POWER?

What if the ICN has power by effect, if not purpose? What if the ICN is becoming the international antitrust standard-setting (norm-setting) organization for the world? The answer has bearing on all three of the factors examined: effectiveness, legitimacy, and (in part) sufficiency.

---

50. *See* Daniel Sokol, *Monopolists Without Borders: The Institutional Challenge of International Antitrust in a Global Gilded Age*, 4 BERKELEY BUS. L.J. 37, 106–07 (2007). Sokol notes that the concern is mitigated by membership of several developing countries on the ICN steering committee. Indeed, in January 2009, David Lewis of South Africa became the interim chair of ICN, succeeding Sheridan Scott of Canada upon her stepping down as Competition Commissioner of Canada.

51. *See* Eleanor Fox & Janusz Ordover, *Internationalizing Competition Law to Limit Parochial State and Private Action: Moving Towards the Vision of World Welfare*, 24 INT'L Bus. Law. 458 (1996); WTO 1997 Report, supra note 10; Heimler, *supra* note 8.

52. The degree of divergence of the law of the various nations was cited as one reason why the world was not ready for an antitrust regime in the WTO. *See* Douglas Melamed, *Promoting Sound Antitrust Enforcement in the Global Economy*, in INTERNATIONAL ANTITRUST LAW & POLICY: 2000 FORDHAM CORPORATE LAW INSTITUTE ch. 1. (Barry Hawk ed., 2001).

53. These accomplishments, however, do not imply that the ICN meets the unfilled need for a coherent trade-and-competition perspective. *See* Fox & Ordover, *supra* note 51; WTO 1997 Report, *supra* note 11. *See* Chris Noonan, THE EMERGING PRINCIPLES OF INTERNATIONAL COMPETITION LAW (2008) Noonan suggests that "[t]he work of the ICN could formally and informally feed into the WTO processes." *Id.* at 563.

We have seen in other fields, such as banking, the migration of soft law standards set by discrete and even secretive bodies into harder international standards.[54] We have noted the use of soft antitrust law to influence legislators and jurists. And we have noted the claim that if the ICN does not achieve convergence, it has failed. More particularly, the ICN merger recommendations have influenced and continue to influence the drafting and revision of merger laws of member nations,[55] and they informed an OECD recommendation on merger notifications.[56] It is therefore not fanciful to consider that the ICN's output may develop into soft law with some influence.

On this hypothesis, we might wish to consider two points. First, in setting the agenda, is more deference due to the ideas and preferences of the "outer group"? If more deference is accorded, might more issues surface that are of particular interest to the less mature and smaller nations and other jurisdictions that are less like the United States and Europe? Second, might the ICN wish to balance the benefits of consensus against the benefits of freedom to diverge? After debate has failed to convince all members that a proposed standard or methodology is good for it, might the ICN, rather than pressing for consensus and thus tending to discount outliers, give the nod to a diversity of perspectives?[57] To consider this balance between convergence and recognition and appreciation of diversity, I present below two examples, and then ask, how important to "global antitrust" is the emergence of one rule for the world?

At the first annual conference in Naples 2002, the Mergers Working Group presented recommended practices regarding merger notifications: what mergers must be notified to reviewing authorities, when, and in what form. The proposed recommended practices required (among many other things) a significant nexus between the merging parties and the reviewing jurisdiction, so that transactions that were unlikely to have an appreciable anticompetitive effect in a potential reviewing jurisdiction would be screened out of the process. One of the recommended practices stated that the nexus (e.g., sales in the jurisdiction) should be measured by the local activities of at least two parties to the transaction or by reference to the acquired firm's business in the local territory.

The director general of a competition authority of a small country argued that sales of the *acquiring* business in the local territory should also, independently, satisfy the nexus requirements, since a domestic acquiring company might harm competition in that nation by acquiring a foreign potential entrant. He proposed amending the language of the recommendation so that nexus could be satisfied by the activity of the acquired company "or the acquiring company." The amendment was opposed on grounds that the addition would pick up too many non-problematic mergers, and that nations could, as does the

---

54. Roman Grynberg & Sacha Silva, *Harmonization Without Representation: Small States, the Basel Committee, and the WTO*, 34 WORLD DEV. 1223 (2006) (noting that small states, excluded from the process, were put at a competitive disadvantage by banking standards).

55. *See* Tritell, *supra* note 38; Rowley & Wakil, *supra* note 41.

56. OECD, Recommendation of the Council on Merger Review, OECD Doc. C(2005)34 (Mar. 23, 2005), *available at* http://webdomino1.oecd.org/horizontal/oecdacts.nsf/linkto/c(2005)34.

57. *See* Dani Rodrik, *Institutions for High Quality Growth: What Are They and How to Acquire Them?*, STUD. IN COMP. INT'L DEV., Sept. 2000, at 3, 5 ("I emphasize the importance of 'local knowledge' and argue that a strategy of institution building must not overemphasize best-practice 'blueprints' at the expense of local experimentation."). Yet, there are trade-offs between blueprints and experimentation; there is opportunity for "institutional arbitrage"; much technical legislation can be borrowed wholesale or at least be a source for learning. *Id.* at 13-14.

United States, address the problem by allowing the authorities to challenge even non-notifiable mergers. The proponent of the amendment was later accommodated.[58]

Smaller and transitional jurisdictions may have preferred the wider net for merger control (although they also may be relieved by a smaller pool of transactions to vet). The ICN recommendation was advantageous the business communites, which worried about the business costs of a wider net more than the public costs of mergers that might slip through the holes in the net.[59]

The second example involves abuse of dominance. There was, as to be expected, some diversity of point of view on how to analyze and apply abuse-of-dominance law. The first important issue was how to prove "substantial market power"—which is a first step in the proof of whether the economic power was abused. In proving substantial market power, may significant or even controlling weight be appropriately given to the putative dominant firm's large market share? May and should proof of a large market share satisfy the plaintiff's prima facie case?

Most mature jurisdictions and their NGAs argued that proof of substantial market power is a very complex matter; that market shares mean very little in themselves, and that significant economic evidence is necessary to hurdle this first stage in an abuse of dominance case. They expressed concern that a simplistic market share test for market power would unjustly label too many firms "dominant," the label of dominance would focus a spotlight of suspicion, and the effect would be to cause the firms to pull their punches and thus to chill their pro-competitive, inventive behavior.

The South African representative, David Lewis, Chair of the South African Competition Tribunal, strongly disagreed with the rejection of the market share proxy. He especially disagreed with the proposed recommendation as applied to South Africa. He argued that developing countries cannot bear a heavy burden of proof at this first stage of proceedings against an apparently dominant firm; that authorities should be able to use high market share as a proxy for market power; and that a rule requiring complex economic evidence and analysis to determine whether a firm with a high market share was indeed dominant would tend to put beyond the ability of developing countries' competition authorities the power to challenge the persistent monopolistic conduct that blights their economies.[60]

---

58. The ICN addressed the problem by adding to the recommendation. Notification thresholds may be based on the acquiring firm's local activities but only if 1) the authority would otherwise be deprived of jurisdiction over the merger, and 2) additional jurisdictional screens are added to minimize filing requirements for non-problematic acquisitions. *See* ICN Document Library, Document Type: Guidelines/Best and Recommended Practices, http://www.internationalcompetitionnetwork.org/index.php/en/library/doc-type/1 (last visited Apr. 5, 2009).

59. Of course, if business is paying unnecessary costs, this also harms their customers—the consumers. Under either proposal, filing thresholds based on sales or assets in the jurisdiction are arbitrary. A larger quantum of sales is no indication of anticompetitive effects. Market share in the jurisdiction would be better correlated with anticompetitive effects, but market share as the benchmark was rejected as too subjective and giving less certainty.

60. David Lewis, *Chilling Competition*, *in* INTERNATIONAL ANTITRUST LAW & POLICY: 2008 FORDHAM COMPETITION LAW INSTITUTE (Barry Hawk ed., 2009). Under South African competition law, "[a] firm is dominant in a market if – (a) it has at least 45 percent of that market. . . ." Competition Act of 1989 s. 7. *See* Michal S. Gal, *Extra-territorial Application of Antitrust—The Case of a Small Economy (Isreal)*, *in*, COOPERATION, COMITY, AND COMPETITION POLICY (A. Guzman ed., forthmocimg Oxford 2009) (noting that ICN rejection of the market share proxy may imply that small jurisdictions will not have the practical ability to

A document emerged from the process and was adopted at the annual conference. It states that proof of substantial market power is a complex inquiry; "[a] firm should not be found to possess dominance/substantial market power without a comprehensive consideration of factors affecting competitive conditions in the market under investigation."[61] "Market shares should be used" as a starting point for analysis. "However, since market shares fail to reflect certain important features of the competitive environment, in particular market dynamics, they should be put into perspective by consideration of other factors, such as potential entry. . . ."[62] The recommendation identifies the various indicia that should influence analysis.

South Africa lost the battle. The mature jurisdictions and their NGAs, however, lost their claim that large market share is no sign at all of economic power and should never be a basis for burden-shifting.

Developing countries and poorly-resourced authorities might have been better satisfied by an ICN endorsement of the use of a high market share, or persistent high market share in the context of a high-barrier market, as a proxy for substantial market power. They might have been better satisfied by an ICN document stating that a high market share accompanied by barriers to entry may give rise to a presumption of economic power, which is in fact the law in many jurisdictions.[63] The recommendation is more conservative than the law.

An unastounding observation can be drawn from these vignettes. The voices of the major players in the developed world are likely to be more influential than the voices of developing and small economies. Even so, the leaders of the ICN have shown consistent resolve to include, involve, and respond to all voice.

E.   IMPLICATIONS OF THE HYPOTHESIS OF ICN's POWER OR INFLUENCE: THE
     IMPORTANCE OF CONVERGENCE VERSUS THE IMPORTANCE OF
     RECOGNIZING DIVERSITY

How important to a linked world is commonality of rules, standards, and procedures? How important is recognition of diversity?

To explore these questions, we might take three examples. The first example is one of the ICN merger recommendations: the recommendation of flexibility in the required timing of filings so as to permit early merger notification—e.g., merger notification may be made upon the parties' certification of a good faith intent to consummate the transaction. This recommendation addressed the problem that jurisdictions specified different triggering dates, resulting in a situation in which the same merger could not be filed on the same

---

bring abuse of dominance cases; "in reality small jurisdictions are mostly, once again, rule takers rather than rule makers.").

61. ICN, Unilateral Conduct Working Group, *Dominance/Substantial Market Power Analysis Pursuant to Unilateral Conduct Laws* 2 (May 9, 2008), *available at* http://www.internationalcompetitionnetwork.org/media/library/unilateral_conduct/Unilateral_WG_1.pdf.

62. *Id.* at 3.

63. Caselaw in most jurisdictions, including the United States, provides that very high market shares (such as in excess of 70 percent) shifts the burden to the putative dominant firm to show that it does not have significant market power. *See Market Share as an Indicator of Monopoly Power, in* 2002 ANNUAL REVIEW OF ANTITRUST LAW DEVELOPMENTS 53, 53-54 (5th ed. 2002). For Europe, see Case C-62/86, AKZO Chemie BV v. Commission, 1991 ECR 3151.

day in the many regulating jurisdictions. Uniform implementation of the recommendation would simplify the filing process and save millions of dollars for the merging firms. Also, it would enable agencies to coordinate reviews. Retaining divergences would serve no purpose. Nothing was at stake for a nation faced (merely) with changing its permissible filing date to accord with the recommendation.

The second example is the nexus requirement, discussed above. Mature jurisdictions and the business community preferred a rule limiting the set of mergers subject to notification in a jurisdiction to those in which both merger partners or at least the acquired partner had sufficient sales or assets in the jurisdiction. At least one small jurisdiction expressed preference for a more copious rule that would have allowed the nexus requirement to be fulfilled by the significant presence of either merging partner. Adopting the smaller net would go some distance in helping to solve the recognized problem of excessive reach of merger filing laws. It would help grease the wheels of business efficiency in the world. It would also relieve agencies of the burden of vetting large numbers of probably non-problematic mergers. Yet (at least arguendo for purposes of this example), for some jurisdictions the larger net would enhance the quality of their antitrust enforcement, catching acquisitions of potential entrants. Would the wider reach significantly disrupt and unduly burden business? Experts may disagree. In any event, mere advocacy for conformity with an ICN recommendation such as this seems harmless.[64] The *principle* requiring an appreciable nexus is not fairly contestable. The recommendation brings home the importance of the principle in a potentially unruly world. One may hope that all nations will take cognizance of the principle. If some nations object to its restrictive application, they may simply design their nexus rules as they see fit.

Third is the proof-of-dominance example from the unilateral conduct project. The problem here is much more complex because it is about substantive principles of law, claims of "sound economics," practicalities in enforcement, market contexts, and agency capabilities. Economies differ from one another. Some economies have been historically monopolized by state enterprise, others boast merit-grown businesses in robust markets and no historic statism. Some agencies are well funded and staffed with teams of economists; others are resource starved. The different characteristics may call for different formulations of law.[65]

This third example is the one example in which ICN outputs are susceptible to becoming soft and maybe harder law for the world. Common substantive principles of law for the world are good and useful for coherence, efficiency, and guidance, all other things being equal, as the developing country experience constantly affirms.[66] But all other things are not equal. Especially if ICN standards might become an influential source for antitrust standards in the world, it seems to this writer that, in the third situation, recogni-

---

64. Such advocacy is especially harmless in view of the amendment to the proposed nexus recommendation. *See supra* note 57.

65. *See* John Fingleton & Ali Nikpay, *Stimulating or Chilling Competition, in* INTERNATIONAL ANTITRUST LAW & POLICY: 2008 FORDHAM COMPETITION LAW INSTITUTE (Barry Hawk ed., 2009) (noting that economies with sluggish markets might need more aggressive antitrust).

66. *See* Commission on Growth & Development, *The Growth Report: Strategies for Sustained Growth and Inclusive Development* (2008), *available at* http://www.growthcommission.org/index.php?option=com_content&task=view&id=96&Itemid=169.

tion of diversity is more important than conformity. Thus, the ICN might usefully adopt Slaughter's "norm of legitimate difference."[67]

V. CONCLUSION

In conclusion, the ICN has been dramatically successful. Its limits have also been its success. It has carved out a space for itself that no other enterprise or project could have achieved. Its own success may have overtaken calls for a global framework for antitrust proper, suggesting that a future WTO project might limit itself to the trade-competition issues left unaddressed.[68] The agenda of "all antitrust all the time" has paid off.[69]

The exuberance comes with two big caveats, based on inconsistent scenarios. First, the ICN's roots are only virtual roots. Virtual roots are easily pulled up. If the leaders and networkers stop pedaling the ICN bicycle, the bicycle will fall. This amazing virtual organization is fully in place, and its movers are unusually hard working and productive (and open and inviting). But ICN depends on continuous devoted leadership and engaging and useful projects. While there is almost no end to global competition problems, the ICN has picked much of the low-hanging fruit. The problems yet to be tackled are more controversial and harder to solve.

To address these problems, a productive future might encompass three aspects: First, the agenda. Some projects might be chosen even when the problems appear intractable. For example, future projects might include nationalistic aspects of financial rescues; cumulative regulation (where laws of many nations are applied to the same cross-border conduct) that becomes over-regulation; jurisdictional clashes; and needs of developing countries in addition to technical assistance and capacity building. Discussing these problems with new sympathy and in new light might lead to an architecture for building bridges over persistent gaps.

Second, testing effectiveness. The ICN might take inventory to examine its apparent successes and shortcomings.[70] What do the representatives at the ICN annual conferences do when they return home? Do they brief their fellow officials and staff? Do they examine their nation's state of compliance with ICN recommended practices, and consider how to comply (or why not to comply)? Do they do nothing? How well do the working groups function, and how useful is their output? How useful are the workshops for learning techniques and ideas that can be implemented at home? What can be learned from networks in other disciplines, such as are examined in this symposium issue?[71]

---

67. *See* Slaughter, *supra* note 1, at 247-50, 259. The norm of legitimate difference mandates "respect . . . to national officials unless a specific reason exists to suspect that they will chauvinistically privilege their own citizens." *Id.* at 248. "It enshrines pluralism as a basis for, rather than a bar to, regulatory cooperation . . . ." *Id.* at 249.

68. These include the flanking issues of dumping/predatory pricing, market access, export cartels, and state shields that protect private anticompetitive conduct.

69. The circumscribed mandate need not deter the ICN from addressing global questions that *are* "all antitrust"–such as a world clearing house for filings of international mergers, methodologies and priorities to modulate systems clashes, and the role of the financial crisis in the application and enforcement of antitrust laws.

70. *See generally* Kovacic, Achieving Better Practices, *supra* note 48, for a wise presentation of the virtues of self-examination.

71. Other networks, however, are more ambitious and by their very ambition they confront challenges that the ICN avoids. By working towards rules and world governance, other networks may confront two types of

Third: movers and leaders. Inspired and hard-working movers and leaders are critical. The ICN has been blessed with such leaders from scores of countries for all of its nine years. The inspirational flame must keep burning. It is most likely to keep burning in a world in which the ICN matters.

While the first caveat was that the ICN could fall apart, the second caveat is: the ICN might have power. The ICN is a vehicle for soft-law formation, and soft law has a tendency to become hard law. For that reason, more acknowledgment might be made of the needs and context of developing countries, small economies, and indeed all jurisdictions other than the United States and the EU. This can be done seamlessly within existing frameworks. Work product, even in the form of recommended practices, can acknowledge differences among nations in analytical methodologies and in preferred rules—differences that may stem from stages of development, unequal agency capacities, and weakness of competition in local markets. Moreover, the power scenario means that the ICN must pay continued attention to transparency, process, and participation and indeed might consider a greater voice for consumer groups, plaintiffs' lawyers, and other under-represented stakeholders.

The ICN has far surpassed expectations. It fills a real need in global antitrust. As Joel Klein said in the months before the birth of the ICN, if it did not exist, it would have to be invented. It is a model worth exploring by other disciplines in the cohort of national economic law that applies to conduct in global markets and yet resists internationalization.

---

problems, as identified by Pierre-Hugues Verdier, *supra* note 2 at 115. First, domestic political pressures may be brought to bear to constrain regulators' autonomy to pursue wise global policy. Second, tighter cooperation is likely to raise significant conflicts over distributive consequences, for the costs and benefits of proposed standards may fall differently on different states. In view of these problems, Verdier questions Slaughter's claim that networks offer an alternative to regulatory races to the top or bottom. *Id.* at 143. By rejecting the pursuit of binding rules, the ICN by-passes these problems.

[12]

What can we really learn from the competition provisions of RTAs?

SIMON J. EVENETT

1. Introduction

When considering the negotiation of international binding rules on competition law, competition policy, and associated enforcement matters, something of a paradox has emerged in recent years. On the one hand, the members of the World Trade Organization (WTO) decided not to negotiate a binding multilateral framework on competition policy during the Doha trade round. Yet, many of the same countries have signed, in principle, binding international rules on competition law and policy in regional trade agreements. Even though it did not claim to be comprehensive, one analysis (OECD, 2005a) identified competition policy-related provisions in 47 recently concluded regional trade agreements (RTAs). Relatedly, the number of RTAs has mushroomed in recent years, and

Professor of International Trade and Economic Development, Department of Economics, University of St Gallen and Research Affiliate, CEPR. The author thanks Ana Maria Alvarez and Lucian Cernat for their guidance in the preparation of this Chapter. Comments from Stefan Amarasinha, Oliver Solano Castro, Pierre Horna, Anestis Papadopoulos, John Preston, and David Round were gratefully received. The views expressed in this Chapter are those of the author and do not necessarily reflect the views of the UNCTAD Secretariat.

40

What we can really learn from competition provisions in RTAs

competition provisions are often part of such initiatives. This seemingly paradoxical outcome raises a number of questions not all of which, admittedly, will be pursued here. One question that is considered here, however, is what are the implications of the recent proliferation of competition law provisions in RTAs for the negotiation of potential future multilateral agreements on competition law and policy? This chapter examines various possible answers to this question and offers a note of caution about what lessons can be properly drawn from the recent experience with rule making on competition law and policy in RTAs.

Section 2 of this chapter summarizes the principal components of competition provisions in RTAs and makes some comparisons with a leading proposal for a multilateral framework on competition policy advanced in 2002-03. Section 3 poses a number of questions that might help establish the implications of rule making in RTAs for future multilateral decision making. Section 4 attempts to answer some of those questions, drawing on the factual record established in Section 2. Concluding remarks are offered in Section 5.

2. An overview of the competition provisions of recent RTAs

Depending on how one counts RTAs in 2005, the cumulative number of such agreements signed lies between 225 and 275 (World Bank, 2005:27).[1] The number of such agreements that were concluded rose sharply after 1990 with 10-20 agreements typically signed annually. In certain years in the mid- to late-1990s, the number of RTAs signed exceeded 25, indicating that a significant amount of rule making was taking place outside the auspices of the WTO.

Many of the recently signed RTAs contain provisions on competition law and policy. Recently the OECD Secretariat analysed the competition provisions of 47 RTAs and this has shed considerable light on their prevalence and content (OECD, 2005a). Notwithstanding concerns about the representative nature of this sample of 47 RTAs, a point the OECD Secretariat properly acknowledges, in what follows here extensive reference is made to this OECD study. Readers are cautioned that the interpretations given here to the evidence presented are the author's own and any criticism of these interpretations should be directed at the author and not at the OECD Secretariat.[2]

The OECD analysed 47 RTAs, 36 per cent of which are between developing countries (which are often referred to as South-South agreements), 3 per cent were between industrialized economies (the so-called North-North agreements), and the remainder have signatories from developing and industrialized economies (the so-called North-South agreements.) Eight types of competition policy-related provisions were identified in these 47 RTAs. It is important to appreciate that not every agreement contained all eight types of competition provisions, although to be included in the OECD study presumably at least one such provision must have been present. The classification of competition provisions in the OECD study was as follows:[3]

1. 'Measures'[4] relating to the adoption, maintenance, and application of competition law;
2. Provisions relating to the cooperation and coordination of activities by competition law enforcement bodies;
3. Provisions relating to anti-competitive acts and measures to be taken against them;
4. Provisions relating to non-discrimination, due process, and transparency in the statement and application of competition law;
5. Provisions to exclude the use of anti-dumping measures against the commerce of signatories;
6. Provisions concerning the circumstances and conditions under which recourse to trade remedies (such as anti-dumping measures, countervailing duties, and safeguards) are permitted;
7. Provisions relating to the application of dispute settlement procedures in competition policy-related matters;
8. Provisions relating to flexibility and progressivity, sometimes referred to as special and differential treatment (SDT) provisions.[5]

It should be evident from the above list that certain provisions are related to others. For example, the first and third provisions could be similar, and the fifth and sixth provisions address similar (but not identical) matters. Care must therefore be taken when interpreting

42

What we can really learn from competition provisions in RTAs

the summary statistics concerning the prevalence of different types of provisions that are presented below. Any analysis of this kind is likely to raise questions about the nature of the classifications used, misclassification errors, and double-counting, points that the reader may want to bear in mind.

As the OECD study notes, the overwhelming impression is that of the substantial diversity in the competition provisions adopted in RTAs. Having said that, one common feature of the agreements analysed was that statements that anti-competitive acts, orchestrated by both the state and the private sector, could frustrate the broad liberalizing objectives of the RTA in question. It seems, therefore, that the competition provisions were included not for their own sake, or because of their own intrinsic value or merit to signatories, but rather as an important measure to support the barrier-reducing objectives of the RTA. This is a statement about the purported rationale for including competition provisions in RTAs and not about the effects of such provisions which, in principle, need not be confined to influencing cross-border commerce.

Broad agreement on the ends, however, does not imply agreement on the means. As the OECD study shows, the types and prevalence of competition commitments taken on vary markedly across RTAs. The following provisions were found in at least 35 of the 47 RTAs considered in the OECD (2005a): provisions relating to the exchange of evidence and information, provisions relating to the abuse of dominance or monopolization, provisions relating to anti-competitive agreements between firms such as cartels, provisions relating to non-discrimination (in particular as they relate to state monopolies), and provisions establishing, or encouraging, consultation mechanisms for the resolution of disputes on competition policy-related matters.

In contrast, the following provisions were found in five or fewer of the 47 RTAs studied: provisions relating to negative comity, provisions relating to positive comity, provisions relating to anti-competitive mergers, provisions relating to the elimination and use of anti-dumping measures between signatories, provisions relating to less-than-full reciprocity of commitments for lesser developed signatories,[6] and provisions directly related to exemptions and exceptions for lesser developed signatories.

It would seem, then, that the recent batch of RTAs contains relatively more provisions on anti-competitive practices than on forms of special and differential treatment, as well as more provisions on consultations and broader cooperation mechanisms between competition enforcement agencies than specific obligations relating to negative and positive comity, the latter often being thought of as 'deeper' forms of inter-agency cooperation on competition matters.

Given that a majority of the agreements analysed in the OECD study are North-South agreements, and that the Northern parties are often the United States, Canada, or the European Communities and its Member States (EC), the diverse picture alluded to above does include certain similarities across distinct groups of RTAs.[7] The OECD (2005a) notes that agreements involving the EC tend to be oriented more around substantive rules than around cooperative provisions, the latter being found more in agreements involving Canada and the USA. Two broad 'families' of competition provisions can, therefore, be identified (OECD, 2005a:14).[8] Having said that, readers should note that a clear majority of RTAs in the OECD study do not include the EC, the USA, or Canada as a signatory, and these RTAs do not necessarily fall into the two families identified above. Diversity, it would seem, is the dominant attribute of RTA provisions on competition law and policy.

Since the principal matter to be addressed in this chapter is the potential lessons of rule making in RTAs for future multilateral initiatives on competition law and policy, it would be remiss not to compare the above findings with the ill-fated proposals for a multilateral framework on competition policy that were advanced before the Cancun Ministerial Meeting of WTO members in 2003. Although a number of WTO members made submissions concerning the potential elements of such a multilateral framework, the European Community and its Member States advanced the most comprehensive set of proposals in this respect and here they will form the comparator to the RTAs analysed in the OECD study.

The EC proposed that a binding multilateral framework on competition policy should have the following components: a commitment to ban so-called hard-core cartels and to take measures at national or regional level to give effect to such a ban, a commitment to adhere to so-called core principles (of non-discrimination, due

44

What we can really learn from competition provisions in RTAs

process, and transparency) in the statement of national competition laws, modalities for voluntary cooperation between agencies responsible for the implementation of competition law, and progressivity and flexibility, including technical assistance and capacity building, for developing country members of the WTO. It was also argued that dispute settlement would only apply to the first two of the above elements. This, in turn, implies that the application of competition law would not be subject to the Dispute Settlement Understanding (DSU) of the WTO, at least under the provisions of the multilateral framework proposed by the EC.

In a few respects, the proposed multilateral framework would have gone further than the competition provisions negotiated in RTAs in recent years. Special and differential treatment provisions are relatively scarce in the latter[9], as are provisions relating to the core principles (although, in so far as they concern state monopolies and state aids, they are quite common in recent RTAs.) The dispute settlement provisions of the proposed multilateral framework stand in contrast to the consultation mechanisms and arbitration procedures found in most RTAs.

Conversely, most recent RTAs do not confine their provisions on anti-competitive practices to hard-core cartels and typically refer also to abuses of a dominant position and to state monopolies and enterprises. Indeed, in this respect, it is worth noting that the substantive provisions that the EC proposed for inclusion in a multilateral framework are in fact narrower than those they often negotiate in RTAs with trading partners.[10] It would be unwise, therefore, to conclude that the principal proponent of a multilateral framework on competition policy was seeking to 'multilateralize' the provisions that it had agreed to in numerous bilateral and regional trade agreements. Rather, the proposed multilateral framework on competition policy would have taken international rule making in yet another direction. This framework would have added to the diversity of international rules on competition law and policy rather than replicated or merely extended those competition provisions found in RTAs.

In the light of the recent competition policy-related rule making in RTAs, it is interesting to note the objections from developing country officials and analysts to the ill-fated proposals for a multilateral framework on competition policy.[11] At first some argued that hard-core cartels were not a concern for developing countries, a view that was tempered once the range and extent of the international cartels prosecuted in the 1990s began to be better understood. Later, some argued that the multilateral framework would not do enough to tackle the harm done by such cartels to developing countries. Others argued that abuses of a dominant position, rather than cartels, were more important for developing countries and that the proposed multilateral framework did not reflect this priority. A different group argued that rule making of this nature was not directly related to the market-opening objective of the multilateral trading system, while others saw such proposals as attempting to prise open markets in developing countries 'through the back door' (presumably through tackling import-impeding anti-competitive practices.)

Some opponents in developing countries felt that the proposed non-discrimination provisions would compromise their government's ability to influence mergers and acquisitions on the grounds of industrial policy and the like. Concerns about implementation costs worried others, as well as fears that developing countries did not have enough expertise to negotiate in 'new' areas such as competition policy. Insufficient attention to special and differential treatment in the proposed framework, it was said, was another ground for opposition. The proposed cooperation provisions of the multilateral framework, essentially being voluntary, were felt to offer little benefit to developing countries. Others argued that negotiations on a multilateral framework should not advance because of a lack of progress in other areas of the Doha Round. Moreover, those WTO members that never really wanted the Doha Round in the first place, which according to some careful observers in Geneva could account for over half of the WTO membership, were a natural constituency to oppose negotiations on multilateral rules on competition policy or on any of the Singapore Issues for that matter.

It might be useful to ask what the grounds for opposing the multilateral framework might reveal about the true level of support by developing countries for rule making on competition policy in RTAs. For the sake of argument, let us take the criticisms of the multilateral framework at face value,[12] putting aside the possibility that some of these criticisms were advanced merely for tactical reasons. It would seem that developing countries' emphasis on the

46

What we can really learn from competition provisions in RTAs

abuse of dominant position does manifest itself in the competition provisions in recent RTAs. Of the RTAs involving developing country signatories in the OECD study (OECD, 2005a) only COMESA omits such provisions.[13] In contrast, more RTAs involving a developing country—five in fact—omit provisions on anti-competitive agreements, including hard-core cartels. (Interestingly, most of those five agreements involve Chile as a party.)

Moreover, developing country concerns about general non-discrimination provisions do seem to find counterparts in recent RTAs. Only the agreements between Bulgaria and Israel, between Canada and Costa Rica, between the members of CARICOM, and between Chile and the USA appear to contain broad non-discrimination provisions. The other RTAs involving poorer countries do not. These two considerations may account, in part, for the opposition of developing countries to a multilateral framework, yet their willingness to sign RTAs with competition provisions. (If this is the case then the paradox alluded to in the Introduction of this chapter may well be resolved.[14])

Yet, if their opposition to a multilateral framework is anything to go by, certain aspects of the competition provisions in recent RTAs cannot surely find favour with developing countries. First, the special and differential treatment provisions of most RTAs are limited or non-existent. Where they do exist, according to the OECD (2005a) study, almost all refer to transition periods and to technical assistance, not to less-than-full reciprocity.[15] This is true of both North-South and South-South agreements.

Developing country opposition to a multilateral framework on the grounds of market opening sits very oddly with the fact that most RTA competition provisions are explicitly motivated by the desire to support other market-opening measures, such as tariff reductions. Moreover, developing country agreement to take on substantive provisions on hard-core cartels in RTAs (and in other areas of competition law for that matter) is hard to square with their concerns about implementation costs. Furthermore, as noted earlier, the voluntary cooperation provisions of many RTAs are pretty limited, yet developing countries agreed to them while they opposed what they regarded as insufficiently robust provisions on voluntary cooperation in the proposed multilateral framework. It could be argued, of course, that unsatisfactory experiences in RTAs were the reason why developing countries opposed similar provisions at the multilateral level. If this is the case, then one also ought to see greater opposition to such provisions in negotiations over future RTAs.

A further perspective on these matters can be obtained by asking, given the arguments made by developing country officials against a multilateral framework, what they imply for their 'real' view of the two families of competition provisions in RTAs identified in the OECD study.[16] The broader range of substantive obligations that is a characteristic of RTAs in which the EC is a signatory is, on the basis of what was said about the proposed multilateral framework, a mixed blessing. The inclusion of abuse of dominance provisions would appear on this metric to be a plus, but concerns about the implementation costs of taking on a number of substantive provisions (many of which are based on intra-EU experience) is a negative. Meanwhile, the so-called North American family of agreements, with their emphasis on cooperation provisions and on fewer substantive provisions, and a tendency to exclude competition provisions from dispute settlement, might be attractive to developing countries in saving them implementation costs and limiting the enforceability of the competition provisions. But such agreements are unlikely to allay any fears about the likelihood of precious little cooperation actually resulting from these RTAs.

To summarize, this section has described the principal characteristics of competition provisions in RTAs and contrasted them with the components of the ill-fated multilateral framework on competition policy, which was proposed by the EC. Even though there is a broad agreement on the goal of the former, there was significant diversity in their legal content. It was also argued that the latter was neither a direct expansion, nor a multilateralization, of the competition provisions that the EC has negotiated in recent RTAs with its trading partners.

Moreover, the grounds stated by many developing countries for opposing the multilateral framework on competition policy were used to assess what they might reveal about the developing country's preferences concerning competition provisions in RTAs. It would seem that the recent batch of RTAs contains provisions that do not match up with the stated preferences of many developing countries,

48

What we can really learn from competition provisions in RTAs

a finding that may reflect the give and take of commercial diplomacy. This finding also holds in RTAs among developing countries, and therefore cannot be attributed solely to the limited bargaining power of developing countries when negotiating with industrial countries over the terms of an RTA.[17] This finding concerning South-South RTAs is unfortunate, as there appears to be no set of current RTAs whose experience, if deemed over time to be satisfactory, could satisfy the developing country critics of the previous multilateral initiative on competition policy.

3. Questions raised by the recent rule making in RTAs on competition policy

The purpose of this section is to describe the questions that might arise in thinking through the implications for future multilateral rule making on competition law and policy of the recent proliferation of RTAs containing such rules. The next section will go some way to answering those questions. The separation of the discussion of questions from answers is deliberate as readers may be more persuaded of the arguments made in one section than in the other.

A number of important preliminary comments are in order as they provide some context and boundaries to this investigation. First, in thinking through the lessons for possible future multilateral rule making, one should be clear what institutional parameters a new multilateral initiative might add to. For example, have the lessons drawn taken account of the potential future relationship between a multilateral initiative and the set of RTAs that prevail at that time?[18] A number of logical possibilities present themselves here. Do the lessons drawn imply that a future multilateral agreement would substitute for or strengthen the competition provisions in prevailing RTAs? Or, implicitly, are the lessons being drawn on the assumption that the potential multilateral initiative will operate independently of the prevailing set of RTA provisions? A related matter would concern the sequencing of any potential future multilateral and non-multilateral initiatives on competition law and policy. Moreover, the standing of the latter's provisions in any future multilateral agreement would have to be thought through.[19]

Another preliminary comment is that, *a priori*, the circumstances of WTO members differ so markedly and this ought to condition the lessons we draw from the competition provisions in existing RTAs. A competition provision in a given RTA may be successful, but to what extent is the success due to the characteristics of the RTA signatories, the circumstances that those signatories have faced, or the provision itself? Likewise, a competition provision in a given RTA may be barely used or used with few positive results, but does this imply that the provision would perform as well in every RTA or indeed if incorporated into a future multilateral framework? Separating out the effects of different influences to draw generalizable lessons is very difficult, especially as little is known about the operation of competition provisions in more than a few RTAs. (Hopefully initiatives such as this book and others will remedy this deficiency over time.[20]) We should not be surprised, therefore, that most of the arguments made are of a conceptual nature or involve reasoning by analogy.

When discussing lessons from RTAs, it is worth noting that multilateral initiatives could differ along (at least) the following important dimensions: membership, the inclusion and nature of substantive provisions to enact or enforce certain competition laws (recognizing that there are a variety of anti-competitive acts, including state-induced acts), the inclusion and nature of cooperation provisions, the inclusion and content of provisions for special and differential treatment, mechanisms for the resolution of disputes, and provisions relating to the statement and enforcement of competition laws in general. The fact that a multilateral initiative could differ along any of these dimensions suggests that there is a wide range of logical possibilities that readers should bear in mind. Therefore, if an analyst argued that an RTA's experience with competition provisions undermined the desirability or viability of one type of multilateral initiative, this does amount to a case against all multilateral initiatives. Moreover, readers might ask themselves whether the multilateral initiatives or initiatives being considered by an analyst are comprehensive, representative, or illustrative of the potential future set of such initiatives.

In interpreting recent experience another factor to bear in mind is that many bilateral, regional, and cross-regional initiatives on competition law and its enforcement between 1996 and 2003 have been influenced by the discussions in the WTO concerning the possible negotiation of a multilateral framework on competition policy. Some opponents, often found in the community of competition law practitioners and enforcers, preferred to see international cooperation take place outside of international trade fora.[21] As a result, the amount of effort that went into designing, negotiating, and eventually using the competition provisions in RTAs was almost surely less than could have been the case. Indeed, the growing number of bilateral accords between competition enforcement agencies and the prominence of the International Competition Network stand as evidence of where many in the competition law community have placed their efforts in recent years.[22]

Related factors were at work when RTAs including competition provisions were negotiated. It has been said that some developing country negotiators were well aware of the potentially precedent-setting nature of competition provisions in RTAs for discussions on a multilateral framework in the WTO. In addition, others have noted that linkages between competition provisions and trade remedies, such as anti-dumping, that were found in some earlier RTAs were avoided in subsequent RTAs precisely because such linkages might be explored in a multilateral context.

In short, it would be unwise to evaluate the content and performance of the current set of competition provisions in RTAs without bearing in mind the multilateral context in the run-up to the Cancun meeting of WTO ministers in September 2003, when a decision on the modalities for negotiations on competition policy in the WTO was made. To the extent that that decision and the prior debate condition current discussions on the efficacy of competition provisions in RTAs, including, in particular, the Economic Partnership Agreements between the European Union and selected African, Caribbean, and Pacific countries, the drawing of appropriate lessons from experiences after Cancun can be challenging too.

So what are the questions raised by the competition provisions in RTAs that may be relevant to the design of potential future multilateral initiatives on competition law and policy? In what follows, these questions have been organized around four themes.

The first theme concerns the *rationale for multilateral rules*. Here the following questions arise: What do the actual and stated rationales for competition provisions in RTAs imply about the appropriate rationale, or rationales, for a multilateral framework? 'Appropriate' here could be taken to mean 'widely acceptable', 'coherent', 'economically important', 'consistent with the long-standing goals of the multilateral trading system', and 'value adding', all of which are distinct, yet in some cases related, criteria for evaluating a proposed rationale for multilateral rules. The value-added criteria, for example, should make an analyst ask whether future multilateral rules are needed, given the current set of RTAs and other inter-governmental or inter-agency accords on competition law and related matters. Analysts should also be open to the possibility that the appropriate rationale differs across different types of anti-competitive activity. Moreover, the logical possibility that a rationale may be appropriate for a multilateral initiative without being an appropriate rationale for competition provisions in an RTA cannot be ruled out.

The second theme concerns the *impact of competition rules in RTAs on non-signatories* and whether this provides a rationale for multilateral action. Ever since the path-breaking research of Jacob Viner, RTA analysts have considered the possibility that these accords effectively discriminate against non-signatories, with possibly detrimental effects. In the present context, the question arises as to whether competition provisions in RTAs introduce discrimination (differential treatment) between WTO members? If so, what form does that discrimination take? Does it represent a violation of the Most-Favoured Nation (MFN) principle? Moreover, is there any evidence, or means to suppose, that the discrimination harms the commercial interests of non-signatories? If so, are there any non-discriminatory alternatives to the discriminatory provision that can attain the same legitimate goals as the latter? Or, is there another discriminatory provision that attains the same goals as the latter but does less harm to the commercial interests of non-signatories? Should any plausible alternatives exist to the discriminatory provision, can a ranking be established among them in terms of their desirability for inclusion in a multilateral initiative?

Analysts should also be open to the logical possibility that the commitments to non-discrimination in competition provisions are, in fact, implemented in such a way as to benefit all WTO members.

52

What we can really learn from competition provisions in RTAs

In which case one might ask whether, given the prevailing set of RTAs, there is much additional bite from implementing generalized non-discrimination provisions in a multilateral initiative on competition policy? Here much would turn on the nature of the non-discrimination provisions in prevailing RTAs, whether there are differences in such provisions across RTAs, as well as the substantive content of non-discrimination provisions in a multilateral framework.

A third theme concerns the *effectiveness of certain competition policy-related provisions of RTAs* that the debate over the proposed multilateral framework on competition policy from 1996 to 2003 revealed to be of particular interest to developing countries such as the provisions that relate to cooperation between signatories and the provisions relating to special and differential treatment. With respect to voluntary cooperation, the nature and likely extent of such cooperation is of interest, as are the factors conditioning the degree of such cooperation. It would be useful in this respect to know if 'harder' (that is more demanding) obligations to cooperate actually induce more cooperation, or at least make non-cooperation more costly or more transparent.

With respect to special and differential treatment, the following questions arise. In any particular RTA, were the transition periods appropriately tailored to the circumstances of, and technical assistance received by, the developing country signatory?[23] Did the transition periods merely postpone compliance to the last minute or were the transition periods used to nurture capacity (perhaps through programmes of capacity building and technical assistance) in the developing country? What factors, perhaps unrelated to the RTA itself, affected this outcome? Concerning less-than-full reciprocity provisions, to what extent, if at all, were the benefits of the RTA compromised by the signing of such provisions? For example, are there reasons to believe that certain anti-competitive practices exist that reduce the value of the RTA to its signatories and that could only effectively be tackled by full reciprocity on the part of a developing country signatory or signatories? Analysts should also be open to the possibility that the effective types of special and differential treatment vary across developing countries, and that the effects of different types of special and differential treatment depend critically on the other provisions contained in an RTA or in a future multilateral initiative.

The fourth theme concerns the *lessons for the political economy of successfully negotiating a potential future multilateral initiative.* Within signatories to an RTA it would be useful to know which interest groups, if any, were galvanized to support the inclusion of, and subsequent compliance with, the competition provisions of an RTA? The answer to this question might provide important clues as to the circumstances under which such interest groups would support a similar multilateral initiative. (The word 'similar' is used here with care, as surely any multilateral initiative must add value along some dimension to the set of prevailing RTAs for interest groups to support the former.) Analysts should be open to the possibility that an RTA indirectly strengthens the popular or interest group-based support for the enforcement of competition law in a signatory country through reinforcing the legal status of the competition enforcement agency and the resources that the national legislature gives to such an agency. Thus, the political economy linkages within signatories may be more varied than support for, or opposition to, a competition provision in an RTA at the time of negotiation or ratification.

There are also political economy factors at international level worth exploring. It would be useful to know which signatories to an RTA were keen on the inclusion of competition provisions, and which were opposed. How 'deep' was the opposition of any signatory and, relatedly, what if anything did these parties obtain in return for acquiescing to the inclusion of the competition provisions? Did proponents of such provisions come to regret their inclusion and, if so, why? Did initial opponents or sceptics change their view after the RTA was signed and, if so, why? How significant were concerns about negotiating and implementation costs in determining the level of support for competition provisions? Were concerns about implementation costs assuaged by the provision of technical assistance, capacity building, aid, or by weak dispute settlement provisions? Are there concerns that multiple RTA negotiations have placed too great costs on developing country parties and have increased the potential for adopting conflicting, or at least inconsistent, obligations? Alternatively, have trade negotiators in developing countries become more comfortable with competition provisions in RTAs as they have negotiated more such RTAs?

Other political economy questions relate to the relationship between existing provisions in RTAs and potential multilateral

54
What we can really learn from competition provisions in RTAs

initiatives. To what extent has the emergence of two families (recall the OECD Secretariat's finding of the so-called EU and US families) of competition provisions in RTAs imposed additional costs on signatory countries? What multilateral initiatives, if any, would be consistent with both families of RTA provisions? To what extent, if at all, would negotiators of a multilateral initiative be willing to substitute one set of competition provisions in RTAs for another set of provisions?

This section has argued that, while there is a wide range of interesting questions concerning the lessons for multilateral rule making of competition provisions in RTAs, there are a number of important factors that condition our ability to effectively answer them. Moreover, the efficacy of any future multilateral initiative on competition policy is likely to depend on some factors wholly independent of the experience of competition provisions in RTAs. These points ought to be borne in mind when considering the arguments advanced in the next section and in the rest of this book.

4. Some thoughts on the lessons from competition provisions in existing RTAs

As the OECD (2005a) study made clear, the often-stated motivation for competition provisions in RTAs is to ensure that the gains from implementing such agreements are not undermined by anti-competitive practices. Often this is articulated in market access terms, where the fear is that state-erected impediments to local markets are replaced by private anti-competitive acts.[24] It is worth dwelling on this rationale for international collective action, exploring what multilateral initiatives it appears to be consistent with and also those it is inconsistent with. In this respect the following points could be made. First, this motivation could be interpreted as being only concerned with a subset of the possible cross-border spillovers created by anti-competitive practices. Specifically, it is concerned solely with the effects of those acts on a country's export interests in so far as those interests can, or are attempting to, supply overseas markets. From this perspective, therefore, such a rationale would not consider as relevant the effects of anti-competitive practices in markets where a country's export interests source parts, components, or services.

Nor would this rationale place any weight on anti-competitive acts that harmed a country's consumers, including its government (which is typically a large purchaser of goods and services.)

Arguably, such a narrow conception of the purpose of multilateral competition rules would sit well with the long-established practice in trade negotiations whereby reciprocal exchanges of market access take place. Moreover, such multilateral rules would, in preserving or ensuring that previously agreed market access is secured, not be out of place with other WTO provisions that discourage Member States from nullifying or impairing the effects of reductions in border barriers.

Such a narrow conception would logically focus on those anti-competitive acts that block the entry into, or that directly impair the competitive position of those firms attempting to enter, overseas markets whether by direct exporting, by foreign direct investment, or by other legitimate means. Arguably, therefore, the focus here would be on some of the anti-competitive practices that fall under the heading of abuse of a dominant position and on anti-competitive vertical restraints. Cooperation provisions, including negative and positive comity provisions, could reinforce presumptions to take enforcement action against market access blockages.

A challenge faced by this approach is that the same mercantilist calculus that might encourage a government to seek the removal of privately inspired market access impediments abroad is the same calculus that seeks to delay, avoid, or prevaricate in investigating such practices at home. This consideration places a significant burden on the dispute settlement provisions of an agreement based on this narrow motivation for multilateral competition rules. Any arbitration or dispute resolution mechanism would have to judge the degree of inaction, or the ineffectiveness of action, of a signatory against an alleged blockage to market access. Judging whether a signatory has gone far enough, or has acted in good faith, is a lot harder than judging whether a government has done something at all. The nature of such disputes would be extremely contentious. These concerns would be exacerbated if the agency tasked with enforcing the competition law and associated international obligations rejected the mercantilistic calculus in favour of a welfare standard. Employing either a total welfare standard or a consumer welfare standard is

56

What we can really learn from competition provisions in RTAs

unlikely to satisfy the demands of a trading partner whose sole interest in any market access-related investigation is going to be the interests of its exporters.

It would be useful to examine how well the current set of RTAs has fared in the face of these challenges. In particular, in jurisdictions with independent competition agencies, many of whose officials would openly reject a mercantilistic calculus, surely there are doubts as to how effective the competition provisions have been in clearing market access blockages? This is an empirical question and it would be helpful to know more about the factual record in this regard.

Another way of looking at this matter is to note that a multilateral framework based on a narrow market access perspective would almost surely require a change in the competition laws of signatories so as to entrench the market access objective. In this way, even independent competition agencies would be forced to consider market access objectives when examining complaints of firms in the import-competing sector. (Of course, if the competition agency has multiple objectives, as many do, the agency could still find reasons to demote the market access objective.) These points are mentioned not because competition agencies should as a general proposition take on market access-related objectives, but because it seems that the logic of the narrow market access conception of multilateral rules would almost surely require that steps be taken to ensure that competition agencies take those objectives seriously. These considerations, and the others detailed above, would surely become important if the market access objective of current RTAs was to be generalized into a multilateral agreement.

Although a narrow market access motivation for a multilateral framework aligns well with the traditional emphasis on border barrier reduction in the WTO system and its predecessor, developments during the latest round of multilateral trade negotiations suggest that an exclusive focus on market access may no longer command universal support. At the Doha Ministerial meeting in 2001, WTO members added promoting economic development as an explicit objective to the multilateral trading system. Without doubt the export opportunities of developing countries, and the private anti-competitive acts that may impede them, have some bearing on the economic development prospects of poorer countries. But other cross-border competition-related knock-on effects do too, and a development focus might therefore provide a rationale for a multilateral initiative on competition policy that goes beyond securing market access. (Of course, what is logically possible need not be uppermost in the minds of trade negotiators at the moment, or indeed at any future point in time, and the following remarks should be seen in that light.)

The first point to be made in this regard is that many developing country exporters do not sell directly to customers in industrialized countries. Instead, they often sell to intermediaries, some of which are large oligopolistic trading companies. These intermediaries may have good access to the markets of industrialized countries while at the same time exerting considerable buyer power over suppliers located in developing countries. The potential for abuses of a dominant position by these intermediaries could motivate a different type of multilateral initiative on competition policy. Very recent World Bank research that has tried to demonstrate how little benefit non-reciprocal preferences are to the African, Caribbean, and Pacific countries has placed considerable weight on buyer power-related arguments. In their discussion of the determinants of the value of non-reciprocal preferences Hoekman and Prowse (2005:5) argue that:

> "to the extent there is market power on the part of either importers/distributors (Francois and Wooton, 2005) or the transport and logistics sector (Francois and Wooton, 2001), the benefits of preferential tariff reductions will be captured at least in part by those intermediaries with market power rather than the exporters. If preferences apply to highly protected sectors in donor countries, they will result in high rents for those able to export free of trade barriers. However, the existence of these rents will be known to buyers, and if they have the ability to set prices (have market power), the rents may predominantly be captured by distributors or other intermediaries (Tangermann, 2002). There is evidence, based on the African Growth and Opportunity Act, AGOA preference scheme, that the pass through of preference margins is indeed partial at best. Olarreaga and Özden (2005) find that the average export price increase for products benefiting from preferences under AGOA was about 6 percent, whereas the average MFN tariff for these products was some 20 percent. Thus, on average exporters received around one-third of the tariff rent. Moreover, poorer and smaller countries tended to obtain lower shares — with estimates ranging from

58

What we can really learn from competition provisions in RTAs

> a low of 13 percent in Malawi to a high of 53 percent in
> Mauritius. In the case of market power, the result is a simple
> redistribution of the benefits of preferences: rents are
> transferred to importers."

It would be useful to see if other research and experience reinforce these findings.

The second non-market access-related spillover that could influence the development prospects of poor countries is that related to cartels with cross-border consequences. There is now a growing body of literature on these matters, which is quite well known, and there is no need to repeat all of the findings here.[25] National decisions about cartel enforcement can generate two cross-border spillovers, which may form the basis for international collective action. Non-enforcement of a cartel law, or more simply non-enactment of such a law, may encourage internationally minded cartels to organize and hide evidence in that jurisdiction — so harming those trading partners whose consumers and producers source goods from cartel members. In contrast, the successful prosecution of an international cartel by a jurisdiction may result in the cessation of its activities in other jurisdictions, either directly through the collapse of the cartel or indirectly through other jurisdictions taking measures to prosecute the cartel and to demand an end to its anti-competitive acts. Either way, the latter jurisdictions have benefited from the prosecution in the original jurisdiction. Both spillovers imply that, in the absence of a global norm to enact and seriously enforce a cartel law, there will be a sub-optimal degree of cartel enforcement. To the extent that the victims of such sub-optimal enforcement are the poor and the defenceless, then a development-related rationale for a multilateral initiative could be advanced.

The third cross-border spillover created by anti-competitive acts that could motivate international collective action relates to mergers and acquisitions that have international reach. The effects of consolidation on markets need not be confined to the jurisdictions where the headquarters of the participating firms are located. Given the resurgence in merger and acquisitions activity after the first quarter of 2005, and the last wave of such activity between 1995 and 2000, these matters deserve at least some thought, even if action is unlikely to result in the foreseeable future. Now, it could be argued that, like industrialized economies, developing countries could undertake merger reviews that evaluate the effect of the proposed transaction within their jurisdiction and, where appropriate, place conditions on the approval of the transaction. This argument is not without its problems, however. Leaving aside concerns that developing countries may not have the technical expertise to evaluate complex transactions, from the perspective of the merging parties and their legal counsel surely there are concerns that the decisions of many competition agencies might conflict, that the total impact of the remedies sought by such agencies individually are sub-optimal compared to other alternatives, and that delays and expenses are greater than otherwise.

These factors suggest that firms with international operations may have an interest in some international coordination and cooperation on merger enforcement (that arguably goes well beyond the current approaches pursued by members of the International Competition Network). Competition enforcement agencies may see advantages in coordinating and sequencing investigations, and even in specializing in certain types of investigations, much in the same way that certain national competition law enforcement agencies in the same jurisdiction cooperate with one another. Arguably, the current discussions on international cooperation on competition law and enforcement are a long way from this type of outcome, but the goal here is not to show what is practicable immediately but where the logic of internalizing cross-border spillovers leads to in terms of international collective action.

To summarize, so far in this section it has been argued that the narrow market access-related perspective that has apparently motivated many competition provisions in RTAs would face significant (principally implementation-related and political economy-related) challenges if generalized at the multilateral level. The first challenge is created by the fact that market access objectives are not entrenched in the competition laws of many countries. Difficulties are likely to arise in reconciling — or at least accommodating — a new objective with existing ones. The second challenge relates to the fact that preserving and expanding market access is no longer seen as the sole legitimate goal of the multilateral trading system. The inclusion of development objectives implies that, as far as anti-competitive acts are concerned, a multilateral initiative that is confined to market access-related cross-border spillovers is likely to be seen now as too limited in scope. Indeed to the extent that, as a general proposition, multilateral competition provisions stimulate inter-firm rivalry within national markets then one should expect non-trade-related developmental benefits to accrue also.[26]

Turning now to a different matter, what are the implications for multilateral initiatives on competition policy of the fact that many RTAs involving developing countries have few competition-specific provisions relating to special and differential treatment? Should we infer from this that developing country calls for such treatment at the multilateral level are all smoke without fire? One should be cautious about drawing this conclusion as the following four explanations could account for the factual record in this regard.

First, developing countries may have found in negotiations on RTAs that they could not persuade richer counterparts to accept special and differential treatment provisions on competition matters. Relatedly, developing countries may well feel more confident of successfully demanding these provisions in multilateral negotiations where there are more like-minded parties arguing together. Second, the generalized special and differential treatment provisions of RTAs may, from the perspective of developing countries, satisfactorily cover the competition obligations of those agreements and so additional competition-specific SDT provisions are unnecessary. Third, developing countries may not have demanded strong special and differential treatment provisions in RTAs, or at least acquiesced in having few of them, precisely because the binding competition obligations in an RTA were covered by limited dispute settlement provisions. Finally, developing countries may well have acquiesced in having few SDT provisions in RTAs precisely because they received something valuable in return somewhere else in the agreement (which might include preferential market access to the large economy of another signatory.) In the absence of a significantly large non-competition-related payoff in ongoing multilateral negotiations, this may well account for developing countries sticking to their demands for elaborate provisions on special and differential treatment.

Likewise, does the fact that few RTAs have strong dispute settlement provisions relating to their commitments on competition policy imply that a future multilateral framework on competition policy must have similarly weak (often taken to mean limited in scope and non-binding) mechanisms for resolving disputes between parties? Here it is worth noting that, with a few exceptions, generally RTAs have much weaker dispute settlement procedures than WTO agreements. Therefore, there may not be anything intrinsic about competition provisions in trade agreements that call for alternative, weak, or no dispute resolution methods. Second, the strength of dispute settlement procedures required is often a function of the nature of the provisions taken on in a trade agreement, not the least of which is whether the provisions are binding at all. To the extent, therefore, that competition provisions in RTAs contain few binding commitments of what to do, and what not to do, by signatories, there may be little point in seeking strong dispute settlement procedures for these provisions. An ambitious future multilateral initiative would, based on this logic, probably have to include robust dispute settlement provisions, and there may be little to learn from the current set of RTAs in this regard.

5. Concluding remarks: some notes of caution

It is not surprising that policy makers, government officials, practitioners, and scholars are interested in establishing lessons from one type of international rule making on competition law and policy for other potential international initiatives, especially given the differential rates of progress in agreeing competition-related measures in bilateral, regional, cross-regional, and multilateral fora. Indeed, as suggested in Section 2 of this chapter, there are a substantial number of policy-relevant questions that arise, in particular if one is exploring the lessons for future multilateral rule making from recently agreed RTA.

It has also been argued repeatedly, however, that our ability to draw solid inferences may at the moment be more limited than one might otherwise think. Not only is the available evidence on the operation of competition provisions in RTAs limited — arguably a concern that will be mitigated over time by research projects, such as those assembled in this book — but it must be recalled that many such provisions were negotiated at a time when the ultimately ill-fated proposals for a WTO multilateral framework on competition policy was being discussed. The legacy of those proposals is being

62

What we can really learn from competition provisions in RTAs

felt to this day, not least in negotiations over the Economic Partnership Agreements between the European Commission, on behalf of the European Union Member States and their former colonies. Furthermore, the nature and extent of one set of competition provisions agreed to in an RTA may well have depended on the nature of the other competition provisions in that agreement, and on other factors; this consideration again qualifies what conclusions we might draw about the preferences of signatories concerning international competition commitments and the associated implications for multilateral rule making.

It is also worth bearing in mind that the case for future multilateral rule making may well be made independently of developments in RTAs. Although there may be relationships between decision making in different international fora, and potential lessons to be learned from initiatives in each fora, care should be taken not to focus on these matters to the exclusion of other factors that might independently account for future international collective action on competition law and its enforcement.

NOTES

[1]The number of reported RTAs varies across studies for the following reasons: not all RTAs are reported to the WTO; RTAs involving countries that accede to the European Union are not always treated the same way by researchers; some RTAs that do not involve the creation of a free trade area on 'substantially all trade' are nevertheless included in some counts. For further discussion of the number of RTAs notified to the WTO in recent years, see the contribution of Alvarez et al. to this volume (Chapter 4).

[2]Readers may also want to bear in mind that this OECD study focuses on the nature of the competition provisions in RTAs and not on whether those provisions have been used, whether the parties to RTAs are satisfied with their use, or on other analyses of the effectiveness of such provisions. Generally, limitations in data availability seem to constrain the ability to address the latter points.

[3]It should be noted that the OECD study further sub-divided the following eight types of provision into component provisions, providing an even richer taxonomy of the competition provisions of RTAs.

[4]The word 'measures' here is taken to mean 'best endeavour' clauses and other promises as well as formal commitments to enact and enforce certain competition laws.

[5]The question does arise as to whether special and differential treatment (SDT) as traditionally understood in the context of trade negotiations and agreements is the appropriate way to think about the potential role and form of special and differential treatment in the competition law context. For example, some have argued that, in the trade context, SDT is motivated by the goal of deferring or avoiding international obligations and that, in the competition law context, SDT is motivated by the goal of furthering the effective implementation of competition law. The differences in goals, it is argued, may have implications for the different types of SDT deemed appropriate in a given situation.

[6]Here the phrase 'lesser developed signatory' is taken to mean a signatory to an RTA that is at an earlier stage of development than another signatory, and should not be confused with the United Nations classification of Least Developed Countries.

[7]Of the just under 30 North-South RTAs analysed, at least 18 include the USA, Canada, or the EC as one of the signatories.

[8]The differences between these two families may be less than they appear at first because many of the RTAs involving the EC, in fact, tend to refer to existing legislation and the anti-competitive practices referred thereto. The author thanks Stefan Amarasinha for drawing attention to this point.

[9]Readers may wish to note that, in Chapter 5 of this volume, Brusick and Clarke find that 13 per cent of the 157 RTAs that they examined include some type of flexibility for the less-developed partners. Brusick and Clarke also provide an interesting discussion on the difficulties in classifying provisions as being related to special and differential treatment, which ought to be borne in mind when counts of such provisions are presented.

[10]These points can be inferred from the statistics presented in the OECD (2005a) study.

[11]In what follows a pretty comprehensive list of the objections raised is presented. Readers should not assume that every critic of the proposed multilateral framework subscribed to each of the objections listed here.

[12]In doing so it should not be assumed that this author endorses those criticisms.

[13]Information provided in Dean (2004) and on the relevant web page of COMESA would, however, seem to contradict this finding of the OECD study. (The competition policy web page of COMESA is http://www.comesa.int/trade/issues/policy/). If the latter information is correct, then it reinforces the point made here, namely, that the concerns of developing countries about abuse of a dominant position have found themselves incorporated into the RTAs that they have signed. This is not to say that those RTA provisions have

64

What we can really learn from competition provisions in RTAs

satisfactorily addressed those developing country concerns, just that those provisions exist in the first place.

[14]The author thanks Pierre Horna for drawing attention to this point.

[15]Again, the manner in which legal provisions are classified appears to matter. In their contribution to this volume (Chapter 5), Brusick and Clarke found 14 instances of provisions in RTAs that 'safeguard [the] interests of less-developed partners', seven provisions relating to exemptions and exceptions, another seven provisions relating to transitional time periods, and only one provision relating to technical assistance (see Table 5.1 of Brusick and Clarke).

[16]Here readers are encouraged to bear in mind the point made in Footnote 11.

[17]The matter of asymmetries in bargaining power is taken up again under the fourth theme addressed in Section 3 of this chapter.

[18]A similar question might be asked of the relationship between any future multilateral initiative and the bilateral agency-to-agency cooperation agreements on competition law and enforcement matters. The author thanks Stefan Amarasinha for drawing attention to this point.

[19]The author thanks David Round for the reminder about these important points concerning sequencing.

[20]Marsden and Whelan (2005a,b,c) and Acevedo (2005) are promising examples of the latter.

[21] Amarasinha (2004) evaluates the criticisms levelled by some in the competition law community towards the proposals for a multilateral framework on competition policy.

[22]In less than five years the International Competition Network (ICN) has undertaken work on a number of important competition law and enforcement-related matters, including merger notification and review, cartels, the implementation of competition law (including analyses of technical assistance and capacity building programmes), and antitrust enforcement in regulated sectors. In the coming year, a working group will be established on matters relating to abuse of a dominant position, a long-standing concern of certain prominent developing country participants in the ICN. The rate of progress made in the ICN stands in contrast to the developments in other non-binding fora. Having said that, it is too early to say whether the ICN membership can sustain the current level of momentum or whether all of its membership is satisfied with the resulting degree of international cooperation and convergence on competition law and enforcement matters.

[23]In answering this question, analysts might consider the views of private-sector practitioners and scholars. These parties may view the transition times and technical assistance necessary to meet the obligations in an RTA differently

from the trade negotiators representing a given country.

[24]One's view of the merits of such arguments may depend on whether the competition provisions are supposed to ensure that previously agreed to market access concessions are not impeded by private anti-competitive practices or whether such provisions are supposed to expand market access beyond previously agreed levels.

[25]See, for example, Levenstein and Suslow (2003).

[26]The author thanks Oliver Solano Castro for the reminder about this important point.

[13]

Journal of International Economic Law (2003) 3–21

LEGAL ASPECTS OF A POVERTY AGENDA AT THE WTO: TRADE LAW AND 'GLOBAL APARTHEID'

*Joel P. Trachtman**

INTRODUCTION

This introductory essay is intended as a somewhat speculative examination of issues expected to shape the international economic law field in coming years. The issue of poverty is the overwhelming moral, economic, legal, and political issue facing us. It should, and will, transform the international economic system, and with it, the field of international economic law. It is chastening that this issue has been a part of the trade system since at least the founding of the GATT in 1947.

It is an appropriate moment to review the relationship between trade law and poverty. The Doha Development Agenda has begun with a pro-development ministerial declaration, and recent meetings in Monterrey on financing for development and in Johannesburg on sustainable development have advanced discussions of the problems of development. Oxfam has prepared a report on trade and poverty, and other NGOs have become active in this area.[1] Developing countries are showing increasing assertiveness in WTO dispute settlement. In addition, social scientists are exploring the relationship between poverty and terrorism, while some political leaders are proclaiming a link.

In 1999, 2.8 billion people lived on less than $2 each day, while 1.2 billion people lived on less than $1 each day – measures of extreme poverty.[2] This is not the place to offer further statistics on other measures of poverty, relating to nutrition, health, education, environmental degradation, etc. However, it is worth noting that many of these measures indicate degradation of capacity: these afflictions reduce not only the quality of life, but also the productive capacity of the afflicted, resulting in a vicious cycle of poverty.

Prior to the September 2002 Johannesburg Summit, Thabo Mbeki, the President of South Africa, described the present international distribution of wealth in terms of 'global apartheid'. We might understand this statement as

---

* Manley O. Hudson Visiting Professor of Law, Harvard Law School; Professor of International Law, The Fletcher School of Law and Diplomacy.

[1] 'Make Trade Fair, Rigged Rules and Double Standards: Trade, Globalisation and the Fight Against Poverty' (2002), available at www.maketradefair.com [hereinafter, the 'Oxfam Report'].

[2] United Nations Development Program, Human Development Report 2002, chap 1 at 17–18.

4   *Journal of International Economic Law (JIEL) 6(1)*

a reference to a circumstance in which the legal system is used to lock certain people into a position of poverty, inequality, and disenfranchisement, or to artificially separate groups of people. Under apartheid, the accident of birth into a particular race radically affected one's life opportunities. Under the international system as it exists, the accident of birth into a particular nationality has a similar effect.

To what extent is the trade law system complicit in the creation of a system of 'global apartheid'? Trade liberalization, at its core, involves the reduction of barriers to equal participation in commerce, so we must say at the outset that the trade law system holds promise for reducing global apartheid. Trade law can be revised to further extend the competitiveness of the *market* – to allow poor people to compete for better wages and better livelihoods. This would be an important component of the destruction of global apartheid, and it can be achieved using familiar trade law tools. The Doha Ministerial Declaration refers to a number of important market access and other issues of interest to poor people in poor countries. And yet, history suggests a degree of skepticism, as often in GATT and WTO history, efforts to assist poor countries have been limited to cheap talk.

Furthermore, there are two possible arguments that the trade law system may perpetuate global apartheid. First, if we consider the trade law system not so much in terms of its requirements of liberalization, but in terms of its *permission* for national barriers to movements of factors, including goods, services, labor, and capital, in both wealthy states and poor states, we may understand the trade law system as limiting the ability of the poor to trade out of poverty. Is the glass half full or half empty? Second, turning to the requirements of liberalization, if these requirements limit the ability of poor states to choose policies that will maximize growth, and best ameliorate poverty, do they not have the effect of perpetuating poverty? Even though the global system does not have the racist basis that South African apartheid did, it may have the effect of limiting the ability of poor people to overcome poverty, inequality of life opportunities, and disenfranchisement.

Let us move into a twilight zone. Looking beyond the traditional trade concern of contestable markets, the remit of trade law has not yet run in any significant way to *non-market* governance in the poverty-reduction sense: to redistribution. Indeed, the general international legal system has little redistributive capacity. However, if there is a need for redistribution, and the trade law system – the WTO – is viewed as responsible for the management of international economic relations, the WTO will be subject to criticism until the needed redistribution is implemented, at the WTO or elsewhere. To what extent is this criticism – similar to the environmentalists' criticism that the WTO does not do enough for the environment – justified?

If we compare the domestic sphere in wealthier states to the international system, we see that domestic politics includes a substantially greater capacity for redistribution than does international politics. The purpose of redistribution may be understood in terms of distributive justice, of social cohesion or of the 'price' of avoiding disruption of the market. To what extent do these goals apply equally in the global system? To the extent that they do, what institutional or legal mechanisms are needed to achieve them?

Thus, there are three main areas for work to improve the position of poor people in the international trade system:

1. *Market Access in Wealthy Countries.* It is clear that opening markets to poor country products, including agricultural products, textiles, and tropical products, is a useful and necessary means to reduce poverty, although the magnitude of the effects of these measures is disputed. Opening developed country markets to services and labor from poor countries would also help many poor people. Of course, while there may be winners in poor countries, there may be losers among the poor in wealthy countries. We must also recall that liberalization in wealthy countries may have the effect of raising the costs of some goods to poor people in poor countries, while it reduces the costs of some goods to poor people in wealthy countries.

2. *Reform in Poor Countries.* As many leading trade economists have pointed out, poor countries may achieve substantial benefits from domestic reform, including trade liberalization. Dani Rodrik has raised concerns about the correct sequencing of trade liberalization reforms, and has insisted that poor countries need sufficient flexibility to devise and implement reforms that are most suitable for their growth.

3. *Global Redistribution.* Providing more money to poor people to pay for needed medicine, food, and education would also help, but has remained outside the trade regime. Other methods to help poor people, including trade discrimination in favor of products of poor countries, are relatively inefficient ways to assist the poor, but may be justified where more direct redistribution is politically impossible. Finally, linked to point 2 above, appropriate policy adjustments must be made by poor countries themselves as a condition of assistance.

What may lawyers add to the debate about poverty and its alleviation? The legal profession is skilled in determining what the law is. However, the discipline of law alone cannot tell us what kind of law there ought to be. A broader social scientific approach, using economics and other tools, examines the relationship between institutions – including laws – and particular outcomes, such as poverty reduction. Nor does law alone tell us *why* poverty should be reduced. Rather, our own values, informed by ethical theory, tell us how to think about the need to reduce poverty, and how to determine our individual obligations. Finally, law tells us little about whether our compatriots and those in other countries will join us in an effort to alleviate poverty. This is the domain of politics.

6   *Journal of International Economic Law (JIEL) 6(1)*

So, what can a legal analyst do? In litigation, lawyers can argue for interpretations of law that may benefit the poor, but this seems like a marginal
strategy at best. More valuably, lawyers can participate in research to evaluate
the consequences of particular legal rules, and assist in institutional design.
Research can serve a critical purpose. Research informed by a complete
understanding of legal rules, and providing information about their consequences, can guide us as to the most effective legislative, or international
treaty-based action to take. Research can empower negotiators and can form
the basis for suggesting revised institutions. Furthermore, and this is an area
in which international lawyers can contribute greatly, analysis of the role of
artificial and real international legal constraints on action – mostly in the form
of assertions of the inviolability of sovereignty and of the false necessity of the
legal structure that contributes to 'global apartheid' – can help to overcome
or remove those constraints.

Part I of this essay outlines ethical and selfish bases for greater assistance to
the poor. Part II reviews some of the arguments from economics and political
economy that market access for poor country goods and services, economic
reform in poor countries often including trade liberalization,[3] and redistribution to poor people, are critical to poverty alleviation. Part III suggests in very
rough terms the types of legal and institutional structures and rules that seem
required in order to overcome these obstacles.

I. ETHICAL AND SELFISH FOUNDATIONS: COSMOPOLITANISM AND EMBEDDED LIBERALISM

Do we have an ethical obligation to assist the poor in our own countries;[4]
does this obligation extend to the poor in other countries? What is the nature
and extent of this obligation? If we do not have an obligation to assist the
poor, would it nevertheless be useful – to us – to do so? This is not a question
we can answer in any reliable way here, or perhaps anywhere. Below, I
describe a Rawlsian rationale for redistribution. I also provide an analysis
of the requirements of 'embedded liberalism', as well as its inadequacies,
broadening the embedded liberalism[5] critique to suggest the need for more

---

[3] While the predominant view among economists seems to be that liberalization can promote growth
in developing countries, there is at least some argument that the timing and scope of liberalization
might be structured in different ways to enhance growth. See Francisco Rodriguez and Dani Rodrik,
'Trade Policy and Economic Growth: A Skeptic's Guide to Cross-National Evidence', NBER
Working Paper No W7081 (1999). For a response, see Jagdish Bhagwati and T. N. Srinivasen,
'Trade and Poverty in the Poor Countries', working paper dated 2002, available at http://
www.econ.yale.edu/~srinivas/trade_poverty.pdf.

[4] See G. A. Cohen, *If You're an Egalitarian, How Come You're So Rich?* (Harvard University Press
1999).

[5] John G. Ruggie, 'International Regimes, Transactions, and Change: Embedded Liberalism in Postwar Economic Order, 36 Int'l Org., 379 (1982). Ruggie modernizes and adapts a perspective earlier
elucidated by Karl Polanyi, *The Great Transformation: The Political and Economic Origins of Our Time*

than adjustment assistance. This argument depends on a kind of global social contract, and the possibility of 'backlash'[6] by poor elements if they are not given a sufficient stake in the operation of global society.

I refer to a Rawlsian[7] analysis of the foundation of ethical responsibility to assist the poor. As is well known, Rawls uses the heuristic of an original position, in which the members of a society decide its structure under a 'veil of ignorance', in which they are ignorant of the actual position and endowments they will enjoy in society. Rawls then seeks to develop an understanding of the principles of justice on which individuals would agree in such a position. His second principle of justice (the first deals with equal liberty) postulates that inequality is only justified to the extent that it is necessary to improve the position of the least well-off members of society. If applied globally, this principle, known as the 'difference principle', would have revolutionary effects. In fact, Rawls, perhaps tragically, argues that this principle of justice only applies within a domestic society – for Rawls, international society lacks the solidarity that is a necessary predicate for its application.

On the other hand, political philosophers such as Charles Beitz[8] and Thomas Pogge[9] argue for a cosmopolitan approach, in which each individual, regardless of borders, enters into a global original position. Under this global original position, individuals, fearing that they might in the real world reside in one of the poorest states, or, more accurately, that they might be among the poorest persons, would decide on a difference principle, in the same way that they would in a domestic original position.

This difference principle-based approach is in very broad terms comparable to an approach to distribution based on 'embedded liberalism', drawing on the work of Polanyi and Ruggie. Polanyi and Ruggie believe that states must

---

(Beacon Press 1944). Dani Rodrik has considered the application of this perspective to modern global markets. Dani Rodrik, *Has Globalization Gone Too Far?* 7 (1999). See also Robert L. Howse, *From Politics To Technocracy – and Back Again: The Fate of the Multilateral Trading Regime*, 96 Am J Int'l L 94 (2002).

[6] For an application of this concept in the corporate law field, see Mark J. Roe, 'Backlash', 98 Colum L Rev 217 (1998)

[7] See *Global Justice* (Thomas W. Pogge (ed), Blackwell 2001); Frank J. Garcia, 'Trade and Inequality: Economic Justice and the Developing World', 21 Mich J Int'l L 975 (2000). See also Joel P. Trachtman, 'Review Essay: The Law and Economics of Global Justice', Am J Int'l L (2002).

[8] See Charles R. Beitz, 'Review Essay: International Liberalism and Distributive Justice: A Survey of Recent Thought', 51 World Pol 269, 290 (1999), stating that 'I believe that the philosophical weakness most characteristic of cosmopolitan theories – although not found equally in all of them – is a failure to take seriously enough the associative relationships that individuals do and almost certainly must develop to live successful and rewarding lives.' However, Beitz accepts a federal possibility: 'it is hardly clear that a sophisticated cosmopolitanism *cannot* explain how local affiliations might give rise to special responsibilities. Such a view would recognize the value to individuals of their associations with domestic or local communities and argue that ethically significant properties of these associations justify internal distributive arrangements that are different from, although not inconsistent with, what is required by global principles.' Id (citations omitted) (emphasis in original).

[9] Thomas W. Pogge, *Realizing Rawls* (Cornell University Press 1989).

8   *Journal of International Economic Law (JIEL) 6(1)*

regulate the distribution of gains from trade in order to avoid political discontent, and, ultimately, a 'backlash' that would destroy the liberal system. In Ruggie's interpretation, individual states must cushion the domestic 'losers' from the loss of wages, livelihoods, and investments that results from liberalization – Ruggie extends Polanyi's approach to relate free international trade to a domestic welfare state. The embedded liberalism 'bargain', in short, is one in which the state takes care of its own through regulatory intervention in order to maintain its political ability to liberalize. But, importantly, embedded liberalism calls for national regulatory intervention, not global regulatory intervention. Its call for redistribution is state-centered, and limited by domestic politics and budgetary capacity.

Further, it is important to recognize[10] that global liberalism embedded within a domestic welfare state is not quite analogous to the system described by Polanyi. Polanyi saw the need for society-wide regulatory intervention to make adjustments in connection with a society-wide market. The true analog in connection with global markets is global regulatory intervention – a global welfare state. Thus, if the scope of the market is to some degree global, then it would seem appropriate that the scope of regulatory intervention in the market would need to be roughly commensurately global.[11] After all, what would be the purpose of artificially constraining the possible funding for adjustment, or of other redistributive regulation, to sources within a particular *geographic segment* of the market?

It is important to recognize, with Polanyi's original work and Ruggie's extension, that the regulation that they are concerned with is best understood as implicitly redistributive. The point is not necessarily to provide a certain quality of regulation, but to provide a certain quality of life. It may be that labor regulation, health regulation, environmental regulation, and others are the best means to do this under particular circumstances. But, as Kaplow and Shavell have pointed out,[12] if redistribution is the goal, then taxation and explicit redistribution are the most efficient means, subject to what we might call political transaction costs. That is, there may be circumstances in which regulation is used to redistribute because direct redistribution will be too difficult in political terms. This technique, of course, has its ethical and practical

---

[10] As Ruggie does in more recent work. See John G. Ruggie, 'Taking Embedded Liberalism Global: The Corporate Connection', Miliband Public Lecture on Global Economic Governance, The London School of Economics and Political Science, 6 June 2002, available at www.globaldimensions.net/articles/ruggie/globalliberalism.html.

[11] It is a question of subsidiarity. For a brief statement of this issue, see David Trubek, 'Book Review: Governance in a Globalizing World', 96 Am J Int'l L 748 (2002). On a related point, see Howse, above n 5, at 116.

[12] Louis Kaplow and Steven Shavell, 'Should Legal Rules Favor the Poor? Clarifying the Role of Legal Rules and the Income Tax in Redistributing Income', 29 J Leg Stud 821 (2000); Louis Kaplow and Steven Shavell, 'Why the Legal System is Less Efficient than the Income Tax in Redistributing Income', 23 J Leg Stud 667 (1994).

problems. But it has even greater problems in the global setting, where these regulatory policies are dependent on different national economic, legal, and political systems and cultures. Suppression of differences in order to embed liberalism may be too costly in terms of legitimate regulatory diversity. Moreover, the scope for transnational externalization – for transnational redistribution – may be too greatly constrained by a requirement to act through regulatory means.

So, a true global embedded liberalism would extend to poor countries and would allow them, as well as wealthier countries, to attenuate the risks and costs of liberalism to which their citizens are exposed. The transfers could occur on a global basis, and would seem to require global institutions to overcome collective action problems in order to make them effectively.

Once extended in this way – in terms of both geographic reach and redistributive scope – the embedded liberalism idea seems to have more in common with the cosmopolitan ethical perspective described earlier. Of course, its motivations are not based on ethics, but on prudent self-interest: the embedded liberalism concept suggests that in order to protect liberalism from destruction by those who lose, it is necessary to compensate them through regulatory intervention. One way in which the Rawlsian difference principle and Polanyi's embedded liberalism can be merged is through recognition that, to some extent, each of us lives our lives in a 'real' veil of ignorance. That is, over time, we are uncertain to which group we will belong – whether we will be among the lucky few who hold wealth, or among the poorest wraiths. Under these circumstances, the difference principle is simply a hypothetical constitutional arrangement that we might actually enter into under uncertainty.[13]

The embedded liberalism concept calls for redistribution in order to forestall a backlash. On a very speculative, and perhaps even a counterfactual, level, we can at least imagine a relationship between poverty and terrorism along these lines. That is, even though there has not yet been identified a causal relationship between poverty and terrorism, we may, at least in our imaginations, consider whether terrorism could become the way that the poor disrupt global liberalism. Is the rise of terrorism a kind of 'backlash' against liberalism?[14] Is the correct response to 'embed' liberalism in a regulatory regime?

A more peaceful 'backlash' – or threat to withdraw from or disrupt the international trade rules system – took place in the early 1960s, when developing countries threatened to leave GATT as a bloc, and were able to obtain

---

[13] See Geoffrey Brennan and James M. Buchanan, *The Reason of Rules* 28–31 (Cambridge University Press: Cambridge 1985); James M. Buchanan and Gordon Tullock, *The Calculus of Consent* 77–80 (University of Michigan 1962); Dennis Mueller, *Constitutional Democracy* 61–64 (Oxford University Press: New York 1996).

[14] See Ruggie, above n 10.

10   *Journal of International Economic Law (JIEL) 6(1)*

substantial concessions from the developed countries.[15] A more peaceful 'backlash' may be said to be taking place now, and has resulted in the development focus of current negotiations at the WTO and elsewhere.

II. GATT/WTO LAW AND POVERTY: CONTINUITY IN THE DOHA DEVELOPMENT AGENDA

Given the desperate and urgent circumstances of so many, the Doha Development Agenda seems rather modest in its scope.[16] It may be that the WTO is not the place to engage in the more extreme measures needed, and there are certainly other important contexts in which poverty is addressed, but there still may be room to contemplate further action. Furthermore, as noted above, to the extent that the WTO is identified with global economic management, it may be that the WTO will be subjected to increasing criticism for failure to address poverty issues more completely.

A. Special and differential treatment

Although it features prominently in the Doha Development Agenda, it appears that the concept of 'Special and Differential Treatment' (S&D), at least as applied so far, has limited utility.[17] S&D is a complex phenomenon – some aspects of S&D are undoubtedly beneficial. However, this concept seems to mask the fact that the international trade system has done little

---

[15] Robert E. Hudec, *Developing Countries in the GATT Legal System*, 39, 40 (Gower: Aldershot 1987); See also John H. Jackson, *The World Trading System* 319–20 (MIT Press 1997) ('a number of developing countries, dismayed with rules that had evolved [at the 1948 Havana conference], opted to stay out of the GATT system for years and even decades.').

[16] For a contrary perspective, or at least an admittedly optimistic perspective, see Peter Gerhart, 'Slow Transformations: The WTO as a Distributive Organization', 17 Am U L Rev 1045 (2002). Prof. Gerhart suggests that in the Doha Ministerial Declaration there is evidence of a move toward greater emphasis on balanced outcomes, and toward a vision of the WTO as motivated not just by efficiency, but by redistribution.

[17] Paragraph 44 of the Doha Ministerial Declaration calls for a review of S&D, with a view toward making the relevant provisions more precise, effective, and operational. For a proposal to revise S&D in order to make it more favorable to poor countries, see Communication from Cuba, Dominican Republic, Honduras, India, Indonesia, Kenya, Malaysia, Pakistan, Sri Lanka, Tanzania, Uganda, and Zimbabwe, Proposal for a Framework Agreement on Special and Differential Treatment, WT/GC/W/442 (2002). For the history of the concept of S&D, see John H. Jackson, *World Trade and the Law of the GATT: A Legal Analysis of the General Agreement on Tariffs and Trade*, 625–71 (Bobbs-Merrill: Indianapolis 1969). For an analysis of the S&D principle, see Peter Lichtenbaum, ' "Special Treatment" vs. "Equal Participation": Striking a Balance in the Doha Negotiations', 17 Am U Int'l L Rev 1004 (2002). See also John Whalley, 'Special and Differential Treatment in a Millennium Round', CSGR Working Paper 30/99, May 1999, available at http://www.warwick.ac.uk/fac/soc/CSGR/wpapers/wp3099.PDF; Constantine Michalopoulos, 'The Role of Special and Differential Treatment for Developing Countries in GATT and the World Trade Organization', working paper dated 2000, available at http://www.worldbank.org/research/trade/archive.html.

specifically intended to alleviate poverty: it is not special and differential enough. S&D includes several specific rules and approaches that can be placed in three categories: non-reciprocity, preferential market access, and permissive protection.[18]

First, S&D includes the concept, initially expressed in the mid-1960s, that poor countries will not be expected or requested to make reciprocal concessions in trade negotiations.[19] This vague principle was later incorporated in Part IV of GATT.[20] However, as several have noted, those who are not required to reciprocate often find that few concessions are accorded to them – even under conditions of MFN.[21] This is because, of course, the products of export interest to developing countries often differ from those of interest to other countries, and so are not included in the give-and-take of negotiation over concessions.

Second, S&D includes the aspiration to provide enhanced market access to developing country products. Partly because of the principle of non-reciprocity, this aspiration was often ignored. The area in which S&D has had its greatest effect is in connection with the Generalized System of Preferences (GSP), which provides for reduced tariff treatment for certain developing country products. While the GSP has provided modest benefits, it has not been applied to provide greater market access for many of the most important poor country products,[22] and the US and EC have imposed substantial conditions on access to their GSP programs.[23] 'Graduation' policies including ceilings on eligible exports have also diminished the utility of GSP. Furthermore, as developed country tariffs have decreased to an average of less than 5 percent, and with the formation of more free trade areas and customs unions, the preferences under the GSP have been greatly eroded, and will be further eroded in future. The magnitude of the 'differential' has declined substantially. If benefits are unstable and are a wasting asset, they cannot form a sound basis for investment that would allow poor countries to actually achieve market access. Furthermore, the principle of non-reciprocity, as implemented

---

[18] See Committee on Trade and Development, Implementation of Special and Differential Treatment Provisions in the WTO Agreements and Decisions, WT/COMTD/W/77 (25 October 2000).

[19] BISD, 13th Supp. (1965).

[20] See Hudec above n 15, at 58.

[21] See, e.g., Constantine Michalopoulous, 'Developing Country Strategies for the Millennium Round', 33(5) J World Trade 1, 25 (1999); Hudec, above n 15, at 46.

[22] Paragraph 42 of the Doha Ministerial Declaration provides a commitment to the *objective* of duty-free, quota-free market access for products originating from least developed countries. If realized, this commitment could be of some importance.

[23] Hudec above n 15, at 210–15. India has begun dispute settlement proceedings against the EC in connection with the EC's conditions applicable to its generalized system of preferences. Request for Consultations by India, European Communities – Conditions for the Granting of Tariff Preferences to Developing Countries, WT/DS264/1, 12 March 2002.

12   *Journal of International Economic Law (JIEL) 6(1)*

through GSP, seems to have the effect of diminishing incentives for liberalization by beneficiary countries.[24]

Third, S&D includes greater permission for protection, in particular under Articles XII and XVIII of GATT,[25] relating to balance of payments. As Michael Finger has pointed out, '[p]erhaps the least development-friendly side of the Doha Declaration is its willingness to ladle out 'special and differential treatment' without a perception of where developing Members would be better off if *they themselves* observed the disciplines the negotiations aim to establish'.[26] For much of the past 20 years, a consensus – part of the 'Washington Consensus' – developed that poor countries would benefit from liberalization of their domestic markets. The debate about whether protection of domestic markets is good or bad for poor countries has recently been revived.[27] However, there still seem to be solid reasons for poor countries to liberalize at some point in their development path. Furthermore, there would seem to be little basis for questioning liberalization as to goods and services, such as financial and telecommunications services, that provide infrastructure for other productive activities.

B. Market access for poor country products

There is a strong consensus that liberalization by the wealthy states in agriculture, textiles, and tropical products, even on an MFN basis, would assist growth in poor countries.[28] For example, exports from developing countries are limited by continuing developed country tariffs (including quotas that were tariffied in the Uruguay Round), domestic supports, and export subsidies. And indeed, market access in products of export interest to poor countries would be an important way to enhance livelihoods in those countries, although it is not unambiguous. Easier exports to wealthy countries could mean higher prices at home. Reduction of wealthy country export subsidies on agriculture could hurt consumers in food importing states.

Furthermore, reduction of barriers in wealthy states would have adverse effects on domestic persons involved in production of competing goods, often

---

[24] Caglar Ozden and Eric Reinhardt, 'The Perversity of Preferences: GSP and Developing Country Trade Policies, 1976–2000', working paper dated 24 May 2002, available at http://userwww. service.emory.edu/~erein/research/gsp2.pdf.

[25] See Chantal Thomas, 'Balance-of-Payments Crises in the Developing World: Balancing Trade, Finance and Development in the New Economic Order', 15 Am U Int'l L Rev 1249, 1256 (2000).

[26] J. Michael Finger, 'A Diplomat's Economics: Development and Trade Perspectives on the Doha Agenda', working paper dated 10 May 2002 (emphasis in original).

[27] See Dani Rodrik and Francisco Rodriguez, 'Trade Policy and Economic Growth: A Skeptic's Guide to the Cross-National Evidence', in *Macroeconomics Annual* 2000 (Ben Bernanke and Kenneth S. Rogoff, (eds), 2001).

[28] See Oxfam Report, above n 2.

hurting the poorest segments of wealthy countries.[29] On the other hand, barriers often disproportionately raise the costs of basic goods to poor consumers. Poverty is a cosmopolitan phenomenon. Bhagwati has suggested that as agriculture in wealthy countries is principally the occupation of wealthier agribusinesses, it is less ethically ambiguous to liberalize in agriculture than in textiles or other manufactured goods.[30]

Tariff peaks and tariff escalation in connection with goods of export interest to poor countries have restricted market access not only in agriculture, textiles, and tropical products, but also in other manufactured goods.[31] While developed country tariffs now average less than 5 percent, Hoekman points out that tariff peaks – higher tariffs – are 'often concentrated in products that are of interest to developing countries'.[32] Many of these apply to agricultural products, and they are often associated with tariff escalation, by which the tariffs on unprocessed products are disproportionately less than the tariffs on processed products, providing perverse incentives against manufacturing in poor countries. Tariff peaks may be a result of the principle of non-reciprocity, or may be the result of 'simple political economy',[33] and of a desire to protect the jobs of the relatively poor in rich countries.

While it is necessary, and will be efficient, for developed states to reduce barriers to developing country products on an MFN basis,[34] it is also necessary to recognize the ethical and political need to take care of workers in competing industries in wealthier countries, as well as consumers in poor countries. Thus, while it is difficult to reduce these barriers because of the harm liberalization would do in wealthy countries, we also must recognize that trade barriers are not the most efficient means to help the poor in wealthier countries. It has long been understood that it would be more efficient globally to provide adjustment assistance to the poor in wealthier countries. However, the cost of adjustment assistance would be domestic, direct, and relatively transparent, whereas the cost of trade barriers is more dispersed, less direct, and relatively opaque.

Thus, it will not be easy, or ethically unambiguous, to achieve change. This is part of the political and ethical conundrum of poverty relief through trade.

---

[29] See Alan O. Sykes, 'Comparative Advantage and the Normative Economics of International Trade Policy', 1 JIEL (1998), at 69.

[30] Jagdish Bhagwati, 'The Poor's Best Hope', *The Economist* (20 June 2002), at 24.

[31] Paragraph 16 of the Doha Declaration calls for the reduction of tariff peaks and tariff escalation.

[32] Bernard Hoekman, 'Strengthening the Global Trade Architecture for Development: The Post-Doha Agenda', working paper dated January 2002, at 5.

[33] Bhagwati, above n 30.

[34] Furthermore, developing countries themselves constitute an important export market for other developing countries. Under the Enabling Clause, developing countries may be able to provide enhanced market access to other developing countries, without benefiting wealthy countries on an MFN basis. Of course, opening developing country markets to imports from other developing countries will hurt some people, and will hurt some countries, again putting pressure on adjustment.

14   *Journal of International Economic Law (JIEL) 6(1)*

In order to open markets to products of poor countries, it may be necessary to make transfer payments to those harmed in both wealthy and poor countries. While from a welfare standpoint it would likely be more efficient to do so, this assumes relatively low political transaction costs allowing these transfer payments to be made. Otherwise, the low political cost solution may be simply to continue protection.

C. Immigration and GATS

One way of ending 'global apartheid' would be to allow workers from poor countries to take jobs in wealthier countries – the current global system of restricted migration may be understood in at least one dimension as a macrocosm of the internal passport system that was used under apartheid. Dani Rodrik has pointed out that substantial benefit could be derived from liberalization of immigration to allow greater trade in labor.[35]

Market access for services, including unskilled labor, of export interest to poor countries should also be liberalized. The General Agreement on Trade in Services (GATS) focused on services in which wealthier countries are more competitive: financial services, telecommunications, professional services, etc., and concentrated on modes of delivery of services other than those that require immigration.[36] By contrast, poor countries have tremendous advantages in unskilled and semi-skilled services, which were largely excluded from GATS, both because their subject matter was not covered, and because the mode of delivery by which these services may be traded is physical movement of the service provider.

Of course, the adjustment issues mentioned in the prior section are applicable and are more intense in connection with immigration. Immigration also raises more intense political issues, partly because it involves issues of access to host country social welfare programs, as well as issues of participation in host country politics.

D. Border measures, internal measures, and domestic policy flexibility

Leading economists including Jagdish Bhagwati, Michael Finger,[37] Dani Rodrik, and T. N. Srinivasen[38] have suggested that one of the problems with

---

[35] Dani Rodrik, 'Feasible Globalizations', working paper dated May 2002.

[36] See, e.g., WTO Secretariat, 'GATS, Mode 4 and the Pattern of Commitments', dated 12 April 2002, available at http://www.wto.org/english/tratop_e/serv_e/symp_apr_02_carzaniga_e.doc.

[37] See J. Michael Finger and Julio J. Nogues, 'The Unbalanced Uruguay Round Outcome: The New Areas in Future WTO Negotiations', working paper dated December 2001.

[38] T. N. Srinivasen, 'Developing Countries and the Multilateral Trading System After Doha', Yale University Economic Growth Center Discussion Paper No 842, dated February 2002, available at http://www.econ.yale.edu/egcenter/research.htm.

the post-Uruguay Round trade system is the intrusion of trade law into areas that were previously viewed as within domestic prerogatives, such as intellectual property rights, technical standards, and phytosanitary standards, and extending to some of the post-Uruguay Round agenda, including environmental protection and labor rights.

Bhagwati and Srinivasen suggest that we can only be confident that agreements will promote welfare when they are tariff-reducing – as tariff reductions, in neo-classical economic theory, promote the welfare of both the exporting state and the importing state, there is little risk of a welfare reduction. While this may generally be true as a matter of wealth maximization, trade policy is not limited to wealth maximization. Rather, as Avinash Dixit has suggested, wealth maximization may be sacrificed for a broader welfare calculus wherein preferences are transmitted through the political system.[39] Furthermore, in these public choice-oriented terms, even tariff reductions can cause harm to one side. Thus, in this broader welfare calculus, there is little difference between tariff reduction agreements and agreements that address domestic prerogatives.[40]

Rodrik, on the other hand, is concerned about domestic policy flexibility, and the need for poor states to have flexibility to tailor their economic policy to meet their own needs.[41] However, this concern does not appear to be implicated so much by restrictions on standards, and is not greatly implicated by labor or environmental measures. It is implicated by restrictions on subsidies and protection – imposed by traditional trade law applied to poor countries. It is also implicated by TRIPS, which is discussed further below.

E. Technical assistance in negotiations, implementation, and dispute settlement

The role of technical assistance in the trade sphere is in some respects comparable to legal aid in the domestic sphere. It can play an important role in assisting poor states to negotiate, or to bring claims to dispute settlement, or to implement their obligations. However, this role is notably interstitial, and its utility to poor people depends on the substantive rules to be negotiated, enforced, and implemented, respectively. So, it would be wrong to suggest that technical assistance does not help, and it certainly can be useful in addressing certain problems. Technical assistance for research and negotiation, allowing developing countries to understand and argue their positions more accurately and persuasively, is of critical importance.

---

[39] Avinash Dixit, *The Making of Economic Policy: A Transaction Cost Politics Perspective* (MIT Press 1996).

[40] I address the distributive effects of the TRIPS agreement in greater detail below.

[41] Rodrik, above n 35.

16   *Journal of International Economic Law (JIEL) 6(1)*

F. TRIPS and poverty

It is clear that TRIPS has imposed significant costs on poor countries, and on poor people. Viewed alone, TRIPS was a bad deal for poor countries. It may be that even as part of the Uruguay Round package, TRIPS was a bad deal for poor countries. However, the problem of poor countries, and more specifically of poor people, in relation to TRIPS is not the rules of TRIPS themselves,[42] but the poverty of these individuals. One strategy that some have explored to seek to reduce the costs of AIDS and other medicines, and relieve the burden of TRIPS on poor people, is to argue for the modification or termination of TRIPS.[43] If all other things remained equal, this would redistribute wealth from the wealthy to the poor (or would reverse the redistribution effected by the original TRIPS from the poor to the wealthy). But it would change the global level of intellectual property protection.

It is not for me to say what the efficient global level of intellectual property protection is.[44] However, I would offer a view that in ideal circumstances, the efficient global level of intellectual property protection should not be modified to provide greater access to medicines for the poor. It would be much more efficient, if we had the institutional infrastructure to do so, simply to transfer resources to the poor to enable them to acquire needed medicines. Srinivasen concludes that 'compared to a policy of income transfers to the poor to enable them to buy drugs at a common world price, market segmentation is an inferior policy.'[45]

Thus, it appears that the TRIPS-AIDS problem might be optimally addressed by redistribution. However, we lack effective institutions for redistribution. Under these circumstances, there may be stronger arguments to modify TRIPS obligations themselves, or even to use human rights-based arguments to procure effective redistribution through abrogation of intellectual property rights. But we should be clear that this technique amounts to a global expropriation of the existing ownership rights[46] of pharmaceutical companies.

G. Summary

This part has suggested some of the limitations of trade law in connection with poverty alleviation. Measures taken thus far have been of limited effect-

---

[42] See Alan O. Sykes, 'TRIPS, Pharmaceuticals, Developing Countries and the Doha "Solution"', John M. Olin Law & Economics Working Paper No 140 (2d series) (2001), University of Chicago Law School, available at http://www.law.uchicago.edu/Lawecon/index.html.

[43] This type of redistribution through abrogation or renegotiation of agreements has some precedent in the periodic renegotiation of foreign debt, or expropriation of foreign direct investment. See Joel P. Trachtman, 'Foreign Investment, Regulation and Expropriation: A Debtor's Jubilee?', 82 Proceedings of the American Society of International Law 103 (1995).

[44] See Sykes, above n 42; see also Frederic M. Scherer, *Industry Structure, Strategy and Public Policy* (HarperCollins 1996) 362–66.

[45] Srinivasen, above n 38, at 13.

[46] This argument is made more complicated, but is not refuted, by the fact that these rights are generally only recently acquired.

iveness. In order to make progress, it is necessary to open rich country markets to products, services, and workers of poor countries, and to encourage appropriate liberalization in poor countries. Opening rich country markets will require redistribution within rich countries. In order to increase the export capacity of poor countries, and in order to alleviate poverty, especially in light of TRIPS, it is necessary to engage in greater redistribution from rich countries to poor countries.

III. WHAT IS TO BE DONE?

Part I has provided an ethical and rationalist argument for greater assistance to the poor. It has recognized the political barriers to action. Part II has shown the potential and limitations of the trade law system as it stands, recognizing the political barriers to action. Obviously, it is uncertain whether any action can be taken, and any action that is taken will be shaped by many factors relevant to negotiations. The purpose of this section is to engage in a relatively conjectural exercise as to what types of actions may be considered, and subjected to further research.

A. Liberalization and redistribution

There are two kinds of tools available to help the poor. The tool that comes most naturally to the trade system is improved market access and domestic reform. The second type of tool is international redistribution. Both tools seem appropriate to be used, and they can reinforce one another.

Enhanced market access would allow the poor to increase their incomes through competition with people in wealthy states. Immigration by poor persons to wealthier states may allow them to achieve greater incomes, and can also allow them access to the internal redistributive mechanisms available in wealthy countries. Increased investment in poor countries can provide the capital necessary to increase the returns to labor within poor countries. The point is factor mobility: breaking down the barriers of global apartheid.

The WTO has the capacity and mandate to coordinate reductions in barriers that impede flows of poor country goods and services, but has not yet addressed issues of labor mobility. While the WTO has not yet engaged in significant efforts to enhance flows of investment (outside of the relatively modest efforts in the GATS and TRIMS agreements), it is not out of the question that the WTO would become more involved in liberalizing investment flows, as recognized in the Doha Ministerial Declaration. The types of investment flows that are needed, of course, are steady flows of capital that would provide a stable basis for enhancing local productive capacity.

However, the TRIPS-AIDS problem described above illustrates too well that the fundamental problem of poor people and countries is that they are poor. Taxation and redistribution would often be a more efficient means to

18   *Journal of International Economic Law (JIEL) 6(1)*

assist the poor in this case, as well as in other policy contexts, compared to modifying what would otherwise be the most efficient intellectual property protection regime, or the most efficient trade policy regime.

At the same time that the poor are accorded greater opportunities to compete, greater aid is needed to provide the tools of competition: food, education, health care, and infrastructure. Given that many people in poor countries lack the nutritional, educational, health, and capital infrastructure to take advantage of enhanced market opportunities, transfers of resources are required to establish these conditions for participation in the global economy.

It is easy to say that more money should be transferred to the poor, but the greatest barrier to poverty alleviation in many cases is weak or predatory government. Recent research suggests that domestic institutional quality is a more significant determinant of growth than geography or trade liberalization.[47]

Finally, let us emphasize the connection between liberalization and redistribution based on the cosmopolitan nature of poverty. In many instances, trade liberalization gives rise to substantial political costs. These costs may be paid through selective protectionism: dissenting interests may be 'paid off' through protection against competing imports. This is despite the fact that it might enhance global social welfare to simply pay direct compensation. However, direct compensation is more readily criticized, and allows costs to fall fully on local taxpayers. On the other hand, protection often raises costs only to presumably more dispersed consumers, and also diminishes the welfare of foreign persons, whose interests are not directly taken into account in the domestic political system. The point is that domestic redistribution is critical to efficient liberalization, just as international redistribution is necessary to poverty relief more generally.

While many states have domestic institutions capable of facilitating redistribution, we lack global institutions capable of facilitating international redistribution. That is, redistribution may be impeded, or at least rendered inefficient, by the lack of appropriate institutions to allow individuals or states to engage in redistribution with confidence and efficiency. Institutional development can assist in overcoming collective action problems in connection with individual decisions to engage in redistribution.[48]

B. Institutional reform and the role of international economic lawyers

As noted at the outset, international economic lawyers can assist by participating in research efforts, with economists and other social scientists, to better

[47] Dani Rodrik, Arvind Subramanian, and Francesco Trebbi, 'Institutions Rule: The Primacy of Institutions over Geography and Integration in Economic Development', Harvard Center for International Development Paper No 97, October 2002, available at http://www.cid.harvard.edu/cidwp/pdf/097.pdf. Rodrik *et al.* refer to Daron Acemoglu, Simon Johnson, and James A. Robinson, 'The Colonial Origins of Comparative Development', 91(5) Am Econ Rev 1369 (2001).

[48] See Leif Wenar, 'Contractualism and Global Economic Justice', in Thomas W. Pogge (ed), *Global Justice* (Blackwell 2001), at 84.

understand the consequences of particular international economic law rules, as they are applied. They can also participate in exercises of institutional imagination, in order to evaluate what substitute legal rules and institutions are available, and to develop predictions regarding their consequences. This work should be particularistic; that is, it should recognize that different countries are at different stages of development, have different social and institutional structures, and have different goals.

In addition, international economic lawyers can participate with economists to develop methods to review the international economic policy, and also the domestic policy, of particular poor countries in terms not of trade liberalization but of poverty reduction. In this regard, a variant of the WTO's successful Trade Policy Review Mechanism, perhaps including support from the WTO, UNCTAD, the IMF, and the World Bank,[49] may be in order. This development policy review mechanism would require careful customized analysis.[50] It would be driven by the particular circumstances and institutional structure of the subject state, rather than by a more general Washington Consensus-type prescription.

Finally, and most speculatively, lawyers can assist in structuring appropriate international institutions to collect resources and redistribute them to poor countries. This is not a new proposal in international relations. As part of the 'Millennium Development Goals', wealthy countries have agreed to urge one another to 'make concrete efforts towards the target of 0.7 per cent of their GNP as [official development assistance] to developing countries and 0.15 to 0.20 per cent of GNP of developed countries to least developed countries ...'.[51] Obviously, this is an intergovernmental and loose institutional structure. The proposals of the 1970s for a Deep Seabed Authority to reap the harvest of manganese nodules and other seabed resources as a common trust for development may serve as a more transnational and institutionalized precedent. The fact that the wealth of the seabed is to a large extent not economically feasible to exploit does not prevent us from identifying other

---

[49] The World Bank's International Development Association (IDA) administers a 20-factor 'Performance Based Allocation' system, which reviews a number of different features of development policy as a basis for lending. However, this system does not provide substantial room for country-specific determinations of appropriate policies. See 'Linking IDA Support to Country Performance: Third Annual Report on IDA's Country Assessment and Allocation Process', April 2002, available at http://siteresources.worldbank.org/IDA/Resources/PBA2002.pdf.

[50] See Michael Massing, 'Challenging the Growth Gurus: A Bitter Feud Is Heating up over Development Policy', *NY Times* (19 October 2002), A19, 21. In that article, Dani Rodrik is quoted as saying 'Trade reform is something that has to be tailored to each country's circumstances, taking into account its geographic advantage, its institutional needs, its relations with its main trading partners.' The article goes on to say that 'Such an approach troubles Jagdish Bhagwati, a colleague of Mr Stiglitz' at Columbia and a strong advocate of free trade. Joe assumes that there's a monolithic view at the fund and the bank, but that's not the case.' Thus, there seems to be agreement that a 'monolithic' approach would not make sense.

[51] Monterrey Consensus, UN Doc A/Conf.198/3, 22 March 2002, para 42. Even these minimal goals are not being met.

20   *Journal of International Economic Law (JIEL) 6(1)*

bases for aggregation of resources. The European Community funds its operations, including its redistribution, through customs duties, levies on agricultural imports, a portion of each member state's value added tax, and an additional resource based on member state GNP. Perhaps a start toward global reform would see wealthy states agree to turn their tariff revenue, including revenue from countervailing duties and anti-dumping duties, over to a redistributive mechanism. Presumably, such a structure would result in some tariff reduction, and would therefore have the collateral effect of increasing net global welfare.

Under circumstances of weak governance in many poor countries, in order to ensure that resources are not misapplied, some international institutional monitoring and conditionality arrangements are necessary. This will have the beneficial effect of causing governments seriously to examine their development policy, by removing moral hazard problems. If citizens could rely on unconditional global redistribution, they would lack appropriate incentives to cause their own state efficiently to achieve their goals – in economic terms, there would be a 'soft market constraint'.[52]

A development policy review mechanism along the lines mentioned above could be established to recommend a wide range of domestic and international policy prescriptions. For example, it could be authorized to recommend non-application of particular WTO legal rules by poor countries, and it could recommend particular domestic reforms. The WTO arrangements for balance of payments exceptions could be modified to serve as an institutional foundation for this type of structure. This would be a form of interventionism, and some will call it a form of neo-colonialism. But sovereignty, in the form of absolute state control over its own affairs, has been oversold to poor small states. First, these states have little control simply because of their weak economic position. Second, local control is not of benefit to individuals when it is in the hands of predatory governments – we must be open to a post-post-colonial possibility of intervention, in cases of failed domestic governance. If predatory governments can be disciplined, through a regime of analysis, transparency, and conditionality, it is possible to improve the lot of their citizens.

It may seem strange to be advancing greater international intervention and conditionality, at a time when the policies underlying World Bank and IMF conditionality are being hotly criticized.[53] While international governance is quite imperfect, to the extent that it can engage in a policy dialog with poor countries, it is possible that useful measures will result, and will be less imper-

---

[52] Rawls makes this argument explicitly at John Rawls, *The Law of Peoples* 8 (Harvard University Press 1999).

[53] See, e.g., Joseph Stiglitz, *Globalization and Its Discontents* (W.W. Norton 2002). But see, 'Letter from Kenneth Rogoff to Joseph Stiglitz', dated 2 July 2002, available at http://www.imf.org/external/np/vc/2002/070202.htm.

fect than the alternatives. Mechanisms need to be created to ensure and facilitate reasoned dialogue, rather than diktat.

Much will depend on the quality of governance in global institutions. What sort of 'constitutional moment' would it take for wealthy states (and poor ones) to accept that these decisions take place outside of national politics? For example, recent proposals for a bankruptcy reorganization-type procedure for states, presumably administered by the IMF, in order to be attractive to wealthy states, might require poor states contingently to give up further control over their domestic policies, and could require wealthy states to provide additional resources, in order to be attractive to poor ones.[54]

CONCLUSION

Apartheid in South Africa was both separate and unequal. Traditional liberalization can reduce the separation between the poor in poor countries and the rich in rich countries. However, greater equalization – greater redistribution – is needed also, especially as both legal and informal separation will both endure for some time. Apartheid did not end immediately upon the world's recognition that it was wrong, and we cannot expect that global apartheid will end immediately.[55] But understanding must precede action.

To what extent can the trade law system be harnessed to dismantle the barriers that form 'global apartheid' and to redress inequality and poverty? While liberalization fits into the core tasks of the WTO, redistribution does not. This essay cannot address the question of whether the WTO, the World Bank, the IMF, the UN, or some new institutional structure would be the best way to proceed to attack the problem of poverty. However, it is increasingly obvious that the trade law system must not be seen to stand in the way of poverty reduction.

---

[54] See, e.g., Anne Krueger, 'International Financial Architecture for 2002: A New Approach to Sovereign Debt Restructuring', 26 November 2001, available at http://www.imf.org/external/np/speeches/2001/112601.htm; Richard N. Cooper, 'Chapter 11 for Countries, Foreign Affairs' (July/August 2002), at 90.

[55] 'Nobody made a greater mistake than he who did nothing because he could do only a little.' Edmund Burke.

Part IV
Selected Country Experiences

A
China

[14]

The New Anti-monopoly Law in China from a European Perspective

Giacomo Di Federico*

The present paper addresses the recent Chinese Anti-monopoly law, in force since 1 August 2008. A brief overview of the events, which led to the adoption of this new discipline, is necessary to appreciate its groundbreaking nature. The normative framework will be analyzed with a view to single out its main goals, scope of application, positive outcomes, and shortcomings. In assessing the overall suitability of the envisaged control regime, reference will be made to EC antitrust law (and policy), highlighting similarities and differences between the two enforcement systems. This comparative approach is intended to act as an efficiency and effectiveness gauge from both an institutional and operational viewpoint.

1. THE ADOPTION OF THE 2008 ANTI-MONOPOLY LAW: RETROSPECTIVE ANALYSIS

On 1 August 2008, China introduced its first comprehensive competition law. The many special regulations passed in this field since the late 1970s have proven inadequate to cope with the globalizing economy. The transition toward a socialist market economy led to the adoption, in 1993, of the Law Against Unfair Competition, which is mainly concerned with the protection of intellectual property (for items not covered under previous trademark legislation) and of trade secrets.[1] A plethora of regulations ranging from company law to foreign trade law, from consumer protection to insurance law, from price law to electric power law, from countervailing to antidumping, have followed.

Overregulation and legislative inconsistency have spawned uncertainty and, ultimately, unenforceability. The multiple control agencies and the respective laws under which they operate are all but efficient and often generate conflicting decisions. Moreover, factors such as 'public interest' (i.e., State nationalist interests) and 'honesty'[2] play an important role in the normative and implementing phases. From a European standpoint, the need to balance competition against other legitimate goals pursued within the relevant legal order is not surprising – suffice it to recall the concept of 'workable competition'

---

* PhD, Senior Researcher of International Law, and Lecturer of European Union Law in the Faculty of Law, University of Bologna. The author would like to thank Mr Alton Cheung for his translation into English of all the official documents, statements, laws, regulations and decisions available only in Chinese.
    [1] Notably, the Law Against Unfair Competition does not provide for a system of merger control.
    [2] See, for instance, Art. 125 of the 2006 Enterprise Bankruptcy Law.

Di Federico, Giacomo. 'The New Anti-monopoly Law in China from a European Perspective'. *World Competition* 32, no. 2 (2009): 249-270.
© 2009 Kluwer Law International BV, The Netherlands

developed by the Luxemburg courts[3] – but the emphasis placed upon these elements is quite different as emerges from the reading of the provisions and the examination of the practice thereof. In this regard, the encouragement of monopolistic activity under the Electric Power Law is particularly revealing of the underlying rationale.[4]

The impressive economic growth of China finds no equivalent in the social and political context.[5] The will to regulate anti-monopoly conduct is the result of a combination of factors,[6] last but not least the accession, in 2001, to the World Trade Organization (WTO). Indeed, membership was not conditional upon the adoption of a comprehensive antitrust law but it is interesting to observe that, while reassuring that state pricing would be applied 'in a WTO-consistent fashion', the Chinese representative reminded the relevant Working Party that above and beyond the Unfair Competition Act of 1993, a new Anti-monopoly law (AML) was in the process of being formulated.[7]

Of course, issues of paramount importance were to be tackled and solved: from the high number of State-owned enterprises to the existence of administrative monopolies. But mostly, it was a question of establishing – with a sufficient degree of legal certainty – the goals of the new framework law and the principles governing conflicts between the latter and other existing and emerging policies (such as international trade, environmental law, energy supply, and so forth).

It is in this rather complex and unclear scenario that, after more than a decade of debates, international cooperation[8] and an intensive drafting exercise, the AML was adopted. The discussions, which accompanied the reform process, revealed the 'desire for competition in the marketplace' but could not hide 'the existence of a total monopoly in the political arena'.[9]

Broadly speaking, public awareness has consistently grown and the government has progressively acknowledged the importance of learning from the US and EU experiences. This is particularly evident in observing the resources recently devoted to executive coaching and professional training: a clear sign that China is already preparing the future generation for the challenges posed by the development of an antitrust policy in the years to come.

---

[3] Case 26/76 *Metro SB-Großmärkte GmbH & Co. KG v. Commission of the European Communities* [1977] ECR 1875, para. 20.

[4] Pursuant to Art. 22 of the 1995 Electric Power Law of the People's Republic of China: 'The State encourages the merger of power-generating enterprises with power networks and of networks with networks. Requests by power-generating enterprises in the status of qualified independent legal persons to incorporate the power they generate into a network shall be accepted by the enterprise that operates the network.'

[5] On the lack of economic and social justice in China, see C. Guidi & W. Chuntao, *Zhongguo Nongmin Diaochao (A Survey of Chinese Peasants)* (Beijing: The People's Literature Publishing, 2004).

[6] See further J.A. Barry, 'Anti-Monopoly in China: A Socialist Market Economy Wrestles with Its Antitrust Regime', *International Law and Management Review* 2 (2005-2006): 129.

[7] See *Report of the Working Party on the Accession of China*, November 2001, accessible at <www.cecc.gov/pages/selectLaws/WTOimpact/wkptrptPRCWTO.php>, paras 64-65. In this regard, it should also be noted the promulgation of a comprehensive antitrust law has been on the 2003-2008 Agenda of the National People's Congress.

[8] X. Wang, 'Highlights of China's New Anti-Monopoly Law', *Antitrust Law Journal* 75 (2008): 134.

[9] M.M. Dabbah, 'The Development of Sound Competition Law and Policy in China: An (Im)possible Dream?', *World Competition* 30 (2007): 344. See also M. Lorenz, 'Guarding the Pass – The Forthcoming Chinese Competition Legislation', *World Competition* 30 (2007): 137.

The AML — an admirable synthesis (in substantial and procedural terms) of the struggle between marketplace needs and the socialist regime — is anything but flawless though it is considered to have ferried the Chinese economic system 'from a command economy to a market economy'.[10]

2. THE AIM AND SCOPE OF THE AML

In light of the described transitional phase, it would be quixotic to envisage a 'system of competition law that is appropriate to a fully marketised modern economy'.[11] In fact, the new law falls short of the expectations the academic and professional environment had developed during the drafting of the AML. Regardless of the many technical problems, which will be referred to shortly, the main concerns pertain to its goals.

Pursuant to Article 1, the AML is intended to (1) prevent and prohibit monopolistic conduct; (2) protect fair market competition; (3) promote the efficiency of economic operation; (4) safeguard the interests of consumers and the public interest; and (5) promote the healthy development of the socialist market economy.

The provision is somewhat troubling as it assumes that 'true' competition already exists in China. Of course, a number of reasons can be (and have been) adduced in order to justify this bold normative attitude. On the one side, the desire to harmonize the legal framework bringing it in line with that of China's international economic partners (i.e., the United States and the EU) might be viewed as an attempt to attract foreign investments. On the other side, it could be argued that the multivalent objectives operate as a limit to administrative and judicial discretion.[12] However, the inclusion of potentially conflicting goals seems to point in the opposite direction, especially since the precise meaning of expressions such as, for instance, 'economic efficiency', 'public interest', and 'healthy development of the socialist economy' is no where to be found. Moreover, even admitting that competition does perform a variety of functions and must be balanced with other policies (and country-specific priorities), many claim that, for the time being, Chinese authorities are not able to carry out this delicate task with the necessary degree of expertise and independence.[13]

Although it is suggested that these deficiencies are the (inevitable) result of the struggle among the various forces (notably, governmental and academic) which contributed to the drafting of the AML,[14] it is a matter of fact that future implementation will undoubtedly suffer the consequences thereof.

---

[10] Wang, n. 8 above, at 134.

[11] M. Furse, 'Competition Law Choice in China', *World Competition* 30 (2007): 323, 340.

[12] In this respect, it should be observed that in China laws are normally applied to the letter. See Wang, n. 8 above, at 144.

[13] See Dabbah, n. 9 above, at 356; Wang, n. 8 above, at 144; Furse, n. 11 above, at 334.

[14] See N. Bush, 'The PRC Anti-monopoly Law: Unanswered Questions and Challenges Ahead', online publication accessible at <www.antitrustsource.com>. The author singles out the different stances taken with respect to the purpose of the AML (consumer protection, promotion of small and medium enterprises, defense against misuse of official power, shield from foreign undertakings, and so forth).

Despite its garbled goals, the AML clearly defines the material, subjective, and territorial scope of application of the new provisions. The regulation applies to the production and distribution of goods and to the performance of services. It also covers anticompetitive conduct on the part of trade associations[15] and the abusive exploitation of intellectual property rights[16] but 'shall not apply to the alliance among or concerted actions by farmers and the farmers' economic organizations in connection with the production, processing, sales, transportation and storage of agricultural products and other business activities related to agricultural products'.[17]

Article 3 reads: 'Monopolistic conduct referred to herein includes: a) conclusion of monopoly agreements by undertakings; b) abuse of dominant market positions and c) concentrations of undertakings that have or are likely to have the effect of eliminating or restricting competition.' Notwithstanding a general ban on anti-competitive behaviour, exceptions are provided for 'industries that are controlled by the State-owned economy and that are crucial to the wellbeing of the national economy and national security' as well as for 'industries in which exclusive operation and exclusive sales are the norm of business in accordance with the law'.[18]

Lastly, it should be noted that the AML is deemed to be applicable to monopolistic activities which are carried out within the territory of the People's Republic of China or that, although implemented abroad, limit or eliminate competition in the domestic market.[19]

3. The Core Areas of the AML: Substantive Provisions

Although largely inspired by Articles 81 and 82 of the EC Treaty (TEC) and EC Regulation No. 139/04, the normative framework presents distinctive features. The notions of 'Undertakings' and 'Relevant Market' provided under Chapter 1 ('General Provisions') are quite similar to those elaborated by the EC courts. Unfortunately, because of the broad definition offered by Article 12 of the AML, they might be easily misconstrued (or deliberately misapplied) by the judicial and administrative enforcement authorities in light of the specific goal (among the many purported by the AML) which is deemed to prevail in a given case. In order to address these concerns, the Anti-monopoly Bureau, which was created within the Ministry of Commerce (MOFCOM),[20] has recently published Draft Market Definition Guidelines, currently in the process of being reviewed

---

[15] Article 11 of the AML.
[16] Article 55 of the AML. The complex relation between antitrust law and IP rights falls outside the scope of this article. For an overview of the relevant Chinese legislation on the latter aspect, see P. Ganea, T. Pattloch, & C. Heath, *Intellectual Property Law in China* (New York: Kluwer Law International, 2005) and D. Yang & P. Clarke, 'Globalisation and Intellectual Property in China', *Technovation*: 25 (2005).
[17] Article 56 of the AML.
[18] Article 7(1) of the AML.
[19] Article 2 of the AML.
[20] On the institutional framework established by the AML, see Section 4.1 below.

by the interested parties before final enactment.[21] Finally, as will be seen, Chapter 5 of the AML presents some interesting analogies with the rules on the functioning of the European internal market and on anticompetitive practices ascribable to public/private authorities entrusted with exclusive or special rights.

3.1. ANTICOMPETITIVE AGREEMENTS

As far as anticompetitive agreements are concerned, the AML does not follow the three-fold structure of Article 81 TEC, though it preserves its main elements. Both vertical and horizontal agreements, decisions and concerted practices are prohibited inasmuch as they restrict or eliminate competition on the relevant market.

With reference to the latter category of agreements, Article 13 of the AML acknowledges that price-fixing, limiting or controlling production, technical development or investment, and sharing markets are prohibited. Moreover, the provision explicitly refers to collective boycotting. In the European Community, this practice is not mentioned in the Treaty but is nonetheless considered a severe violation of the competition rules, inasmuch as it is directed to eliminate a troublesome competitor.[22] The choice of the Chinese legislator is perhaps not accidental, as suggested by recent commercial surveys.[23] It has been reported by domestic newspapers that Eastern Airlines is being boycotted for lowering prices on the Chengdu-Shanghai route. The dissatisfaction of competing companies International, Sichian, and Shanghai Airlines resulted in a ban on associated travel agencies to sell Eastern Airlines' tickets under threat of severe countermeasures (e.g., limiting computer access, denial of authorizations, and so forth). Apparently, price-fixing is common practice in the air transport market, particularly when travelling to or from Shanghai. In this regard, civil aviation sources denounce the phenomenon of 'same route, same flight, same price'. All the above reveals a blatantly anticompetitive combination of horizontal and vertical agreements the competent enforcement authority will have to determine and remedy.

As to vertical agreements, Article 14 mainly targets distribution agreements fixing resale prices. This seems to indicate that, by contrast with the wording of Article 81(1) EC, applying 'dissimilar conditions to equivalent transactions with other trading parties, thereby placing them at a competitive disadvantage' or making 'the conclusion of contracts subject to acceptance by the other parties of supplementary obligations which, by their nature or according to commercial usage, have no connection with the subject of such contracts' will not prima facie be regarded as unlawful.

---

[21] The text of the guidelines (in Chinese) is accessible at <www.mofcom.gov.cn>. Unfortunately, official translation of the document into English is not available. For the purposes of this contribution, the author has obtained an unofficial translation by a native speaker with a legal background.

[22] See Decision 74/431/EEC, *Belgian Wallpaper* [1974] OJ L 237/3, point IV, 3; and, more recently, Decision 1999/60/EC, *Pre-Insulated Pipe Cartel* [1999] OJ L 24/1, point 147.

[23] See Chengdu Commercial, 7 January. 2009, A16.

Without entering into the economic debate on the harmfulness of vertical agreements, it is somewhat disconcerting that exclusive distribution agreements and tying arrangements are not expressly targeted. Both these conducts may prove to be very dangerous in terms of market foreclosure and ultimately consumer welfare.[24] This becomes even more evident when considering that vertical agreements are often used as a means of ensuring the success of a cartel. In this sense, the described Eastern Airlines case is again revealing.

The lists that identify unlawful (vertical and horizontal) agreements finish with a catchall clause, enabling the antitrust authorities to extend their scope of application. Future practice will tell whether the mentioned shortcomings will be appropriately addressed.

Similarly to what happens in Europe, the AML envisages exceptions to the rule and singles out possible causes for exemption. Among them, the need to pursue public interests (including but not limited to achieving energy saving or protecting the environment), to mitigate the severe decrease in sales volume or excessive overstock during economic recession, and to safeguard the interests in foreign trade deserve particular attention, as they prove that the AML is a flexible instrument allowing for other policies to be taken into consideration in the implementation process. On the other hand, admitting a cartel in order to combat economic depression could have fatal long-lasting consequences. In this regard, unlike Article 81(3) TEC, the AML is silent as to the requirement that, objective justification and consumer benefit aside, the result cannot be the elimination of competition on the relevant market.

Furthermore, no reference is made to the adoption of block exemption regulations, which have in turn been an important factor in limiting the Commission's workload, allowing it to concentrate on the most serious antitrust infringements.

Finally, as to the civil legal consequences of an unlawful practice, Article 50 of the AML states that: 'undertakings that cause loss to others as a result of their monopolistic conduct shall be liable for civil liabilities in accordance with the laws'.[25] The possibility to bring lawsuits against national and multinational companies in China is indeed one of the most interesting features of the AML, and it will be further investigated when addressing the enforcement regime thereof.[26]

3.2. ABUSE OF A DOMINANT POSITION

The rules on abusive exploitation of a dominant position also reflect the influence of EC antitrust law but, from a normative perspective, are more detailed. The definition offered of dominance appears to be more stringent than that developed by the Community

---

[24] In particular, exclusive distribution agreements (with territorial protection clauses) may have disruptive effects in terms of market structure, especially if part of a wider net of similar agreements implemented throughout the country's regions and provinces.

[25] Article 50 of the AML.

[26] See Section. 4.2 below.

courts.[27] The multifactor analysis that will have to be carried out in ascertaining dominance is very similar, if not identical, to what the European Court of Justice (ECJ) found appropriate in *Hoffmann-La Roche v. Commission of the European Communities*.[28] Nevertheless, by contrast with what happens in the EC, where the ability to 'prevent effective competition being maintained on the relevant market'[29] is determined on a case-by-case basis, the AML fixes presumptions of dominance.[30]

The solution is intended to facilitate the work of the competent agencies and courts, but overlooks three key variables: (1) it is often difficult to calculate the relevant market share; (2) the number of competitors (and, consequently, the structure of the market concerned) can vary substantially according to the nature of the goods or services in question; and (3) a market economy may be extremely dynamic (or even volatile). Although it can be argued that flexibility is ensured by the rebuttable nature of the presumptions,[31] the indicated factors make an a priori, one-size-fits-all approach questionable, especially in the absence of a sufficient understanding of economics.

The mentioned market definition guidelines are precisely intended to address these concerns: the assessment of the product, geographic and 'temporal' market is largely consistent with the European practice, taking into account substitutability both on the demand and on the supply side. Similarly to what is stated in the Commission's Notice on the subject matter,[32] the latter aspect will only be considered when it has a constraining effect on the conduct of the undertakings operating on the concerned market.[33] In identifying the range of interested products (and the territorial boundaries of the relevant market[34]), the Small but Significant and Non-transitory Increase in Price (SSNIP) (or Hypothetical Monopolist) test will be applied, but only in particularly complex cases. This specification is rather unfortunate for it implies that, save in exceptional

---

[27] Article 17(2) of the AML reads: 'Dominant Market Positions ... mean market positions held by undertakings who are able to control the price or quantity of commodities, or other transaction terms in the Relevant Market or block or affect the entry of other undertakings into the Relevant Market.' According to the European Court of Justice (ECJ), dominance is 'a position of economic strength enjoyed by an undertaking which enables it to hinder the maintenance of effective competition on the relevant market by allowing it to behave to an appreciable extent independently of its competitors and customers and ultimately of consumers'. Case 322/81 *NV Nederlandsche Banden Industrie Michelin v. Commission of the European Communities* [1983] ECR 3461, at para. 30.

[28] Compare Art. 18 of the AML and Case 85/76 *Hoffmann-La Roche v. Commission of the European Communities* [1979] ECR 461, where the Court recognized that very large market shares are highly significant evidence of the existence of a dominant position. Other relevant factors are the relationship between the market shares of the undertaking concerned and of its competitors, especially those of the next largest, the technological lead of the undertaking over its competitors, the existence of a highly developed sales network and the absence of potential competition.

[29] Case 27/76 *United Brands Company and United Brands Continentaal BV v. Commission of the European Communities* [1978] ECR 207, para. 65.

[30] See Art. 19 of the AML. However, the temptation to introduce presumptions of dominance based on market share is detectable in cases such as Case C-62/86 *AKZO Chemie BV v. Commission of the European Communities* [1991] ECR I-3359 (hereinafter '*Akzo*') and Case C-497/99P *Irish Sugar plc v. Commission* [2001] ECR I-5333, where the Court of Justice considered that a market share of 50% could be held to be 'indicative' of a dominant position.

[31] See, in particular, Art. 19(3) of the AML.

[32] See Commission Notice on the definition of relevant market for the purposes of Community competition law [1997] OJ C372/5, points 13 and 20 to 23.

[33] See the Anti-monopoly Bureau Draft Market Definition Guidelines, n. 21 above, Art. 8.

[34] It is noteworthy that the relevant geographical area will also be determined considering factors such as trade barriers, transportation costs, and consumers' preferences. Compare the Draft Market Definition Guidelines, n. 21 above, Art. 8 and points 30, 31, and 41 of the Commission Notice on the definition of relevant market, n. 32 above.

circumstances, the determination of competing/substitutable products will be based on intuition instead of on sound economic analysis.

As to the specific practices prohibited under the AML, illustrative (i.e., non-exhaustive) abuses of dominance are listed in Article 17. The differences with respect to Article 82 TEC are minor[35] and in any case compensated by a catchall provision.[36] Moreover, it should be underlined that dominant undertakings are allowed to adduce justification for their (potentially) abusive conduct. If their arguments are upheld by the enforcing agency, the practice will be considered legitimate.

3.3. MERGERS AND ACQUISITIONS

The AML creates an ex ante control system on Mergers, which, if the relevant thresh-olds are met,[37] must be notified to the competent authorities and await authorization before they can be implemented. Unlike the previous rules on Mergers and Acquisitions (M&A), the AML covers both domestic and foreign parties, which again confirms the comprehensive scope of the latter regulation.[38] Still, worries for possible acquisitions of national firms by foreign investors have prompted the legislator to foresee a special 'national security review'.[39]

The factors to be taken into account when determining the admissibility of a merger operation are very similar to those indicated in Regulation No. 139/04.[40] The two-stage procedure laid down in Articles 25 and 26 is aimed at guaranteeing flexibility while ensuring a speedy handling of notifications.[41] The latter aspect needs further con-sideration. Article 23 sets out the information to be provided when requesting approval

---

[35] The definition of predatory pricing included in Art. 17(1), 2nd indent, departs from the notion elaborated by the ECJ in *Akzo* and Case 333/94 *Tetra Pak International SA v. Commission of the European Communities* [1996] ECR I-5951, where the judges clarified that the sale below cost must be aimed at forcing competitors out of the market.

[36] See Art. 17(1), 7th indent.

[37] It is worthwhile noting that the AML leaves the State Council the task of fixing these thresholds. Two days after the enactment of the AML, an order (no. 529) was passed setting the following thresholds: (1) the aggregate global turnover of all business operators to the concentration for the preceding financial year exceeds CNY 10 billion, and there are at least two business operators whose turnover in China for the preceding financial year each exceed CNY 400 million; or (2) the aggregate turnover of all business operators to the concentration in China for the preceding financial year exceeds CNY 2 billion, and there are at least two business operators whose turnover in China for the preceding financial year each exceed CNY 400 million. By contrast, Art. 22 of the AML allows undertakings not to file any notification if: (1) one undertaking participating in the concentration owns more than 50% of the voting shares of the other participating undertakings *or* (2) more than 50% of the voting shares or assets of every undertaking participating in the concentration are owned by a single undertaking that does not participate in the concentration.

[38] The equal footing of indigenous and foreign firms under the AML does not in itself prevent protectionism. The favour of national authorities for domestic undertakings can be appreciated by analyzing the report published by the State Administration of Industry and Commerce in May 2004, 'Behaviour and countermeasures for anti-competitive practices of multinational undertakings in China'.

[39] See Art. 31 of the AML.

[40] Compare Art. 27 of the AML and Art. 2 of EC Regulation No. 139/04 on the control of concentrations between undertakings [2004] OJ L24/1.

[41] After a preliminary review, the competent authorities might need to gather further information before granting or denying authorization. The maximum review period is 180 days (although no guidance is offered as to whether these are intended to be business days or calendar days). These time limits are notably longer than the ones set out in Regulation No. 139/04, whereby the Commission has ninety days to take a final decision. This period might be extended up to twenty working days in complex cases.

of a concentration. A series of documents related to merger filing were recently published, indicating the procedural steps available to parties wanting to engage in pre-filing consultation with the competent enforcement authority, the factors to be addressed when representing the possible impact of the operation, and the additional documents and materials to be submitted.[42] Although consistent with the information demanded in the Form CO, annexed to EC Regulation No. 802/2004,[43] practitioners consider the data required too burdensome. Their concerns are even greater in the absence of effective guarantees as to the respect of legal professional privilege.[44]

The amount of documentation to be forwarded is not the only problematic issue. The lack of a clear deadline for the acceptance of the notification has also been denounced for it enables the competent agency to freely delay the procedure. The ongoing practice reveals risks of potential abuses. By the end of 2008, thirteen notifications were formally accepted but many others are still being processed. In this regard, the new guidelines state that the MOFCOM, which is responsible for the review of concentrations, will issue an information registration form upon receipt of the notification, but such statement does not imply the documentation is complete[45] and the filing stage might last weeks or even months.[46] Although the possibility to require further detailed information is certainly appropriate, it is feared that the Ministry might use this power to discourage concentrations it does not consider to be 'politically viable' (e.g., the acquisition of a national firms by foreign investors).

Furthermore, by contrast with what happens in Europe, the acceptance of a notification will not be publicized, excluding interested third parties from the procedure.[47] This is unfortunate as it deprives the enforcement authority of potentially relevant data concerning the existing degree of competition on the market and the actual impact of the proposed operation.

Concentrations that have or may have the effect of eliminating or restricting competition will be prohibited. Nonetheless, a 'rule of reason' has been introduced and the

---

[42] The following documents were published in Chinese on the web site of the Ministry of Commerce (<www.mofcom.gov.cn>) and are effective as of 1 January. 2009: Working Guidelines for Anti-monopoly Investigation of Concentrations of Business Operators (Working Guidelines); Guiding Opinion on Reporting of Concentrations of Business Operators (Opinion on Reporting); Guiding Opinion on Documents and Information Required for Reporting of Concentrations of Business Operators (Opinion on Documents); and Flowchart for Anti-monopoly Investigation of Concentrations of Business Operators. Since official translation into English is not available, the author has obtained an unofficial translation by a native speaker with a legal background.

[43] Compare Opinion on Reporting and Opinion on Documents, n. 41 above, and Annex I of Regulation No. 802/2004 implementing Council Regulation No. 139/2004 on the control of concentrations between undertakings [2004] OJ L133/1.

[44] See 'Ministry Publishes New Anti-monopoly Law Guidelines', online publication accessible at <www.chinalawandpractice.com/Article/2081356/Ministry-publishes-new-Anti-monopoly-Law-guidelines.html>.

[45] Opinion on Reporting, n. 42 above, Art. 5.

[46] The Coca-Cola Company filed a notification for the acquisition of China Huiyuan Juice Group Ltd in early September and had to wait until early December for formal acceptance of its submission. See S.G. Harris, P. Wang, & Y. Zhang, 'China's Antitrust Agency Provides Insights into the Merger Review Process under the New Anti-Monopoly Law', online publication accessible at <www.mondaq.com/article.asp?articleid=71236>.

[47] Under Art. 18(4) of the EC Regulation 139/04, the Commission is compelled to hear any third party who applies and shows a sufficient interest. If specifically requested, the latter may also be admitted to present observations during the oral hearing (see Regulation No. 802/2004, n. 43 above, Art. 16(2)).

Anti-Monopoly Enforcement Authority (AMEA) is empowered to authorize a merger when the positive effects outweigh the negative effects thereof *or* when issues of public interest arise.[48] The alternative raises some concerns as it leaves great discretionary power in the hands of the public enforcer (notably when state-owned undertakings are involved in the operation) to the detriment of competitors and, ultimately, consumers.

Moreover, pursuant to Article 29 of the AML, the approval may be conditional upon the imposition of restrictive conditions to reduce the adverse effects on competition. To be sure, in the first formal decision since the adoption of the AML, the MOFCOM accepted InBev's takeover of Anheuser-Busch Cos Inc AB, but stipulated that neither of the undertakings may increase its ownership stakes in domestic beer companies without prior authorization.[49] At closer scrutiny – notwithstanding the creation of an Economic Division within the Anti-monopoly Bureau – the decision does not contain in-depth competition analysis and its legal reasoning leaves a lot to be desired. Decision-making transparency is instead of the utmost importance to ensure effective judicial protection. The Ministry appears to have (partially) acknowledged the problem by issuing, shortly after the reported decision, a document providing some insights into its approach to merger cases, with ample references to the steps taken in the InBev case.

3.4. Services of general interest

According to Article 7 of the AML: 'With respect to industries that are controlled by the State-owned economy and that are critical to the wellbeing of the national economy and national security, as well as industries in which exclusive operation and exclusive sales are the norm of business in accordance with the law, the State shall protect the lawful business activities of the undertakings in such industries.'

The provision is reminiscent of Articles 16 and 86 TEC for it addresses those activities entrusted to undertakings (private or public) with special or exclusive rights, which normally are not conducted under free market principles. Universal service, continuity, quality of service, affordability, as well as user and consumer protection would be impossible to guarantee in markets, such as postal delivery, electric supply, public transportation, social and health services, and so forth, without the possibility of derogating from competition rules.

Within the EU legal order, the derogation is admissible only in so far as the application of such rules would obstruct the performance, in law or in fact, of the particular tasks assigned to them and provided the development of trade is not affected to such an extent as would be incompatible with the interests of the Community.[50] In the words of the ECJ, the provision 'seeks to reconcile the Member States' interest in using certain undertakings, in particular in the public sector, as an instrument of economic or fiscal

---

[48] Article 28 of the AML.

[49] See China Daily, 19 November, 'MOFCOM approves InBev, AB merger', accessible at <www.chinadaily.com.cn/bizchina/2008-11/19/content_7219360.htm>.

[50] Article 86(2) TEC. See, also Case C-320/91 *Criminal Proceedings against P. Corbeau* [1993] ECR I-2533, para. 13.

policy with the Community's interest in ensuring compliance with the rules on competition and the preservation of the unity of the Common Market'.[51] Needless to say that, inasmuch as it allows a departure from the general Treaty provisions, the Commission, responsible for monitoring the respect of Article 86 TEC,[52] will closely weigh the relevant interests. On its part, the ECJ has affirmed that the norm is to be interpreted narrowly.[53]

It is essentially the responsibility of public authorities, national or supranational (in the exercise of their respective competences[54]), to decide on the nature and scope of a Service of General Interest (SGI). In recent years, the EU has devoted considerable attention to the elaboration of principles and conditions for the operation of these services. Most notably, the Commission envisages a mix of sector-specific and issue-specific actions aimed at consolidating the EU framework applicable to SGIs: (1) providing legal guidance on cross-cutting issues; (2) modernizing and developing sector-specific policies through positive actions in the fields of energy, transport, e-communication and postal, social and health services; and (3) monitoring and evaluating to guarantee quality and transparency, through comprehensive analysis and progress reports.[55] Furthermore, the Community legislator has adopted directives for the liberalization of markets in energy, telecommunications, and so forth, which, while ensuring a sufficient degree of competition, enable or require Member States to impose public-service obligations on suppliers relating to the security, continuity, quality, and price of supply.[56]

In China, benefits from growth are not yet shared by the whole population (in particular, in rural areas). It is true that, *from* the 1990s, there has been a shift from a purely economic policy to a more social policy and that the State has developed health and education policies, but those sectors are still problematic.[57] By contrast with what happens in Europe, where access to services of general economic interest is conceived as a fundamental right,[58] in China, the social unit of reference for users appears to be the

---

[51] Case 202/88 *French Republic v. Commission of the European Communities* [1991] ECR I-1223.

[52] According to Art. 86(3): 'The Commission shall ensure the application of the provisions of this Article and shall, where necessary, address appropriate directives or decisions to Member States.'

[53] Case C-340/99 *TNT Traco SpA v. Poste Italiane SpA and Others* [2001] ECR I-4109, para. 19.

[54] This shared responsibility is apparent from Art. 1(3) of Directive 2006/123/CE on services in the internal market ('This Directive does not affect the freedom of Member States to define, in conformity with Community law, what they consider to be services of general economic interest, how those services should be organized and financed, in compliance with the State aid rules, and what specific obligations they should be subject to') and is also reflected in the Protocol on SGIs annexed to the Treaty of Lisbon [2008] OJ C115/9.

[55] Communication from the Commission to the European Parliament, the Council, the European Economic and Social Committee, and the Committee of the Regions, of 20 November 2007, accompanying the Communication on 'A single market for 21st century Europe' – Services of general interest, including social services of general interest: A new European commitment [COM(2007) 725 final – not published in the Official Journal]. Also see Communication from the Commission to the European Parliament, the Council, the European Economic and Social Committee, and the Committee of the Regions of 12 May 2004 entitled 'White Paper on services of general interest' [COM(2004) 374 final] and Commission Green Paper of 21 May 2003 on services of general interest [COM(2003) 270 final – Official Journal C 76 of 25 March 2004].

[56] See, for instance, Directive 2002/22/CE on universal service and users' right relating to electronic communications networks and services [2002] OJ L108/51.

[57] The housing sector also appears to raise concerns (see 2007 China Europe Forum, accessible at <www.china-europa-forum.net>).

[58] See Art. 36 of the Charter of Fundamental Rights of the European Union [2007] OJ C303/1.

family (rather than the individual). Moreover, whereas in the EU, the performance of SGIs is left to national laws and practices, in accordance with the Treaties, in China, the regulation (and funding) of such activities is left to the State.[59]

Despite these important and somewhat physiological differences, some lessons could be drawn from the European experience. Firstly, the AML does not seem to frame the criticalities peculiar to SGIs in terms of necessary exceptions to the general rule (i.e., free competition). To be sure, Article 7 reads: 'The State shall regulate and supervise the business activities of such undertakings and regulate the prices of commodities and services provided by such undertakings in accordance with the law so as to protect the interests of the consumers and to promote technological progress.' Although the 'interest of consumers' is normally safeguarded by enhancing competition – an interpretation that would help bring the provision in line with the aims of the AML – the expression 'in accordance with the law' indicates that specific regulations will apply. This conclusion is supported by the circumstance that none of the authorities responsible for the application of the AML are mentioned in the provision.[60]

Secondly, in the absence of a framework legislation on SGIs containing their definition and the general applicable principles, the risk of abuses, both at a centralized and decentralized level, is particularly high.[61]

Thirdly, a breach of Article 86(1) TEC presupposes the violation of some other Treaty provision (in particular, Articles 12 and 81–89 TEC) and the liability of the undertakings concerned will be determined accordingly, save when the exception laid down in Article 86(2) applies. Article 7(2) of the AML, instead, merely requires that 'Undertakings in the industries referred to in the preceding paragraph shall conduct their business in accordance with the law, shall be honest and reputable in their business dealings, and shall maintain strict self-discipline and accept public supervision. They shall not harm the interests of consumers by utilizing their controlling positions or their status as the exclusive provider of certain services or products.' As already anticipated, the concept of honesty is capable of generating confusion and, mostly, of escaping sound administrative and judicial review, especially taking into account that no reference is made to Article 17 of the AML (i.e., abuse of a dominant position).

It follows from the above that the AML does not tackle with sufficient vigour the many problems connected to the performance of SGIs. The potential negative effects of the provision in question have been clearly described by N. Bush: 'given the prevalence of state ownership in some energy, mining, communications, and manufacturing sectors, Article 7 may, ironically, derail general competition rules in many of the most inefficient sectors of the economy'.[62]

---

[59] Although there seems to be a growing questioning of the transfer of tax resources from the State toward local authorities in charge of SGIs.

[60] As to the institutional framework created by the AML, see Section 4.1 below.

[61] These problematic issues are closely linked to the provisions laid down in Ch. 5 of the AML. See Section 3.5 below.

[62] Bush, n. 14 above, at 5.

3.5. THE ABUSE OF ADMINISTRATIVE POWER

However, the most distinctive feature of the AML is the explicit prohibition of administrative monopolies.[63] According to the provisions laid down in Chapter 5 (Articles 32 to 37), Administrative agencies and organizations empowered by laws and regulations to have the function of administrating public affairs shall refrain from abusing their governmental powers to (1) require (or demand in a disguised form) organizations or individuals to deal in, purchase, or use the commodities supplied by the undertakings designated by them; (2) hinder the free flow of commodities among different regions;[64] (3) exclude or restrict the participation of undertakings from other regions in local bidding activities by means such as prescribing discriminatory qualification requirements or standards or by not publishing information according to law; (4) exclude or restrict investment in their region or establishment of branches or subsidiaries in their region by undertakings from other regions, by applying means such as treatment not equal to what local undertakings are entitled to;[65] (5) compel undertakings to engage in any monopolistic conduct; and (6) make regulations that contain provisions eliminating or restricting competition.

The provisions are aimed at combating two specific phenomena that are likely to jeopardize the effectiveness of the AML. On the one hand, the possible distortion of competition resulting from the sectorial legislation/regulation; on the other, the risk that China's provinces and cities engage in protectionism by supporting local enterprises vis-à-vis competitors coming from outside that area.[66]

Surprisingly, no exception is mentioned in Chapter 5. The reason for this becomes clear when reading Article 51(2). Because the AML is conceived as a *lex generalis*, the norm provides that any abuse restricting or eliminating competition pursuant to specific laws and regulations shall be governed by the latter. This circumstance would not in itself be so troublesome if the *leges speciales* (e.g., postal services, telecommunications, and so forth) had been updated concomitantly with the elaboration of the AML. Unfortunately, this does not seem to have occurred, making it difficult to assess the overall impact of

---

[63] Chapter 5 of the AML (Arts 32-37). The notion of administrative monopoly is believed to cover situations where the abuse of the administrative power by an administrative agency restricts competition and hinders the proper functioning of the Socialist Market economy. See H. Ruyin, *Competition and Monopoly: Socialist Microeconomic Analysis* (Shanghai: Sanlian Publishing, 1998) and, more recently, Z. Pengcheng, *Research on Legal Control and Administrative Monopoly* (Beijing: Peking University Press, 2002).

[64] More precisely, Art. 33, nos 1 to 4, of the AML illustrate possible measures harming intra-regional trade: (1) to charge discriminatory fees under separate fee categories or at different rates, or fix discriminatory prices for commodities originating in other regions; (2) to impose on commodities originating in other regions technical requirements or inspection standards different from those applied to similar local commodities, or cause commodities originating in other regions to be subject to discriminatory technical measures such as duplicate inspection or certification, so as to restrict the entry of commodities originating in other regions into the local markets; (3) to implement special administrative licensing measures applicable only to commodities originating in other regions, so as to restrict the entry of commodities originating in other regions into the local markets; and (4) to set up checkpoints or take other measures to block the entry of commodities originating in other regions or the flow of local commodities out of the region. The list ends (5th indent) with a catchall clause ('other actions that may impede the free flow of commodities among different regions').

[65] Chinese law requires most domestic firms to establish branches in the various localities where they do business.

[66] Legal commentators have long been advocating the adoption of an AML in China confronting the problem. See, for instance, Hu Weiwei, 'Antimonopoly law is a necessity in China', *Jurisprudence* 3 (1995): 35.

the newly adopted law in the following years.[67] In addition, it should be noted that the rules on industries in which exclusive operation and exclusive sales are the norm of business in accordance with the law could offer a 'legal safeguard' for abusive administrative monopolies.[68]

From a European perspective, Chapter 5 is interesting since the provisions contained therein recall to a certain extent norms of the EC Treaty. Firstly, Articles 28, 43, and 49 TEC should be considered. Although, unlike the mentioned provisions, the AML is applicable to a one-party State, the decentralized exercise of governmental powers needed to be brought in line with the spirit which animated the reform and demanded the insertion of what is normally referred to as a standstill obligation.[69] On the contrary, no duty to remove the existing barriers is foreseen. The inclusion of such an obligation, possibly combined with a duty to adjust any State monopoly of a commercial character (so as to ensure that no discrimination regarding the conditions under which goods are procured and marketed exists between the different regions, provinces, and cities),[70] would probably have contributed to limit the future coordination problems between the AML and the plethora of existing sectorial rules potentially incompatible (in the absence of objective justification) with the former.

Secondly, it can be argued that Article 37 of the AML is capable of covering public anticompetitive practices such as subsidies and other preferential conditions granted to local champions by means of specific regulations. In other words, the provision could be used (but is not likely to be invoked) to prohibit State aids with no objective justification, similarly to what happens pursuant to Articles 87-89 TEC.[71] And yet, the absence of any specific rule (or official statement) on the subject matter makes it practically impossible to imagine any development in this direction.[72]

Lastly, it should be noted that Article 36 can be associated with the case law of the ECJ on the joint applicability of Articles 81 and 10 TEC. The latter court has in fact consistently claimed that a State will be considered in breach of the principle of loyal cooperation, read together with the prohibition of anti-competitive agreements when it 'requires or encourages the adoption of agreements, decisions or concerted practices contrary to Article 81 EC or reinforces their effects, or where it divests its own rules of

---

[67] Actually, it appears that many sectorial laws are currently under review. Let it suffice here to recall the envisaged amendment of the PRC's Postal Law (the deadline for submitting comments on the draft has expired on the 30 November. 2008). It should however be noted that foreign firms have manifested great dissatisfaction with regard to the draft rules governing access to the postal market (see online article accessible at <www.chinaeconomicreview.com/dailybriefing/2008_10_30/Courier_companies_worried_by_postal_law.html>).

[68] In this sense, Bush argues that: 'Article 7 … may also gut the rules against administrative monopoly in the sectors where they are needed most' (Bush, n. 14 above, at 5).

[69] See, in particular, Arts 33 and 35 of the AML.

[70] See Art. 31 TEC.

[71] For a shared opinion on the issue, see Dabbah, n. 9 above, at 358.

[72] On the rules applicable to State aids and the policy developed by the EU in recent years, see, A. Biondi, P. Eeckhout, & J. Flynn (eds), *The Law of State Aid in the European Union* (Oxford: Oxford University Press, 2004) and J. Flett, *EC State Aid Law* (Alphen aan den Rijn: Kluwer Law International, 2008).

the character of legislation by delegating to private economic operators responsibility for taking decisions affecting the economic sphere'.[73]

4. The Enforcement of the AML

Another controversial aspect of the AML is the suitability of the enforcement regime it foresees. A first glance at the law is sufficient to single out three main questions which deserve further attention: (1) the need for a more coherent institutional framework, (2) the distinction between public and private enforcement, and (3) the risk of administrative abuse remaining substantially unpunished. These aspects will be addressed in the following paragraphs with a view to highlight the distinctive (and problematic) features of the application system considered as a whole.

4.1. The 'multifunctional' enforcement agencies: regulation, control, and procedural guarantees

The implementation of the AML is entrusted to (1) the Anti-Monopoly Commission (AMC), operating under the State Council, entitled to formulate competition policies and guidelines, coordinate the enforcement activities, and evaluate market competition;[74] and (2) the AMEA, responsible for the enactment of the Law (carrying out inspections, ordering searches and seizures, imposing fines, and so forth).[75] The enforcement duties will be shared by three existing agencies: the State Administration for Industry and Commerce (SAIC), the National Development and Reform Commission (NDRC), and the MOFCOM,[76] all empowered to apply sectorial regulations.

Moreover, Article 10(2) allows the AMEA to delegate the corresponding agencies at the level of province, autonomous region, and municipality. It is for the State Council to lay down a unified framework coordinating the respective activities.[77] Legal commentators agree that the current situation is unsatisfactory and reflects a loss-making administration.

The shortcomings of this multifunction/multilevel enforcement regime are twofold and pertain to (1) possible conflicts of jurisdiction under the AML and/or under other regulations and (2) possible conflicts of competencies under the AML and/or other implementing regulations. On the one side, it is possible to envisage a situation where the same practice is caught by the AML and by specific industry regulations.[78] On the

---

[73] See Case C-250/03 *Giorgio Emanuele Mauri v. Ministero della Giustizia and Commissione per gli esami di avvocato presso la Corte d'appello di Milano* [2005] ECR I-1267, para. 30 and in Joined Cases C-94/04 and C-202/04 *Federico Cipolla and Others v. Rosaria Fazari, née Portolese, and Roberto Meloni* [2006] ECR I-11421, para. 47.

[74] Article 9 of the AML.

[75] Article 10 of the AML. On the enforcement powers granted to the AMEA, see Arts 38-54 of the AML.

[76] As already noted (see *supra*, text accompanying n. 20), an Anti-monopoly Bureau has been created within the Ministry of Commerce.

[77] A Restructuring Plan concerning the tasks to be assigned to SAIC, NDRC, and MOFCOM under the AML began in March 2008, following the 11th Session of the National People's Congress.

[78] Possible 'conflicts of jurisdiction' may arise, for instance, when the practice also falls under the scope of application of the 2000 Telecommunications Regulation or the 1995 Insurance Law.

other, a given conduct (e.g., predatory pricing) might be evaluated by the NDRC's as a monopolistic pricing behaviour and by the SAIC as an abuse of a dominant position. The allocation of enforcement functions can also cause implementation problems when considered in its vertical dimension: a decentralized agency might be tempted to favour local state-owned firms regardless of the degree of competition on the relevant market.[79]

The AML offers no guidance as to what law should prevail and on how to avoid political bias and, ultimately, prevent conflicting decisions. It follows that key elements for the success of the reform, such as legal certainty, the neutrality of the relevant agency, and the uniform application of the AML, remain unsettled.[80] In this sense, the envisaged adoption of the described guidelines on the definition of the relevant market, regarding in particular conducts falling under Articles 13, 14 (anticompetitive agreements[81]), 17 (abuse of a dominant position), and 19 (mergers) of the AML, certainly represent an important step in the right direction.

From the public enforcer's perspective, institutional questions aside, there are many technical issues that call for closer examination when assessing the suitability of the new regime. For reasons of brevity, only a few will be mentioned. Firstly, the circumstance that the AMEA will be fully equipped to perform its investigative functions.[82] Secondly, the fact that Article 45 allows for the development of a leniency policy, which in the US and EU experiences has proven to be effective and cost-efficient. Thirdly, the possibility to avoid a long and expensive procedure by accepting commitments on the part of undertakings engaged in anti-competitive conducts.[83] Of course, all these issues deserve further attention, especially in consideration of the practice that will develop over time.

As far as sanctioning powers are concerned, the AML punishes both substantial and procedural violations. Within the first category, the law draws a distinction between the breach of the rules on monopoly agreements and on abusive conduct, on the one side, and the unlawful implementation of a concentration, on the other. In cases covered by Articles 13, 14 and 17 of the AML, the AMEA is entitled to stop the illegal act, confiscate illegal gains, and impose fines of 1% to 10% of the offenders' total turnover from the preceding year. The only exceptions concern those agreements that have not been implemented and those resulting from the direct involvement of trade associations governing undertakings within their industries.

In both cases, the fine will not exceed CNY 500,000. Albeit for different reasons, these derogations are hard to explain. On the one hand, non-implementation could be assimilated to an attenuating circumstance. Why the legislator felt the need to single out this specific circumstance remains unclear, taking into account that Article 49 of

---

[79] Wang, n. 8 above, at 149.

[80] Although, according to the draft submitted by the State Council to the Standing Committee in 2006: 'If there are relevant laws and administrative regulations stipulating that the monopolistic conducts prohibited by this Law shall be investigated and handled by the relevant departments or supervisory organs, the law and regulations are to be applied'.

[81] In particular, the guidelines will be applied in order to determine whether two or more undertakings should be considered competitors.

[82] Article 39 of the AML.

[83] Article 45 of the AML.

the AML enables the Anti-monopoly authorities to fix the amount of the fine having regard to the nature, the extent, the duration of the violation and to '*other factors*'. On the other hand, it is curious to say the least that the infringement of the law on the part of trade associations, particularly powerful within their industries, should determine the imposition of a fine which is fully assimilated to that imposable on single undertakings entering into an non-implemented agreement. Perhaps fortunately, the apparent *favour* for such entities is counterbalanced by the fact that 'if the circumstances are serious, the authority in charge of registration and administration of social organizations may revoke the registration of the trade organizations in accordance with the law'.[84]

By contrast, should the undertakings implement a concentration in violation of Articles 21, 25(2) or 26(2) of the AML, the AMEA, in addition to a fine of less than CNY 500,000, shall order them to stop implementing the operation and adopt structural remedies, such as (but not limited to) compulsory disposal of equities or assets in limited time, with a view to revert to the condition of the undertakings before the concentration.[85]

As to procedural violations (e.g., supplying the enforcement authority with false or misleading data during the procedure), the AML provides for a fine of less than CNY 20,000 to be imposed on individuals and for a fine of no more than CNY 200,000 on organizations. In the event the breach is deemed to be serious, save the criminal relevance of the act in question, Article 52 foresees a substantial increase in the amount of the pecuniary sanctions.[86]

From the undertakings' perspective, the AML establishes a number of guarantees, notably, the protection of commercial secrets (which must be kept confidential),[87] the right to submit written observations (although no access to the file is expressly stated),[88] and the right to challenge the measures adopted by the enforcement agencies. In this regard, the aggrieved parties have two possible courses of action:[89] (1) seeking reconsideration by a higher administrative office[90] or (2) initiating administrative litigation in court.[91] It appears that only the area of mergers will depart from this general rule. Under Article 53(1) of the AML, in fact, individuals or organizations objecting to a prohibition or authorization of a given merger 'may first apply for administrative review in accordance with the law; if they object to the decision of the administrative review, they may file an administrative lawsuit in accordance with the law'. In addition, the exception laid down in Article 31 should be remembered: if the merger with or acquisition

---

[84] Article 46(2) of the AML.
[85] Article 48 of the AML.
[86] More precisely, Art. 52 of the AML envisages a fine of more than CNY 20,000 and less than CNY 100,000 for individuals and a fine of more than CNY 200,000 and less than CNY 1,000,000 for organizations.
[87] Article 41 of the AML.
[88] Article 43 of the AML.
[89] Article 53(2) of the AML.
[90] The time limit for administrative reconsideration is sixty days (starting from the acceptance of the complaint), which can be extended to ninety days in complicated cases. See Administrative Reconsideration Law, Art. 31. The law is available at <www.china.com.cn/law/flfh/txt/2006-08/08/content_7063886>.
[91] Administrative lawsuits are to be filed with the Administrative Disputes Tribunal pursuant to the Procedural Law on Administrative Litigation (and other relevant laws).

of domestic enterprises by foreign investors should raise concerns for national security, it shall undergo a special review procedure conducted in accordance with the relevant State regulations.

Some additional remarks on the possible courses of action following an AML decision are needed. Although the possibility to apply for administrative reconsideration is certainly to be welcomed, the chances of success are, de facto, very limited. Pursuant to Article 14 of the Administrative Reconsideration Law (ARL), decisions by the ministries under the State Council are to be reconsidered by the ministry that issued the decision with the paradoxical result that measures adopted by MOFCOM, SAIC, and NDRC, as ministries operating under the State Council, will be reconsidered by the same agency that issued the original decision.

Appeals against the administrative decisions are brought before the intermediate administrative tribunals,[92] pursuant to specific procedural laws. As previously mentioned, the measures taken by the enforcement authorities might be concise thereby making it difficult for the parties to argue in court that the administrative act is ill-founded. Still, in early November 2008, the Supreme Peoples' Court (SPC) affirmed that in judicial reviews of Anti-monopoly decisions the competent AMEA agency will bear the burden of proof in determining the substantive grounds and the reasonableness of the contested act.[93] As to the complainants, the document released by the SPC provides for access to the relevant administrative file thus enhancing their chances of success. Last but not least, it should be observed that, despite their potential interest, nothing is said about the possibility for third parties to contest the administrative decision approving a merger operation, finding no abuse of a dominant position or admitting what is believed to be an anticompetitive agreement pursuant to Article 13 or 14 of the AML.

4.2. PUBLIC VERSUS PRIVATE ENFORCEMENT

Article 50 of the AML entitles private applicants to seek redress vis-à-vis firms responsible for breaching competition rules. By contrast with the 'wavering' institutional framework, the AML draws a clear distinction between public and private enforcement. This should not be underestimated, both from a theoretical and practical perspective.

In the former sense, pursuant to the latest trends emerging in EC competition policy,[94] it demonstrates that consumers are recognized as the ultimate victims of

---

[92] See 'Strengthening AML Judicial Review and Protecting Fair Competition', accessible at <http://chinaiprlaw.cn/file/2008112113943.html>.

[93] See P.J. Wang, H.S. Harris, & M. Allen Cohen, 'PRC Courts Beginning to Establish Procedural Framework for Anti-Monopoly Litigation', online publication accessible at <www.jonesday.com/pubs/pubs_detail.aspx?pubID=S5771>.

[94] On 19 December 2005, the Commission published a Green Paper on damage actions for breach of the EC antitrust rules. The purpose was to stimulate debate on a number of possible options favouring private enforcement of Arts 81 and 82 EC. This document was followed by a White Paper, released on 2 April 2008, suggesting specific policy choices and measures (ranging from standing rules, to access to evidence, from fault requirements, to limitation periods) capable of ensuring that victims of anticompetitive practices have access to effective redress mechanisms and that they be fully compensated for their losses. Both documents are accessible at: <http://ec.europa.eu/competition/antitrust/actionsdamages/documents.html>.

anticompetitive behaviour. Although the solution can be considered (theoretically) viable from a Law and Economics standpoint, from the undertakings' point of view, it remains to be seen whether: (1) Chinese courts are equipped for antitrust litigation and willing to grant individuals the necessary protection, (2) the existing procedural hurdles (standing limitations, evidence standards, rules governing compensation and damages, and so forth) allow private litigation in practice, and (3) the administration of justice is sufficiently efficient to cope with the consequent workload.

This line of investigation falls outside the scope of the present contribution but certain crucial aspects should nevertheless be taken into account when examining the scope of Article 50, namely: (1) whether lawsuits can be brought directly to the courts or whether a prior finding of infringement by the AMEA is required, (2) the judicial bodies competent to apply the AML, and (3) the relevant standing requirements.

In addressing these problems, it should be borne in mind that the AML is mainly a substantive law: procedural issues such as competence, admissibility, evidence standards, and damage calculations will be governed by Civil Procedural Law and, if necessary, settled by SPC through a judicial interpretation. So much so that even before the entry into force of the new law, the SPC released a Regulation on cause of action in civil cases (1 April 2008) and a Notice on study and adjudication of the AML disputes (28 July 2008), indicating that private parties are entitled to act simultaneously before the courts *and* the AMEA.[95] This undoubtedly increases the risk of inconsistent rulings by the agencies and the courts, calling for further indications as to the cooperation between the former and the latter. In this regard, it has been suggested that depending on the nature of the case – i.e., primarily civil or administrative – preference should be given to one course of action, while staying the other proceeding in order to preserve uniformity.[96] On the other hand, it cannot be ruled out that the complex and overall unsatisfactory institutional framework, with multiple enforcement (administrative) authorities, might boost private litigation as the primary avenue of action against anticompetitive behaviour.[97]

The latter consideration leads us to the second problem mentioned above. It appears that jurisdiction over any anti-monopoly case will be set at an intermediate level and,

---

[95] It is interesting to observe that in other domains the Supreme Court has opted for a different solution, conditioning the admissibility of private claims to an administrative finding that the contested behaviour was in breach of specific regulations. Pursuant to a judicial interpretation issued by the SPC in 2003, damages in securities fraud cases will be granted only after the China Securities Regulatory Commission (CSRC) has found the practice in question unlawful, or following a criminal conviction. See 'Some Provisions of the Supreme People's Court on Trying Cases of Civil Compensation Arising from False Statement in Securities Market, Interpretation' [2003] No. 2. Art. 5, *available at* <www.court.gov.cn/lawdata/explain/civilcation/200303200005.htm>. Moreover, it should be noted that the suggested solution had been envisaged in a 2005 draft of the AML.

[96] See 'Strengthening AML Judicial Review and Protecting Fair Competition', n. 91 above.

[97] As a matter of fact, multinational companies such as Intel and Sony have in recent years been brought to court under the Anti-Unfair Competition Law of the PRC. See Intel Accused of Monopoly in Beijing Court, available at <www.chinatechnews.com/2005/04/04/2472-intel-accused-of-monopoly-in-beijing-court/> and Sony sued for unfair competition, February 2007, available at <www.chinalawandpractice.com/Article/1690375/Channel/16143/SONY-SUED-FOR-UNFAIR-COMPETITION.html>.

in principle, be handled by the relevant special Intellectual Property Tribunal.[98] This has been confirmed by the SPC in its Notice on Study and Adjudication of the AML, which, due to the complexity of the issues arising in competition cases, also exhorts courts to adopt a cautious approach in handling such matters, eventually bringing new and unclear aspects to the attention of the Supreme Court. An alternative could be the creation of specialized AML courts. This is indeed the solution adopted by the Shanghai Intermediate Court, where a seven-judge panel was established in December 2008, with specific competence to hear AML lawsuits and related actions, both civil and administrative. Although beneficial to the coherence of the enforcement regime, these adjustments do not solve the issue of uniformity, which in the absence of a central appellate court can hardly be ensured.

Finally, the AML fails to specify whether *locus standi* will be granted to consumers *and* competitors or limited to the former.[99] In previous drafts, the expression 'party with interest' was used and intended to cover both so that the adoption of the term 'others' in the final version of the AML has led commentators to anticipate a restrictive interpretation of the provision in this respect. A viable explanation for such an approach is the risk of abuse and expensive litigation (particularly against State-owned undertakings), a phenomenon well known in the United States. Nevertheless, this does not seem to be true in practice, as indicated by the SPC and demonstrated by the first cases filed under the AML.[100] Moreover, in order to ensure predictability, the Notice states that civil actions brought under the AML will be governed by the ordinary rules set out in the Civil Procedure Law.[101]

4.3.   Enforcing the AML vis-à-vis administrative agencies

As previously seen, administrative agencies and other organizations empowered by laws and regulations to have the function of administrating public affairs shall refrain from abusing their powers in breach of the AML.[102] By reason of their special status under Chinese law, the infringement of this obligation will not result in a sanction but, rather,

---

[98] As noted by P. Wang, S.G. Harris, & Y. Zhang, 'China: Filing Antitrust Suits in Chinese Courts', online publication available at <www.mondaq.com/article.asp?articleid=64680>: 'In China, not every level of local court has IP Tribunals. IP Tribunals usually reside within intermediate courts, although some sophisticated and experienced first-level local courts also have jurisdiction over such cases, including the Beijing Hai Dian District Court.'

[99] Previous versions of the AML recognized standing to any 'party with interest'. This expression was understood to cover both competitors and consumers. This can be seen as a mindful choice precluding competitor standing. See further M.X.Y. Zhang, 'Private Civil Lawsuits under China Anti-Monopoly Law', online publication accessible at <www.antitrust-lawblog.com/2008/04/articles/article/private-civil-lawsuits-under-china-antimonopoly-law/>.

[100] For a concrete example, see Section 4.3 below.

[101] See, in particular, Art. 108 of the CPL, prescribing that: 'The following conditions must be met before a lawsuit is filed: (1) The plaintiff must be a citizen, legal person, or an organization having a direct interest with the case; (2) there must be a specific defendant; (3) there must be a concrete claim, a factual basis, and a cause for the lawsuit; and (4) the lawsuit must be within the scope of civil lawsuits to be accepted by the people's courts and within the jurisdiction of the people's court to which the lawsuit is filed.'

[102] Save where the measures are adopted in compliance with specific laws and regulations (Art. 51(2)). See Section 3.5 above.

in formal admonition by their superior authority. Pursuant to Article 51(1), in fact, the latter 'shall order them to make correction'.

The chances that such a behaviour will actually be condemned to the benefit of competition are indeed quite limited. As argued by Professor Wang, the reason for this is twofold: on the one side, 'political', as 'any administrative restriction on competition usually reflects treatment in favour of the State-owned entity' shared throughout the hierarchical structure; on the other, 'technical', for the superior authority is not necessarily equipped to conduct the necessary legal and economic analysis. In order to compensate this lack of expertise, the AMEA is entitled to act as an amicus curiae suggesting to the superior authority how to address the issues at stake. Nonetheless, the absence of a binding opinion and of further regulations governing the cooperation mechanism cast doubts on the effectiveness of the provision.

Despite the reported shortcomings, on 1 August 2008 (date of the entry into force of the AML), four companies filed a lawsuit against the State Administration for Quality Supervision, Inspection and Quarantine (AQSIQ) in the Beijing Intermediate People's Court contesting an abuse of administrative power. More precisely, the plaintiffs alleged that AQSIQ had requested consumer product manufacturers to subscribe to Product Identification, Authentication, and Tracking System services from a company designated by it (and in which the agency has direct interests) with the result of restricting their ability to provide competing product verification services.[103]

For the sake of completeness, it should be added that Article 51(1) of the AML also contemplates personal liability and the agents directly responsible for the violation may be subject to disciplinary sanctions. However, the scope of the provision is quite limited as it will find application only when it can be proved that the administrative abuse is the immediate result of the individual conduct.

5. An Overall Assessment of the AML: Problematic Issues and Future Perspectives

As noted by J.O. Haley: 'the enactment of competition legislation has indeed become a global phenomenon. Competition law has, in effect, become the latest fashion'.[104] Whether competition law will be able to affirm itself in China and develop according to international standards is yet to be seen. In analyzing the newly adopted AML, this article has tried to highlight the many factors capable of affecting antitrust enforcement in China. The complex normative and institutional framework constitutes a major limit but on its face offers the necessary instruments to enhance a 'competitive culture' among the economic and legal operators.

---

[103] See further P. Wang & S.G. Harris, 'China: The Anti-Monopoly Law Becomes Effective', online publication accessible at <www.mondaq.com/article.asp?article_id=65184&lk=1>. To the author's knowledge the case is still pending as AQSIQ is in the process of negotiating a withdrawal of the complaint.

[104] J.O. Haley, 'Competition Law for the Asia-Pacific Economic Cooperation Community: Designing Shoes for Many Sizes' *Washington University Global Studies Law Review* 1 (2002): 1.

Despite the specificities of the socialist market economy, it is a matter of fact that State-owned entities (under the administration of the Government) are likely to escape the application of antitrust law. The existence of administrative monopolies is detrimental to the promotion of fair competition throughout the country and does not encourage foreign investment. The same can be said for the plethora of sectorial rules, which on many occasions will prevail over the AML.

It has also been stressed that the AML often uses broad (or even vague) language requiring further implementing regulations. This circumstance hardly matches the legal certainty that should have accompanied the groundbreaking reform professed by the AML. This is particularly true for foreign multinational companies willing to invest in China and for local private companies operating or trying to have access to markets dominated by State-owned firms.[105] Some important documents, such as the market definition and merger notification guidelines, have already been adopted but many gaps still remain allowing for ample discretionary power on the part of enforcement agencies and courts.

Lack of independence and scarce professional training are another important limit to the full operability of the AML, as recognized by the SPC in its 2008 Notice on Study and Adjudication of AML Disputes. Both aspects need to be tackled promptly if sound economic analysis is to prevail over 'intuitions of fairness or industrial policy'.[106] Competition cases require a high level of expertise and an adequate understanding of economics. The creation of an economic division within the Anti-monopoly Bureau and the establishment of a specialized AML panel by the Shanghai Intermediate Court prove that the problem has been partially acknowledged, although more comprehensive measures are certainly needed.

Conversely, many actions have been taken to promote private enforcement and guarantee judicial protection vis-à-vis decisions by the AMEA agencies. The fact that, to date, most AML cases are settled at an informal level at very early stages of the proceedings[107] makes it difficult to formulate any general conclusion on the courts' interpretation of the AML, but it indicates that the latter has already produced positive results, deterring potential violators from persisting in their anti-competitive practices. The counterargument could of course be that the defendants are keener to negotiate an amicable solution than to sustain the costs of litigation, whose result is still highly unpredictable. Only time will tell whether China is capable of developing a consistent body of jurisprudence on the application of the AML, but the absence of a central appellate review (with the consequent forum-shopping phenomenon) heavily reduces the chances that this will take place in the near future.

---

[105] As pinpointed by Wang & Harris, n. 103 above, 'Many outsiders fear that Chinese anti-monopoly enforcers will be pressured to apply the new AML unfairly … Certainly, the law provides at least some room for the enforcers to do so.'

[106] Bush, n. 14 above. See further Furse, n. 11 above, at 339.

[107] For an exhaustive review of the private actions brought to date under the AML, see A. Bobrow et al., untitled online publication accessible at <http://meetings.abanet.org/webupload/commupload/IC860000/newsletterpubs/China CommitteeSubmission.2008final.pdf>.

B
India

[15]

Journal of Competition Law & Economics, 4(3), 609–638
doi:10.1093/joclec/nhn021
Advance Access publication 16 July 2008

INDIA'S NEW COMPETITION LAW: A COMPARATIVE ASSESSMENT

*Aditya Bhattacharjea**

ABSTRACT

This paper critically examines India's new Competition Act. I begin by examining the working of its predecessor, the 1969 Monopolies and Restrictive Trade Practices Act. Earlier studies, as well as a survey of recent cases undertaken for this paper, show that most cases under that Act involved consumer complaints and contractual disputes unrelated to competition. Very few cartels were prosecuted, the development of a rule of reason for vertical agreements was hamstrung by the legislature, and merger review was terminated in 1991. Thereafter, judgments increasingly tried to enforce "fair" business conduct "in the public interest," often protecting competitors rather than competition. India thus has little relevant experience for the many technical economic criteria in the Competition Act. Although the new Act has several positive features, it is riddled with loopholes that might condone hard-core cartels, predatory pricing, and potentially anticompetitive cross-border mergers, while it also perpetuates the earlier tendency to penalize "unfair" behavior with no bearing on competition. I argue that several institutional limitations will also impair the Act's effectiveness and conclude with a plea for capacity building and phased implementation.

JEL Codes: K21; L40; O25

I. INTRODUCTION

After a long and troubled gestation, India's new Competition Act[1] is soon to take effect. It is not that new, having been passed by both Houses of the Indian Parliament in December 2002 after several years of discussion and drafting. Some of its administrative clauses were brought into force by government notification, and the Competition Commission of India (CCI) was formally constituted with one member and a skeleton staff in October 2003. But further expansion of the CCI, and enforcement of the competition-related provisions of the Act, was held up by a writ petition in the Indian Supreme

* Professor of Economics, Delhi School of Economics, University of Delhi, Delhi 110007, India. E-mail: aditya@econdse.org. I would like to thank Avinash Sharma for excellent research assistance, Manish Agarwal and David Round for very helpful comments on earlier drafts, and the East Asian International Law and Policy Programme of the University of Hong Kong for financial support. The usual disclaimer applies.
[1] Act 12 of 2003. See http://www.competition-commission-india.nic.in for the full text of the Act, as well as draft regulations and advocacy literature.

610   *Journal of Competition Law & Economics*

Court (SC). The petitioner contended that the CCI would exercise judicial functions, and therefore the doctrine of separation of powers under the Indian Constitution required that it be headed by a judge chosen by the Chief Justice of India (CJI), not a bureaucrat chosen by the executive. The SC expressed its displeasure over the exclusion of the judiciary, and the government then promised to amend the Act so as to have the Chairman and members of the CCI chosen by a committee headed by the CJI or his nominee.

The SC passed its orders in January 2005, declining in the context of a hypothetical amendment to answer the questions that had been raised in the petition, leaving them open until Parliament amended the Act.[2] But the Competition (Amendment) Bill was passed only in September 2007 after a Parliamentary committee had suggested several modifications to an earlier version tabled in 2006. The amendments not only sought to meet the Supreme Court's objections, but also altered several of the substantive sections of the original Act dealing with mergers and anticompetitive practices. Posts in the CCI were advertised only in May 2008, and it seems unlikely that enforcement will begin before 2009. Meanwhile, the sole member and staff of the CCI have been actively engaged in capacity building and competition advocacy through workshops and newspaper articles.

Throughout this period of uncertainty, the 1969 Monopolies and Restrictive Trade Practices (MRTP) Act[3] has remained India's operative competition law. Even though it is to be repealed when the substantive sections of the new Act are brought into effect, Section II of this paper discusses its working at some length. This is because a proper understanding of the kind of problems that may arise for the new regime requires a retrospective examination of India's experience with its predecessor. I focus in particular on two aspects of the MRTP era that are likely to carry over into the new dispensation. First, the nature of cases brought before the MRTP Commission (MRTPC) tells us a good deal about the constituency for competition litigation in India. It turns out that the majority of cases decided by the MRTPC in the last two decades has been in the area of consumer protection rather than antitrust, and many of the Act's antitrust provisions were interpreted to interdict practices and settle contractual disputes that had no bearing on competition. Thus, although India has one of the oldest competition laws in the developing world, there is very little relevant experience or expertise to draw on for implementing the Competition Act. Second, rulings by the MRTPC, and by the Supreme Court on appeals, provide an insight into Indian jurisprudence in competition matters that may influence the interpretation of similar clauses of the Competition Act.[4]

---

[2] Brahm Dutt v. Union of India (2005) 2 SCC 431. (Here and in subsequent footnotes, SCC refers to the standard Indian reporting journal, *Supreme Court Cases*.)

[3] Act 54 of 1969.

[4] A less important reason for studying the old Act is that all pending cases will continue to be decided under its provisions even after repeal. I therefore refer to it in the present tense.

Section III of the paper points out various ambiguities and loopholes in the new legislation that may allow some of the distortions of the MRTP era to resurface in a new guise; in some respects, it is worse than the earlier law. It also departs in significant ways from international practice. For example, cartels may be subject to a rule of reason and predatory pricing may be condoned, whereas "abusive" conduct having no bearing on competition will be condemned *per se*. I also flag concerns about conflict with sector regulators, autonomy from the government, and delays in deciding cases. Section IV concludes the paper by drawing on lessons from the earlier sections and makes a plea for capacity building and phased implementation.

This paper is likely to be of interest to the international antitrust community for three reasons. First, cases involving foreign firms will inevitably arise in the growing Indian market with its rapidly expanding international linkages, both through trade and foreign direct investment. In particular, merger review, which was deleted from the MRTP Act by an amendment in 1991, has been revived in the Competition Act, which explicitly covers mergers involving firms located abroad. It also reinstates jurisdiction over foreign conduct with domestic effects, which was read out of the MRTP Act by the Supreme Court in 2002. Second, an Indian case study may be relevant to international antitrust scholarship because India follows a system of common law in which judicial interpretation is crucial; judgments sometimes cite British and American precedents; and both the old and new competition laws draw on their foreign counterparts, but with crucial modifications. Instances of each of these features will appear below. Finally, there are lessons that go beyond the Indian context, involving the relationship between the actual working of a competition law and its institutional setting. The paper thus provides a cautionary tale for those who are eager to see competition laws enacted in developing countries: the result may be very different from that intended.[5]

II. THE MRTP ACT

The MRTP Act was passed in 1969 in response to growing evidence of concentration of economic power in Indian industry, manifested in the large absolute size and market dominance of family-controlled business groups. However, the mechanism created by the Act to address this problem was very different from the exercise of competition law as usually understood. It added another layer of approvals to the system of industrial licensing that had been in existence since the wartime controls of the British colonial

---

[5] I have dealt with the debate over inclusion of clauses relating to national competition laws in multilateral and regional trade agreements in Aditya Bhattacharjea, *The Case for a Multilateral Agreement on Competition Policy: A Developing Country Perspective*, 9(2) J. OF INT'L ECON. LAW 292 (2006).

612   *Journal of Competition Law & Economics*

government in the 1940s that the Industries (Development and Regulation) Act of 1951 had vastly extended.[6] This Act required central government permission for capacity creation, expansion, relocation, and diversification by enterprises in all sectors of manufacturing. In the 1960s, several official committees found evidence of substantial industrial concentration, widespread restrictive business practices, and large industrial houses using their clout to preempt licenses and thereby block entry. In response, Chapter III of the MRTP Act required firms that were either "large" (those that had, along with their "interconnected undertakings," assets above a certain threshold) or "dominant" (having assets above a lower threshold as well as a minimum market share) to register themselves with the central government. These "MRTP companies" had to obtain government approval for substantial expansion, establishment of new undertakings, mergers, and appointment of their directors in other undertakings. The government could refer applications to the MRTP Commission, but did not do so in most cases, and was not bound by the Commission's advice. Restrictions on the size and dominance of large firms induced many of them to set up nominally independent units in the same industry, or to diversify as conglomerates.

In the 1980s, economic reforms began to undo the command-and-control system of economic governance (known in India as the "license-permit raj"), whose ill effects had become too obvious to ignore. The threshold defining "large" firms was quintupled in 1985, taking most of them out of the ambit of MRTP approval, and the requirement for such approval was abolished altogether when the MRTP Act was amended in 1991, deleting almost all of Chapter III as part of the far-reaching liberalization in 1991 that also abolished licensing for all but a handful of industries. One immediate consequence was a wave of mergers. The erstwhile MRTP companies were actively involved, often merging firms under the same business group and in the same industry, undoing the overdiversification and fragmentation of capacities that they had resorted to in the pre-reform years.[7] Despite the merger wave, there was no unambiguous increase in market concentration, which rose in some sectors but fell in others.[8]

---

[6] Act 65 of 1951.

[7] Manish Agarwal and Aditya Bhattacharjea, *Mergers in India: A Response to Regulatory Shocks*, 42(3) EMERGING MARKETS FINANCE & TRADE 46 (2006). That paper was based on a uniquely comprehensive merger database for India.

[8] Suma Athreye and Sandeep Kapur, *Industrial Concentration in a Liberalising Economy: A Study of Indian Manufacturing*, 42 J. OF DEVELOPMENT STUDIES 981 (2006); K.V. Ramaswamy, *State of Competition in the Indian Manufacturing Industry*, in TOWARDS A FUNCTIONAL COMPETITION POLICY FOR INDIA 155–65 (Pradeep S. Mehta ed., 2006); T.A. Bhavani and N.R. Bhanumurthy, *The State of Competition in the Indian Manufacturing Sector* (2007), report of a research project commissioned by the Competition Commission of India, available at http://www.competition-commission-india.nic.in. A caveat: the last two studies use the largest firm-level database available in India—but this is limited to companies registered with the Bombay Stock Exchange, so it excludes fully state-owned enterprises and fully

This was because concurrent reforms in 1985 and 1991 also substantially relaxed entry barriers in the form of investment licensing, restrictions on foreign direct investment, and reservation of several sectors for state-owned enterprises.

Research on the implementation of the remaining provisions of the MRTP Act is hampered because judgments of the MRTP Commission (MRTPC) are irregularly and selectively published in a number of different journals. In what follows, I shall therefore draw upon the work of earlier authors who tabulated all of the MRTPC decisions under its various sections for different periods. As they used different data sources and definitions, intertemporal comparisons are only indicative. I supplement this with the results of a survey, undertaken specifically for this paper, of recent cases regarding Restrictive Trade Practices (discussed below). I also cite significant recent decisions by the Supreme Court, which has reversed some earlier decisions of the MRTPC and placed severe curbs on its interpretation of the law.

Chapter IV of the MRTP Act deals with "Monopolistic Trade Practices" (MTPs), which are defined in §2(i) to include maintaining prices at an "unreasonable" level, "unreasonably" preventing or limiting competition, limiting technical development or capital investment, or allowing quality to deteriorate. An amendment in 1984 added to this list "unreasonably" increasing cost of production, prices, or profits. What was "unreasonable" was left dangerously open-ended. The clause on preventing competition faintly resembles provisions on abuse of dominance in modern antitrust, but its application was not limited to firms in dominant positions. In fact, according to §32 of the original Act, an MTP was presumed to be "prejudicial to the public interest" only if it was practiced by a monopolistic undertaking, defined as one that, together with two independent undertakings, had a market share of one-half. But the 1984 amendment deleted the concept of a monopolistic undertaking and rewrote this section to provide that, except when authorized by law or government order, "every monopolistic trade practice shall be deemed to be prejudicial to the public interest." Thus, the practices listed in §2(i) were condemned *per se*, regardless of the market share of the perpetrator. With MTPs being defined so indiscriminately, almost any business conduct could have come into the net.

---

foreign-owned affiliates of multinational corporations, which are large and dominant in various industries. Their exclusion would bias concentration measures downwards. The database also excludes a much larger number of private limited companies, the vast unincorporated sector, and imports, resulting in a bias in the opposite direction. Athreye and Kapur use an even smaller dataset, confined to medium and large nongovernment corporations. All of these databases, moreover, use their own classification of industries, rather than economically defined product markets. The absence of reliable data on market shares is a major obstacle for competition analysis in India.

614   *Journal of Competition Law & Economics*

Table 1. Distribution of Cases before the MRTP Commission, 1972–2006

(1) Type of practice	(2) Inquiries instituted	(3) Cases reported	(4) Inquiries pending	(5)
	1972–1991	1991–1998	End-2001	End-2006
Monopolistic	16	4	5	5
Unfair	c. 1,900[a]	327	654	583
Restrictive	3,474	250	530	307
Of which instituted by				
(a) consumers and their associations	171		299	230
(b) central or state governments	2		2	1

[a]As the Unfair Trade Practices chapter was included in the MRTP Act only in 1984, these inquiries are for 1984–91.
Sources: for column (2), Sandesara (as note 14 below); for column (3), Basant and Morris (as note 14 below); for columns (4) and (5), computed from the Annual Reports of the Department/Ministry of Company Affairs for 2002 and 2007.

Fortunately, there have been very few inquiries under this chapter (see Table 1), and in any case, the Commission could only report its findings to the central government, which alone could take action on monopolistic trade practices. But I shall demonstrate below that complaints against "unreasonable" conduct were entertained under a different section of the MRTP Act, and are likely to be entertained again under a section of the Competition Act.

The 1984 amendment of the MRTP Act also inserted a new Chapter V-B that created a category of "Unfair Trade Practices" (UTPs), dealing with misleading advertising and prize schemes and noncompliance with product standards. The same amendment gave the Commission the power to issue injunctions and award compensation for any loss or damage resulting from monopolistic, restrictive, or unfair trade practices. Despite the enactment of a Consumer Protection Act (COPRA) in 1986, with identical provisions on UTPs and a mechanism to compensate consumers for defective goods and deficient services, several advantages ensured that the MRTPC remained the favored forum for such complaints, at least in the area around Delhi.[9] Since the 1990s, the majority of cases pending before the Commission has concerned such matters (see Table 1). It seems that the majority of compensation applications was of this nature as well.[10] Dealing with such

---

[9] COPRA has the advantage of having adjudicatory forums in each state and district, whereas the MRTPC sits only in Delhi. But unlike the consumer forums, the MRTP Commission has its own investigative and legal staff to aid complainants, has powers of injunction, and can award compensation to firms as well as to consumers.

[10] Their number fell from 2,272 at the beginning of 2001 to 1,110 at the end of 2006, according to the *Annual Reports* of the Department/Ministry of Company Affairs for 2002 and 2007.

consumer cases inevitably stretched the Commission's resources and diluted its ability to deal with the kind of anticompetitive business practices that are usually the focus of antitrust law. As I shall show below, even some of the clauses in the MRTP Act that were designed to deal with such practices were used to entertain consumer complaints or contractual disputes for which remedy should have been sought under the COPRA or in civil courts.

With the Act's sections on aggregate concentration only patchily enforced (and deleted in 1991), the sections on monopolistic practices falling into disuse, and the irrelevance of the sections on unfair trade practices for a study of competition law, I shall focus in the remaining part of this section on Chapter V of the Act (renumbered V-A by the 1984 amendment that created V-B), which covers restrictive trade practices (RTPs). These are defined in broad terms in §2(o) of the MRTP Act. According to this awkward "definition clause,"

> "Restrictive trade practice" means a trade practice that has, or may have, the effect of preventing, distorting, or restricting competition in any manner and in particular–
>
> (i) which tends to obstruct the flow of capital or resources into the stream of production, or
>
> (ii) which *tends to bring about manipulation of prices, or conditions of delivery* or to affect the flow of supplies in the market relating to goods or services *in such manner as to impose on the consumers unjustified cost or restrictions.* [Emphasis added.]

The phrases in italics have created considerable confusion, as will be shown in the case studies below. Another section (§33[1]) lists several types of agreements that must be registered with the MRTP Commission. These cover a range of restrictions, both horizontal (price fixing, output restriction, collective boycotts, and collusive tendering) and vertical (tying, full-line forcing, dealer discounts or rebates, exclusive dealing, territorial allocation, resale price maintenance), as well as price discrimination, limit pricing, and predatory pricing. In the early years of the Commission's operation, these were treated as restrictive *per se*, but a Supreme Court judgment in 1977 held that a rule of reason based on the definition clause 2(o) had to be applied even to such agreements.[11] The number of registrations and inquiries dropped dramatically as a result. However, they rose sharply again after an amendment to §33 in 1984, which stated that *every* agreement in the list would be deemed to be restrictive and subject to registration, effectively restoring the earlier position. The Supreme Court later held that, although the practices listed in §33(1) were deemed to be restrictive, other practices also could be examined in light of the general definition

---

[11] TELCO v. Registrar of Restrictive Trade Agreements, 2 SCC 55 (1977), especially ¶ 29–32.

in §2(o).[12] Apart from these sections, §§39 and 40 prohibit (minimum) resale price maintenance and its enforcement via discriminatory treatment of dealers.

According to §38, an RTP is deemed to be prejudicial to the public interest unless the MRTPC is satisfied such that one or more specified requirements are fulfilled. These so-called "gateways," mostly taken verbatim from §21 of the UK Restrictive Trade Practices Act of 1956,[13] include the countering of anticompetitive practices by some other party, prevention of a fall in employment or exports, competition not being affected to any material degree, and instances where restrictions are needed to maintain essential services or the security of the State. As in the UK Act, the section concludes with a "tailpiece" requiring the Commission to balance these circumstances against any loss to persons not party to the agreement. Unlike cases of concentration of economic power in which the MRTPC could only review mergers referred to it by the government and recommend action, in the case of RTPs, it can entertain complaints, initiate inquiries by its Director General, order temporary injunctions, and pass its own final orders, which can either require the violator to "cease and desist" from the practice or modify it suitably so that it is no longer prejudicial to the public interest. Fines and jail terms can be imposed by a sessions court if the respondent fails to comply with these orders or to furnish information sought by the Commission, but such penalties have never been imposed in RTP cases as far as I am aware. Parties harmed by the impugned practice may also claim compensation under §12A, but I shall show that most such cases have not involved antitrust injuries.

Four earlier studies have tabulated RTP cases under different heads.[14] These reveal that a growing proportion—reaching 80 percent in the 1990s—was filed under the general definition in §2(o). Many of these cases were brought by consumers against dealers for delayed delivery or other contractual disputes, especially concerning cooking gas cylinders, cars, or real estate. These were not competition concerns at all and should have been taken to the forums established under the Consumer Protection Act or to civil courts for breach of contract. However, they were raised before the MRTP Commission under the clause in 2(o)(ii) referring to "manipulation of prices, or conditions of delivery ... in such manner as to impose on the

---

[12] Voltas Ltd. v. Union of India, Supp. 2 SCC 498 (1995).

[13] 4 & 5 Eliz. 2, ch. 68 (now repealed).

[14] P.V. Krishna Rao and K.P. Sastry, *Restrictive Trade Practices Policy in India*, 37 J. OF INDUSTRIAL ECONOMICS 427 (1989), covering 1970 to 1984; J.C. Sandesara, *Restrictive Trade Practices in India, 1969–91*, 29 ECONOMIC AND POLITICAL WEEKLY 2081 (1994); Jaivir Singh, Some Aspects of Industrial and Labour Markets in India: Perspectives from Law and Economics (1999) (unpublished Ph.D. dissertation, University of Delhi), covering the same period but with a different classification; RAKESH BASANT AND SEBASTIAN MORRIS, COMPETITION POLICY IN INDIA: ISSUES FOR A GLOBALISING ECONOMY, ch. 5 (Ahmedabad: Indian Institute of Management, 2000), covering 1991 to 1998.

consumers unjustified cost or restrictions." These allegations were seldom successful, but the protracted inquiries caused considerable harassment. Horizontal restrictions were involved in a declining proportion of cases, falling to less than 4 percent in the 1990s, and most of these failed to result in a finding of prejudice to the public interest. Most of the remaining cases involved vertical restrictions, especially tying, resale price maintenance, and discriminatory dealing. There was a sharp drop in the number of RTP cases after 1991—the year in which India took a decisive turn towards market-friendly policies.

Looking at the RTP cases from another angle, Table 1 above shows that the proportion resulting from complaints by consumers and their associations rose from around 5 percent between 1972 to 1991 to over half in 2001, to about three-fourths in 2006. Pulling all of these observations together, combining them with the proliferation of UTP cases discussed above, and assuming that a similar proportion of compensation applications was of the same nature, it seems that consumer complaints were increasingly taking up the bulk of the Commission's workload, although the data do not permit cross-tabulation to establish this conclusively.

My own study of all RTP cases decided by the Commission since 2001 involving §§2(o) and 33(1) of the MRTP Act shows that such cases continued to predominate. Of the 52 cases, only five involved seller cartels. Three arose from collective boycotts by distributors, 10 from complaints by dealers alleging discriminatory discounts, and four alleging other kinds of discriminatory treatment by manufacturers.[15] Most of the rest involved miscellaneous consumer complaints. Litigation was thus largely driven by dealers and individual consumers.

I now turn to the kind of reasoning given in some significant cases, beginning with those on vertical agreements. Although exclusive dealing and territorial restrictions were among the agreements required to be registered under §33(1), the Supreme Court held as early as 1977 that, in the particular circumstances of the commercial vehicles industry, such clauses did not restrict competition. In reasoning that was remarkably contemporary for its time, the judgment held that territorial allocation of dealerships was necessary to encourage dealers to invest in after-sales services that were necessary for trucks to ply in remote areas of the country, and that exclusive dealerships promoted what today would be called inter-brand competition.[16]

---

[15] In the interest of economy, citations are provided only when I mention individual cases.

[16] TELCO v. Registrar of Restrictive Trade Agreements, *supra* note 11. This judgment was delivered in January 1977, five months before the U.S. Supreme Court's famous decision in Continental T.V. v. GTE Sylvania, Inc., 433 U.S. 36 (1977), which used similar reasoning to revolutionize the antitrust treatment of nonprice vertical restrictions on intra-brand competition that promote after-sales service and inter-brand competition. Two years later, another bench of India's Supreme Court strongly reaffirmed TELCO, noting its similarities with the rule of reason expounded by the U.S. Supreme Court in a series of early decisions,

The Court later held that franchising was an acceptable means of facilitating distribution, and could not be regarded as a restraint of trade.[17] Subsequently, the Commission applied a sensible rule of reason to vertical restraints that promoted orderly distribution, quality assurance, and after-sales service, without requiring the respondent to invoke the "gateways."[18] More recently, however, the Supreme Court has held that instructions to a distributor to restrict the area of sales, or a clause in a contract disclaiming responsibility in case of failure or refusal to supply the distributor, came under the practices listed in §33(1), and therefore had to be regarded as restrictive in light of the *Voltas* judgment.[19]

RPM has always been treated as restrictive *per se*, but firms could escape simply by including a clause in their dealership agreements to the effect that distributors were free to sell at lower prices than those recommended. Discriminatory discounts given to dealers without rational justification attracted cease and desist orders in three of my sample of 52 recent cases, although no analysis of secondary-line injury to competition was conducted. In five other cases, discrimination was held to be justified on grounds of dealer performance, creditworthiness, etc. In another five such cases, respondents were allowed, on the basis of their minuscule market shares, to pass through the "gateway" provided by §38(h) for restrictions that do not "restrict or discourage competition to any material degree."

I now turn to horizontal restrictions. The MRTPC had a dismal track record on action against hard-core cartels, which are usually the prime targets of competition agencies. As mentioned earlier, only five of the 52 post-2001 cases in my survey involved cartels, to which perhaps the three involving collective boycotts by distributors seeking better terms from manufacturers can be added. That this is not a recent development is shown by De's comprehensive study of all cartel cases from 1970 to 2004 reported in different journals or summarized in law textbooks.[20] She found that there had been a drastic fall in cases reported after 1991. Even before that, the Commission at best passed cease and desist orders, or even accepted assurances from the respondent firms that they would not indulge in cartelization. In several cases, there were renewed complaints of cartelization against the same firms, yet the

---

especially Chicago Board of Trade v. United States, 246 U.S. 231 (1918). *See* Mahindra and Mahindra Ltd. v. Union of India, 2 SCC 529, ¶ 15 (1979).

[17] Gujarat Bottling Co. Ltd. v. Coca Cola Co., 5 SCC 545, ¶ 30 (1995).

[18] *E.g.* Director General (I&R) v. Godrej-GE Appliances and Others, I(2002) CPJ 48 (MRTP), Director General (I&R) v. Godrej-GE Appliances and Another, I(2002) CPJ 13 (MRTP).

[19] Peico Electronics and Electricals v. Union of India, 3 SCC 358, ¶¶ 10, 12 (2004) (citing Voltas, *supra* note 12, ¶¶ 8, 10).

[20] Oindrila De, *Identifying Cartels in India*, (2005) (unpublished M. Phil. dissertation, University of Delhi).

Commission refrained from seeking fines for noncompliance with its earlier orders. Although in a very few instances cartelization was inferred from identical prices or bids, in many more cases, citing international practice, the Commission held that mere evidence of parallel price movements was not sufficient to prove cartelization: evidence of collusion was necessary. This position was strengthened by a Supreme Court ruling in 1993, which held that quotation of identical prices constituted reasonable grounds for suspecting cartelization, but was not conclusive in the absence of "a specific agreement by way of a concerted action suggesting conspiracy."[21]

Although that case concerned collective predatory pricing, in subsequent decisions the MRTPC explicitly adapted the ruling in the form of a three-pronged test for cartelization, requiring evidence of price parity, agreement suggesting conspiracy, and intent to restrict or eliminate competition.[22] This is more stringent than the EC or U.S. "parallelism plus" approaches, in that it requires evidence of conspiracy as the only "plus factor"; the role of facilitating practices such as exchange of price information was not recognized.[23] With its growing caseload of consumer and UTP cases, limited investigative resources, and no provision for an amnesty scheme to induce cartelists to report their activities, the Director General's office was consistently unable to establish conspiracy. Updating De's study with the research undertaken for this paper, it appears that only seven cartel cases have been decided by the Commission since 1991, and these were only decided after inordinate delays ranging from 6 to 18 years after initiation of the inquiry. Three cases were dismissed because no evidence of conspiracy was found; another case (against members of the Indian Banks' Association for fixing service charges) was dropped because the Reserve Bank of India (the country's central bank) directed the Association to desist from the practice. In one case, the Commission did find evidence of cartelization by a foreign export association, but its orders were overturned by the Supreme Court. I shall return to this very significant judgment below. In these last two cases, formal price-fixing agreements could be easily established on the basis of publicly available documents of the concerned associations. But covert agreements went largely undetected: cease and desist orders have been issued in only two cartel cases since 1991.

On the other hand, §2(o)(ii) (quoted above) cast its malefic shadow even on one of the cases in which the Commission found "not an iota of evidence" of collusion. It nonetheless continued the inquiry into an abnormal

---

[21] Union of India v. Hindustan Development Corporation and Others, SCC 499, ¶ 16 (1993).

[22] Director General (I&R) v Modi Alkali and Chemicals Ltd. and Others, II (2002) CPJ 19 (MRTP); Director General v Reliance and Another, I (2003) CPJ 80 (MRTP).

[23] The Indian government unwittingly enforces a facilitating practice through the Weights and Measures (Packaged Commodities) Rules (1977), which require manufacturers of packaged commodities for retail sale to print the quantity and maximum retail price on the package. Obviously, this makes it easy for cartelists to detect deviations from a collusive price.

increase in prices by the firms, as there was a "strong inference in regard to manipulation of conditions of delivery or prices leading to distortion and restriction of the competition in the market."[24] As the Commission itself noted, the industry comprised 42 manufacturers, so it is difficult to see what kind of competition issue was at stake here.

Earlier orders passed by the Commission under §2(o)(ii) have been set aside by the Supreme Court in recent years for not having a clear connection to competition. The Commission had held against a private school for not giving interest on a student's security deposit; against a state housing agency for delay in delivering possession of a house; and against a state government for implementing a scheme for rotating supplies of irrigation water.[25] In each case, setting aside these orders, the Supreme Court held that the main clause of §2(o), regarding "preventing, distorting or restricting competition in any manner" defined a restrictive trade practice. Subclause 2(o)(ii) only provided an example that could not be read independently of the main clause.

These reversals had a salutary effect on the Commission, which discharged (after hearing) dozens of long-standing RTP inquiries against firms for practices that did not have a competition dimension. Many of the 52 recent decisions that I surveyed were of this nature. Three involved delayed supply of gas cylinders, and eleven terminated inquiries against firms for high or rising prices or profits, quantity reductions, or underutilized capacity. In some cases, the Commission pointed out that the manufacturers concerned were selling in a manifestly competitive market, or pricing their products in accordance with price control regulations.[26] The most disturbing aspect of these cases was that the complainant was usually the Commission's own Director General, a civil servant on deputation, who should have had a better understanding of competition issues. In one of the earlier cases, the MRTPC declared that it was "unable to accept the argument of learned counsel for the Director General that any increase in the price of a product without a corresponding increase in the cost of inputs would *ipso facto* have the effect of preventing, distorting or restricting

---

[24] Director General (I&R), *supra* note 22, ¶ 16.

[25] *See*, Principal, Apeejay School v. MRTP Commission 2 SCC 474 (2001); Rajasthan Housing Board v. Parvati Devi, 6 SCC 104 (2000); State of U.P. v. Gir Prasad, 3 SCC 152 (2004), which cite and summarize the relevant MRTPC decisions. In an even more disturbing case, in 2001 the Supreme Court set aside a 1987 MRTPC order, resulting from an inquiry initiated in 1983, against termination of a dealership, holding that the Commission had not established a violation of *either* prong of §2(o), nor apprised the respondent of the nature of the case which it had to meet. Hindustan Lever Ltd v. Director General (I&R), 2 SCC 474 (2001).

[26] *See*, Director General (I & R) v. Jay Engineering Works Ltd, III (2002) CPJ 4 (MRTP) (2001), and Director General (I & R) v. Biddle Sawyer Ltd., II (2002) CPJ 66. The latter case also involved a rare allegation of monopolistic trade practices. Both cases involved conduct during 1989 to 1990, and the inquiries were ultimately terminated only in 2001.

competition."[27] In another decision, the Commission forcefully reiterated the Supreme Court's *Rajasthan Housing Board* judgment[28] over the Director General's objections; it also dismissed a simultaneous allegation of monopolistic trade practices with the declaration that "[i]t is settled law that mere high prices and high profits are not enough to sustain the charge of monopolistic trade practices. Highly profitable ventures are not always a bane to the society, they can be a bliss from the point of their positive contribution to employment and the State revenues."[29]

The Commission's willingness to dismiss irrelevant charges was not, unfortunately, matched by a greater focus in prosecuting and upholding relevant ones. We have already seen that its record on cartels was dismal. My survey reveals that, of the 45 other recent cases, cease and desist orders were passed in only nine. Of these, only four, involving refusal to deal by distributors or manufacturers, perhaps had a competition dimension. As mentioned above, three others involved discriminatory discounts offered by manufacturers to dealers, with no case made that they were exclusionary. The remaining two involved delayed allotment of a residential flat and incorrect calibration of petrol pumps. It remains to be seen how the Supreme Court rules on a pending appeal by Monsanto against an MRTPC injunction ordering it to reduce the excessive and discriminatory royalty that it charges for Bt Cotton seeds.[30] In this case, the Commission pointed to the fact that Monsanto charged a much lower price in China.

As the earlier studies cited above had noted, a large number of RTP cases involved delayed delivery or changes in payment conditions for flats, cars, or gas cylinders. Even after the Supreme Court put a stop to this, my own perusal of recent cases shows that such complaints continued to be entertained as "misrepresentation" under the UTP chapter of the Act, adding to the Commission's workload. It remains to be seen whether this too is halted by a more recent Supreme Court decision, involving disputes between a property developer and two buyers. The Court observed that the "power of the Commission to award compensation, therefore, is restricted to a case where loss or damage had been caused as a result of monopolistic or restrictive or unfair trade practices. It has no jurisdiction where damage is claimed for mere breach of contract."[31]

---

[27] Director General (I&R) v. Heinz India, 2001 CTJ 205 (MRTP).

[28] *See supra* note 25.

[29] Director General (I & R) v. Hindustan Lever Ltd., III(2002) CPJ 46 (2001), ¶ 9. Interestingly, even when accepting that high profits might have some social justification, the Commission used arguments reminiscent of the preliberalization era, rather than pointing to the role of profits in guiding resource allocation or promoting innovation.

[30] RTPE No. 2 of 2006.

[31] Saurabh Prakash v. DLF Universal Ltd., 1 SCC 228 (2007).

This review of RTP cases has shown that the MRTP Commission had a record of settling litigation involving essentially contractual disputes, or ordering inquiries or injunctions against prices or practices that it regarded as "unfair," even though they had nothing to do with competition. Ironically, although the specialized competition agency repeatedly decided cases on criteria other than competition, the Supreme Court, with no such special mandate, set aside most of these orders and redirected the Commission's attention to competition.

However, the Supreme Court's own interpretation of competition and "fair" pricing has been ambivalent, especially in matters concerning cross-border RTPs. A landmark in this context was the 2002 *Haridas Exports* judgment, which terminated the extra-territorial operation of the MRTP Act and also stated far-reaching principles on the regulation of competition that transcend the particular cases involved, or indeed the moribund MRTP Act itself.[32] The unanimous decision was delivered by the then-Chief Justice, and his two colleagues on the bench both rose to that position subsequently, one being the current Chief Justice. Also, coming from a three-judge bench, the decision is binding on the two-judge benches that normally hear appeals. I shall therefore discuss it at some length.

Some American soda ash manufacturers had formed an export association named ANSAC, and registered it under the Webb–Pomerene Act,[33] giving it qualified exemption from U.S. antitrust law. In 1996, an association of Indian soda ash manufacturers complained to the MRTPC that ANSAC was a cartel that was charging *low* prices for its exports to India. The Commission ordered an *ex-parte* injunction against the import of ANSAC's soda ash. After a regular hearing, the Commission confirmed the injunction, citing authority under the "effects doctrine" to regulate anticompetitive conduct by firms based abroad but having adverse effects within the country; this authority is now commonplace in almost all antitrust jurisdictions. ANSAC appealed to the Supreme Court. Clubbing this appeal with another in which the Commission had ordered an injunction against imported Indonesian float glass on grounds of predatory pricing, the Supreme Court held that the Act did not provide for extra-territorial operation. The Commission could not take action against foreign cartels or the pricing of exports to India, nor could it restrict imports. Action on the basis of the effects doctrine could be taken only if a restrictive trade practice involving an Indian party could be proved, and that too only after the goods had been imported into India. The MRTPC orders were decidedly peculiar, for here was a competition authority restricting competition from imports. But

---

[32] Haridas Exports v. All India Float Glass Manufacturers' Ass'n, 6 SCC 600 (2002). A summary of the case appears in Bhattacharjea, *Export Cartels: A Developing Country Perspective*, 38(2) J. OF WORLD TRADE 331, 342–4 (2004).

[33] 15 U.S.C. §§61–64.

by altogether removing the anticompetitive practices of firms based abroad from the coverage of the MRTP Act, the Supreme Court threw the baby out with the bathwater, making it impossible for India to act against international cartels, whose activities have been extensively documented.[34]

Apart from the question of extra-territorial operation, the Supreme Court's decision in *Haridas Exports* dealt with broader issues raised by the MRTPC orders. The complainants had also alleged predatory pricing by the foreign suppliers. The MRTPC did not attempt to establish whether the suppliers were dominant. In the float glass case, the Chairman of the Commission had brushed aside the respondents' argument that the imports in question constituted less than 2 percent of the total turnover of float glass in India. This, he said, "may look like a trickle at present but in the long run this trickle will be transformed into a flood." Further, "people of this country can very well afford payment of about 12% higher cost of float glass production manufactured and marketed by Indian companies rather than allowing them to go for that imported from Indonesia. A marginal difference of 12% in price of float glass might not be prejudicial to any public interest."[35] Continuing in this vein, he declared

> It would be a colossal loss to the nation if the Indian float glass industry is allowed to be ruined on account of liberal import of float glass production from Indonesia at predatory prices. As transpiring from the material on record, at least one float glass manufacturing company in India has already become sick. One more is likely to be so. If this trend is allowed to continue, a day would come that the Indian float glass industry will be completely ruined and the funds invested by investors would go waste. To cap it all, thousands of people thriving on the Indian float glass industry will be deprived of their sustenance and might have to look for alternative means for livelihood in these days of the alarming proportion of unemployment. Even if the ban on import of float glass from Indonesia at predatory prices might not be in consumer interests, it is certainly in public interests for the simple reason that the public interests should certainly outweigh consumer interests.[36]

The Chairman's views did not prevail immediately, for the other member of the two-member bench gave a diametrically opposing order, finding no evidence of pricing below costs or intent to eliminate competition, and pointing out that antidumping measures were the appropriate remedy for injury caused by low-cost imports. A third member to whom the matter was referred supported the Chairman, arguing among other things that there was no reason to expect that Indonesia, as a developing country, had a cost advantage in float glass production as compared to India!

[34] *See* Margaret Levenstein and Valerie Y. Suslow, *Contemporary International Cartels and Developing Countries: Economic Effects and Implications for Competition Policy*, 71 ANTITRUST LAW JOURNAL 802 (2004).

[35] All India Float Glass Manufacturers' Ass'n v. PT Mulia Industrindo, 2000 CTJ 252 (MRTPC), ¶ 21 of the Chairman's order.

[36] *Id.* at ¶ 22.

624   *Journal of Competition Law & Economics*

Although it set aside the MRTPC injunctions on grounds of extra-territorial application of the Act, the Supreme Court left some scope for ambiguity on the broader issue of competition versus protection, and the "public interest." The Court held that the Commission could act if the importation of goods involved an RTP *within* India, but

> [f]or the Commission to have jurisdiction to pass such an order, whether interim or final, it must come to the conclusion that it is in the public interest to do so. It is to be borne in mind that public interest does not necessarily mean interest only of the industry. Unless and until it can be demonstrated that an efficient Indian industry would be forced to shut down or suffer serious loss resulting in closure or unemployment, the Commission ought not to pass an injunction restraining an Indian party from importing goods from a cartel at predatory prices. Importing goods at a price lower than what is available in India is not *per se* illegal. We have provisions under the Customs Act which enable the Government to impose anti-dumping duties with a view to protect the Indian industry. Nevertheless, the era of protectionism is now coming to an end. The industry has to gear up to meet the challenges from abroad. If the cartel is selling goods to India and is still making profit then it will not be in the interest of the general body of the consumers in India to prevent the import of such goods. The remedy of the Indian industry, in such an event, is to take recourse to the provisions under the Customs Act in relation to the levy of anti-dumping duties.[37]

Thus, although the judgment did assert the primacy of competition over the other concerns articulated by the MRTP Commission in the specific cases under appeal, it did leave some room for imposition of import restrictions in future cases. Further, the Court consciously refused[38] to rule on the question of predatory pricing. From the lengthy paragraph quoted above, it seems that it would regard a price above cost as nonpredatory, but this begs the question: which concept of cost? Its statement endorsing the protection of an "efficient Indian industry" from the threat of predatory pricing also leads to ambiguities. The Court did not go into the question of whether entry barriers would permit the alleged predator to recoup the profits sacrificed through predation. An earlier Supreme Court judgment had approvingly quoted the very paragraph in which its American counterpart had laid down this standard in its landmark *Matsushita* decision,[39] but missed its significance regarding the importance of market structure: the Indian judgment used it only to assert that a low price was not necessarily predatory, and that therefore it could not be concluded that the manufacturers who offered such a price formed a cartel.[40] Subsequently, the MRTP Commission used this formulation to hold that a price below an appropriate measure of costs would not be regarded as predatory unless intent to drive out competitors was also established.[41]

---

[37] Haridas Exports, *supra* note 32, ¶ 74.
[38] *Id.* at ¶ 78.
[39] Matsushita Elec. Indus. Co. v. Zenith Radio Corp., 475 U.S. 574 (1976).
[40] Hindustan Development Corporation, *supra* note 21, ¶¶ 14–16.
[41] Director General (I&R) v. Modern Food Industries, 3 COMP LJ 154 (1996).

Another troubling aspect of the Supreme Court's views in the long quotation above is its endorsement of antidumping. Especially since 1998, India has emerged as one of the leading (ab)users of this provision of the GATT. As in the U.S. and the EC, a few highly concentrated industries disproportionately use the antidumping mechanism.[42] In several cases, the Indian Director General of Anti-Dumping (DGAD) has determined the level of antidumping duties as the difference between the landed value of imports in India and a "noninjurious price" (NIP) that would permit a reasonable rate of profit to the competing Indian industry. A recent Supreme Court judgment has increased the likelihood of protectionist abuse of this mechanism. The DGAD had assessed the NIP on the basis of costs that included the actual cost of electric power generated by a captive power plant owned by a manufacturing firm. This resulted in a lower antidumping duty that, the Court held, would be discriminatory against other producers who had to buy power. The NIP should therefore be determined for the industry as a whole, not for individual firms.[43] This implies, however, that even the least efficient producers in an industry are guaranteed protection, and the more efficient ones stand to benefit from their existence. The Court further observed that the purpose of the antidumping mechanism

> was that our industries which had been built up after independence with great difficulties must not be allowed to be destroyed by unfair competition of some foreign companies. Dumping is a well-known method of unfair competition which is adopted by the foreign companies. This is done by selling goods at a very low price for some time so that the domestic industries cannot compete and are thereby destroyed, and after such destruction has taken place, prices are again raised.[44]

In short, the judgment conflated dumping with predatory pricing. And like the previous judgments by the Court and the MRTP Commission, it did not recognize the importance of establishing the actual or potential dominance of the alleged predator, much less the likelihood of its being able to recoup the losses incurred by predatory pricing.

To conclude this review of the working of the MRTP Act, I must note that the Indian government has itself displayed a distressing lack of faith in it. According to one study, in 2000 the MRTP Commission's budget as a proportion of government expenditure was much less than those of the competition agencies of Pakistan, Sri Lanka, Brazil, Kenya, or South Africa.[45]

---

[42] Samir K. Singh, *An Analysis of Anti-dumping Cases in India*, 40 ECONOMIC AND POLITICAL WEEKLY 1069, 1071 (2005). According to statistics reported on the WTO website, between 1995 and mid-2006 India initiated 474 antidumping cases. The U.S. and EC were far behind, with 375 and 363 initiations respectively. http://www.wto.org/english/tratop_e/adp_e/ad_init_rep_member_e.pdf visited 14 May 2008.

[43] Reliance Indus. Ltd. v. Designated Authority, 10 SCC 368, ¶¶ 26–35 (2006).

[44] *Id.* at ¶ 10. The same position is articulated in ¶ 12, stating that lower prices benefit consumers only in the short term.

[45] *Approaches to Competition Policy in South Asian Countries* (Jaipur: CUTS-CIER 2003).

Further, as the last row of Table 1 shows, the government has hardly ever filed complaints against RTPs. And recently the Prime Minister, addressing the Confederation of Indian Industry, asked his audience to "desist from non-competitive behaviour," and in that context to keep profit maximization "within the bounds of decency and greed" and show "self-restraint."[46] He did not hold out even a veiled threat of using the MRTP Act, or mention the soon-to-be-enforced Competition Act, to which I now turn.

III. THE COMPETITION ACT[47]

The new Act improves upon the MRTP Act in many ways. It covers the usual three areas of anticompetitive agreements between firms, abuses of a dominant position by a single firm, and "combinations" (that is, mergers and acquisitions above specified asset or turnover thresholds). It wisely avoids areas such as monopolistic pricing and "unfair trade practices," to which the MRTP Act devoted entire chapters, although I shall show that they may reappear in a different guise. Unlike the MRTP Act, anticompeti-tive practices such as cartels and predatory pricing are now defined, and the latter is now explicitly regarded as an abuse of a dominant position. Unusually, the statute itself lists several economic criteria that the Competition Commission of India (CCI) "shall have due regard to" in arriv-ing at a decision, although there are some inconsistencies in these criteria that I shall point out below. Criteria for determining the relevant geographi-cal or product market are also listed. Detailed steps have been laid down to guide the process of adjudication, with time limits for merger reviews. Firms violating the new law can be fined substantial amounts (10 percent of their turnover, or one-third of the profits of a cartel), and face much bigger monetary penalties for noncompliance with orders as compared to those provided for in the MRTP Act, as well as prison terms. Regulations drafted by the CCI lay out an impressive leniency program that allows for complete amnesty to the first participant who provides information about a cartel, reduced penalties for others on a sliding scale, and stipulated decision times

---

[46] "PM's address at CII annual general meeting – 2007", 24 May 2007, http://pmindia.nic.in/speech/content.asp?id=548 (visited 9 April 2008).

[47] Taking into account the amendments passed in 2007 and some rethinking on my part, this section modifies and updates my earlier assessment in Bhattacharjea, *India's Competition Policy: An Assessment*, 38(34) ECONOMIC AND POLITICAL WEEKLY 3561 (2003). It focuses on key aspects of the Competition Act and does not purport to be a comprehensive introduction. *See* S. Chakravarthy, *India*, in COMPETITION POLICY AND DEVELOPMENT IN ASIA, 107–60 (Douglas H. Brooks and Simon Evenett eds., 2005), and Vinod Dhall, *Competition Law in India*, 21 ANTITRUST 73 (2007) for earlier descriptions of the (unamended) Act by senior officials involved in its drafting, and Subhadip Ghosh and Thomas Ross, *India's New Competition Law: A Canadian Perspective*, 23 CANADIAN COMPETITION RECORD 23 (2008), for a recent discussion of the amended Act. On various points, my analysis differs from all of these authors.

and confidentiality guarantees. Various sections of the Act authorize the CCI to hire professional consultants, to engage in competition advocacy, and to advise the government and sector regulators on competition-related matters. All of these are welcome developments.

The new Act explicitly provides (§32) for its application against firms or persons located abroad whose practices have an anticompetitive *effect* in India. This will remedy the problem caused by the Supreme Court's judgment in the *Haridas Exports* case (discussed above), which held that the MRTP Act had no such extra-territorial application. The Act also provides (§18) for the CCI to enter into arrangements with foreign competition agencies. Both sections will help in dealing with anticompetitive practices of foreign firms.

There are, however, several loopholes and inconsistencies in the Act, which will create problems once actual enforcement begins.

A. The "Development" Criterion

The list of objectives prefacing the Act was amended when the Competition Bill was moved in Parliament to include the phrase "keeping in view of the [*sic*] economic development of the country." Correspondingly, the following new clause 19(4)(l) was inserted into the list of criteria for determining whether a firm enjoys a dominant position: "relative advantage, by way of the contribution to the economic development, by the enterprise enjoying a dominant position having or likely to have an appreciable adverse effect on competition." A similar clause 20(4)(m) was inserted into the list of criteria for determining whether a combination would have an adverse effect on competition.

These clauses are meaningless and potentially dangerous. Unlike the other listed criteria, they in no way help to determine dominance or the effect of a combination on competition; instead, they invite the competition authority to condone blatantly anticompetitive activities by large corporations that purport to promote development. The relationship between competition and development, and even the meaning of development itself, are controversial even amongst economists who have been studying these matters for years. Section 38 of the MRTP Act at least listed specific circumstances (the so-called "gateways") that could be adduced to rebut the presumption that a particular RTP was against the public interest. In the Competition Act, however, the CCI's interpretation of "development" will lead to inconsistent verdicts and legal uncertainty.

B. Anticompetitive Agreements

Section 3(1) of the Competition Act prohibits any agreement "which causes or is likely to cause an appreciable adverse effect on competition within India," and §3(2) holds such agreements to be void. According to §3(3), certain agreements (price-fixing, output restricting, market-sharing, or bid-rigging, generally known as "hard-core" cartels) are *presumed* to have an appreciable adverse effect on competition (hereafter AAEC). Does this amount to a *per se* prohibition? There are divergent views on this, even amongst those responsible for the Act. The sole member of the present CCI, who as a senior civil servant was involved in shepherding it through Parliament, observes that it is "similar, but not necessarily identical to, the per se rule in the United States," because there is a long-established tradition in Indian law to treat a "presumption" as rebuttable.[48] I may point out that if a *per se* prohibition was intended, §3(3) would have stated that such agreements were *deemed* to have an anticompetitive effect. Indian courts defer to the legislative intent behind such "deeming clauses" or "statutory fictions," unless they violate the Constitution. As we have seen above, the Supreme Court made this quite clear in respect of the provision in §33(1) of the MRTP Act whereby certain agreements— including those involving hard-core cartel activities—were deemed to be restrictive.[49]

On the other hand, a former MRTPC member who was associated with the drafting of the Competition Act believes that it does make the agreements described in §3(3) *per se* illegal, and there is "almost no scope for errant enterprises to rebut the presumption of illegality."[50] However, matters are not that straightforward, for §19(3) further muddies the waters. To understand why, it needs to be quoted in full:

> 19(3): The Commission shall, while determining whether an agreement has an appreciable adverse effect on competition under section 3, have due regard to all or any of the following factors, namely:—
>
> (a) creation of barriers to new entrants in the market;
> (b) driving existing competitors out of the market;
> (c) foreclosure of competition by hindering entry into the market;
> (d) accrual of benefits to consumers;
> (e) improvements in production or distribution of goods or provision of services;
> (f) promotion of technical, scientific and economic development by means of production or distribution of goods or provision of services.

Now, criteria (a)–(c) help to determine whether an agreement has an AAEC, but (d)–(f) do not: they instead provide various arguments that can be used to justify such agreements. Note that §19(3) is applicable to *all* of §3, including the hard-core cartel activities listed in subsection 3(3). It might seem that the phrase "while determining whether an agreement has an appreciable adverse effect on competition" steers §19(3) away from such

[48] Dhall, *supra* note 46, at 74.
[49] *See supra* notes 12, 19 and surrounding text.
[50] *See* Chakravarthy, *supra* note 46, at 115.

activities, which are presumed to be anticompetitive. But if this presumption is rebuttable, then even if the rebuttal is unsuccessful, the words "while determining..." open the door to applying criteria (d)–(f) even to an anticompetitive cartel. Further, an "Explanation" attached to §3(3) excludes from the presumption of an AAEC those joint ventures that increase "efficiency in production, supply, distribution, storage, acquisition or control of goods or provision of services." A hard-core cartel that operates through a common sales or buying agency that results in cost savings could exploit this proviso along with the clauses in §19(3). One way or another, therefore, many cartels are likely to escape *per se* prohibition.

As for vertical restrictions, §3(4) of the Act holds that any such agreement, including five specific types (tying, exclusive supply, exclusive distribution, refusal to deal, and resale price maintenance), shall be in contravention of the prohibition in §3(1) if it results in an AAEC. Recall that these are treated as restrictive *per se* in the MRTP Act. Section 3(5)(i) provides that nothing in §3 shall restrict the right of any person to impose "reasonable" conditions to protect the intellectual property rights (IPRs) recognized by six listed IPR laws.

In devising a rule of reason for this entire range of potentially anticompetitive agreements, the CCI will presumably be guided by criteria (d)–(f) of §19(3). But these are problematic. They appear to be a simplistic adaptation of Article 81(3) EC, which permits exemptions for efficiency-enhancing agreements and concerted practices. The EC provisions, however, impose additional conditions: they require that the agreement or practice allows consumers to share in the benefits, does not impose restrictions that are unnecessary to attaining the efficiency objective, and does not substantially eliminate competition. All of these conditions are mandatory, whereas those in the Indian Competition Act are permissive. The European Commission, moreover, has given "block exemptions" to certain kinds of agreements. In India, under §54 of the Competition Act, the government (not the CCI) can exempt "any class of enterprises if such exemption is necessary in the interest of security of the State or public interest," or "any practice or agreement arising out of" any obligation under an international treaty. Efficiency-enhancing agreements do not figure here, so they can only be subject to case-by-case consideration, in a context in which there is very little comprehension of the economics of such agreements.

C. Abuse of Dominance

The Competition Act's treatment of abuse of dominance represents another, and more dangerous, adaptation of EC law. Section 4(2) of the Act lists several practices that constitute abuse, and as Table 2 shows, its subsections (a), (b), and especially (d) are clearly inspired by the corresponding sections

Table 2. Comparison of Abuse of Dominance Provisions in the Indian Competition Act and the EC Treaty

Competition Act, §4(2)	Article 82 EC
There shall be an abuse of dominance under subsection (1), if an enterprise—	Such abuse may, in particular, consist of:
(a) directly or indirectly, imposes unfair or discriminatory—	(a) directly or indirectly imposing unfair purchase or selling prices or other unfair trading conditions;
(i) condition in purchase or sale of goods or service; or	
(ii) price in purchase or sale (including predatory price) of goods or service, [...] or	
(b) limits or restricts—	(b) limiting production, markets, or technical development to the prejudice of consumers;
(i) production of goods or provision of services or market therefore; or	
(ii) technical or scientific development relating to goods or services to the prejudice of consumers; or	
(c) indulges in practice or practices resulting in denial of market access in any manner; or	(c) applying dissimilar conditions to equivalent transactions with other trading parties, thereby placing them at a competitive disadvantage;
(d) makes conclusion of contracts subject to acceptance by other parties of supplementary obligations that, by their nature or according to commercial usage, have no connection with the subject of such contracts; or	(d) making the conclusion of contracts subject to acceptance by the other parties of supplementary obligations that, by their nature or according to commercial usage, have no connection with the subject of such contracts.
(e) uses its dominant position in one relevant market to enter into, or protect, other relevant markets.	

of Article 82 EC, but with a crucial difference that I shall point out below. Section 19(4) lists 13 "factors" the CCI "shall have regard to" while determining "whether an enterprise enjoys a dominant position." Ten of these are standard economic indicia, but there is also the "development" criterion, "social obligations and social costs," and "any other factor which the Commission may consider relevant for the inquiry." Unlike the sections on anticompetitive agreements and combinations, *no AAEC test is required* for establishing abuse of dominance, other than for the exclusionary behavior described repetitively by §4(2)(c) and (e). That this was no oversight is clear from the fact that it is pointed out by one of the Competition Act's architects. He observes that the listed activities cover "exploitative" abuses such as unfair or discriminatory prices, as well as exclusionary abuses such as predatory pricing, as in Article 82 EC.[51]

As is apparent from Table 2, this comparison is inaccurate, for Article 82 makes a crucial distinction between unfair and discriminatory practices.

[51] Dhall, *supra* note 46, at 75.

Article 82(a) deals with unfair prices or selling conditions, but 82(c)—which has no analog in the Competition Act—makes it clear that discrimination is a violation only if it affects competition, with injury being caused to other firms.[52] In a trenchant review of actual decisional practice regarding Article 82(c), Geradin and Petit have shown that the Commission and the appellate courts have frequently disregarded the need to establish equivalence of transactions or exclusionary effects, have ignored possible welfare-enhancing effects of discrimination, and have inappropriately targeted primary-line injury and discrimination between national markets in Europe.[53] But these are interpretational stretches of the law that have been condemned by most scholars. In contrast, §4(2)(a) of the Competition Act is worded from the start so as to run together unfair, discriminatory, and predatory behavior, with no mention of competition, trading parties, or equivalence of the impugned transactions.

Moreover, charges of exploitative abuse have been infrequently made and even less frequently sustained in the EC, and that is as it should be, because of the probability of wrong convictions.[54] But the wording of §4(2)(a) and (b) will almost certainly invite complaints against "unfair" prices, discriminatory treatment of dealers, contractual breaches, and capacity underutilization, of the kind that were entertained earlier under the MRTP Act's chapter on "monopolistic" trade practices and more recently under §2(o)(ii) defining restrictive trade practices. Such complaints will divert the CCI from its role as a competition watchdog. At least the main clause of §2(o) of the old Act (quoted in full in Section II above) had a clear reference to competition-restricting practices, enabling the Supreme Court to put the MRTPC back on the right track; the Competition Act does not.

True, unlike the MRTP Act's §2(o), §4 of the Competition Act is applicable only to a firm in a dominant position, but it also contains an "Explanation" that defines that as a "position of strength" which enables a firm to "(i) operate independently of competitive forces prevailing in the relevant market, or (ii) affect its competitors or consumers or the relevant market in its favour." Contractual disputes of the kind that frequently came before the MRTP Commission, involving buyers locked in to a relationship with a large supplier, would fit this definition. Some of the criteria in §19(4), such as "size and importance of the enterprise" or "dependence of consumers on the enterprise," would also come to complainants' aid. Most daunting of all, §28 arms the CCI with the power to break up a firm to

---

[52] As is the case in the U.S. under §2(a) of the Robinson-Patman Act, 15 U.S.C. §13(a).

[53] Damien Geradin and Nicolas Petit, *Price Discrimination under EC Competition Law: Another Antitrust Doctrine in Search of Limiting Principles?* 2 J. COMPETITION L. & ECON. 479 (2006).

[54] The reasons and cases are neatly summarized by Bruce Lyons, *The Paradox of the Exclusion of Exploitative Abuse*, CCP Working Paper 08-1, University of East Anglia, 2007, http://www.ccp.uea.ac.uk/publicfiles/workingpapers/CCP08-1.pdf (visited 12 February 2008).

ensure that it does not abuse its dominant position—without requiring proof that it has already done so.

Although the foregoing arguments suggest that the CCI has been given excessive authority to penalize a range of legitimate business practices as well as dominance *per se*, it has been emasculated in dealing with predatory pricing. A further "Explanation" after clause 4(2)(a) (indicated by the ellipsis in Table 2) excludes from its purview unfair or discriminatory conditions or prices if they are adopted to "meet the competition." Desirable though it may be to qualify the Act's condemnation of price discrimination without an AAEC, this exclusion explicitly covers *predatory* pricing, which is defined in a subsequent "Explanation" as pricing below cost "with a view to reduce competition or eliminate the competitors." In this, too, the Competition Act departs from the EC script, which does not allow meeting the competition as a defence of predatory pricing.[55]

This carve-out will allow firms that have the financial resources to incur temporary losses to drive out more efficient rivals. The usual Chicago-style dismissal of this "deep pockets" story assumes that the prey has equal access to the capital market, enabling it to finance its losses and thus survive the predator's campaign if it is otherwise competitive. However, the Indian capital market is far from perfect, and small and medium firms have been credit-constrained by a banking system that systematically ignores future profitability in lending decisions.[56] In sum, then, the sections on abuse of dominance will condemn normal business practices that have nothing to do with competition, and on the other hand exculpate genuine abuse in the form of predatory pricing.

D. Merger Review

Abandoned in 1991 under the MRTP regime, the revival of merger control has been the most controversial feature of the Competition Act. Indian business interests opposed any kind of merger review during the early discussions on the Act, and even though it prescribes relatively high thresholds for reviewable mergers, they continue to do so, arguing that they need to be allowed to grow and achieve economies of scale to compete internationally.[57] The government has not yielded on this, but the CCI has recently (January 2008) posted draft merger regulations that indicate considerable

---

[55] As confirmed recently in CFI, France Télécom SA v. Commission of the European Communities, Case T-340/03 (2007).

[56] *See* Abhijit Banerjee, Shawn Cole and Esther Duflo, *Bank Financing in India*, in INDIA'S AND CHINA'S RECENT EXPERIENCE WITH REFORM AND GROWTH 138–57 (Wanda Tseng and David Cowen eds., 2005).

[57] *Indian industry against regulation of mergers*, ECONOMIC TIMES, 24 Dec. 2007, at 1 (based on a statement by the Confederation of Indian Industry).

backtracking in the face of domestic and foreign criticism.[58] As these are still being debated, with even the CCI's legal authority to issue them being questioned, I shall not deal with the merger regime in detail. However, a brief comment is required on the possible foreclosure of potential competition, which neither the CCI nor its critics have recognized.

First, some background. The Act defines a "combination" as any merger, acquisition, or acquiring of control in which the *combined* assets or turnover of the firms exceed specified thresholds: INR 10,000 million (roughly US$250 million) in assets or INR 30,000 million (roughly US$750 million) in turnover in India, or respectively US$500 million and US$1,500 million worldwide. Thresholds four times as high are specified for business groups to which the combining firms belong. A combination that crosses any of these thresholds would be subject to review, after which the CCI can block it or require it to be modified. The original Act provided for voluntary notification of combinations to the CCI, but the Parliamentary committee reviewing the 2006 Amendment Bill recommended a mandatory notification requirement. This provoked a memorandum from the International Bar Association (IBA) recommending that voluntary notification be retained and that foreign mergers with little or no "effective local nexus" should not be brought into the net.

The revised Amendment Bill passed in 2007 did make notification mandatory, but qualified the thresholds, now requiring that at least INR 5,000 million (about US$125 million) or INR 15,000 million (about US$375 million), respectively, of the combining parties' joint worldwide assets and turnover would have to be in India to fall within the purview of the Act. The amendment also extended the period after which CCI approval would be deemed to have been granted from 90 to 210 days after notification. No merger will come into effect until the expiry of 210 days or CCI approval, whichever is sooner. The IBA then issued another memorandum (with sections of the American Bar Association issuing one along similar lines) protesting this lengthy timeline, and also pointing out that, even with the new local nexus condition, a merger involving a firm with no business in India would still need to be notified if the other party alone has assets or turnover in India exceeding the threshold. It called on the CCI to devise appropriate implementing regulations to deal with this anomaly.[59] The CCI's draft Regulations respond to this. They specify

---

[58] "Proposed draft of the Competition Commission of India (Combination) Regulations, 200_", accessed from http://www.competition-commission-india.nic.in on February 13, 2008. *See* Regulations 5(1) and 5(2)(iii). The website has also posted extremely critical comments received from business groups and from the U.S. Federal Trade Commission on various aspects of the Regulations.

[59] For the IBA memoranda, see http://www.ibanet.org/legalpractice/AntitrustWGIndia.cfm; for the ABA letter, http://www.abanet.org/antitrust/at-comments/2007/11-07/Comments-IndianCompetition.pdf, both visited 13 February 2008. Large Indian firms, which have recently begun making high-profile overseas acquisitions, were also reported to be lobbying along the same lines.

thresholds for assets (INR 2,000 million, or about US$50 million) or turnover (INR 6,000 million, or about US$150 million) within India for *each* of at least two parties to the combination. Combinations involving parties below these thresholds are among those that will be regarded as "not likely to cause an appreciable adverse effect on competition in India."

Automatic approval of such combinations is not, however, as harmless as it appears. Foreign firms with no current business in India may enter the Indian market after trade and regulatory barriers are dismantled by the economic cooperation agreements that India is currently negotiating with various countries. Preemptive mergers with their likely competitors (Indian or foreign) already present in India can lessen potential competition in the Indian market.[60] A sounder justification for the new regulation would be similar to that for high basic thresholds: the need to prevent the inexperienced CCI from being overwhelmed by having to review mergers with a lower (but certainly not zero) probability of posing competition problems.

E. Institutional Deficiencies

Concerns have been expressed over potential conflicts between the CCI and sector regulators, many of whom are also mandated to adjudicate on competition issues in their sectors.[61] Sections 21 and 21A of the amended Competition Act now provide for reciprocal references between the CCI and statutory authorities on aspects of decisions that might be contrary to each other's governing Acts. The opinion sought from the other agency has to be provided within 60 days, and the originating agency must consider it and record its reasoned response. This may not be sufficient to preclude jurisdictional conflicts and forum shopping. There are also concerns about autonomy. The government has the power under §55 of the Act to issue binding policy directives to the CCI, and under §56 to supersede and reconstitute it altogether if it fails to discharge its functions or comply with policy directives, or even "in the public interest."

The extensive amendments passed in 2007 to get around the Supreme Court's strictures (recall the opening paragraph of this paper) will have

---

[60] This argument has been developed in Manish Agarwal and Aditya Bhattacharjea, *Are Merger Regulations Diluting Parliamentary Intent?*, 43(26) ECONOMIC AND POLITICAL WEEKLY 10, 28 June 2008 available at http://papers.ssrn.com/abstract=1158359. Ghosh and Ross (*supra* note 46 at 35–36) are of the opinion that India's Competition Act would not preclude a forward-looking, "but for" test of anticompetitive effects of a merger, as is applied in Canada. Their paper, however, was written before the new Regulations became available.

[61] *See* T.C.A. Anant and S. Sundar, *Interface between Regulation and Competition Law, in* TOWARDS A FUNCTIONAL COMPETITION POLICY FOR INDIA 95–104 (Pradeep S. Mehta ed., 2006). Some other chapters in this book deal with specific sectors. Regulators already exist for telecommunications, financial markets, port tariffs, pharmaceutical prices, petroleum and natural gas, and power. Ministries exercise regulatory functions in respect of airlines, airports, and shipping and sometimes take decisions that bypass the regulatory agencies in other sectors.

several negative consequences for the implementation of the Act. To restore the role of the judiciary, the Act creates a Competition Appellate Tribunal (CAT) that must be headed by a current or former Judge of the Supreme Court or Chief Justice of a state High Court. The CCI need not be headed by a judge, but it has been deprived of the power to adjudicate between private parties and to award compensation; these powers have been reserved for the CAT. CCI orders on monetary penalties can be executed through the income tax authorities, and jail terms for noncompliance can now be imposed only by a designated magistrate's court. The CCI will now take decisions collectively as a collegium of up to seven members, rather than in benches of at least two members as originally intended. Consequently, the provisions for regional benches and at least one specialized merger bench in the original Act were deleted by the amending Act, which is unfortunate. A body sitting only in Delhi is inaccessible to parties elsewhere in such a vast country, and mergers do require specialized expertise. Moreover, the collegial approach mandated for the CCI, and the interposition of the Appellate Tribunal, sector regulators, tax authorities, and a magisterial court, howsoever necessary to preserve institutional balance, will lead inevitably to costly litigation and delayed resolution of cases.

IV. CONCLUSIONS

In Section II of this paper, I reviewed India's experience with its extant competition law, the MRTP Act, pointing out various problems and distortions that have arisen in the course of its implementation, particularly the displacement of competition regulation by consumer protection and "public interest" considerations. In Section III, I discussed various lacunae in the 2002 Competition Act that will invite many of these problems to reappear and create some new ones. In particular, in a striking inversion of international practice, cartels may be subject to a rule of reason, and predatory behavior may be condoned, whereas "abusive" conduct having no bearing on competition will be condemned *per se*. The delay in bringing the new law into effect may not, therefore, have been such a bad thing.[62] Ideally, another comprehensive overhaul would be desirable before it is activated. The amendments that need to be considered are implicit in the analysis of Section III. However, the government has passed an amending Act to take care of all of the problems that it is willing to fix. The question then is what should be done so as to make the best of a bad piece of legislation?

Priority must be given to strengthening the capacity of the CCI to implement the many technical provisions in the new Act. As I explained in Section II, the MRTP Act used very different criteria, and the Commission

---

[62] And, I might point out, it was precisely in this period (2003–2008) that the Indian economy witnessed its highest-ever growth rates.

often side-stepped them by resorting to *per se* condemnation or the overarching concepts of "public interest" and "manipulation of prices" that proved decisive in many cases. The promising development of a rule of reason was thwarted by the 1984 amendment that condemned *per se* the "monopolistic" practices listed in §2(i) and the agreements in §33(1).[63] The same amendment inserted the chapter on Unfair Trade Practices into the Act, and over the next two decades the limited resources of the MRTPC were diverted to dealing with the large number of cases of individual consumer complaints that did not involve competition issues. Its record on establishing collusion in cartel cases has been poor. Lack of expertise is likely to create special problems for merger review, which was deleted from the MRTP Act in 1991, and has been reintroduced by the Competition Act.

Although the 2007 Amendment Act requires the chairman of the Appellate Tribunal to be a judge, no such background is required for the chairman and members of the CCI. Given the government's track record with all of its other regulatory agencies, most of these posts, as well as that of the Director General and subordinate staff, will probably be filled by generalist civil servants. The prospect of retiring or being transferred after a few years will inhibit their incentive to acquire the relevant skills, and whatever skills they do acquire will be lost to the CCI when they move out. Already, most of the officers who underwent capacity building after the CCI was set up in 2003 have left the agency before handling a single case.

Members of the CCI and CAT, whether they come from the judiciary or bureaucracy, will also need to be sensitized to the techniques of modern competition analysis, to prevent judicial activism unrelated to the purpose of the Act. According to its preamble and §18, its purpose is the promotion of competition and protection of consumer interest, but I also showed that the lacunae in the new Act will permit idiosyncratic ideas about "fair" pricing and intervention in contractual disputes to reappear. The Commission and its Director General must stand ready to dismiss at the threshold complaints unrelated to restrictions on competition: as I showed above, such complaints caused much harassment under the MRTP regime during the 1990s.

The urge to protect competitors rather than competition will also have to be tempered. Although some scholars have tried to make a case for "pro-poor" competition policy,[64] it has to be recognized that competition often hurts the poor. In a country with no unemployment benefits, this can be devastating. There will inevitably be pressure to restrain rather than

---

[63] Although, as I have shown, there were very few cases under the former section, and the amendment to the latter began to bite only after a Supreme Court judgment two decades later.

[64] For an eloquent, well-informed, and empathetic statement, *see* Eleanor M. Fox, *Economic Development, Poverty and Antitrust: The Other Path*, 13 SOUTHWESTERN JOURNAL OF LAW AND TRADE IN THE AMERICAS 211 (2007).

promote competition.[65] What needs to be kept in mind is that helping one industry can harm another. The two MRTPC injunctions that were set aside (on other grounds) in the *Haridas Exports* judgment are instructive in this context. By imposing an injunction on imports from ANSAC, the Commission helped the Indian soda ash industry, but deprived the float glass industry of cheap supplies of a vital input, and made it vulnerable to imported Indonesian float glass. The injunction on the latter would in turn have harmed user industries, notably the labor-intensive construction sector. Adjudicators must also recognize that even "fair" competition will inevitably result in unemployment and force some firms to close down, and that such a churning of the industrial structure can be a source of productivity growth in developing countries.[66] There is a tradeoff involved, and each country has to decide how to deal with it, but the competition agency cannot resolve such conflicts on a case-by-case basis.

Instead, such public interest issues can be dealt with by *exempting* certain categories of enterprises from provisions of the Act, for example, cartels to promote small firms, or to save jobs in a declining industry. But under §54 of the Act, authority for granting exemptions for "any class of enterprises" has been given to the central government, not the CCI. These exemptions should be granted on the basis of sound criteria, rather than political favoritism. In many countries, the statute itself lists exempted sectors, or the power to grant certain types of exemption is delegated to the antitrust agency.

A related problem springs from the unreliability of data on market shares in India (see note 8 above). This will make it impossible to devise EC-style block exemptions with *de minimis* provisos for certain kinds of agreements among small firms, U.S.-style "safe harbors" for mergers based on the Hirschman-Herfindahl concentration index, or thresholds for defining dominance. Absent these "bright line" rules, it will be up to the fledgling CCI to make its own assessment of dominance or an appreciable adverse effect on competition in the relevant market.

In conclusion, a statute riddled with loopholes and unfamiliar technical provisions, little useful experience carried over from the preceding MRTP regime, inexperienced staff, and lack of reliable data make for an unpropitious beginning for enforcement of the Competition Act. In view of the

---

[65] India is not unique in this respect. As I argued in my earlier article (*see* Bhattacharjea, *supra* note 46, at § III), the enactment of competition laws in developed countries was primarily motivated by distributional objectives and the need to legitimize the operation of a market economy by giving the impression of curbing its worst excesses. These remained major influences on the operation and interpretation of the laws for several decades, well after these countries had attained levels of development and social safety nets far more advanced than India has today.

[66] Although the evidence on this is modest: *see* James R. Tybout, *Manufacturing Firms in Developing Countries: How Well Do They Do, and Why?* 38 J. OF ECONOMIC LITERATURE 11, 26–28 (2000).

638   *Journal of Competition Law & Economics*

complexity of merger review, the unsettled state of the merger regulations, and the bad drafting of the sections on abuse of dominance, it might be best for the government to bring into effect only the provisions on anticompetitive agreements.[67] Even then, the CCI will have its work cut out in developing the nebulous rule of reason provided by §19(3), operationalizing §3(5)(i) on "reasonable" restrictions to protect the statutory IPRs, defining relevant markets, and calculating overcharges. In short, there will be several difficult analytical problems for the CCI to cut its teeth on, and it should not overreach itself.

This article was submitted for publication in mid-2008. The new Competition Commission was appointed in May 2009, with a small staff drawn from other government agencies. Simultaneously, the remaining sections of the Act were brought into force, with the exception of those governing merger review, for which the Regulations discussed in this article were yet to be finalized as of January 2010. Several cases pertaining to anti-competitive agreements and abuse of dominance have been filed, but no decisions have yet been handed down. The issues discussed in this article are yet to be resolved.

---

[67] §1 of the Act provides for different sections to be brought into force at different dates.

C
Chile

[16]

Building Trust in Antitrust: The Chilean Case

ELINA CRUZ* AND SEBASTIAN ZARATE**

I. Introduction

A. Overview

Chile is among the most economically stable countries in Latin America. In some areas, it is viewed as a pioneer in competition law and policy in the region. In spite of a general market-based economic orientation, the problem of Chilean antitrust is one based on a broad trust in competition, but mistrust in the antitrust system.[1] This mistrust manifests itself in at least two areas: collusion enforcement and institutional design. Some of the problems with competition law and policy that will be discussed in this paper are common to other jurisdictions. However, we believe that there are at least two elements that characterize the Chilean case that are not present in similar countries.

First, the process of trade liberalization, deregulation and privatization started in 1973 was relatively early compared with other countries in the region. In the process of market liberalization, Chilean policy-makers understood the freedom to compete as a core value, and consequently the 1980 Chilean Constitution protects the right to develop any economic activity. This principle of freedom to

* Assistant Professor, Pontificia Universidad Católica de Chile. Center of Competition Law at the Pontificia Universidad Católica de Chile. Associate Researcher, Institute of Regional Applied Economics, Universidad Católica del Norte.
** Assistant Professor, Pontificia Universidad Católica de Chile. Center of Competition Law at the Pontificia Universidad Católica de Chile. We would like to thank Ricardo Jungmann, the Executive Director of the Center of Competition Law at the Pontificia Universidad Católica de Chile, for his helpful comments and suggestions on earlier drafts. Any remaining errors are ours.

[1] The Organization for Economic Co-operation and Development (OECD) suggests the need for greater antitrust enforcement in Chile, stating: '[T]he tradition of caution, including an apparent reluctance to find violations and to impose fines, has in part reflected a view in Chile that economic offences against the public are not serious and that the costs of monopoly may not exceed the costs of competition law enforcement.' OECD and Inter-American Bank, Competition Law and Policy in Latin America: Peer Reviews of Argentina, Brazil, Chile, Mexico and Peru (Sao Paulo, OECD Publishing, 2006), at 192–93.

compete was probably the one that at first inspired Chilean competition law and competition authorities. For example, it explains why, even in the context of a country strongly influenced by Chicago School economics, competition authorities viewed vertical restraints initially as anti-competitive. In this sense, Chilean competition law has gradually moved towards an approach based on efficiency considerations and consumer welfare, but even today freedom to compete and to develop economic activities seems to be a powerful motive. For instance, in February 2008, the Competition Tribunal (TDLC) rejected a large retail merger. The public debate that the decision caused was based not so much on efficiency or consumer welfare, but rather on the questions of whether it was constitutional for the TDLC to reject a merger and whether the TDLC actually had the power to make such a decision without affecting economic freedom and private property. This view of competition as a way to achieve the freedom to compete had a strong influence on each of the practices challenged by the Chilean competition authorities. However, under this view, collusion is naturally a conduct that is given less importance than other practices, which is why its study is particularly interesting.

A second element that shapes the Chilean case is the fact that it is a relatively small economy compared with other countries in the region, and its industries are highly concentrated. While it is generally understood that concentration potentially may be a factor that facilitates collusion, in Chile this has worked as a disincentive towards collusion enforcement. For example, according to the OECD Chilean country review on competition policy, there seems to be agreement that a leniency program could fail because a person who came forward with information about collusion would have trouble finding future employment. The reason for this is that concentration produces little job mobility, and consequently informants would face social sanctions in future employment. We believe that this could be an overstatement, but nevertheless it shows a characteristic of Chilean reality which is not necessarily true about other jurisdictions, and that affects the enforcement of competition policy.

The starting point for this chapter (in section II) is an analysis of Chilean case law on collusion from 1973 until 2007. From this analysis we detect a key finding: the fact that almost no collusion claim has been successful in Chile, and that certainly this topic has not been a relevant focus of competition authorities. Nevertheless, the case study also illustrates the second finding: that after the major amendment of the Competition Act in 2003 (Competition Act 2003), the attitude towards collusion has changed towards a far more proactive approach; and for the first time, stronger infringement decisions have been issued by competition authorities.

From an institutional viewpoint, in section III this chapter analyzes two problems of trust that the Chilean competition system has experienced since the application of the Competition Act 2003. The first one is the lack of effective investigatory tools of the Office of the National Economic Prosecutor (FNE), particularly in collusion cases. This problem, currently subject to parliamentary debate in a proposed amendment, is partly due to confusion with regard to the legal nature of competition infractions under Chilean law. The second problem is more serious, and relates to role of the Supreme Court. Instead of building an appeal process before an upper tribunal composed of experts in the topic, the Competition Act 2003 opted for a review by non-specialized Supreme Court judges. In other words, the Supreme Court has been conceived in the institutional design as the *ultimate decision-maker of the competition system*. As such, the Supreme Court has overruled important decisions made by the TDLC (including specialized reasoning in competition law and economics). This weakness is aggravated by what we consider an ill-defined concept of the review powers of the Supreme Court, ie conceiving the review process, the *Recurso de Reclamación*, as an appeal instead of as a judicial review, which has enormous consequences in the level of deference and scope of control of the Supreme Court. In *the last part of* section III, we propose solutions to overcome these elements of distrust displayed towards competition institutions.

B. Chilean Competition Law and the 2003 Amendment

Chile enacted its first competition law in 1959,[2] but this statute was barely used until 1973, the year in which a new Competition Act came into force (hereinafter the 'Competition Act 1973') in the context of trade liberalization and market deregulation. The Competition Act 1973 made no express mention of its goals (eg, promoting efficiency or enhancing welfare), and its substantive provisions consisted basically in punishing 'any deed, act or contract that prevents, restricts or hinders free competition or tends to produce such effects'.[3]

A list of examples of practices that could potentially harm competition followed this general provision, and such a broad set of examples left most of the development of antitrust to the case law handed down by the competition authorities. Consequently, competition case law was an exception: in the context of a civil law jurisdiction, where generally precedents and decisions are non-binding, the legal community viewed the decisions issued by competition commissions as extremely relevant. This factor also explains why it is useful to study the case law produced by competition authorities. The penalties for violation of competition law consisted of imposing fines, dissolving legal entities, and imposing prison sentences (although the third option was almost never used). Fines, although few were actually applied, were the most commonly used sanction, but their amounts were small, averaging US $13,500.[4]

---

[2] Chilean Law 13,305 (April 6, 1959), <http://www.bcn.cl/lc/bleyes/>.
[3] Competition Act of 1973, <http://www.bcn.cl/lc/bleyes/>.
[4] OECD and Inter-American Bank, above n 1, at 210.

160   *Elina Cruz and Sebastian Zarate*

The Competition Act 1973 created several antitrust institutions, of which the FNE is the only that remains in use. Among other tools, the FNE may undertake investigations and enforcement. The Finance Ministry oversees the FNE but the FNE has budgetary independence. The President of Chile appoints the head of the FNE, the National Economic Prosecutor, who may be removed by her at any time. The Competition Act 1973 set up a Resolutive Commission, which was an administrative body equivalent to an antitrust commission. The Resolutive Commission no longer exists and was replaced by the TDLC. The Resolutive Commission had both judicial and non-judicial powers. Among the former, it deliberated cases brought by the Prosecutor's Office or by private parties, as well as appeals of decisions made by the Preventive Commissions. Among the latter, it could recommend the amendment of laws or regulations that were considered to interfere with competition law. The Resolutive Commission was chaired by a Supreme Court judge, chiefs of service from the Finance Ministry, a law school dean and a dean from an economics department. The decisions issued by the Resolutive Commission were subject to review before the Supreme Court, but this procedure was restricted only to those cases that established the dissolution of a business, the prohibition of a person to hold certain posts, or the imposition of fines. Lastly, there were Preventive Commissions (Central and Regional), which the TDLC also replaced, which mostly had consultative powers. Their main role was to answer questions regarding competition law in Chile, and they had the power to issue orders to stop anti-competitive practices temporarily and to require the intervention of other authorities when they considered that competition law was being affected. Commissions were formed by a member from the Ministry of Finance, one from the Treasury, a law professor, an economics professor and a member of the Local Community Association.[5] The case law developed by the Preventive Commissions was probably the most elaborate, hence its relevance for establishing precedents in competition matters.

While the Government granted the FNE a moderate budget, the members of the Resolutive and Preventive Commissions worked *ad honorem* and met once a week. Given this structure, an amendment seemed necessary to improve the enforcement and application of competition law. In November 2003 a new Competition Act came into force,[6] and by 2004 there was full implementation. The Government sponsored this amendment with the aim of improving competition law and enforcement in Chile through the strengthening of the antitrust authorities. It created a Competition Tribunal, the TDLC, which replaced both

---

[5] According to Art 1 of the Local Communities Act 1997, a community association is 'a local organization representing the residents of a local community with the aim of promoting community welfare, protecting the interests and rights of its members, and cooperating with the Council and Governmental authorities'.

[6] Between 1973 and 2003, Chile amended its competition law under several regulations: Law Decree 2,760 from 1979, Law Decree 2879 from 1979, Law Decree 3,057 from 1980; and Law 19,336, Law 19,610 and Law 19,806. However, the most important change in this law was made by the Law 19,911—the Competition Act 2003—published in the *Official Gazette* in Nov 2003.

the Resolutive and the Preventive Commissions. In particular, the main objectives pursued by the Government through this amendment were:

a) changing the selection process for members of the competition authority, based on a transparent and open call for candidates to ensure they had the necessary expertise to apply competition law;
b) establishing a salary for the members of the TDLC and increasing the number of sessions of the tribunal;
c) separating the roles of the FNE and the TDLC by granting the latter entity budgetary independence;
d) ensuring the independence of the TDLC from the rest of government; and
e) strengthening the powers given to the TDLC in order to enforce competition law.

While the Competition Act 2003 eliminated criminal penalties (in reality these penalties were almost never used), the new law drastically increased the possible amount of the fines (by December 2007 the maximum fine established by the law was approximately US $16,500,000). Moreover, the Competition Act 2003 allowed settlements between the FNE and the parties (unlike in the previous Competition Act). However, the TDLC must call for conciliation and must later approve the settlement between the parties.

The substantive terms of the new law remained basically the same, but the new Article 1 states the objective of Chilean competition law: 'This law intends to promote and defend free market competition.'[7] Nevertheless, the Competition Act 2003 effectively changed competition enforcement in Chile: the decisions issued by the newly created TDLC reflect the expertise of its members, and the sanctions imposed so far by this authority for anticompetitive violations have been stronger than before, with the TDLC imposing fines of over US $6 million.[8] Yet there were some unintended effects of the amendment. The most important of these has been the role played by the Supreme Court in the new institutional design. Little parliamentary debate (if any) was devoted to this topic, especially considering that until the amendment, the Supreme Court had almost no influence within the competition law system. As explained in section III below, judicial review of the rulings made by the TDLC was no longer restricted to certain types of decisions (ie, those that ordered the dissolution of a corporation, disqualified people from holding certain posts or imposed fines). In other words, the new law allowed all decisions of the TDLC that impose any kind of sanction or punishment to be challenged by judicial review before the Supreme Court. This legal change passed silently in a Congress whose debate focused on the creation of an independent tribunal and the increase in punishments for anticompetitive violations, with no awareness of the unexpected power that was being granted to the Supreme Court in this matter. Moreover, because there was an increase in the sanctions that

---

[7] Competition Law 2003, above n 6, at Art 1.
[8] *Falabella-Paris*, Competition Tribunal (2008), 63/2008.

could potentially be imposed by the TDLC (in particular the amount of fines) and because enforcement became more effective through this more specialized authority, the incentives for the parties to use judicial review increased as well.

Consequently, through the extension of judicial review plus the increase in incentives to use this review that stem from more active competition enforcement, the Competition Law 2003 granted the Supreme Court the role of the ultimate decision-maker in the competition law system. One of the problems with this role is that the Court does not have the expertise to decide on competition law matters, a problem that is common to other jurisdictions. However, what is perhaps particular to Chile is that because of the interpretation that the Court and the parties have given to judicial review, there is no deference whatsoever from the Supreme Court towards the TDLC in technical competition matters. This explains why (as discussed further in section III) what we propose is not to redesign the competition institutions or to pass another legal amendment, but to rethink the interpretation of the nature of the TDLC and of the judicial review procedure.

Overall, the current institutional model is close to what has been called a 'bifurcated agency model'[9] in which there are two separate bodies—one that conducts investigations and brings complaints before a second body that adjudicates. Under Chilean law, there is no doubt that the FNE is an autonomous administrative agency. The situation of the TDLC is more complex. Some scholars argue that the Tribunal is a judicial body, and as such must be treated as a court of the judiciary.[10] They argue that this is because it is subject to the supervision of the Supreme Court.[11] Our position, however, is that the TDLC is an autonomous administrative agency, exercising adjudicative administrative powers, in dispute and non-dispute cases. The reason that the TDLC is subject to the supervision of the Supreme Court is the constitutional requirement that every public body adjudicating in dispute cases must be supervised by the Supreme Court, according to Article 82 of the Constitution. Nonetheless, in the case of the TDLC, this supervision is limited because it is an autonomous agency and because the supervision is only applicable to dispute cases. Therefore, under Chilean law it is possible to have an autonomous administrative agency adjudicating, with the only consideration being that as far as dispute cases are concerned, they are subject to the limited supervision of the Supreme Court.

---

[9] M J Trebilcock and E M Iacobucci, 'Designing Competition Law Institutions' 25 *World Competition* 361 (2002).

[10] See, eg, T Menchaca, 'Evolución del antiguo al nuevo sistema' *Revista Anales de Derecho UC. Temas de Libre Competencia* (2007). Another example is the case of the former Senator Augusto Parra, a legal academic who was by then one of the members of the Senate committee that undertook the reform in 2002. He insisted on the judicial nature of the TDLC during the parliamentary debate (see Chilean Senate, Second Report of the Joint Committees of Constitutional Affairs and Finance, Bill No 2.944-03, p 53).

[11] Chilean Constitution, Art 82, first para: 'The Supreme Court is entrusted with the executive, correctional and economic supervision of all the courts and tribunals of the nation. The Constitutional Court, the Electoral Commission, the Regional Electoral Commissions and the Military Courts in time of war are excepted from this norm.'

From this brief account, it can be concluded that the Competition Act 2003 has effectively given an impulse to competition law and enforcement in Chile. However, several issues still need to be resolved. For this reason, there is a Bill currently being debated in Congress that introduces amendments to the Competition Act 2003. The main proposals contained in this Bill[12] are the following:

a) the addition of the term 'or effect' to restrict competition (as explained later) and the extension of the law to cases of collective dominance;
b) the incompatibility between holding the post of member of the tribunal and holding other posts, compensated by a salary increase for members;
c) the introduction of a new mechanism to order the dismissal of the National Economic Prosecutor;
d) the granting of new powers to the FNE (as discussed in section III) and the possibility of reaching extra-judicial settlements through the FNE, as well as the possibility of establishing preventive measures to maintain market transparency; and
e) an increase in fines and the introduction of a leniency policy.

II. Collusion in Chile

This section discusses how the lack of trust in antitrust has been reflected in collusion cases and enforcement. The analysis will be divided into two stages: the past and present of competition law and policy in connection to collusion in Chile. The past will be explained through a time-series study of Chilean case law from 1973 onwards. The present is defined as the events that have taken place since 2004, when the Competition Act 2003 came into force. The future of collusion cases lies in the Bill that is currently being debated in Congress about the introduction of a leniency policy, the strengthening of the powers of the FNE and other amendments.

A. The Past: 1973–2003

As mentioned earlier, Article 1 of the Competition Act 1973 punished in general 'any deed, act or contract that prevents, restricts or hinders free competition or tends to produce such effects'.[13] Article 2 contained a list of illustrative practices that could potentially harm competition. Among these practices, the one closest to collusive agreements was the prohibition against determining the prices of goods and services. However, because Article 2 merely contained a list of examples, any

---

[12] As of Jan 2008.
[13] Competition Act 2003, above n 6, at Art 1.

conduct that was considered anti-competitive and was not covered in Article 2, could be prosecuted under Article 1 of the statute.

This was the extent of the substantive legal provisions of Chilean competition law, which meant that the Chilean competition authorities, the Preventive and Resolutive Commissions, were left with the role of developing the principles and ideas of competition in the country. For this reason, the following is an analysis of the cases reviewed by these competition institutions.

In selecting the cases relevant to collusion, we have considered different issues. The period chosen was 1973 to 2003. The year 1973 was used as a starting point for the analysis because this is the date on which the Competition Act 1973 came into force; and in turn the year 2003 saw the last collusion case reviewed by the previous competition authorities (replaced by the Chilean TDLC under the Competition Act 2003).

As for the search mechanisms employed, the main resource used was the FNE's website,[14] which contains a link to all decisions issued by Chilean competition authorities before the change to the Competition Act. The practices searched for, selected from the 28 categories available in the website, were the following:

a) cartels;
b) horizontal agreements regarding prices;
c) horizontal agreements regarding production; and
d) horizontal agreements regarding exclusive markets.

The search produced 15 results for a), 110 for b), 7 for c), and 39 for d). However, some of these results were repeated in more than one category, so the total number of cases actually used in the database was 127.

Each result corresponds to one decision issued by the Resolutive Commission or by the Preventive Commissions. According to the Competition Act 1973, some cases were first decided by the Preventive Commissions and then reviewed before the Resolutive Commission, which had the power to issue a completely new ruling. In these type of situations, which represent 15.5 per cent of the total number of cases contained in the study, to maintain clarity, the database shows two separate decisions (even though they refer to the same matter).

The resource used to find Supreme Court decisions issued before 2003 was *Legal Publishing*, and the criterion used for the search was the quotation of the Chilean Competition Act, commonly referred to as 'DL 211' in the decision. The search produced 35 results. Because of the limited powers of the Supreme Court in the review procedure under the Competition Act 1973, as will be explained in section III, none of these results are relevant in this section. The reason is that in the great majority of cases—all of them when it comes to collusion—the Supreme Court confirmed the decisions of the Chilean competition authorities. Hence, in

---

[14] www.fne.cl.

this subsection the discussion focuses exclusively on the case law produced by the Resolutive and Preventive Commissions, excluding the Supreme Court. The institutional setting changes dramatically when the Supreme Court appears as a relevant actor in the system.

The most striking fact reflected in the time series data is the relative lack of importance of collusion cases in Chilean case law: only 6.3 per cent of the total number of competition cases from 1973 until 2003 are related to this topic. Graph 1 shows the proportion of collusion cases in relation to total number of cases in each year[15]:

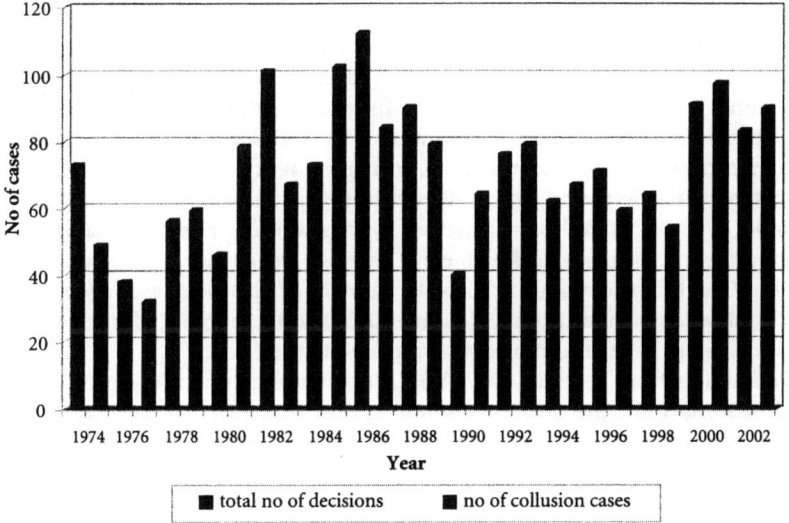

Graph 1 Total number of cases reviewed/number of collusion cases 1974–2003

It is clear from these numbers that a small number of cases from competition case law have been related to collusion. The reason for this may be partly found in the strong focus of Chilean enforcers on the freedom to compete. There is no straightforward set of data which serves as a baseline and shows exactly which proportion of cases corresponds to each of the other potentially anticompetitive practices. However, based on the 2004 OECD *Peer Review of Competition Policy*, in the period 1973–93 the competition authorities focused first on monopolization (abuse of dominance) cases, particularly on infrastructure monopolies, and secondly on vertical restraints.[16] This report categorizes Chile as a pioneer in the

---

[15] Source: National Economic Prosecutors Office.
[16] OECD (Terry Winslow), *Chile—Peer Review of Competition Policy* (2004), <www.pecd.org/dataoecd/7/41/35908641.pdf>.

field of dealing with infrastructure monopolies as part of the trade liberalization and privatization process carried out since 1973. Vertical restraints cases were initially considered anti-competitive, but the case law evolved and eventually became consistent with the generally accepted view that these practices are pro-competitive. Mergers also followed strong efficiency considerations and, similar to what happens with collusion, the authorities found very few cases to be anti-competitive. Overall, while it is true that the resources devoted to competition enforcement as from 1973 were scarce, and that this area was not a priority for public policy, competition policy developed alongside the process of privatization and deregulation of the economy, having its focus on the freedom to compete; a criterion which left out practices of collusive behaviour.

From the existing 127 cartel-related decisions, it is possible to observe an evolution in the criteria used to analyse these cases, as well as two different trends over time. The first trend corresponds to the period between 1973 and 1987, and is characterized by a relatively high number of collusion cases and a relatively high number of decisions involving an infringement of the law. The second trend corresponds to the period from 1988 onwards, and shows a decline both in the number of cases of collusion reviewed by competition authorities and in the infringement decisions issued by them. These two trends may be clearly appreciated in Graph 2 below, which shows the number of collusion cases reviewed by competition authorities from 1974 until 2003, and the number of infringement decisions issued by the commissions from among these cases.

Period 1 is from 1973 to 1987. This is the stage at which the competition commissions took the strongest stand against collusion (in relative terms) before the enforcement of the Competition Act 2003. It is important to note

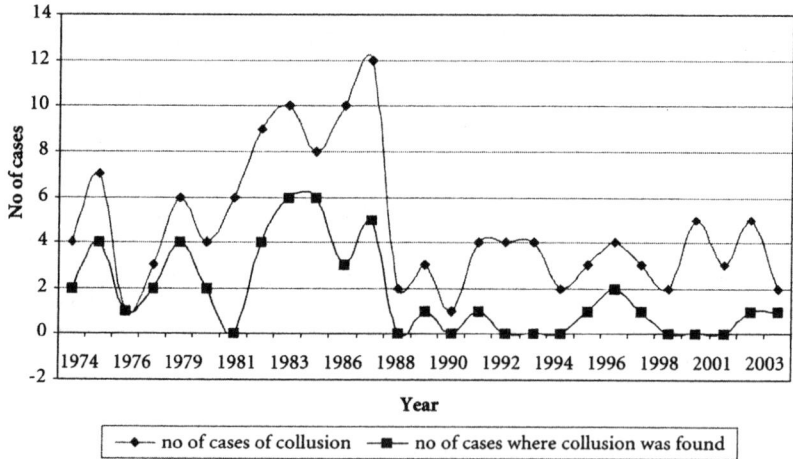

Graph 2 Collusion cases reviewed by Chilean competition authorities 1974–2003

that this stand was not always based on strong legal or economic theory, and that it was not particularly consistent among cases. Despite these difficulties, from the analysis it is clear that there were at least two relevant concepts developed by the competition authorities during this time frame regarding collusion: the prohibition of market sharing agreements, and the 'price identity rule'. Other types of collusion agreements, not based on price or market sharing, received little or no attention, so they must be excluded from this analysis.[17] The prohibition of market sharing agreements is perhaps the only practice that has clearly received strict enforcement by competition authorities. An example of the prohibition of market sharing is *Coca-Cola*,[18] in which the Commission vetoed part of a contract subscribed by the undertaking and its bottlers, which created a geographic division of the country into exclusive territories among the bottlers. Moreover, by 1976 the Central Preventive Commission asserted that market sharing agreements were objectively or 'per se' illegal.[19] This approach towards market sharing agreements has not seen any major changes since then, and it was maintained during the second period (post-1988) as well.[20]

With regard to price agreements, the approach during these early years was also stronger than after 1988, but it was always more inconsistent, and even erratic, when compared with what happened with market sharing agreements. An example of the stronger approach towards price agreements is found in *Airline-Exchange Rate*,[21] in which the Commission issued an infringement decision against airline companies for overcharging an equal amount above the exchange rate to their customers. In connection with price agreements, a primitive 'price identity rule' was developed, establishing that price identity was an indication of collusion.[22] The application and use of this rule varied significantly among cases and within its scope.

The second period is from 1987 to 2003. In 1987, the Resolutive Commission, overturning a decision taken by a Regional Preventive Commission, declared that price identity was not a certain indicator of collusion; rather, price identity may also indicate perfect competition in the market.[23] This was one of the decisions that represented a new approach towards collusion cases: while in the first period 39 infringement decisions were issued, only seven infringement rulings were issued in the second period. Graph 3 below shows a comparison between the number of collusion cases in the first and the second period, as

---

[17] The other type of agreements reviewed by competition authorities (worth mentioning) were related to collusive tendering or bid rigging, but they amount to a total of 8 cases for the whole period 1973–2003.

[18] *Coca Cola*, Central Preventive Commission (1975), 69-6.

[19] *Aluminio*, Central Preventive Commission (1976), 129.

[20] However, there are very few cases post-1988 that deal with market sharing agreements.

[21] *Airline Exchange Rate*, Central Preventive Commission (1982), 346/792.

[22] See, eg, Concepción Regional Preventive Commission (1974), 5.

[23] *Dirinco con Estaciones de Servicio*, Central Preventive Commission (1987), 244.

well as a comparison of the number of infringement decisions issued in both periods of time:

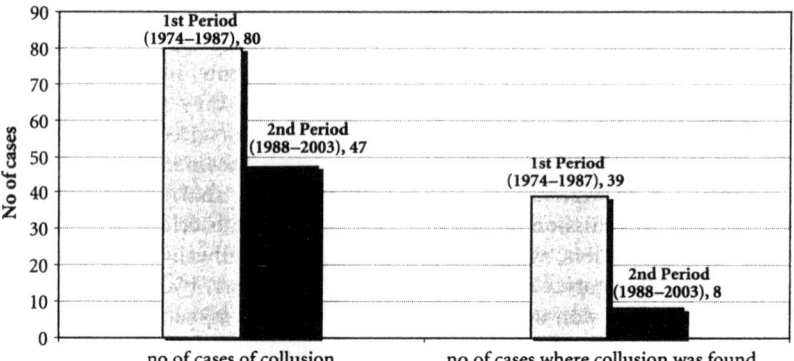

Graph 3 Comparison of no of collusion cases in Chile over two periods: 1974–87 and 1988–2003

From the seven infringement decisions issued in the second period, five of them are related to the public transport industry, and the fines imposed in these cases were insignificant. The remaining two cases refer to different industries: one of them fined pharmacy chains for colluding in retail prices, and the other one fined airlines for colluding to stop entry into the industry using a simultaneous and identical decrease in price.[24] The former decision was accompanied by abundant evidence, including witnesses and confessions. The latter decision is the only precedent for tacit collusion practices, stating that 'it is clear that they acted, at least, tacitly colluded',[25] hinting that the proof of tacit collusion is not as strict as is demanded today by the Supreme Court, as explained below.

Having described the existence of these two periods in the approach of Chilean case law to collusion, we next offer a hypothesis that explains the change in this approach. The hypothesis for the change of criteria in these periods is that we believe that the position adopted from 1973 until 1987 was to a great extent explained by the economic, political and social context of the country during those years. More specifically, as mentioned above, the economy was being liberalized and deregulated, which meant competition authorities needed to deal with industries that were just learning how to react to market forces, and with new law decrees that aimed to govern certain activities in these new circumstances. Hence, during this time, many of the decisions issued by the competition commissions had more to do with contributing to liberalization and adapting to a new

---

[24] Resolutive Commission (1995), 432.
[25] Consideration 9 of Resolutive Commission (1995), 432.

economic reality than with a strong enforcement against collusion itself. Chile completed the liberalization process for the most part by the end of the 1980s. This led to a more stable market economy. This date coincides with the change of criteria used by competition authorities when reviewing collusion cases.

Some examples of how the economic context influenced collusion cases during the first period, which support our hypothesis, are as follows:

a) Nearly 10 per cent of all collusion cases in both periods are related to the bread industry, and almost 80 per cent of these were reviewed in the period 1973–87. Before the first period, the bread price was fixed by the Government, so the first cases that the competition commissions reviewed were related to structuring cost models for bread without entering into a collusive agreement.[26]

b) Another 10 per cent of all cases (and again 80 per cent of these occurred in the first period) are related to certain law decrees issued by the Government, and their compatibility with competition law and collusive agreements. For example, the commissions reviewed many cases relating to the new laws applicable to the taxi industry and whether these laws facilitated or encouraged collusion practices in the market.[27]

c) During the period 1973–87, 10 per cent of all collusion cases were based on surveys carried out by the DIRINCO. The DIRINCO was the National Bureau of Industry and Trade, created in 1980 in order to preserve market transparency and ensure consumer protection. In 1990 DIRINCO was replaced by the National Consumer Service. The importance of this organization for competition was that it carried out price surveys in different areas of the country, particularly focused on food-related products, and if it found that there was a price identity among sellers, it filed a competition claim. The cases initiated by the DIRINCO constituted an important part of the caseload of the competition commissions during the first period, and these had the advantage of containing some form of pre-prepared evidence like the above-mentioned surveys. The DIRINCO disappeared completely in 1990, which coincides with the change of criteria from competition authorities. In regard to this point, note that the surveys carried out by the DIRINCO were usually limited to a few sellers from a particular region, and on average they referred to three- or four-day periods. Consequently, we believe that any decision issued exclusively according to this evidence was insufficient to establish collusion.

The examples mentioned above show how the decisions issued by competition commissions were strongly influenced by factors related to the economic background of the country, perhaps more than they were influenced by competition concerns. After 1987 most collusion cases seem to fit better into the 'traditional

---

[26] See Central Preventive Commission (1978), 191/312.
[27] Central Preventive Commission (1981), 5/434-278*bis.*

competition case' scenario, in which a company or the FNE filed a claim against two or more undertakings for engaging in collusive behaviour. It is during this second period when the number of cases of collusion, as well as of infringement decisions, experienced a rather drastic decline and the lack of trust in antitrust in collusion decisions began to show more clearly.[28] Perhaps the exception to this lack of trust is in market sharing agreements, which have produced infringement decisions by competition authorities.

B. The Present: 2003 to Date

The Competition Act 2003 produced dramatic changes in competition law and enforcement in Chile. This amendment encouraged a more active and stronger approach towards potential anti-competitive practices, and collusion has been no exception to this rule. The TDLC meets regularly and has members that specialize in competition matters, which has meant more and better enforcement of competition law in the country. However, while it is true that the TDLC has taken important steps towards a more consistent legal and economic approach to cases, there is still a gap in economic arguments, particularly in the empirical evidence submitted in the cases.

In relation to collusive agreements, the Competition Act 2003 is more explicit than its predecessor in forbidding collusion, punishing:

> [e]xpress or implied agreements between business agents or concerted practices between them having the intent of fixing sale or purchase prices, limiting production or assigning themselves market zones or quotas, abusing the power conferred upon them by such agreements or practices.[29]

Again, the substantive provision of the law is quite short, leaving its exact determination to the case law produced by competition authorities. As of July 2008, there have been seven TDLC decisions regarding collusive agreements, plus three cases that are still pending on this matter. This case load represents just 8 per cent of the total case load of the tribunal, but we believe that this percentage is highly influenced by two facts. First, there is currently a Bill being debated in Congress that introduces a leniency program and gives more powers to the FNE to prosecute cartel cases. It is very likely that potential claimants in collusion cases are waiting for this Bill to be approved. Secondly, there is a strong deterrent in the fact that the Supreme Court has managed to overturn *every* decision of the TDLC in which collusion was found, as explained below. As discussed below, as a result of the Supreme Court intervention, the TDLC has established that the determination of a collusive agreement is possible only if there is an abuse of dominant position.

---

[28] Other possible explanations for the cautious approach towards collusion adopted by Chilean competition authorities have been given by the OECD in its *Peer Review*, based on the fact that Chilean case law has focused on infrastructure and natural monopolies, and consequently other anti-competitive practices have been overlooked.

[29] Competition Act 2003, above n 6.

In reality, this new approach to collusion is already having effects: collusion claims are being filed as monopolization (abuse of dominance) cases, and the collusive agreement is treated as a secondary issue.

Despite the encouragement given to competition law by the amendment, once again the lack of trust in antitrust appeared, this time under the form of an empowered player in the competition system—the Supreme Court. The nature of the new powers conferred on this institution will be discussed in detail later; for now, suffice it to say that the Supreme Court can overturn the decisions made by the TDLC. This aspect of the new Act has represented a strike against competition law and policy, particularly since November 29, 2006, the date on which the Supreme Court handed down the first decision to overturn the findings of the TDLC.[30] Moreover, two out of the three overturning decisions made by the Supreme Court (in a six-month period) have been connected to collusion, so the impact has been particularly severe as regards this issue.

As mentioned before, seven cases of collusion were decided by the TDLC in the period of 2004 to January 2008, from which:

— The TDLC rejected three cases; from these three, the Supreme Court permitted one appeal, in which it confirmed the decision taken by the TDLC.
— Two cases involved infringement or violation decisions issued by the TDLC. The Supreme Court overturned both of these decisions. In these two cases, the TDLC had imposed significant fines.
— The TDLC rejected one decision (Isapres), and a decision of the Supreme Court recently confirmed the TDLC's ruling. The difference between this decision and the three rejected decisions already mentioned is that this one shows the influence that the Supreme Court's overturning of decisions has had on the TDLC. Had these overturning decisions had not taken place, the TDLC probably would have issued an infringement decision.
— One decision was an infringement ruling issued by the TDLC, and as of July 2008 it was still pending before the Supreme Court. This decision was based, first, on abuse of dominance and, secondly, on collusion.

Given their importance for this chapter, we will discuss the two infringement decisions overturned by the Supreme Court, as well as the last two cases mentioned above.

1. Asoex[31]

The Chilean National Association of Exporters filed a claim against several shipping agencies (which represent the shipping companies), alleging, among other things, that these agencies had colluded to impose a tariff for an additional

---

[30] In *James Hardie*, Supreme Court (2006), 3449/2006. This was the first time the Supreme Court overturned a decision made by the Competition Tribunal regarding a predatory pricing case.
[31] *Asoex*, Competition Tribunal (2006), 38-2006; *Asoex*, Supreme Court (2006), 33715.

approval for bills of lading. The TDLC determined that this mandatory tariff was the consequence of a collusive agreement between the shipping agencies. The main factors used to reach this conclusion were the simultaneity in the start of this tariff, as well as the similarity of tariff amounts between shipping agencies. The TDLC also considered the existence of facilitating factors for collusion, such as the fact that exporters had no choice of shipping agencies, the existence of barriers to entry, and market concentration.

A crucial point needs to be made: as in all the other cases to be described, in this one there was no direct or hard evidence of an agreement between the undertakings. However, this lack of evidence should be interpreted cautiously in the context of current Chilean law. The FNE has no powers to inspect the premises of the undertakings; it can only request information from the parties involved in the investigation. In turn, there is no leniency policy to rely on for obtaining further proof of collusion. Considering these two points together, plus the fact that collusive agreements are usually secretive and parties try to hide any evidence of their existence,[32] it could be asserted that it is highly likely that competition authorities in Chile will never be able to obtain direct evidence of collusion agreements. This will be true, however, only until the approval of the Bill that lies in the Chilean Congress, which addresses this issue (among others).

In this context, a lack of direct evidence in a case may signal two possibilities. The first possibility is tacit collusion in the form of conscious parallelism, but the illegality of this practice, according to international competition law, is questionable (for example, in Europe it has been considered that parallel behaviour is punishable only if there are no other alternate plausible explanations for the conduct of the undertakings, among other conditions). In Chile the law is clear: implicit agreements are an offense to competition law. The second possibility is that it may be a function of explicit collusion, but with no direct evidence to prove the agreement. Whatever the scenario, the chances of having the evidence necessary to demonstrate collusion are very low. Keeping this in mind, we describe the Supreme Court decision which overturned the *Asoex* case.

The Supreme Court decision concluded that there was no agreement between the shipping agencies. The main argument used by this institution to reach this result was that there was a lack of evidence. The Court stated that, in a collusion case, the following conditions should be shown:

a) that the behaviour of the undertakings is a result of a concerted practice; and
b) the existence of intent (*mens rea*).

Hence, the standard of proof for collusion was elevated by the Supreme Court. This new standard of proof has produced several reactions in the legal community, which have taken the form of proposals contained in the Bill being debated in Congress.

---

[32] A Jones and B E Sufrin, *EC Competition Law: Text Cases and Materials* (Oxford, Oxford University Press, 2008).

Building Trust in Antitrust: The Chilean Case   173

2. Oxígeno[33]

The FNE filed a claim against oxygen providers for bid rigging in an auction held by the Government to provide oxygen products for the public health system. The TDLC considered this to be a case of collusive tendering for different reasons:

a) the fact that the prices offered by the oxygen providers to public hospitals before the auction were lower than those offered in the auction itself; and
b) that the market incentives existed in the opposite direction (prices should have been lower after the auction).

There was a dissenting vote in this decision from one of the judges, and this is relevant because it anticipates the criteria to be used in the *Isapres* decision (described below). The *Oxígeno* dissenting vote stated that there was not enough evidence to prove the agreement between the undertakings, and that Article 3 of the Competition Act required:

a) an agreement;
b) with an anti-competitive objective; and
c) market power and abuse of this market power.[34]

The vote asserted that condition c) had not been met. This is the first glimpse we get of the new trend followed by Chilean case law towards demanding the existence of an abuse of dominant position to establish collusion. When overturning this decision, the Supreme Court agreed with the dissenting vote, asserting that there was not enough evidence to prove a collusive agreement.

3. Isapres[35]

The FNE filed a claim against several *Isapre* companies (privately run health insurers), accusing them of a collusive agreement which resulted in simultaneously reducing their health coverage from 100–80 per cent (100 per cent of hospital care and 80 per cent of ambulatory procedures) to 90–70 per cent. The Tribunal held that the three conditions mentioned in the minority vote in *Oxígeno* (above) were necessary to establish collusion. The TDLC also analyzed the existence of barriers to entry and other facilitating factors of collusion, such as concentrated markets, frequent interaction between undertakings and information exchange. Despite the fact that all these factors were found to exist, the TDLC decided that there was no agreement among the parties because there might be an alternate explanation for the practice: that of an oligopoly's parallel behavior. This decision was issued with 3 votes in favor

---

[33] *Oxigeno*, Competition Tribunal (2006), 43-2006; *Oxigeno*, Supreme Court (2007), 5057-2006.
[34] *Oxigeno*, Competition Tribunal (2006), 43-2006.
[35] *Isapres*, Competition Tribunal (2007), 57/2007; Isapres, Supreme Court (2008), 4052-07.

and 2 votes dissenting. This case had abundant evidence (although indirect) to prove collusion, and hence it is likely that the TDLC would have reached a different conclusion if it believed that the Supreme Court would not overturn its decision. Consequently, the effects of the Supreme Court intervention in the system may have had an anticipatory effect in shaping the rulings issued by the TDLC.

The TDLC was right in its anticipation—the Supreme Court recently confirmed its decision by three votes to two.[36] In doing so, it reproduced the conditions required by the TDLC as proof before sanctioning a collusive agreement:

a) the existence of an agreement;
b) the influence of such agreement in a relevant element of competition; and
c) that the agreement should enable the parties to abuse the market power they obtain, maintain or increase through it.[37]

The intervention of the Supreme Court in the competition system has turned out to be particularly damaging to the fight against collusion by the Competition Act 2003. The influence of the Supreme Court is probably related to the fact that the first collusion case was accepted with 5:0 votes, the second one was accepted by 4:1 votes and the third was rejected by 3:2 votes.

However, it is important to note that while the Supreme Court has raised the standard of proof for collusion, the TDLC, perhaps in an attempt to avoid having its decisions overturned, has reacted by developing the theory that collusion cases also need to demonstrate an abuse of dominant position. The effects of the former doctrine might be even more harmful than the Supreme Court intervention if it this is interpreted as the need to add a claim of an abuse of dominant position to the collusion claim. This development is extremely confusing: does this mean that collusion by itself is not enough?

We believe that these questions lead to a lack of clarity as to what practice is being punished (collusion, dominant position or both) and which conditions should be met to evidence them. Moreover, this interpretation leaves no room for a 'per se' approach to collusive agreements, making the evidentiary issue of proof of this conduct more difficult to obtain. The TDLC dissenting vote in *Isapres* (2008) argued that the abuse of a dominant position should not be part of the conditions required by law to establish a collusive agreement. However, the Supreme Court rejected the dissenting vote when it confirmed the TDLC ruling. The result of this new approach towards collusion can clearly be appreciated in the next decision analyzed.

---

[36] For the first time there was as divided decision from the Supreme Court in collusion matters. The minority vote asserts that the only condition that should be met is that the act has the potential to harm competition in the market (or effectively does).

[37] *Isapres*, Supreme Court (2008), 4052-07.

4. Falabella-Paris[38]

The FNE filed a claim against two big retail chains for stopping their electronic suppliers from participating in a technology fair organized by a banking institution. The allegation was that the retail chains had stopped their suppliers because the terms of sale offered in the fair were better than the ones offered in their retail stores, so these retail chains threatened their suppliers with sanctions if they participated in the fair. The FNE alleged that both retail chains had communicated with each other and jointly agreed to threaten their suppliers. Probably because of the new approach developed by the TDLC, the main allegation of the prosecutor in this case was that there was an abuse of dominance by the retailers. According to the allegation, such abuse was made worse because of the collusive agreement between the parties. The TDLC, following the allegation, condemned the parties for abuse of dominance aggravated by collusion, and imposed the highest fine ever applied in a competition case in Chile, over US $6 million. The TDLC focused its analysis on abuse of dominance, devoting almost no analysis to collusion. This decision seems to show that collusion enforcement is stepping away from a 'per se' approach. In any case, the parties have used the judicial review procedure to file a claim against this ruling before the Supreme Court, which to date is pending.

The Supreme Court's overturning of decisions and the new approach to collusion developed by the TDLC as a response to the Supreme Court have meant that collusion enforcement in Chile has been deterred once again. The role given to the Supreme Court in the institutional design has been particularly damaging for competition law overall and, within competition law, for collusion cases.

III. Institutional Reforms in the Chilean Antitrust System

A. Introduction

Effectively, the Competition Act 2003 has created more powerful institutions to enforce competition policy, but the lack of investigatory tools given to the FNE and the key role granted to the Supreme Court as an ultimate decision-maker both demonstrate that trust has been excessively limited in Chilean competition policy. Also, there are problems as regards the institutional communication between the TDLC and the Supreme Court.

This section will discuss two main points. First, there is a Bill in Congress that proposes granting more powers to the FNE to investigate collusive agreements, which is a signal of trust in this institution. Secondly, these new powers, as well

---

[38] *Falabella-Paris*, Competition Tribunal (2008), 63/2008.

as the general encouragement given to the law by the Competition Act 2003, may be overshadowed by the institutional design in terms of the role played by the Supreme Court.

However, we believe that the answer to this problem is not the re-design of the system, but rather the correct interpretation given to Chilean competition law and, consequently, to the judicial review procedure. In this sense, the understanding of competition law in Chile as part of Administrative Criminal Law and the categorization of the TDLC as an administrative agency will lead to the conclusion that judicial review, established in competition law, grants the Supreme Court the power to overturn decisions only when due process has not been followed. It does not grant the Supreme Court the right to overturn decisions based on technical issues of competition law and economics. In other words, this interpretation leads the way towards the use of the principle of deference by the Supreme Court towards the TDLC. Moreover, we believe that this deference could be further improved by adequate communication between competition institutions.

Before analyzing this, there are several improvements which have been made in Chile since the Competition Act 2003, worth mentioning as relevant steps towards the development of antitrust enforcement and the creation of a competition culture. There are elements incorporated into the Competition Act 2003 that appear as clear signs of trust in the system, in the sense that they improve the autonomy and expertise of the TDLC. First, it can be observed that one of the most important claims against the structure of the institutions established by the Competition Act 1973 was the lack of personal independence from the Government of the members of the commissions.[39] In the past there have been controversies surrounding members of the commissions appointed by the Government, who at the same time were civil servants or held other posts in the gift of the President.[40] This changed with the Competition Act 2003, and now the members of the Tribunal are appointed after an open process in which anyone meeting the expertise and legal requirements can participate, and civil servants are excluded. An additional aspect in relation to the personal independence of the members of the Tribunal is the fact that they are currently paid, changing the unusual previous situation of serving *ad honorem*.

[39] Menchaca, above n 10.

[40] A case that captured attention was that of the price caps in relation to the incumbent telecom company, in which one of the members of the old Tribunal (the *Comisión Resolutiva*), who also was the energy regulator appointed by the Government, was going to vote against the position expressed by the Government (favoring the telecom company's position). At the time, Mr Espejo, who later served as a Secretary of State of Transport and Telecommunications, resigned from the Tribunal. His resignation was interpreted as a response to the pressure he received from the Government to change his vote. The Chilean Congress investigated this case, and the Deputies approved a non-statutory proposal which recommended that the Government should not impose any pressure or intervention in the regulatory processes.

A second way in which the position of competition authorities has been strengthened is by the fact that the TDLC has been given complete budgetary independence; formerly it was funded by the Ministry of Finance. Moreover, there has been a separation between the TDLC and the FNE, which is a way to mirror the success of the Criminal Procedure Reform implemented in the country in 2000. In this sense, following the institutional typology of Trebilcock and Iacobucci,[41] the current system is close to a *bifurcated model.*

B. Investigatory Powers and Judicial Review Design: Blocking the Trust?

So far, it seems that this has been a happy tale, and that after 30 years of experience in competition policy enforcement, it was time for the institutions to develop and show signs of growth, together with relative economic and political stability. Nevertheless, two problems with the Competition Act 2003 have become evident. Analyzed as a whole, the 2003 Act tries to protect the right to a fair trial by extending the 'appeal'[42] procedure, but it forgets that the nature of the TDLC is highly specialized, and that the Supreme Court is unlikely to have enough knowledge and expertise in competition law and economics. The second issue, mentioned in the next subsection, is that according to the Competition Act 2003, in reality, the investigatory powers given to the FNE have been limited, particularly as regards collusion cases. Overall, the problem has been that both issues of combine to frustrate the efforts of the rest of the team.

The key question here is whether these two problems stem from an imperfect institutional design, or from something deeper. At first sight, the answer seems to be the latter, given the experience with other important reforms implemented in Chile. To take an example, the Criminal Procedure Reform was managed in a similar way, and the result of the whole amendment can be considered to have been fairly successful. In that case, the Congress first approved only the most important provisions changing the former criminal system, including an amendment to the Constitution. It was a year after the approval that it agreed to undertake the further necessary reforms, in what was called the Adaptation Bill. This legislative technique was indeed innovative for Chile in implementing important changes.

Was the intention to follow the same legislative technique for competition policy? There is no mention of this in the discussions of the Competition Act 2003, but it might be arguable that this was the case—after the reformed institutions had been in practice for two years, a new Bill (about leniency policy and others) was introduced.

---

[41] Trebilcock and Iacobucci, above n 9.

[42] As we will argue later, the existing judicial review procedure has been treated, improperly, as an appeal.

1. *Investigatory powers*

At the time of the Competition Act 2003, it seemed that the powers of the FNE were sufficient for undertaking any investigation about a competition offense. The Competition Act 2003 gave the FNE the power to:

a) require the collaboration of any public servant or anyone employed by municipalities or nationalized industries;
b) require from any person the information or documents necessary for conducting the investigation; and
c) issue subpoenas to those who might have knowledge of the investigated practices.

All of these powers carried the possibility of issuing an arrest warrant if there is a failure to comply with the prosecutor's order. Apart from these, however, there were no further provisions concerning investigatory powers; at the time of the Competition Act 2003, though, these powers were considered proportionate and sufficient for the FNE.

Nevertheless, as discussed above, collecting the evidence has proved to be a difficult task, particularly in tacit collusion cases. Additionally, as has been already mentioned, the TDLC and the Supreme Court have dismissed tacit collusion,[43] which means that under the current legislation they would be unlikely to punish any collusion at all. For this reason, Congress introduced a Bill in 2006, amending various aspects of the Competition Act 2003.

According to this Bill, it would be possible that on certain conditions, in collusion cases, the FNE could make a request to a judge of the Court of Appeal (the one on duty corresponding to territorial jurisdiction). The request would allow the existing police institutions, under the direction of staff members of the FNE, to undertake dawn raids. In this regard, the Bill makes applicable to competition law the conditions and procedure of the Criminal Procedure Act.

These tools were heavily criticized by some people who testified before the Select Committee of Economy of the Chamber of Deputies in the first phase of the Bill's proceedings.[44] For example, a representative of a policy institute linked to right-wing political parties, *Libertad y Desarrollo*, stated that:

> [I]t does not seem convenient to empower the Office of the Economic Prosecutor with faculties that simply belong to a criminal investigation, which—in any case—affect constitutionally protected rights, such as people's privacy and intimacy, and the protection of privacy of forms of communications. ... In any case, the interception of communications does not seem justified.[45]

---

[43] *Oxigeno*, Supreme Court (2007), 5057-2006.
[44] Chamber of Deputies, Report of the Select Committee of Economy, 2006, Bill No 4324-03-1.
[45] *Ibid*, at 23.

Building Trust in Antitrust: The Chilean Case   179

This is indeed a very central point in the way that it focuses the debate on the nature of legal provisions concerning competition enforcement, ie whether they fit into a civil or criminal law category. This is an important consideration, particularly under Chilean law, in which a clear division between these two areas has been vital to the application and enforcement of the entire legal system. This separation causes procedural systems, rights and enforcement to differentiate dramatically, and thus it is critical to investigate the civil or criminal nature of Chilean competition law, not only to analyze the powers granted to the Prosecutor's Office but to deduce further relevant elements that may help to solve other issues.

Some scholars argue that competition offences under Chilean law have a civil nature, or at least that they do not have a criminal connotation. In so arguing, they are mainly influenced by some of the provisions of the Competition Act 2003 that prescribe that in the absence of an express procedural rule, the Civil Procedure Code should be applied. However, these references do not indicate the legal nature of the competition offenses, but rather are procedural rules with a general scope.[46]

We believe that competition offenses under Chilean law are a somewhat special situation, which cannot be classified exactly as civil or criminal in nature. As with other regulatory areas, this is a mixed area, which fits better into the sub-discipline of administrative law or *administrative criminal law*. Indeed, the norms belong to administrative law, because they are enforced by an administrative agency, the TDLC, and the TDLC's function is of an administrative nature. This function consists in responding to binding consultations in non-dispute cases and in deciding dispute cases; and the exact object of this administrative activity is a manifestation of the power of the State to punish offenses: what is called in Chile the *ius puniendi* of the state.

In this regard, the Chilean system of administrative criminal law, the *Derecho Administrativo Sancionador*, applies core principles of criminal law on the grounds that administrative offenses are manifestations of the *ius puniendi* of the State, as the Constitutional Court, the Supreme Court and other national courts of appeals have ruled.[47] Despite the differences between 'truly' criminal law and administrative criminal law, Chilean judicial decisions have not evidenced any lessening in the application of the general principles of criminal law

---

[46] One of the references of the Competition Act 2003 (Art 22) to the Civil Procedure Act is in relation to the evidence produced: 'There shall be admissible all the evidence indicated in Article 341 of the Civil Procedure Code.' However, this does not imply that this is the only form of evidence admissible, as the Competition Act adds: '... and any other evidence or record that, in opinion of the Tribunal, might be relevant for establishing the facts'. The second reference is a generic one, in relation to the procedure as a whole, filling possible procedural regulatory gaps with the 'General Rules for Judicial Procedures' and 'Ordinary Dispute Resolution Procedure', contained in the Civil Procedure Act.

[47] STC 389-2003, Spanish Constitutional Court (2003), STC 376-2003, Spanish Constitutional Court (2003), STC 479-2006, Spanish Constitutional Court (2006), STC 480-2006, Spanish Constitutional Court (2006), Administradora de Fondos de Pensiones con Superintendencia, Santiago Court of Appeal (2005), 2078-2005, Castillo con Inspección del Trabajo, Temuco Court of Appeal (2007).

to administrative offences. This situation may be compared with that in other jurisdictions, both civil law countries and common law countries, as shown below.

In Spain (another civil law jurisdiction) there has been a slightly different trend in this area. The Constitutional Court and the Supreme Court have ruled that the same set of principles from criminal law must be applicable to administrative offenses, but adapted and attenuated.[48] However, some core principles, such as *mens rea*, are not affected by this attenuation, and it has been ruled that it is against the Spanish Constitution to apply an administrative penalty if the required intent is absent.[49] This is particularly relevant for the Chilean case. As mentioned before, there, *mens rea* is required to the same degree as intent in a criminal offence.

Comparing this area of law in a common law jurisdiction (Canada), it is possible to match this requirement to the decision in *R v Wholesale Travel Group Inc.*[50] One of the arguments behind this decision was the distinction between 'regulatory offences' as opposed to 'truly criminal' ones, the former having a lesser degree of protection than the latter for the purposes of the requirement of *mens rea*. Canadian courts applied the same criteria in another leading case, *R v Nova Scotia Pharmaceutical Society*,[51] which addressed the requirements of collusion.

These references are made with a solely comparative purpose, taking examples from both civil and common law jurisdictions,[52] highlighting that under Chilean law, even if the scholarship has not paid too much attention to the legal nature of competition law infractions, the courts are starting to interpret similar conduct according to the category of administrative criminal law. Under such a label, it has been recognized that there is no less protection than in the case of criminal offences. Particularly in the case of collusion, the Supreme Court has played an important role, requiring the same *mens rea* called for in criminal offenses. We agree with this approach of the Chilean Supreme Court, despite the fact that the Court has not always deferred to the TDLC with regard to the analysis of proof.[53] In other words, we believe that requiring intent for collusion cases, as the Supreme

---

[48] STC 169/1998, Spanish Constitutional Court (1998); STC 129/2003, Spanish Constitutional Court (2003); STC 18/1981, Spanish Constitutional Court (1981); STC 56/1998, Spanish Constitutional Court (1998); STC 54/2003, Spanish Constitutional Court (2003); STC 9/2003, Spanish Constitutional Court (2003); STC 146/1994, Spanish Constitutional Court (1994); STC 316/2006, Spanish Constitutional Court (2006), among other rulings.

[49] STC 76/1990, Spanish Constitutional Court (1990).

[50] [1991] 3 SCR 154R, Supreme Court of Canada.

[51] [1992] 2 SCR 606, Supreme Court of Canada.

[52] The nature of legal concepts and institutions matters in both common and civil law systems. It has been commonplace to criticize civil law jurisdictions as being too concerned about the nature of institutions, instead of applying them to cases in practice. Here, however, the consideration of whether a public body is an administrative institution or not, or whether a grievance mechanism is properly an appeal or judicial review, changes all the analyses and consequences.

[53] Although the Supreme Court is not the only one to blame for this lack of deference, as the TDLC has not put forward convincing arguments when giving its reasons for accepting the facts as proved.

Court has done, is consistent with general legal principles existing in Chile under administrative criminal law; but this does not mean that the evidence threshold necessary to demonstrate such intent is nearly as high as pretended by the Supreme Court. As long as the TDLC is clear in proving the facts of the offense, the Supreme Court will restrain its control.

Considering that the transgression and the proceedings for investigating and penalizing that conduct are of an administrative criminal nature, this enables the FNE to use a set of tools, ie legal mechanisms, sufficient to undertake its functions.

When the granting of these investigative tools was debated in Congress, it was alleged that giving them to the FNE might affect constitutionally protected rights, ie the right to a fair trial and investigation,[54] and, as in this particular case, those fundamental rights related to the protection of privacy.

These allegations can be interpreted as evidencing an element of distrust in competition enforcement, due to the building of a culture in which these types of illegal conduct have not been perceived negatively as offenses to society. They can also be interpreted as distrust in this kind of institution (FNE), as opposed to the trust shown when dealing with criminal offenses that are handled by the judiciary and the National Criminal Prosecutor.

In Chile, it would not be lawful for the FNE to undertake investigations employing certain investigative mechanisms (eg, intercepting communications) without its being empowered to do so by an Act of Parliament, particularly in the case of the exercise of fundamental rights, according to what Chilean constitutional law calls the doctrine of 'statutory reserve' (*principio de reserva legal*). Therefore, the only realistic way of bringing cases of collusion before the TDLC would be by enhancing the powers vested in the Office of the National Economic Prosecutor.

To sum up this point, it seems that putting into practice the Competition Act 2003 has been positive for building trust. This trust has been tested by the parliamentary discussion of the reform that will extend the powers of the FNE to act in a way similar to the Criminal Prosecutor. More than the discussion of the nature of the offenses contained in the Competition Act, the acceptance that fighting cartels requires more power is indeed a demonstration of a growing confidence in the competition system. However, this somewhat optimistic conclusion cannot compensate for the effects left by the institutional designers in establishing the Supreme Court as the ultimate decision-maker of the system.

2. Judicial Review: the Recurso de Reclamación

The new system of judicial review, *Recurso de Reclamación*, established by the Competition Act 2003, has been considerably extended in comparison with the review procedure applicable under the Competition Act 1973. Under the 2003

---

[54] Chilean Constitution, at Art 19 No 3.

Act, where there is dispute between the parties (non-consultative cases), the TDLC is entitled to:

a) modify or terminate acts, contracts, agreements, systems or arrangements entered into contrary to the provisions of the Competition Act;
b) order the amendment or dissolution of partnerships, corporations and other legal entities of private law involved in acts, contracts, agreements, systems or arrangements referred to in a); and
c) apply fines.[55]

In all these situations it is possible to apply for judicial review of the decision of the TDLC. The standing rules state that the FNE or the parties in the case are the only possible applicants.

The new system also entitles interested parties to seek judicial review in non-dispute cases, in which the applicant requires binding advice from the TDLC (as a preventive mechanism) and[56] the Tribunal's binding response to that consultation consists in meeting certain conditions in order to comply with the Competition Act 2003. Here, the standing rules require that only the FNE and interested parties can apply for review.[57]

Under the Competition Act 2003, the Supreme Court can examine a broader range of decisions. In practice this means that the Supreme Court has tended to analyze every detail of the TDLC's reasoning, without consideration of whether this require any economic or specific legal expertise. In other words, the Supreme Court has been 'invited' to be the ultimate decision-maker in the competition system, and the Court has warmly accepted this invitation. As might be expected, the result is that when the decisions of the Supreme Court are related to the rights of the parties in the proceedings before the TDLC, the Court's rulings have been satisfactory and consistent with legal principles; but in those parts of the decisions involving competition law and economics, the Court has struggled to make sensible arguments.[58]

We estimate that the causes of this failure in design can be traced back to a lack of trust in competition policy by the legislators, together with the ill-defined nature of the TDLC and of the *Recurso de Reclamación* itself. All of the above can be explained if the TDLC is considered a judicial body, with all the characteristics

---

[55] Competition Act 2003, Art 26.

[56] Function formerly performed by the Preventive Commissions (one in each region of the country, plus the Central Preventive Commission).

[57] The current criterion of the Supreme Court is that the interest will exist when the party is directly affected by the decision of the TDLC. It has been understood that competitors in the relevant market always have sufficient interest to use the judicial review procedure, as does the FNE as guardian of the public interest in this area. However, standing is denied when the interested party seeking judicial review has not acted as an opposing party before the TDLC.

[58] E Cruz, 'Precios Predatorios y Libre Competencia' *Revista Anales de Derecho UC. Temas de Libre Competencia* (2007).

of a court of the judiciary, and not as an adjudicating administrative agency. In this scenario the *Reclamación* is conceived of as an appeal in which there is no deference whatsoever from the Court towards the TDLC. However, we argue that the real nature of the *Recurso de Reclamación* is a judicial review mechanism, established primarily in the Constitution.

It is necessary first to understand the logic behind the *Recurso de Reclamación*, as it is commonly forgotten in this area. The *Reclamación* is intended to cover what is known as 'judicial review'; it is not an appeal procedure: not even an appeal on a point of law is allowed. The Competition Act states that the decisions of the Tribunal described above can be challenged through the *Reclamación*, and apart from the standing rules, the Act does not make any other mention of it. In this sense, since these are decisions from an administrative body principally adjudicating dispute cases (which are the majority of cases, as opposed to binding consultations), they are subject to review through the *Reclamación* originating in Article 38 of the Chilean Constitution, which in the second paragraph declares:

> Any person whose rights shall have been adversely affected by the Administration of the State, the Bodies thereof or the Municipalities, is entitled to file a complaint in the courts established by law, without prejudice to the responsibility which might affect the officer who caused the harm.[59]

The purpose of the judicial action is thus to permit a person who has experienced a violation of his constitutional rights through an administrative act to seek a remedy. In that sense, the Competition Act 1973 was intended to protect constitutional rights whenever there was a risk that the former Resolutive Commission was able to cause such damage. If the three cases in which the affected parties were permitted to seek judicial review are analyzed, it is possible to match each one of them with a possible risk of violation of constitutional rights, as has been shown above.

However, in practice, this constitutional protection by the courts was understood as an appeal procedure, and by the time of the Competition Act 2003, the institutional designers considered that it was necessary to make this 'appeal' procedure available to most of the decisions issued by the TDLC. Unfortunately they did not take into account that the TDLC, as an administrative autonomous body created for an administrative function, was not a court of the judiciary. If the legislator wanted to grant a proper appeal, the two options would have been allowing an appeal before a specialized upper tribunal, or or referring the decision back to the TDLC for an appeal on points of law only.[60]

Again, given the nature of anti-competitive infractions, the difference in names is not a purely terminological issue. The Supreme Court will need to display

---

[59] Chilean Constitution, Art 38.

[60] The latter was the solution adopted in the Criminal Procedural Reform, in which, because of the costs and time expected for each trial, it was opted not to repeat the trial before an appeal court but instead to permit a review only on points of law.

less deference to the decisions of another body in an appeal-like situation than it would have to show when considering an application for judicial review of an administrative body, as is required in the case of the *Reclamación*. Thus, the attitude of the Supreme Court towards the TDLC has not been in any way deferential, and the Court has entered into the technical competition aspects of the considerations of the TDLC.

This is particularly important, because judicial restraint is part of the generally accepted constitutional principle in Chile of the 'deference of public institutions'.[61] Therefore, if there is no clarity regarding the nature of the TDLC, and if it is treated as a court of the judiciary, the expectation of deference cannot be very high either. Conversely, if it is accepted that the TDLC is an autonomous administrative agency exercising adjudicative powers, and that its decisions are subject to judicial review, the scope, attitude and powers of the Supreme Court change dramatically, and the deference principle is more likely to be applied.

There is certainly agreement that the participation of the Supreme Court has not been in the best interests of the system. This does not mean that Supreme Court judges are exclusively at fault in this matter. As has happened in other areas of constitutional law where the role of the Supreme Court has been crucial, as in the case of the *Recurso de Protección*, another constitutionally regulated action of judicial review, it has been easier to blame the Supreme Court for the constitutional imperfections than to ask for the involvement of the other participants in order to change the situation. Supreme Court judges only speak through their decisions, as it is commonly said, and most of the time they are subject to criticisms from people who do not consider the collective responsibilities of other policy makers and the scholarship on the issue.

In this particular case, the lack of clarity in the scholarship, and to a great extent the Government and the legislature, aggravate the distrust in the system. Supreme Court judges have responded to the unrestrained power given to them in competition cases by 'speaking through their decisions' in these cases, but with their language based on an extensive expertise in civil and criminal law (and the procedural aspects of both) instead of antitrust law or economics. Supreme Court judges are not required to be specialists in antitrust, much less in economics, but the designers of the system trusted them instead of the members of the Tribunal, whose expertise has not been questioned. In the parliamentary debate, it is noticeable that the intention behind this was to protect the right to a fair trial within the Tribunal's proceedings.

Notwithstanding the imperfections introduced into the design, we propose—as a solution to the unintended effect of involving the Supreme Court—the interpretation of the *Recurso de Reclamación* in its original form: as a mechanism for the protection of constitutional rights when they are violated by the Tribunal

---

[61] P Zapata, *La jurisprudencia del Tribunal Constitucional. Parte general* (Santiago, Biblioteca Americana, 2002).

(Article 38 of the Chilean Constitution). This would mean that the scope of the Court would be limited, as the Constitution states, to remedying the violation of fundamental rights; it would not be able directly to amend the decisions of the Tribunal (in their substantive competition aspects). Using this method, the principle of deference of the public institutions would be upheld.

Chile is arguably a very legalistic country, in which culture mandates that every problem must be solved by an Act of Congress. Sometimes a correct interpretation of current laws is a much more feasible and proportional form of solving institutional problems. Therefore, we are unconvinced that what we need is yet another legal reform; rather, we support better interpretation of the already existing institutions. Indeed, what we have attempted to argue here is that the legal community needs to acknowledge the administrative nature of the TDLC, and to consider the *Recurso de Reclamación* as a judicial review procedure instead of an appeal. The current situation demonstrates that on a strictly legal basis an incorrect interpretation sets up an obstacle in the system. Moreover, beyond the debate of what should be the best interpretation on a point of public law, what lies behind this common understanding among Chilean scholars and the rest of the legal community is distrust in the competition system itself. We believe that strengthening the competition institutions will not be effective if the Supreme Court continues to display a non-deferential attitude towards these institutions.

C. Building the Trust: Effective Communication and Better Interpretation

The designers of the system have shown their distrust in competition by nominating the Supreme Court the 'ultimate decision-maker in competition policy', without being the most expert in competition law and economics. Instead of limiting its functions to the already crucial role of constitutional guardian of fundamental rights, the Supreme Court has been given the principal role of guardian of the competition system as a whole. The result of the current situation is that the Court is overturning the decisions of the TDLC by providing arguments on competition law, but from the perspective of an expert in civil and criminal law.

What is being proposed here is that, without the need for further legal reforms, it is possible to overcome the situation by:

a) interpreting infractions of competition law as breaches of administrative criminal law;
b) restating that the TDLC is an administrative adjudicative body; and
c) ensuring that judicial review is available whenever a fundamental right has been violated by the TDLC.

All of this is a matter of interpretation, but building trust in competition would also mean adopting an effective system of communication between the actors.

The adoption of a common 'code' or 'language' will enhance enormously communication between the actors.

Let us illustrate some of these failures of communication in two important areas. The first is action required before the Supreme Court. There are only two cases—*IP Telephony* (2007)[62] and to a lesser extent *Chiletabacos* (2006)[63]—in which the applicants sought the protection of the Supreme Court on the grounds of constitutional rights. In these cases, the decision of the Court was to dismiss most of the arguments put forward by the applicants. The Supreme Court upheld the TDLC's decision and only agreed to the reduction of the fine. Both cases can be considered an example of the real nature of the debate in a *Recurso de Reclamación*. The remaining applications to the Supreme Court have used the *Reclamación* as a regular appeal, under the general formula of requiring the Court to 'amend the decision of the Tribunal according to the rule of law', which is precisely the legal definition of an appeal under the Civil Procedure Act.[64]

The second area of concern relates to proof of *mens rea* (and proof in general). Under Chilean law, since a competition violation is an administrative offence, constitutional and criminal law require the existence of intent and its proof. Communication between the TDLC and Supreme Court has not been at its best in this regard. The rulings of the TDLC sometimes fail to use the same language the courts employ to refer to the facts and proved elements of the conduct. In this regard, we believe that the problem lies not in the requirement of intent itself, but rather in the interpretation of the proof itself required to demonstrate such intent, as discussed above.

The Supreme Court will show less judicial self-restraint towards the Tribunal regarding issues of general law (criminal, civil and procedural law), for example the reasoning of the TDLC on the legal deductive process as to how the proof of the facts convinced them in order to declare the elements proved. In this area, the TDLC still employs a form of argument that does not really fit with the language used by members of the judiciary (even given that one of the members of the TDLC is a Supreme Court judge). This situation led the Court in *Oxígeno* to criticize the way in which the Tribunal reached its decision, the terminology and the text of the argument being implicitly considered inappropriate by the Supreme Court.

In the most recent decision of the Court,[65] the trend for requiring a correct form of argument from the Tribunal is more evident. In that case, Justice Gálvez (in the majority opinion) is quite severe when referring to the procedural arguments of the TDLC. The Tribunal described different possible scenarios, concluding

---

[62] *Telefonia IP*, Supreme Court (2007), 6236-2006.
[63] *Chiletabacos*, Supreme Court (2006), 4332-2005.
[64] Civil Procedure Act, Art 186.
[65] *Isapres*, Supreme Court (2008), 4052-07.

that a collusive agreement was unlikely in comparison with other possibilities. In the decision, Justice Gálvez states:

> 11°) That the disquisitions in the last four paragraphs above, seem to have a lack of precision and certainty that is improper of the reasoning that must be adopted by judges of the Republic. Indeed, these statements are vague, ambiguous, contradictory and less enlightening by the time of the definition of whether exactly there is a collusive agreement as it has been argued in this case. It is not enough to mention the concurrence of elements that would eventually be suitable for establishing the facts, but it is necessary to conclude with certainty if they prove this circumstance or not.

One of the most valuable aspects of Justice Gálvez's opinion in this case is that he engages in a dialogue between the TDLC and the Supreme Court. In a way, this ruling opens the door to a more restrained Supreme Court, as long as the Tribunal adopts a more 'judicial style' in writing its decisions and expressing the way it reaches them. By establishing a fluent degree of communication, the Supreme Court, as the *ultimate decision-maker in competition policy*, will veto fewer decisions, and this will help build a richer culture of competition policy between institutions.

D. Conclusion

From a time-series study of collusion case law from 1973 until 2003, it is clear that little attention has been given to these collusive practices, particularly from 1987 onwards, by the Chilean Supreme Court. The Competition Act 2003 initially represented a shift in this trend, producing the first rulings issued against hard-core cartels; these rulings were based on sound economic and legal standards. However, an unexpected problem appeared: the role of the Supreme Court. This institution overturned all the infringement decisions relating to collusive agreements handed down by the newly-created TDLC, leaving in evidence the need for a change in order to detect and punish collusion successfully in the market. Moreover, as a consequence of the Supreme Court intervention, the case law of the TDLC has been altered, requiring an abuse of dominant position on top of a collusive agreement. The effects of this recently developed theory, which is quickly moving away from a 'per se' approach to collusion, are yet to be seen.

We believe that the strengthening of collusion enforcement in Chile requires several conditions. First, following Chilean law, it is essential that the Supreme Court has more flexibility when interpreting the evidence submitted by the parties in these types of cases. Secondly, it would be beneficial to introduce a leniency program and to grant the FNE more powers to investigate collusive behavior; both elements are contained in a Bill currently being debated in Congress. Thirdly, it would be useful to clarify, through case law, that the objectives of competition law are not limited to efficiency and, more importantly, that consumer welfare should be one of its goals.

From an institutional viewpoint, there are elements of the Competition Act 2003 that appear as clear signs of trust in the system, ie the independence and expertise of the TDLC's members, budgetary independence, and complete separation between the tribunal and the enforcement agency. However, in reality there are also signs of distrust: the lack of powers granted to the FNE, and the extension of the procedure of review of TDLC decisions by the Supreme Court. Additionally, there is a serious problem with communication between the TDLC and the Supreme Court.

We believe that the answer to this problem lies not the re-design of the system, but rather in giving the correct interpretation to Chilean competition law and, consequently, to the judicial review procedure. In this sense, the understanding of competition law in Chile as part of administrative criminal law, and the categorization of the TDLC as an administrative agency, will lead to the conclusion that judicial review, established in competition law, grants the Supreme Court the power to overturn decisions only when due process has not been followed. It does not grant the Supreme Court the right to overturn decisions based on technical issues of competition law and economics. In other words, this interpretation leads the way towards the use of the principle of deference by the Supreme Court towards the TDLC.

Moreover, we believe that deference could be further improved by adequate communication between institutions. Paradoxically in order to achieve effective communication, the TDLC must tend towards a more 'judicial' style when weighing evidence and preparing decisions.[66]

Overall, we believe that building trust in antitrust does not require the introduction of new laws to change the role granted to the Supreme Court but, in the context of an already over-legalized country, the proper and better use of existing regulation, and the consequent improvement of competition culture and awareness.

---

[66] In this process, under the 1973 Competition Act (repealed in this part by the Competition Act 2003), the contribution of the Supreme Court judge who was at the same time the President of the former Tribunal (the Resolutive Commission) was key to achieving such an objective, helping to move this process forward by sharing his expertise in judicial procedures with the other members of the tribunal. In the Explanatory Notes to the Bill containing the current Competition Act 2003, it was stated that the role of the Supreme Court judge would be essential for maintaining the procedural protections of the cases, given his judicial expertise, and for that reason his appointment and position was maintained (it would be the President of the TDLC). However, during the parliamentary debate this was considered inadequate for the independence and role of the Supreme Court itself, and an amendment to the Bill was approved, under which the Supreme Court participates in the appointment process, without appointing one of its members. We agree with the reform on this point, but recognize at the same time the value of the Supreme Court judge as far as importing a judicial style is concerned. See Competition Act 1973, Art 16 (repealed); Explanatory Notes to the Competition Bill (now Competition Act 2003), Presidential Bill No 136-346, p 7; Chilean Senate, Second Report of the Joint Committees of Constitutional Affairs and Finance, Bill 2944-03, pp 17–20.

D
Mexico

[17]

Competition and Equity in Telecommunications

Rafael del Villar

The lesson drawn from both theory and experience is that an economy's incentive structure is critical to its performance. An economy with a healthily competitive incentive structure is likely to lead to

- a more efficient use of resources, and consequently greater aggregate output
- a wider variety of higher quality goods and services available to consumers at lower prices
- the availability of more job opportunities with remuneration in line with productivity
- the availability of more possibilities for entrepreneurs to turn their creativity into material returns and successful projects.

For markets that do not operate under conditions of competition, welfare losses can often significantly exceed the rents being received by the sheltered sectors. This leads to less efficient allocation of resources and, to the extent that rents accrue to wealthier groups, worse income distribution.

The author would like to thank Eduardo Martínez, Everardo Quezada, and Arcelia Rodríguez for the excellent assistance provided in preparing this chapter. He would also like to thank Roger Noll, Jessica Serrano, and Michael Walton for valuable comments. The opinions expressed in this chapter are those of the author and do not necessarily represent those of the Bank of Mexico or the Ministry of Communications and Transport.

321

The concept of equity goes beyond income distribution. As Bourguignon and Dessus discuss (chapter 1 in this volume), the concept refers to the ability of members of society to access opportunities that allow them to lead productive lives. As society grants more equity (ex ante), this will be reflected, over time, in improved distribution (ex post) of income and wealth and an improvement in the overall standard of living.

Equity and competition are closely linked. These concepts are particularly relevant for broadly used inputs such as labor, telecommunications, and energy. Any change in these sectors affects not only consumers, but also the activities for which they are inputs. Where lack of competition leads to restrictions in access, this amounts to an inequitable outcome: those firms or individuals with influence or connections have preferential, exclusive, or cheaper access to inputs than others. The other side of this is that for certain activities, the social rate of return is greater than the private rate of return (for example, ensuring an educated and healthy society and providing basic infrastructure). In the context of this chapter, ensuring extensive broadband penetration in Mexico is essential for both efficiency and equity reasons, and should be a priority objective of public policy. Thus, the purpose of this chapter is to analyze several issues that have a bearing on competition and equal opportunities as they relate to the telecommunications sector.

Economic Overview of the Privatization of Teléfonos de Mexico

The telecommunications sector has been among the economy's most dynamic over the past 40 years. The key event during this period was the privatization of Teléfonos de Mexico (TELMEX) in 1990, which continues to influence and mold the sector.

Between 1965 and 1980, the number of telephone lines increased more than 12 percent per year. During the 1980s, Mexico underwent a serious external debt and macroeconomic crisis that led to economic stagnation: annual gross domestic product (GDP) growth fell from 6.7 percent between 1965 and 1980 to just 1.8 percent in the 1980s. During that same decade, the average annual increase in the number of telephone lines fell to 7 percent. The precariousness of the economy and public finances not only had an effect on the sector's growth, but also on the quality and reliability of telephone services. The government viewed TELMEX's revenues as a source of funds to be used for other areas of the economy and for servicing its debt (Casasús 1994). Thus, the necessary investments to support

TELMEX operations were not made, and it had to rely on increasingly obsolete technology. The 1985 Mexico City earthquake paralyzed the telecommunications system and revealed the frailness of its infrastructure and the growing need for investment.

All led to the development of a modernization policy for the sector that included the privatization of TELMEX. In September 1989, the government announced its intent to privatize the company. The government's strategy was based not only on improving the company's efficiency, but also on possibly improving its public finances basically by decreasing government subsidies.

In August 1990, the government changed TELMEX's license (known as a title of concession under Mexican law), giving the company an ambitious set of obligations. These were aimed at preventing the privatized company from engaging in monopolistic or excessive practices and ensuring that third parties would have nondiscriminatory access to the company's key facilities and infrastructure, such as interconnection.

The government's overriding goals were, however, to maximize revenues from the privatization and to do so as quickly as possible so it could proceed with other privatizations. This approach ultimately meant that the privatization took place without a sound institutional framework. Indicative of this was the fact that the Ministry of Finance was responsible for the privatization and not the Ministry of Communications and Transport.

To maximize revenues from the privatization, the government sold a package of firms to a single group of investors. It included TELMEX and Teléfonos de Noroeste (the telephone carrier in northwest Mexico), both state-owned fixed telephony companies that operated in exclusive geographic zones; the only existing nationwide cellular telephony concession; the federal microwave network; and several frequency bands.

To eliminate subsidies and make the company more attractive to potential buyers, the government allowed TELMEX to credit up to 65 percent of the special tax on telephony (equal to 29 percent of the company's revenues) against its investments. This implied lowering the effective tax from 29 percent to 10 percent. Before the privatization, it also increased rates considerably. As a result, annual revenues per line rose from US$440 in 1989 to US$710 in 1990, a 61 percent increase (Casanueva and del Villar 2003).

In addition, the government negotiated with the Telephone Workers' Union of the Republic of Mexico (Sindicato de Telefonistas de la Republica Mexicana, or STRM) to modify the collective bargaining agreement to make labor conditions more flexible. In exchange, the workers received stockholding interest in the privatized company.

In 1989, months before the federal government announced the privatization, the STRM and TELMEX agreed to change the collective bargaining agreement and decrease STRM interference in the company's modernization (for example, the STRM had had the right to intervene in the implementation of technological changes and the startup of new services).

Improved labor flexibility was achieved by eliminating the previous structure that regulated all details of labor relations through so-called department agreements. These were now replaced by position profiles, which were much less regulated and gave much more general definitions of workers' duties and categories. It also allowed TELMEX to have more say about moving its personnel internally among departments without having to be subject to STRM approval.

The government guaranteed that TELMEX would not face competition in domestic and international long distance for the first six years following its privatization. At the time of privatization, revenues from international and domestic long distance telephony represented slightly more than twice the revenues the company earned from local telephony (this market was left open to competition after privatization). The share of local telephony in the company's overall revenues increased drastically, rising from a little more than 20 percent of total revenues in 1989 to slightly more than 41 percent in 1992.

The owner of the television monopoly in Mexico was barred from acquiring TELMEX because of the government's concerns about this type of concentration. In exchange, the government blocked the possibility of TELMEX offering television and video services indefinitely in its title of concession.

Finally, although the government had stipulated obligations for the privatized company regarding coverage and network expansion in the modification to the title of concession, the main responsibilities concluded in 1994—for example, the requirement that telephone lines had to increase a minimum of 12 percent annually. (Other requirements, such as reducing the period of time consumers must wait before being serviced or increasing the number of public telephone booths, which extended beyond 1994, are not as economically important.) This was the last year in office of the administration of President Carlos Salinas, which was responsible for carrying out the privatization of the company. In an example of political opportunism, the authorities did not set conditions regarding the growth of the company, considering them not to be particularly relevant, even though monopolies are motivated to restrict supply in order to increase prices.

Thus, even though the concession forbids monopolistic practices and discrimination against third parties and obligates TELMEX to provide interconnection and nondiscriminatory access, the administration did not take the necessary steps to ensure that competition would materialize. It did not grant concessions or set interconnection conditions so that third parties could enter the local telephony market that, on paper at least, had been left open to competition, and even though third parties were indeed interested in competing in this market.

The government's actions and omissions turned TELMEX into an extremely profitable quasi-monopoly and its owners into economically powerful people virtually overnight. By 1993, TELMEX's gross profits were roughly equivalent to 1 percent of GDP, while the added value was only 2 percent of GDP. The administration that carried out the privatization essentially ignored the problems this enormous private economic power would, in all likelihood, pose in the future for the authorities responsible for regulating the company.

Importance of Telecommunications

The impact of telecommunications services and information technologies in the economy has been thoroughly documented and discussed. According to Jorgenson and Vu (2005), the adoption of information and communication technology explains more than 15 percent of the growth the world economy experienced from 1995 to 2003. The contribution of information and communication technology to growth varies among countries: although it accounted for almost 30 percent of economic growth, on average, in the Group of Seven countries (and 47 percent in Germany), it accounted for only 8 percent in Eastern Europe and 10 percent in Sub-Saharan Africa.

In Mexico, national account statistics also confirm the increasing contribution of information and communication technology to the economy. The share of telecommunications has increased drastically in recent years, rising from 1.1 percent in 1990 to 5.0 percent in 2005, while the weight of telecommunications service rates in the national consumer price index has risen to 2.16 percent for local telephony, similar to that of electricity (2.27 percent) (figures 9.1 and 9.2).

All population deciles in Mexico account for significant consumption of telecommunications services. In 2006, household expenditure on telecommunications in the poorest income decile accounted for 2.9 percent of total household expenditure, whereas for the second-richest decile telecommunications expenditure represented 5.7 percent of household expenditure, the highest of any decile (table 9.1). This high percentage is explained primarily by the high rates consumers pay for telecommunications services.

Figure 9.1 Weight of Telecommunications Services Rates in the Consumer Price Index, Selected Years

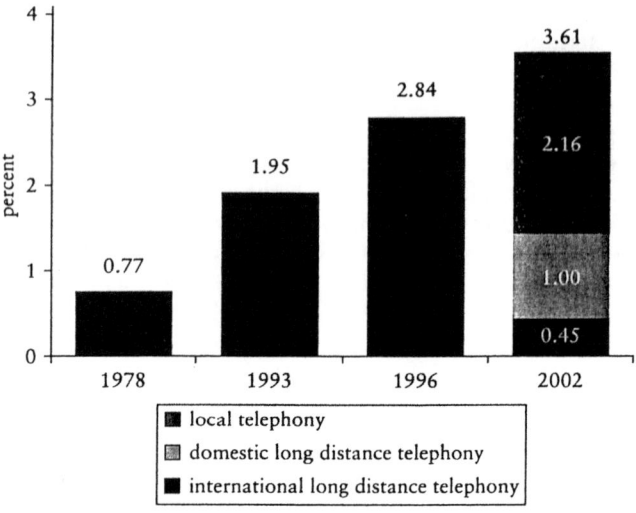

Source: Bank of Mexico data.

Figure 9.2 Share of Communications Services in Gross National Product, Selected Years

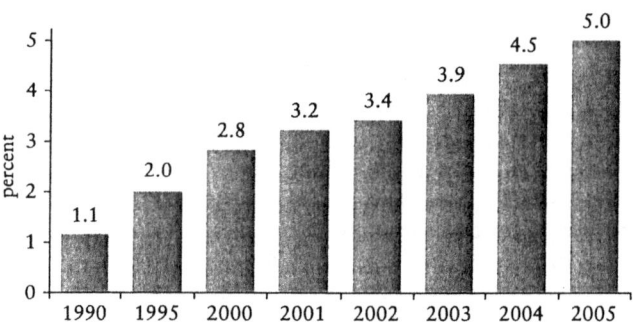

Source: President, Fifth State of the *Union* address, September 2005.

In addition, according to household income and expenditure surveys, since 2004, households from all population deciles have stated that they spend money on Internet services, but the disparity in expenditure between the highest-income decile and the two lowest

Table 9.1 Household Expenditure on Telecommunications Services by Population Decile, 2006
(percentage of household expenditure)

| Category | Total | Poorest | | | | Household deciles[a] | | | | | Richest |
		1	2	3	4	5	6	7	8	9	10
Total communications[b]	4.8	2.9	3.2	3.5	3.9	4.3	4.7	4.7	5.6	5.7	5.0
Local service[c]	1.7	1.3	1.4	1.5	1.6	1.8	2.1	2.0	2.1	2.0	1.4
Long distance service	0.6	0.3	0.4	0.5	0.5	0.5	0.5	0.6	0.7	0.8	0.7
Mobile telephony[d]	1.9	0.8	1.0	1.0	1.3	1.5	1.5	1.7	2.3	2.4	2.3
Internet service	0.3	0.1	0.1	0.2	0.1	0.2	0.2	0.2	0.3	0.4	0.5

Source: Author's estimates are based on the 2006 national survey of household income and expenditures.
a. According to monetary income.
b. Includes public telephony and other services such as mail, telegraph, public fax, beeper, and others.
c. Includes telephone installation and local calls.
d. Includes initial payment, equipment acquisition, prepaid cards, and mobile telephony service.

Table 9.2 Penetration of Telecommunications Services by Population Decile, 2006
(percentage of households)

Population decile	Fixed telephony	Mobile telephony	Internet
1 (poorest)	11.34	7.56	1.13
2	17.62	14.68	2.55
3	25.09	20.28	4.65
4	31.14	29.54	6.25
5	39.70	38.53	7.66
6	46.56	40.54	7.73
7	52.02	48.00	10.06
8	62.15	58.83	14.96
9	71.18	69.57	20.22
10 (richest)	84.68	82.11	39.03
Total	44.15	40.96	11.42

Source: 2006 national survey of household income and expenditures.

income deciles is 87 to 1, whereas the difference between the income of the highest decile and the lowest is 33 to 1. Moreover, Internet penetration in the seven lowest income deciles is still low (table 9.2). Ninety percent of households have little or no Internet access, with the main reason cited for lack of access being a lack of resources.

The TELMEX Price Cap

This section discusses TELMEX's pricing regime and its impact on competition and consumers.

Evolution of Telephone Rates

Telephone rates—in real terms—have behaved irregularly. Thus, figure 9.3 shows that real telephone rates increased 50 percent between 1988 and 1994, remained stable until late 1997, and exhibited a downward trend as of December 1997. The decreases in rates have occurred primarily in the markets that have faced stiffer competition, such as long distance telephony and local business telephony.

In addition, tables 9.3 and 9.4 show the significant discrepancy between the evolution of the real rates for residential and business telephony services and the drop in costs from 1990 to 2005. For example, whereas residential and business service rates fell 24.8 percent

Figure 9.3 Evolution of Telephone Rates Relative to the Consumer Price Index, Selected Months and Years

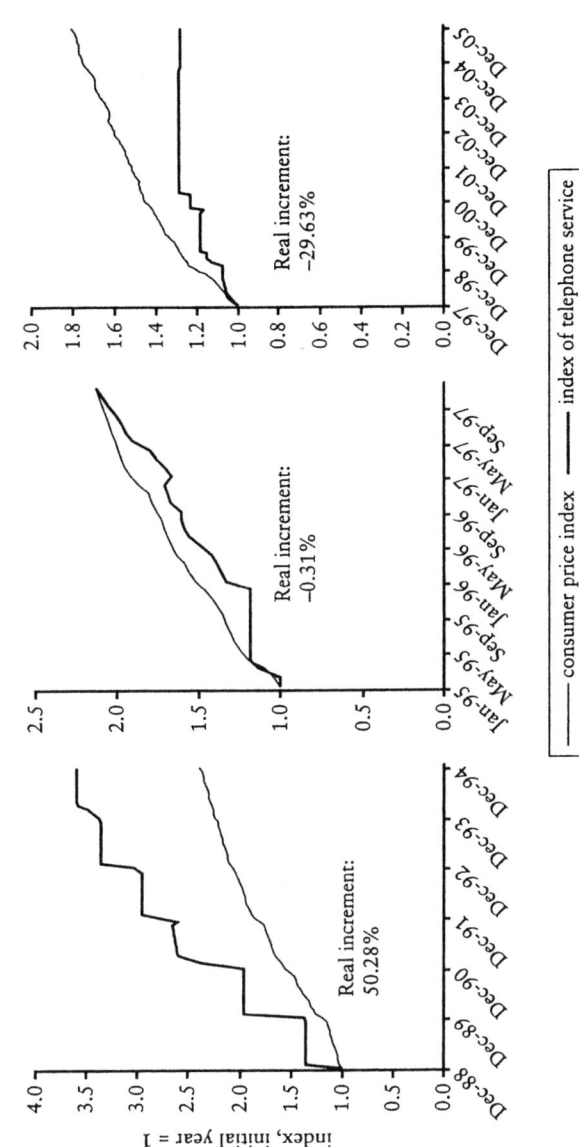

Source: Bank of Mexico data.

329

Table 9.3 Evolution of TELMEX Rates, 1990–2005
(percentage change)

Category	Residential	Commercial
Local service	13.9	−27.7
Connection charge	−79.9	−88.4
Monthly rent of fixed line	83.7	−8.4
Average service charge	−28.5	−28.5
National long distance	−79.0	−79.0
International	−80.8	−80.8
Weighted average	−24.8[a]	−48.3[b]

Source: Author's estimates based on TELMEX data.

a. Telephone services for residential customers are based on the weights that local, national long distance, and international long distance each have in the consumer price index (basis: last two weeks of June 2002).

b. Telephone services for business customers are based on the weights that local, national long distance, and international long distance each have in the producer price index (basis: December 2003).

Table 9.4 Indicators Explaining the Drop in TELMEX Costs, December 1990–December 2005
(percentage change)

Indicator	Change
Employees per telephone line	−74.0
Employees per local call	−80.1
Employees per minute of domestic long distance	−78.2
Employees per minute of outgoing international long distance	−78.0

Source: Author's estimates based on TELMEX annual reports.

and 48.3 percent, respectively, cost indicators decreased between 74.0 percent and 80.1 percent.

Establishment of the Price Cap

TELMEX's title of concession establishes a price cap mechanism for controlling basic services (local telephony, domestic long distance, and outgoing international long distance for residential and business users). As specified in the concession contract, as of January 1999 and in four-year cycles thereafter, the price cap mechanism contemplates two types of adjustments to the controlled services basket. First, the Federal Telecommunications Commission (Comisión Federal de Telecomunicaciones, or COFETEL) must set the price level that will be in force at the start of the new cycle for the controlled services basket. Second, every quarter COFETEL must apply a productivity gains adjustment factor to the index of the rates of the controlled services so that the latter does not increase more than inflation, as measured by the consumer price index, minus this adjustment factor (called X).

Condition 6–7 of the title of concession states that a technical-economic study will be carried out every four years, following the established methodology, to determine long-term incremental costs and to specify the initial level of the basket and adjustment factor X that will produce sufficient revenue levels to obtain an internal rate of return on the controlled services basket equal to the weighted average cost of capital.

Estimation of the Initial Price Increase and Adjustment Factor X

Incremental cost studies for controlled basic services are considered confidential, and only the Ministry of Communications and Transport, COFETEL, and TELMEX have access to them. For the purposes of this section (which draws on del Villar and Serrano 2003), the calculation methodology used publicly available information related to the mandated accounting separation of local telephony, domestic long distance, and international long distance.

The study made two assumptions to estimate the initial increase that the price cap must have undergone in early 2003. First, that COFETEL fixed the initial level of the basket at the correct level in early 1999 during the review of the price cap for the 1999–2002 cycle. Second, that between 1999 and 2002, TELMEX operated with a reasonable degree of efficiency, and therefore the costs it reported for the period did not evolve very differently from the incremental costs. These assumptions entail that the implied initial 2003 change in the price cap can be estimated by the cumulated difference between the annual 4.5 percent adjustment factor X established for 1999–2002 and the annual adjustment factor X estimated on the basis of the information reported by the company during this period. According to these data, the price cap should have undergone a 17.67 percent downward adjustment in 2003. Contrary to this result, COFETEL decided that the price cap would not have to be adjusted.

After the initial change in the level of the price cap for controlled services for 2003 was determined, a cash flow model was developed to endogenously establish the productivity adjustment factor X for the 2003–06 basic services basket such that the internal rate of return equals the weighted average cost of capital. The annual adjustment factor X that resulted from the relevant cash flow model was 5.28 percent. Contrary to this result, COFETEL decided on an annual adjustment factor of 3.00 percent.

The same steps were taken to estimate the required initial change in the price cap for the next cycle in early 2007 by cumulating the difference between the estimated adjustment factor and the established adjustment factor from 1999 to 2006. The result (table 9.5) was that the price cap should have been adjusted down 33 percent in 2007. Contrary to this result, COFETEL decided again that the price cap would not be adjusted.

Impact of the Initial Changes in the Price Cap on Consumer Expenditure

From 1999 to 2006, TELMEX lowered its real rates faster than required by the price cap that COFETEL defined. This change means TELMEX could increase the rates of the controlled services basket by roughly 9.5 percent without violating the price cap. A 33 percent drop in the price cap would have forced TELMEX to reduce the price-controlled services basket by approximately 24 percent.

The direct impact of a 24 percent decrease in TELMEX's basic service prices on the consumer price index would have been between 0.4 and 0.5 percent, because the controlled services basket has a 2.7 percent weight in the consumer price index. Although TELMEX does not account for the entire market, other basic telephone service providers would have likely found themselves obliged to lower their rates if the rates of the main carrier had.

Table 9.5 Estimate of Required and Established Initial Price Increases, 1999–2006
(percent)

Year	Estimated X factor	Established X factor	Difference
1999	14.0	4.5	9.47
2000	4.6	4.5	0.05
2001	15.7	4.5	11.17
2002	1.1	4.5	−3.36
2003	6.0	3.0	2.99
2004	9.4	3.0	6.40
2005	6.7	3.0	3.68
2006[a]	2.5	3.0	−0.48
Cumulated difference			33.04

Source: Author's estimates based on TELMEX and COFETEL annual reports.
a. Figures for the fourth quarter are estimates.

Dominance

This section discusses how TELMEX's economic and political power affects its relationship with its regulatory authorities and the impact of TELMEX's behavior on competition in the industry.

Difficulties of Establishing Healthy Competition in the Telecommunications Sector

The lack of competition in the telecommunications sector has occurred in part because the resolutions issued by the Federal Competition Commission (Comisión Federal de Competencia, or CFC) have in large measure been turned down in the courts (see also chapter 4 in this volume). The CFC determined that TELMEX had engaged in monopolistic practices in nine instances; however, TELMEX has not complied with any of the CFC's resolutions either because the courts have taken too long to hand down their rulings or because TELMEX has been granted *amparos* (injunctions or stays of action) that have prolonged procedures and even prevented the substance of the litigation from being resolved.[1]

The most important case the CFC and COFETEL have lost so far is probably the one regarding Article 63 of the Federal Telecommunications Act. According to this article, the Ministry of Communications and Transport is empowered to establish specific obligations on concessionaires holding substantial power over the market in accordance with the Federal Antitrust Act. The ministry could exercise this power through COFETEL, a decentralized agency of the Ministry of Communications and Transport. In December 1997, the CFC determined that TELMEX held substantial market power in five fixed telephony markets (local telephony services, access or interconnection services, domestic long distance service, interurban transportation services, and international long distance service). TELMEX immediately started an *amparo* to prevent any action in this regard.

In sum, almost nine years after the CFC issued its declaration of substantial market power and six years after COFETEL established specific obligations,[2] the courts overruled the substance of the CFC resolution. Even though the CFC has appealed the decision, it might have to start from scratch in defining TELMEX as a dominant player.

TELMEX filed a motion before the CFC for reconsideration of the 1997 ruling, but the CFC confirmed it in 1998. TELMEX delayed implementation of the decision by means of several *amparos*. COFETEL ultimately issued a resolution that established certain obligations on TELMEX in 2000, but TELMEX appealed it through an *amparo* that held up implementation of the said obligations. In 2001, the courts annulled the original CFC decision, and as a consequence, TELMEX was able to reverse all the resolutions that had derived from the original decision, including the one issued by COFETEL. The CFC later issued a new ruling declaring TELMEX to be a dominant player, but the company once again appealed and won an *amparo* in May 2004. In August 2004, the CFC promulgated another decision that TELMEX also appealed. In October 2006, the courts overturned the substance of the CFC decision.

Article 63 of the Federal Telecommunications Act implies that for COFETEL to impose obligations on a company, the CFC first must declare that the company has substantial power in the relevant market. This system is inefficient in practical terms and poses problems as follows:

- The delays it causes are considerable, because decisions by CFC and COFETEL are sequential and TELMEX can appeal the decisions of both before the courts. This hinders COFETEL from imposing pro-competition regulations in a timely manner, because it has to wait for the CFC to issue a resolution on the matter.
- The authorities have to make public their intent to regulate and affect private interests, thereby allowing TELMEX to take measures to preempt the acts of the authorities.
- The resolutions issued by the CFC are not guaranteed the expected reaction by COFETEL.

Note that the CFC's annual budget is equal to two days worth of profits by TELMEX and RadioMóvil Dipsa (TELCEL) combined. The disparity in the economic power of the authority and that of the regulated entity has probably contributed to the CFC's low effectiveness. Antitrust agencies need resources to hire the best law firms because of the economic power wielded by the companies they face.

Foreign Investment

Foreign direct investment (FDI) is recognized as a key mechanism for the diffusion of new technologies among countries. The relationship between FDI and competition is complex. Companies on the receiving end of FDI can put significant competitive pressure on sectors that had previously been dominated by large domestic companies, or they can come to hold a dominant position in a segmented market. That, is why competition policies are fundamental in realizing the benefits of FDI. Restrictions on FDI are particularly counterproductive when they are asymmetric in closely linked markets. This is the case of fixed telephony and mobile telephony. FDI is limited to 49 percent for the former, where competition is limited, whereas there is no limit for the latter, where levels of competition are high.

This situation has led to low levels of investment in the sector. Between 1990 and 2003, average investment as a share of total industry revenue was 30 percent, which does not compare favorably with other countries with similar per capita income levels. Figure 9.4 shows that the level of investments in telecommunications in Mexico was below the average of selected emerging countries of the Organisation for Economic Co-operation and Development (OECD) between 1991 and 2003. As the constant drop in investment levels between 1990 and 1995 indicates, investment performance in Mexico worsened after the privatization of TELMEX.

By its nature, the telecommunications sector requires huge investments, profound market knowledge, and access to specialized equipment. Opening the fixed telecommunications market to FDI would promote the entry of foreign carriers that have the financial leverage, knowledge, and technology needed either to start up new companies or to acquire or enter into partnerships with existing companies.

Figure 9.4 Investments by Telecommunication Companies, Mexico and Selected Emerging OECD Countries, 1991–2003

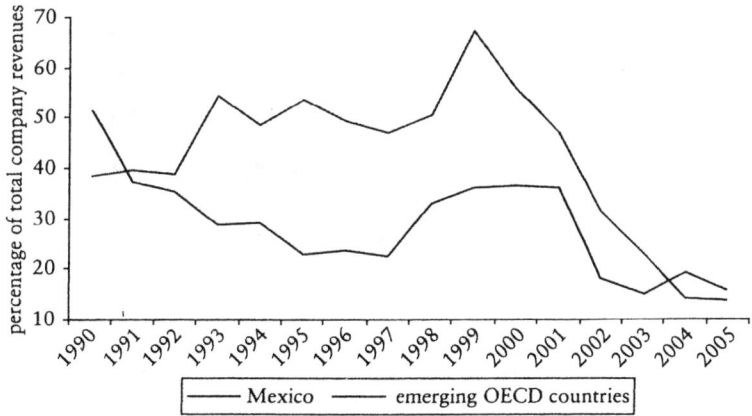

Source: OECD telecommunications database.

Note: The emerging countries include the Czech Republic, Greece, Hungary, Poland, the Republic of Korea, the Slovak Republic, and Turkey.

Importance of TELMEX's and TELCEL's Main Shareholders on the Stock Exchange

TELMEX has earned net profits of US$2.0 billion to US$2.5 billion per year since 1990, earning roughly US$30 billion in profits between 1991 and 2003. (Note that TELCEL was split from TELMEX in 2000.) These earnings are being shared by fewer shareholders over time. In December 1990, the Grupo Carso, TELMEX's main shareholder, held 5.7 percent of TELMEX's shares and currently holds 48 percent of the voting shares of TELMEX and 71 percent of the voting shares of TELCEL. Furthermore, companies associated with

Figure 9.5 Market Value of TELMEX and TELCEL Controlling Group Companies, November 2006

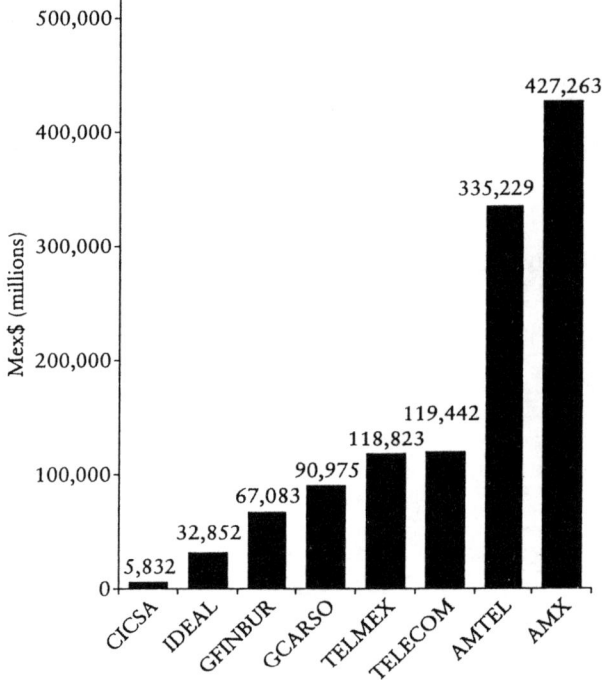

Source: Mexican stock exchange data.

Note: AMTEL = Axtel; AMX = America Movil, CICSA = Carso Infraestructura y Construccion; GCARSO = Grupo Carso; GFINBUR = Grupo Financiero Inbursa; IDEAL = Impulsora del Desarrollo y el Empleo en America Latina; TELECOM = Carso Global Telecom.

Figure 9.6 Weight of TELMEX and TELCEL Controlling Group Companies in the Mexican Stock Index, November 2006
(percent)

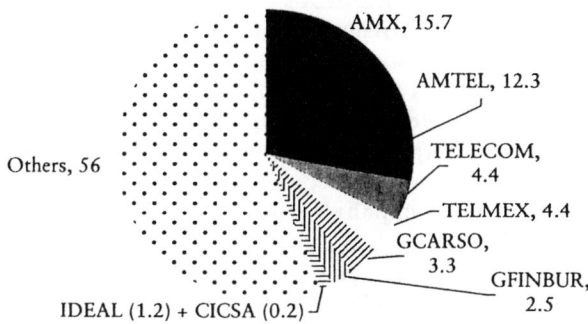

Total weight of the
group in the stock index = 44%

Source: Mexican stock exchange data.

Note: AMTEL = Axtel; AMX = America Movil, CICSA = Carso Infraestructura y Construccion; GCARSO = Grupo Carso; GFINBUR = Grupo Financiero Inbursa; IDEAL = Impulsora del Desarrollo y el Empleo en America Latina; TELECOM = Carso Global Telecom.

the Grupo Carso have substantial weight in the Mexican stock exchange (figures 9.5 and 9.6).

Even though TELCEL's market value was 3.6 times greater than TELMEX's in November 2006 (US$38.9 billion compared with US$10.8 billion), TELMEX's earnings before interest, taxes, depreciation, and amortization were 50 percent greater than TELCEL's in 2005. Both companies generate large profits, but even though it operates in a less competitive market, TELMEX apparently has a much higher profit rate.

Commercial and Financial Ties with Competitors

In 1995, TELMEX's main shareholder bought 49 percent of Cablevisión—the cable television company that serves the Mexico City area and is owned by Televisa, Mexico's largest television broadcasting company. In 2000, the CFC forced TELMEX to divest itself of these shares. Nevertheless, the Grupo Carso later bought 25 percent of the shares of Televisa through Inbursa Bank (another company of the Grupo Carso) that, according to a CFC ruling, it should also have sold off a few years ago.

At the same time, close financial connections also exist between TELMEX owners and other carriers, which weaken competition. In 2001–02, TELMEX bought 20 percent of Alestra's debt, worth US$80 million, before Alestra carried out its restructuring plan in November 2003. Later, TELMEX's partner, the Southern Bell Company, acquired American Telephone and Telegraph (better known as AT&T) in the United States.

In 2002 and 2003, TELMEX bought MCI debt worth approximately US$340 million, which it recently sold to Verizon for US$1.1 billion after it was converted into stock. (MCI holds 49 percent of Avantel's stock.) TELMEX became MCI's main stockholder, with 13.8 percent of the company's stock, when MCI emerged from bankruptcy in 2004.

Another example is the purchase of Unefon debt and the sale of radio-electric spectrum to TELCEL in late 2003 for US$288 million. In addition, Inbursa (the Grupo Carso's bank) granted Televisión Azteca a US$300 million credit in 2004. Televisión Azteca is Mexico's second-largest television broadcasting company.

Status of Interconnection between Carriers

The interconnection framework has played an important role in shaping the current market structure of the industry. When TELMEX was privatized, mandatory interconnection was incorporated into its title of concession to allow the development of competition. This condition was later extended to all carriers when the Federal Telecommunications Act was enacted in 1995, but this obligation has not been enforced in a cost-effective and timely manner for three main reasons. First, COFETEL, perhaps because of regulatory capture, has been reluctant to enforce the time frame and conditions specified in the law. Carriers have used this lack of enforcement to delay interconnection, sometimes for years. The same holds true for dispute resolution. According to the Federal Telecommunications Act, disputes should be resolved within 60 working days, but this does not happen. The CFC and COFETEL can also intervene by imposing special conditions on dominant carriers, but this avenue has not yet been applied because TELMEX has been successful in using the courts to reverse all CFC decisions (for more details, see Solano, del Villar, and García-Verdú 2006).

The second reason why mandatory interconnection has not been effectively enforced is that the law does not recognize key issues such as collocation and billing and collection services as interconnection services. This has allowed TELMEX to soften competition by denying interconnection services such as collocation.

The third reason is that COFETEL and market participants have poor access to commercial and technical information about carriers. Interconnection agreements and information about the location and technical specifications of a carrier's network are not publicly available. This allows discriminatory treatment among carriers and inhibits the development of business plans, because firms have no certainty about the required investments for entry. For example, the lack of transparency has allowed TELMEX and TELCEL to engage in agreements with preferential conditions.

To address some of these loopholes, COFETEL recently issued a set of interconnection rules for public consultation, but they still have to undergo a lengthy review process before becoming effective.

Long Distance Interconnection

On July 1, 1994, when Mexico decided to open up long distance telephony, the authorities established that, as of January 1, 1997, new carriers could interconnect with TELMEX in 60 cities and that interconnection would gradually be increased until all facilities with switching capabilities were covered by January 1, 2001. This has not happened.[3] Of the 397 local service areas the country has been divided into, non-TELMEX long distance carriers can interconnect in only 198. The 199 areas not open to competition hold 18.7 percent of all lines and are home to 25 percent of the population, most of whom have relatively low incomes. To terminate calls in non-open areas, the competition has to pay TELMEX a so-called resale tariff. Even though the interconnection rate (which is equivalent to the termination rate in local areas open to competition) has dropped from US$0.03 or US$0.05 per minute (depending on how it is measured) to slightly less than US$0.01 per minute, the resale tariff has remained well above the interconnection rate and is currently US$0.07 per minute.

Although COFETEL recognized resale services as an interconnection service and, hence, subject to regulation, in a resolution issued in 2001, TELMEX obtained an *amparo* against this decision. An alternative avenue taken recently by COFETEL to lower the resale tariff was to merge non-open areas with open areas; however, a decision that merged 70 non-open areas with other open areas made in early 2007 has not yet been implemented because TELMEX obtained an *amparo* from the courts.

In relation to international traffic and despite a regulatory scheme aimed at maintaining high international settlement rates, growing bypass practices have led to significant drops in these rates. In 2000, the United States brought Mexico before a World Trade Organization panel. As a result, on August 11, 2004, Mexico eliminated the exclusive privilege of the long distance carrier with the highest share of the outgoing long distance market (TELMEX) to negotiate settlement rates, proportional return systems, and the uniform settlement rate scheme. The reduction in international settlement rates has been huge, falling from approximately US$0.40 per minute in 1997 to approximately US$0.02 in 2007, provided that the calls terminate in areas open to long distance competition. In the 199 areas not open to competition, rates are US$0.08 to US$0.09 because of the high resale charges.

Interconnection among Local Carriers

With the dawn of competition in local telephony in 1999, COFETEL made a distinction between local telephony carriers that would be subject to symmetric interconnection rates because they had certain coverage obligations, on the one hand, and local telephony carriers that would not be subject to coverage obligations and that would therefore be subject to asymmetric interconnection rates, on the other hand. The former initially consisted of Axtel, Maxcom, and TELMEX, among others. They were later joined by other companies that were granted long distance telephony concessions such as Alestra and Avantel. The latter group included a consortium from the cable television sector, Megacable.

COFETEL promoted a bill-and-keep regime to interconnect new carriers in the first group with TELMEX. According to this strategy, carriers would not charge each other for interconnection. The carriers originally negotiated with TELMEX to continue with the bill-and-keep scheme as long as the imbalance in incoming and outgoing traffic was not more than 40 percent. If it were more, then long distance interconnection rates for calls exceeding the allowed imbalance would apply. If, however, the imbalance was greater than 70 percent, interconnection rates would apply for the total imbalanced traffic. Over time, TELMEX lowered the allowed traffic imbalance, which currently stands at only 5 percent, on the ground that part of the domestic and international long distance traffic is introduced into the TELMEX network as if it were local traffic and, therefore, avoids paying long distance interconnection fees. This may be hampering competition, because it increases the interconnection costs of new entrants, which usually generate more outgoing traffic than incoming when starting operations. It also facilitates price collusion among carriers, because it penalizes price reduction strategies that create traffic imbalances and because it limits the expansion of services such as public telephony that would generate traffic imbalances (public-telephone-booth traffic is exclusively outgoing in Mexico).[4]

As for the Megacable interconnection with TELMEX, COFETEL decided that Megacable would pay TELMEX the domestic long distance interconnection rate and TELMEX would pay Megacable a little less than 40 percent of that rate (Gil 2000). Because of this policy, cable television companies were, in practice, excluded from the market. In late 2003, the Ministry of Communications and Transport issued agreements that allowed cable television companies to lease their infrastructure to concessionaires that had been authorized to provide local telephony services. The ministry did not permit cable television companies to provide telephony services directly. This ban was not consistent with the Federal Telecommunications Act and was eliminated in late 2006. At the same time, cable television companies were allowed to negotiate bill-and-keep agreements, enabling them to compete in the market.

Interconnection on Mobile Networks

Initially, a decision was reached whereby TELMEX would not pay the interconnection rate for termination of calls on mobile networks, although mobile telephony carriers had to pay an interconnection rate for calls terminated on the TELMEX fixed telephony network. In 1999, when the calling party pays (CPP) scheme for local calls came into force, a decision was reached whereby fixed networks would pay mobile networks a US$0.19 per minute interconnection fee. In exchange, fixed networks were allowed to charge users a US$0.06 per minute fee for billing and collection on calls made to mobile networks. COFETEL decided that it would review the billing and collection charge each year, but has not done so for the past eight years. Most important, the billing and collection charge represents a double charge for fixed telephony users, because the monthly fixed telephony rent already includes billing and collection (see Noll, chapter 10 in this volume). This charge represented close to US$0.4 billion annually in revenues for TELMEX during 2002–05 (figure 9.7).

At the same time, in 1999 a decision was reached that the US$0.19 fixed-mobile interconnection rate would also apply to the interconnection rate that mobile telephony carriers would pay each other. This rate remained constant in nominal terms during 1999–2004 and then fell 10 percent over 2005 and 2006.

TELMEX does not allow competitors to interconnect directly with TELCEL within its facilities where TELCEL is collocated. TELMEX charges US$0.3 per minute, which is the same as the mobile termination rate, to interconnect other carriers with TELCEL.

As figure 9.8 illustrates, in recent years interconnection fees from fixed networks to mobile networks have been less important for

***Figure* 9.7** TELMEX Revenues from Billing and Collection Charges, 1999–2005

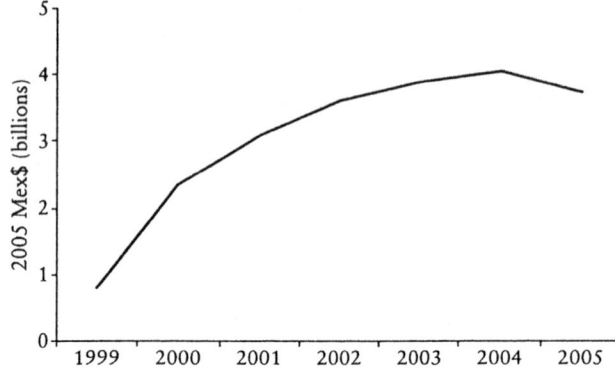

Source: Author's estimates based on TELMEX annual reports and Merrill Lynch 2006.

Figure 9.8 Mobile Carrier Revenue from Fixed-Mobile Interconnections, 2000–2005

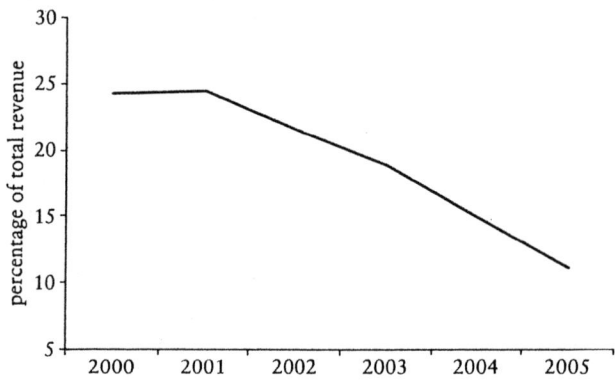

Source: Author's estimates based on TELMEX annual reports and Merrill Lynch 2006.

mobile carriers. This is because the relative size of fixed networks in relation to mobile networks has decreased and because users often make their calls from mobile networks instead of fixed networks because doing so is less expensive.

Table 9.6 Tariffs, Lines, and Network Traffic, 1999–2006

Category	1999	2000	2001	2002	2003	2004	2005	2006
General tariff (U.S. cents)								
Fixed-mobile	2.50	2.50	2.50	2.50	2.50	2.50	2.25	2.03
Interconnection tariff (U.S. cents)								
Fixed-mobile	1.900	1.900	1.900	1.900	1.900	1.900	1.710	1.540
Mobile-mobile	1.900	1.900	1.900	1.900	1.900	1.900	1.710	1.540
Mobile-fixed	0.300	0.316	0.117	0.094	0.105	0.110	0.106	0.106
Lines (millions in service)								
Mobile network	7.7	14.1	21.8	25.9	30.1	38.5	45.1	56.4[a]
Fixed network	10.9	12.3	13.8	15.0	16.3	18.1	19.2	20.9[a]
Network traffic								
Mobile network (millions of minutes)	5,152	10,975	15,919	19,990	26,386	38,188	50,236	73,000[a]
Fixed network (millions of TELMEX calls)	23,426	24,738	25,567	25,679	26,494	26,782	26,680	26,666[a]

Source: COFETEL and TELMEX data.

a. January–November.

Distortions Caused by High Mobile Interconnection Rates

Table 9.6 suggests that high fixed-mobile rates for users have had a significant impact on the development of fixed and mobile networks. Fixed network traffic only increased slightly more than 10 percent between 1999 and 2006, whereas the number of fixed lines almost doubled. The opposite is the case for the mobile network. Between 1999 and 2006, mobile network traffic increased 14-fold, even though the number of mobile lines increased only 7-fold. This is because with the introduction of the CPP scheme, making calls from fixed telephones to mobile telephones became more expensive than making them from mobile telephones, which tended to reduce fixed network traffic and increase mobile network traffic. The spike in the number of fixed lines during this period seems to be associated with the low penetration of telephone service in the country. That is, it reflects the fact that fixed telephony is still reaching many households for the first time given the large coverage lags in Mexico. In addition, fixed telephone lines are the main vehicle for access to the Internet.

Fixed-to-mobile and mobile-to-mobile interconnection rates are much higher than mobile-to-fixed rates. To compare the mobile termination rate with the fixed termination rate, one must add an additional 25 percent to the former, because mobile termination services are billed on a full per-minute basis. As a result, the mobile termination rate is 15 times higher than the fixed termination rate.

The high mobile termination rate has generated important price differences between calls that originate and terminate on the same mobile carrier network (on-net) and those that originate on one network and terminate on another (off-net). This is because high termination rates put a floor on off-net prices while channeling competition through on-net prices.

High termination rates dissuade healthy competition. They let TELCEL (the incumbent carrier) offer rates that, although high, discourage consumers from belonging to the competitors' networks. That is, elevated interconnection rates disproportionately increase costs for smaller mobile competitors, which is why the incumbent is able to fix relatively costly on-net rates.

Consider the example of a mobile telephony user who makes calls to mobile telephones only. Assume that call traffic is uniformly spread out between all the companies, that is, it is in the same proportion as the companies' market share.[5] TELCEL's market share is 80 percent and Telefónica's is 13.6 percent. Assume that the final fee TELCEL and Telefónica charge their users for their on-net calls is US$1.00 and US$0.00 per minute, respectively. As far as the off-net calls are concerned, assume that TELCEL charges US$2.00 per minute whereas Telefónica charges its users the interconnection rate of only US$1.54 per minute. Even if TELCEL charges more than Telefónica for on-net and off-net calls, the average cost per minute for users would be less if they opted for TELCEL over Telefónica because of the high interconnection rate (note that under this scheme, Telefónica would not be earning revenue from its users).

If one assumes that calls are distributed in accordance with the overall market shares in the population, the average cost per minute for TELCEL users is $0.8 \times US\$1.00 + 0.2 \times US\$2.00 = US\$1.20$. The average cost per minute for Telefónica users is $0.136 \times US\$0.00 + 0.864 \times US\$1.54 = US\$1.30$. If the mobile interconnection rate were lowered to cost, competition among mobile carriers would be on a level playing field. In addition, resources would no longer be transferred from fixed telephony users to mobile networks and users. Fixed telephony rates would drop, and increased competition in mobile telephony would also tend to lower mobile telephony rates.

Even though this would decrease the interconnection revenue these carriers received, the subsequent fall in rates for consumers would significantly increase the use of mobile services, which could more than compensate for the decline in revenues from interconnection rates. This effect can be seen in table 9.7, which shows that economies with lower mobile termination rates have higher minutes of use per mobile subscriber.

Table 9.7 Revenues, Usage, and Termination Rates, Selected Economies, 2005

Economy	Average revenue per minute (US$)	Average number of minutes of use per subscriber per month	Average revenue per user (US$)	EBITDA margin (%)	Mobile termination rate (US$)
Argentina	0.10	116	11	23.6	0.134
Chile	0.14	106	14	34.6	0.124
China	0.02	323	10	49.2	0.010
Hong Kong (China)	0.05	399	21	19.6	0.006
India	0.02	445	9	36.2	0.007
Korea, Rep. of	0.11	315	44	33.9	0.044
Mexico	0.14	115	18	41.0	0.140
Peru	0.16	68	14	28.7	0.168
Singapore	0.08	320	32	44.3	0.006
United States	0.06	822	53	33.2	0.010

Sources: Merrill Lynch 2006; Sárl Switzernet data.
Note: EBITDA = earnings before interest, taxes, depreciation, and amortization.

CPP Scheme in Long Distance

In November 2006, the CPP scheme was extended to domestic and international long distance calls, which, until that time, had been under the receiving party pays (RPP) scheme. With the exception of TELMEX, fixed telephony carriers have filed to nullify implementation of this scheme and some have been granted permanent injunctions.

The benefits of operating under a CPP scheme in long distance are being hotly debated. The literature and international evidence has shown that in many countries, particularly in Europe, use of the CPP scheme makes the price per minute of calls to mobile telephones high, because interconnection rates are much higher than costs. This is evidenced by interconnection rates under the CPP scheme more than compensating for the air time charged to users in the RPP scheme.

In Mexico, the CPP scheme in long distance has led to an increase in the price of domestic and international long distance calls to mobile telephones. In domestic long distance calls made from fixed telephones to mobile telephones under the previous RPP scheme, the user originating the call and the user receiving it together paid an average of US$0.24 per minute (not including the cost of the local call that is charged to the fixed telephone consumer). Under the new CPP scheme, these calls cost US$0.30 per minute, not including the cost of the local call.

When one compares charges included in long distance calls from fixed telephones to mobile telephones under the CPP and RPP schemes, the cost of domestic long distance service is the same under both. The average price differs because a billing and collection fee was introduced under the CPP scheme, which constitutes a double charge and was presumably added because of TELMEX's demands to ensure it would accept the new scheme.

Moreover, the interconnection rate is higher than the average air time rate that mobile carriers charge to their users under the RPP scheme. The difference between the air time rate and the interconnection rate is probably due to the air time rate being determined by each mobile telephony company in competition with other mobile telephony companies, whereas carriers reach agreement as to the interconnection rate.

As far as the long distance CPP interconnection rate is concerned, it was essentially agreed upon by TELMEX and TELCEL, which belong to the same group of shareholders. Even though the negotiation of interconnection rates between two connected companies with different concessions does not constitute a violation of the Federal Telecommunications Act, it is contrary to its spirit and objectives.[6] The objectives of the Federal Telecommunications Act are

(a) to promote the efficient development of telecommunications, (b) to set the basis for the government's regulatory functions, and (c) to foster healthy competition. Hence, fixing high interconnection rates, and thereby establishing elevated rates, is contrary to the law's goals of efficiency and competition.

Even though, as noted earlier, some fixed telephony carriers have been granted *amparos* by the courts that allow them to continue operating under the RPP scheme, mobile carriers have introduced systems that make completing calls difficult (for example, voice mail). In highly competitive markets, such as the incoming international market, this type of restriction tends to displace those carriers that were granted *amparos* by the courts. International traffic is being passed through TELMEX or other carriers that follow the CPP strategy for long distance.

Coexistence of the RPP and CPP Schemes for Incoming Domestic and International Long Distance Service

Letting long distance calls to mobile telephony users operate under both schemes without any type of restriction to completing calls would be advantageous. Each time users want to make long distance calls to a mobile phone, they would choose the preferred billing scheme, either the CPP with the 045 prefix or the RPP scheme with the 01 prefix. Users receiving calls would know, thanks to caller identification, when a call was made under the RPP scheme and would have the option of not taking the call. Current technology could allow the coexistence of the two regimes.

This proposal would be efficient, because it would let the maximum number of calls be completed. Calls not made under the CPP scheme would be made under the RPP scheme. In addition, because the RPP is cheaper, most traffic would be made under this scheme, which would eventually force CPP rates down.

The coexistence of both strategies would benefit both low-income mobile telephony users by means of the CPP scheme and mobile service users who value being connected to mobile telephony and fixed telephony users and who would thus be willing to pay the air time rate, as is mainly the case for companies.

Factors that Influence the Performance of Mobile Telephony

This section includes an econometric analysis using panel data of the main variables that affect mobile telephony (Eduardo Martínez

Chombo prepared the econometric model estimation). The mobile telephony performance variables employed in this analysis were average revenue per minute, average minutes of use per user, and mobile telephony penetration. The explanatory variables were GDP per capita in thousands of U.S. dollars (as the economic performance proxy for each economy), the percentage of prepaid lines, a dummy variable for the payment modality (CPP scheme = 1, other schemes = 0), a dummy variable for number portability, the market share of the two major carriers, and the number of carriers in the market. (Note that for the market share of the two largest telephone companies and the telephone number portability dummy, the coefficients were insignificant.) The analysis used annual information (calculated as the average of quarterly values) from 50 economies for 2001–05 as reported by Merrill Lynch (2006). In the case of information on dichotomous variables that do not vary over time, such as payment mode and number portability, the estimation used the random effects method. Table 9.8 summarized the results of the estimations. The estimate was performed on unbalanced panel data. In the final report, variables with less than 10 percent significance were sequentially eliminated.

The main results are as follows:

- When compared with the RPP scheme, the CPP scheme tends to reduce the use of mobile telephony while increasing revenues per minute.[7] This confirms that the CPP scheme is linked to

Table 9.8 Panel Data Regression Results

Variable	Revenue per minute (U.S. cents per minute)	Minutes of use (minutes per month)	Penetration of mobile telephones (percentage of all calls)
Number of companies	–1.4643*	—	4.7284*
CPP	6.2210*	–95.792*	17.416*
Prepaid	—	–0.7933*	—
Per capita GDP	0.2719*	1.7808*	1.9039*
Constant	13.165*	260.06*	–5.3488
R²	0.33	0.39	0.52
Number of observations	224	176	247
Number of countries	48	46	50

Source: Author's calculations based on data from the International Monetary Fund's world economic outlook database and Merrill Lynch 2006.

Notes: * = 1 percent significance. — = Not included in the regression.

high interconnection rates. High rates lead to a decreased use of mobile telephony, which is particularly inefficient because of the high price of terminal devices and the tendency of mobile carriers to replace them periodically, regardless of how much they have been used. When the cost of the terminal device has to be amortized in fewer air time minutes, the cost of providing air time increases.

- Penetration levels are higher with the CPP strategy. Interconnection rates place limits on off-net rates, so the competition focuses on offering subsidized terminal devices, replacing the devices frequently, and/or maximizing on-net call rates. In addition, this payment scheme fosters the connection of terminal devices whose main objective is to receive calls.

- GDP per capita has a positive relationship with minutes of use and mobile telephony penetration variables. GDP per capita also has a positive effect on revenue per minute, which is explained by the presence of 16 European countries in the sample (32 percent of the total). In those high-income countries, interconnection rates were elevated, which was evidenced by high usage per minute prices.

- Of the two variables used to measure competition in the market (number of companies in the industry and market share of the two largest companies), the results suggest that the number of participating companies is the most relevant. This is probably explained by the high entry barriers to the telephony market that make competition dependent on the number of current competitors. The results also highlight that the fewer the number of companies, the more revenue they earn (negative sign of the coefficient). They also indicate that countries with few mobile telephony companies have less penetration (positive sign of the coefficient). All this suggests that in countries with few participants in the industry, the companies hold market power.

- As concerns the existence, or not, of the portability of mobile numbers, this variable did not significantly affect any of the three mobile telephony indicators analyzed.

- The prepayment variable was important only in the regression of the minutes of use. Extensive use of a prepayment system reduces the time of use of mobile telephony. This might be because prepayment system prices are higher than those of postpayment systems and prepayment users face temporary liquidity limitations, and thus, when they are recurrently left without credit, prepayment users are briefly compelled to reduce their consumption.

Development of Broadband

The telecommunications industry has undergone rapid technological change in recent decades. Network capacity has been doubling every 6 to 12 months since 1997. This change has allowed the introduction of new and better quality services, including those related to the Internet, that require huge amounts of bandwidth. These services have improved business productivity and welfare, as Crandall and Charles (2001) find for the United States, estimating an annual consumer surplus gain of between US$270 million and US$420 million because of more rapid adoption of broadband services.

As defined by the OECD, broadband is an Internet connection at one-way speeds greater than 256 kilobits per second where the user is permanently connected. Broadband development has been strongly linked to that of the Internet, because the delivery of new content demanded greater bandwidth.

The positive impact of broadband use on economic performance has been well documented (Crandall and Charles 2001; Ford and Thomas 2005; Jorgenson 2004; Lehr and others 2005; Litan and Rivlin 2001; Minges 2006). For the United States, Lehr and others (2005) show that broadband use is connected to favorable economic development, employment, wages, and investment. In the case of developing countries such as Mexico, the benefits of this technology are significantly higher, because it can be a valuable instrument for educating and training large and scattered segments of the population. By promoting broadband penetration, governments could foster equity as well as growth within society. In addition, broadband could help make public administration more efficient by enabling the provision of public services, facilitating the payment of taxes, fostering greater transparency, and improving accountability.

Broadband in Mexico

Until 2001, TELMEX introduced broadband Internet services over its copper lines, known as digital subscriber lines. Broadband adoption in Mexico has been slow compared with countries that started to introduce broadband at the same time, such as the Czech Republic, Hungary, and Poland, and with countries where it started later, such as Ireland and the Slovak Republic (figure 9.9).

Mexico's delay in adopting broadband is a consequence of several factors, among which the following stand out: (a) the lack of a policy to increase competition by unbundling or leasing local subscriber loops, (b) the delayed authorization to cable television companies to

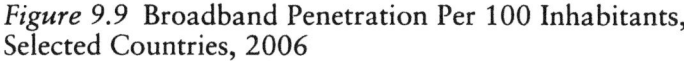

Figure 9.9 Broadband Penetration Per 100 Inhabitants, Selected Countries, 2006

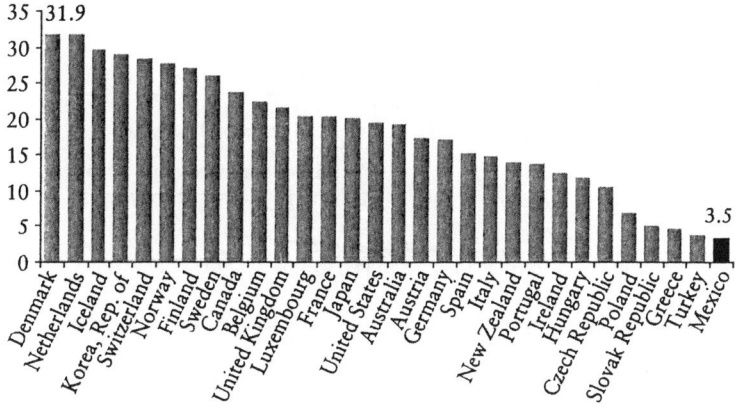

Source: OECD 2006.

provide broadband services, and (c) the restrictions that TELMEX has imposed on broadband use.

Local loop unbundling is particularly useful in fostering competition in countries with few broadband access alternatives where conventional telephony networks dominate. Unbundling allows users with telephone service to access broadband through providers that lease the local loop from the dominant carrier's network. Mexico is the only OECD country that has not introduced broadband competition by unbundling or leasing local loops. In light of TELMEX's opposition, the possibility of unbundling local loops has not even been discussed. By contrast, TELMEX has backed unbundling outside Mexico, notably in 2004, when the Chilean government asked for responses to its proposed framework for network unbundling.

One example of the impact that unbundling could have on telephone rates and quality of service is Orange in Spain, a subsidiary of France TELECOM. This carrier leases local loops from Telefónica and is currently offering a €39 (US$54) package per month that includes ultra-broadband service (20 megabits per second) that is five times faster than the fastest service TELMEX offers (4 megabits per second) at one-tenth the price, unlimited local and long distance calls, and 1,000 minutes of international long distance calls to 25 countries.

Another clear example can be seen in figure 9.10. Even though both Japan and Mexico introduced digital subscriber line offerings at roughly at the same time, Mexico has far fewer broadband users.

Figure 9.10 Evolution of Number of Broadband Internet Subscribers, Japan and Mexico, 2000–05

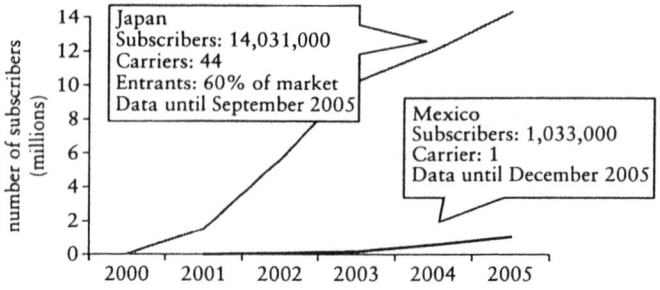

Japan
Subscribers: 14,031,000
Carriers: 44
Entrants: 60% of market
Data until September 2005

Mexico
Subscribers: 1,033,000
Carrier: 1
Data until December 2005

Sources: OECD, COFETEL, and Japan Ministry of Public Management data.

One of the reasons for this difference is that Japan allowed the unbundling of loops whereas Mexico did not.

Even though the 1995 Federal Telecommunications Act did not restrict public telecommunications networks from providing new services, the authorities did not let cable television companies begin to supply Internet access until 2003. In contrast, by 2002, cable television companies in 26 other OECD countries were already offering their users broadband Internet access.

The entry of cable television companies into the broadband market in Mexico could have significant effects on welfare, because their networks cover up to 55 percent of the population. These effects include the following:

- Cable television companies would offer the same services TELMEX does but at lower prices. Cable television companies have entered the market with lower rates: a 2 megabits per second connection costs residential cable television users between 8 to 35 percent of what TELMEX charges and business users 28 to 47 percent of what TELMEX charges.
- By competing, the cable television industry would stimulate lower rates, faster speeds, more innovation, and/or better quality of services. TELMEX recently decided to increase its users' broadband Internet speed without raising its rates, probably because of increased competition from cable television companies.
- Users would have more options to choose from. Note that TELMEX's slowest residential speed is 512 kilobits per second, whereas several cable television companies offer slower speeds at much lower prices, which would help an important segment of the population be incorporated into the market, especially

lower-income users, and would let users select the price and speed combination that is best for them.

Finally, TELMEX has limited the applications and services offered over the Internet. TELMEX's service contracts ban customers from using broadband for voice over Internet protocol (VoIP) services, which are much less expensive than traditional switchboard network technology. TELMEX has also forbidden broadband resellers from providing VoIP through its network.

Broadband and Content

Demand for broadband depends on the applications and content available to users. The more applications broadband can offer, such as VoIP, the greater the demand and, therefore, the faster it is adopted.

A connection exists between broadband supply and broadband providers' access to content such as television channels, and it is in the interests of broadband providers to obtain exclusive content to have a competitive edge on the market. If a broadband provider has limited or no access to content or must operate under unfavorable conditions in relation to another provider, it might be unfairly pushed out of the broadband market. For example, one of the main reasons Direct TV left the pay television market in Mexico was because it could not have access to Televisa's free-to-the-air programming, while its rival SKY could.

So far, the Internet has fostered free distribution of content and applications, which has led to a boom that has benefited users and that has, in turn, spurred broadband demand. However, the possibility that Internet access providers might follow discriminatory practices is high, particularly given the enormous concentration of broadband provision and content in Mexico whereby two television broadcasting companies dominate the content market. This could lead to agreements among the major broadband and content providers that would limit both content offerings and competition in the broadband market. The economic costs could be high in terms of lower broadband penetration, little content variety, and higher prices.

Concern is not limited to agreements between two or more broadband and content providers, but also applies to vertically integrated companies such as TELMEX, because it is not always in their interests to allow users to have unlimited access to applications and content. As noted earlier, this is particularly true for services that compete with those broadband providers offer such as VoIP services. Thus, the service contract of TELMEX's broadband offering bans customers from simultaneously using other available applications.

In relation to this issue, the U.S. Federal Communications Commission defined its stance in its Internet freedom principles published in 2005. These principles stated that to foster broadband penetration and to preserve and advance the open and interconnected nature of the public Internet, consumers have the right to use the applications of their choice. Allowing telecommunications service providers to make unrestricted offerings to broadband users may have a similar effect to that of local loop unbundling. Indeed, the U.S. Federal Communications Commission forbade AT&T the privilege of degrading any applications transmitted through its broadband.

More recently, as a result of a lawsuit by an Internet service provider and the Office of the National Economic Attorney, the Chilean Court for the Defense of Free Competition fined the dominant fixed telephony carrier approximately US$1 million for blocking VoIP providers. The court ordered the carrier to eliminate any clauses from its contract that banned or limited the use of services provided by independent vendors. It also ordered the company to abstain from restricting or hampering broadband use, in any manner, contractually or in practice, in the future.

Broadband access providers can restrict or discriminate against content or applications on their networks in several ways. For example, they can prioritize certain types of services or applications on the network, thereby affecting the quality of the content or services provided by third parties. Network providers can also use a variety of tools to block content. For instance, bit caps limit the number of bits a user can send out per month, notwithstanding bandwidth, while so-called walled gardens block third party's content or services (as is currently the case for the VoIP provider Skype), which the authorities in Mexico justify by noting that these providers require concessions that the authorities have not been willing to grant.

The following is a list of alternative measures the government could use to foster access to telecommunications content and services and, thereby, stimulate Internet demand:

- Ban Mexican companies from making exclusive or discriminatory arrangements with content or broadband providers. Free content, such as local television and radio, should also be available for free on the Internet (maintaining the restriction that local television advertising must be broadcast). The aim would be to increase Internet content, attract users to the Internet platform, and avoid the traditional television platform from being favored over the Internet.

- Encourage alternative broadband access platforms.
- Introduce competition by unbundling loops on TELMEX's network.
- Counteract the market power of Televisa and Televisión Azteca in the field of content by promoting competition in the television industry and allowing entry by foreign companies that broadcast in Spanish and are committed to creating domestic content.
- Require structural separation between providing broadband services and providing access to content, at least for the major content and broadband providers.

Municipal Use of the Radio-Electric Spectrum to Provide Broadband Services

One way to encourage broadband is to allow cities, municipalities, or states to offer this service jointly with telecommunications carriers. Several municipal projects to deploy wireless broadband networks are currently under way in cities such as San Francisco, Philadelphia, and Singapore. The governments of these cities plan to offer broadband Internet access for free at speeds of 256 to 512 kilobits per second and at reasonable prices at speeds above 1,000 kilobits per second.[8]

Development of these types of projects is partially due to the emergence of new wireless access technologies, namely, Wi-Fi and Wi-MAX, that allow entrants to deploy citywide networks in a short period of time and with only a small investment. Compared with wire-line networks, wireless deployments are faster and cheaper, because a single antenna may cover large areas. Chaska County, Minnesota, for example, installed a wireless network that covers the whole county with an investment of only US$600,000. As a result, the monthly rate consumers pay for broadband service is US$15.99 (Tropos Networks 2004).

Another driver of such municipal projects is the availability of unlicensed frequency bands. Experts have indicated that designating a greater portion of the radio-electric spectrum as unlicensed, particularly in the low frequency bands, would trigger broadband service offerings and innovation in mobile technologies and applications (Lehr 2004). The availability of unlicensed spectrum and relatively inexpensive equipment has led to an increase in the number of hotspots: public sites with wireless Internet access such as coffee shops, airports, and universities. The United States, for example, has more than 150,000 hotspots serving close to 30 million users (Federal Telecommunications Commission 2006).

POTENTIAL BENEFITS OF MUNICIPAL WIRELESS BROADBAND NETWORKS

According to a report by the U.S. Federal Telecommunications Commission (2006), municipalities should provide broadband services for three basic reasons. First, dominant telecommunications carriers have restricted broadband service offerings; thus, municipalities could represent an alternative for consumers. Second, municipalities could use the networks to improve the services they provide. Third, wireless broadband services could produce positive externalities, such as attracting or keeping companies or accelerating the adoption and use of new, beneficial technologies in a community.

Wireless networks could also let states and municipalities offer long distance health and educational services, thereby lowering coverage costs. Other services for which wireless networks might prove useful are consulting criminal, driving license, and fingerprint databases; providing wireless communication services for fire fighting and ambulance operations; and undertaking distance metering and billing of public utilities such as water and power.

Another argument for municipal wireless broadband networks is that installing wireless networks could be less expensive than installing wire-line networks, especially in areas with low population densities. In addition, public provision of wireless broadband could be more efficient than private provision, because it avoids costs related to the negotiation of rights of way to install antennas. Note that municipalities should consider equity issues when deciding to provide services; subsidies may be justified to provide service in unprofitable areas.

Finally, municipal wireless networks could represent an alternative to the dominant carrier network; thus, telecommunications carriers could offer telephony services to the community.

STATUS OF WIRELESS BROADBAND IN MEXICO

Mexico currently has few wireless broadband providers. Multivision is a wholesale and retail wireless broadband service provider that provides service to the three main cities using pre-Wi-MAX technology in the 2.5 gigahertz band. Another carrier that recently started offering wireless broadband services is Iusacell in the personal communication system band. Some frequency bands have already been assigned, but concessionaires are not using them. In 1998, TELMEX and UNEFON each obtained access to 50 megahertz in the 3.5 gigahertz band, which has been declared suitable for providing broadband services based on Wi-MAX technology, but have not yet provided any service on it.

Unlicensed spectrum could represent a means for encouraging wireless broadband deployments. In Mexico, certain spectrum ranges were declared unlicensed for broadband services according to a 2006 agreement (*Federal Official Gazette* 2006). TELMEX is currently using the 2.4 gigahertz unlicensed band to offer wireless broadband services to its clients through its Prodigy Móvil (Wi-Fi) brand.[9]

Under current regulations, states and municipalities could operate broadband networks on unlicensed frequency bands, as occurs in other countries. These networks should offer nondiscriminatory access to all carriers interested in providing services through them. In the United States, bills to this end have already been introduced. Because Mexico's Federal Telecommunications Act allows only concessionaires to negotiate interconnection agreements, municipalities will have to strike alliances with concessionaires so that they can offer not only wireless broadband Internet services, but also telephony services.

Aside from the unlicensed bands, the federal government could assign dedicated-use frequency bands, through the social coverage mechanism of the Federal Telecommunications Act, to public–private partnerships in municipalities or cities. For example, some frequencies in certain bands have not yet been assigned. Those bands could operate with Wi-MAX equipment, which transmits data at faster speeds and over longer distances than Wi-Fi (OECD 2006).

With the advent of digitalized television signals, the United States has begun to auction off spectrum in the 700 megahertz band to companies offering wireless broadband services, among others. Although Mexico is also transitioning toward digital television, the government has still not established a policy to release spectrum as soon as possible for other uses. The policy for the transition to digital television in Mexico sets deadlines for television station concessionaires to make digital replicas of the analog channel, but does not specify a date for turning off the analog channels (*Federal Official Gazette* 2004).

Consumer-Related Issues

This section discusses the impact of Mexico's telecommunications regulatory framework on consumer welfare.

Empowering Consumers

Class action suits are important to lower the costs of legal representation to dispersed clients, each of whom may have only a small claim. Mexico has made progress in this regard, because the 2004 Federal Consumer Protection Act states that the Federal Consumer Advocate's Office can file class action suits before the courts without needing to present any guarantees. However, the office is constrained by the need for interested parties to prove that they have suffered damages, which, in some cases, makes the class action nonviable (for example, in the case of gas stations or distributors that cheat consumers by charging for full liters but do not dispense full liters). Why the Federal Consumer Advocate's Office is the sole legal entity that can file these types of suits is still unclear.

Double Billing Calls

On November 30, 1994, the Ministry of Communications and Transport authorized TELMEX to charge the cost of a local call to all long distance calls, to calls to 1–800 numbers, and to mobile telephones, which means customers are being billed twice for using the local network. In the case of long distance calls, consumers pay for the long distance call to the long distance carrier that, in turn, pays two interconnection rates: one to the local carrier originating the call and another to the local carrier terminating it. Interconnection rates cover the costs local carriers incur for originating and terminating long distance calls. In addition, local carriers of originating calls charge their customers for a local call, which once again covers the cost of originating and terminating the call. Therefore, local infrastructure is paid for twice; that is, both the long distance carrier and the subscriber pay.

For international long distance calls originating in Mexico, essentially three payments are made for using the local infrastructure of origin, one by the long distance carrier and two by the subscriber. In 2005, TELMEX revenues from double billing long distance calls amounted to US$0.48 billion (figure 9.11), or 3.9 percent of its total revenues in Mexico.

On calls to 1–800 numbers, the subscriber pays the carrier providing the service for the calls it receives, whether local or long distance. The local carrier also charges the subscriber for a local call when these numbers are dialed. In addition to this charge to the consumer, carriers also have to pay TELMEX for billing and collection services.

Rounding Up Minutes or Charging Per Minute

In Mexico, calls to mobile telephones and long distance calls are charged per minute, and these charges are rounded up to the next minute. For example, if a customer makes a 1.5-minute call, the

Figure 9.11 TELMEX Revenues from Charges to Fixed Telephone Consumers on Long Distance Calls, 1999–2005

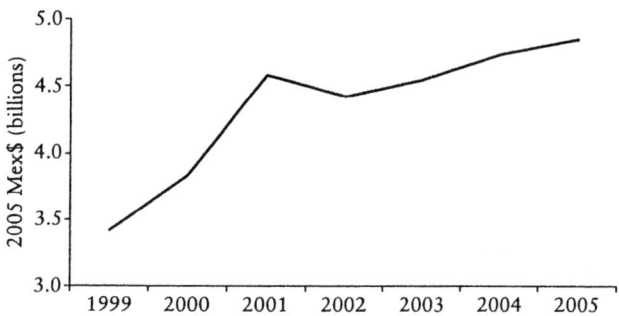

Source: Author's estimate based on TELMEX annual reports.

customer is billed for a 2-minute call, representing a surcharge of 33 percent. In other words, consumers pay an additional percentage on top of the cost of their call for time they never used. This kind of rounding up is not transparent for consumers and violates the Federal Consumer Protection Law, which prohibits charging users for a service that is not used. Technology permits tracking calls by the second.

Enabling Portability of Numbers

In Mexico, number portability is technologically feasible and has been legally binding for a number of years. At present, however, subscribers are made to change telephone numbers when they switch carriers, which is extremely inconvenient and poses a barrier to making the change.

The benefits of number portability include the following:

- cost savings for subscribers who switch service providers, because portability eliminates the expense of having to inform third parties of the new number and subscribers do not miss possible business opportunities or other calls;
- cost savings for subscribers making calls to users who have switched providers, because portability eliminates the costs and time connected with users who have to obtain the new number; and
- enhancements to service efficiency and quality, as well as price reductions because of increased competition.

COFETEL began a process to allow for the portability of geographic and nongeographic numbers. Portability is expected to be implemented by late 2007. Users would incur a charge for administrative expenses only.

Conclusions

When TELMEX was privatized in late 1990, a significant part of the country's infrastructure was concentrated in the hands of this one company, which was also granted a substantial rate increase and tax reduction. Moreover, when TELMEX was privatized it was shielded from competition for six years in the profitable domestic and international long distance markets. For all practical purposes, the company was also sheltered from competition in local telephony, because the government failed to establish interconnection rules until 1999. Furthermore, the more relevant coverage obligations were imposed on TELMEX until only 1994.

TELMEX has exercised its substantial market power unchecked. With the privatization, the Ministry of Communications and Transport took on key supervision, sanction, and control functions for which it was poorly prepared. Improving its skills in these areas was discouraged, because each time ministry technical departments tried to impose sanctions on TELMEX for noncompliance, they were rejected by their superiors. This rejection obviously frustrated the ministry staff, which, in turn, led to no follow-up of TELMEX's compliance with its concession-related obligations.

When the 1995 Federal Telecommunications Act was enacted, the government had an opportunity to create an agency with technical autonomy to supervise and regulate TELMEX and the industry. Initial drafts envisaged a telecommunications commission with that authority, but the articles dealing with the detailed enforcement powers of the regulatory entity were deleted. COFETEL was set up by a general article as an agency of the Ministry of Communications and Transport in such a way that it lacked the power required for effective regulation.

Mexico was also short of other institutions that could countervail TELMEX's market power. For example, in November 1994, when the Ministry of Communications and Transport authorized TELMEX to charge both the long distance rate and the cost of a local call for long distance calls, no consumer advocacy groups were in place that could have challenged the authorization. The opaque manner in which this charge was introduced meant that for years most consumers were unaware of what they were being charged for. The Federal Consumer

Advocate's Office was not involved in the problem and, in any case, would probably have been unable to disallow the charge.

The defense of consumers' rights before the federal courts faces two significant limitations. First, *amparos* do not have effects on all parties, but rather are binding only upon the parties involved in the proceedings. Second, contrary to the custom in other countries, when juridical proceedings are filed before the federal courts regarding regulatory measures issued by the telecommunications regulating agency, users (individually or collectively) cannot participate in the corresponding *amparo*. This is the case for the suits currently filed against the CPP scheme in long distance. The rationale is that— according to judicial criteria—users have only an economic, not juridical, interest in COFETEL's rulings and, therefore, cannot be party to the suit.

As for competition policies, even though Mexico's constitution bans monopolies, it did not have both the legislation and the agency to deal with economic competition issues until mid-1993, plus the CFC's capacity to enforce its resolutions before the courts has been limited. It has been unable to implement many of the sanctions it has imposed, as was the case with the declaration of TELMEX's dominance in the market in late 1997, which the courts recently rendered null and void.

Because of the country's institutional weaknesses, it has been unable to prevent practices that harm competition and consumers. In light of the huge technological changes in the sector and to foster competition, preventing existing dominant carriers from forming monopolies with new technologies or standards is extremely important. This would be the case for Wi-Fi, power line communications, digital subscriber lines, VoIP, and so on, because these technologies have the potential of opening increasingly important telecommunications markets to competition. To date, the authorities' performance has been lackluster. TELMEX has monopolized digital subscriber line technology, which uses telephone-line copper pairs to provide broadband access, because no policy regarding local loop unbundling is in place. Power line communications technology runs a similar risk of monopolization if, instead of being operated by the Federal Electricity Commission, a decision is reached for its commercial applications to be undertaken by a dominant company.

Mexico can, however, overcome its tardiness in embracing broadband and place itself on the cutting edge. Proper management of the radio-electric spectrum by the state is crucial. So far, allocation of the spectrum has been concentrated among just a few players. Those players sometimes seem to acquire the spectrum either to warehouse it and prevent it from falling into the hands of third parties who would then offer services or to secure it so they can resell it to major carriers. In the case of Wi-Fi standards, because equipment operates on bands that have recently been declared unlicensed, cities or municipalities, in association with concessionaires, might be able to develop low-cost broadband networks for offering competitive tele-communication services to citizens.

The underlying question is therefore how Mexico can change the status quo. It now has the Telecommunications Law, which, although obsolete in certain regards, has fundamentals that are still valid. In addition, Mexico has signed international agreements such as the World Trade Organization's Fourth Protocol to the General Agree-ment on Trade in Services. The protocol includes a reference paper on basic telecommunications that clearly stipulates key issues regard-ing proper interconnection of networks, anticompetitive practices, and even appropriate operation of a regulatory agency. The paper notes that regulatory agencies are to be independent of all basic services vendors and that agency decisions must be impartial with regard to market participants.

Mexico could achieve a good deal simply by complying with the provisions of the Federal Telecommunications Act and the reference paper, as well as by ensuring clear separation between the major carriers and the regulatory agency.

Notes

1. Condition 8–4 of the concession certificate requires that if TELMEX engages in monopolistic practices in any or several of the services it provides and cannot prove otherwise, the Ministry of Communications and Trans-port can (a) revoke authorization according to the terms and conditions established in the law or in regulations in effect, or (b) ban TELMEX from providing services for a five-year period or for an undefined period of time.

2. In 2000, COFETEL established 39 specific obligations for TELMEX: 18 pertaining to rates, 12 to quality of service, and 8 to information, and 1 stating the goal of the regulation and the relevant markets it covered.

3. According to the July 1, 1994, resolution and the long distance rules of June 20, 1996, all local areas are open to competition through the presub-scription service (whereby competitors interconnect with TELMEX in areas where it has digital connections). TELMEX's network has been entirely dig-ital since 2000. Thus, it could provide this presubscription service through-out the country, but has yet to do so.

4. Apparently, some local carriers are unwilling to enter the market to avoid payment of the long distance interconnection rate, and so to provide public telephony services, they lease lines from TELMEX.

5. The assumption that call traffic is uniform overestimates the average cost if we consider that users prefer to make more on-net calls than off-net calls. The Telefónica average cost per minute would decrease by a smaller proportion than the TELCEL average cost, because Telefónica users cannot minimize their off-net calls as much as TELCEL users. In this scenario, the negative effects of high interconnection rates on the competition could be greater than estimated.

6. The act assumed that negotiations would be carried out to determine interconnection rates because one of the parties would want to lower the rates while the other party would want to keep them high. The law did not consider the case in which both parties would be willing to keep interconnection rates high for the benefit of one or both of the companies involved, albeit to the detriment of competition and consumers.

7. There is a double accounting of minutes per user in countries using the RPP system. This is because on-net calls are billed twice, once for the calling party and again for the receiving party. Under the CPP system, only the party making the call is billed. Data for countries using the RPP system have been adjusted downward by 20 percent as a way to compensate for the double billing.

8. For more information, visit http://www.sfgov.org/site/tech_connect_index.asp?id=36612; http://www.wirelessphiladelphia.org/; http://www.ida.gov.sg/idaweb/marketing/infopage.jsp?infopagecategory=factsheet:wireless&versionid=2&infopageid=I3928.

9. For more information, visit http://www.telmex.com/mx/hogar/ai_pdgyMovilInicio.html.

References

Casanueva, C., and R. del Villar. 2003. "Analysis of the Reform in the Basic Telecommunications Industry in Mexico (1990–2000)." In *Critical Infrastructures: State of the Art in Research and Application*, ed. W. A. H. Thissen and P. M. Herder, 179–207. Kluwer Book Series, International Series on Operations Research and Management Science, vol. 65. Boston: Academic Publishers.

Casasús, C. 1994. "Privatization of Telecommunications: The Case of Mexico." In *Implementing Reforms in the Telecommunications Sector: Lessons from Experience*, ed. B. Wellenius and P. Stern, 177–84. Washington, DC: World Bank.

Crandall, R., and J. Charles. 2001. *The $500 Billion Opportunity: The Potential Economic Benefit of Widespread Diffusion of Broadband Internet Access*. Washington, DC: Criterion Economics.

del Villar, R., and J. Serrano. 2003. *Estimate of Teléfonos de México 2003 Controlled Services Rate Level and the Adjustment Factor for 2003–2006.*

Mexico City: Banco de México, Departamento de Investigación Economica.

Federal Official Gazette. 2004. "Agreement to Adopt the Technological Standard of Terrestrial Digital Television and Establish the Policy to Transition to Terrestrial Digital Television in Mexico." First section, July 2.

————. 2006. "Agreement to Establish Policies for Broadband Services and Other Applications." First section, March 13.

Federal Telecommunications Commission. 2006. *Municipal Provision of Wireless Internet.* Staff Report. Washington, DC: Government Printing Office.

Ford, G., and K. Thomas. 2005. "Broadband and Economic Development: A Municipal Case Study from Florida." *Review of Urban and Regional Development Studies* 17 (3): 219–22.

Gil, J. 2000. "La interconeccion en el sector Mexicano de telecomunicaciones desde la privatizacion de TELMEX: Un analisis teorico y empirico," B.A. thesis, Instituto Tecnológico Autónomo de México, Mexico City.

Jorgenson, D. W. 2004. "Accounting for Growth in the Information Age." In *Productivity and Cyclicality in Semiconductors: Trends, Implications and Questions.* Washington, DC: National Academies Press.

Jorgenson, D. W., and Khuong Vu. 2005. "Information Technology and the World Economy." *Scandinavian Journal of Economics* 107 (4): 631–50.

Lehr, W. 2004. *Economic Case for Dedicated Unlicensed Spectrum Below 3 GHz.* Cambridge, MA: Massachusetts Institute of Technology, Research Program on Internet and Telecoms Convergence.

Lehr, W., C. Osorio, S. Gillett, and M. Sirbu. 2005. "Measuring Broadband's Economic Impact." Paper presented at the 33rd Research Conference on Communication, Information, and Internet Policy, October, Arlington, VA.

Litan, R. E., and A. M. Rivlin. 2001. "Projecting the Economic Impact of the Internet." *American Economic Review* 91 (2): 313–17.

Merrill Lynch. 2006. *Global Wireless Matrix 2Q06.* New York: Global Securities Research and Economics Group, Research Department.

Minges, M. 2006. *Revisiting Jipp.* Research report. Washington, DC: Telecommunications Management Group.

OECD (Organisation for Economic Co-operation and Development). 2006. *The Implications of WiMax for Competition and Regulation.* Paris: OECD. http://www.oecd.org/sti/ict/broadband.

Solano, O., R. del Villar, and R. García-Verdú. 2006. "Challenges to the Effective Implementation of Competition Policy in Regulated Sectors: The Case of Telecommunications in Mexico." *Northwestern Journal of International Law and Business* 26 (3): 527–46.

Tropos Networks. 2004. *Metro-Scale Wi-Fi as City Service.* Chaska Case Study. Minnesota: Tropos Networks.

E
Sub-Saharan Africa

[18]

THE ROLE OF COMPETITION LAW AND POLICY IN ALLEVIATING POVERTY – THE CASE OF ZAMBIA

Thulasoni Kaira*

1. Introduction

Definitions of poverty are normally debatable but have increasingly taken an economic rationalization approach where a standard quantifiable figure of "less than a dollar a day" has been used as the rule of the thumb. Arguments may arise as to the determination of poverty levels in a country and the variables thereto, more so when such determination has been done by foreign expertise. Some of the more developed countries refuse to accept the existence of poverty in their countries; while the lesser developed countries usually acknowledge its existence but often tend to argue against higher statistics thereto. This is because poverty is an embarrassing phenomenon to acknowledge. A discourse on causes of poverty would also produce varying answers ranging from wrong Government policies to "laziness" of the poor. Whichever the case and whatever the answers to the many more questions that may be posed about poverty, the presence of some less or extreme levels of poverty is a reality in almost each country and denial in any context and to any extent would likely impede the efforts to address the issue. Inevitably, poverty alleviation and/or eradication is a subject and source of wealth for a lot of other people who study the phenomenon in less developed countries either through research organizations or through personal individual consultancies. For this reason, poverty is big business anywhere, more

* The author is the Acting Executive Director of the Zambia Competition Commission. He has worked at the Commission since 1998 and has risen through the ranks to his current position. The author is gratefully indebted to Mr John Preston of DFID and Emily Mburu of UNCTAD who made very insightful and inspiring comments, and Mr George Lipimile of UNCTAD, Chilufya Sampa, Wesley Kalapula and Kelvin Kamayoyo of the Zambia Competition Commission for their useful comments (e-mail: zcomp@zamtel.zm (corporate); Thulasonikaira@yahoo.com (private)).

133

so in Africa. Evidently, the way to a poor man's mouth is through a rich man's hand.

Whatever the causes of poverty, the solution to alleviating them would ordinarily have to lie in pragmatic policy interventions. Precisely, there is a need to know who the poor are and where they are to be found. For example, as far back as 1998, in a report for the Zambia Central Statistical Office (CSO)[114], it was shown that 84.4 per cent of the small-scale farmers (who are concentrated in the countryside) were living in extreme poverty. This was at a time when the overall national poverty levels were at 84 per cent. According to this same study, the population living in the high-cost areas experienced a significant increase in their poverty level between 1996 and 1998, but they continued to have the second smallest incidence of poverty next to the large-scale farmers. On the whole, life was good for the large-scale farmers.

The prevalence of high poverty levels in less developed countries such as Zambia is not only embarrassing but one that requires serious attention in terms of feasible or result-oriented policy formulation as well as realising the intended objectives and/or refocusing the same. Dealing with poverty in the Third World is a mammoth task that often appears to dog the most prudent of policies, competition policy notwithstanding.

A casual observation shows that where there is stable political leadership, there is likely to be sustainable macro-economic indicators, which are a prelude to any meaningful poverty eradication efforts. There would appear to be some indications of such positive strides in countries within the region such as Namibia, Botswana, Mauritius, and to a notable extent, Zambia and South Africa.

The road to poverty reduction in Zambia was ably formulated under the auspices of the Ministry of Finance and National Planning in the *Poverty Reduction Strategy Paper* –PRSP (2002). An outline representation of its implementation is given in Appendix 1. The PRSP considered poverty in the following ways:

---

[114] *Living Conditions in Zambia*, Zambia Central Statistical Office, 1998.

- *Income perspective:* A person is poor if his/her income falls below a defined moneymetric poverty line, e.g. $1 a day.
- *Basic needs perspective:* A person is poor if he/she falls short of the material requirements for minimal acceptable fulfilment of human needs. This concept goes beyond the lack of income.
- *Capability perspective:* A person is poor if he/she lacks certain basic capabilities to function. Such 'functionings' range from physical ones such as adequate food, clothing, and shelter to more complex social achievements such as participation in the life of the community. The merit of the capability approach lies in its ability to reconcile the notions of relative and absolute poverty. Relative deprivations in incomes and material requisites can lead to absolute deprivation in capabilities.

A truly holistic measure of poverty needs to encompass elements from all three perspectives. The PRSP recognised that the traditional measures (such as the headcount index) that capture only income deficiency are simply not adequate. One such holistic measure is the Human Poverty Index (HPI), developed by the United Nations Development Programme (UNDP)[115]. The HPI, which intends to gauge a broader notion of 'human poverty' as opposed to just income poverty, appears to be a composite index that measures deprivation in three broad dimensions: deprivation of a long and healthy life measured by the percentage of newborns not expected to survive to 40 years of age; deprivation of knowledge measured by illiteracy; and deprivation in economic provisioning measured by the percentage of the population lacking access to health services and safe water as well as the number of children who are moderately or severely underweight.

Even the HPI, however, does not measure all aspects of poverty. It excludes, for instance, lack of political freedom and personal security and the inability to participate in decision making and in the life of the community. Notably, the Government acknowledged in the PRSP that these facets of poverty are of course not easy to measure.

While the PRSP has been implemented in some measure, its success is a subject of continued debate. In an attempt to contribute to this debate, this study analyses the causes of poverty in Zambia and its

---

[115] *Human Development Report,* United Nations Development Programme, 1997.

location, what is being done to address poverty, and how competition law and policy has and/or can be used to address poverty, before presenting conclusions.

In the context of competition law and policy, it is essential to hypothesize that any poverty alleviation efforts have to create wealth (i.e. through efficiencies), create jobs (i.e. through new entry), and/or reduce prices (through competition). Where competition enforcement efforts do not lead to these results, then the existence of this law should be questioned and answers given as to why these results are not self-evident. There is a public demand that all institutions that depend on the taxpayer for their existence must be able to demonstrate their benefit to the general public, more so in terms of facilitating the creation of wealth. In the conclusion, there is an attempt to explain any observed failures of competition law and policy to function as an effective tool for poverty alleviation strategies.

2. Literature review on interface between competition policy and law and poverty alleviation

It is now common knowledge in the domain of the average competition student that the primary objective of competition policy is to enhance consumer welfare by promoting competition. Economic efficiency is generally enhanced by encouraging competition, and thus one of the key links between competition policy and development has been the role that competition policy plays in increasing economic efficiency. The efficient use of resources is especially important in the development context where resources are particularly scarce. Less developed countries such as Zambia would fall into this category.

The main static effects of competition are to reduce the ability of firms to raise prices above marginal cost and to ensure that firms produce at the lowest possible costs. The dynamic consequences of competition can include incentives to innovate, to imitate, and to invest in the development of new technologies and know-how. Competition policy reinforces economic efficiency by preventing or providing

136

remedies for market structures and business practices that weaken the degree of inter-firm rivalry in markets[116].

   While the above statements appear quite abstract, there are some scholars and experts who have attempted to actually directly link competition policy and law implementation efforts to poverty reduction *per se*. For instance, Fox (2007)[117] submitted that market tools are a very important part of the panoply of tools needed to address world poverty and that they should be used liberally. These market tools include market-freeing measures that reduce prices. They also include antitrust priority setting that targets conspiracies that raise the price of staples, such as milk, bread, transportation and utilities, helping the poor as well as those who are better off. Perhaps the critical challenge to the traditional efficiency advocacy for competition law and policy was best rephrased by Fox when she asked this pertinent question: If you were a policy maker in a country whose principal economic problem was deep systemic poverty, aggravated by corruption, cronyism, selective statism, weak institutions, and often unstable democracy, what is the foundational perspective on which you would formulate your country's antitrust law? In particular, would you choose a foundational principle that trusts liberalization and free enterprise ("first model") or would you choose a foundational principle that centrally takes account of the opacity, blockage and political capture of your markets, and includes some measure of helping to empower people economically to help themselves ("second model"). In the face of the disparities in wealth and opportunity to the harm of some of the poorest people caused by globalization, Fox considered the second model to be the other path through which developing countries can use competition law to ensure that the free market policies do not disproportionately advantage the already advantaged in every game played. It is clear than even in the face of liberalization, developed countries liberalized where convenient

---

[116] OECD Conference, *Investment for Development: Making it Happen*, Background Information in Support of the Global Forum on International Investment *Putting the Policy Framework for Investment into Action* – a Policy Framework for Investment: Competition Policy, 25–27 October 2005, Rio de Janeiro, Brazil, Hosted by the Government of Brazil. Organized by the OECD Investment Committee in partnership with the World Bank.

[117] Prof Eleanor Fox, *Economic Development, Poverty and Antitrust: The Other Path*, New York University Public Law and Legal Theory Working Papers, Paper 57, 2007.

and resisted liberalization where inconvenient. Fox attempted to link deep systemic poverty to inequality in world trade.

Freeing the markets has been shown to hold great economic benefits for developing and transition countries. For this, Fox is convinced that antitrust can help, although she is mindful of the form such an antitrust law should take.

Khemani has observed that the World Bank's *Global Economic Prospects Report* (2003) points to the pro-growth and pro-poor benefits of competitive markets. Research conducted for the report indicates that economies with competitive domestic markets generally tend to have higher levels and rates of growth in *per capita* income. Entry of firms plays an important role in the competitive process and such economies also have lower rates of poverty and attract more domestic and foreign investment. Accordingly, these research findings are considered to be consistent with the theory that barriers to competition impede innovation, growth and prosperity[118]. While enactment of a competition law does not necessarily result in competition, Khemani has acknowledged that with a competition law in place, it signals to firms and markets that certain business behaviours and commercial practices, as defined in the law, are illegal. It confers rights and obligations on transacting parties and provides for due process to resolve disputes and obtain relief from anti-competitive practices. Findings from the World Economic Forum's *The Global Competitiveness Report 2006–2007* provides further evidence of the importance of competition, and competition law and policy, in fostering higher incomes, broad-based markets (less dominant firms) and global competitiveness.

The Department for International Development (DFID)[119] has recognized that fair competition in markets is crucial for economic and social development, and for reducing poverty yet anti-competitive practices diminish the opportunities for innovation and growth, making consumers worse off. Recognition is made (p. 38) of the contribution

---

[118] R. S. Khemani, *Competition Policy and Promotion of Investment, Economic Growth and Poverty Alleviation in Least Developed Countries,* Occasional Paper 19, the World Bank, FIAS, 2007.
[119] *Competition Assessment Framework – An operational guide for identifying barriers to competition in developing countries,* Department for International Development, Zambia, January 2008.

that competitive markets can make to economic growth and to poverty reduction.

The development of the micro, small and medium-sized enterprises (MSMEs) may also appear to be one area where competition law and policy may facilitate growth and thus reduce poverty. Hallberg[120] has observed that imperfectly competitive markets for products produced by SMEs are certainly a distortion that creates a bias against small firms. In addition, imperfect competition in markets for products and services used by SMEs (for example, financial markets) can discriminate against them. The first-best solution would be to deal directly with the market failure (e.g. enforcing competition policy).

Hallberg argued that SME promotion is justified on the grounds of the greater efficiency of small firms, their contribution to a more equitable distribution of income, and their role in generating employment. However, she was sensitive to the fact that empirical evidence supporting these claims was very mixed. The real reason that developing country governments should be interested in SMEs was not because of the benefits of smallness, but because "they are there", and account for a large share of employment.

3. The poverty levels in Zambia

According to the latest statistics from the Zambia CSO, Zambia has a population of about 11 million. Of this population, about 500,000 are formally employed while the rest are either children, retirees, or are self/informally employed. A walk in the streets of Lusaka, more so in the unplanned settlements (or "compounds" as they are commonly referred to), shows a large proportion of the self-employed, notably women. These are arguably the visible urban poor. Those in rural settlements are considered to be arguably worse off[121] because of the volatile nature

---

[120] Kristin Hallberg, *Small and Medium Scale Enterprises: A Framework for Intervention,* Small Enterprise Unit, Private Sector Development Department, The World Bank, May 21, 1999.

[121] On the other hand it may be argued that although materially poorer, those in rural areas, in the absence of drought and animal disease, are better off in that they are spared the squalor of urban settlements which are often incubation spots for disease and societal rot.

139

of their economic lifelines, e.g. crop yield and livestock rearing may be susceptible to drought and disease.

While poverty levels in Zambia remain unacceptably high, there has been tremendous progress made in terms of macroeconomic stability since 2002, which has had positive effects on the microeconomic variables. While there is a lot to be done in terms of developing a culture of competition in public procurement and private business dealings, there is still a lot that has been done in terms of realigning the economy from a State-controlled economy to a market economy.

Table 1 shows the relatively commendable growth rates that have been achieved since 2000, with relatively higher growth rates registered since 2002 onwards.

Table 1: Key macro-statistics 1996–2006

	1996	1997	1998	1999	2000	2001	2002	2003	2004	2005	2006
Total GDP at current prices (ZK'billion)	3,950.2	5,140.2	6,027.9	7,477.7	10,071.9	13,132.7	16,260.4	20,479.2	25,997.4	32,456.3	38,676.5
Total GDP at constant (1994) prices (ZK'billion)	2,328.1	2,404.9	2,360.2	2,412.7	2,499.0	2,621.3	2,707.9	2,846.5	2,999.2	3,155.9	3,343.3
GDP per capita at current prices (kwacha)	444,059	564,127	645,869	782,201	1,028,587	1,301,621	1,562,085	1,906,038	2,344,290	2,836,723	3,278,034
GDP per capita at constant (1994) prices (kwacha)	261,707	263,935	252,886	252,384	255,213	259,806	260,138	264,930	270,450	275,830	283,365
GDP growth rate at constant (1994) prices	6.9	3.3	−1.9	2.2	3.6	4.9	3.3	5.1	5.4	5.2	6.2

Source: CSO, National Accounts Statistics.

With the growth rate, the poverty levels appear to have also diminished, as shown in Table 2:

140

Table 2: Poverty trends 1991–2006

Total/Residence	1991	1993	1996	1998	2004	2006
Zambia	70	74	69	73	68	64
Rural	88	92	82	83	78	80
Urban	49	45	46	56	53	34

Source: CSO, *Living Conditions Monitoring Survey V* (2006).

Despite the liberalization and commercialization of the economy from 1991, the biggest challenge to Zambia's efforts to reduce poverty have been years of high inflation in the 1990s. It was not until 2002, when the "New Deal" policies[122] of the present Government were announced, that Zambia appeared to show great strides in this regard, which culminated in a single-digit figure in 2006. With reduced inflation, this has seen interest rates decrease and provided affordable finance capital to business, more so the SME segment that provides critical supply linkages to the growing mining industry.

Graph 1 shows the inflationary trend from December 2006 to December 2007.

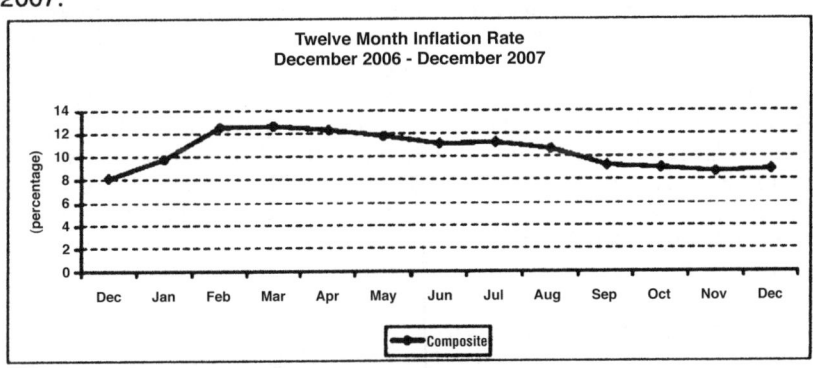

Source: Consumer Price Index (CPI), December 2007

Graph 1: Inflation rate December 2006 to December 2007

While stabilisation of inflation has been a significant success story of the New Deal policies – and admittedly other macro-economic

---

[122] At his inaugural Presidential speech in January 2002, current President Levy Mwanawasa, enunciated "New Deal" policies that he promised his government would follow in order to change the economy and reduce poverty levels.

statistics show some good news – the figures would appear to still be far from the reality on the ground in so far as extreme poverty levels are concerned. A consideration of those that are poor shows that they are to be found somewhere in the

- small informal businesses sector (largely street vendors and market traders), and
- agriculture sector (largely the rural areas, where the poverty levels are about 80 per cent).

It would be in these areas that competition law should show itself active in ensuring that any interventions yield efficiencies that trickle downstream.

4. Why there is still extreme poverty in Zambia

Having identified where the majority of the poor are, it is a natural consequence to ask the question: Why do we have poverty, especially extreme poverty? Various reasons have been advanced by both Government and external development partners on the causes of extreme poverty levels in Zambia. Whatever the causes, they should be the primary mischief that competition law and policy should, directly, and/or indirectly, be engaged actively and otherwise to resolve. Various writings including those of the CSO and the PRSP (pp. 28–29) have posited hypotheses as to why there is poverty in Zambia. These have been considered as follows:

4.1. Lack of economic growth

At the time that the PRSP was being drafted and finalized (in 2002), the economic reality of Zambia was uninspiring in many ways. This was perhaps true at the time of formulation of the PRSP, when the economy was marginally growing. The trend has been different since 2002. For now, this has been sustained above 5 per cent and it is hoped that policy stability shall continue. However, much of the growth is attributed to the discovery of new mines and the increased copper prices as a result of the high Chinese demand. Bottlenecks such as

HIV/AIDS continue to be a toll on the human capital although there has been a drastic reduction.

Significant poverty reduction requires a substantial injection of resources into poverty reduction activities and that is not possible without growth. In its absence, there can be little increase in domestic resources either through savings or tax revenues. Fortunately, there has been a remarkable improvement in macroeconomic statistics from 2002, with a reducing trend in inflation and an increasing trend in GDP. For instance, Table 3 shows that international reserves have increased by almost 50 per cent between 2006 and 2007, which is exceptionally good for Zambia considering where it is coming from.

Table 3: International reserves 2006–2007

International reserves	December 2007 (ZK billion)	December 2006 (ZK billion)	End-period exchange rate Dec. 2007: US$1=ZK3,845 Dec. 2006: US$1=ZK4,407
Gross official foreign assets	7,251	5,334	
Foreign currency reserves	4,110	3,054	
SDRs holdings	38	59	
IMF reserve position	3,086	2,220	
Other foreign assets	17	1	

Source: adapted from CSO, *Zambia National Summary Data Page, External Sector 2007*[123].
SDRs - Special Drawing Rights; IMF - International Monetary Fund.

4.2. High inequality

Increased economic development inevitably leads to more wealth for the wealthy and/or more money for those who are able to exploit the opportunities. The prospects for growth as well as the subsequent impact of any growth on poverty reduction are thwarted by a

---

[123] Figures on http://www.zamstats.gov.zm/extern.php captured on 3 March 2008.

143

high level of inequality. Rural-urban, interprovincial, and inter-social strata disparities are already evident from the tables presented so far. Another crucial conclusion of empirical research has been that a historically unequal situation might perpetuate itself unless changed by government policy, such as asset redistribution.

It is possible for competition law and policy to influence or facilitate measures that would be aimed at expanding the base of entrepreneurship through modification and/or outright prohibition of anti-competitive arrangements by dominant firms and trade associations. The provisions for small business promotion in the Australian *Trade Practices Act 1974* provide a relevant model that countries such as Zambia may also opt to include in their legislations.

4.3. Debt burden

Another major factor that has reduced resources for poverty reduction is the heavy debt burden, which has exerted a significant crowding-out effect on social expenditures. Over the years up to 2003, debt service has on average accounted for 10 per cent of the GDP, while all the social sectors together have accounted for only 5 per cent. With Zambia reaching the "Highly Indebted Poor Countries" (HIPC) benchmarks set by the International Monetary Fund (IMF), debt relief has come as a major boost to economic activity as it has freed resources. Overt evidence of this has been a strengthened local currency and reduced interest rates due to less Government borrowing from the domestic financial institutions.

Considering that not more than three years ago the country had an external debt of over US$6 billion (ZK24 trillion), a reduction to US$1 billion (K4 trillion) lays good ground for using resources for development rather than for debt serving.

Table 4: External debt 2006–2007

External debt	December 2007 (ZK billion)	December 2006 (ZK billion)	End-period exchange rate Dec. 2007: US$1=ZK3,845 Dec. 2006: US$1=ZK4,407
Total debt (stock)	3,923	4,350	
Official debt (stock)	3,496	4,077	
Multilateral	2,392	2,336	
Bilateral	1,104	1,741	
Private debt, incl. parastatals (stock)	427	273	

Source*: adapted from CSO, Zambia National Summary Data Page, External Sector 2007[124].*

4.4. Excessive external dependence

The absence of growth and the huge debt burden have made external funding a necessity. External funding constituted, for instance, 89 per cent and 84 per cent, respectively, of the total spending in the water and sanitation sectors in 1995 and 1996, compared to 31 per cent in 1990. In 2001, 53 per cent of the national budget was expected to be funded from outside.

By 2007, this was reduced to about 30 per cent, which is a commendable drop within a period of five years. It is likely that the trend is going to be downwards although such dependence may easily fluctuate in higher realms where international factors adversely affect the balance of payments, e.g. oil prices.

---

[124] *Ibid.*

145

4.5. Other causes

Other causes include inappropriate prioritization; inadequate social safety nets; and HIV/AIDS, and rural-urban migration. CSO statistics show that rural-urban migration has led to congested urban areas, overburdened social amenities and a pressure on jobs that has in turn led to a burgeoning informal sector. Migrants formally of an occupation in agriculture, fisheries and animal husbandry accounted for the highest percentages in all provinces compared to other occupations. In Eastern Province they accounted for 46 per cent followed by Luapula at 39 per cent and Western Province with 36 per cent (CSO, 2003).

5. What needs to be done to address poverty in Zambia?

It is evident that most of the poor in Zambia are in the agricultural sector. Thus, policy interventions in agro-related industries would likely have the greatest impact on improving the extreme levels of poverty. It is already a known fact that agriculture is expected to be a key sector for the future development of the Zambian economy, together with mining and tourism. This perhaps is true for most of sub-Saharan Africa. Infrastructural issues normally come to mind in terms of accessing the rural with farming implements as well as the rural farmer accessing markets with his harvest. Transportation of agricultural inputs and outputs is a major constraint each year, a constraint that the unscrupulous and opportunistic trader has taken advantage of to abuse the rural farmer. The condition of rural roads is of key importance to farmers as is wider agricultural and regional development, especially in trying to bring subsistence or marginally commercial farmers into the cash economy[125]. The competition law would ordinarily come in handy to ensure that the bidding process for such critical infrastructure is not marred by anti-competitive practices such as bid rigging or collusive tendering[126].

---

[125] United Nations, *Zambia Country Profile*, Johannesburg Earth Summit, p. 89, 2004.
[126] Section 9 of the *Competition and Fair Trading Act,* CAP 417 of the Laws of Zambia.

146

In the 2006 *Living Conditions Monitoring Survey (V)*, households were asked to indicate which developmental projects they would like provided or improved in their communities. The results show that 30 per cent of the respondents desired projects related to road infrastructure. Provision or improvement of education facilities was the second preferred project with 18 per cent of the households followed by health facilities with 13 per cent. The least desired projects were credit facilities, employment issues, police/security facilities, and sanitation at one per cent each (CSO, *The Monthly,* 2007).

Even the rural poor know that infrastructure development will be a decisive factor in their socio-economic transformation. The role of competition policy in infrastructural development is critical to its success. The bid-rigging or collusive tendering instances would be minimized in the wake of competition for public works. This has actually been a major problem in capital-intensive projects such as road and bridge construction where contractors are given a contract to do the same job, one after the other fails to complete it. The following section shall deal with how competition has been used in agro-related sectors to stimulate or sustain wealth creation.

6. Using the competition law and policy to deal with poverty

A competition law has a specific sphere of operation and objectives that may in many ways contribute to the alleviation of poverty by ensuring that failing firms are taken over by more vibrant competitors or new entrants. The competition law may also be used to break cartels that constrain freedom of trade and business expansion as is shown later in a poultry case study. Further, this law may also be used to ensure that there is no exclusive dealing that is anti-competitive and that leads to the failure of other market actors to penetrate markets and/or thrive competitively. It is in, *inter alia,* these areas that a competition authority would directly and/or indirectly contribute to wealth maintenance and wealth creation, which are key to any strategy to alleviate poverty.

The United Nations system in Zambia has recognized the role of competition law in economic development. The Zambia Country Profile notes that the *Competition and Fair Trading Act* regulates the

147

market to ensure fair trading practices and prevent market domination through the Competition Commission[127].

The report noted that the Ministry of Commerce, Trade and Industry has come up with initiatives to foster industrial development, including:

- promoting institutionalized consultative dialogue with the business community
- regional and multilateral agreements
- bilateral agreements
- competition policies – promote fair trading
- investment promotion
- a privatization programme
- establishing export processing zones.

The PSRP does not mention promotion of competition in any precise way. However, on its p. 62 there is an outline of *Industrial Development Programmes for Poverty Reduction*, of which the basic principles and goals were adopted from the 1994 *Industrial, Commercial and Trade Policy*[128]. In order to align manufacturing growth to poverty reduction, it is necessary to ensure a strategic focus on poverty both in the medium and long term in the manufacturing growth strategy. In this regard, the following vision was to guide Zambia's industrial development over the next 25 years[129]:

"To attain a dynamic, competitive, and environmentally sustainable industrial sector in both urban and rural areas as a means of reducing poverty through sustained economic growth and employment creation."

In order to attain this vision, the specific objectives for manufacturing development were presented as to:

---

[127] United Nations, *Zambia Country Profile*, Johannesburg Earth Summit, Country Profile Series, CP2002-Zambia, p. 79, 2002.
[128] Competition Policy has been given prominence in a revised *Draft Industrial, Commercial and Trade Policy*, which is yet to be adopted. At the time of writing this report, the Ministry of Commerce, Trade and Industry had set up a committee to draft a distinct and comprehensive national competition policy.
[129] Per 2004 *Industrial, Commercial and Trade Policy*.

148

- Promote investments in both urban and rural areas that primarily utilize local raw materials.
- Encourage output and employment expansion in the sector by promoting growth in manufactured exports especially in areas where Zambia has comparative advantage.
- Promote growth in small- and medium-scale enterprises.
- Promote an enabling environment and even the playing field with respect to competing imports, efficient utilities in energy, transport and telecommunications, skills training, science and technology development, and a legal and regulatory framework that is conducive to the growth of manufacturing.

The 2004 *Industrial, Commercial and Trade Policy*, however, lacked programmes targeted at poverty reduction and did not give concrete indications as to how to involve the poor and the disadvantaged in manufacturing activities aimed at stimulating growth and reducing poverty. The policy also lacks strategies for encouraging new investments, establishing competitiveness in industry, and economic diversification. Efforts to establish strategic export niches also need strengthening. Cross-cutting issues of gender, the youth, HIV/AIDS, environment, and energy will form a critical pillar to attaining industrial development[130].

While competition policy has been tacitly mentioned in various policy documents in Zambia, the enactment of the *Competition and Fair Trading Act* in 1994 was a major milestone in having a comprehensive law that dealt with improving the *"efficiency of production and distribution of goods and services"*[131]. It is a general expectation that one of the key objectives of competition policy and law is to preserve and promote competition as a means to ensure the efficient allocation of resources in an economy. This preservation and promotion of competition should result in tangible (and not hypothetical) growth, equitable distribution, and lower prices and adequate supplies to consumers. For a developing economy handicapped by resource

---

[130] An acknowledgment made in the *Poverty Reduction Strategy Paper*, 2002.
[131] One of the statements in the preamble to the *Competition and Fair Trading Act*, 1994.

constraints, efficient allocation of resources is absolutely essential to enable optimum utilization of limited resources[132].

Addressing the ills brought about by market power (i.e. control of abuse of dominant position) is a likely good starting point to ensure that the benefits of competition accrue to all the market actors. This would thus maintain business momentum, jobs, and wealth creation, which are cardinal to poverty alleviation.

To illustrate the contribution of competition law enforcement efforts in alleviating poverty, the following key areas are identified where interventions appear to have yielded positive results in Zambia:

- The cotton sector
- The horti- and floricultural sector
- The poultry sector
- The beef sector.

These sectors are deliberately chosen because they are agricultural based, an area where 80 per cent of the poor find their socio-economic livelihood. Therefore, efforts aimed at improving efficiencies, equitable market benefits, grass-root growth in these sectors are most likely to have the greatest impact in alleviation of poverty.

6.1. Interventions in the cotton industry

The Commission was moved to intervene in a major case in the cotton industry after an article that appeared in the *Post* of Saturday, 28 October 2006 entitled *"Katete women farmers call for review of cotton contract"*. The complainants contemplated *"to fight unfair trade practices"* in the Zambian cotton industry[133]. The women[134] alleged that

---

[132] World Bank & OECD, *A Framework for the Design and Implementation of Competition Law and Policy*, Washington D.C., 1999.

[133] In *Competition Assessment Framework – An operational guide for identifying barriers to competition in developing countries*, January 2008, at page 42, DFID has recognized that contract farming is not necessarily either good or bad for farmers, or for competition. The system can be mutually beneficial to the farmer and the company purchasing the output. It can be particularly useful for higher

multinational companies stole their money during the 2005/2006 cotton-marketing season by reducing the price of grade A cotton from the previous ZK1,220 per kilogram to ZK850[135].

The ginners through the Zambia Cotton Ginners Association contended that the low prices were as a result of the strong kwacha experienced in 2005. The farmers were reported to have claimed that it was unfair for the ginners to transfer the burden of the kwacha's appreciation onto the local farmers, and appealed to the Government through the Ministry of Agriculture and Cooperatives to investigate such issues and ensure that there was equity and fairness in the business. One of the strategies proposed for the following season was that outgrower agreements should be entered into between farmers and ginners and the elimination of third parties who previously appeared to gain more than the farmers.

The Zambia Competition Commission had been closely monitoring the developments and growth of the cotton industry through its interventions pertaining to mergers and acquisitions as well as other industry-related anti-competitive trade practices since 1998. The matter of cotton contracts has been an issue that has been of concern since the liberalization of the economy in 1991 and the sale of the then State-owned enterprise LINTCO to Lonrho Cotton.

After considering the market dynamics, the Commission's view was that all economic activity has to translate into economic efficiency and ultimately enhance the welfare of the citizens. It was observed that despite growing cotton under contract for some time, the socio-economic welfare of most of the contract cotton farmers did not appear to show that the benefits accrued to farmers, whose poverty levels have remained high.

Since the initiation of major agricultural reforms in the early 1990s, Zambian cotton production and processing has grown rapidly and now ranks as one of the most important sources of crop income

---

value crops, and can provide the farmers with access to reasonable terms for finance, technical information and markets. However, there are sometimes situations where the terms imposed by the buyer are unnecessarily restrictive.
[134] Women are reckoned to account for 51 per cent of the population in Zambia.
[135] US$1 = ZK4,000.

among small farmers and agribusiness firms in key agricultural production regions of the country[136]. The subsequent report by the Food Security Research Project (FSRP) under the Ministry of Agriculture, Food and Fisheries revealed that cotton production in Zambia has doubled since the dismantling of the cotton parastatal monopoly LINTCO and the introduction of outgrower programmes supported by private agribusiness firms in the mid-1990s. In spite of these achievements, the cotton sector was still faced with the following key challenges:

- Sustaining and building upon previous success and remaining competitive in the face of a projected long-term decline in world cotton prices as well as shorter price cycles;

- Bringing about more transparent practices and less volatility in prices for farmers;

- Maintaining agribusiness firms' provision of supply inputs and extension of support to smallholder farmers to achieve productivity growth while addressing ginners' and other firms' problems with farmer loan repayment; and

- Financing necessary investments in agricultural research and extension systems to achieve long-term productivity growth in an environment where the public sector is not likely to provide these investments.

The Commission's findings showed that the outgrower schemes under the smallholders are a critical strategic link to the merchants/ginners. Large-scale commercial farms do not necessarily have all the land they need to meet market demand for their produce in the rainy season. Neither would it be profitable for them to have large areas of land lying fallow in seasons when the market demand is low. It has thus been acknowledged that it is more economic to meet the expansion/contraction cushion effect by utilizing the services of small- and medium-scale farmers who have the ability to change crops quickly. For this reason, it is a matter of course that the ginners invest heavily in

---

[136] *Key Challenges and Options Confronting Smallholder, Agribusiness and Government Leaders in Zambia's Cotton Sector*, Food Security Research Project (FSRP) Team 2000.

the crop and do what is in their power to recover their cost. However, such recoveries do not appear to be effected in an equitable manner. The ginners ruthlessly attempt to recover all their fixed and variable costs as well as ensure a profit even where the farmers themselves are left with nothing. To attain this, the ginners engage court-certified bailiffs to salvage the little chattels that the farmers may have and/or threaten them with blacklisting them from future financing arrangements[137].

The outgrower scheme principally creates a monopsony buyer, who determines the price at the signing of the outgrower contract. In 2006, market share estimates showed a duopolistic market of which Dunavant held 53.49 per cent and Cargill Cotton held about 30 per cent, with the rest fragmented amongst five on-and-off players. The two-firm concentration ratio (CR2) was 83.49 per cent.

During the same period, the cotton farmers found their feet in the name of the Cotton Association of Zambia (CAZ), which advised all its member farmers not to collect inputs from ginners for the 2006/7 farming season before the price for the commodity was agreed upon. With the Commission knocking on its door, Dunavant was reported to have increased its 2006/7 planting price at ZK1,000/kg for grade 'A' seed cotton from the ZK850/kg offered during the 2005/06 marketing season. The company further reduced the input prices to ZK36,000 per pack from the ZK40,000 set for the previous farming season and promised to revise the ZK1,000 price if circumstances changed positively at harvesting time[138].

In the ensuing unfair pricing complaints in the agricultural sector, under the headline *"Peasant Farmers Call for Better 2007 Crop Marketing Strategy"* the *Post* reported that the National Association for Peasant and Small-Scale Farmers of Zambia (NAPSFZ) had called on

---

[137] The world prices for cotton are an important element in the pricing of the seed cotton at the local level. James Tefft in his paper entitled *Building on Successes in African Agriculture; Mali's White Revolution: Smallholder Cotton from 1960 to 2003* has noted thus *"subsidies to cotton farmers in the United States currently depress world prices by about US$0.11 per pound. If these subsidies were removed and the price increase transmitted to Malian farmers, the typical farm would increase earnings"*.

[138] Business Post , Tuesday 14 November 2006, *"Dunavant Raises 2006/2007 Pre-Planting Cotton Price"*.

government to come up with a better crop marketing strategy for the 2006/7 farming season[139].

According to a report that was subsequently produced by the Commission[140], the outgrower schemes have the potential to greatly contribute to reducing poverty and contribute to the efforts being made by Zambia as a country to achieve the Millennium Development Goals (MDGs) but the current (lower) prices in these outgrower schemes undermine this potential. The MDGs represent a global partnership that has grown from the commitments and targets established at the world summits of the 1990s. Responding to the world's main development challenges and to the calls of civil society, the MDGs promote poverty reduction, education, maternal health, gender, equality, and aim at combating child mortality, AIDS and other diseases[141].

Table 5: "Dunavant pledges not to reduce prices next year"

Dunavant assured farmers of no reductions in prices next marketing season (2006/7), regardless of the performance of the local currency and world market situations.

Mr Richard Laurin, the company's chairman based in Geneva Switzerland, explained the circumstances to price changes in the previous marketing season and apologized for a sharp decline in prices after the kwacha appreciated against the US dollar. During meetings with farmers in Sinazongwe, Mobola and Monze, Mr Laurin repeatedly assured the farmers that the guaranteed pre-planting price of ZK1,000 per kilogram of seed cotton would not be reduced as was the case during the previous marketing season.

Mr. Laurin is reported to have admitted that in 2005 Dunavant had announced that they would buy a kilogram of seed cotton at ZK1,220 but after the kwacha appreciated, the price of cotton came down to ZK850. The paper reported that Mr. Laurin admitted this and said that it was his personal failure. Mr Laurin apologized to the farmers for the situation.

Source: *The Business Post, Tuesday, 12 December 2006.*

---

[139] Saturday Post of 18 November 2006.

[140] Zambia Competition Commission, *Report on Competition & Fair Trading regarding Outgrower Cotton Farmers*, August 2007 (Case Officer – Willard Mwemba).

[141] United Nations Development Programme; Millennium Development Goals. http://www.undp.org/mdg/

The Commission reviewed the imbalance of power in the negotiation of prices of cotton in outgrower schemes. Multinational entities such as Dunavant and Cargill Cotton were actually disproportionately benefiting, compared to the farmers, whose economic gains were stagnant against the huge profits that the merchants were making. Not surprisingly, the cotton association and Dunavant could well afford to offer ZK 1,120 per kilogram of grade seed cotton this marketing season[142]. The offer price of ZK1,120 included an additional ZK50 per kilogram premium for deliveries up to 14 July 2007.

In the same period, Cargill Cotton also took steps to correct its pricing system. The input prices for the 2006 planting season were reduced by 28 per cent year on year making Cargill's complete input package cheaper than that of any other ginner. This dramatic reduction in input costs was part of a conscious effort by Cargill Cotton to offset the impact of low global cotton prices on the incomes of small-scale Zambian farmers. In line with its previously stated strategy to pay a competitive seed cotton price, Cargill Cotton announced a buying price for the 2007 crop of ZK1,120/kg, an increase of 32 per cent over the previous year. Considering the reduced input cost, Cargill Cotton reported that their farmers were to enjoy the largest increase in net revenue in comparison to other cotton farmers throughout the country. This was to give the average farmer an additional net income of 75 per cent compared to the previous year[143]. It was a desirable outcome that the ginners were finally using higher promised returns to the farmers as a competitive advantage.

What began as an ordinary newspaper article and an investigation by the Commission ended up being one of the biggest poverty alleviation stories in the Zambian agricultural sector, with the cotton association calling on the farmers it had previously dissuaded to encourage them to grow cotton[144]. Cargill Cotton had become a founding member of the Zambia Cotton Outgrower Association (ZCOPA), which aimed to provide an industry-wide forum to promote

---

[142] Post, Friday, 11 May 2007: *"CAZ, Dunavant sign agreement"*.
[143] The Post, 13 June 2007: *"Cargill Cotton Information Bulletin"*.
[144] The Post, Wednesday, 27 June 2007 *"Continue growing Cotton, CAZ appeals to farmers"*.

cotton production and enforce sanctity of contract with a stated goal to eradicate the practice of side-marketing.

In its report, the Commission made recommendations that included continuous monitoring of this very dynamic industry by bringing to the attention of the relevant stakeholders that include, *inter alia*, the Cotton Association of Zambia, the Government, the Ginners Association of Zambia and the National Association for Peasant and Small-Scale Farmers of Zambia, the following advisory opinions: the ginners and the smallholders should come up with a mechanism for sharing the risks that may arise due to the appreciation of the kwacha, the fall in the world prices and other production risks involved in the cotton industry.

In addition, better access by farmers to information on market trends, including the pre-planting price for cotton. Such information could be provided by the CSO and the Ministry of Agriculture and Cooperatives, thus making it easily accessible. Efforts are also required to improve farmers' marketing skills, coupled with the cultivation of long-term relations between the farmers and the ginners. This could be achieved by holding seminars, workshops and field days whereby farmer associations (such as CAZ) and ginners associations will interact.

Furthermore, it was also recommended that the existing cotton cooperatives, such as the Cotton Development Trust, be strengthened. If the objectives of the cooperatives were well formulated, they could benefit both the farmer and the ginners. The following objectives were recommended for the cooperatives:

(i)   To encourage members to be thrifty and to establish a fund from which could be given loans for agricultural purposes.
(ii)   To encourage farmers to adopt modern farming methods.
(iii)   To help farmer members market their produce at lucrative prices as well as helping them process their produce if necessary.
(iv)   To supply members with agricultural equipment and seeds.

At the time of writing this report, all the parties had reached what appeared to be a "win-win" arrangement where principally the ginners were not to pass on their losses to the farmers, notably the smallholder "peasant" farmers. The Commission has continued to monitor the situation through information links with the cotton association and the Zambia National Farmers Union. It is likely that with the formation of distinctive formal associations to represent their interests, the cotton farmers will have a better platform through which to express and/or channel their grievances.

6.2. Horticultural sector

At the point of merger and acquisition notification, the mandated competition authority is given an opportunity to influence the structure of markets through structural undertakings and/or influence behaviour of market players through behavioural undertakings aimed at ensuring that a particular player does not abuse its market power *vis-à-vis* other players, notably smaller players. This inherently assists in assuring that small businesses can exist in their niche markets and that they are not unduly encumbered when trying to access markets.

On 6 December 2004, Agriflora Limited (Agriflora) and Chalimbana Fresh Produce Limited (Chalimbana)[145] (herewith referred to as "the parties") submitted a joint notification to the Zambia Competition Commission for the transfer of controlling ownership of Agriflora to Chalimbana. At the time, Agriflora was highly in debt and on the verge of being declared bankrupt by the creditors. Its expatriate Chief Executive Officer even fled the country, leaving the company in a serious limbo[146].

---

[145] At the time, Chalimbana was reported to be a start-up company with the major shareholder being Plantation and General Investments Plc (UK) (P&G) and Arthur Gregory Barnes of Khal Amazi Farm of Lusaka as the minority shareholder. P&G is majority owner of Khal Amazi Limited - a rose-growing farm in Lusaka. In Malawi, P&G is involved in horticultural, floricultural products, dairy farming, wheat and maize farming. Chalimbana shall engage in similar activities in Zambia.

[146] Agriflora Limited started operating in 1994. By 2001/2002 it had 22 hectares of roses and 1,000 hectares of vegetables. Agriflora had processing factories with 7000 tonnes capacity of fresh produce per year, drip irrigation systems and a refrigerated transport fleet. It had an outgrower scheme that had over 3,000 workers. There are about 25 players in the market. Agriflora had the largest market share of 80 per cent while the second was York Farm. The market share for the other competitors including York Farm was 20 per cent. 60 per cent of

157

Agriflora was mainly involved in the growing of fresh vegetables and flowers for the export market. In the case of *The Acquisition of the Assets of Agriflora by Chalimbana Fresh Produce Limited*[147], the Commission authorized the takeover of the assets of Agriflora by Chalimbana on the basis of assurances from Chalimbana that the takeover was envisaged to provide the continuity of the viable and lucrative business of Agriflora, with supply linkages to the small to medium scale farmers. Agriflora needed to be revitalized in order to revamp the business and assure the continuity of the outgrower scheme. Therefore, the takeover was necessary to keep the vibrant business going, with the assurance that:

"*the transaction will create 3000 jobs; contribute to Government revenue through taxes; contribute to national economic development through foreign exchange in export earnings; and put Zambia on the world map through horticultural and floricultural produce from Zambia selling on the international market*".

The takeover has contributed to a thriving flori- and horticultural export market that is somehow managing to compete with the regional market leaders, South Africa and Zimbabwe. The resuscitation of operations and repositioning of Agriflora after the takeover authorization by the Commission has seen the enterprise continue to forge linkages with small-scale farmers in the horti- and floricultural industries.

The role of Agriflora[148] in the sector is perhaps exemplified through the USAID captioned story in Table 6:

---

the produce for Agriflora was vegetables while flowers accounted for 40 per cent of Agriflora's exports.

[147] Zambia Competition Commission, Staff Paper No. 211, February 2005.

[148] The Multilateral Investment Guarantee Agency (MIGA) of the World Bank issued a US$3.6 million guarantee to the Industrial Development Corporation of South Africa Limited (IDC), of South Africa, to cover its US$4 million equity investment in Zambia's Agriflora, the second largest food production company in the country, Keith Nuthall, June 2003, http://www.just-food.com/article.aspx?ID=90513.

Table 6: Irrigation technology: small-scale farmer enters international export business

On retirement from the Zambian Civil Service in 1988, Mike Phiri settled on his four-hectare smallholding just 60 kilometres from the capital, Lusaka. Since any type of pension is negligible in Zambia, Mike cultivated his land during the rainy season producing enough corn to feed his family. Occasionally, he grew vegetables for subsistence. He lived simply, well aware that given the low local maize prices, he would be losing money if he tried to grow maize or other crops for the local market. In March 2000, everything changed. Under a new loan scheme, the Zambia Agribusiness Technical Assistance Centre (ZATAC) would supply irrigation equipment for the production of baby corn, runner beans, and mangetout peas. **The vegetables would be contracted for sale to the country's largest horticultural exporter, Agriflora Ltd. The firm, near the Lusaka International Airport, had over the years exported a wide range of fresh vegetables to Europe. Interested in expanding production beyond its own farms, Agriflora saw the attractiveness of working with various smallholders in the vicinity of its pack house located just outside the airport. This would only be possible if the small producers overcame the constraint of rain-dependent agriculture and were organized by some other organization to act as a group.** At ZATAC's request, CLUSA, with their group-mobilizing techniques, began working with the small farmers.

Within three months, Mike's drip irrigation equipment was installed by ZATAC while Agriflora Ltd. installed a small refrigeration warehouse next to his house. By September 2000, nine months after his irrigation equipment was installed, Mike had delivered 1.3 tons of fresh vegetables to Agriflora and received US$1,500 payment for the produce. Over the next 12 months Mike's net income target was US$4,000. Mike remarked, *"Things have moved very fast. We are very happy with ZATAC. Both my neighbours and I have been occupying this land for over a decade. We did not know that we would one day be in the international export business. The vision of ZATAC and Agriflora in mounting this project is simply phenomenal. We have now broken clear of the vagaries of seasonal agriculture. We grow crops all year round for the European market and we receive an all year round income"*.

Source: USAID, *Human Resources Development Project (HRDP) Newsletter April/May 2000 – Success Stories*
http://www.usaid.gov/regions/afr/success_stories/zambia.html

A further success story with linkages to the horticultural sector was the Commission authorization of the takeover of the assets of the previously State-owned and privatized Sunripe Products Limited, whose

159

primary business was food processing and canning. Following numerous bidders and a blockage by the Commission to have the assets relocated to South Africa, the Commission eventually authorized the takeover of the assets by Fresh Pikt Limited, which has since resuscitated the plant and restored linkages with the smallholder farmers. The company produces 18 different canned products which include baked beans, mixed beans, pineapple chunks, tomato puree, tomato and onion mix and whole peeled tomatoes[149]. Table 7 shows the current economic lifeline role that Fresh Pikt is playing in the economy, more so as it relates to small-scale farmers:

Table 7: Fresh Pikt out to fight poverty in rural areas
Most rural communities in Zambia are hard-working, a trait honed out of decades of subsistence existence on the land where survival has been a function of production from the land…One of the companies that are turning around this gloomy scenario, at least on the current scale is Fresh Pikt.
In an effort to encourage citrus fruit production, Fresh Pikt Limited has just signed a contract with farmers in Mwinilunga for the supply of 40 tonnes of pineapples to its Lusaka plant on a weekly basis. The development would enable more than 1,000 farmers in the area to expand both the pineapple production and earnings from their produce.
Choice Nuts Zambia Limited, a sister company to Fresh Pikt, has set up a network to access the abundant groundnuts from Eastern Province which it exports after treatment at its Lusaka plant. The company will this season export over 2,000 tonnes of raw dried groundnuts worth approximately US$2 million.
Both Fresh Pikt and Choice Nuts are companies that have shown a practical approach to a quick way of tackling poverty in the rural areas.

Source: *Times of Zambia, Wednesday, 6 February 2008.*

---

[149] Times of Zambia, Monday, 3 March 2008.

160

6.3. Poultry sector

The poultry sector is one of the largest employers in the country and is highly fragmented downstream, with a large informal sector thereof. The industry has increased from 16 million birds in 2000 to about 26 million in 2007, with enquiries and orders for mainly processed eggs and hatching eggs coming from as far away as the Comoros Islands, the Democratic Republic of Congo, Angola, Tanzania and Uganda among other countries in the region[150].

Interventions by the Commission have assisted in creating, maintaining, and sustaining competition and employment. This has been done in several ways as explained in the following paragraphs.

During a series of meetings involving management of the then largest day-old chick supplier in Zambia, Hybrid Poultry Farm Zambia Limited (Hybrid Poultry), and the Zambia Association of Manufacturers (ZAM) with the Zambia Competition Commission in the second quarter of 1999, it was revealed that Hybrid Poultry and Galaunia Holdings Limited (Galaunia) had earlier agreed to effect a sale of a farm (Mariandale Farm) and a poultry processing factory thereon to Galaunia, subject to agreed exclusive dealing clauses and conditions (Galaunia was the largest customer for Hybrid Poultry and specialised in raising day-old chicks to table broilers). Upon this discovery, the Commission advised the parties to notify the said exclusive agreements for assessment under Section 7[151] of the *Competition and Fair Trading Act*. In January 2000 Hybrid Poultry notified the said agreements[152].

Through this agreement Hybrid Poultry was to sell to Galaunia its Mariandale Farms comprising fixtures and fittings, stock-in-trade

---

[150]*Times of Zambia*, 14 November 2007, quoting Matthews Ngosa, Chairman of the Poultry Association of Zambia. See also quoted at http://www.thepoultrysite.com/poultrynews/13331/zambian-poultry-attracts-world-market.

[151] Which states that: *"Any category of agreements, decisions and concerted practices which have as their object the prevention, restriction or distortion of competition to an appreciable extent in Zambia or in any substantial part of it are declared anti-competitive trade practices and are hereby prohibited"*.

[152] Zambia Competition Commission, Annual Report, 2000.

(chickens) and the goodwill of the business and the premises subject to anti-competitive terms. The Commission was concerned that Hybrid Poultry required Galaunia to only purchase day-old chicks from itself. Further, Galaunia was also required to offer Hybrid Poultry right of first refusal should it intend to resell Mariandale Farm. Galaunia was also not allowed to raise any type of poultry at the farm, apart from broiler chickens, including the provision not to go into the business of a chicken hatchery. The parties also agreed that Galaunia was to be accorded the right of first refusal in the event that Hybrid Poultry sold some of its shares. In return, Hybrid Poultry was given the first right of refusal to participate in an outgrower scheme in the event that Galaunia came up with one. These are highlighted in Table 8 below:

Table 8: Salient clauses from the sale and purchase agreement between Hybrid Poultry Farms Limited (HPF) and Galaunia Holdings Limited:
Clause 11: The consideration, selling price, Hybrid Poultry property was US$250,000 for the goodwill, chattels, chickens and premises, payable on completion.
Clause 13: That Galaunia would not raise any type of poultry on Mariandale Farm other than broiler chickens.
Clause 14: That Galaunia and any subsidiary or associate company would not enter into the business of a chicken hatchery or breeder broiler production in Zambia.
Clause 15: That Galaunia would only procure its day-old chick requirements exclusively from Hybrid Poultry.
Clause 16: That Galaunia shall purchase DOC from Hybrid Poultry at short notice.
Clause 17: That Galaunia shall have the exclusive right to collect all chicken manure from HPF chicken houses located in the Lusaka-Chisamba area at a cost of US$0.30 per 90-kg bag.
Clause 19: That Galaunia should give Hybrid Poultry the right to first refusal to purchase, within five years of completion date, should it decide to sell the business.
Clause 21: Should Galaunia develop and implement an outgrower scheme to

Source: *The Sale and Purchase Agreement between Hybrid Poultry Farms Limited and Galaunia Farms Limited.*

In another agreement pertaining to the formerly Hybrid Poultry owned Poultry Processing Company Limited that was purchased by Galaunia, it contained restrictive clauses. Principally, in the sale of the poultry factory, the parties agreed that they would keep out of each other's business, i.e. that Hybrid Poultry would not set up a poultry processing factory and that in the event that Galaunia intended to sell the factory, Hybrid Poultry was to be accorded the right of first refusal. The poultry processing factory was viewed as a third-stage downstream operation after the Hybrid Poultry hatchery and the broiler farms under Galaunia. This was a vertically integrated and restrictive arrangement that had been a complete foreclosure of the Zambian poultry market. These are highlighted in Table 9 below:

Table 9: Restrictive clauses in the sale and purchase agreement of the poultry processing company

Clause 11: The purchaser agrees that should it within five years of the completion date wish to dispose of the business then it will give the Vendor right of first refusal to purchase the Business at cost plus the value of any improvements that the purchaser has made to the Business such value to be mutually agreed failing which to be assessed by a registered valuation surveyor mutually appointed by the head of the Valuation Surveyors Institute of Zambia. Should the Vendor not exercise its right to purchase the Business within 30 days then the Purchaser will be at liberty to dispose of the Business to any other person.

Clause 12: In the event that the Management buy-out (MBO) wishes to sell its shares to the vendor then the Purchaser shall be accorded the right of first refusal to purchase the shares from the MBO. Should the Purchaser not exercise its rights to purchase the shares within 30 days then the MBO will be at liberty to sell the shares to any other party.

Clause 13: The Vendor hereby agrees that it and its subsidiaries and associates will not at any time in the future in Zambia enter into the business of processing or selling of frozen chickens of any type except in collaboration with the Purchaser as mutually agreed in writing.

(**Source:** *The Sale and Purchase Agreement.*)

In defence of the agreements, Hybrid Poultry argued before the Commission that the terms of the agreement did not restrain competition nor did they have any adverse effect on trade or the economy in general. The condition for Galaunia to buy day-old chicks exclusively from Hybrid Poultry was arguably there in order to "protect" the chicken industry as a whole in the country. According to Hybrid Poultry, the nature of the product was such that genetically, the day-old chicks of two or more different breeds could not be put together at the same chicken run. This was purportedly for fear of an outbreak of disease.

While this was scientifically arguable, the exclusive dealing effectively excluded competition as Galaunia could not buy day-old chicks from Hybrid Poultry's only formidable competitor at the time, Tamba Chicks.

At the time, it was evident from the Commission's analysis that Hybrid Poultry was a dominant firm both in the quantitative and in the qualitative sense in the relevant product market.

6.3.1. Market shares for day-old chick suppliers

Hybrid Poultry	–	60 per cent
Tamba Chicks	–	30 per cent
Others	–	10 per cent

6.3.2. Major buyers

Table 10 shows the major buyers of day-old chicks in 1999. The position of Galaunia was significantly higher than that of its nearest rival, who trailed at 10,000 chicks per week:

Table 10: Major buyers of day-old chicks - 1999

Company	Chicks per week	%
Galaunia (Diamondale & Mariandale)	42,000	24%
Eureka	10,000	6%
Jonken	5,000	3%
Mapepe	5,000	3%
Others (11,000 farmers)	115,500	65%
Total	177,200	

Source: *ZCC Assessment Report on the proposed takeover of Tamba Chicks by Hybrid Poultry Farms Limited.*

164

Galaunia was by far the most important customer for day-old chicks in the country. Hybrid Poultry's exclusive deal was a source of its dominance to which Galaunia was tied. These agreements led to higher prices of day-old chicks for Galaunia, and affected the operations of Tamba Chicks and effectively constrained entry both upstream and downstream.

6.3.3. Effects of the agreements

The parties seemed to have taken advantage of their dominant market positions upstream and downstream where either party was dominant. The parties were, both by motive and concerted practices, excluding competition both in the day-old chicks, table birds (broiler) and broiler chickens markets.

The signing of these exclusive supply arrangements adversely affected the operations of the other only notable day-old chicks supplier at the time, Tamba Chicks Limited. The problem went so far as to have Tamba Chicks facing liquidity problems and its owner decided to sell the company to avert actual liquidation. During the same investigations, the Commission discovered that Hybrid Poultry had used its economic power to facilitate a loan for Tamba Chicks, which facilitation compelled Tamba Chicks to sign a "Right of First Refusal" with Hybrid Poultry in the event that Tamba Chicks was put up for sale. The Commission nullified these agreements under Sections 7 and 9 of the *Competition and Fair Trading Act*. When Tamba Chicks was finally advertised for sale, the Commission blocked the bid by Hybrid Poultry and instead allowed a new entrant, Ross Breeders, who is still around and providing the relevant market checks and balances in the industry that are desirous to the Commission.

The result of the competition intervention is that the general downstream industry has grown to more than ten notable players, with almost a new entrant every year. Ross Breeders has been able to sustain and in many ways outcompete Hybrid Poultry in the day-old chicks segment. Ross Breeders is reckoned to have about 50 per cent market share now, with Hybrid Poultry trailing at about 40 per cent.

Currently, the poultry industry is the largest livestock industry in Zambia and is very competitive. The sector has seen an inflow of high investment and the market players in the industry have benefited from rapid returns on their investments. With barriers to entry such as that instigated by Hybrid Poultry in the 1990s gone, there are reasonably low start-up capital costs especially in the broiler segment with production cycles of 6 to 7 weeks. The numbers of broiler chicks marketed have increased from 16 million birds in 2000 to about 26 million in 2007. As for the pullets, 1.7 million pullet layer chicks are marketed per annum and populations of pullet layers inlay stands at 1.25 million per annum[153]. A phenomenal growth of 30 per cent has been experienced since liberalization, and growth is envisaged to reach 50 per cent in the next two years due to increasing demand from international markets.

This segment has seen intensive investment on aggregate and has allowed for generation of income in the economy standing at Zambian Kwacha 195.7 billion (about US$ 51,578,947)[154]. Approximately 24.4 million broiler chickens are produced per annum – 15.86 million and 8.54 million in the formal and informal sectors, respectively. Of the broilers sold at wet markets, 65 per cent are dressed while 35 per cent are live chickens[155]. Large producers of chickens are promoting broiler contracts in collaboration with small-scale farmers to meet the demand for processed chickens on the market and these have helped this sector to grow at an astonishing rate with both formal and informal providers[156].

Since 1999, the market has seen a number of entrants in the day-old chicks sector. Hybrid Poultry has repositioned itself over the years following the entry of a vigorous competitor, Ross Breeders, who took over the assets of Tamba Chicks. Both entities claim to have a larger market share than the other. The figures in Table 11 are based on a survey by the Commission as well as sales figures registered by the Poultry Association of Zambia:

---

[153] Poultry Association of Zambia, 2008.
[154] US$1=ZK3,800.
[155] *Ibid.*, 2007.
[156] Zambia Competition Commission, *A Study of Competition in the beef, poultry and dairy retail sector in Zambia* (financed by the International Development Research Centre (IDRC) of Canada), January 2007.

Table 11: Day-old chicks market shares - 2007

Producer	Brand name	Market share
Hybrid	Cobb/Bovans	40%
Ross Breeders	Ross	35%
Bokomo	Ross/Lonhman	20%
Panda	Hubbarb	5%
Total		100%

Source: Figures estimated from Zambia Competition Commission Survey 2006,PAZ 2007 report as well as findings from survey[157].

As regards the processed chicken segment, the competition is as shown in Table 12:

Table 12: Market shares for processed chicken brands

Producer	Brand name	Market share
Hybrid	Verino	25%
Galaun Holdings	Crest	20%
Zambeef	Zamchick	15%
Eureka Chickens	Eureka	10%
Savannah Chickens	Savannah	5%
Zambezi Nkuku	Zambezi Nkuku	5%
Informal sector	Traditional	20%
Total		100%

Source: Figures estimated from Zambia Competition Commission Survey 2006,PAZ 2007 report as well as findings from survey[158].

6.4. Beef sector

Cattle ranching is one of the most lucrative rural businesses and occupations in most of the countryside, notably in Southern and Western provinces. It is thus a source of livelihood for most of the rural dwellers that constitute part of the 80 per cent of the population that falls into the poverty bracket. Besides the natural hazards of animal disease outbreaks, most of the traditional cattle owners are vulnerable to commercial traders, abattoirs, and processors. The market is

---

[157] *Ibid.*
[158] *Ibid.*

167

predominantly under the control of one dominant firm, Zambeef. As observed in a recent Commission report, the Zambian beef sector has large economic potential for the country. Not only has it been a major source of employment in the formal context, but it has also been a source of income for the informal sector[159].

The socio-economic role of cattle in the traditional sector dates back to the pre-colonial days. In this sector cattle has multiple roles. Cattle ownership has always been regarded as a symbol of family wealth. It is known from Zambian history that tribes such as Tongas (Southern Province), Lozis (Western Province), Chewas (Eastern Province), Namwangas and Mambwes (Northern Province) were traditional cattle keepers. As far back as 1993, it was estimated that about 70 per cent of the Zambian cattle is found in this sector, which underlines its importance[160]. The areas where such cattle is found actually have registered high poverty levels. Table 13 shows the areas.

Table 13: Overall and extreme poverty by residence and province, Zambia, 1998

Residence	Overall poverty	Extreme poverty
Rural	83	70
Urban	56	36
Central Province	77	63
Copperbelt Province	65	47
Eastern Province	**80**	**66**
Luapula Province	81	69
Lusaka Province	52	34
Northern Province	**81**	**67**
North-western Province	76	63
Southern Province	**76**	**60**
Western Province	**89**	**78**

Source: *CSO: Living Conditions in Zambia, 1998.*

Table 13 shows that there are higher levels of poverty in the provinces where traditional cattle ranching is practiced. This is of

---

[159] *Ibid.*
[160] Chindo Hicks, *The role of Zambian cattle populations in socio-economic development*, Royal Veterinary and Agricultural University, Department of Animal Science and Animal Health, Bülowsvej 13, 1870 Frederiksberg C. Denmark.

concern when taking into account that the growth that entities such as Zambeef have achieved from buying cattle from the same provinces, notably in Southern Province and Western Province, where poverty levels are relatively higher[161]. Furthermore, the market shares in processed beef show the imbalance of economic power even amongst the market players, as shown in Table 14.

Table 14: Market shares in the beef sector

Beef producer	Brand name	Ownership status	Market share
Zambeef	Zambeef	Publicly owned	65%
Galaun Holdings	Luscold	Privately owned	10%
Northern Zambezi Traders	Pama	Privately owned	7%
Dar Farms	King Quality	Privately owned	3%
Best Beef Company	Best Beef	Privately owned	3%
Savannah Beef	Savannah	Privately owned	2%
Others	Traditional	Privately owned	10%
Total			100%

Source: *Figures estimated from Zambia Competition Commission Survey 2006 and from primary data collected.*

As shown in Graph 2, the prices of the various beef products have actually continued to rocket since 1993, and have made Zambeef in particular one of the most prosperous enterprises in the Zambian economy[162]. The same cannot be said of the "Others" in the chain.

---

[161] Which posted a 26 per cent growth in turnover in 2006 with US$55 million, with a net profit of US$8 million (which increased by 78 per cent from 2005). For Zambian-owned companies, this is in the blue-chip category. Source: Zambeef Annual Report 2006.

[162] Zambeef Products PLC Group is a major agribusiness whose core activity is the production, processing, distribution and retailing of beef, chickens, eggs and dairy products through its own retailing network throughout Zambia and Nigeria. It has since expanded into Ghana (trading under the name "Master Meats"). The conglomerate controls key abattoirs in major cow-belts. It slaughters 60,000 cattle per annum and produces 12,000 grain-fed cattle per annum from its feedlots. It had a turnover of US$56 million (ZK223 billion) in 2006 – *2006 Annual Report.*

Graph 2: Prices of selected beef products 1993 to 2007

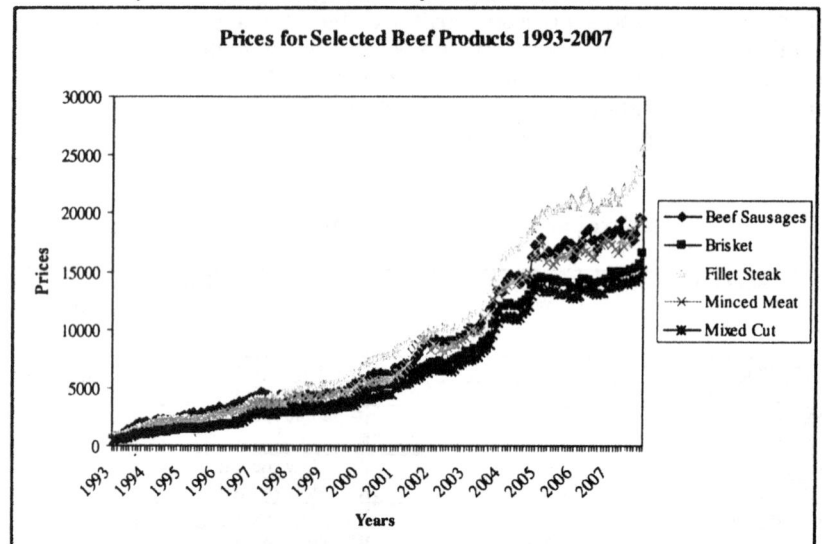

Source: Central Statistical Office.

Thus, the Commission has been vigilant in its consideration of matters in the sector driven by Zambeef. In the assessment of *The proposed takeover of Rumcortin Meat Processors by Zambeef Products PLC*[163], the Commission was concerned with allegations that Zambeef's strategic objective in taking over the Rumcortin abattoir, which was the only usable abattoir in the Southern and surrounding Western Province areas, was to have the abattoir certified as the only one that meets the national and/or international Sanitary and Phytosanitary (SPS) standards or other such specifications. In effect, this was feared to lead to a situation where all the other competing abattoirs in Livingstone and surrounding areas would be closed, especially during animal disease outbreaks. Such a situation would lead to entrenching Zambeef's monopoly position in the major cattle belt in the country. Similar allegations were made during cattle disease outbreaks in Mongu (Western Provincial capital) in the late 1990s and in Namwala (key cattle area in Southern Province) and surrounding areas in 2004/2005.

---

[163] Zambia Competition Commission, Staff Paper No. 267.

170

Zambeef was alleged then to have monopolized the cattle trade by insisting that all cattle slaughtered at the only abattoir in the area (which it controlled) had to be sold to them. The carcasses were then transported by Zambeef in refrigerated trucks for processing. Other commercial competitors would also be put in a difficult position to deal with a vertically integrated operator who had first access to the best cattle brought for slaughter.

It was with this background in mind that the Commission required undertakings from Zambeef to address the competition and unfair trading concerns. While it was understood that Rumcortin was not operational, the Commission was aware of both the financial, technical and vertically aligned abilities of the Zambeef conglomerate to turn the company around and make it viable. The Commission supported efforts made to resuscitate a failing firm while at the same time it was desirous to ensure that the resuscitated firm was not used to prevent, restrict or distort competition leading to the exit of other market players and/or create a barrier to entry for prospective players. The long-term effects of the latter scenario were likely to lead to market stagnation and the desired holistic investment results not being attainable.

Further, through the competition law's objective of expanding the base of entrepreneurship and ensuring that no single entity unduly dominated, through abuse or acquisition of a dominant position of market power, the Commission has advised the parties to provide undertakings essentially to guarantee third-party access to the abattoir in the event that it is the only abattoir permitted to operate. The Commission was also concerned about the livelihood of the rural poor whose primary source of wealth was cattle. Zambeef gave undertakings to the Commission as shown in Table 15.

Table 15: Undertakings given by Zambeef Products PLC to the Zambia Competition Commission

1. In the event of a major disease outbreak and upon formal written notification by the relevant authority, if Rumcortin Abattoir is declared to be the only SPS certified abattoir and all other slaughter facilities in the relevant geographic area/district are closed, Zambeef shall allow third-party access to the Rumcortin abattoir on an objective criteria and without discrimination.
2. For third-party access to the abattoir in a period of disease outbreak, Zambeef will charge an access fee set at a reasonable economic and competitive rate that takes into account the prevailing rates for similar services, which rates shall be negotiated entirely between Zambeef and the third parties.
3. Zambeef shall not insist on third-party cattle slaughtered at the abattoir to be sold to Zambeef but shall allow the cattle owners/traders to exercise their freedom of trade.
4. The first priority for slaughter and storage of carcasses in the cold room will always be for Zambeef cattle. However, Zambeef will make efforts to consider third-party slaughter and storage as provided above.
5. Zambeef shall appoint a senior management official within its ranks who shall be the "Trade Practices Compliance Officer" and who shall liaise with the Commission from time to time on matters of compliance with the undertakings and/or the *Competition and Fair Trading Act*, 1994, CAP 417 of the laws of Zambia.

Source: *Memorandum of Undertakings given by Zambeef Products PLC to the Zambia Competition Commission, February 2007.*

The Commission has thus continued to monitor the situation and ensure that Zambeef adheres to the undertakings through regular contact with the compliance officer. The undertakings afford ease of access to this key facility in the cattle-belt and principally, guarantee the freedom of trade of the village level and other small scale farmers. A good return on their cattle investment is a step in alleviating the levels and effects of poverty.

6.5. Tobacco sector

The tobacco industry is one of the most lucrative sectors in the Zambian agriculture sector. As in the cotton sector, it is dominated by multinational merchants who operate outgrower schemes. Competition-related interventions in this sector are thus necessary in order to ensure that the rural poor are not exploited in the pricing and distribution of the tobacco they grow under contract. During the latter months of 2005, the Commission was handling the merger of Dimon Incorporated (Dimon) and Standard Commercial Corporation (Stancom) into Alliance One[164]. The Commission raised concerns about the possible anti-competitive trade practices in the industry that would arise as the two merging firms were going to create a monopoly undertaking with a likely chance of abuse. Stancom was at the time the third largest independent leaf tobacco merchant in the world while Dimon was the world's second largest dealer, both of which had operations in more than 30 countries. The merger was to create the second largest tobacco merchant in the world, and the largest in Zambia, i.e. actually a monopoly.

The Commission thus demanded undertakings that would address the competition concerns that had been raised during the investigations. Alliance One contracted lawyers from America who responded and disputed the finding of the Commission that Alliance One was going to be a monopoly undertaking, since there were other players in the Zambian tobacco industry. The Commission argued in turn that under the Zambian competition legislation, a monopoly was a firm with at least 50 per cent market share and since Alliance One was going to have 55 per cent market share, this raised competition concerns.

Employing its usual analytical framework, the Commission had defined the general relevant market as the processing, storage, shipping and marketing of leaf tobacco, but the actual relevant product market as made up of flue-cured, burley and oriental tobacco.

The main competition issue of the Commission was that there appeared to be no effective countervailing power from the leaf tobacco farmers in the outgrower schemes who were under contractual arrangements with Stancom and Dimon. The merger into Alliance One

---

[164] Case File ZCC/CO/383.

173

meant that the farmers would have no choice of contract between the two, despite the presence of other alternative merchants already existing in the market. The Commission further argued that the merger of Stancom and Dimon would definitely result in the removal of a vigorous competitor from the market. Apart from Stancom (40 per cent) and Dimon (15 per cent), the rest of the market (45 per cent) was made up of a fragment of small to medium-sized leaf tobacco dealers who were not likely to offer effective competition to the merged entity.

After being convinced of the monopoly status of Stancom in the tobacco industry in Zambia and likely competition issues affecting the outgrower farmers, the parties finally agreed to give the undertakings outlined in Table 16.

Table 16: Undertakings given by Alliance One on the occasion of the merger between Stancom and Dimon

1.   Alliance One shall continue to use multiple transportation providers and shall not engage in exclusive dealing in the relevant market without seeking the express authorization of the Zambia Competition Commission.
2.   Alliance One shall continue to promote and develop better tobacco farmers through the outgrower scheme and encourage local entrepreneurs.
3.   After the merger approval, Alliance One shall identify a suitable senior officer who shall act as a Fair Trade Compliance Officer with the Commission on competition and fair trading matters.

Source: Undertakings given by Alliance One to the Zambia Competition Commission, 2005

This case demonstrated the use of undertakings or commitments from the industry as one of the enforcement tools available to a competition authority to ensure that the gains of market liberalization are not unduly concentrated in one entity. There would appear to have been no incidence of complaints on prices since 2005.

7. Conclusions

The role that competition law and policy plays in poverty alleviation cannot be overemphasized. While there is no claim that such a law and policy would be the "cure-all" in terms of poverty as found in countries such as Zambia, it is a major step in combating extreme poverty levels as has been evidenced in the Commission's interventions in the cotton, poultry and other sectors.

There is a need to identify areas where poverty levels are high and to use appropriate interventions in those areas, and perhaps with more than ordinary vigilance and focus. There is a lot to be done by the Commission and perhaps said by the public in terms of the contribution of competition law and policy in their daily lives. While some results may not be tangible, others are clearly tangible.

The effective implementation of competition law and policy clearly assists in the attainment of efficiencies in the production of goods and services as has been demonstrated through the prohibition of cartels and attempted anti-competitive acquisitions in the poultry sector in Zambia. There is of course need for in-depth research that would empirically show whether or not the changes explained in the horticultural, poultry, beef and tobacco industries in Zambia are solely due to competition enforcement efforts. It is not likely that competition law enforcement is the only force behind the resuscitation of some sectors, but there is a strong correlation shown in the intervention against the cartel activities of Hybrid Poultry and the opening up of the day-old chicks market as well as the broiler segment to more entrants, which have in turn created employment and, through outgrower schemes, facilitated the continued growth of the micro and small enterprises.

This is perhaps even more so in the horticultural sector, where a firm that was almost on the verge of collapse was resuscitated through an acquisition authorized by the Commission and vertical linkages created with small-scale farmers (Fresh Pikt and Agriflora).

As a way forward, there would be need to have deliberate provisions in a competition legislation that support small business growth and development, as explicitly provided for in the *Trade*

175

Practices Act 1974 of Australia. For developing countries, the growth of the micro and small businesses into medium, larger and perhaps even into more formalized business organizations would provide a better base for industrial renaissance. Competition law and policy may be effectively used in this regard, contemporaneously with other pro-business/pro-consumer policies.

Suffice it to state that it remains a highly debatable though saleable idea in Zambia that the implementation of competition law and policy actually does contribute to poverty alleviation. To sale this idea, there would be need to raise the extremely low levels of competition law-policy culture that exist at policy formulation stage. The visibility of the competition authority and its programs and achievements must be self-evident, even to the "small" citizen striving to sell cotton or cattle in the rural areas. This is no easy task and Zambia may not be unique in this regard.

Appendix 1

SUMMARY OF THE ZAMBIAN PRSP

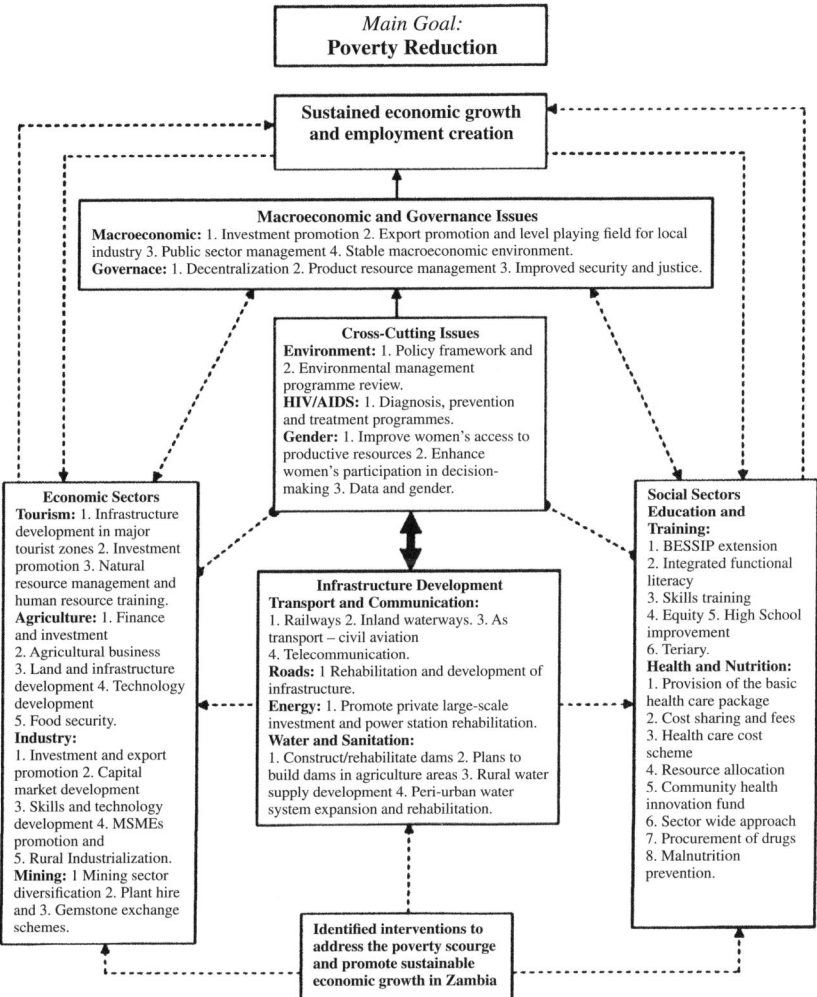

177